programming`.java`

An Introduction to Programming Using Java™

Second Edition

Rick Decker
Stuart Hirshfield

Hamilton College

Brooks/Cole
Thomson Learning™

Australia • Canada • Mexico • Singapore • Spain • United Kingdom • United States

Sponsoring Editor: *Kallie Swanson*
Marketing Team: *Nathan Wilbur,*
 Christina De Veto, Samantha Cabaluna
Editorial Assistant: *Grace Fujimoto*
Production Coordinator: *Kelsey McGee*
Production Service: *Publishers' Design and*
 Production Services, Inc.
Manuscript Editor: *Connie Day*

Permissions Editor: *Mary Kay Hancharick*
Cover Design: *Laurie Albrecht*
Typesetting: *Publishers' Design and Production*
 Services, Inc.
Cover Printing: *Phoenix Color Corporation*
Printing and Binding: *R. R. Donnelley and Sons/*
 Crawfordsville

For more information, contact:
BROOKS/COLE
511 Forest Lodge Road
Pacific Grove, CA 93950 USA
www.brookscole.com

Printed in United States of America

10 9 8 7 6 5 4 3 2

Library of Congress Cataloging-in-Publication Data

Decker, Rick.
   Programming.Java : an introduction to programming using Java /
Rick Decker, Stuart Hirshfield.—2nd ed.
     p.   cm.
   ISBN 0-534-37109-4 (pbk.)
   1. Java (Computer program language) I. Hirshfield, Stuart.
II. Title.
QA76.73.J38D44   1999   99-38991
005.13'3—dc21

To our students,
understanding as we do the ups,

Many are our joys
In youth, but oh! What happiness to live
When every hour brings palpable access
Of knowledge, when all knowledge is delight
And sorrow is not there!

—William Wordsworth, *The Prelude*

And the downs,

My life is one demd horrid grind.

—Charles Dickens, *Oliver Twist*

CONTENTS

PREFACE

This second edition of "programming dot java" (like the first) is intended to be used in a one- or two-semester introduction to programming using the Java™ language. We assume no prior programming experience on the part of our audience. In the tradition of new releases of software, we'll begin with a revision history of this product, describing the features of the original version ("edition," if you prefer), and the changes we have made.

Revision History

`programming java 1.0`

Hands-on experience. In a separate lab manual—available in print and on-line formats—we provide students with detailed, directed, experimental exercises which help them to explore firsthand the principles of OOP and Java in a controlled fashion. These exercises are integrated precisely with the textual material and bring the static text material to life. The text introduces students to new concepts. As they read the text, students encounter a number of sample programs that illustrate the new concepts. Then, in the laboratory, they experiment with "Lablet" programs and extend them using what they have learned from the text. All the sample programs will be provided on a disk that will accompany the lab manual.

Objects from the start. It's almost impossible to avoid classes, objects, and inheritance in a Java program. This means that we could build in an object-oriented approach from the very beginning, rather than just tacking it on later. Specifically, this text introduces students to Java and OOP from the top down. That is, we start by presenting the empowering features of Java and OOP—classes, packages, and inheritance—and defer the algorithmic details until later. After a quick generic introduction to computers and programming, roughly the first third of the text is devoted to using and experimenting with Java's Abstract Windowing Toolkit (the "AWT"). Doing so allows us to provide students with lots of algorithmically simple code to read and to use, all of which emphasizes basic OOP notations and ideas while providing tangible graphical output. Our overriding motivation in this approach is to make sure our students are introduced to object-oriented design early, before any bad habits can set in. By the end of this section of the course, students will be able to use the AWT to describe arbitrarily complex graphical user interfaces (GUIs). More important, they will be completely conversant in the basics of OOP and the use of Java packages.

Graphical orientation. Java contains a rich class library containing complete, platform-independent support for event-driven, graphically-oriented programming.

That is, users can interact with Java programs in a modeless manner by means of a contemporary graphical user interface, rather than by responding to program prompts by typing text into a console window. Just as the language dictates a reliance on object-oriented design, the class library makes it virtually impossible to avoid an approach that emphasizes code reuse. From the instructor's point of view, we gain a natural context for discussing important principles of software design, and our students can build visually interesting programs from the very start. After all, our audience has been raised on programs that have a rich graphical user interface: Java allows them to build the kind of programs they're used to seeing.

programming java 2.0

Java 2 compatibility. When we were writing version 1.0 of this text, the Java language was in the process of a major change, placing us in the uncomfortable position of releasing a book that was aimed at a moving target. Realizing that it would be a while before compiler writers caught up with the language change, we gritted our teeth and wrote it so that it discussed both the old and the (then) new versions of Java. Just to keep us on our toes (or so it seemed), as we were writing the current version, Sun Microsystems introduced yet another version—Java 2. Fortunately, this change entailed only the smallest of modifications, other than a decision to omit—for the moment—any detailed coverage of the new library packages (particularly Swing) that comprise Java 2. This means that the labs, lablets, and language features covered here are compatible with any version of Java with number 1.1 or higher.

New Lablets, new labs. We've streamlined many of the sample Lablets and completely replaced some, in the interest of not clobbering our readers with too much detail. The new model of event handling introduced in Java 1.1 necessitated changes in most of the Lablets, and, most important, we squashed a number of bugs that cropped up in the earlier programs. Of course, the changes in the Lablets resulted in a number of changes in the associated labs, as well.

New features. This version of the text includes review self-test questions at the end of nearly every section, with answers provided near the end of each chapter. We've also added end-of chapter reference sections that describe in compact form all the classes introduced in the chapter. In the back of the book, we've included a glossary of new terms and a complete rewrite of the atrocious index that came with the first version.

Coverage

You won't find the traditional CS 1 chapters, "Loops" and "Selection Statements," here. Our approach, as we've explained, is to cover object-oriented design and programming from the beginning, and to adopt a "just in time" approach to the algorithmic language features. **Chapter 1** provides a background context, discussing the evolution of programming, the Internet and the Worldwide Web, and providing an overview of Java.

The next three chapters introduce the AWT fundamentals. **Chapter 2** discusses the Applet class and graphical programming. **Chapter 3** introduces the basic graphical user interface components, such as buttons, labels, textfields, and checkboxes. The Lablet for this chapter uses all the components in the front end of an online ordering program. **Chapter 4** continues the investigation of the AWT classes by discussing containers, layouts, windows, frames, dialogs, and menus.

Chapter 5 begins our transition from using the AWT classes for visual design to writing programs that actively interact with the user. Here we introduce the Java language features that students will need, discussing primitive types, identifiers, scope, access, expressions, and statements. **Chapter 6** introduces event-driven programming and, now that they're necessary, the Java selection statements. **Chapter 7** recapitulates everything that we've introduced and then explores the design process in detail, moving from a vaguely-worded description of a problem to a fully functional simulation of an automatic teller machine. **Chapter 8** discusses arrays and the String class, introducing loops. We begin to discuss algorithmic programming by producing a visual sorting demonstration.

The remaining four chapters cover the other classes needed to produce all but the more arcane Java programs. **Chapter 9** introduces exceptions. **Chapter 10** discusses file input and output, culminating with the design and exploration of a word processor. **Chapter 11** introduces threads. **Chapter 12** concludes the book, describing how to make an applet interact with the Web, using sounds, images, and animation.

programming.java contains more material than most instructors will wish to introduce in a single semester. Many people we've talked to indicate that they cover most of Chapters 1 through 8 and then, depending on their interests and the interests of their students pick a topic or two from the remaining four chapters. We've heard that some schools have what might be called a "CS 1.5" course—covering Chapters 8 through 12 along with a healthy dose of software engineering—either as a requirement or an elective between CS 1 and the traditional Data Structures course that usually follows CS 1.

Thanks

programming.java, second edition wouldn't exist were it not for the efforts of a number of diligent and helpful people, many of whom we're proud to count among our friends. Our heartfelt thanks go out to the people at Brooks/Cole, especially Kallie Swanson, our editor; Grace Fujimoto, Brooks/Cole's editorial assistant for computer science titles; and Kelsey McGee, the production coordinator; Nathan Wilbur, senior marketing manager for engineering and computer science; and Mark Bergeron, of Publishers' Design and Production Services, Inc. Thanks also go to Connie Day, for reading the manuscript and magically transforming our sow's ear into a silk purse of accepted standards of punctuation, grammar, and orthography, and to Michael Fry of Lebanon Valley College, Kent Jones of Whitworth College, Robert Kline of West Chester University, J. Richard Rinewalt of Texas Christian University, Celia Schahczenski of Montana Tech of the University of Montana, and Susanne Steiger of Massachusetts Bay Community College for their detailed, thorough, and enormously helpful reviews of this edition. Special thanks, finally, go to our families for putting up with frequently absent and always bemused husbands and fathers. As Brian Dennehy said about his family in his Tony acceptance speech, "they paid for this with that most precious of coins, time." Writing and producing a book is a process that ranks right up there on the misery scale with cholera, except that it takes longer. It can never be called a pleasant experience, but the help, support, and warmth of all involved at least made it bearable.

Rick Decker
Stuart Hirshfield

■ **CHAPTER ONE** ■

BACKGROUND

So what's all this fuss about Java™? In this chapter, we'll put Java in historical and technological context. We'll describe briefly what programming languages are, how they evolved in the past 50 years, how they work, and what sets Java apart from the scores of other programming languages, both ancient (well, as ancient as anything can be in the short history of computers) and modern. Along the way, we'll touch on the development of graphical user interfaces and describe the burgeoning of the Worldwide Web, an aspect of modern computer use that is closely tied to the growing popularity of Java.

Objectives

In this chapter, we will

■ Discuss the history of programming, from the earliest days to the development of Java.
■ Learn about the development of the Internet and the Worldwide Web and see how Java came to be associated with Web pages.
■ Outline the process of creating a Java program and placing it in a Web page.
■ Explore the nature of Java and see what makes it different from other programming languages.

1.1 The Evolution of Programming

In simplest terms, programming is the process of designing a collection of instructions that a computer can execute to solve a problem. This sounds like a straightforward exercise—if we replace the word *computer* with *person,* we do this sort of thing every time we give a passing motorist directions to the local Post Office. All we have to do is provide an unambiguous list of commands that the recipient can perform: "Go down this road for three miles, turn left at the first light, and keep going until you see the school. The Post Office is just past the school on the left." The difference is that the person to whom you give these directions speaks the same language you do. Computers don't. In fact, the only language a computer "understands" (in the sense of being able to execute statements in that language) is about as far as we can imagine from a natural language like English. Indeed, you could hardly invent a language more difficult for people to understand than the machine language used by a computer. It is not unreasonable to view the entire history of programming as a series of attempts to facilitate the process of communicating with computers. Let's take a look at the problems of communicating with computers and the solutions that have evolved.

Figure 1.1

ENIAC[1], the first electronic computer, 1946. © CORBIS/Bettmann

The Not-So-Good Old Days

Electronic computers were invented independently in the United States, Germany, and England during the 1930s and 1940s. The first successful computers were huge, were expensive, and had roughly the same computational power as a modern digital watch. Still, for all their limitations, the computers available by the end of World War II (see Figure 1.1) were thousands of times faster than human calculators, and these "giant brains" found many eager buyers at the research centers, government facilities, and the private corporations that could afford the million-dollar-plus price tag. Programming in those days was very different from what we do today—the instructions for the computer were written in the language of the machine itself. As a result, the only people who could write programs were those few who had mastered the daunting task of speaking the machine's own dialect.

The language of a computer is determined by the way the computer is designed. In essence, a computer is nothing more than an enormous collection of on–off switches connected to each other. Everything a computer handles, whether data or instructions, must be represented internally as a collection of electric currents that are either on or off. For example, if we wanted to build a computer that was capable of performing arithmetic operations on whole numbers, we would have to design it so that each number we wanted to manipulate was represented by a suitable collection of "on" and "off" values. Such a two-value encoding of information

binary   is known as *binary* representation.

---

[1]ENIAC stands for Electronic Numeric Integrator and Computer. It was designed at the University of Pennsylvania's Moore School of Electrical Engineering and was first used to produce artillery firing tables. It was recently restored to working condition to celebrate its fiftieth birthday.

We might, for instance, decide to use two wires to represent numbers and represent zero as "off, off," one as "off, on," two as "on, off," and three as "on, on." To simplify the description, let's use 0 to represent "off" and 1 to represent "on," for no other reason than that it saves typing. Then, with this two-wire representation, we might decide on the representation $00 \rightarrow 0, 01 \rightarrow 1, 10 \rightarrow 2, 11 \rightarrow 3$. Of course, this is a pretty limited coding scheme, because only four values can be represented by the on–off combinations of two switches. We would probably design our computer using groups of 8 or 16 switches, but the principle would be the same.

Having decided how to represent numbers, we would then have to design a collection of other switches and wires that would perform operations, such as addition, on these values. We would have to put together a circuit that would have four wires coming in (for the two pairs of number wires) and three coming out (for the two digits of the sum, plus one more for the carry), as we illustrate in Figure 1.2. The details of what goes on in the adder circuit are unimportant to us here. What is important is that we would design circuits to provide all the operations we deemed necessary, such as subtraction, multiplication, and comparison. We would also have to set aside a collection of groups of switches for storage of incoming, intermediate, and final data values, to serve as the memory of our computer.

To complete our design, we would include switches to control which of the possible operation circuits would be activated on which values in memory. In our simple example, we might decide to use three control switches arranged so that "off, off, on" would turn on the adder, "off, on, off" would turn on the subtracter, and so forth. These design choices, then, would dictate the language of our machine. A machine language instruction might take the form illustrated in Figure 1.3, using 3 binary values to determine the operation, 4 each for the memory locations to be used, and 4 more for the memory locations where the results will be stored. With this representation, we could refer to any of 8 instructions acting on any of 16 memory locations (do you see why?). For example, the machine instruction 001 0000 0001 0010 would add (the 001 code) the values in memory locations 0 (0000 code) and 1 (0001 code) and place the result in memory location 2 (0010 code).

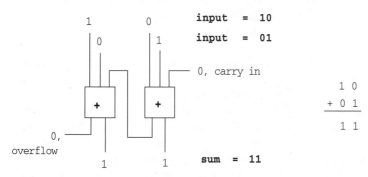

Figure 1.2

A simple addition circuit, computing 1 + 2 = 3.

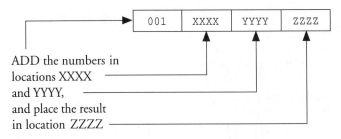

ADD the numbers in
locations XXXX
and YYYY,
and place the result
in location ZZZZ

Figure 1.3

A (highly simplified) machine language instruction format.

Finally, we'd be ready to write a program for our computer. Here's what it might look like, in part:

```
001000000010010
110001000011010
011101000010000
111000100010000
001000010100010
```

Obviously, no one who had any choice would want to instruct a computer in this language. First, we have the problem that stems from the fact that a computer can perform only a very small collection of operations. There were only eight possible operations in our sample computer, and even modern computers are limited to several dozen fundamental operations, simply because it is costly and difficult to design and build a computer with more. This means we have to express a problem like "sort a list of numbers stored in memory locations 0 to 1000" by using only the few simple operations, like COMPARE and MOVE, that have been provided for us.

As if that weren't bad enough, imagine how unlikely it would be—even if you correctly figured out which instructions to employ and in what order they should be used—that you would be able to produce the hundreds of necessary machine language instructions without once mistakenly placing a 1 where a 0 should be, or vice versa. Not only would your program be almost certain to contain a host of such small errors, each potentially fatal to its success, but it would also be nearly impossible difficult for you to track down the errors you had made among such a sea of ones and zeros.

Finally, and most important in the long run, the fact that machine language is dictated by the machine's design implies that a machine language program is no more "portable" than a set of dentures. Different machines use different languages, and there's nothing we can do about it. If a company were to buy a new computer, all its old programs would have to be rewritten from scratch to run on the new machine, and if the Des Moines office had a different model from the one used in Philadelphia, there would be no hope of cutting costs by sharing programs. This pretty well describes the state of the programming art in the 1950s, a sorry state indeed. There had to be a better way to get the job done, and there was. The solution was right there in the building, downstairs in the big air-conditioned room.

Help Arrives

In those early days, writing programs required a near-inhuman precision, flawless mastery of a host of details, and a powerful resistance to boredom and frustration. Let's see now—computers are inhumanly precise; when properly programmed, they have no difficulty keeping track of far more details than we can; and they are innately immune to boredom and frustration. It wasn't long before computer scientists came up with the idea of enlisting the help of the very machines that were responsible for the problem.

Because the instructions that make up a program can be stored in memory just like any other data[2], the computer can manipulate program instructions just as it manipulates numbers, strings of characters, pictures, sounds, and anything else that can be represented in binary. With this insight, we can free ourselves from the tyranny of the machine's architecture-dictated language and can design a language that is far easier for human programmers to work with.

The earliest steps in making the programming process easier were simple extensions of some of the techniques that machine language programmers did manually. Imagine for a moment that you were faced with the task of writing a machine language program. Just as we used 0s and 1s to symbolize OFF and ON switches, you could develop simple mnemonics to replace the binary notation, saying something like "I'll represent memory locations 0000, 0001, and 0010 by A, B, and C. What I want to do here is ADD A and B and store the result in C." In fact, you might actually write that down, producing a representation of a program that looked like this, complete with notes to yourself:

```
ADD A B C ; C contains A + B
MUL C C D ; now D contains (A + B) * (A + B)
```

This is much easier to understand than the binary version. What we can do now is write a (machine language) program that takes as its input a collection of characters like the ones above and translates it, line by line, into the corresponding binary instructions. If this *assembler* program, as it is called, sees ADD, it produces the operation code 001. Seeing A for the first time, it would find a memory address it hadn't used, such as 0000, and append that to the operation code it had produced; then it would continue similarly. We could even write our assembler program so that everything from the semicolon to the end of the line would be recognized as a comment and ignored in the translation process.

assembler

The task of programming now simultaneously becomes simpler for the human and more complex for the machine: You would program in the easier assembly language, feed the program into the assembler, and get executable machine language as output, which the computer could then run. This process would be more or less invisible to the programmer; in fact, one could imagine that the assembly language program was actually running on a *virtual machine* that somehow was wired to execute assembly language, rather than binary.

virtual machine

---

[2]The notion of the *stored-program computer* is credited to John von Neumann. The original ENIAC didn't store its programs in memory and was "programmed" by plugging in wires and setting switches.

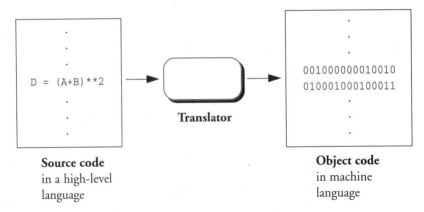

Source code
in a high-level
language

Object code
in machine
language

Figure 1.4

Using a program to translate programs (considerably simplified from reality).

The next step in the evolution of programming languages, one that continues to this day, was to invent languages even easier for humans to use, known as *high-level languages.* Obviously, people are happier working at much higher conceptual levels than a machine is capable of. Our example above, for instance, could be captured in the single instruction D = (A + B)**2, where the algebraic symbols (,), and + have their customary meanings, ** denotes raising to a power, and = is interpreted as "evaluate the expression on the right and store it in the location named on the left."

Of course, the translation from high-level *source code* into machine language *object code* is much more complicated (Figure 1.4), because one statement in source code might very well translate into a dozen or more instructions in object code. For example, the FORTRAN (FORmula TRANslator) language, introduced in 1954, was among the first high-level languages invented, and it took 18 person-years to complete the translator program. Since then, we've learned enough about language design and the translation process so that the design of a translator for a high-level language is now a common semester-length project in computer science graduate schools.

Because we'll be using the terms frequently in what follows, it's worth mentioning that the translation process from high-level language to machine code comes in two flavors. An *interpreter* translates a single source code statement into its machine code equivalents, executes the machine code, and then goes on to the next source code statement, translates and runs it, and so on. A *compiler,* on the other hand, translates the entire source code program, producing an object code file that can then be executed. Interpreted programs tend to run more slowly than their compiled equivalents, because execution is interleaved with the translation process. On the other hand, it is generally easier to write an interpreter than a compiler, and, all things being equal, it is easier to debug a program (find and fix errors) in an interpreted environment than when one is using a compiler. Languages like LISP and BASIC are often interpreted; more complex languages like C++ are generally compiled. Java, as we will see, is compiled and then interpreted.

high-level
language

source
code,
object
code

inter-
preter
compiler

Using a high-level language frees us from the dictates of the underlying machine. A language designer can concentrate on designing a language that is as easy as possible to use, subject only to the constraint that it can be translated into machine code (which is why, at least at present, we can't write programs in English). Studies have shown that the number of lines of debugged code a programmer can produce in a day is pretty much independent of the language used, so working at a high conceptual level tends to be more efficient, because a 200-line Java program might very well translate into a 1000 or more machine code instructions. We get another benefit, as well, when using a high-level language. Although the machine languages used in a Sun workstation, a Pentium-based IBM PC, and a PowerPC Macintosh are completely different, the same Java source code will run on all three, as long as each has a suitable translator program installed. As far as the programmer is concerned, all three computers are just Java machines with different logos on the box.

Review Questions

Answers to the review questions can be found at the end of the chapter, where answer 1.1 refers to review question 1 in Section 1.1, and so on.

1.1 What do we mean by the "binary representation" of information?
1.2 How many values can be represented by a collection of three binary digits?
1.3 What is an assembler? Why were assemblers invented?
1.4 Explain the difference between a compiler and an interpreter.

1.2 The Internet and the Worldwide Web

By the 1960s, computers were commonplace in government installations and scientific laboratories throughout the United States. While computers were growing more powerful and programming languages were growing more sophisticated, developments of interest to us were taking place on another front. Recognizing the importance of computers, both for research and for what is known in the jargon as C3 (command, control, and communication), the U.S. Department of Defense proposed a network connecting computers at government facilities, research labs, and universities. As a result, what we now call the Internet was born on Labor Day in 1969, connecting host computers at UCLA, the Stanford Research Institute, the University of California at Santa Barbara, and the University of Utah at Salt Lake City.

The Internet was designed from the beginning with security and robustness in mind. The Department of Defense required that the network be resistant to a "point of failure attack"; that is, in the event of a nuclear attack, the destruction of a few host computers would not compromise the communications capabilities of the remainder of the network. This requirement had important and unforeseen consequences. It meant that the network could not be designed like the existing telephone network, with a few centralized switching centers responsible for routing all messages. Instead, the proposed network had to be decentralized, with each host computer responsible for routing any messages it received, whether the message was for use by a computer in a local network connected to the host site or was to be passed along to another location.

Such decentralization implied that it was quite simple to add other sites to the network. A location with its own local network could simply designate one of its computers as an Internet host, install the necessary routing software, and connect the host computer to one or more routing computers at other sites that had agreed to the connection. This connection was more or less transparent to the local computers; even though the Internet is in fact a network of local networks connected by routing computers, it appears to the local machines as though each is connected directly to all others anywhere on the net.

Because the routing computers were responsible for managing network traffic, another consequence was that every communication over the Internet was in effect a local call. Distance over the Internet was a meaningless concept from the very beginning. To send a message from San Francisco to Pasadena, the routing computers may decide that the most efficient path (in terms of current net traffic) would be from San Francisco via satellite to Norway, then over landlines to London, by satellite again to West Virginia, and finally by wire and microwave to Pasadena.[3]

The fact that it was so easy to connect to the Internet, no matter where you were located, led to an amazing and completely unexpected growth. Fired by the desire for electronic mail (another unexpected use of a network that was originally designed with collaborative projects in mind), the number of hosts doubled each year, reaching 1024 in 1984, 28,174 in 1987, and over 1 million by 1992. Today, as this is written, there are over 8 million host computers serving 50 million users worldwide with a total traffic of well over 30 trillion bytes per month. (A *byte* is a group of 8 binary digits, the amount needed to encode a single character.) This traffic is roughly equivalent to transmitting the entire contents of the Library of Congress electronically each month. Pretty impressive, especially when you consider that in 1973, the designers of the Internet anticipated a maximum of 256 sites.

byte

The Worldwide Web

In its early years, the Internet was used primarily for electronic mail, newsgroups, remote log-in to computers, and access to information stored in files at other sites. Using the Internet was a fairly technical and somewhat daunting process back then. Not only did transferring information from one computer to another require mastery of one or more software packages, but even locating the information in the first place was by no means easy, even with the help of programs designed to search out the needed data. The anarchic, decentralized nature of the Internet meant that there was no central directory where you could look up information on, for instance, colobus monkeys.

---

[3]This is not a far-fetched example. It is, in fact, the path used for an early demonstration of the network.

Partly to address these problems, researchers at CERN, the European laboratory for particle physics, proposed the notion of distributed hypermedia in 1989. A hypermedia system is one that mixes text, graphics, animation, and sound in a single document. A *hypertext* document (as it is also known) about colobus monkeys might contain a textual description of their habitat, physical characteristics, and social behavior, along with pictures of a family group, the sounds of their calls, and a video clip of their threat behavior. You may be familiar with hypermedia if you have ever seen a computer-based encyclopedia. Of course, the concept of hypermedia originated long before 1989; what made the CERN proposal so important was that it included the idea of having a hypertext document include *links* to others, even those stored at other computers. This is why we use the term *distributed hypermedia:* A Web page may appear as a single visual entity, but the information it contains may come from a number of files, stored on computers spread across the globe.

Such a project was clearly a substantial undertaking. Not only did there have to be standards for the way text, pictures, and sounds were to be represented in binary, but there also had to be programs, known as *browsers,* to support the display of all this information and to handle the process of calling up hypertext documents from other computers on the Internet. By 1993 the first browsers had been developed and the Worldwide Web was born, with some 50 sites supporting these linked hypertext documents by January of that year. Within just 9 months, Web messages represented 1% of all Internet traffic. By June 1994 there were about 1500 Web sites, and today the number is over a million.

It's important to realize that, unlike the Internet or a purely local network (known as an *intranet*), the Worldwide Web is not a physical entity. Rather, it is a concept we use to refer to the documents, their links, and the browsers used to view and interact with this collection. In a sense, the Web lives on top of a computer network like the Internet.

It would be difficult to overestimate the impact of the Worldwide Web, which abruptly made it possible for every user to become an information source. All you need is access to a Web server (a computer with the appropriate software and Internet connections), and anyone in the world can access your Web pages. The ease with which Web pages can be generated and accessed has led to millions of pages across the global network, all densely interconnected. Information access became far easier, as well, with the invention of search engines. These programs, such as Yahoo, Lycos, and Excite, spend their free time jumping from one link to another and recording references to what they find in a database that is used to handle user queries. To find information on colobus monkeys, again, you no longer need to know where the information is located. Instead, you can point your browser to one of these search engines and tell it to look for the keyword *colobus.* The engine then looks in its database and returns the Net addresses of all the locations where it had found the word colobus. Just for fun, we tried this with several search engines; the results ranged from a low of 50 sites to a high of 709. We found enough text, photographs, video clips, and sounds in the space of a few minutes to satisfy anyone's curiosity about *Colobus abyssinicus.*

HTML

One of the nicest features of the Worldwide Web is that all you need to make a Web page is a computer, a text editor, and a browser (you can even dispense with the browser if you don't care to see what your creation looks like when displayed). Web browsers are all designed to recognize a purely text-based language known as HTML   *Hypertext Markup Language,* or HTML for short. The elements of HTML are known as *tags,* which consist of keywords and other information enclosed between pointy brackets, < and >.[4] Anything that's not a tag is considered to be plain text, and is displayed appropriately by the browser.

One important feature of HTML is that it is exceedingly easy to learn. There are only a few dozen tags to learn, and most of them are simple enough to be almost self-explanatory. For example, if you enclose text between the paired tags <B> and </B>, the enclosed text will be displayed in boldface. If you were to write

```
This is <B>really</B> easy.
```

The browser would see the tags and display

This is **really** easy.

Statistics indicate that there's a good chance you have already used a browser like Netscape Navigator or Microsoft's Internet Explorer to wander around the Web. When you do, what happens is both very simple and very complex. If you instruct your browser to go to a location like this (which happens to be one of our home pages),

```
http://www.cs.hamilton.edu/~rdecker/
```

the browser sends a message over the network to the *Web server* computer www, located at the domain cs.hamilton (our department), in the wider domain edu of all educational institutions. The message tells the host computer to find the HTML document index.html (this is assumed by the browser because we didn't specify it) in the directory ~rdecker and to send a copy back to your computer. Once there, your browser reads the document, interprets the tags, and displays the result, all nicely formatted, on the monitor of your computer, as we indicate in Figure 1.5. The concept, then, is quite simple.

The actual process of getting the document, interpreting the tags, and displaying the result is, of course, quite complicated. For example, decisions about which font to use for displaying plain text or how to size a page to fit the monitor on which it is to be displayed are left to the programmers who write Web browsers. This complexity stems in part from the fact that HTML is a platform-independent standard: As long as you have a Web browser that is designed for use on your com-

---

[4]*Technical term alert:* The characters < and > were originally placed on computer keyboards to represent the mathematical operators "less than" and "greater than," but for us they are just special angular forms of parentheses. In geekspeak, they're known as brockets, for "broken brackets."

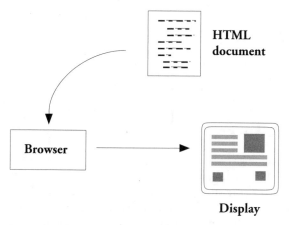

Figure 1.5

An HTML document displayed by a Web browser.

puter, it doesn't matter who makes the computer; the Web page is guaranteed by the HTML standards to communicate the same information, even if it might look a little different from one browser to another.

Most browsers offer you the option of inspecting the underlying HTML code of any document. You can use this feature to inspect the HTML source code Rick used to make his Web page. Try it! Find a Web-connected browser, open Rick's page, and explore the code.

Pay particular attention to the tag in lines 29–32:

```
<IMG
    src = "common/graph.gif"
    align = right
    width = 258
    height = 169>
```

This line instructs the browser to go to the computer where the HTML document is originally stored, find the image graph.gif in the directory common, and draw the image aligned with the right side of the browser window. If you wished, you could even copy this image for use in an HTML document of your own.[5] The point of all this is to illustrate how easy it is in the Worldwide Web to find information on other computers and download it for use by a browser. We'll use this feature quite a lot in the chapters to come, both for searching for online Java information and for looking at Java programs that other people have written.

---

[5]A word of caution is in order here. In spite of the open nature of the Web, *everything* you see while browsing is owned by someone, and copyright laws do indeed apply in cyberspace. You can legally copy anything you find for your own personal use, but it's both immoral and illegal to copy and publish someone else's work without permission.

Review Questions

2.1 Are you younger or older than the Internet? Than the Worldwide Web?
2.2 What is a browser?
2.3 What is "platform independence" and why is it valuable?
2.4 What is HTML?

1.3   Along Comes Java

For all its visual and auditory appeal, an HTML document appears in a browser as a fairly static object with limited functionality, beyond the important ability it gives a user to click on links and see documents stored elsewhere. The Worldwide Web provides access to an unimaginably vast storehouse of information, but Web pages, at least as originally conceived, don't offer much in the way of user interactivity. That's all changing now, largely because of a project launched at about the same time as the Web, nearly half a world away.

Smart Toasters

In 1990, at Sun Microsystems in California, James Gosling was working on a new programming language. Unlike many traditional languages, this one was designed for use in control systems of consumer electronics devices such as toasters, microwave ovens, and television sets. Because of the nature of such appliances and the economics involved, languages that were standards in data processing and scientific use, like C++, were inappropriate choices. They were simply too large for the problem at hand. Most of the languages current at the time were designed for industrial-strength programming and so were intended to make the programmer's life easier, regardless of the computational costs involved. For many, the cost of the memory and processing chips needed to run them exceeded the cost of the appliance itself. Although they certainly could have handled tasks like setting a microwave to cook at full power for three minutes and then at half power until the temperature probe measured a heat of 185°F, using them in this way would have been equivalent to chartering a nuclear-powered aircraft carrier for a day's fishing trip. What was needed was a language that was designed from the start to be fast, small, reliable, and universal.

The traditional solution to this problem had been around for two decades in digital watches and electronic calculators.[6] A manufacturer of microwave ovens, for instance, would decide on an inexpensive processor chip, build it into the appliance, and hire someone to write its program in machine code. There were several problems with this approach, however. First, machine language, as we have noted, is machine-specific. If the manufacturer were to change brands of control processors,

---

[6] In fact, the first microprocessor, or computer-on-a-chip, the Intel 4004, was developed for use in electronic calculators.

they would have to pay for new machine code; the older code would almost certainly be incompatible. This would also make upgrading or repairing the old appliances more difficult, because the manufacturer would have to keep a stock of the old control processors, and microprocessors are usually superseded by new models far faster than appliances wear out.

Gosling and his team decided that the solution would be to make a small language, but not as small or hard to use as machine language, that would run on any kind of computer chip. As we saw in Section 1.1, the only way to do that would be to make the new language easy to compile. With such a language, the hardware would no longer be an issue. A manufacturer who upgraded to a new control processor could use exactly the same programs it had on hand and would need only to buy or design a new compiler to translate its programs into the machine code for the new model chips. In effect, the programmers could write the control code once and be done with it, never giving a thought to what kind of chip the code would eventually run on.

Java, Meet Web; Web, Meet Java

The first use of this new language[7] was in a device designed to act as a master control for a number of household appliances such as televisions, lights, telephones, and so on. That product never made it to store shelves, but shortly thereafter the design team hit upon a "virtual appliance" that seemed to provide a perfect match for Java's speed, simplicity, and robustness: a Web page. Why not embed Java code in HTML documents? Web pages were designed to be device-independent; Java was designed to be device-independent (to view a Web page on an Intel-based PC, a Macintosh, or a Sun workstation, all one needed was the right browser); and Java was simple enough that a Java interpreter could be embedded in a browser without a prohibitive amount of extra programming. All that was needed was to get a browser developer to agree, and in 1995 that happened when it was announced that Netscape Navigator 2.0 would support Java. To appreciate the difference this made, take a look at

```
http://www.acm.uiuc.edu/webmonkeys/juggling/index.html
```

With Java, you can make a Web page come alive with animation and user interactivity. Properly designed, the Java portion of a page can instruct, inform, amuse, explain, entertain, and emphasize. Of course, as with all design decisions, you can also make a Java program that will bore, irritate, or outrage your audience. We would encourage the former choices, naturally, but we'll point out enough of the latter that you'll be able to make an informed decision about what to do.

---

[7]Trivia: The language was originally named Oak, but the design team learned that that name was already taken by another language. The more-or-less official story about the final name, Java, was that it was selected during a visit to a local coffee shop.

Applications and Applets

Applica-
tion

Java programs come in two flavors, depending on their eventual use. *Applications* are traditional stand-alone programs designed to be compiled and then run, like this one:

```
public class Hello
// Just about the simplest Java application anyone can write.
{
    public static void main(String argv[])
    {
        System.out.println("Hi!");
    }
}
```

method

The heart of this program is the line containing main. That line and the three below it are known as a *method*, which is nothing more than jargon for "a named section of a program that contains code instructing the computer to take some action." In this example, the action that takes place is the single statement

```
System.out.println("Hi!");
```

which, in turn, causes the message "Hi!" to be displayed. Every Java application must have a main method, called, appropriately enough, main. The rest of this application is easy to understand; the braces serve the same punctuation purposes for the compiler as for people—they collect the code into groups.

comment

The line starting with two slashes[8] (//) is a *comment*—it is ignored by the compiler and is solely for the edification of the person reading the code. Finally, looking at the top line, you can see that the whole thing is part of a *class*. Classes are an essential aspect of Java. In any language, human or computer, there are rules for correct grammar that may make little sense when you first see them. We'll have lots more to say about classes in the next section.

For applications, Java is just one choice among many. We could write the program above in any of a number of languages. Here's what it would look like in Pascal:

```
program Hello(output);
{Just about the simplest Pascal program anyone can write.}
begin
    writeln("Hi!");

end.
```

and here's what it would look like in C (or in C++, with some minor changes):

```
main()
/* Just about the simplest C program anyone can write */
{
    printf("Hi!\n");

}
```

---

[8]The character / is also known as *virgule* or *solidus,* although no programmer calls it by those names.

Although Java is just one of many language choices for writing applications, it is at present the only choice available if you want to embed a program in a Web page. A Java *applet* is a program that is not intended to be run on its own but, rather, is supposed to live at some location in a Web page, in much the same way as a graphic image might. Applets are a trifle more complicated to write than applications, but not much more. Here's an applet that does the same thing as the application we listed above:

applet

```
import java.applet.*;
import java.awt.*;

public class Hello extends Applet
// Just about the simplest Java applet anyone can write.
{
    public void paint(Graphics g)
    {
        g.drawString("Hi!", 20, 10);
    }
}
```

This looks a lot like the application, and they do just about the same thing in different contexts. There's a class, `Hello`, containing all the code for the applet, which in this case is the single method `paint`. The body of the `paint` method contains the single statement

```
g.drawString("Hi!", 20, 10);
```

which causes the "Hi!" message to be displayed. We could even have used the same statement

```
System.out.println("Hi!");
```

that we used in the application—it just would have just placed the message in a different location (in a separate window known as the *Java console*). The two `import` statements at the top are instructions for the system to look up two *packages* of additional code, where the definitions of `Applet` and `Graphics`, respectively, are stored.

We'll talk about packages in Section 1.4.

To use this applet in a Web page, we have two tasks to perform. One task is to compile the text-based Java source code into Java *bytecode*. Bytecode is an easy-to-translate, low-level language that can be interpreted by any Java-aware browser, such as Netscape Navigator or Internet Explorer. The other task is to prepare an HTML document that describes the Web page in which the applet will live. Figure 1.6 illustrates what we have to do to display an applet in a Web page.

bytecode

Let's take a more detailed look at the steps we sketched in Figure 1.6. We mentioned earlier that Java is both compiled and interpreted. We'll see why when we look at what must be done to bring a Java program to life in a browser.

Step 1. Write the program. This is by far the hardest part of the process and, in fact, is what we'll spend the rest of the book teaching you to do.

Step 2. Compile the program. The next step is to produce the bytecode by sending your Java source to a compiler. For example, the method

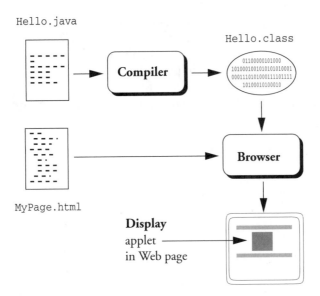

Figure 1.6

Applets, from source code to display.

```
public void paint(Graphics g)
{
    g.drawString("Hi!", 20, 10);
}
```

is compiled into the sequence of numbers 43, 18, 1, 16, 20, 16, 10, 182, 0, 6, 177, with the following mnemonic codes and meanings:

43	aload_1	*(load the Graphics object g)*
18, 1	ldc 1	*(load the first constant, "Hi")*
16, 20	bipush 20	*(load the value 20)*
16, 10	bipush 10	*(load the value 10)*
182, 0, 6	invokevirtual	*(call the "drawstring" method)*
177	return	*(leave the "paint" method)*

This bytecode would be saved in a file named `Hello.class`. Bytecode file names must end with a `.class` extension and must start with the same name as the class they contain (`Hello`, in this instance). We'll have more to say about naming conventions in the lab for this chapter.

Step 3. Let the browser know where your bytecode is. You do this by producing an HTML document that refers to the `.class` file produced by the compiler. For this part, you'll need a text editor. Any word processor will do; it doesn't have to be fancy or expensive, because all you need is to produce raw text, without any style information. You can even use the one that came with your computer, like SimpleText for the Macintosh or Write for a Windows environment. You would type the following HTML, without the italicized comments.

```
<HTML>                              The HTML code starts here.
    <HEAD>                          Nothing in the HEAD is displayed,
        <TITLE>
            My Applet Page          except for the title, which will show
        </TITLE>                    up in the window's title bar.
    </HEAD>
    <BODY>                          The BODY part will be displayed:
        Here's my applet. . .       Any old HTML can go here,
        <HR>                        like this horizontal rule
        <APPLET code = "Hello.class"  The applet comes next,
                width = 60          with specified width and height
                height = 60>
        </APPLET>
        <HR>                        More HTML can go here
    </BODY>                         The end of the BODY part
</HTML>                             The HTML code ends here.
```

You can be pretty careless when typing HTML. Although misspellings can hurt you (browsers will ignore any tag they don't recognize, like <BIDY>), HTML is *case-insensitive,* so <BODY>, <body>, and even <bOdY> all represent the same tag. In addition, browsers will ignore any repeated *whitespace* (spaces, tabs, and returns), so you can format your HTML in any way that you find makes it easier to read.

When you're done, you save the document as text (your editor might also call this format ASCII) and save it under the name MyPage.html. (The last dot is a period at the end of the sentence and shouldn't be used in the file name.) You can name the document anything you wish, as long as it ends with the .html extension. Finally, at this stage you should make sure that the MyPage.html and Hello.class files are stored in the same directory or folder. There are ways to avoid this, but you'll have to wait a bit before we're ready to describe them.

Step 4. Use the browser to open the HTML page. The browser will look at the HTML and format it appropriately on the screen. When it comes to the <APPLET> tag, the browser will invoke its own Java interpreter and execute the bytecode line by line, translating each line into the machine code that's appropriate for the computer on which it's running, telling the computer to execute the machine code, and continuing on to the next line of the bytecode, where the whole translate–execute process begins anew.

You're finished. If you've typed everything in correctly, you should now be able to start your Web browser and use it to open the file MyPage.html. The result should appear as we've illustrated in Figure 1.7 (though, of course, it may look somewhat different if you're using a different browser from the one we used to generate the picture).

Review Questions

3.1 What is the difference between an applet and an application?

3.2 The translation from Java source code involves two steps: compiling the source code into bytecode and then interpreting the bytecode into machine language. What programs are responsible for each step?

Figure 1.7

Your first applet.

3.3 Why does Java have comments?

3.4 What two kinds of files does a browser need to run an applet?

1.4 An Overview of Java

Java represents an evolutionary change from earlier programming languages, rather than a radical departure. In many ways, Java is like its predecessors Pascal, C, and, especially, C++. In this section we'll explore the important features of Java, and show how these features make it similar to, and different from, other programming languages that came before it.

Syntax

syntax

The *syntax*—the collection of grammar rules—of Java is extremely close to that of its big brother, C++. C++, originally known as C with Classes, was conceived in 1979 by Bjarne Stroustrup of Bell Laboratories. Designed as an improved successor to the language C, it had substantially attained its present form in 1986.[9] It was adopted rapidly and enthusiastically by industry, and somewhat less rapidly and enthusiastically by educational institutions. The reason for this difference in enthusiasm has a lot to do with the invention of Java.

C++ is a good choice for a wide variety of real-world programming projects. It is a very high-level language, allowing programmers to design programs without initially having to keep track of a host of minor details. At the same time, it is a

---

[9]The name C++ was chosen in 1983 and is something of an inside joke, as you'll see in a later chapter.

highly expressive language, allowing a programmer to think in very low-level terms (that is, to think about what the underlying machine is doing) when necessary. It has a very rich set of features, which provide many different ways of performing the same task.

The features that made C++ so suitable for large-scale work by teams of experienced programmers also made it a very large and complex language and a rather daunting prospect for compiler designers (this is why Gosling's team at Sun ruled it out for their embedded-systems project). Another result of C++'s expressiveness is that it is fairly easy for a novice programmer to write code in C++ that compiles without error but actually runs in a way that the author never intended. In the words of the title of Allen I. Holub's delightful book, C++ gives you *Enough Rope to Shoot Yourself in the Foot* (New York: McGraw-Hill, 1985).

Java was designed from the start to retain the core parts of C++ syntax, while trimming away as much of the rest as possible. Many of the powerful but nasty features of C++ (like pointers) were axed, along with some (like templates) that were elegant but gave compiler designers nightmares. The result was a language that should look very familiar to those experienced in C++ but is far leaner and smaller.

Language Features

Java programs, like any others, manipulate information. Java has a rich and extensible collection of data types that it can deal with: *integers* (like −1, 600, or 788402), *floating-point* numbers (like 3.1415926535 and −2887.0), *boolean* values, representing `true` and `false`, *characters* (like A and ?), strings of characters (like the "Hi!" you saw in our sample applet), and *class types* (like the `Graphics` object `g` in the sample applet).   **data types**

Information in a Java program can be expressed as a *literal* value, like the "Hi!", 20, and 30 in the sample, or can have a symbolic *variable* name, like the `g` in the sample, which stands for a place in memory where a `Graphics` object (whatever that is) can be stored.   **literal**   **variable**

Of course, being able to represent information in a program is pretty much useless without some way to operate on it. As you progress through this book, you'll learn about Java's *operators*, which take one or more pieces of data, do something to them, and return a result. This is just a fancy way of saying that in a Java program you can do things like adding, subtracting, multiplying, and dividing two numbers, using familiar operator symbols like +, −, *, and /. You can assign a piece of data into a variable of the right type, and you can combine operators into *expressions*, such as   **operator**   **expression**

```
fahrenheit = (9.0 / 5.0) * celsius + 32
```

where we're using the assignment, division, multiplication, and addition operators, along with the numeric literals 9.0, 5.0, and 32, to convert a value stored in the variable `celsius` to another value, which we store in the variable `fahrenheit`.

At the lowest level, a Java program, like programs in most languages, is just a sequence of statements, the basic units of execution. You'll discover that there are just a few different kinds of statements, like these: **statements**

```
// An expression statement: evaluate this expression
// (which increases the value stored in "counter" by 1).
counter = counter + 1;

// An if statement: if the condition in the parentheses is
// true, execute the statement in the braces, otherwise skip it
if (number > 0)
{
    average = sum / number;
}

// A method call: execute the method drawString(), belonging
// to the object g, giving it the three values "Hi!", 20, and
// 30 that it needs to draw the string at a certain location.
g.drawString("Hi!", 20, 30);

// A declaration statement: establish a new integer variable
// named "mySum," initially containing the value 0.
int mySum = 0;
```

You'll also discover how to make methods of your own by specifying the information the method receives, the statements it uses to manipulate its information, and the value (if any) that it sends back when it is finished. Here is an example:

```
// This function takes in two integers, p and q, and
// returns the larger of the two.
int maxValue(int p, int q)
{
    if (p > q)
    {
        return p;
    }
    else
    {
        return q;
    }
}
```

Objects and Classes

object-oriented language

Early in the history of programming languages (up to the early 1970s), programmers were restricted to building their wares out of nothing but statements, perhaps collected into methods (which were called *functions* or *procedures* then). Like a house builder restricted to using boards, nails, bricks, and mortar, one can do a lot with just the raw materials, but it's certainly not the most efficient way of working. The house builder's job is much easier if the materials include prefabricated doors, windows, and stairways. Not only do these complicated objects not have to be built from scratch, but having them on hand also enables the contractor to plan the day's work at a higher conceptual level, thinking "An AF44–3 window will go here," rather than "I'll need to make the sill and the mullions, put the stop here, mortice in the twelve panes of glass. . . ."

The essence of Java, like that of C++ and Smalltalk, is that it is an *object-oriented language.* In such languages, the basic conceptual building block is the object, an entity that has its own data and its own methods for manipulating that data and interacting with the world around it. In programming terms, for example, we might consider a `Point` object, designed to represent a two-dimensional location. Such an object would need data to describe its coordinates (two numbers would suffice, for the *x*- and *y*-coordinates). A `Point` object, like any other, needs *constructors* to set its initial values, and it might need to be able to compare itself to a pair of coordinates, set its coordinate values, and translate itself by adding offsets to its coordinates. The description of a `Point` might look like this (in fact, Java's built-in `Point` class looks exactly like this):

constructor

```
DATA
    int x                               the x-coordinate (an integer)
    int y                               the y-coordinate (an integer)
CONSTRUCTORS
    Point()                             Make a point by setting its coordinates to 0, 0.
    Point(int x, int y)                 Make a point by specifying its coordinates.
    Point(Point p)                      Make this point a copy of p.
METHODS
    boolean equals(int x, int y)        Return "true" if this point has coordinates x, y.
    void move(int x, int y)             Set this point's coordinates to those specified by x and y.
    void translate(int dx, int dy)      Add dx and dy to the x and y coordinates, respectively.
```

An object contains its own data and has methods for manipulating its data.

In Java everything is an object, with the exception of *primitive types* of information as integers, floating-point numbers, boolean data, and characters. We should think of every Java program as being made of a collection of cooperating objects, passing requests to others to perform their methods and responding to similar requests from other objects.

A Java program is a collection of cooperating objects.

When we spoke of `Point` objects, we were operating under the assumption that a program might have more than one. It would be a waste of effort to redo all the descriptions above for each such object, so Java, like other object-oriented languages, provides us with the notion of the *class*. A class is nothing more than a collection of objects, or, equivalently, every object is a single instance of a class. If you wish, you can think of a class definition as providing a prototype for all of its objects.

class

Two `Point` objects might have different values for their coordinates, but they—along with all other `Point` objects—would still have two numbers for data and the constructors and methods listed above, as we illustrate in Figure 1.8.

The notion of classes of objects provides us with a natural way of solving problems by extending the programming language we're using. The designers of Java—or of any other programming language—couldn't possibly have anticipated all the needs of all programmers, so making our own classes allows us to pretend, at least for the life of the program, that the language has the features we need. For example, although Java has a predefined class for representing two-dimensional points, it doesn't have a class for points in three-dimensional space. However, the language allows us to design our own and use it, just as though it had been part of the language right from the start.

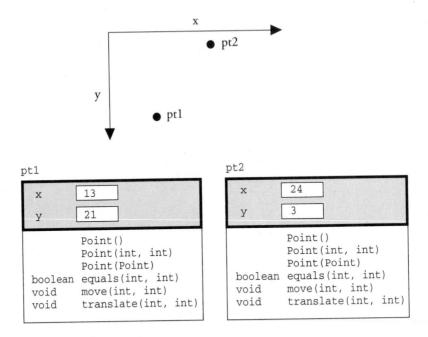

Figure 1.8

A conceptual view of two `Point` objects, along with their descriptions.

Inheritance

Even though Java has its own `Point` class, there's no guarantee that it will meet our needs. We might, for instance, have to write a geometry program that would require us to be able to find the distance between a point and the (0, 0) origin and to produce a new point that was the component-wise sum of two others. The `Point` class we described above, however useful it might be for other applications, lacks the extra methods we need. Fortunately, object-oriented languages such as Java have just the capability we require.

We can define a class in such a way that it *inherits* all or most of the definition of another and then go on to add whatever features we need. In our example, we might define a new class, `GeometricPoint`, that has the two data members `x` and `y` of the `Point` class, along with the `Point` constructors and methods. We could then add two new methods, `magnitude()` and `add()`. If nothing else, this saves us a lot of typing. In Java, if we say in the definition of a class that it *extends* another class, we get all of the methods and data of the original class without ever having to make explicit mention of them.[10] In Java we do that by starting the definition of `GeometricPoint` as follows:

---

[10]That's not entirely true, as you'll see when we discuss *access*. It is possible to tag some of the data and methods of a class so that they are not available to any inheriting class.

```
class GeometricPoint extends Point
{
    // The definitions of magnitude() and add() would go here.
}
```

Then, if myPt was a GeometricPoint object, we could invoke its methods magnitude() and add(), but we could also have it perform a move() method, because a GeometricPoint "is-a" Point, under the rules for inheritance. In one sense, *extends* is a less than perfect word choice: Although GeometricPoint extends the functionality of Point, it could equally well be argued that we should write GeometricPoint **restricts** Point, because the GeometricPoint objects form a subset of the Point objects.

To say class B **extends** class A is to say, roughly speaking, that

1. Every B object is also an A object.

2. B objects may have information and abilities that A objects don't.

Libraries

We might, after lots of arduous effort, put together a whole collection of classes for the geometry program we've begun to create. It's easy to imagine that we'd need a GeometricPoint class, along with the classes Line, Segment, Ray, Triangle, and so on. If we wanted to make efficient use of our time, we might consider saving these classes for later use, in case we were ever called upon to design a different geometry program. As you'll see later, Java provides a mechanism to group a collection of logically related classes into a *package*, so the classes in the package can be made part of another program by using the import statement.

This is just what we did when we wrote import java.applet.* at the start of our Hello applet. In doing so, we instructed Java to make available to our program all the classes in the java.applet package (there's just one, the Applet class, along with three class-like things called *interfaces*, which we'll discuss later).

Java provides a rich collection of library packages. Strictly speaking, none of them are parts of the language itself, but they contain such useful extension classes that it is a rare Java program indeed that doesn't use at least some of them.[11] The packages that Sun supplies with Java include

▲ java.applet, which we've already mentioned
▲ java.awt, which contains many useful classes, such as Button and TextField, for making graphical user interfaces
▲ java.io, with 58 classes for file reading and writing
▲ java.lang, which has classes like Object, Math, and String that are of general use

---

[11]No useful applet can be written without importing java.applet. and the sample application we gave in Section 1.2 is just about the most that can be accomplished without importing some package.

▲ java.net, with 18 classes for working with computer networks, like the Internet
▲ java.util, which contains utility classes such as Date and Random, along with data containers such as Hashtable and Vector

We'll spend much of the first third of this text discussing the classes in java.awt, and we will eventually cover many of the classes in the other packages (except for java.net, which is beyond the scope of this text).

Review Questions

4.1 Name two of Java's primitive types. Name two class types.
4.2 What is a statement? Name three kinds of statements.
4.3 What is the difference between an object and a class?
4.4 What benefits do we gain from inheritance?
4.5 Is the Graphics class a part of the Java language?

1.5 Hands On

We'd be the first to admit that the Hello applet we gave you is pretty silly. What's the point of taking the time to write, debug, and error-test it when all it does is display the string "Hi!"? We could have saved a lot of time by typing the message in the original HTML, rather than having the computer do it for us. In this, our first "Lablet," we'll walk you through a simple applet that actually does something.

Don't expect to understand all the Java code you'll see below—we have plenty of time to explore Java's vocabulary and rules of grammar in the chapters to come. Instead, we present here a sample that demonstrates some of the things a Java applet can do and that you can use to explore your particular Java development environment.

On the screen, our Lablet takes the following form:

Clicking on the buttons will cause the colors of the background or text to be changed. In this chapter's lab, we take you through some exercises to give you practice in entering, compiling, running, and correcting a Java applet. This would be a good time to turn to the lab manual and work through the exercises. If you can't spare the time right now, here's what the Java source code looks like. Read through it and look first at the overall structure: The applet subclass `Colors` contains three data members (a Font, `f`, and two integers, `bgCode` and `txtCode`) and three methods, `init()`, `actionPerformed()`, and `paint()`. Once you've detected the structure, see whether you can deduce what some of the statements, like `if` or `switch`, are accomplishing.

```
//=================================================================
// PROJECT:         _programming.java_
// FILE:            Colors.java
// PURPOSE:         Chapter 1 lablet, new version
// VERSION:         1.2
// TARGET:          Java v1.1 or higher
// UPDATE HISTORY:  1.2 5/18/99 changed to action commands
//                  1.1 8/27/98 changed to v1.1 compliance
//                  1.0 4/21/96
//=================================================================
//-------------------------- NOTES --------------------------
/*
   This example demonstrates some of the features of a Java applet. We
   obviously don't expect you to understand all (or even most) of the
   details—think of this as a prototype of what a typical applet looks
   like. For example, this text is a comment—since we've enclosed it in
   a "slash-star...star-slash" pair, the compiler will completely ignore
   it. There are three different kinds of comments in Java, all of which
   are used in the first 40 lines of this file.
*/
//-------------------------- IMPORTS --------------------------
/*
   A lot of what a Java program does depends on packages of classes that
   the nice people at Sun have written for us. If we're using any of
   these classes we have to "import" their packages so the compiler
   knows what words like "Applet" and "Button" mean.
*/
import java.applet.*;
import java.awt.*;
import java.awt.event.*;

//======================= Colors CLASS =========================
/**
 * The Colors class is an extension of the Applet class, meaning
 * that it has all the properties of the Applet class, along with
 * whatever data and methods we've added. The "implements
 * ActionListener" clause means that we've implemented a method
 * named actionPerformed(), so that our applet will respond to
 * actions like button clicks.
 */
public class Colors extends Applet implements ActionListener
{

//-------------------------- DATA --------------------------

   int  bgCode = 0,
        txtCode = 0;
   Font f = new Font("Helvetica",Font.BOLD,18);
```

```
//--------------------------- METHODS ---------------------------
    /**
     * This function is called into action when the applet first
     * starts running and is used to lay out all the objects and
     * initialize them if needed. Almost all applets have an init()
     * method. Here, we generate two new buttons, add them to our
     * applet, and register the fact that "this" class will be the
     * listener for button clicks.
     * Notice that here and throughout, we're calling a lot of
     * functions like add() and addActionListener() that are
     * defined elsewhere (which is why we needed the "import"
     * statements above).
     */
    public void init()
    {
       Button backButton = new Button("Background Color");
       add(backButton);
       backButton.setActionCommand("BKG");
       backButton.addActionListener(this);

       Button textButton = new Button("Text Color");
       add(textButton);
       textButton.setActionCommand("TXT");
       textButton.addActionListener(this);
    }

    /**
     * Respond to any click on a button. We've registered the
     * applet as an ActionListener for both buttons, so whenever an
     * action takes place this method will be invoked. What it
     * does is find out which of the two buttons triggered the
     * event and then execute the appropriate code for the button.
     */
    public void actionPerformed(ActionEvent e)
    {
       String cmd = e.getActionCommand(); // Who was clicked?
       if (cmd.equals("BKG")) // if backButton was, ...
       {
          bgCode = ++bgCode % 4;
          switch (bgCode)
          {
             case 0: setBackground(Color.cyan);     break;
             case 1: setBackground(Color.orange);   break;
             case 2: setBackground(Color.red);      break;
             case 3: setBackground(Color.green);    break;
          }
       }
       else if (cmd.equals("TXT")) // if textButton was...
       {
          txtCode = ++txtCode % 3;
       }
       repaint(); // Make the new colors show up.
    }

    /**
     * Perform any graphic updating that's needed. Buttons already
     * "know" how to draw themselves, for example, but the system
     * has no way of knowing that we intend to change the
     * background and text colors, so we have to provide that
     * functionality ourselves.
     */
```

```
public void paint(Graphics g)
{
    switch (txtCode)
    {
        case 0: g.setColor(Color.blue); break;
        case 1: g.setColor(Color.magenta); break;
        case 2: g.setColor(Color.black); break;
    }

    g.setFont(f);
    g.drawString("Goodbye world! Hello Java!", 30, 120);
}
}
```

1.6 Resources Online

Because of the intimate connection between Java and the Worldwide Web, you'll discover that there are abundant Java resources available on the Web. Here are some of the most important and useful ones. Crank up your browser and check them out.

- *http://java.sun.com/* Sun Microsystem's Java home page. Go to the source!
- *http://www.javasoft.com/nav/read/tutorial.html* Sun's own Java tutorial.
- *http://www.javasoft.com/products/jdk/1.1/docs/api/packages.html* Index of all Java packages. If you need the official word on any of the Java classes, this is where you should look.
- *http://www-a.gamelan.com/index.shtml* The Gamelan home page. A huge collection of links to Java sources.
- *http://sunsite.unc.edu:80/javafaq/links.html* Java links. Very nicely done.
- *http://www.javasoft.com/applets/* Java Applets. Javasoft is Sun's Java promotion arm. This is its source for applets. You can try them out (with a Java-enabled browser) and inspect the source code.
- *http://www.yahoo.com/Computers/Languages/Java/* Yahoo's Java sources.
- *http://infoweb.magi.com:80/~steve/java.html* The Programmer's Source. Another nice collection of Java links.

1.7 Summary

- A computer can execute programs only in its own machine language, and machine language is unsuitable for humans.
- A high-level language is designed for ease of use by programmers. To run a high-level language on a computer, we employ a translator program to translate the high-level source code into machine-executable object code.
- There are two forms of program translators: A compiler translates all of the source code into object code, which then can be executed. An interpreter interleaves translation with execution on a statement-by-statement basis. Compilers are generally harder to write than interpreters, but a complied program generally runs faster than an interpreted one, because translation is separated from execution.

- Worldwide Web pages are produced by making an HTML text document and then having the document displayed by a Web browser.
- A Java applet is a program that is designed to be embedded in a Web page. A Java application is an ordinary stand-alone program.
- A Java applet is first compiled into bytecode, a simple intermediate language, and the bytecode is then interpreted by the browser.
- A Java source file's name is given a `.java` extension; the complied bytecode file has the same name but has a `.class` extension.
- An applet is marked in an HTML document by using the APPLET tag, which provides the location of the `.class` file.
- HTML is not case-sensitive; Java source code is.
- The major organizing unit of a Java program is the class. A class is a collection of objects, entities with data, and methods for manipulating their data.
- In an object-oriented language like Java, a program is considered a collection of cooperating objects.
- One class can inherit the data descriptions and methods from another. In Java, inheritance is indicated by the keyword extends.
- The Java language may be augmented by including packages of classes. A programmer can create packages, and Java provides a collection of useful packages such as `java.awt`.

1.8   Exercises

1. What is a computer? According to your definition, which of the following are "computers"?

    a. A dog.

    b. A toaster.

    c. The solar system.

    d. You.

    e. "Malzel's Chessplayer," a nineteenth-century automaton shaped like a man sitting at a chessboard, purportedly constructed of clockwork gears, rods, cams, and levers, and reliably reported to be able to play chess as well as most people. Edgar Allen Poe wrote an essay about The Turk, as it was also known, but it was a real device (now lost), not one of Poe's fictions.

    f. A newborn baby.

2. We mentioned at the beginning of this chapter that using three binary digits to represent the operation of a machine language statement would allow us to have as many as eight operations.

    a. Why?

    b. How many different sequences of ten binary digits can we make?

    c. Many modern computers access memory locations by using 32 binary digits for the addresses. How many memory locations could a computer have if it used 32-bit addresses? How does this compare with the amount of memory in the computer you use?

3. We concentrated on two-value binary notation because modern electronic computers have two states that their hardware components can take: "on" and "off." Suppose someone were to discover a practical method for making hardware with the three states "foo," "bar," and "baz." Call a three-value digit a *trit*.

   a. If we used three trits to encode operations, how many different operations could our new computer have?

   b. How many trits would we need to provide at least as many sequences as we could make with 10 binary digits? (See Exercise 2.)

   c. With off-the-shelf components available today, we could build three-value hardware. We might decide that 0–2 volts would represent one state, 3–5 volts would represent another, and 7–9 volts would represent the third (assume that the hardware could be designed so that there would be no ambiguous voltages, such as 4 volts). What would be the advantages and disadvantages of such a three-value computer?

4. Java represents characters, such as q or Æ using a 16-bit code called *unicode*. Using 16 bits gives unicode the ability to encode any of 65,536 different characters. If you look at a keyboard, you'll see that even accounting for characters modified by shift or control-shift combinations, we still come up with under 300 possible characters. Explain why unicode seems to permit almost 200 times as many characters as we'll ever need.

5. Digital encoding of information is particularly useful for the Internet, because the same net hardware can be used for anything that can be encoded with 1s and 0s. Invent a protocol for encoding graphical information in binary form. In terms of your protocol, how true is the statement "a picture is worth a thousand words?"

6. Computer manufacturers and programmers count in a different way than ordinary people do. Whereas in English, K can be understood as an abbreviation of "kilo" (1000) and M as an abbreviation for "mega" (1,000,000), in computer-speak K represents 2^{10} (10 copies of 2, multiplied together) and "M" represents 2^{20}. Exactly how big are computer K's and M's?

7. Why do you suppose the designers of Java decided to employ a two-step translation process, using bytecode as an intermediate step?

8. What is a program? In terms of your definition, which of the following (if any) could be made into programs? Why or why not?

   a. 1. Go to Hollywood.
      2. Get a contract with a movie studio.
      3. Star in a hit movie.
      4. Become rich and famous.

   b. Given a list of numbers, do the following:
      1. Start with a number, *sum,* initially zero, and start at the beginning of the list.
      2. Add the current number in the list to *sum.*
      3. If there are any more numbers in the list, move to the next one and go back to step 2. Otherwise, go to step 4.
      4. Divide *sum* by the number of numbers in the list.

   c. Given a whole number, *n,* greater than zero, do the following:

     1. If *n* is even, divide it by 2. If *n* is odd, multiply it by 3 and add 1 to the result. In either case, replace *n* by the result.

     2. If the result isn't 1, go back to step 1.

9. There are dozens of computer languages in use today, ranging from the popular ones like COBOL, FORTRAN, BASIC, Pascal, C, and C++, to "niche" languages like Prolog and FORTH. How do you account for this multiplicity of languages? If you became King or Queen of the World and dictated a single language for all programs, how might your subjects respond?

10. What is a high-level language? Why do we have them?

11. Here is the syntax for braces, { and }, in Java. A brace expression is defined by these and only these rules.

   (1) { } is a brace expression.

   (2) If B is a brace expression, so is { B } .

   (3) If A and B are brace expressions, so is A B.

Which of the following are brace expressions?

   a. { { } { } }

   b. { { { } { }

   c. } { { { { } } }

   d. { { { } { } { { } } } }

12. Why is it redundant to say "Java applet"?

13. Can you write a Java applet or application without using classes at all?

14. Consider two classes of a single model of cars, Standard and Loaded. Cars in the Standard class are the cheap versions, and Loaded cars are the fancy ones, with six-way power seats, computerized navigation systems, walnut burl veneer, and so on. Which class would be an extension of the other?

15. Design a class hierarchy for motor vehicles, as we did for geometric objects.

In Exercises 16–21, provide descriptions of the classes you would use in programs that would perform the indicated tasks. These descriptions are very much like those you might get at the start of a programming job—vague and open-ended—so feel free to make any reasonable assumptions you want.

16. Control a conventional soda machine.

17. Implement an on-screen calculator. The user would "press" the buttons by moving the pointer to the necessary location and clicking the mouse button.

18. Control the action of a bank of elevators.

19. Manage the inventory of a fast-food restaurant.

20. Manage the payroll of a fast-food restaurant.

21. Operate a traffic light attached to sensors that could tell whether a car was waiting at the light.

1.9   Answers to Review Questions

1.1 To encode data in binary representation, we use a sequence of two-value symbols, often written 0 and 1.

1.2 Three binary digits can represent eight distinct values: 000, 001, 010, 011, 100, 101, 110, and 111.

1.3 An assembler is a program that makes a line-for-line translation from statements in a symbolic assembler language to statements in machine language.

1.4 Compilers and interpreters both translate from one language to another. A compiler translates an entire file, which then can be executed, much as you would do if you had to translate a short story from English to Spanish. An interpreter, on the other hand, translates in a statement-by statement fashion, somewhat like what goes on at the United Nations during a speech to the delegates.

2.1 If you were born after 1969, you are younger than the Internet. It's not likely that you are younger than the Worldwide Web; it was 4 years old at the time this book was written.

2.2 A browser is a program that fetches Web documents and displays them on the screen.

2.3 Platform independence, advertised by Sun as "write once, run anywhere," denotes an environment, like Java applets on the Web, in which one program will run on different kinds of computers with no additional effort on the part of the programmer. This saves the programmer from having to write one version of a program for Windows environments, an entirely different one for Macintoshes, another for computers running in a UNIX environment, and so on.

2.4 HTML is an acronym for "Hypertext Markup Language," a text-based language used to produce Web documents.

3.1 An applet is designed to be run in a Web browser or applet runner program; an application is a traditional "stand-alone" program that requires no "helper" program to run.

3.2 A compiler (like Sun's `javac`) translates Java source code into bytecode. Then a browser or applet runner interprets the bytecode into machine code.

3.3 Comments are ignored by the compiler; they are used by the programmer to explain what the source code is supposed to do.

3.4 To run an applet, a browser needs one or more bytecode files and an HTML document that refers to the bytecode file where execution will begin.

4.1 Java primitive types include integers, floating-point numbers, characters, and boolean types. Some examples of class types are `Graphics`, `Button`, `TextField`, and `Applet`.

4.2 A statement is the fundamental unit of execution in a program. Statements include expression statements, `if` statements, method calls, and declaration statements.

4.3 An object is an entity that contains its own data and methods for inspecting and manipulating its data. A class is a collection of objects—we could look at a class as providing a specification for all of its objects.

4.4 By extending one class from another, we can give the extending class access to all of the data and methods of the parent class, just as though they had been written into the extending class. This not only saves typing but also enables us to organize our thinking by considering one class as "a kind of" another.

4.5 Strictly speaking, no. The `Graphics` class is defined in the `java.awt` package and isn't part of the Java language itself, in the sense that method calls are, for example.

CHAPTER TWO

APPLETS

If you've had some experience with programming languages like BASIC, C, or Pascal, you'll discover that programming in Java is somewhat different from what you're used to. First, as we mentioned earlier, Java is an object-oriented language. This means that we think of a Java program as a collection of cooperating objects, rather than primarily as a list of instructions to be executed in some clearly defined order. In addition, Java comes with a rich collection of classes that we can use to make our programs visually interesting. We'll explore these two themes in this chapter.

Objectives

In this chapter, we will

- Use the `Applet` class to illustrate the properties common to all Java classes.
- Discuss the way we use classes and their methods to design object-oriented programs.
- Begin our discussion of the classes in the `java.awt` package.
- Introduce several of the Java classes that can be used to produce graphical images.

2.1 The `Applet` Class

As we saw in Chapter 1, an applet is a kind of program that is designed to be run within a Java-aware environment like a Web browser or an applet runner. An applet, unlike a Java application, isn't a traditional stand-alone program but, rather, is a class that is loaded and executed by another program. We begin our discussion of Java programming by talking about applets—first because they serve as the source of every Java Web program and second because applets illustrate the fundamental properties of all Java classes. In what follows, we'll build several applets, explaining what we've done and gradually adding features.

Learning from a Simple Applet

We'll begin by recalling the ultrasimple applet we used in Chapter 1.

```java
import java.applet.*;
import java.awt.*;

public class Hello extends Applet
// Just about the simplest Java applet anyone can write.
{
```

```
   public void paint(Graphics g)
   {
      g.drawString("Hi!", 20, 10);
   }
}
```

As we saw, all this does is display the string "Hi!" in the space the browser has reserved for the applet. This is something of an abuse of the power of Java, we'll admit. The applet is completely static, and it doesn't do anything (except consume computer resources) that we couldn't do far easier with basic HTML. It does, however, illustrate quite a lot about Java classes and is worth studying for that reason alone. Let's go through it line-by line.

The first two lines,

```
import java.applet.*;
import java.awt.*;
```

inform the Java compiler that we will be using classes from the packages `java.applet` and `java.awt`. The first package contains the definitions for the `Applet` class, along with some other classes (`AppletContext`, `AppletStub`, and `AudioClip`) that are of no concern to us here. We need these `import` declarations for a somewhat subtle reason: Because a Java program is composed of a collection separately compiled files, there would be no reason to expect that the compiler would recognize any of the externally defined names, such as `Applet`, while translating our program file. All we're doing here is saying to the compiler, "If you come across a name in this file that you don't recognize, try looking for its definition in the `java.applet` and `java.awt` packages."

The star (*) at the end of the package name is simply a "wild card" marker, telling the compiler to look for names among all the classes in the package. Our sample never used any of the names from `AppletContext` or the other definitions, so we could have made the `import` statement clearer by writing

```
import java.applet.Applet;
```

Some people prefer this form; the only downside is that in a big package like `java.awt`, it's easy to leave out a class name inadvertently, thereby confusing the compiler. We prefer the wildcard form because it doesn't add any overhead to the running of the applet and makes mistakes less likely.

The **import** statement allows you to use names of classes and methods defined in other packages. It takes the form

```
import packageName.*;
```

or

```
import packageName.className;
```

The semicolons at the end are required, and the **import** statement must appear before any of the names defined in the package are used (this is why we always place all **import** statements at the beginning of the file).

The next line in our program,

```
public class Hello extends Applet
```

is the beginning of the definition of our `Hello` class, the rest of which is enclosed in the pair of braces `{` and `}`. The keyword `public` allows access to this class from outside the file. We'll have more to say about access control later. The remainder of that line indicates that what follows is the definition of a class of our own, named `Hello`, which is an extension of the library `Applet` class. This means that our `Hello` class is in fact an `Applet` and inherits all 22 of the `public` methods of the `Applet` class, along with any additional ones we decide to define.

We named our class `Hello`, but we could have chosen any legal Java name we wished, as long as it hadn't already been defined. For example, we could have called our class `Fred`, although that's not very descriptive, but we would have gotten into big trouble with the compiler if we had chosen to call our class `Panel`, `false`, or `if`, because those names have predefined meanings in Java.

> Names of Java classes, methods, and variables (collectively known as identifiers) can be any strings of letters, digits, and the underscore character, as long as they start with a letter.

For example, `limitValue`, `x`, `switch72b`, and `a_long_name` are all legal identifiers, whereas `2wayStreet`, `my variable`, and `#*&!!` are not. Java identifiers are case-sensitive, so `limitValue`, `LIMITVALUE`, `limitvalue`, and `lImItVaLuE` are all considered different names.

The next line,

```
// Just about the simplest Java applet anyone can write.
```

is a comment. The Java compiler ignores everything from the two slashes to the end of the line, and this gives us a way us to put in explanatory notes. Remember that every program has two audiences: the compiler and the person reading the source code. The compiler quite literally is blind to comments, but they are invaluable to people reading your code (including yourself a week or more later—it's amazing how often you can find yourself saying, "Now what in the world did I intend here?").

Comments in Java can be inserted in two different ways.[1] A single-line comment begins with two slashes, `//`, and extends to the end of the line, like this:

```
// Set up the initial values
height = 0.0; // Measured in meters above sea level
```

Note in the second line how we follow a statement with an explanation. For longer

---

[1] There is also a third type, known as the *documentation comment,* which we use before every class and method definition. These comments allow a program called `javadoc` to produce HTML documentation of your classes, just as you see when you look at Sun's online documentation.

comments, Java will also ignore anything between the pair /* and */, no matter how far apart the markers are. Here's an example:

```
/* This method will return the maximum of the
   values of its three arguments x, y, and z. */
```

Style Tips

1. It is possible to go overboard with comments, but it's far better to err on the side of too many than too few.

2. Some comments, however, are not worth including, like this one:

```
x = 0;     // set x to zero
```

Well-written programs should be *self-documenting* as much as possible, which means that the code should explain itself.

3. Get in the habit of including comments while you're writing code. This way, you don't run the risk of later forgetting what you intended to say.

You can't nest comments within comments of the same type, but you can enclose a // comment within a /* . . . */ pair. This is useful if you want to remove code from your program temporarily for test purposes. Rather than deleting the questionable lines, simply enclose them between /* and */, as long as the lines you enclosed didn't contain those delimiters.

Review Questions

1.1 What is the purpose of an import statement?

1.2 What is an identifier? What are the rules for legal Java identifiers?

1.3 What is the difference between // and /* . . . */ comments?

2.2 Methods, Inheritance, and Overriding

Having completed the import portion, the head of the Hello class definition, and a comment line, we come to the body of the class itself:

```
{
   public void paint(Graphics g)
   {
      g.drawString("Hi!", 20, 10);
   }
}
```

In this simple example, the class definition consists of a single method definition for the paint() method. What's going on here? We're providing our applet with a method that will control what appears whenever the browser or applet viewer decides that the applet needs to be drawn. To do that, our `paint()` expects to be given a `Graphics` object named `g` and invokes `g`'s `drawString()` method to draw the appropriate message on the screen at the coordinates provided.

That's pretty confusing. If you're thinking of any of the following questions, pat yourself on the back for diligence and rest assured that we'll explain everything shortly.

▲ What's the purpose of the parentheses?
▲ What's a `Graphics` object?
▲ `void`? What's that?
▲ What are the braces for?
▲ What's the `g`. doing before the `drawString()`?
▲ Is it too late to drop this course?

Java Methods

A method in Java is a named sequence of statements that perform some task. A method takes in a (perhaps empty) collection of information and uses that information to do its job, optionally sending back a piece of information. Think of a method as a small factory: In the right end (the arguments, that part enclosed in parentheses) you put some raw materials and some money, the factory grinds away noisily, and out of the left end comes a custom-built toaster.

There are two slightly different kinds of methods in Java. In the first kind, the method is intended to take in whatever arguments it needs, do the statements in its body, and then return control to that part of the program where it was first invoked. Such a method is characterized by the fact that its header begins with the keyword `void` and is defined in this form:

```
void methodName(list of arguments)
// Nothing comes out the left end--we're only interested in the
// noise the factory makes
{
    list of statements, enclosed by braces
}
```

The second kind of method acts almost exactly as the first. The only difference is that this kind of method returns to its point of invocation with some information. The type of information it returns is indicated by placing a type name at the start of the method head, like this:

```
returnTypeName methodName(list of arguments)
// Something comes out the left end, which we'll use later.
{
    list of statements, enclosed by braces
}
```

For the moment, we'll devote our attention to the first form, the one with the `void` return type. Such a method is *called* into action by telling an object to perform

method call

its method, using the object's name, a dot, and the name of the method, along with any arguments the method needs to do its job. That's what we're doing in the line

```
g.drawString("Hi!", 20, 10);
```

> Every method is defined in some class. To call a method, we must specify the object whose method we'll use by writing
>
> ```
> objectName.methodName(argument list);
> ```
>
> The arguments used in the call have to match those in the method definition in order, number, and type.

`drawString()` is a method that belongs to the `Graphics` class (part of the `java.awt` package). Because `g` is a `Graphics` object, we are requesting `g` to execute its own `drawString` method. In doing so, we're giving the method the string we want it to draw on the screen, along with two integers that tell the method how many pixels[2] from the left and top edges of the applet we want the drawing to start.

In Figure 2.1 we provide an illustration of (roughly speaking) the interaction between a method call and its definition in a class. When we call a method, execution jumps from the place of calling to the place where the method is defined. As this happens, the actual arguments are sent to fill in the placeholder formal arguments in the method definition. Then the method code is executed, and upon completion, execution returns to the statement immediately following the method call.

In Java, every method definition consists of a collection of calls to other methods, along with some other statements that are invoked in place, without hopping out to another method.

We've answered all the questions we posed earlier, but there's still one we've avoided until now. Where is `paint()` called? You'll come to see that a lot of action in a Java program, particularly in an applet, takes place behind the scenes. In our sample applet, it's the responsibility of the browser or applet runner to decide when `paint()` should be called. It might be when the applet first appears on the screen, or when the user decides to scroll or resize the browser window—the applet doesn't know and we shouldn't care. All we have to do is understand that there will be times when a method named `paint()` will be called and to take steps to make sure that when it is, it will do the right thing. We leave it to the applet runner to decide when to call `paint()` and to provide the necessary `Graphics` object as the argument.

Inheritance and Overriding

As we have said, the system that's running our applet will from time to time decide to call a method named `paint()` and will pass it a `Graphics` object on which to do

---

[2]A pixel (from *pic*ture *el*ement) is one dot on the screen. The size of a pixel varies from monitor to monitor but is generally about 1/72 of an inch (or 0.39 millimeter).

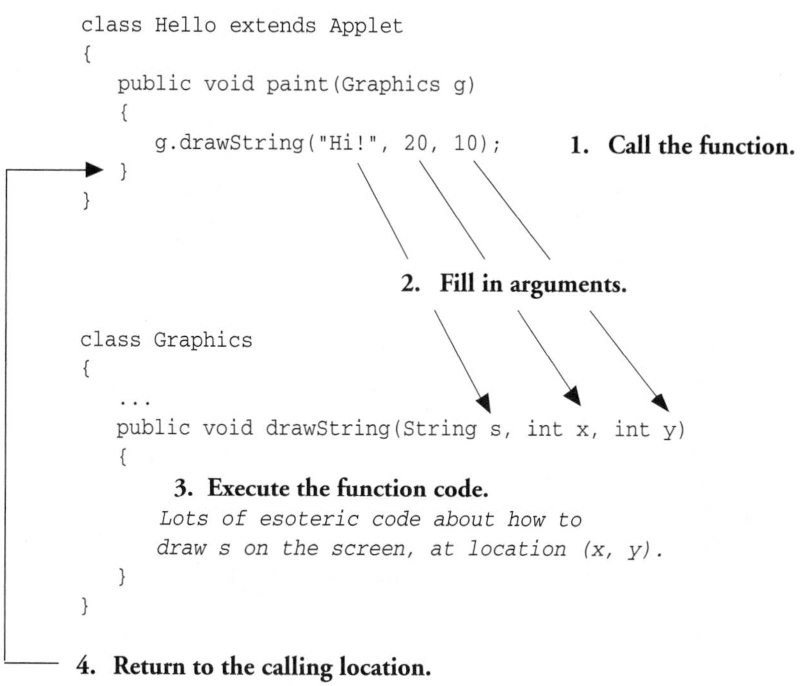

```
class Hello extends Applet
{
    public void paint(Graphics g)
    {
        g.drawString("Hi!", 20, 10);
    }
}
```

1. Call the function.

2. Fill in arguments.

```
class Graphics
{
    ...
    public void drawString(String s, int x, int y)
    {
```
3. Execute the function code.
```
        Lots of esoteric code about how to
        draw s on the screen, at location (x, y).
    }
}
```

4. Return to the calling location.

Figure 2.1

What happens when a method is called.

the painting. We obviously have to provide the statements inside the paint()
method, because the system has no way of knowing what we want to happen when
painting is required. Let's consider what would happen if we forgot to write a
paint() method, or if we had an applet that didn't need to do any on-screen painting, like this:

```
import java.applet.*;
import java.awt.*;

public class NoPaint extends Applet
{
    Button bttn = new Button("Click me");

    /**
     * init() is an Applet method that's called when the
     * applet is first loaded. Here, we're adding the
     * button to the applet, so it will be visible.
     */
    public void init()
    {
        add(bttn);
    }
}
```

This is another somewhat silly applet, (it contains a button that doesn't do anything), but it's perfectly legal, as you can demonstrate by entering, compiling, and running it. How does the system deal with the fact that we haven't provided a `paint()` method? Calling a method that isn't defined is an error and will bring the compiling to a screeching halt, so the fact that this sample compiles and runs must mean that somewhere there's a `paint()` method that's being called. Where is it? Is it in the `Applet` class? You can look through the documentation of the `Applet` class at the end of this chapter to see that it is not.

If you look through the documentation, though, you'll discover that the `Applet` class extends something called the `Panel` class, whatever that is, so an `Applet` object has access to all of `Panel`'s accessible methods. We'll describe the `Panel` class in Chapter 4. But is `paint()` defined there? No. Continuing our search, we find that every `Panel` object is also a member of the `Container` class, but `paint()` isn't among the `Container` methods, either. Finally, we discover that the `Container` class extends `Component`, and that's where we find the first mention of `paint()`.

If you think about it, that's where we'd expect `paint()` to be, way up near the top of the class hierarchy, part of which we illustrate in Figure 2.2.

class hierarchy

Because drawing an object to the screen is such a fundamentally important task, it makes good sense that it should be in a method that would be inherited by all the classes that contain drawable objects, such as buttons, fields to hold text, panels to hold other components, and (finally) applets.

override

Each of these "paint-able" objects, though, has to be drawn in an entirely different way, so we can't expect there to be an ultraclever `paint()` method up in `Component` that knows how to draw everything. Instead, what we have to do is *override* `Component`'s `paint()` method, describing what it is expected to do for our particular class, `Hello`. That's exactly what we did—and that's all we did—in the

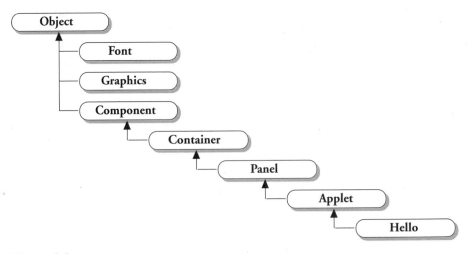

Figure 2.2

A portion of Java's class hierarchy.

definition of our `Hello` class. Accordingly, when our applet is asked to draw itself, the call will be to `paint()`, but it will be our own `paint()` method, if any, that's invoked. That's why our `NoPaint` applet didn't need a `paint()` method. The system looked for the definition, didn't find it, and then started looking upward in the class hierarchy until it found a `paint()` method, in the `Component` class. `Component`'s `paint()` method doesn't do anything, but it exists, and that's enough to keep the compiler happy.

> If a method definition cannot be found in an object's class definition, it will be sought by looking upward in the class hierarchy.

In what is to come, we'll be doing a lot of this overriding of methods from super-classes. As a matter of fact, for the first four chapters, this activity will occupy a considerable portion of our time. Rest assured that we won't expect you to memorize several dozen classes and their several hundred methods. A lot of the methods out there are never overridden and are called behind the scenes, so the methods we'll actually have to deal with are fairly few in number. To give you a sample of what's to come, the next section offers an introduction to a few of the classes we'll use just as they come "out of the box."

Review Questions

2.1 What is a method?

2.2 Methods appear in two places: in a class definition, where they are defined, and in a statement in a method, where they are called. In which of these two places do we use formal arguments and in which do we use actual arguments?

2.3 Describe the inheritance hierarchy of the classes from `Applet` to `Object`.

2.3 Graphical Programming

The `java.awt` package contains 61 classes and interfaces, all of which are devoted in one way or another to producing applets and applications with graphical user interfaces (GUIs). In this section, we'll introduce some of the classes that can be used in an applet's `paint()` method to spruce up the applet's look. In this and all subsequent chapters, we will provide, in a reference appendix at the end of the chapter, detailed summaries of each class we discuss.

GUI

Class references

Before we get into describing some of the graphics-related classes, we should mention how Java measures locations for drawing purposes. Every pixel on the screen is described by two integer coordinates, a horizontal one (often called x), measured from the left edge of the applet frame (or from the left edge of whatever object we're drawing in) and a vertical one (often called y), measured from the top of the applet frame or component, as we illustrate in Figure 2.3.

If you've had any experience with the Cartesian coordinates used in analytic geometry, this will take a bit of getting used to, because in Java the origin, the (0, 0)

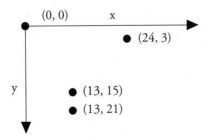

Figure 2.3

Java's graphical coordinate system, using (**x**, **y**) pairs.

point, is in the upper-left corner, and the vertical coordinates increase, rather than decrease, as you move down.

The Graphics Class

This class consists of objects that are used to draw on the display. As we have noted, an applet will have a Graphics object associated with it, which you can access within paint() because it is provided as an argument. Once you have the Graphics object, you can use its methods to draw anything you want, limited only by your creativity (and your patience). Here's a list of the more useful Graphics methods. There are several we've omitted, either because they're not often used or because we have to lay some additional groundwork before we can fully explain them. You can find most of the omissions at the end of the chapter.

```
void clearRect(int x, int y, int width, int height)
```

This clears a rectangle by painting it in the background color. The arguments are integers, like 2 and 450, and represent the coordinates of the upper-left corner of the rectangle and the width and height of the rectangle. See Figure 2.4 on page 49 for an illustration of the meanings of the coordinates of a rectangle.

```
void draw3DRect(int x, int y, int width, int height, boolean raised)
```

This draws a rectangular border of the specified dimensions, shaded in the background color to look three-dimensional. If the argument raised has the value true, the border is painted as though it were raised out of the surface; if it has the value false, the border appears as though it is depressed.

```
void drawLine(int x1, int y1, int x2, int y2)
```

This draws a line from the point with coordinates (x1, y1) to the point with coordinates (x2, y2).

```
void drawOval(int x, int y, int width, int height)
```

This draws an unfilled oval within the bounding rectangle specified by the arguments.

```
void drawRect(int x, int y, int width, int height)
```

This draws an unfilled rectangle with position and size given by the arguments.

```
void drawString(String s, int x, int y)
```

This draws a string of characters with its baseline (the lower edge of letters like m and A that have no "descenders") starting at coordinates x and y.

```
void fill3DRect(int x, int y, int w, int h, boolean raised)
void fillArc(int x, int y, int w, int w, int stA, int arcA)
void fillOval(int x, int y, int w, int h)
void fillRect(int x, int y, int w, int h)
void fillRoundRect(int x, int y, int w, int h,int aW, int aH)
```

These five work just like their "draw" counterparts, except that they also fill the enclosed region in the current drawing color.

```
void setColor(Color c)
```

This sets the current drawing color to the color specified in the argument. The drawing color stays fixed until it is changed by another call to setColor(). We'll see shortly how the Color class is defined.

Using the Graphics Class
(and Learning Some Programming in the Process)

Here's a simple example of what we can do with the Graphics methods. One drawback to the drawing routines is that they don't provide us with any way of changing the line width. Suppose we want to make an applet that draws a logo consisting of three squares like this:

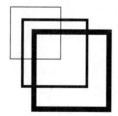

A clever way of increasing the line width is to draw several rectangles, one inside the other. To do this, all we have to do is increase the x- and y-coordinates by 1 at each stage, while reducing the width and height by 2. We do this as many times as we need to make the desired thicknesses of lines. For example, to draw a 100-by-100-pixel square with its upper-left corner at (50, 80) with line thickness 3, all we have to do is use the following three method calls

```
g.drawRect(50, 80, 100, 100);
g.drawRect(51, 81, 98, 98);
g.drawRect(52, 82, 96, 96);
```

Here we show what the complete applet would look like. We encourage you to start up your Java compiler and try it out.

```java
/**
 * This is a sample applet to try some of the
 * Graphics methods. It draws a sequence of three
 * squares with increasing sizes and border
 * thicknesses.
 */
import java.applet.*;
import java.awt.*;

public class Logo extends Applet
{
    public void paint(Graphics g)
    {
        // Draw the first square
        g.drawRect(50, 80, 100, 100);

        // Draw the next square, offset from the first
        // by 25, 50 pixels larger, with line width 2.
        g.drawRect(75, 105, 150, 150);
        g.drawRect(76, 106, 148, 148);

        // Draw the last square, offset from the second
        // by 25, 50 pixels larger, with line width 3.
        g.drawRect(100, 130, 200, 200);
        g.drawRect(101, 131, 198, 198);
        g.drawRect(102, 132, 196, 196);
    }
}
```

This certainly does what we need, but there's a wide gulf between a program that merely works and one that's easy to read and modify. One problem with this program is that it has entirely too many "magic numbers"—numbers with no immediately obvious meaning. Observe that the second and third squares are offset from the first and second by a common amount, 25, and that the size likewise increases by a common amount, 50. We can provide named storage for these two numbers. While we're at it, let's also use three more *local variables* to hold the x- and y-coordinates of the upper-left corner of the first square and the initial size. Our paint() routine would now look like this:

```java
public void paint(Graphics g)
{
    int x = 50;         // x coord. of first square
    int y = 80;         // y coord. of first square
    int size = 100;     // size of first square
    int OFFSET = 25;    // x, y offsets of squares
    int INCREMENT = 50; // size increases of squares
    // Draw the first square
    g.drawRect(x, y, size, size);

    // Increment the start coordinates and size
```

```
        // and draw a border-width-2 square.
        x = x + OFFSET;
        y = y + OFFSET;
        size = size + INCREMENT;
        g.drawRect(x, y, size, size);
        g.drawRect(x + 1, y + 1, size - 2, size - 2);

        // Do it again, for the third square
        x = x + OFFSET;
        y = y + OFFSET;
        size = size + INCREMENT;
        g.drawRect(x, y, size, size);
        g.drawRect(x + 1, y + 1, size - 2, size - 2);
        g.drawRect(x + 2, y + 2, size - 4, size - 4);
    }
```

Granted, it's quite a bit longer than the original, but it's a lot easier to read and modify. To change the start coordinates, size, OFFSET, and INCREMENT would require modifying five numbers and almost no thought, whereas in the original version, we would have to modify carefully 24 different numbers!

Programming Tip

> Avoid magic numbers as much as possible. It's generally much better to devote a variable to the task of storing a value, rather than "hard-wiring" it in.

All we're doing is providing five integer variables within the paint() method to hold the numbers we need. We'll talk more about variables in Chapter 5; for now, all we need to do is mention that we must declare a variable before we use it. Declaring a variable requires us to specify what type of information it will hold, which is why we preface each variable with the type name int: (whole numbers in Java are called ints). If we want, we can set the initial value stored in the variable, too, as we do above, by using = and the initial value at the end of the declaration.

the int type

> A variable declaration looks like
>
>   *typeName identifier;*
>
> or
>
>   *typeName identifier = initialValue;*
>
> Variables must be declared before they are used, and a variable declared in a method has meaning only within that method (and so wouldn't be recognized in some other method).

Note that Java allows you to perform arithmetic operations, like x + 2, and that the *assignment* operator, =, evaluates whatever expression is on the right and stores the result in the variable on the left. In our example, the statement

```
x = x + OFFSET;
```

computes the value of x + OFFSET and then places that value in the variable x. In simple terms, this statement increases the value of x by the amount OFFSET.

Before we leave this example, note that we used lowercase names for the variables x, y, and size, which changed during the method's execution, and uppercase names for INCREMENT and OFFSET, which didn't. This is a fairly common convention.

Style Tip

Build as much information as you can into your program by adopting consistent standards of naming. Many programmers use ALL_CAPS for variables that are not going to change their values during execution and lowerCase or lower_case_with_underscores for variables whose values might change.

The Color Class

This class's objects represent colors. It contains 13 constant values that can be used when you want black, blue, cyan, darkGray, gray, green, lightGray, magenta, orange, pink, red, white, or yellow. To use one of these constants, you need to inform the compiler that the identifier belongs to the Color class, so you attach the class name to the front of the color name, along with a dot. In other words, to draw a green rectangle, we could use Graphics' setColor() method, along with the color name, and then make a call to fillRect(), like this

```
g.setColor(Color.green);      // assuming g is a Graphics object
g.fillRect(10, 20, 100, 200); // draw a rectangle (in green)
```

Colors in Java are described by a model that specifies the amount of red, green, and blue, as though the color were made by shining three lights of the given base colors. To specify a color, you can specify the brightness of each of the components as an integer between 0 and 255, where 0 represents none of the component (the light is off). The color 0, 0, 0 in this RGB model, then, is black, 128, 128, 128 is a medium gray, and 255, 0, 128 is fuchsia (a red with a bit of blue in it). For reasons that will be clear in the next chapter, you declare a Color variable by using the operator new. In our example above, for instance, we could have painted a fuchsia rectangle by using a Color variable myColor:

```
Color myColor = new Color(255, 0, 128);  // a new Color object,
g.setColor(myColor);                     // used here
g.fillRect(10, 20, 100, 200);
```

We could have accomplished the same thing, by the way, by defining the color "on the fly," just as we sent it into the argument of setColor():

```
g.setColor(new Color(255, 0, 128));
g.fillRect(10, 20, 100, 200);
```

The Font Class

Just as the `Color` class is used to represent colors, objects in the `Font` class represent the fonts used for textual displays. There are five basic fonts that will be supported on any platform on which Java is running; their names are SansSerif, Serif, Monospaced, Dialog, and DialogInput. Because of copyright considerations, version 1.1 of Java changed the names of some of the fonts, but you can probably get away with using Helvetica for SansSerif, TimesRoman for Serif, and Courier for Monospaced. Although the older names are still supported, they have become *deprecated*, which means that they may not be recognized in future versions of the language. Installed fonts vary from computer to computer, so you shouldn't expect a particular font to look exactly the same on all systems, but they should be close to the appearances below.

Old Name	Appearance	New Name
Helvetica	Helvetica	SansSerif
TimesRoman	TimesRoman	Serif
Courier	Courier	Monospaced
Dialog	Dialog	
DialogInput	DialogInput	

Just as with colors, there are some `Font` class constants, used in this case to specify the style of the font. These are `Font.BOLD`, `Font.ITALIC`, and `Font.PLAIN`. Also as with colors, you make a `Font` object by using the `new` operator and a `Font` *constructor*, to which you send as arguments the font name, style, and size. Newly constructed `Font` objects are often used with `Graphics`' `setFont()` method, like this:

```
g.setFont(new Font("SansSerif", Font.BOLD, 12));
g.drawString("This is Helvetica bold-12", 10, 20);
```

You can combine styles by adding them, so if we used the expression `Font.BOLD` `+ Font.ITALIC` as the second argument in a `Font` constructor, the text would be displayed as ***bold italic***. The size argument is (more or less) the height in pixels. Finally, if you specify a font name that isn't installed, Java will choose a default font on its own. Unfortunately, there is no way for an applet to determine what fonts are resident on the machine on which it is running.[3]

Positions and Sizes: The Classes `Point`, `Dimension`, and `Rectangle`

Because drawing often requires a considerable amount of coordinate calculation, Java provides three classes that are useful for manipulating collections of dimensional values. These are the classes `Point`, `Dimension`, and `Rectangle`.

---

[3]You could test for the presence of a particular `font` by using the Font method `getFont()`, but the details are beyond the scope of this text.

The `Point` class is the simplest of the three. As we saw in Chapter 1, a `Point` object contains two integers, `x` and `y`. As with the rest of the dimensional classes, the purpose of the `Point` class is to allow us to make a single object that contains several pieces of information. There are three constructors used with the new operator to make a new `Point` object.

Point()
Constructs a new `Point` object with both `x` and `y` coordinates equal to zero.

Point(int x, int y)
Constructs a new `Point` object by specifying the `x` and `y` coordinates.

Point(Point p)
Known as a *copy constructor*, this makes a new `Point` object with coordinates equal to those of the argument `p`.

There are a few methods we can use to manipulate points. They're far less often used than the constructors and the `x` and `y` values, so we'll tuck their descriptions away in the end-of-chapter reference.

In one respect, the `Point` class is somewhat unusual. As you'll see when we talk about access in more detail, we nearly always make an object's data `private` so that it can't be seen except by an object in the same class. In the case of `Point`'s `x` and `y` data, though, Java has departed from this rule and has made both data members `public`. This means we can write code like this:

```
Point myPoint = new Point(0, 3);
myPoint.x = 2;   // unusual--we can get to the data directly
myPoint.y = -1;
```

The `Dimension` class is very much like `Point` in that it contains two integer data members, both of which are publicly accessible. The only real difference between the two classes is in their intent: The two integers in `Point` are supposed to represent coordinates of a point, whereas the integers in a `Dimension` object, named `width` and `height`, are intended to represent the horizontal and vertical extent of some geometric object. This class has even fewer methods than `Point`. As with our discussion of `Point`, we've left the method descriptions for the references section.

Like the `Point` class, the `Dimension` class has three constructors:

Dimension()
Constructs a new `Dimension` object with both `width` and `height` equal to zero.

Dimension(int w, int h)
Constructs a new `Dimension` object with data members `width = w` and `height = h`.

Dimension(Dimension d)
Another copy constructor, this builds a new `Dimension` object having the same `width` and `height` values as those of the argument `d`.

The `Rectangle` class is a combination of the two we've already discussed. A `Rectangle` object is described by a point (the x and y coordinates of the upper-left corner) and a dimension (its width and height). These four member data are named x, y, `width`, and `height`, and all are publicly accessible via the usual dot notation. Figure 2.4 illustrates how these four member data combine to describe a `Rectangle` object.

There are seven constructors for `Rectangles`—and hence a good deal of flexibility in how we can make a new `Rectangle` object. The three you'll use most are

`Rectangle``(int x, int y, int w, int h)`
Constructs a `Rectangle` from four `ints`, specifying the upper-left corner (x and y), the width (w) and height (h).

`Rectangle``(Point p, Dimension d)`
Constructs a `Rectangle` anchored at the `Point` given by p and having `width` and `height` given by d.

`Rectangle``(Rectangle r)`
Makes a new `Rectangle` having the same anchor and dimensions as r.

Rectangles are used quite a lot in Java programs to describe bounding regions of many objects and to set the *clipping region* in which drawing is allowed to take place. For that reason, this class is provided with a rich collection of methods for inspecting and manipulating its objects.

`boolean` **`contains`**`(int x, int y)`
Tests whether the point (x, y) is in this rectangle. If it is, returns `true`; otherwise returns `false`.

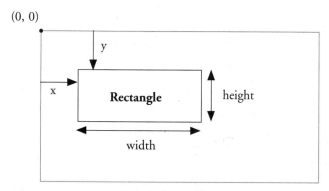

Coordinate system

Figure 2.4

Member data describing a `Rectangle`.

Point **getLocation()**
Returns a Point with the same coordinates as the anchor of this rectangle.

Dimension **getSize()**
Returns a Dimension object with the same width and height of this rectangle.

void **grow**(int h, int v)
Changes the size of this rectangle by expanding the width by h on both sides and expanding the height by v on the top and bottom, Note that *expanding* isn't quite accurate: If either h or v is negative, this rectangle will contract in the appropriate direction.

void **setBounds**(int x, int y, int w, int h)
Changes this rectangle's anchor and dimensions to those specified by the arguments.

void **setLocation**(int x, int y)
Changes this rectangle's anchor to (x, y).

void **setSize**(int w, int h)
Changes this rectangle's dimensions to w by h, keeping the anchor fixed.

Review Questions

3.1 If g is a Graphics object, what is accomplished by the following method call?
g.fillRect(0, 10, 20, 30);
3.2 What color is represented by the RGB triple 255, 255, 255?
3.3 How would you declare a new Point object, pt, representing (10, 20)?
3.4 What four variables are owned by every Rectangle object?

2.4   Hands On

In the Lablet for this chapter, we'll use some of the classes we've discussed to build an applet that will do some simple drawing on the display. The applet draws a blue vortex on a black background, along with a text message in white with a drop shadow. Unlike most of the Lablets to come, this one has several parts and thus provides a case study of program development.

Pass 1: Painting 101

If you look at Figure 2.5, you'll see that the basic idea is pretty simple—we'll draw a black background, then draw a collection of nested ovals in different shades of blue, and finish by drawing a message with a drop shadow, white on blue. To give fairly smooth shading while keeping the programming (and exposition) to a reasonable level, we decided to use ten ovals.

   The only tricky part was deciding how to size the ovals. We began with an applet of 500 by 350 pixels and decided to leave left and top margins of 50 and bot-

Figure 2.5

The Wormhole applet in action.

tom and right margins of 100. This gave us an outer oval of width 350 and height 200, anchored at (50, 50), as in Figure 2.6.

We decided to align the rest of the ovals so that they would have the same right-end coordinate and would be centered vertically. After some fiddling, we decided that each inner oval would be offset 30 pixels right and inset 10 pixels top and bottom from the immediately outer one. This gave us the bounds we list in Table 2.1.

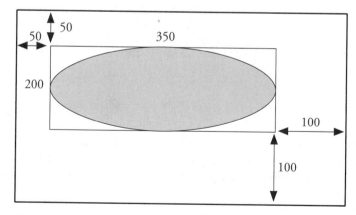

Figure 2.6

Aligning the outer oval.

Table 2.1   Bounds for the ten nested ovals

x	y	Width	Height
50	50	350	200
80	60	320	180
110	70	290	160
140	80	260	140
170	90	230	120
200	100	200	100
230	100	170	80
260	110	140	60
290	120	110	40
320	130	80	20

As always, we begin with a documentation block describing the purposes of the class definition it contains (in this case, just the class Wormhole).

```
//================================================================
// PROJECT:          _programming.java_
// FILE:             Wormhole.java
// PURPOSE:          Chapter 2 lablet, first pass
// VERSION:          1.0
// TARGET:           Java v1.1 or above
// UPDATE HISTORY:   1.0   4/3/99
//================================================================

//-------------------------- NOTES --------------------------
/*
    This works best if the applet size is set to 500 x 350.
*/
```

The customary collection of import statements refers to the ones we expect.

```
import java.applet.*;
import java.awt.*;
```

Next, we come to the definition of the only class in this file, the subclass, Wormhole, of Applet. It's worth pointing out here that we've decided to adopt the same naming convention that Java does: Class names have initial capitals, whereas other identifiers, such as variable and method names, do not. The class definition contains just a paint() method.

```
public class Wormhole extends Applet
{
    /**
```

```
* Do all the drawing.
*/
public void paint(Graphics g)
{
    // Draw the black background.
    g.setColor(Color.black);
    g.fillRect(0, 0, 500, 350);

    // Draw ten nested "holes."
    g.setColor(new Color(0, 0, 25));
    g.fillOval(50, 50, 350, 200);

    g.setColor(new Color(10, 10, 50));
    g.fillOval(80, 60, 320, 180);

    g.setColor(new Color(20, 20, 75));
    g.fillOval(110, 70, 290, 160);

    g.setColor(new Color(30, 30, 100));
    g.fillOval(140, 80, 260, 140);

    g.setColor(new Color(40, 40, 125));
    g.fillOval(170, 90, 230, 120);

    g.setColor(new Color(50, 50, 150));
    g.fillOval(200, 100, 200, 100);

    g.setColor(new Color(60, 60, 175));
    g.fillOval(230, 110, 170, 80);

    g.setColor(new Color(70, 70, 200));
    g.fillOval(260, 120, 140, 60);

    g.setColor(new Color(80, 80, 225));
    g.fillOval(290, 130, 110, 40);

    g.setColor(new Color(90, 90, 250));
    g.fillOval(320, 140, 80, 20);

    // Draw the text, in white with a blue drop shadow.
    g.setColor(Color.blue);
    g.setFont(new Font("TimesRoman", Font.BOLD, 36));
    g.drawString("On to Cydonia!", 22, 300);

    g.setColor(Color.white);
    g.drawString("On to Cydonia!", 20, 298);
    }
}
```

Note that we've set the color before each call to the `Graphics` method `fillOval()`, defining each time a color of our own. At each step, we turn up the red and blue components by 10 and the blue component by 25, obtaining successively brighter blues. The text message "On to Cydonia!" is painted by first drawing the shadow, at location (22, 300), and then drawing the white text on top of it, offset up and right by two pixels.

Pass 2: Clarifying by Complicating

Looking at what we wrote, we see that there are 70 unexplained numbers in the oval-drawing portion of the program alone. The program works—it compiles and runs to give just the picture we wanted—but there's a big difference between a program that runs and one that runs *and* is easy to understand and modify. First, without explanation, it's a fair amount of work just to figure out what all the numbers do, and second, even with judicious use of the text editor's cut-and-paste facility, it would be somewhat strenuous to change the *x*-offset from 30 to 25, for example. We can deal with this in the same way we did with the Logo applet in the previous section: by identifying some important values, storing them in variables, and expressing the "magic numbers" in terms of the values stored in the variables.

Let's take the *x*-coordinates of the anchor points of each oval as an example. Table 2.1 gives us 50, 80, 110, 140, 170, 200, 230, 260, 290, and 320 for the *x*-values of the anchors of the ovals. Each of these is obviously just 50 plus a multiple of the *x*-increment, 30, so we'll set up two integer variables, X0, containing 50, and X_INC, containing 30. Then the bounding *x*-coordinate of each oval is nothing more than X0 + n * X_INC, for n values 0 through 9.

If we do the same analysis for the other numbers in each call to setColor() and drawOval(), we'll have

x-coordinate:	X0 + n * X_INC
y-coordinate:	Y0 + n * Y_INC
Width:	W0 - n * X_INC
Height:	H0 - n * 2 * Y_INC
Color red, green:	n * RG_INC
Color blue:	n + 1) * BLUE_INC

Where Y0 is the initial y-coordinate, 50; Y_INC is the *y*-increment, 10; W0 is the initial oval width, 350; H0 is the initial oval height, 200; RG_INC is the increment for the red and green components of each color, 10; and BLUE_INC is the increment for the blue component, 25.

Our applet now starts like this (omitting the comment blocks for simplicity):

```
public class Wormhole extends Applet
{
    int X0 = 50,       // x-anchor: from left of applet
        Y0 = 50,       // y-anchor: from top of applet
        W0 = 350,      // initial width
        H0 = 200,      // initial height
        X_INC = 30,    // x-anchor increment
        Y_INC = 10,    // y-anchor increment
        RG_INC = 10,   // red-green increment
        BLUE_INC = 25; // blue increment
```

Immediately after the class header, we come to what are obviously the declarations of eight variables, of type int. These variables are not declared in any method but instead are declared at the topmost class level. Declaring them that way makes them what are known as *instance variables*, such as x and y in Point, rather than the local variables they would be if they had been declared in some method.

instance
variable

> Every variable must be declared within some class. If a variable is declared within some class's method, it is called a local variable and has meaning only within the nearest pair of enclosing braces, { and } . If a variable is declared within a class but not within any of the class's methods, it is an instance variable and may be accessed by any method in the class.

These are the only choices we have for variables; either they are declared "globally" in a class or they are local variables. Instance variables can be used by any method in the class, whereas local variables are—at best—valid only within the method in which they are declared.

By the way, the declaration of the eight variables is a single statement in this case: a comma-separated list of variables of the same type (int, for integer), along with their initial values. Because the compiler can't see the comments, the declaration appears to the compiler to look like this:

```
int X0 = 50, X_INCR = 30, Y0 = 50, and so on;
```

a perfectly ordinary declaration of eight variables.

Now that we have eliminated most of the "magic numbers," the paint() method looks like this:

```
public void paint(Graphics g)
{
    // Draw the black background.
    g.setColor(Color.black);
    g.fillRect(0, 0, 500, 350);

    // Draw ten nested "holes."
    g.setColor(new Color(0 * RG_INC, 0 * RG_INC, 1 * BLUE_INC));
    g.fillOval(X0 + 0 * X_INC, Y0 + 0 * Y_INC,
               W0 - 0 * X_INC, H0 - 0 * 2 * Y_INC);

    g.setColor(new Color(1 * RG_INC, 1 * RG_INC, 2 * BLUE_INC));
    g.fillOval(X0 + 1 * X_INC, Y0 + 1 * Y_INC,
               W0 - 1 * X_INC, H0 - 1 * 2 * Y_INC);

    g.setColor(new Color(2 * RG_INC, 2 * RG_INC, 3 * BLUE_INC));
    g.fillOval(X0 + 2 * X_INC, Y0 + 2 * Y_INC,
               W0 - 2 * X_INC, H0 - 2 * 2 * Y_INC);

    /* Steps 3 through 8 omitted for simplicity. */

    g.setColor(new Color(9 * RG_INC, 9 * RG_INC, 10 * BLUE_INC));
    g.fillOval(X0 + 9 * X_INC, Y0 + 9 * Y_INC,
               W0 - 9 * X_INC, H0 - 9 * 2 * Y_INC);

    // Draw the text, in white with a blue drop shadow.
    g.setColor(Color.blue);
    g.setFont(new Font("TimesRoman", Font.BOLD, 36));
    g.drawString("On to Cydonia!", 22, 300);

    g.setColor(Color.white);
    g.drawString("On to Cydonia!", 20, 298);
}
```

This new version is quite a bit more verbose than the original, but look at what we've gained. It's far easier to understand than the original, and if we want to change the *x*-increment, we need change only one number, the initial value of X_INCR, rather than the 20 we would have to change in the original.

Pass 3: Methods of Our Own

Writing the second version was easy, once we decided to use variables to store repeatedly used information. In fact, with judicious use of copy and paste, the whole process took less than 2 minutes, because the ten pairs of statements differed only in the numbers 0 through 9 that we used as multipliers. What a waste of typing, though! We have 20 statements that are almost exactly the same. This happens so often that programming languages all have a feature designed just for such situations.

You will recall that a method (called a procedure or function in other programming languages) is nothing but a collection of statements that can be called into action by using its name. So far, our methods have been overrides of existing library methods, but we can also write our own if we need to. Let's try it here.

Step 1. Decide what the method should do (its statement body).

That's easy here—the repeated tasks are to set the drawing color and draw an oval, using the Graphics object g and the multiplier, which we'll denote by n.

```
g.setColor(new Color(n * RG_INC, n * RG_INC, (n + 1) * BLUE_INC));
g.fillOval(X0 + n * X_INC, Y0 + n * Y_INC,
          W0 - n * X_INC, H0 - n * 2 * Y_INC);
```

Step 2. Decide what the method needs to know (its local variables) and what has to be supplied to it from outside (its arguments).

Looking at the statements above and the applet itself, we see that the eight variables are used only in the drawing statements, so they don't need to be instance variables in the applet class but, rather, can be local variables inside the method itself. On the other hand, the Graphics object, g, and the number, n, that controls the color and the size of the ovals have to be supplied from outside the method. This means they have to come from arguments supplied when the method is called.

Programming Tip

Declare variables as locally as possible.

Step 3. Decide what information, if any, has to be sent back to the program when the method is complete (its return type).

In this case, the paint() method (where we'll call our method) has no need to know what the method does, only that it does its task and returns, so we can give the method a void return type.

Step 4. Give the method a descriptive name.

How about using `drawHole` as a name? This indicates that something is being drawn, and it's a legal Java identifier, as we saw in Chapter 1. Methods are commonly given verb-phrase names, reflecting the fact that they do something.

Putting it all together, our method definition will look like this:

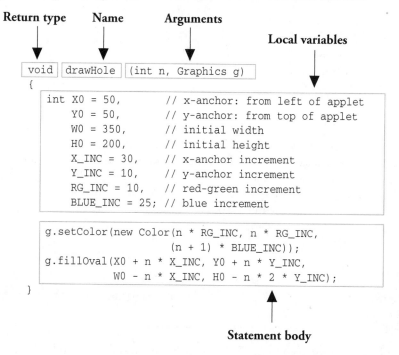

Here's what our applet looks like now. It includes our `drawHole()` method at the end and calls `drawHole()` ten times in the body of `paint()`.

```
public class Wormhole extends Applet
{
    /**
     * Do all the drawing.
     */
    public void paint(Graphics g)
    {
        // Draw the black background.
        g.setColor(Color.black);
        g.fillRect(0, 0, 500, 350);

        // Draw ten nested "holes," calling a method of our own.
        drawHole(0, g);
        drawHole(1, g);
        drawHole(2, g);
        drawHole(3, g);
        drawHole(4, g);
        drawHole(5, g);
        drawHole(6, g);
        drawHole(7, g);
```

```
        drawHole(8, g);
        drawHole(9, g);

        // Draw the text, in white with a blue drop shadow.
        g.setColor(Color.blue);
        g.setFont(new Font("TimesRoman", Font.BOLD, 36));
        g.drawString("On to Cydonia!", 22, 300);

        g.setColor(Color.white);
        g.drawString("On to Cydonia!", 20, 298);
    }

    void drawHole(int n, Graphics g)
    {
        /* Details omitted--see the definition above. */
    }
}
```

This is a considerable improvement. To see this, compare the paint() methods in Pass 2 and Pass 3—the latter is considerably easier to read, because we've hidden a lot of the detail in a single method. In Pass 3, we're not bogged down with a lot of code verbiage; we've encapsulated the oval-drawing code in a method of its own, where it belongs. In addition, the full file of Pass 2 is 97 lines long, containing 3213 characters, whereas the Pass 3 version is 81 lines long, containing 2229 characters. We've saved 16 lines of code and shortened the file by a third.[4]

Design Tip

> Whenever you have repeated code, consider encapsulating it in a method of its own.

Oops! It looks as if there's an error here, though. So far, every method call we've seen has begun with a reference to some object, like the Graphics object g in g.setColor(Color.black). Here, however, the call to drawHole() is simply the naked drawHole(7, g), for instance. What object's drawHole() method is being called here? It's clearly the Wormhole applet itself, because that's where the method is defined, but how do we get an object to call one of its own methods—by using something like this.drawHole(7, g)? That's exactly what we can do!

> An object can call one of its own methods, or any inherited method of one of its superclasses, by either (1) not using any object name in front of the method name or (2) using the name this, which is always understood by Java to mean the object itself.

---

[4]When we introduce repetition statements in Chapter 8, you'll see how we could simplify this Lablet even further.

Review Questions

4.1 What is the difference between a local variable and an instance variable?

4.2 What is `this`?

4.3 Which class owns the method `paint()`? Objects of which classes can call it?

2.5 Summary

- We discussed the following classes:

`Applet`	`Font`
`Color`	`Graphics`
`Component` (briefly)	`Point`
`Dimension`	`Rectangle`

- The `import` statement is used to indicate to the compiler that a file may contain names of classes, methods, and data that were defined in packages located in other files. We discussed the packages `java.applet` and `java.awt`.

- Comments in Java come in two forms. Any text from `//` to the end of the line is ignored, as is anything between the pairs `/*` and `*/`. Comments of the same type cannot be nested within each other, though any `//` comments within a `/* . . .*/` pair are ignored. Comments are Good Things; use them.

- An identifier is a class, variable, or method name. Java identifiers must start with a letter and, after that, may contain any combination of letters, digits, or underscore characters.

- Java identifiers are case-sensitive: Lower- and uppercase letters are considered different by the compiler when looking up names.

- A class definition always looks like this:

```
class Name extends OtherClassName
{
    Instance variable declarations
    Method definitions
}
```

  Although we often derive a class from a superclass, the `extends` part of the header is optional—classes do not necessarily have to be derived from other classes.

- When we declare a variable, we are indicating to the compiler that it should remember the variable name and should associate that name with a type, either a primitive type such as `int` and `boolean`, or a class type, such as `Applet` and `Graphics`.

- Variable declarations take one of two forms:

```
TypeName variableName;
TypeName variableName = expression of the correct type;
```

- Any variable must be declared in some class. The *scope* of a variable—the locations in the program where the compiler will recognize its name—is limited to the portion of the program between the nearest pair of braces that enclose the declaration. In addition, a variable has meaning only in that part of its scope that occurs after its declaration.

■ When we construct an object for use in a declaration, we must use the new operator in front of the constructor, like this:

```
ClassName variableName = new ClassName(argument list);
```

■ Declaring a non-class-type variable, such as an int or boolean, does not use the new operator.
■ A method definition takes one of two forms, depending on whether it returns a value to the location it was called.

```
void methodName(formal argument list)
{
    list of statements
}

TypeName methodName(formal argument list)
{
    list of statements
}
```

■ The argument list of a method is a (possibly empty) list, separated by commas, of terms of the form *TypeName formalArgument*. When a method is called, the formal arguments are set equal to the actual arguments provided by the method call. Formal arguments are local to the function.
■ If a void method belonging to class T is called, the call forms a single statement and looks like

```
T-typeObjectName.methodName(actual arguments);
```

In all method calls, regardless of return type, the actual arguments must match the formal arguments of the method definition in order, type, and number.
■ If an object calls one of its own methods or a method from one of its superclasses, the call can take one of two forms:

```
methodName(actual arguments)
this.methodName(actual arguments)
```

The keyword this is a synonym for "the object itself."
■ We have learned two kinds of statements so far: declarations and void method calls (technically, import is classified as a declaration).

2.6 Exercises

1. In terms of the number of characters (counting spaces and carriage returns, too), what is the smallest possible Java applet? It needn't do anything, but it should compile correctly.
2. Which of the following are legal choices for the name of a variable of your own? For those that aren't syntactically correct (those that would cause problems during compilation), explain briefly what's wrong with them.
  a. FOO
  b. version1.1

  c. two
  d. 2
  e. Supercalifragilisticexpialidocious
  f. O.K.
  g. _temp1
  h. applet
  i. w_i_e_r_d_n_e_s_s

3. Comments are ignored in Java, so is the following a legal declaration? Explain why or why not. Note that we have moved the semicolon.

```
int x = 3      // 0, 1, and 2 are disallowed;
```

4. Each of these variable declarations is fatally flawed. Explain what's wrong in each.

  a. `x = 21;`
  b. `Color c = blue;`
  c. `int x`
  d. `Dimension = new Dimension(200, 100);`
  e. `Point origin = new Point(200);`
  f. `Font titleFont = Font("Dialog", Font.BOLD, 24);`
  g. `int x = new int(145);`
  h. `rectangle r = new rectangle(5, 10);`

5. In some applet method, could you make the following method call? Why or why not?

```
this.drawRect(29, 37, 113, 84);
```

6. Can an applet make the call `drawOval()`? Why or why not?

7. Are local variables necessities or conveniences? In other words, if we have a class definition that uses local variables in some of its methods, can we somehow make an equivalent applet that uses no local variables?

8. Describe what would be displayed if the `Graphics` object `artist` were used to make the following calls. You may assume that `artist` would be capable of drawing on the screen. *Hint:* In both cases, the result is probably not what was intended.

  a. This sequence:

```
artist.setColor(Color.red);
artist.drawOval(20, 30, 40, 50);
artist.setColor(Color. black);
artist.fillRect(20, 20, 100, 70);
```

  b. This sequence:

```
artist.drawOval(20, 30, 150, 60);
artist.setFont(new Font("Helvetica", Font.PLAIN, 9));
artist.drawString("Cool!", 35, 55);
```

9. The following applet is a complete mess. Identify all the errors you can. Don't concern yourself with stylistic problems—just pick out and explain the potential compiler errors. Depending on how you count, there are at least a dozen errors here.

```
/*****************************************
My First Applet--I'm sooo proud!
*****************************************
import Java.applet;
public class MyFirstApplet
{
    this.resize();
    private void paint(graphics theGraphics);
    {
        theGraphics.drawstring('Cool!', 20)
    }
}
```

10. Come up with a strategy that would make Exercise 9 a fairly easy problem.

11. Java is a *free-form* language: Like C and C++, it ignores spaces, tabs, and carriage returns, except where necessary to separate linguistic elements. This means we have a considerable amount of flexibility in the way we lay out our programs. Comment on the readability of the following conventions for program layout, some of which are used in actual practice.

a. The layout we use in this text, with braces tab-aligned on separate lines and interior elements one tab to the right of the enclosing braces:

```
public class Hello extends Applet
{
    public void paint(Graphics g)
    {
        g.drawString("Hi!", 20, 10);
    }
}
```

b. A layout like layout (a), but with opening braces on the line above:

```
public class Hello extends Applet {
    public void paint(Graphics g) {
        g.drawString("Hi!", 20, 10);
    }
}
```

c. An extension of layout (b), with the closing braces also moved up:

```
public class Hello extends Applet {
    public void paint(Graphics g) {
        g.drawString("Hi!", 20, 10); } }
```

d. Like layout (a), but with a broken Tab key:

```
public class Hello extends Applet
{
public void paint(Graphics g)
{
g.drawString("Hi!", 20, 10);
}
}
```

e. Java is enough like C and C++ that they share many stylistic conventions. Look at several C or C++ texts for a different style and comment on it. Another good source is the Net. Crank up your browser and go looking for Java sources to critique.

12. There's a difference between the way we refer to data belonging to an object and data belonging to a class. Sometimes, we can refer to the data in an object by using the object name, such as `myPoint.x`, which refers to the `x` instance variable belonging to the point `myPoint`. Other calls require the name of a class, as we saw in the Lablet when we used `Color.red`. This is because nonlocal variables can be either instance variables, belonging to each object in a class, or class variables, which belong to the class rather than to its objects. We'll explore this difference in detail later; for now, see if you can find an example of a method that belongs to a class rather than an object.

13. Give a sequence of statements that would draw the dreaded yellow "smiley face."

14. Modify the Logo applet we wrote in Section 2.3 so that it draws one of the following images. Pick your favorite colors.

a.   **b.**

15. What are the RGB values of bright yellow? *Hint:* If you're not a professional colorist, you might want to write a tiny applet that draws a filled rectangle in colors you choose.

16. What color has RGB values 40, 80, 160?

17. Given a `Rectangle` object `r`, how would you compute the coordinates of its lower-right corner?

18. There's a lot going on behind the scenes in the *Rectangle* class. Provide complete descriptions of what the following methods have to do to perform their tasks. For example, in part (a), a portion of the answer is "If `p.x` is greater than `x + width`, then set `width` to `p.x - x`." You'll find descriptions of these methods at the end of this chapter.

    a. `add(Point p)`

    b. `intersection(Rectangle r)`

19. Suppose you were given a `Graphics` object, `g`, as you would if you were in a `paint()` method, for example. Show the calls to `g`'s methods that you would use to draw a shaded ball, like this:

20. In Exercise 19, did you use any "magic numbers"? How about for the radius or center? Rewrite the calls, assuming you had local `int` variables `x` and `y` for the coordinates of the center and `size` for the radius of the outer ball. You should have code that looks like this:

```
int x = 20;
int y = 40;
int size = 15;
// ... Some code follows that uses g, x, y, and size
// to draw the ball.
```

21. If you haven't tried it yet, put your code in the `paint()` method of an applet and see if it draws as it should.

22. Now comes the fun part. In your applet, define a new method with signature

```
void drawBall(Graphics g, int x, int y, int size)
```

that would, when called, draw a ball of radius `size`, centered at (x, y), using the `Graphics` object g to do the necessary drawing. Basically, all you have to do is pull out the code you had in part (c) from the `paint()` method and place it in your `drawBall()` method. You won't need the declarations of x, y, and `size`, of course. They are formal arguments in your new method, so they are already declared.

23. Try it. Make your paint() method look like this and run the applet.

```
void paint(Graphics g)
{
    drawBall(g, 20, 40, 15);
}
```

24. That was a lot of work and hardly worth it. Or so it seems. Modify your applet to draw ten balls at various locations and sizes. Comment on what the `paint()` method would look like if you hadn't made a helper method.

2.7   Answers to Review Questions

1.1 To alert the compiler that some names used in the file might be found in the package named in the statement.

1.2 The name of a class, variable, or method. Identifiers must begin with a letter, which may be followed by zero or by more letters, digits, or underscores.

1.3 A `//` comment extends to the end of its line; a `/* . . .*/` comment may extend over several lines.

2.1 A named collection of statements that are called into action when the method name and argument list are used in a statement.

2.2 Formal arguments are used in method definitions; actual arguments are used in method calls.

2.3 `Applet, Panel, Container, Component, Object`.

3.1 A filled rectangle is drawn in g's current color. The rectangle's upper-left corner is at (0, 10), its width is 20, and its height is 30.

3.2 White.

3.3 `Point pt = new Point(10, 20);`

3.4 `x, y, width,` and `height`.

4.1 A local variable has no meaning outside the method in which it is declared, whereas an instance variable can be used by any method in its class.

4.2 `this`, when used in a method, is a reference to the object itself.

4.3 paint() is a Component method; paint() can be called by Component or by any Component subclass.

2.8 Class References

In this chapter and those to come, we introduce several new classes. In the body of the text in order not to disrupt our discussion, we typically concentrate on the most commonly used methods. However, we'll provide more detailed (though not always complete) descriptions of the classes in chapter appendices, like this. In the descriptions of the classes, we'll flag the particularly important methods (which often are discussed in detail in the chapter body) with the symbol ♦.

java.applet.Applet

You'll almost never use the Applet class without extending it and overriding its init() and paint() methods. Remember that paint() isn't an Applet method—it belongs to the Component superclass, which is described in detail in Chapter 3.

```
class Applet extends Panel
{
    //---------- Constructor ----------
    Applet();

    //----------- Methods ------------
    AppletContext getAppletContext();
    /* Returns the AppletContext object (see Ch. 12)
       associated with this applet. */

    AudioClip getAudioClip(URL url);
    AudioClip getAudioClip(URL url, String name)
    /* Returns a reference to an AudioClip object (see Ch.
       12) located at the Web address given by the URL, or
       at the file with location relative to the URL. */

    URL getCodeBase();
    URL getDocumentBase();
    /* We'll discuss these in Ch. 12. getCodeBase() returns
       the URL of the .class file of this applet, and
       getDocumentBase() returns the URL of the HTML file
       that loaded this applet. */

    Image getImage(URL url);
    Image getImage(URL url, String name);
    /* Returns a reference to an Image (see Ch. 12) located
       at the given URL or relative to the URL. */

    String getParameter(String parameter);
    String[][] getParameterInfo();
    /* As you'll see in Chapter 12, you can provide information
       in the <APPLET> tag that can be used by the applet.
       These two methods allow the applet to get the provided
       information. */

♦   void init();
    /* This is called by the system when the applet is first
       loaded. It's where we do any needed initialization. */
```

```
        void resize(int width, int height);
        void resize(Dimension d);
        /* Sets the size of the applet's frame to the dimensions
           provided. NOTE: This method is ignored by some browsers.
        */

    ◆   void showStatus(String message);
        /* Displays the string, often in the status line at the
           bottom of the browser window. This is handy for
           debugging, because it allows you to watch a message sent
           while the applet is running. */

        void start();
        void stop();
        /* We'll discuss these in more detail in Ch. 11. start()
           is called by the system when the applet is displayed
           and stop() is called by the system when the browser
           leaves the page containing the applet.

    }
```

java.awt.Color

A Color object represents a color, expressed as a predefined name or a triple of integers (between 0 and 255) representing the red, green, and blue components of the color.

```
class Color extends Object
{
        //---------- Constructors ---------
    ◆   Color(int r, int g, int b);

        Color(int rgb);
        Color(float r, float g, float b);
            // We'll discuss these constructors in Chs. 5 and 12.

        //-------- Class Constants --------
    ◆   black, blue, cyan, darkGray, gray, green, lightGray,
        magenta, orange, pink, red, white, yellow
        /* These are names of predefined Color objects. They are
           always prefixed by the class name, like Color.red. */

        //------------ Methods ------------
        Color brighter();
        Color darker();
        /* Returns a new Color object that is slightly brighter or
           darker than this color. */

        int getBlue();
        int getGreen();
        int getRed();
        /* These return the value of the particular component of
           this color. */
    }
```

java.awt.Dimension

A Dimension object contains two publicly accessible values, width and height.

```
class Dimension extends Object
```

```
{
    //---------- Constructors ---------
    Dimension();
♦   Dimension(int width, int height);
    Dimension(Dimension d);

    //------- Instance variables ------
♦   int width;
♦   int height;

    //----------- Methods -----------
    boolean equals(Dimension d);
    /* Returns true if this object has the same width and
       height values as d does and returns false if not. */

    void setSize(Dimension d);
    void setSize(int width, int height);
        // Sets the width and height values of this object to
        // those specified.
}
```

java.awt.Font

This class represents fonts for textual display. There are five font names that are guaranteed to be recognized by any Java environment: SansSerif, Serif, Monospaced, Dialog, and DialogInput.

```
class Font extends Object
{
    //---------- Constructors ---------
♦   Font(String name, int style, int size);

    //----------- Constants -----------
♦   BOLD, ITALIC, PLAIN

    //----------- Methods -----------
    String getName();
    int getSize();
    int getStyle();
        // These return the name, size, and style of this object.

    boolean isBold();
    boolean isItalic();
    boolean isPlain();
    /* Returns true if this Font object is a particular style and
       returns false otherwise. */
}
```

java.awt.Graphics

This class is used for drawing on the display. You can't construct a Graphics object; instead, you'll use the one provided in the Component paint() method or the one returned by the Component or Image methods getGraphics().

```
abstract class Graphics extends Object
{
    //------------ Methods ------------
◆   void clearRect(int x, int y, int width, int height);

    void clipRect(int x, int y, int width, int height);
        // Limits drawing to the given rectangle. (See Ch. 12.)

    void dispose();
    /* A Graphic object uses a lot of system resources, so it's
       a good idea to dispose() of it when you're finished using
       it. */

◆   boolean drawImage(Image im, int x, int y, ImageObserver ob);
    boolean drawImage(Image im, int x, int y,
        int width, int height, ImageObserver ob);
    boolean drawImage(Image im, int x, int y, Color bgColor,
        ImageObserver ob);
    boolean drawImage(Image im, int x, int y,
        int width, int height,
        Color bgColor, ImageObserver ob);
    boolean drawImage(Image im, int dx1, int dy1,
        int dx2, int dy2, int sx1, int sy1,
        int sx2, int sy2, ImageObserver ob);
    boolean drawImage(Image im, int dx1, int dy1,
        int dx2, int dy2, int sx1, int sy1,
        int sx2, int sy2, Color bgColor,
        ImageObserver ob);
    /* These methods are used to draw a previously produced
       Image object. (See Ch. 12.) */

    void draw3DRect(int x, int y, int width, int height,
        boolean raised);
◆   void drawLine(int x1, int y1, int x2, int y2);
◆   void drawOval(int x, int y, int width, int height);
◆   void drawRect(int x, int y, int width, int height);
◆   void drawString(String s, int x, int y);
◆   void drawArc(int x, int y, int width, int height,
        int startAngle, int arcAngle)
    /* This draws an unfilled arc within the rectangle specified
       by x, y, width, and height. The arc begins at the angle,
       in degrees, specified by the argument startAngle, and
       extends arcAngle degrees. Angles are measured
       counterclockwise from 3:00 o'clock and extend from the
       center of the bounding rectangle.
          A call to drawArc(10, 10, 160, 80, 45, 165) might
       look like this. */
```

```
    void drawRoundRect(int x, int y, int width, int height,
        int arcWidth, int arcHeight);
```

/* This draws an unfilled rounded rectangle with position
   and size given by the first four arguments. The last
   two specify the width and height, respectively, of the
   rounded corners. */

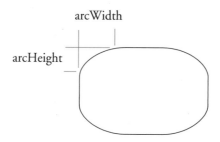

```
    void fill3DRect(int x, int y, int w, int h, boolean raised);
    void fillArc(int x, int y, int w, int w, int stA, int arcA);
◆   void fillOval(int x, int y, int w, int h);
◆   void fillRect(int x, int y, int w, int h);
    void fillRoundRect(int x, int y, int w, int h,
        int arcWidth, int arcHeight);

◆   Color getColor();
        // Returns the current drawing color.

    Font getFont();
        // Returns the Font currently being used by this object.

    FontMetrics getFontMetrics();
    FontMetrics getFontMetrics(Font f);
    /* Returns a FontMetrics object (see Ch. 12) corresponding
        to the current font or the font specified.

◆   void setColor(Color c);
◆   void setFont(Font f);
        // Sets the drawing color or font of this Graphics object.
    void setPaintMode();
    void setXORMode();
        // Sets the drawing mode. We'll discuss these in Ch. 12.
}
```

java.awt.Point

A Point object contains two publicly-accessible values, x and y.

```
class Point extends Object
{
    //---------- Constructors ---------
    Point();
◆   Point(int x, int y);
    Point(Point p);

    //------- Instance variables ------
◆   int x;
◆   int y;
```

```
//------------ Methods ------------
boolean equals(Point p);
/* Returns true if this object has the same x and
   y values as p does, and returns false if not.

void move(int x, int y);
void setLocation(Point p);
void setLocation(int x, int y);
/* Sets the x and y values of this object to those
   specified. */

void translate(int dx, int dy);
/* This changes the point's coordinates by adding dx and dy
   to its x and y coordinates, respectively. */
}
```

java.awt.Rectangle

A Rectangle is a combination of a Point (the upper-left anchor point) and a Dimension (the width and height). As in Point and Dimension, the instance variables are publicly accessible.

```
class Rectangle extends Object
{

    //---------- Constructors ---------
    Rectangle();
    /* Constructs an "empty" Rectangle located at (0, 0) and
       having width and height zero. */

    Rectangle(int w, int h);
    /* Constructs a Rectangle at (0, 0) with width = w and
       height = h. */

    Rectangle(Point p);
    /* Constructs an empty Rectangle (width and height both
       zero) anchored at the Point given by p. */

    Rectangle(Dimension d);
    /* Constructs a Rectangle anchored at (0, 0) with width and
       height given by the argument d. */
 ◆  Rectangle(int x, int y, int w, int h);
 ◆  Rectangle(Point p, Dimension d);
    Rectangle(Rectangle r);

    //------- Instance variables ------
 ◆  int x;
 ◆  int y;
 ◆  int width;
 ◆  int height;

    //------------ Methods ------------
    void add(int x, int y);
    void add(Point p);
    void add(rectangle r);
    /* Expands this rectangle to be just large enough to
       contain the specified point or rectangle also. */
```

```
boolean contains(int x, int y);
boolean contains(Point p);

boolean equals(Rectangle r);
/* Returns true if this rectangle has the same anchor and
   size as r; returns false if not. */

Point getLocation();
Dimension getSize();

void grow(int h, int v);

Rectangle intersection(Rectangle r);
/* Returns the Rectangle consisting of all the points in
   this rectangle that are also in r. */
```

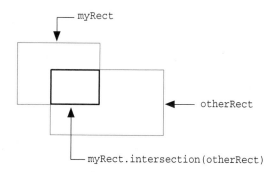

```
boolean intersects(Rectangle r);
/* Returns true if and only if this rectangle contains any
   points of r. */

boolean isEmpty();
/* Returns true if and only if this rectangle is empty;
   i.e., either width or height is zero or less. */

void setBounds(int x, int y, int w, int h);
void setBounds(Rectangle r);
void setLocation(int x, int y);
void setLocation(Point p);
void setSize(int w, int h);
void setSize(Dimension d);

void translate(int dx, int dy);
/* Changes this rectangle's anchor by adding dx to its x
   datum and dy to its y datum. In other words, shift
   this rectangle in the direction (dx, dy). */

Rectangle union(Rectangle r)
/* Returns the smallest Rectangle object containing both
   this rectangle and the argument r.
```

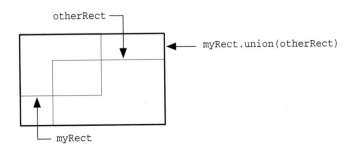

```
}
```

CHAPTER THREE

WIDGETS

Modern graphical user interfaces (GUIs) are built from an increasingly common set of parts, such as buttons for user response, regions for displaying and entering text, drop-down menus, and so on. These parts are called *widgets* in computerspeak. The `java.awt` package (AWT stands for Abstract Windowing Toolkit) provides a platform-independent collection of classes that implement a wide variety of widgets. Using the AWT classes, you can design a useful and visually effective program without having to worry about the low-level details associated with graphical objects. A menu in a Java program, for example, can look like a Windows menu on a PC running Windows, like a Mac menu on a Macintosh, and like a Motif menu on a Unix machine, all with the same code.

Objectives

In this chapter, we will

- Continue our discussion of the `Component` class, which is the parent class for nearly all of the Java widget classes.
- Investigate the look and actions of the most important `Component` subclasses, such as `Label`, `TextField`, `TextArea`, `Button`, `Checkbox`, and `Choice`.
- Begin an exploration of GUI programming that will continue over the next four chapters.

3.1   Components

The `Component` class is unquestionably the most important class in the `java.awt` package (Figure 3.1). With 95 methods, it is also by far the largest. `Component` is the superclass of all the widget classes, with the exception of menus, and serves as the repository of all the methods common to the widgets. We'll talk about some of these methods, especially those that deal with the way components look on the screen, in this chapter, and we'll return to `Component` in Chapter 6 when we talk about making our widgets take action in response to user input.

For all its importance, you'll never see a direct instance of a `Component` object in a Java program. That's because `Component` is an *abstract class,* which means that it is intended as a repository of methods and data and can never be *instantiated* into an object. The notion of an abstract class arises quite naturally when we take an object-oriented view of the world. It's reasonable to think of a class `Car`, for instance, because cars all have features like engines and seats in common, along with behaviors like accelerating, braking, and turning left. In the real world, though, you'll never

abstract class

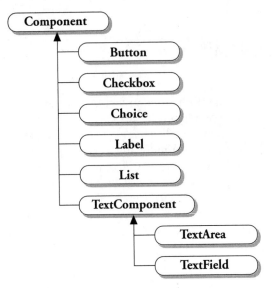

Figure 3.1

A portion of the class hierarchy derived from `Component`.

see a generic `Car` object—instead, you'll see instances of `Car` subclasses, such as the Universal Motors Belchfire 5000.

`Component`'s Graphical Methods

We have no intention of deluging you with all `Component` methods at once, but there's a fairly long list we do have to discuss. After some practice, you'll come to learn the most useful methods and will use them more or less automatically, often not even thinking about the class to which they belong. After having built a few applets, for example, you'll get used to putting in an override of the `paint()` method and won't need to think much about the fact that `paint()` is actually a method that belongs to a class several levels up the hierarchy from `Applet`. Pretty much the only time you need to worry about the hierarchy is when you need a method that you think *should* belong to a class and can't find it in the class documentation. If it should be there but isn't, there's a good chance that it belongs to some superclass.

> When in doubt about where to find a method, look up (up in the class hierarchy, that is).

Let's get the constructor out of the way first. `Component` has one constructor; it has good uses, but they are beyond the scope of this text. The list that follows includes those `Component` methods that have to do with what appears on the screen, like the position, size, and visibility of an object.

Dimension **getSize**()

This returns a Dimension object with width and height the same as those of this Component. This is often used to find the size of an applet, as we'll see shortly.

void **paint**(Graphics g)

We've seen this one. This method causes this Component to be painted, using the Graphics object in the argument. In Component, this is an empty method that does nothing at all. It is intended to be overridden in a subclass, as we did in our applets in Chapter 2. You'll almost never call this method—the system will call it when it is needed.[1] You can, however, cause it to be called by calling repaint().

void **repaint**()
void **repaint**(int x, int y, int width, int height)

You'll use these a lot. These methods tell the system that this Component needs to be redrawn as soon as possible. The second version specifies a rectangular region within which redrawing should take place, for those instances where you don't need to redraw the entire Component.

These methods instruct the system to schedule a call to update() on what we might describe as its "to do" list, along with things like responding to keyboard input and handling requests for access to the disk drive. You can't count on a call to repaint() to result in an immediate screen update. Most times the update will happen quickly, but if you are doing something very time-sensitive, such as animation, you will have to employ some special techniques.

void **setBackground**(Color c)

Sets the background color of this Component. This is the companion to getBackground().

void **setBounds**(int x, int y, int width, int height)
void **setBounds**(Rectangle r)

Changes the size and location of this Component.

void **setFont**(Font f)

Sets the font of this Component to f.

void **setForeground**(Color c)

Sets the foreground color of this Component. This is a companion to getForeground().

void **setLocation**(int x, int y)
void **setLocation**(Point p)

---

[1]The only time you'll ever call paint() is in an override of update().

Moves this `Component` so that its anchor is at the coordinates given by the arguments.

```
void setSize(int w, int h)
void setSize(Dimension d)
```

Changes the size of this `Component`, keeping the current anchor.

```
void update(Graphic g)
```

Just as for `paint()`, you can't call this method. It is called by the system when the screen needs to be redrawn. If you don't override it, this method will erase this `Component` (by painting over it in the background color) and then call the `Component`'s `paint()` method. The erase–redraw combination may cause an annoying flicker unless you override this method.

Review Questions

1.1 What do `Button`, `Checkbox`, `Choice`, `Label`, `List`, and `TextComponent` have in common?

1.2 What is an abstract class?

1.3 When you call `repaint()` in a program, what apparently happens? What actually happens?

3.2   Textual Widgets

There are three widgets that you can use to deal with the display of text: `Label`, `TextField`, and `TextArea`. Along with these three, there's a more or less abstract one, `TextComponent`, that contains many of the methods common to `TextField` and `TextArea`. All are `Components` by inheritance and so have access to the `Component` methods, as well as to their own.

The `Label` Class

This is a simple class. A `Label` is a `Component` that displays a line of text on the screen. The text can't be altered by the user, though it can be modified by the program during execution.

The `Label` class has three constructors.

```
Label()
```

This creates a `Label` object with center alignment and no text.

```
Label(String label)
```

This creates a center-aligned `Label` object displaying the text given in the argument.

```
Label(String label, int alignment)
```

Like the foregoing constructor, this creates a Label with the given text. In addition, the alignment of the text is specified by using one of the three class constants Label.LEFT, Label.CENTER, or Label.RIGHT. For example, if you wished to construct a Label with the text "Future value" aligned to the right, you could use the declaration

```
Label fvLabel = new Label("Future value", Label.RIGHT);
```

Two Label methods (out of a total of six) are of interest to us here.

```
String getText()
```

Returns a String object whose value is the same as that of this Label's text. This and getText() are quite commonly used.

```
void setText(String label)
```

Sets the text of this object to the string given in the argument.

The TextComponent Class

Because TextFields and TextAreas are so similar in their purposes, the data and methods common to both were "factored out" and placed in the TextComponent class, and both TextField and TextArea were then defined to be subclasses of TextComponent. This is a class that does its work behind the scenes; it has no constructors, so you can't initialize a TextComponent object, even if for some reason you ever wanted to use one in a program.

This class, however, does contain quite a few useful methods that are inherited by both TextField and TextArea objects. This, by the way, is a good example of another programming idiom, that of "factoring out" common code: Rather than repeating the same methods in two classes, such as TextArea and TextField, we make them both subclasses of a single class (TextComponent), and put the common methods in that class.

"factor out" idiom

```
int getCaretPosition()
```

Returns the position, measured in number of characters, of the text cursor (which might be a vertical bar, blinking bar, "I-beam," or whatever else the system uses for editing text).

> Java prefers to count from zero.[2] In all TextComponent and TextArea methods that measure positions of characters, the first (or leftmost) character is always in position 0.

---

[2]This "start counting from zero" convention is common to many programming languages, new and old. It seems odd at first, but you get used to it.

```
String getSelectedText()
```

Returns a copy of the part of the text that has been selected. Such text is often highlighted on many systems—think of the way your favorite word processor works, for instance.

```
int getSelectionEnd()
int getSelectionStart()
```

These two methods return the position, in characters, of the end and start, respectively, of the selected text.

```
String getText()
```

Like the method of the same name in Label, this returns a copy of the current contents of the component. As with setText(), you'll use this often.

```
void select(int start, int end)
```

Selects all characters in the text, from position start to position end, highlighting the selected area in whatever way is appropriate for the system in which it is running.

```
void selectAll()
```

Selects and highlights all characters in the text.

```
void setCursor(int position)
```

Moves the cursor to the indicated position in the text. The position argument must be greater than or equal to zero.

```
void setSelectionEnd(int position)
void setSelectionStart(int position)
```

These methods allow the program to set the end and start of the selected portion of the text.

```
void setText(String text)
```

Sets the current text to be that given by the argument. You'll use this a lot.

The TextField Class

A TextField object looks like a box into which one can place a single line of text. The text in the field can be changed by the user (by clicking and typing) or by the program (using the methods below). Here's a sample of what a TextField object might look like on the screen:

Ask for Coupons!

This is a very common and useful class. It is used in many instances where a small amount of text is needed for input or output. Most of the methods you'll call on `TextField` objects will be inherited from the `TextComponent` superclass.

The `TextField` class has four constructors, which we list here, and two methods, which we describe in the References section.

`TextField``()`

Creates a `TextField` object with empty text (that is, containing no characters) and a default width determined by the system.

`TextField``(int columns)`

Creates a `TextField` with empty text, wide enough to hold `columns` characters.

`TextField``(String text)`

Creates a `TextField` object with content given by the argument string.

`TextField``(String text, int columns)`

Creates a `TextField` object with content and width given by the arguments.

Using `TextFields`

Here's an example of using a `TextField`. In this applet, we find the size of the applet, using the `Component` method `getSize()`; display the size in a `TextField`; and use the size to draw a blue rectangle, centered in the applet display. When we run it, the result looks like the illustration in Figure 3.2.

The applet is simple enough, but it does use a method we haven't talked about so far, the `Applet` method `init()`, and it uses a `String` operator we haven't discussed in detail.

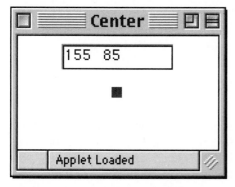

Figure 3.2

Using the applet size in a **TextField** and for painting.

```java
import java.applet.*;
import java.awt.*;

public class Center extends Applet
{
    Dimension appletSize;
    TextField display = new TextField(10);

    public void init()
    {
        add(display);
        appletSize = getSize();
        display.setText(appletSize.width + "  " + appletSize.height);
    }

    public void paint(Graphics g)
    {
        int centerX,
            centerY,
            SIZE = 8;
        appletSize = getSize();
        centerX = appletSize.width / 2;
        centerY = appletSize.height / 2;
        g.setColor(Color.blue);
        g.fillRect(centerX - SIZE / 2, centerY - SIZE / 2, SIZE, SIZE);
        display.setText(appletSize.width + "  " + appletSize.height);
    }
}
```

The init() method, like paint(), isn't called directly; it's one of those methods the system will call when it is needed—in this case, when the applet is first loaded. This is where we do any one-time initialization. Nearly all but the simplest applets will have an init() method override, as you'll see. In our example's init(), we first use the Container method add() to make the display object a visible part of the applet. Without a call to add(), the TextField would still be part of the applet, of course, but it would never show up on the screen. Next, we use the Component method getSize() to get the size . . . of what? This is another of those naked method calls we talked about in Chapter 2, without an object and a dot in front, so it's assumed to be the applet object itself whose size we're getting. Finally, we use the TextComponent method setText() to place some text in the display field.

The String operator +, used here in the argument of setText(), is the *concatenation* operator—it makes a new string by copying its two operators and hooking them together, end to end. For example, the expression "dog" + "food" yields the string "dogfood". Hold on here! The width instance variable of the Dimension object appletSize isn't a String; it's an integer. That's true—appletSize.width is indeed an int, but a nice feature of the operator + is that if one of its two operands is a String, the other will, whenever possible, be converted into its string representation as a collection of characters. In other words, in evaluating "R2D" + 2, the compiler will see that the first operand, "R2D", is a string and will then convert the integer 2 to the String equivalent, "2", and concatenate the two, yielding the String object "R2D2". In our example, the applet width is converted to a String, concatenated with three blanks, and finally concatenated with the String equivalent of the applet height, and the result is placed in the display field.

The paint() method again gets the size of the applet and uses that to find the center point of the applet frame. The center point local variables, centerX and centerY, are in turn used with SIZE to draw a filled blue square in the exact center of the applet and to update the text in the display field. If you're in an environment like an applet runner that supports manual resizing, enter the applet and resize the window—you'll see that the blue square is redrawn correctly and that the display text is changed to reflect the new applet dimensions.

The TextArea Class

If we need more than a single line of text for input or output, we can use a TextArea object. As is the case with all Java widgets, you can be pretty sure about how a TextArea object will work, but you can't guarantee precisely what it will look like. Here's an example from one environment:

There are five TextArea constructors.

TextArea()

Creates a TextArea of system-dependent default size, with empty text (no characters).

TextArea(int rows, int columns)

Creates a TextArea with empty text, with room for rows of text, each of which has room for columns characters.

TextArea(String text)

Creates a default-sized TextArea, containing the argument string.

TextArea(String text, int rows, int columns)

Creates a TextArea containing the argument string, of size specified by the rows and columns arguments.

TextArea(String text, int rows, int columns, int scrollbars)

This acts just like the foregoing constructor, but also allows the program to specify whether the TextArea will have horizontal and/or vertical scrollbars. The class constants that can be used as arguments are pretty much self-explanatory. They are

```
TextArea.SCROLLBARS_BOTH
TextArea.SCROLLBARS_NONE
TextArea.SCROLLBARS_HORIZONTAL_ONLY
TextArea.SCROLLBARS_VERTICAL_ONLY
```

The `TextArea` methods are, as you might expect, somewhat similar to those in `TextField`, though they're more heavily oriented to editing here than in `TextField`.

void **append**(String str)

Change the text of this object by appending the characters in the argument to the end of the current text. For example, if the `TextArea` object `myDisplay` contained the text "In", the call

```
myDisplay.appendText("credible!");
```

would make the current text in `myDisplay` "incredible!" (without the quotation marks, of course).

int **getColumns**()

Returns the current width, in columns, of this `TextArea`.

int **getRows**()

Returns the current height, in rows, of this `TextArea`.

void **insert**(String str, int position)

Inserts the argument string into the current text, at the location given by the position argument. The text is shifted to make room for the new characters. For example, if the `TextArea` `myDisplay` originally contained "mud," then after the call

```
myDisplay.insertText("star", 2);
```

`myDisplay` would contain the text "mustard." As in all the `TextComponent` methods, positions are counted from the left, beginning with 0. Thus, a `position` argument of 0 will result in the argument string being concatenated to the front of the current text. If the position argument is greater than the number of characters in the current text, the additional text will be appended to the immediate right.

void **replaceRange**(String str, int start, int end)

Replaces the current text between positions `start` (included in the replacement) and `end` (*not* included) with the argument string. For example, if the `TextArea` `myDisplay` originally contained "abcdefghi," then after the call

```
myDisplay.replaceText("**", 2, 6);
```

`myDisplay` would contain the text "ab**ghi." You can use this to delete a range of the current text by using as argument the *empty string*, `""`. There are certain conditions on the arguments you should try to satisfy: $0 \leq$ `start` $\leq$ `end` $\leq$ *length of current text*. If you violate any of these, you may get strange results in some Java environments.

```
void setColumns(int columns)
void setRows(int rows)
```

Changes the number of columns or rows in this `TextArea`.

Using `TextAreas`

Here's an applet that includes some of the features we've discussed in this section.

```java
import java.awt.*;
import java.applet.*;
public class WidgetSample extends Applet
{
    // Declare and initialize a pair of text widgets.
    TextArea myArea = new TextArea(4, 12);
    TextField myField = new TextField(15);

    public void init()
    {
        // Put some text into the TextArea.
        myArea.appendText("Here's some text, just for practice.");
        myArea.appendText(" Here's some more text.");

        // Select the text from position 18
        // up to (but not including) 35.
        myArea.select(18, 35);

        // Declare a string for moving text from the TextArea to
        // the TextField and initialize it to the selected text.
        String transferText = myArea.getSelectedText();

        // Use the string to set the text in the TextField
        myField.setText(transferText);

        // Add the area and the field to this applet.
        add(myArea);
        add(myField);
    }
}
```

Let's take a close look at it and see what we can learn. First, we see that the structure is simple and familiar—the class definition begins with the declaration of two new instance variables, `myArea` and `myField`, and includes an override of the Applet method `init()`.

Programming Tip

> When reading a program, concentrate first on the Big Picture and put the details aside for later. This is excellent advice for writing programs, too—get the structure right before you start filling in code.

Looking at the body of `init()`, we see that it begins by using two calls to `appendText()` to put some text into `myArea`. Next, we see a call to `select()`. The documentation reminds us that `select(18, 35)` will select the text in positions

18 . . . 34. Recalling that character positions in `TextAreas` and `TextFields` begin at zero, we count characters in `myArea` and see that the selected text should be "just for practice". Now that we know what to expect, we run the applet.

Programming Tip

> Running a program just to spot potential compile errors is a very useful technique. Even better is to *predict* what the program should do before you run it. Having the wrong mental model of what a language feature does is a common source of error.

The next statements,

```
String transferText = myArea.getSelectedText();
myField.setText(transferText);
```

are supposed to transfer a copy of the selected text from `myArea` into `myField`. It seems straightforward enough at first—use `getSelectedText()` to return a `String` containing the text, and then use `setText()` to put the text into `myField`. We declare a local `String` variable to hold the text, but where's the new operator we're used to?

It's not there because we don't need it. A new `String` is being constructed, but it is constructed by `getSelectedText()`, so we don't have to do anything but use the returned string to initialize `transferText`. We could have done the same thing by omitting any explicit mention of the `String` being used for the transfer and combining the two statements into one:

```
myField.setText(myArea.getSelectedText());
```

> In declaring a class-type variable (as opposed to a nonclass type, like `int` or `boolean`), the right-hand side can be a method call, a variable, or a constructor call. If you use a method call or a variable on the right, don't use the `new` operator; if you use a constructor, `new` is required.
>
> In either case, of course, the type returned by the expression on the right must match the type declared on the left.[3]

Review Questions

2.1 Besides their different looks, what is the major difference between a `Label` and a `TextField`?

2.2 You can't construct a new `TextComponent`, so why have this class at all?

2.3 What is the result of `"1" + 2`? Of `1 + 2`? Of `"1 + 2"`?

2.4 If a `TextField` or `TextArea` contains just the string "ABCDE", which character is in position 3?

---

[3]There are some subtleties at work here that we'll explain in Chapter 5.

3.3   Active Widgets

As useful as `Textfields` and `TextAreas` are, a program nearly always needs to do more than serve as a repository of text. In particular, one of the consequences of modern GUI design is that a program typically spends most of its time waiting for the user to communicate his or her intent. Think of your favorite application and you'll see what we mean: In many cases, nothing at all apparently happens until you click a button or pull down a menu and make a choice. Once you do, the program recognizes that you've done something and take appropriate action. In Chapter 6 we'll talk in detail about how a Java program recognizes and responds to a user-generated event, but we can start by describing the `Components` that are provided for user interaction.

The "active widgets" classes include `Button`, `Checkbox`, `Choice`, and `List`.[4] Like the text widgets, all these are subclasses of `Component`, so they all have access to the `Component` methods to change their size, position, color, visibility, and so on.

The `Button` Class

This class is designed solely to give the user a place to click (and, as we'll see in Chapter 6, to give the program a way to recognize that a mouse click has occurred on the button). A `Button` object can have an optional label string, and because it is a `Component`, it will have a size, a location, a font, foreground and background colors, and an appearance on the screen.[5] As with the other widgets, the appearance of a `Button` object will depend on the system in which its program is running. Here are two examples, taken from screen shots of the Lablet for this chapter, running in two different environments.

There are just two constructors for *Buttons*, depending on whether or not you want to specify a label string.

```
Button()
Button(String label)
```

The `Button` class has ten methods, only two which are of interest to us at present.

```
String getLabel()
void setLabel(String label)
```

---

[4]We left out only the `Dialog`, `Menu`, and `Scrollbar` classes. We'll discuss `Dialog` and `Menu` in the next chapter and `Scrollbar` in Chapter 6.

[5]Actually, a `Button` object is likely to have two appearances on the screen; its normal appearance and the highlighted look it takes while it is being clicked.

These are a now-familiar get/set pair. The former method returns a copy of the label text, and the latter allows you to change the label text. `setLabel()` is often used for *toggle buttons*. A toggle button can be in two or more states and changes its state each time it is clicked. A START/STOP button is a good example; the first time it is clicked, it sends a message to the program to start something, and on the next click, it sends a message to stop something. We could provide visual feedback to the user by altering the label text on each click between the strings "On" and "Off."

Design Tip

> Keep the user informed about what your program is doing and what state it in. Users get very grumpy when a program surprises or confuses them.

The `Checkbox` Class

A `Checkbox` object is a specific kind of toggle button with visual feedback. It has a `boolean` member datum indicating its state and, like a `Button`, has an optional text label. The object has a different look, depending on whether its state is `true` or `false`. The pictures below are typical of the look of a `CheckBox` object. The one on the left is in a `true` state, and the one on the right is in a `false` state.

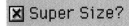 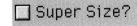

There are four `Checkbox` constructors.

Checkbox`()`

This *default constructor* (a constructor with no arguments) creates a `Checkbox` with no label and `false` state.

Checkbox`(String label)`

Constructs a `Checkbox` with the given label and an initial `false` state.

Checkbox`(String label, boolean state)`

Constructs a `Checkbox` with the specified label and state.

Checkbox`(String label, boolean state, CheckboxGroup group)`

Sets the label and state, and in addition specifies the group of Checkboxes to which this one will belong. We'll talk about the class `CheckboxGroup` in a moment. There are six `Checkbox` methods that we will discuss now.

CheckboxGroup **getCheckboxGroup**`()`

Returns the `CheckboxGroup`, if any, to which this `Checkbox` belongs. Patience! We'll get to `CheckboxGroup` very soon.

`String` **`getLabel`**`()`

Paired with `setLabel()`, this returns a string containing the label text of this `Checkbox`.

`boolean` **`getState`**`()`

Returns the current state (`true` or `false`) of this `Checkbox`.

`void` **`setCheckboxGroup`**`(CheckboxGroup group)`

Sets the `CheckboxGroup` to which this object belongs.

```
void setLabel(String label)
Sets the label of this Checkbox.
void setState(boolean state)
```

Sets the state of this `Checkbox`.

The `CheckboxGroup` Class

You may have seen electronic devices with a row of buttons, only one of which can be down at any time; pushing one down causes any other that is down to pop up. That's just what a `CheckboxGroup` is: a collection of `Checkboxes`, only one of which is in a `true` state at any time. These are often called "radio buttons" (many old radios had such buttons for station selection), and they usually have a distinguishing look, like this:

This class is *not* a subclass of `Component`. It's a subclass of the mother of all classes, `Object`. `CheckboxGroup` has no visual appearance; all it does is provide a way to collect `Checkboxes` into a related group. You can have as many `CheckboxGroups` in a program as you wish.

There is a single default constructor for this class:

`CheckboxGroup``()`

and a pair of get/set methods:

```
Checkbox getSelectedCheckbox()
void setSelectedCheckbox(Checkbox c)
```

`getSelectedCheckbox()` returns the `Checkbox` in this group, if any, which is in the `true` state. The `setSelectedCheckbox()` method has the same effect as if the user had clicked on the `Checkbox` in the argument—it sets the state of `c` to `true` and turns off any other `true` `Checkbox` in this group.

Just for fun, here's an applet you can try, using three Checkbox objects joined in a single CheckboxGroup, to produce the layout illustrated above.

```
import java.awt.*;
import java.applet.*;

public class RadioButtonTest extends Applet
{
    Checkbox fee = new Checkbox("fee");
    Checkbox fie = new Checkbox("fie", true); // set it on
    Checkbox foe = new Checkbox("foe");
    CheckboxGroup giant = new CheckboxGroup();

    public void init()
    {
        fee.setCheckboxGroup(giant);
        fie.setCheckboxGroup(giant);
        foe.setCheckboxGroup(giant);

        // The add() method of Container adds a Component to
        // the Container. In this case, the three Checkboxes
        // will appear when the applet does.
        add(fee);
        add(fie);
        add(foe);
    }
}
```

The Choice Class

When a Choice object is quiescent, it looks like this:

When the user clicks on it and holds down the mouse button, a list of items drops down, from which the user can make a selection. Here are two samples.

The items in the list highlight as the pointer moves over them, and when the mouse button is released, the label changes to the text of the selection. A Choice object has methods that allow you to add new items, determine the number of items and the currently selected item, and inspect the text of the item in a given position.

The Choice class has one constructor,

Choice()

and quite a few methods you can use, some of which we list here.

```
void add(String item)
```

Adds a new item with the given label to the list of this `Choice` object. Items are added to the list from the top down. Don't confuse this with the far more common `add()` method belonging to `Container`, which we have mentioned briefly already. We'll talk about that one in more detail in the next chapter.

```
String getSelectedItem()
```

Returns the text of the current selection.

```
void insert(String item, int index)
void remove(int index)
```

The first of these methods inserts a new item string in the list in the given position, and the second removes the item at the given position. In both, the `index` argument must be valid, which is to say that for `insert()` we must have $0 \leq$ index $\leq$ *itemCount* and for `remove()` we must have $0 \leq$ index $<$ *itemCount*.

```
void removeAll()
```

Removes all items from this `Choice`.

```
void select(int index)
void select(String item)
```

Both of these methods can be used to change the currently selected item (and hence the text that appears in the object when the mouse is not clicked). In the first version, the item is selected by position (which must be from 0 to *itemCount* $-$ 1), and in the second the selected item is the one, if any, that matches the string given in the argument.

The `List` Class

A `List` is somewhat like a permanently expanded `Choice`. A `List` object appears as a `TextArea` with a collection of items, one per line, like this:

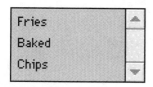 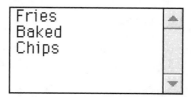

When the user clicks the mouse on one of the lines, it becomes highlighted and serves as the current selection. A `List` object may behave in one of two ways: A click on the item may highlight it without influencing any rows already highlighted (*multiple-selection* mode), or a click on an item may turn off any currently highlighted rows (*single-selection* mode). As with `Choice`, the items are enumerated from the top down, the topmost item having index zero.

There are three `List` constructors. All three construct an initially empty `List` object (one with no items).

`List()`

Creates a default-sized `List` object in single-selection mode.

`List(int rows)`

Creates a `List` object in single-selection mode, with a number of rows given by the argument.

`List(int rows, boolean multipleSelections)`

Creates a `List` object with the specified number of rows. If the boolean argument is `true`, the `List` is in multiple-selection mode, and if the argument is `false`, the created `List` is in single-selection mode.

As you might expect, there is a strong similarity between the `List` methods and those of `Choice`. When we talk about arrays in Chapter 8, we will see what methods are specific to multiple-selection mode.

```
void add(String item)
void add(String item, int index)
void addItem(String item);
```

These add a new item with the given label to this `List` object. If the index is not specified, the item is added to the bottom; otherwise, the existing items at and after position `index` are shifted down one row to make room for the new item.

`void deselect(int index)`

Turns off the selection of the item in position `index`.

`int getItemCount()`

Returns the number of items in this `List`.

`int getRows()`

Returns the number of rows in this `List` object.

`int getSelectedIndex()`

Returns the index of the current selection. This returns –1 if no item is currently selected or if more than one item is selected.

`boolean isIndexSelected(int index)`

Returns `true` if the item in position `index` is selected; otherwise, returns `false`.

```
void remove(int index)
void remove(String item)
```

These methods remove an item from this `List`. In the first, the item in position `index` is removed. The index argument must be valid, which is to say we must have $0 \leq \text{index} < itemCount$. The second form searches for an item matching the `String` argument, and if there is one, it is removed.

```
void removeAll()
```

Removes all items from this List.

```
void replaceItem(String newItem, int index)
```

This replaces the item in position index with the text given by the argument newItem.

```
void select(int index)
```

This selects the item in position index.

```
void setMultipleMode(boolean m)
```

Turns multiple-selection mode on if the argument is true and sets the mode to single selection if the argument is false.

Review Questions

3.1 What is the purpose of a CheckboxGroup?
3.2 How do you add a new item to the end of a List object?
3.3 Besides their different looks, what is the primary difference between a List object and a Choice object?

3.4 Hands On

This chapter's Lablet lays out a screen for online ordering from a fast-food restaurant we've invented (see Figure 3.3). It's not what you'd see from a professional site, but we've designed it to use all the widgets we've talked about in this chapter.[6]

As usual, we begin with a comment block and a collection of import declarations. Note that because we're not responding to any events, we don't need to import the java.awt. event package.

```
//================================================================
// PROJECT:        _programming.java_
// FILE:           Gigobite.java
// PURPOSE:        Chapter 3 lablet
// VERSION:        1.1
// TARGET:         v1.1 and higher
// UPDATE HISTORY: 1.1 9/8/98   new documentation
//                              and 1.1 compliance
//                     1.0 8/21/96
//================================================================
//-------------------- IMPORTS --------------------------------
import java.applet.*;
import java.awt.*;
```

---

[6]For an example of professional food ordering, take a look at the Web site that Pizza Hut has set up. Start at http://www.pizzahut.com/ and go to the demo area. This is not a Java-based site, but it's easy to see how you could design an applet to do what Pizza Hut's site does.

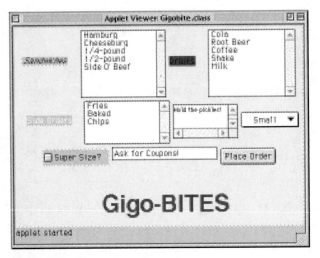

Figure 3.3

The appearance of the **GigoBites** applet.

We continue with the applet class definition, first declaring all the widget variables that we'll use. Note that we used the Tab key to align the initialization parts of each declaration. The compiler doesn't care, of course, but we find that it makes reading easier.

```
public class Gigobite extends Applet
{
    //---------------------- DATA ----------------------------
    private Checkbox    superSize    = new Checkbox("Super Size?");
    private TextField   reminder     = new TextField("Ask for Coupons!",18);
    private List        sandwiches   = new List(5,true);
    private List        drinks       = new List(5, true);
    private List        sides        = new List(3, false);
    private            Choice sizes  = new Choice();
    private TextArea    comments     = new TextArea("Hold the pickles!", 2,
                                           10);
    private Button      order        = new Button("Place Order");
    private Label       sandsLabel   = new Label("Sandwiches");
    private Label       drinkLabel   = new Label("Drinks");
    private Label       sidesLabel   = new Label("Side Orders");
    private Label       title        = new Label("Gigo-BITES");
    private Font        myFont1       = new Font("SansSerif",Font.BOLD,36);
    private Font        myFont2       = new Font("SansSerif",Font.ITALIC,12);
```

Now we come to `Applet`'s `init()` method. You can see from the declaration above that `sandwiches` is a `List` instance variable. In the first few lines, we call its method `add()` to add five items to it. We then do the same thing to the other two `List` objects, `sides` and `drinks`.

```
public void init()
{
    //----- Place the items in the sandwich List object.
    sandwiches.addItem("Hamburg");
    sandwiches.addItem("Cheeseburg");
    sandwiches.addItem("1/4-pound");
    sandwiches.addItem("1/2-pound");
    sandwiches.addItem("Side O' Beef");
    //----- Place the items in the side order List object.
    sides.addItem("Fries");
    sides.addItem("Baked");
    sides.addItem("Chips");
    //----- Place the items in the drinks List object.
    drinks.addItem("Cola");
    drinks.addItem("Root Beer");
    drinks.addItem("Coffee");
    drinks.addItem("Shake");
    drinks.addItem("Milk");
```

Next, we add some items to the `sizes` object, using the `Choice` method `addItem()`.

```
    //----- Place the items in the size Choice object.
    sizes.addItem("Small");
    sizes.addItem("Medium");
    sizes.addItem("Large");
```

We're just about finished with the setup. All we need to do now is a bit of miscellaneous tweaking, more to show that we *can* than for any real design purpose. We set the applet's background color to a blinding yellow and resize it. (We really don't need to resize the applet, but we wanted to allow you to change the size to see how the layout of the widgets is affected by the applet size.) Then we set the fonts and colors of the four `Label`s, again using methods that `Label` inherits from `Component`.

```
    //----- Set the applet's background color and size.
    setBackground(Color.yellow);
    resize(450,300);
    //----- Adjust the properties of some of the widgets.
    sandsLabel.setFont(myFont2);
    drinkLabel.setBackground(Color.cyan);
    sidesLabel.setForeground(Color.red);
    title.setFont(myFont1);
    title.setForeground(Color.blue);
```

At this stage, we've initialized all 12 widgets and the applet itself. We could end the `init()` method here and run the applet. If we did, though, we wouldn't see any of the widgets we've spent so much time designing. They would be instance variables of our applet, but they would never appear, because we hadn't indicated that they should. To make them visible when the applet is drawn, we need the method `add()`. This `Container` method, recall, associates a `Component` with the `Container` for both logical and graphical purposes.

In the next chapter, we'll see that a `Container` object (which is what an applet is, by inheritance) can be used to group other `Components` together. We've seen this sort of behavior already—a CheckboxGroup is a way of collecting logically related Checkboxes into a single entity. In the case of Container, we use add() to indicate that when the Container is drawn, the parts added should also be drawn.

```
        //----- Add all of the widgets to our applet.
        add(sandsLabel);
        add(sandwiches);
        add(drinkLabel);
        add(drinks);
        add(sidesLabel);
        add(sides);
        add(comments);
        add(sizes);
        add(superSize);
        add(reminder);
        add(order);
        add(title);
    }
}
```

The 12 Component widgets are added to our applet in the order in which they appear in the code. Altering the order in which we add the widgets would produce a corresponding visual shuffling when the applet was finally drawn.

If you run the applet, it should look more or less like Figure 3.3. We say "more or less" because the actual look will depend on how large the widgets are in the screen and how well they fit in the 450-by-300-pixel dimension we've set for our applet. In our applet, we haven't specified how the widgets will be laid out on the screen; we really can't in this case, because we have no idea about how large they are.[7] We ran this applet on two different systems on the same computer, for instance, and found that in one system the sides List was 144×72 pixels, whereas on another it appeared as 108×54.

In the next chapter, we'll discuss the LayoutManager classes and show how you can have control over the way Components are placed on the screen. Because we haven't specified any layout here, the default is to "flow" the widgets within the applet frame, from left to right and top to bottom. If you change the values in the setSize() call above and recompile and run the applet, you'll see that the widget Components change their positions. In Figure 3.4, we show how the widgets might be arranged in two different applet frames. Note that in both cases, the overall order is the one in which they were added, but the final result will depend on how they fit the applet.

That's it—we're finished with this applet. Almost. Notice anything peculiar about its structure? *There's no* paint() *method!* What's going on here?

> You don't have to paint() widgets. The system will do it for you.

All of the Components in the AWT library "know" how to paint themselves. The only time you need to worry about painting Components is when you design a cus-

---

[7]We could, though, have used their Component methods setSize(), setLocation(), and setBounds() to place them precisely where we want. We'll see how to do this in the next chapter.

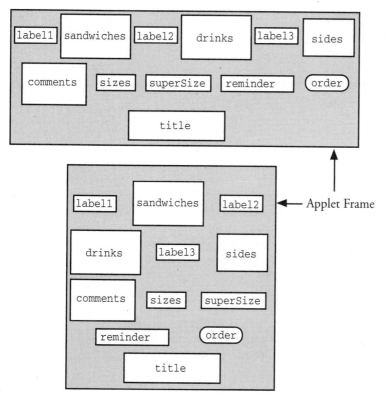

Figure 3.4

Same applet, different dimensions.

tom widget of your own. We weren't doing any Graphics-related drawing on the applet frame, so we didn't need a paint() method here.

3.5 Summary

- We discussed the following classes:

Button	Label
Checkbox	List
CheckboxGroup	String (briefly)
Choice	TextArea
Component	TextComponent
Container (briefly)	TextField

- Among other data, a Component object has information about its bounding rectangle, its foreground and background colors, its font, and its minimum and preferred sizes, along with methods for inspecting and modifying most of these.
- Component is a superclass of Button, Checkbox (but not CheckboxGroup), Choice,

Label, List, TextArea, TextComponent, and TextField. These subclasses have access to all the methods we mentioned in the discussion of Component.

■ Component is an abstract class, which means that it is impossible to declare and initialize a Component object. It is, of course, perfectly legal to declare and construct any of the Component subclasses we mentioned above (except TextComponent).

■ A Button is designed to respond to mouse clicks.

■ A Checkbox is a two-state button with a particular look. A Checkbox has an internal state (true or false) that is mirrored by its visual appearance.

■ Checkboxes can be grouped into "radio buttons" by making them part of a CheckboxGroup. At most one Checkbox in a group can be in the true state at any time.

■ A Choice object is a drop-down menu used for selecting one of a list of items.

■ A List generally looks like a TextArea, containing a collection of items, one per row. The user can select one or more items from the list by clicking on them. A List can be in one of two modes: single-selection, in which at most one item can be selected at a time, and multiple-selection, in which several items can be selected (and hence highlighted).

■ TextComponent is the superclass of TextArea and TextField. You cannot construct a TextComponent—like Component, the TextComponent class is designed to serve as a repository of methods to be used by its subclasses.

■ A TextField is a holder for an (optionally) editable single line of text.

■ A TextArea can contain several lines of text for input by the user or output by the program.

■ When declaring and initializing an object in Java, use the new operator if the right-hand side of the declaration calls a constructor. You don't need new if the right-hand side of the declaration uses a method that returns an object.

■ Constructors in Java always have the same name as the type of object they construct.

■ Java counts from zero. If there is a linear collection of things in Java (such as items in a List or Choice), they are almost always indexed from zero.

■ The AWT classes are platform-independent, which means that the look of a widget will generally differ from one implementation to another.

■ A Container is a Component that is used to contain other Components.

■ To make a Component a visual part of an applet (or any other Container, for that matter, you must use Container's add() method

■ You do not need to write code to paint a widget. All the AWT widgets "know" how to paint themselves. The only time you need a paint() override in a Component is when you are going to perform any Graphics drawing methods in the Component.

3.6 Exercises

1. If you were presented with an unfamiliar applet, how could you tell whether an object on the screen was a List or a TextArea, without inspecting the underlying code? *Hint:* Run the Gigobite Lablet and see.

2. Think about how an applet is displayed and try to guess what the effect would be of calling `this.setLocation(100, 200)` in an applet's `init()` method. After you have made your guess, add the line at the start of the Lablet's `init()` (don't forget that the statement will need a semicolon at the end), run the Lablet, and correct your guess, if necessary, explaining what you observe.

3. Where is the anchor point of a `Component`?

4. Name 11 pieces of information that each `Component` contains. This will take a bit of deduction on your part, because we don't list them in a single place. *Hint:* To get you started, a `Component` object has to know its foreground color.

5. How could an applet test whether two of its components overlap?

6. Can an applet change the size of one of its components while it is running?

7. Can you change the font of just a part of the text in a `TextField`—for example, making just one word italic out of a total of ten?

8. After execution of this code fragment, what text would be in `result`?

```
TextArea entry = new TextArea("Are these");
entry.appendText(" the shadows of things that must be?");
entry.select(1, 21);
TextField result = new TextField(entry.getSelectedText);
```

9. a. Write the code that would delete all but the first and last characters in a `TextArea` named `display`. *Hint:* The `String` class has a method,

```
int length()
```

that returns the number of characters in the `String`. You may assume that `display` contains more than two characters.

  b. Do part (a) under the assumption that `display` is a `TextField`.

  c. Which of parts (a) and (b) is easier? Why?

10. Two-state devices are so common that the AWT contains a class, `Checkbox`, specifically for that purpose. Describe a reasonable situation in which a *three*-state device would be useful.

11. What consumer electronic product commonly contains parts that act like a `CheckboxGroup`?

12. Can a `Checkbox` be in two `CheckboxGroups` simultaneously?

13. Why might you want to `remove()` an item from a list? *Hint:* Think of a program like the Lablet for this chapter.

14. In the Lablet, we used a `Label` for the title, "Gigo-BITE," that appeared at the bottom. We could have used `drawString()` in a `paint()` override to place the title, but we didn't. We wanted to make a point by showing you an applet without a `paint()` override, but that wasn't the only reason.

  a. Why would it not be a good idea, *in general,* to have painted the title directly on the applet frame?

  b. Ignore the reason or reasons you came up with in part (a). What would the `paint()` override for the Lablet look like if you were to eliminate the `title` variable and draw the title string directly on the applet?

15. Write an applet that contains a single `Button` 20 pixels high and 36 pixels wide, containing the label text "Plonk," centered vertically and horizontally in the applet frame. Your code should work correctly regardless of the applet's dimensions. *Hint:* We did something like this in Chapter 2.

16. Run the Lablet in a Java-aware Web browser, such as Netscape Navigator or Internet Explorer, and run it again in the applet runner in your Java development environment. Record the differences in appearance that you notice.

17. In Figure 3.3, we illustrated how the system "flows" widgets from left to right and then from top to bottom. That's the horizontal arrangement. What can you deduce about the apparent vertical alignment of widgets within this flow layout?

18. In the Lablet, do the 12 widget objects need to be instance variables, or could we have made them local variables within the init() method?

19. Write a declaration and any other code you would need to make a TextField named myLCD appear in an applet with the text "Status set" in green on a black background.

20. Which of the following variable declarations are legal Java? For those that would cause compile errors, explain what's wrong with them. You may assume that any other variables have already been declared to be the right type and initialized to some appropriate values.

    a. `Dimension theSize = new myButton.minimumSize();`
    b. `Choice options = new Choice();`
    c. `String contents = theField.getText();`
    d. `TextField field2 = theField;`
    e. `Component myWidget = new Component();`
    f. `int start = new int(theField.getSelectionStart());`
    g. `int end = theField.getSelectionEnd();`

21. This is a screen shot of an applet we wrote, with two Buttons, two Lists, a Textfield, and a Choice. Write an applet that will lay out these items, with their contents as indicated. You may have to adjust the applet size to make it look (more or less) like this.

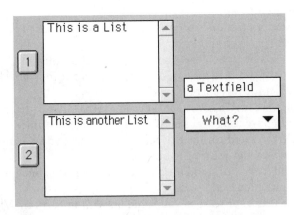

22. Write an applet that contains this calculator, with 18 Buttons, a TextField, and a 2-pixel-wide drop shadow below and to the right of the TextField, all on top of an enclosing round rectangle.

Try to make your applet appear as close to this as possible (get out your ruler and assume that there are 72 pixels per inch). The font for all the button labels is 14-point Courier bold, and the background is medium gray with a black border. We understand you have no control over exactly how the buttons will appear on your system, so don't worry about that part. Do this exercise with the requirement that the calculator should not change its look if the applet frame is resized—in other words, you'll have to anchor the Components in place.

Note: To do this, you'll need to include the following statement at the start of your init() method. We'll explain why in the next chapter.

```
setLayout(null);
```

23. Can a Container contain another Container?

3.7 Answers to Review Questions

1.1 They are all subclasses of Component.

1.2 You cannot make an object from it; an abstract class is a placeholder for methods and data to be used by a subclass.

1.3 A call to repaint() causes the Component to be redrawn. repaint() calls update(), which erases the Component and redraws it by calling the Component's paint() method.

2.1 The user can't edit the text in a Label object but may be able to change the text in a TextField.

2.2 The TextComponent class is an example of the "factor out" idiom—it's a holder for the methods that are common to the TextArea and TextField subclasses.

2.3 "1" + 2 evaluates to the String "12", 1 + 2 evaluates to the int 3, and "1 + 2" is just the String literal "1 + 2". The first + is String concatenation, the second is integer addition, and the third is just an ordinary character in a String.

2.4 D is in position 3.

3.1 To enforce "radio button" behavior among a collection of Checkboxes.

3.2 By calling the List's add() or addItem() method, passing the item name as an argument.

3.3 A List object may allow multiple selections; a Choice object doesn't.

3.8   Class References

java.awt.Button

A Button object is a clickable object with an optional label. Its job is to generate an ActionEvent (see Chapter 6) when it is clicked, which the program can then catch and respond to.

```
class Button extends Component
{
    //--------- Constructors ----------
    Button();
    Button(String label);

    //------------ Methods ------------
◆   void addActionListener(ActionListener lstnr);
    void removeActionListener(ActionListener lstnr);
    /* Add or remove the argument from the list of
        objects that deal with events generated by
        this button. (See Ch. 6.) */
◆   String getActionCommand();
    void setActionCommand(String s);
    /* Unless you've changed the command name associated with
        this button, getActionCommand() will return the label
        of this button. These methods are used in event
        handling. (See Ch. 6.) */

◆   String getLabel();
◆   void setLabel(String s);
}
```

java.awt.Checkbox

A Checkbox object is a two-state widget that is either checked or not. The clause implements ItemSelectable in the class header is used only to indicate that this class contains the method getSelectedObjects(), which we won't use.

```
class Checkbox extends Component implements ItemSelectable
{
    //--------- Constructors ----------
    Checkbox();
◆   Checkbox(String label);
◆   Checkbox(String label, boolean state);
◆   Checkbox String label, CheckboxGroup grp, boolean state);

    //------------ Methods ------------
◆   void addItemListener(ItemListener lstnr);
◆   void removeItemListener(ItemListener lstnr);
        // See Chapter 6.

    CheckboxGroup getCheckboxGroup();
    void setCheckboxGroup(CheckboxGroup grp);
    String getLabel();
    void setLabel(String s);
◆   boolean getState();
    void setState(boolean state);
}
```

java.awt.CheckboxGroup

This is a logical, rather than visual, organizer of Checkboxes. The Checkboxes in one of these groups act like "radio buttons" in that no more than one can be selected at any time.

```
class CheckboxGroup extends Object
{
    //---------- Constructor ----------
◆   CheckboxGroup();

    //----------- Methods -----------
◆   Checkbox getSelectedCheckbox();
    void setSelectedCheckbox(Checkbox c);
}
```

java.awt.Choice

A Choice object is a drop-down list of items, any one of which can be selected by the user. Like Checkbox, this class also contains a getSelectedObjects() method, which you won't use.

```
class Choice extends Component implements ItemSelectable
{
    //---------- Constructor ----------
◆   Choice();

    //----------- Methods -----------
◆   void add(String name);

◆   void addItemListener(ItemListener lstnr);
    void removeItemListener(ItemListener lstnr);
       // Event-related methods, explained in Chapter 6.

    String getItem(int index);
    /* Returns the text of the item in position index in the
       list. Positions are enumerated top-to-bottom,
       starting at zero. The index argument must be in the
       range 0 . . . itemCount-1. */
    int getItemCount();
       // Returns the number of items currently in this object.
    int getSelectedIndex();
    /* Returns the index of the selected item. See getItem()
       for an explanation of how items are enumerated. */

◆   String getSelectedItem();
    void insert(String name, int index);
◆   void remove(String name);
    void remove(int index);
    void removeAll();
    void select(int index);
◆   void select(String name);
}
```

java.awt.Component

This is the root class of nearly all the AWT widgets. You won't need to concern yourself with the clause implements ImageObserver until we talk about Images in Chapter 12.

```
abstract class Component extends Object implements ImageObserver
{
    //---------- Constructor ----------
    Component();
    /* You would call this constructor if you were designing
       your own custom Component (like a triangular button, for
       instance). You cannot use this with new to make a
       Component. */
    //----------- Methods -----------
    void add(PopupMenu p);
    void remove(MenuComponent p);
        // Add or remove a PopupMenu (Ch. 4) from this component.

    void addComponentListener(ComponentListener lstnr);
    void addFocusListener(FocusListener lstnr);
◆   void addKeyListener(KeyListener lstnr);
◆   void addMouseListener(MouseListener lstnr);
◆   void addMouseMotionListener(MouseMotionListener lstnr);
    void removeComponentListener(ComponentListener lstnr);
    void removeFocusListener(FocusListener lstnr);
    void removeKeyListener(KeyListener lstnr);
    void removeMouseListener(MouseListener lstnr);
    void removeMouseMotionListener(MouseMotionListener lstnr);
        // These event-related methods are explained in Ch. 6.

    boolean contains(int x, int y);
    boolean contains(Point p);
    /* These return true if the point (measured in
       coordinates relative to this Component's anchor) lies
       within this Component, and false if not. */

    Image createImage(Image im, ImageObserver io);
    Image createImage(Image im, int width, int height,
            ImageObserver io);
        // These return a new Image object. (see Ch. 12.)

    void doLayout();
        // Forces this Component to be laid out (see Ch. 4).

    Color getBackground();
    Color getForeground();
    /* These return the colors used for painting this Component.
       A Label object, for example, appears as a line of text in
       the foreground color, painted over a rectangle of the
       background color. */

    Rectangle getBounds();
    Point getLocation();
◆   Dimension getSize();

    Point getLocationOnScreen();
    /* The first three return the bounding rectangle, anchor
       point, and size of this Component. The last method
       returns the anchor of this Component relative to the
       screen coordinate system. */

    Component getComponentAt(int x, int y);
    Component getComponentAt(Point p);
    /* Returns the Component containing the specified point,
       measured in this Component's local coordinates. */

    Cursor getCursor();
    Font getFont();
```

String **getName**();
/* These return the Cursor, Font, or Name associated with
   this object. */

◆ Container **getParent**();
/* A Component object may be contained in a Container
   object (as would happen, for instance, if we used
   add() to include a button in an applet). This returns
   the Container that contains this component, if there
   is one, and returns null if this object isn't
   contained in a Container. */

Dimension **getMaximumSize**();
Dimension **getMinimumSize**();
Dimension **getPreferredSize**();
/* Every Component has a maximum, minimum, and preferred
   size, used when laying it out on the screen. We'll
   have much more to say about layouts in Chapter 4. */

boolean **isShowing**();
boolean **isVisible**();
/* isShowing() returns true if and only if this Component
   can currently be seen on the screen. On the other
   hand, isVisible() tests for the *property* of
   visibility. It is possible for a component to be
   visible but not showing--this would happen, for
   instance, when a Button object had been created but
   not yet painted or when a Component was in an
   invisible Container (which we'll talk about in the
   next chapter). */

void **list**()
/* Sends a description of this Component to the standard
   output, System.out. */

◆ void **paint**(Graphics g);
◆ void **repaint**();
void **repaint**(int x, int y, int width, int height);

◆ void **requestFocus**();
/* This method gives focus to this Component, meaning
   that it will respond to textual input from the user,
   if it is capable of doing so. */

◆ void **setBackground**(Color c);
◆ void **setBounds**(int x, int y, int width, int height);
void **setBounds**(Rectangle r);
void **setCursor**(Cursor c);
   // Changes the cursor associated with this object.
◆ void **setFont**(Font f);
◆ void **setForeground**(Color c);
void **setLocation**(int x, int y);
void **setLocation**(Point p);
void **setSize**(int w, int h);
void **setSize**(Dimension d);
void **setVisible**(boolean isVisible)
/* If the argument is true, makes this Component visible
   on the screen; otherwise, makes it invisible. For more
   details, see the discussion of isVisible() above. */

String **toString**();
/* Returns a String description of this object. Although we
   don't mention it in other class descriptions, this is a

very common method name, appearing in no less than 60
classes. */

◆ void **update**(Graphic g)
}

java.awt.Cursor

Though we don't discuss this class in the body of the text, we include it here, because
you can use the Component method setCursor() to change the cursor to a different
look when appropriate. The available cursors depend on what's available on the system—some of the resize cursors, for example, aren't available on some systems.

```
class Cursor extends Object
{
    //---------- Constructor ----------
    Cursor(int type);
    /* This constructs a new instance of a cursor, having the
       appearance specified by one of the class constants listed
       below. You won't use this very often; most of the time,
       you'll make a cursor oject by using the more efficient
       method getPredefinedCursor(). */

    //-------- Class Constants --------
◆  DEFAULT_CURSOR, CROSSHAIR_CURSOR, HAND_CURSOR,
    MOVE_CURSOR, TEXT_CURSOR, WAIT_CURSOR,
    N_RESIZE_CURSOR, S_RESIZE_CURSOR, E_RESIZE_CURSOR,
    W_RESIZE_CURSOR, NE_RESIZE_CURSOR, NW_RESIZE_CURSOR,
    SE_RESIZE_CURSOR, SW_RESIZE_CURSOR
    /* Constants representing the 14 available cursor types. As
       with all class constants, these must be prefixed by the
       class name, as Cursor.WAIT_CURSOR. */

    //-------- Class Methods ---------
◆  Cursor getDefaultCursor();
    /* Returns an instance of the default cursor normally used
       by the system. This is a class method, so rather than
       calling it with an object name and a dot, we call it
       by the class name, as in this example:
       myCursor = Cursor.getDefaultCursor(); */
◆  Cursor getPredefinedCursor(int type);
    /* This returns a new instance of a cursor of the indicated
       type (using one of the class constants above). For
       efficiency, this method keeps a local copy of the new
       cursor, so it can be reused later without having to be
       constructed again. */

    //------------ Methods ------------
    int getType();
    /* Returns the code of this cursor. You could compare the
       returned value against the class constants to find out
       what type this cursor currently is. */
}
```

java.awt.Label

A Label is a widget that consists of nothing but some text on the screen. It can't be
edited by the user, but it can be changed by the program.

```
class Label extends Component
{
    //---------- Constructors ---------
    Label();
♦   Label(String label);
♦   Label(String label, int alignment);

    //-------- Class Constants --------
♦   CENTER, LEFT, RIGHT
    /* These are class constants, so they're always prefixed
       by the class name, like Label.CENTER. */

    //----------- Methods -----------
    int getAlignment();
    /* Returns an integer corresponding to the alignment of this
       Label. This could then be compared against one of the
       three class constants to determine the current alignment
       of this object, for example. */
    void setAlignment(int alignment);
    /* Sets the alignment of this Label to the one given by the
    argument. For example, myLabel.setAlignment(Label.LEFT)
    would make the text of myLabel aligned to the left edge.
    */

    String getText();
♦   void setText(String label);
}
```

java.awt.List

A List object appears like a TextArea: a scrollable collection of items. The user can select one or more items (depending on whether multiple-selection mode is turned off or on) by clicking on them.

```
class List extends Component
{
    //---------- Constructor ----------
    List();
♦   List(int rows);
♦   List(int rows, boolean multipleSelections);

    //----------- Methods -----------
♦   void add(String item);
♦   void add(String item, int index);
    void addItem(String item);

    void addActionListener(ActionListener lstnr);
♦   void addItemListener(ItemListener lstnr);
    void removeActionListener(ActionListener lstnr);
    void removeItemListener(ItemListener lstnr);
        // See Chapter 6.

    void delItem(int index);
    void delItems(int start, int end);
    /* This removes a range of items from this List. The
       removed items are those in the range start ... end,
       inclusive. For example, if the List object myList
       contained these items,
```

```
             A
             B
             C
             D
             E
```
then after the call myList.delItems(2, 3), myList would
contain
```
             A
             B
             E
```
(Remember that positions are counted from zero). */

◆ void **deselect**(int index);

String **getItem**(int index);
String[] **getItems**();
/* The first returns the text of the item in position index
   in this List. The index argument must be in the range 0...
   itemCount - 1. The second method returns an array (Ch.
   8) of all the item names in this object. */
int **getItemCount**();

Dimension **getMinimumSize**();
Dimension **getMaximumSize**();
Dimension **getPreferredSize**();
   // See the Component methods of the same names.

int **getRows**();

◆ int **getSelectedIndex**();
int[] **getSelectedIndexes**();
/* The second of these methods returns an array (Ch. 8) of
   integers, corresponding to the indices of the selected
   items. */
◆ String **getSelectedItem**();
String[] **getSelectedItems**();
/* These act like getSelectedIndex() and
   getSelectedIndexes(), except that they return the names
   of the items, rather than their indices. */

int **getVisibleIndex**();
/* Returns the argument that was used in the last call to
   makeVisible(), or -1 if no call to makeVisible() has been
   made previously. See the discussion of makeVisible() for
   details. */

◆ boolean **isIndexSelected**(int index);

boolean **isMultipleMode**();
/* Returns true if this List is in multiple-selection mode;
   otherwise, returns false. */
void **makeVisible**(int index);
/* A List object is displayed as a scrollable text area,
   because the number of items in the List may be larger than
   the number of rows displayed. This routine scrolls the
   List display so that the item in position index is
   visible. */

void **remove**(int index);
void **remove**(String item);
void **removeAll**();
```
```

```
◆  void replaceItem(String newItem, int index);
   /* This replaces the item in position index with the text
      given by the argument newItem. */
   void select(int index);
      // This selects the item in position index.
   void setMultipleMode(boolean m);
   /* Turns multiple-selection mode on if the argument is true
      and sets the mode to single selection if the argument is
      false. */
}
```

java.awt.TextArea

Objects of this class consist of multiline containers for text, optionally ornamented with scrollbars.

```
class TextArea extends TextComponent
{
   //---------- Constructor ----------
   TextArea();
◆  TextArea(int rows, int columns);
   TextArea(String text);
◆  TextArea(String text, int rows, int columns);
   TextArea(String text, int rows, int columns, int scrollbars);

   //-------- Class Constants --------
   SCROLLBARS_BOTH, SCROLLBARS_HORIZONTAL_ONLY,
   SCROLLBARS_NONE, SCROLLBARS_VERTICAL_ONLY

   //------------ Methods ------------
◆  void append(String str);
   int getColumns();
   int getRows();
   void setColumns(int columns);
   void setRows(int rows);

   Dimension getMinimumSize();
   Dimension getMaximumSize();
   Dimension getPreferredSize();
      // See the Component methods of the same names.
   int getScrollbarVisibility()
   /* Returns one of the four class constants above, indicating
      which of the scrollbars are visible. */
◆  void insert(String str, int position);
   void replaceRange(String str, int start, int end);
}
```

java.awt.TextComponent

A class without a constructor, this is just a holder for the methods that are common to both TextArea and TextField.

```
class TextComponent extends Component
{
   //------------ Methods ------------
   int getCaretPosition();
◆  String getSelectedText();
   int getSelectionEnd();
   int getSelectionStart();
```

```
◆   String getText();
    boolean isEditable();
    /* This returns true if the user can modify the text and
       false otherwise. */

◆   void select(int start, int end);
◆   void selectAll();
    void setCursor(int position);
◆   void setEditable(boolean canEdit);
    /* If the argument is true, the user can modify the text;
       if it is false, the text may not be edited by the
       user. */
    void setSelectionEnd(int position);
    void setSelectionStart(int position);
◆   void setText(String text);
```

java.awt.TextField

A single-line display of text, used for input from the user and output from the program. This is a subclass of TextComponent.

```
class TextField extends TextComponent
{
    //---------- Constructors ----------
    TextField();
◆   TextField(int columns);
◆   TextField(String text);
◆   TextField(String text, int columns);

    //------------ Methods ------------
    void addActionListener(ActionListener lstnr);
    void removeActionListener(ActionListener lstnr);
       // See Chapter 6.

    boolean echoCharIsSet();
    char getEchoChar();
    void setEchoChar(char c);
    /* An echo character is one that will appear in place of
       what the user types, as we'd use in a program that had to
       ask the user for a password. For example, if the echo
       character had been set to '*' and the user typed in
       "booGeymAn," the text "*********" would appear in the
       field. The method echoCharIsSet() returns true if an
       echo character has been set by setEchoChar(), and false
       otherwise. */

    int getColumns();
    /* Returns the current width, in columns, of this TextField. */
    void setColumns(int columns)
    /* Sets the width of this TextField to be enough to hold
       columns characters. The argument must be greater than or
       equal to zero. */
}
```

CHAPTER FOUR

VISUAL DESIGN

In Chapter 3 we discussed how to build an applet by using a collection of buttons, text displays, checkboxes, and other widgets. As you saw, simply adding widgets to an applet gives you very little control over the look of the interface—what looks good in one environment might be completely unacceptable in another. In this chapter, we'll conclude our discussion of the visual design of a Java program by discussing two features that give us the ability to make a GUI look the way we want, regardless of the system in which our programming is running. The Container subclasses permit us to think of visual design in terms of a hierarchical organization, and the layout classes allow us to specify how our hierarchy of Containers and their Components will appear to the user.

Objectives

In this chapter, we will

- Discuss the Container class and its subclasses Panel, Window, Dialog, and Frame.
- Show how to make a Java application.
- Introduce the Canvas subclass of Component.
- Discuss three of Java's layout classes: BorderLayout, FlowLayout, and GridLayout.
- Use what we've learned to produce a complicated user interface.

4.1   Containers

A Container object is used to group Components together for display purposes. There is no limit to the number of Components a Container may hold. As Figure 4.1 illustrates, the Container class is a subclass of Component, which means, first, that any Container object has access to all the Component methods we listed in Chapter 3. In addition, because a Container is a Component, we can put Containers within other Containers. In fact, there's no limit to the number of Components a Container may hold or to how deeply they may be nested. A Container has references to each Component it contains, and each Component also has a reference to its *parent*, the Container to which it belongs. For drawing purposes, a Container has a local coordinate system, measured from the anchor point of its bounding rectangle. This local coordinate system is independent of where the Container is located on the screen.

local coordinates

Every Container has its own LayoutManager that determines how its Components will be arranged within the Container when it is displayed. We'll describe the LayoutManager classes in the next section.

Like Component, Container is an abstract class. You can never have a generic Container object in a Java program—you must use one of its subclasses (or create your own class that extends Container).

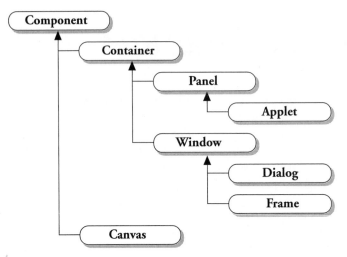

Figure 4.1

Most of the **Container** classes, and **Canvas**.

Container Organization Methods

As you might expect, Container is a fairly large class. It has a single default constructor with no arguments, which is invoked automatically (and invisibly) whenever we create a specific type of Container object. We'll discuss the methods that apply to the Components a Container holds and will defer discussion of methods dealing with layout until the next section.

```
void add(Component c)
void add(Component c, int position)
void add(String name, Component c)
```

These three methods are among the most important and most commonly used of the Container class. Each adds a new Component to those contained by this Container. The first simply adds the argument to the end of the list of Components already in this Container. The second method allows you to specify the position in the list where the new Component will be added. In this version, the position must be valid, which means that it must be between zero and the number of Components currently in this Container. If you don't want to bother counting the Components, a position argument of –1 will always just add the Component argument to the end of the current list. The final add() method has a String argument; this is for the convenience of some LayoutManagers, such as BorderLayout and CardLayout.

You cannot add a Container to itself, and if you attempt to add a Component that is already contained elsewhere, it will be removed and reinserted, generally in a different position.

void **doLayout**()

Forces this Container to be laid out.

Component **getComponentAt**(int x, int y)
Component **getComponentAt**(Point p)

These both return the Component in this Container that contains the given point, measured in the local coordinates. You might want to use these to determine which object the mouse pointer is currently over, for example.

int **getComponentCount**()

Returns the number of Components currently contained in this object. This counts only the top-level components, not those that are contained in any Containers within this object.

Container **getParent**()

This is *not* a Container method. It is a Component method that returns the Container that holds this Component. In the containment hierarchy of Figure 4.2, for instance, choice.getParent() would return panelB.

boolean **isAncestorOf**(Component c)

Returns true if this Container is the parent of c (or is the parent of the parent, and so on). Returns false if c isn't below this Container in the containment hierarchy. In Figure 4.2, for example, the method call

panel_A.isAncestorOf(list_1)

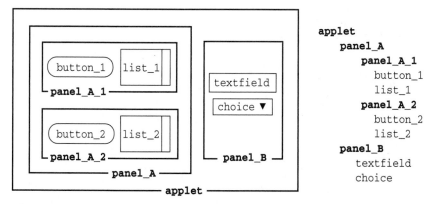

Figure 4.2

Visual organization of an applet and its containment hierarchy.

would return `true`, and

```
panel_B.isAncestorOf(panel_A)
```

would return `false`.

```
void remove(int index)
void remove(Component c)
```

These remove a `Component` from this `Container`'s list. In the first, the `Container` to be removed is specified by its index in the list. These look only at the top-level list and do not search down the containment hierarchy, so in Figure 4.2, the call `panel_A.remove(button2)` would do nothing. The call `panel_A.remove(panel_A_2)`, however, would remove `panel_A_2` from `panelA`'s list and hence would also remove `button_2` and `list_2` from the hierarchy.

```
void removeAll()
```

Removes all `Components` from this `Container`.

The Containment Hierarchy

The containment hierarchy is not determined by the order in which you add `Components` to a `Container`, but rather by which ones are added to which. Consider the example in Figure 4.2. Working from the top level down, we see that `applet` (which, being an `Applet`, is a `Panel`, and hence a `Container`) contains `panel_A` and `panel_B`. `panel_A` itself contains `panel_A_1` and `panel_A_2`, each of which contain a `Button` and a `List`. The actual look on the screen would be determined by the `LayoutManagers` of the separate `Containers`, so if you run this applet as it is, the odds are that it won't look like Figure 4.2. In any case, we would build the containment hierarchy like this:

```java
public class LayoutTest extends Applet
{
    // These declarations could be done in any order.
    Panel panel_A = new Panel();
    Panel panel_B = new Panel();
    Panel panel_A_1 = new Panel();
    Panel panel_A_2 = new Panel();
    Button button_1 = new Button();
    Button button_2 = new Button();
    List list_1 = new List();
    List list_2 = new List();
    TextField textfield = new TextField();
    Choice choice = new Choice();
    /**
     * Now we build the containment hierarchy, from
     * bottom-up.
     */
    public void init()
    {
        panel_A_1.add(button_1);
        panel_A_1.add(list_1);    // done with panel_A_1
```

```
        panel_A_2.add(button_2);
        panel_A_2.add(list_1);   // done with panel_A_2
        panel_A.add(panel_A_1);
        panel_A.add(panel_A_2);  // panel_A is now done
        panel_B.add(textfield);
        panel_B.add(choice);     // panel_B is complete
        add(panel_A);            // add panels to the applet
        add(panel_B);            // finished!
    }
}
```

The Panel Class

The Container of choice for arranging Components is the Panel class. It's simple, small, and easy to use, as you saw in the example above. It has a default constructor, Panel(), that builds a Panel object with its layout set to FlowLayout, and it has a constructor,

Panel(LayoutManager layout)

that allows you to set the LayoutManager that the constructed Panel will use. We'll get to layouts immediately.

A Panel has no additional methods of interest to us here, beyond those it inherits from Container, Component, and Object.

Review Questions

1.1 There are two kinds of relations between classes, "is-a," when one class is a subclass of another, and "has-a," when one class contains an instance of another as part of its data. What are the "is-a" and "has-a" relations between Component and Container?

1.2 How were we able to arrange Components in an Applet in earlier chapters, before we had discussed Containers?

1.3 Why do we use Panel to group objects, rather than Container?

4.2 Layouts

The three layout classes we'll discuss in this section all implement what is known as the LayoutManager interface.[1] In simple terms, this means they are all responsible for positioning components within a Container object; they differ only in how this positioning is accomplished. Some arrange the components in rows, from left to right in each row; some divide the display of the Container into separate regions and allow the programmer to specify within which region a Component will be

---

[1]We'll talk about interfaces in Chapter 6. For now, you can think of an interface as a class and not be too far wrong.

placed. Although it's beyond the scope of this book, it is even possible to design a class of your own that performs custom layouts.

All of the layout classes we will mention[2] have access to the minimum and preferred sizes of the components and may or may not use this information to decide where things should be placed. When a component is resized, the layout is recomputed to compensate for the new size.

Container **Layout Methods**

As we mentioned earlier, every Container has its own LayoutManager, along with some methods that can be used to access and modify the layout.

    void **doLayout**()

This method instructs this Container's LayoutManager to lay out its Components. Generally, you won't have to call this, but you could if you wanted to force layout to take place, rather than waiting for it to be done for you.

LayoutManager **getLayout**()

Returns the current LayoutManager for this Container.

Dimension **getMinimumSize**()
Dimension **getPreferredSize**()

These are overrides of the Component methods of the same names. They ask the LayoutManager to compute the minimum or preferred sizes, respectively, that are necessary to hold all of this Container's Components.

    void **setLayout**(LayoutManager layout)

This method allows you to change the LayoutManager of this Container. You'll use this quite often to switch from the default layout provided for a particular Container.

The **FlowLayout** Class

A FlowLayout positions Components in much the same way as a word processor displays its text: from left to right by rows, arranging the rows from top to bottom. If you look back to Figure 3.4, you'll see an example of 12 Components positioned by a FlowLayout, using two different Container dimensions. As with all the layout classes, FlowLayout will do the best it can to fit all the Components in the visible por-

---

[2]The only AWT layout classes we won't cover here are CardLayout (see the appendix to this chapter) and GridbagLayout. Java 2 introduced the Swing library, which contains a number of new layouts that we also won't discuss here.

tion of their Container. However, if the minimum sizes of all the Components can't be fit in the available space, there's nothing the layout can do—some parts of the Components simply won't appear. You can see this if you run either the Gigobite or the Ovenator Lablet from this chapter in an applet runner and manually resize the window.

FlowLayout contains three class constants: FlowLayout.LEFT, FlowLayout.CENTER, and FlowLayout.RIGHT. These correspond to the three possible alignments that a FlowLayout can have. If the alignment is LEFT or RIGHT, the Components in each row are aligned flush left or flush right, respectively, and if the alignment is CENTER, the Components of each row are centered in the row. In addition, a FlowLayout has two private variables that specify the horizontal gap between objects in each row and the vertical gap between rows. These can be negative integers if you want the Components to overlap.

FlowLayout is the default layout for Panel (and hence, by inheritance, for Applet), so if you don't set the layout for these objects, they will be set automatically to FlowLayout's defaults (center alignment, gaps of five pixels).

The FlowLayout class has three constructors.

FlowLayout()

Creates a FlowLayout object with center alignment and horizontal and vertical gaps of five pixels each.

FlowLayout(int alignment)

Constructs a FlowLayout with the specified alignment and the default gaps of five pixels in each direction.

FlowLayout(int alignment, int hGap, int vGap)

Constructs a FlowLayout with the specified alignment and gaps. For example, you might change the layout of an applet with six buttons from its default alignment by making the following call in its init() method:

```
this.setAlignment(new FlowLayout(FlowLayout.RIGHT, 20, 10));
```

If you did, the result might look something like this (depending on the size of the applet panel, of course).

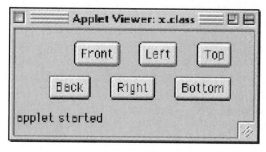

There are six `FlowLayout` methods of interest to us.

int **getAlignment**()

Returns an integer corresponding to the alignment of this `FlowLayout`. This could then be compared with one of the three class constants to determine the current alignment of this object, for example.

int **getHgap**()
int **getVgap**()

Returns the current horizontal or vertical gap, respectively, for this `FlowLayout`.

void **setAlignment**(int alignment)

Sets the alignment of this `FlowLayout` to one of the three class constants.

void **setHgap**(int h)
void **setVgap**(int v)

Sets the horizontal or vertical gap, respectively, of this layout.

The `BorderLayout` Class

In a `BorderLayout`, the `Container` is divided into five regions: North, East, West, South, and Center. Here's an example of an applet with layout set to `BorderLayout`, to which we added five labeled `Buttons`.

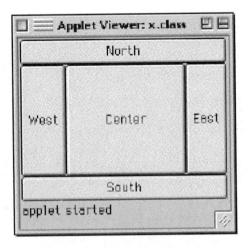

To add `Components` to a `Container` that has a `BorderLayout`, you use the version of the `add()` method that takes an additional `String` argument,

void **add**(String location, Component c)

The location is specified by using the String class constants:

BorderLayout.NORTH

BorderLayout.EAST

BorderLayout.WEST

BorderLayout.SOUTH

BorderLayout.CENTER

For example, if p is a Panel whose layout had been set to BorderLayout (rather than its default FlowLayout), we could add a Button to its East region by calling p.add(BorderLayout.EAST, myButton). You don't have to add Components to each region—any missing region will be treated as a Component of size zero. In some older programs, you might find these class constants replaced by the String literals "North", "South", "East", "West", and "Center", so the method call above might also be written p.add("East", myButton).

Like FlowLayout, BorderLayout allows you to specify horizontal and vertical gaps between regions, though in this layout their values will be zero unless you specify otherwise. This layout is the default for the containers Window, Frame, and Dialog, which we'll discuss shortly.

This layout does a fair amount of work behind the scenes. When a Container is arranged using BorderLayout, the layout manager performs the following tasks, in order:

1. The North and South Components are given their preferred heights, if possible, and laid out at the top and bottom of the Container, leaving a space between. The North and South Components are stretched horizontally to fill the entire Container width.

2. In the portion remaining, the East and West regions are given their preferred widths, if possible, and stretched vertically to fill the space.

3. Finally, the Center Component is placed in the remaining space, stretched both horizontally and vertically to fill the space completely.

Note that unlike FlowLayout, BorderLayout will resize the Components to fill their allotted spaces. This explains why the buttons completely filled the regions in the illustration above.

Design Tip

> If you don't want your Components to be resized during layout, you can place them in Panels and add the Panels to the Container.

We did just that to get the picture below, adding the Center Button to a Panel and then adding the Panel to the Center region. Now, the Panel fills the Center, but the Button does not fill the Panel, because the Panel uses its default FlowLayout.

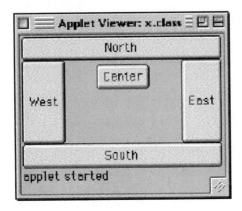

There are two BorderLayout constructors.

BorderLayout()

This creates a `BorderLayout` object with center alignment and horizontal and vertical gaps of zero pixels.

BorderLayout(int hGap, int vGap)

This constructs a `BorderLayout` with the specified gaps.
The methods of this class are quite similar to those of `FlowLayout`.

int **getHgap**()
int **getVgap**()

Returns the current horizontal or vertical gap, respectively, for this layout.

void **setHgap**(int h)
void **setVgap**(int v)

Sets the horizontal or vertical gap, respectively, of this layout.
Using a `BorderLayout` isn't much more difficult than using a `FlowLayout`. For example, we laid out the sample illustrated above like this:

```
public class BorderTest extends Applet
{
    Button northBttn = new Button("North"),
           southBttn = new Button("South"),
           eastBttn = new Button("East"),
           westBttn = new Button("West"),
           centerBttn = new Button("Center");

    public void init()
    {
        // Change the applet's layout from Flow to Border
        setLayout(new BorderLayout());
```

```
        // Place the buttons, with the center one in a panel of
        // its own.
        add(BorderLayout.NORTH, northBttn);
        add(BorderLayout.SOUTH, southBttn);
        add(BorderLayout.EAST, eastBttn);
        add(BorderLayout.WEST, westBttn);

        Panel pCenter = new Panel();
        pCenter.add(centerBttn);
        add(BorderLayout.CENTER, pCenter);
    }
}
```

Notice the last three lines—we declare a local variable pCenter and initialize it to a new Panel (with the default FlowLayout), we add the center Button to the new Panel, and finally we add the Panel (and everything it contains, like the Button) to the Applet. We declared the new Panel locally in the init() method, because it is highly unlikely that it will be referenced anywhere else in the applet, no matter what later modifications we might make.

The GridLayout Class

When you need a "graph paper" layout, with all regions of the same size, use a GridLayout. In this layout scheme, you specify a number of rows and columns and when adding components, they will be placed in the same order in which you're reading this paragraph: left-to-right within rows and top-to-bottom in row order.

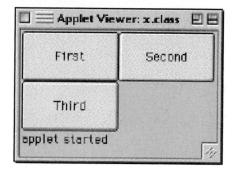

You can construct a GridLayout by specifying the numbers of rows and columns it will have. When the time comes to do a layout, the Components will be placed in equal-sized cells (resizing them, if necessary, to fill the cells) in the order in which they were added. A portion of a row may be left unfilled, as we see above, and if more items are added to the Container than there are cells requested, the layout will allocate enough columns to fit all the Components.

In the Exercises, we will explore exactly how a GridLayout determines the number of rows and columns needed. For now, it's enough to advise you to have enough

Components to result in placing at least one in the last row. For example, with 3 rows of 4 columns each, you shouldn't expect any surprises if you add 9, 10, 11, or 12 Components.

As you might infer from the screen shot above, GridLayout will resize the Components to fill its cells. Like FlowLayout and BorderLayout, this layout allows you to specify the horizontal and vertical gaps between cells (with default value zero).

There are three constructors for this class, depending on how much information you want to provide.

GridLayout()

Creates a new layout with one row, an unlimited number of columns, and zero horizontal and vertical gaps between cells.

GridLayout (int rows, int columns)

This is like the default constructor, except that you can set the number of rows and columns in the layout.

GridLayout (int rows, int columns, int hgap, int vgap)

Here, you can set everything.

If FlowLayout, BorderLayout, and GridLayout were the only LayoutManagers that Java had and would ever have, you could factor out nearly all of the methods of these three classes into a single superclass. That's an indication that you're going to see quite a few methods in GridLayout that you've already seen.

```
int getColumns()
int getRows()
```

Returns the number of columns or rows, respectively, in this layout.

```
int getHgap()
int getVgap()
```

Returns the current horizontal or vertical gap, respectively, for this layout.

```
void setColumns(int columns)
void setRows(int rows)
```

Sets the number of columns or rows, respectively, of this layout.

```
void setHgap(int h)
void setVgap(int v)
```

Sets the horizontal or vertical gap, respectively, of this layout.

No Layout at All

No long list of methods here, we promise. In fact, the last layout we'll discuss has no constructors and no methods, because it isn't a class at all. The layout classes we've discussed so far are powerful and easy to use, but they do so much behind the scenes that they take a lot of control out of the programmer's hands. Most of the time, that's a good idea—we generally wouldn't want to have to deal with the display differences among a dozen or more platforms, browsers, and Java development environments, nor do we want to worry about losing sight of a Component when an Applet is resized.

Still, there are times when you might want to take the reins and lay out widgets to a precise and unvarying specification. You can do this by indicating that no LayoutManager at all should be used in a Container. We do so by using the null layout. We'll have more to say about null in the next chapter. It's the only Object literal, and it is often used as a signal to mean "nothing" in various contexts. For example, if we say

null

```
myContainer.setLayout(null);
```

we are indicating that we don't want to use any LayoutManager to place the Components of myContainer, but, rather, want to position and size them ourselves, using the Component methods setLocation(), setSize(), and setBounds() [particularly setBounds ()]. This can be handy when we're using widgets in combination with on-screen graphics. If, for example, we wanted to group two buttons within an enclosing rectangle, we would want to anchor the buttons in place with respect to the underlying graphic. Let's suppose that we want to achieve a look like this, with two buttons on a colored rectangle, all surrounded by a 2-pixel-wide black border:

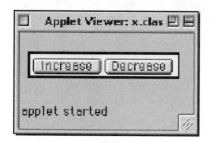

Here's a first stab at the program. Cover up the screen shot, pretend you never saw it, and look the program over carefully. How clear is it?

```
public class Fixed extends Applet
{
    Button increase = new Button("Increase");
    Button decrease = new Button("Decrease");

    public void init()
```

```
    {
        setLayout(null);
        add(increase);
        add(decrease);

        increase.setBounds(12, 24, 70, 16);
        decrease.setBounds(86, 24, 70, 16);
    }

    public void paint(Graphics g)
    {
        // Draw the 2-pixel-wide border
        g.drawRect(7, 19, 156, 26);
        g.drawRect(8, 20, 154, 24);

        // Now fill it with yellow.
        g.setColor(Color.yellow);
        g.fillRect(9, 21, 152, 22);
    }
}
```

It works, more or less, but note that the program has no fewer than *20* magic numbers! Of course, we could cut through some of this fog by declaring extra instance variables, such as ANCHOR_X, ANCHOR_Y, BTTN_HEIGHT, BTTN_WIDTH, VSPACE, and HSPACE, but even if we do, we wind up with something that is, at best, a lot of work to code and, at worst, incomprehensible. The moral is clear:

> The null layout can be useful, but generally it's better to leave the work to a real LayoutManager.
>
> *Caution:* If you ever use a null layout, you'll have to remember to set the sizes and positions of *all* the components that will be used, because there's no LayoutManager to do it for you.

Review Questions

2.1 If you don't specify a layout for a Panel, which do you get?
2.2 Of the layout managers we've discussed, which *don't* resize the Components being laid out?
2.3 Can you setLayout() of a Component object?

4.3 Other Containers, Other Details

The Containers we've discussed so far all "live" in the applet panel. There are also some containers that are far more mobile—in fact, they can be placed anywhere on the screen. In this section, we introduce the Window, Frame, and Dialog classes. We will also talk about using Frames to make Java *applications,* programs that aren't invoked by a browser but are more like traditional "free-standing" programs. Before we get to either of these topics, though, we need to introduce one more class that addresses some of the problems we just saw with mixing graphics and widgets.

The `Canvas` Class

If you want to paint on the screen, there's a `Component` subclass that's made specifically for the purpose, namely `Canvas`. Unless you're using a `null` layout, there's no possible way for any `LayoutManager` to know where you've placed your graphics, so an applet that looks good when you're designing it may be a horrible mess when it is run within a different system.

Java Design Tip

> It's a good idea to try a program in as many different environments as possible. Not only might the look vary considerably, but you might even find that a Java program that runs as expected on one system may produce entirely unexpected results on another.

The `Canvas` class, as we'll see in Chapter 6, also responds to all events, which, when combined with its drawing prowess, makes it the ideal candidate for creating custom `Components`. Want a visual thermometer, a dial, or a fancy button? Make your own subclass of `Canvas` to do the job.

This class has a single default constructor.

`Canvas()`

Creates a `Canvas` object of size zero. Like most other `Components`, a `Canvas` will generally be used within some `Container`, such as a `Panel`. If it is, the `LayoutManager` of the parent `Container` will size the `Canvas` for you. If you want to specify the size, you can always use one of the `Component` size methods, such as `setBounds()`.

`Canvas` also has a `paint()` method, which provides you with a `Graphics` argument that you can use for all of your drawing calls.

Let's see how we can use `Canvas` to produce a class of our own. We'll invent a class, `WarningMessage`, that will display an attention-grabbing message provided by the user of the class. The message will be drawn in bold italics and will be preceded by three red exclamation marks, like this:

!¡! *Really erase hard drive?*

(Trust us, the exclamation marks really are red, however they might look here.)

Let's investigate the class definition by looking first at its structure.

```
class WarningMessage extends Canvas
{
    private String myMessage; // We store the message here.

    public WarningMessage(String message)
    {
        ...
    }

    public void paint(Graphics g)
    {
        ...
    }
}
```

The header indicates that this class is named `WarningMessage` and that it is a subclass of `Canvas` and so inherits all of the available `Canvas` methods (along with all those of `Component`, too). The body of the definition contains one instance variable, where we store the message to be displayed, along with a constructor and an override of the `Canvas` `paint()` method.

Now let's fill the pieces in. Here's the constructor:

```
public WarningMessage(String message)
{
    myMessage = message;
    setSize(60, 25);
}
```

Constructors are very important parts of most class definitions. A class's constructor is invoked when a new object of that type is created. This is the place to do any initialization, and in this case, we get the message provided for us and store it in the instance variable `myMessage`. Having done that, we set the size of our `WarningMessage`.[3]

> A constructor almost always has `public` access (so it can be called in declarations in other classes). It has no return type (not even `void`) and must *always* have the same name as the class. Constructors are intended for any initializations that must be done to build a new object.

The `paint()` method override is simple enough: We set the current color and font of the `Graphics` context `g`, draw three exclamation marks in different locations, change the color and font, and draw the message.

```
public void paint(Graphics g)
{
    g.setColor(Color.red);
    g.setFont(new Font("SansSerif", Font.BOLD, 18));
    g.drawString("!", 10, 20);
```

---

[3]We used magic numbers to set the size of the `WarningMessage`. It would hve been better to find the dimensions of the message and use them to set the size. Look up the `FontMetrics` class to see how that might be done.

```
        g.drawString("!", 16, 24);
        g.drawString("!", 22, 16);
        g.setColor(Color.black);
        g.setFont(new Font("SansSerif",
            Font.ITALIC + Font.BOLD, 10));
        g.drawString(myMessage, 32, 18);
    }
}
```

Now it is clear why we bothered with the instance variable `myMessage`. We had to have it, because we needed to set it in the constructor and use it in the `paint()` method. If we had made it a local variable in either the constructor or `paint()`, it would have been accessible in only one place and would have had no meaning in the other.

> An instance variable is accessible by any method in its class, so it provides a convenient way of sharing information between methods. Instance variables should nearly always have `private` access (so other objects can't inspect or modify them without the class's permission).

That's it—we've built a class all on our own. This is really the heart of almost all "real" programming tasks, especially in object-oriented programming. The designers of Java clearly couldn't have made classes to handle all possible programming situations, so they provided a powerful suite of fundamental classes and gave us the ability to make classes of our own to address our needs. In essence, designing classes allows us to *extend* Java to meet our own needs. If we ever need a graphic warning message in a program, all we have to do is write our own `WarningMessage` class and save it to use whenever we need it. As a matter of fact, this wasn't an empty exercise; we'll use this class in just a few more pages.

> At a fundamental level, programming in Java is nothing more than designing and using classes.

Windows

It's time to return to our discussion of `Containers`. The `Window` class is the superclass of two other classes we'll discuss in this section, `Frame` and `Dialog`. A `Window` appears as a rectangular area that is displayed on top of any existing applet or browser or, in fact, anything that is already showing on the screen. In that respect, a `Window` object acts visually like the windows you're used to seeing on your system, except that a `Window` doesn't have any of the ornaments you're used to, such as scroll bars, a title, and "grow" and "go away" boxes. Because a `Window` is, visually, a naked rectangle, it is most often subclassed to create custom pop-up `Components`. We won't have much to say about the `Window` class here, because it is rarely used on its own. Instead, you'll be much more likely to use the `Window` subclasses `Frame` and `Dialog`.

For layout purposes, a `Window` and its subclasses all default to `BorderLayout` unless you set the layout to something else.

There are three useful `Window` methods that we should mention before we leave, particularly because they are often used in the `Window` subclasses `Frame` and `Dialog`.

void **dispose**()

Once it has been created, a `Window` consumes quite a few system resources. You can't necessarily be sure that these resources will be immediately released when the `Window` vanishes from sight, so it's good programming practice to free up all resources by calling this method after you've finished with the `Window`.

void **pack**()

This method resizes this `Window` to fit the `Components` it contains. You would call this method if you didn't want to call `setSize()` to set the dimensions of a `Window`.

void **show**()

Creating a `Window` (or any of its subclasses) and even adding it to some other `Container` won't make it appear on the screen. To do that, you need an explicit call to `show()`.

Frames

A `Frame` is a `Window` with all the dressing that's appropriate to the system in which it is running. It will have a title, and it may have scroll bars, a menu bar, its own cursor, and system-specific widgets to hide it, minimize it, grow it, and so on. A `Frame` is a `Container` subclass (with default `BorderLayout`), so we can add to it any `Components` we wish.

The default size for a `Frame` is (0, 0), so a `Frame` should call `setBounds()` to size itself and place itself appropriately on the screen. The anchor position is measured in screen coordinates, relative to the upper-left corner of the whole display. In addition, a `Frame` is initially invisible, so you'll need to have it call `show()` to make itself visible.

There are two `Frame` constructors you can use, depending on whether you want to specify a title.

Frame()

Creates a new `Frame` with no title at all.

Frame(String title)

Creates a new `Frame` with the specified title.

`Frame` has the usual `Container` and layout methods, along with two others that are of interest to us here.

```
boolean isResizable()
void setResizable(boolean canResize)
```

The first method returns `true` if the `Frame` can be resized by the user, `false` if it cannot. The second allows you to set whether the `Frame` is resizable.

Below, we provide an example of an applet that pops up a `Frame` asking for information from the user. The North region (remember, `Frame`s default to `BorderLayout`) contains instructions; the Center region contains a `Panel` with two `Label`s and two `TextField`s, arranged in a grid; and the South region contains a `Panel` with a `Button`.

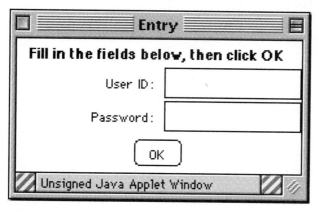

```java
import java.applet.*;
import java.awt.*;
import java.awt.event.*;

public class Framer extends Applet implements ActionListener
{
    Frame myFrame = new Frame("Entry");
    Label explainLbl = new Label("Fill in the fields below, then click
                        OK");
    Label label1 = new Label("User ID:", Label.RIGHT);
    Label label2 = new Label("Password:", Label.RIGHT);
    TextField field1 = new TextField(15);
    TextField field2 = new TextField(15);
    Button okayBttn = new Button("OK");

    public void init()
    {
        // Set the background color of the frame, the
        // font used in the label, and the password echo char.
        myFrame.setBackground(Color.white);
        explainLbl.setFont(new Font("SansSerif", Font.BOLD, 10));
        field2.setEchoChar('*');

        // Add the explanation label to the frame.
        myFrame.add(BorderLayout.NORTH, explainLbl);

        // Build the center panel and add it to the frame.
        Panel pc = new Panel();
        pc.setLayout(new GridLayout(2, 2, 8, 2));
        pc.add(label1);
        pc.add(field1);
        pc.add(label2);
```

```
        pc.add(field2);
        myFrame.add(BorderLayout.CENTER, pc);

        // Put the OK button in a panel and add it, too.
        Panel ps = new Panel();
        ps.add(okayBttn);
        myFrame.add(BorderLayout.SOUTH, ps);

        // For now, pay no attention to these two lines.
        okayBttn.addActionListener(this);

        // Finally, set the location and the size of the frame,
        // and make it visible. We need both of these calls.
        myFrame.setBounds(50, 150, 250, 100);
        myFrame.show();
    }

    /**
     * Handle a click on the "OK" button. For now, don't worry
     * about how this works--it'll be explained in Chapter 6.
     */
    public void actionPerformed(ActionEvent e)
    {
        myFrame.dispose();
    }
}
```

If you run this applet in a Web browser, you might find that the browser adds an alert message to the frame, as it did in the illustration above. This is a security precaution, because it would be fairly easy for an unscrupulous programmer to write an applet that "spoofs" some other program, asking for information that it would then save for later use. In this example, for instance, users might think they are interacting with their own mail server and thus unwittingly reveal all the information necessary to get into their e-mail account.

For now, don't worry about the `implements ActionListener` clause in the class header, the line

```
    okayBttn.addActionListener(this);
```

in the `init()` method, or the `actionPerformed()` method. These are included so that a click on the "OK" button will make the frame vanish. Without them, there is a chance that there will be no way of getting rid of the frame, even by quitting the browser or applet runner. We'll explain event handling in Chapter 6.

Dialogs

A `Dialog` is a `Window` that is intended for simple input and output. In fact, the `Frame` example we just finished would really be better as a `Dialog`, because it gets only two pieces of text and responds to a button click.

If you've spent any time at all using computer applications, you've probably seen dozens of dialogs. You may have also observed that some dialogs are *modal*, which means that while they're up they hog the incoming events. Selfishly, a modal dialog acts as though it, and it alone, should get all the attention: There can be no moving windows, clicking on other buttons, or using menus while the dialog is open. Dialogs in Java can be modal or *modeless,* they may or may not be resizable, and they may or may not be given a title. As we mentioned, each Dialog is also a Window and hence also a Container (and a Component, as well). As we also mentioned, a Dialog has a BorderLayout, unless you set its layout to something else.

A Dialog must be associated with a Frame known as its *parent* frame. This presents a small difficulty for Dialogs associated with applets, because an applet may not have a Frame to act as parent for its Dialogs. Somewhere, either in the browser or the applet runner, there may be a Frame, but getting it isn't easy. Fortunately, there's an easy solution: Simply create a dummy Frame in the applet whose sole purpose is to provide a Frame for the Dialog. Using a null parent sometimes also works.

As with Frame, you must set the size and location of a Dialog, and you must also call show() (an override of the corresponding Window method) to make it appear. In addition, when you're finished with a Dialog, it's a good idea to call dispose() to free up its system resources.

Dialog has four constructors.

Dialog(Frame parent)

Creates a new, untitled, modeless Dialog with the specified parent.

Dialog(Frame parent, String title)

Creates a modeless Dialog with the given title.

Dialog(Frame parent, boolean isModal)

Creates a Dialog with the given title. If the second argument is true, makes a modal Dialog; if the argument is false, makes a modeless Dialog.

Dialog(Frame parent, String title, boolean isModal)

Creates a Dialog with the specified properties.
There is a fairly small collection of Dialog methods of interest to us here.

```
boolean isModal()
void setModal(boolean isModal)
```

The first method of this pair returns true if the Dialog is currently modal, false if it is not. The second allows you to set whether the Dialog is modal.

```
boolean isResizable()
void setResizable(boolean canResize)
```

The first method returns true if the Frame can be resized by the user, false if it cannot. The second allows you to set whether the Frame is resizable.

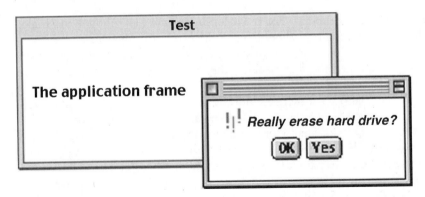

Figure 4.3

A `Dialog`, on top of the application that spawned it.

Figure 4.3 shows an example of using a `Dialog`. When the program opens, it immediately presents a `Dialog` with a warning message and a pair of buttons the user may click. It's a good thing this is just an example, because it's not exactly what we would call user-friendly (in fact, "user-hostile" might be a better description). In the screen shot below, note that the `Dialog` is not tied to the rest of the display. We deliberately set the location of the `Dialog` to extend beyond the application `Frame`, and if we had wanted to, could have placed the `Dialog` completely outside the `Frame`.

The program is interesting not only for its use of a `Dialog` but also for the fact that it is an application, not an applet. As we mentioned earlier, an application is a program that does not need an enclosing program such as a browser or applet runner in which to run. In fact, it's quite possible to compile the classes, link them appropriately, and turn a Java application into a stand-alone program just like your favorite word processor or Web browser.[4] Before we continue, we should alert you to the fact that if you try this on your own, you'll probably be able to compile this example file just as you always have, but you won't be able to run the result in either an applet runner or a browser, because it's not an applet. It will be necessary for you either to find a Java application runner or to check the documentation, if you're using an integrated development environment.

As we did before, let's begin by looking at the structure of the file "DialogAppTest.java." We see immediately that the file contains three class definitions: `DialogAppTest`, `WarningDialog`, and—lo and behold!—our old friend the `WarningMessage` class we just invented a few pages back.

---

[4]Sun's *HotJava* Web browser is just that—a Web browser written entirely in Java. It was one of the earliest Java applications and the first Java-aware Web browser. This provides ample evidence that Java is not just for "toy" programs.

> A Java program is nothing but a collection of class definitions, perhaps spread over several files. Every Java source code file must have a `public` class definition, and the name of the file must be the same as that of the `public` class (with the extension ".java" added).

In this example, the first class, `DialogAppTest`, depends on the second, and the second, `WarningDialog`, obviously uses `WarningMessage`. This ordering was chosen for purposes of readability only.

> The order in which class definitions appear in a file need not have anything to do with dependencies among the classes.

We'll look at the organization of the `DialogAppTest` class first.

```
public class DialogAppTest extends Frame
{
    public DialogAppTest(String title)
    {
        super(title);
    }
    public static void main(String[] args)
    {
        ...
    }
}
```

First, note that `DialogAppTest` is defined to be a subclass of `Frame`. Making it so gives the application a window for display and also provides a parent for the `Dialog`. We don't have to build an application by subclassing `Frame`, but it is very common to do so.

First, we see that this class has a constructor with a single argument, but what's that `super()` in the constructor body? Is it a method we haven't seen before? It sure looks like one, having a parenthesized argument list, but it's not—it's a constructor call. We wanted to get a title in the application's frame, and an easy way to do that is to call the `Frame` constructor that sets the title. The `super()` call is just a call to the appropriate `Frame` constructor!

> In a class that extends another class, you can use a call to `super()` to invoke the constructor of the superclass; "super" is just a synonym for "the next class up in the class hierarchy," just as "this" is a synonym for "this object."
> *Caution:* If a `super()` constructor is used in a subclass constructor, it must be the first statement.

We haven't had to do this before, because Java has always done it for us— the first thing that happens in a subclass constructor is always a hidden call to the no-argument superclass constructor. We needed an explicit `super()` call here precisely because we didn't want to have the compiler insert a call to the default constructor.[5]

Continuing the class definition, we find a call to another method we haven't seen before, `main()`. The `main()` method is the important one here. In a Java application, execution starts at the first statement of `main()` and continues until the method returns (or disaster strikes). In some Java programming environments, you need to specify the "startup file" to be the one containing the `main()` method that controls execution.

> For reasons we'll explain later, every Java application must have a `main()` method. Its header must look like
>
> ```
> public static void main(String[] args)
> ```

We'll finish this class definition by looking at the `main()` method. After the header, we see a local declaration of a `Frame`, `f`. Most applications will want to display something on the screen, so we declare a `Frame` object for that purpose. In this case, as often happens, the class is a `Frame` by inheritance, so we initialize `f` to be a new instance of `DialogAppTest`. We didn't need to do it this way in this simple example, but it serves as a good protocol in many cases.

The rest of the method is simple enough: We add a `Label` to the `Frame`, set the size and location of the `Frame`, and show it. The last thing the method does before expiring is create and show a new `WarningDialog`. Note that we didn't need to add the `Dialog` to the application `Frame`. Can you figure out why?

```
public static void main(String[] args)
{
    Frame f = new DialogAppTest("Test");
    f.add(BorderLayout.CENTER,
      new Label(" The application frame..."));
    f.setBounds(20, 20, 300, 100);
    f.show();

    WarningDialog wd = new WarningDialog(f, "Really erase hard drive?");
    wd.show();
}
```

The next part to explore is the `WarningDialog` class. This class owns a `WarningMessage` widget and two `Buttons`. The constructor for the class is largely the sort of thing we've seen before: calls to `add()` to place the `Components` in the object, followed by a `setBounds()` call to place this `Dialog` where we want it. Excising that lot leaves us with this:

---

[5]If this seems confusing, be patient. We'll go over it in more detail in Chapter 5.

```
public WarningDialog(Frame parent, String message)
{
    super(parent, false);
    // ...
}
```

This constructor has two arguments: the parent `Frame` and the message `String` (which is sent to `WarningMessage` via its constructor). That's clear enough, and we just saw what a `super()` call does—in this case, we're calling the superclass `Dialog` constructor, specifying the parent `Frame` that all `dialogs` have to have, and indicating by the `false` argument that we don't want the `dialog` to be modal.

Finally, we're finished. The only part of the file that remains is the definition of the `WarningMessage` class, and we've already been through that earlier. Here's the complete file, with comments restored:

```
//----------------- File DialogAppTest.java -----------------

import java.awt.*; // Notice, no import java.applet.* !!
import java.awt.event.*;

/**
 * This is an application, not an applet. It extends Frame
 * so there's some place for it to be displayed
 * and has a main() method, which is where execution begins.
 */
public class DialogAppTest extends Frame
{
    /**
     * In this simple application, all constructor has to do
     * is call the superclass constructor to set the title.
     */
    public DialogAppTest(String title)
    {
        super(title);
    }

    /**
     * Set up the application frame and the warning dialog.
     */
    public static void main(String[] args)
    {
        Frame f = new DialogAppTest("Test");
        f.add(BorderLayout.CENTER, new Label(" The application
                                        frame..."));
        f.setBounds(20, 20, 300, 100);
        f.show();
        WarningDialog wd = new WarningDialog(f, "Really erase hard
                                        drive?");
        wd.show();
    }
}

//----------------------------------------------------------
/**
 * This class is an extension of Dialog. It has a graphical display
 * (a WarningMessage object) and two buttons, neither of which
 * (fortunately!) does anything but make this dialog go away.
 */
class WarningDialog extends Dialog implements ActionListener
```

```
{
    private WarningMessage warn;
    private Button okayBttn = new Button("OK");
    private Button yesBttn = new Button("Yes");

    /**
     * Our constructor for this class. We need a Frame argument,
     * since a dialog must know its parent frame.
     */
    public WarningDialog(Frame parent, String message)
    {
        // First, call the Dialog constructor and then set some
        // of the properties of this object.
        super(parent, false);
        setBackground(Color.white);
        setResizable(false);

        // Initialize the warning message and add it to this dialog.
        warn = new WarningMessage(message);
        add(BorderLayout.NORTH, warn);

        // Add the two buttons in a panel of their own
        Panel p = new Panel();
        p.add(okayBttn);
        p.add(yesBttn);
        add(BorderLayout.CENTER, p);

        okayBttn.addActionListener(this);
        yesBttn.addActionListener(this);

        // Finally, set the size and location of this dialog.
        setBounds(200, 80, 190, 75);
    }

    /**
     * Respond to a click on either button (see Ch. 6).
     */
    public void actionPerformed(ActionEvent e)
    {
        dispose();
    }
}

//----------------------------------------------------------

class WarningMessage extends Canvas
{
    // To save space, we've deleted the class definition
    // here, since we discussed it at the start of this section.
}
```

Review Questions

3.1 Why do we recommend doing all drawing on a `Canvas`?

3.2 What is the visual difference between a `Window` and a `Frame`?

3.3 What is the difference between a modal and a modeless `Dialog`?

3.4 What happens when you call `super()`?

3.5 What method distinguishes a Java application?

4.4 Menus

We've all seen and used menus that drop down with a list of choices when we click on them. Java has menus, even though the class structure that implements them is a bit complicated (Figure 4.4).

For all the complexity of the class hierarchy, menus have a straightforward logical structure.

▲ A `MenuBar` holds a collection of `Menus` and must be associated with a `Frame`.
▲ A `Menu` holds a collection of `MenuItems` and separators.
▲ A `MenuItem` may be enabled or disabled, and it may be checkable.
▲ A `Menu` may also be a `MenuItem`, leading to hierarchical menus.

In Figure 4.5 we can see the `MenuBar` at the top of the `Frame`. This `MenuBar` contains a single `Menu`, "File." The "File" `Menu` contains six `MenuItems`: "New," "Open," "Save," "Lose," "Randomize," and "Scatter," along with a *separator* between the "Open" and "Save" items. The "Save" item is *disabled*, which means that it is displayed in a distinguishing way and will not respond to the mouse. The "Lose" item is actually another `Menu` (which is why `Menu` is a subclass of `MenuItem`) containing four items: "Some File," "This Directory," "Hard Drive," and "Mind." The "Mind" item is a `CheckBoxMenuItem`; it initially looks like any other item, and it toggles between a checked and an unchecked state each time it is selected.

`MenuShortcut` is a class that allows you to associate key combinations with menu items so that pressing the Control and N keys simultaneously would have the same

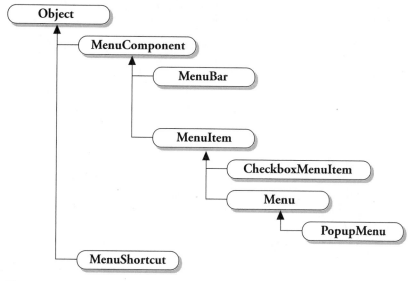

Figure 4.4

The **Menu** class hierarchy.

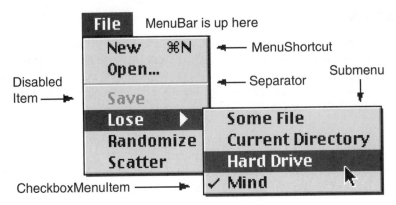

Figure 4.5

The parts of a **Menu**.

result as selecting the "New" item from the "File" menu, in our example. We won't discuss this class in depth; you can inspect it in the Class References appendix to this chapter.

You can designate a Menu as being a *tear-off menu*. On the systems that support this option, you can drag a selected Menu off the menu bar to another location, where it will remain open as a floating *palette*.

Where a MenuBar will appear and what its Menus will look like depend, of course, on the system in which the program is running; it may appear in the frame, or it may appear in the main menu bar at the top of the screen. (We ran the sample applet below on several systems and got both locations.)

MenuComponents

This abstract class is the superclass, directly or indirectly, of all the Menu classes except MenuShortcut, which means that its methods can be called by any of the other Menu classes. The only methods of concern to us here are two get/set pairs.

```
Font getFont()
void setFont(Font f)
```

These get or set the Font used for the name of this component. Setting a Font for a Menu will set the Font for all its items. setFont() can be used creatively to make strikingly ugly Menus.

```
String getName()
void setName(String name)
```

These get or set the name used for this component.

MenuBars

The `MenuBar` class holds `Menus`. You use the `add()` method to add a `Menu` to the `MenuBar`, and you associate a `MenuBar` with a `Frame` by using the `Frame` method `setMenuBar(MenuBar mb)`. This class has a single default constructor, `MenuBar()`, and the following methods, among others.

Menu **add**(Menu m)

This adds a `Menu` to this `MenuBar`. `Menus` are added in the order in which they appear in the program. You can't add a `MenuItem` to a `MenuBar`. `Menus` (and `MenuItems`) are distinguished by name, so a `MenuBar` can have only one `Menu` with a given name.

int **getMenuCount**()

Returns the current number of `Menus` in this `MenuBar`. This count does not include any submenus; it counts only the top-level ones whose names appear in the bar.

Menus

The `Menu` class has three constructors.

Menu()
Menu(String name)
Menu(String name, boolean canTearOff)

The first constructor creates an untitled `Menu` that can't be torn off. The second allows you to provide a name (like "File") for a nontearable `Menu`, and the last permits you to provide a name and indicate whether this `Menu` will be tearable (`true` argument) or not (`false` argument).

The methods of this class are similar in many ways to those of `MenuBar`. You use the `add()` method to add `MenuItems` (which can be `Menus`, you will recall) to the `Menu`. Items are added in order and are indexed from zero.

void **add**(String name)

This useful method creates a new `MenuItem` with the specified name and adds it to this `Menu`. Remember that `MenuItem` names must be distinct. If the argument string has already been used in this or another `Menu`, the existing item is removed and reinserted (often in a different position).

MenuItem **add**(MenuItem m)

Adds a `MenuItem` to this `Menu`.

void **addSeparator**()

Adds a graphical separator to this `Menu`. Separators do not respond to mouse events but are figured in the item count. See also `insertSeparator()`.

```
void insertSeparator(String name, int index)
```

Inserts a separator in the indicated position in this `Menu`. The index argument must be greater than or equal to zero.

```
boolean isTearOff()
```

Returns `true` if this Menu has the "tear-off" property, whether or not the system supports tear-off menus, and returns `false` if this Menu doesn't have the property.

MenuItems

This class describes the items that live in menus. Bear in mind that `MenuItem` is a superclass of `Menu`, so all the methods we describe here are available to `Menus`, too.

There are three constructors for this class. The two of interest to us are

```
MenuItem()
MenuItem(String name)
```

The first constructs an unnamed `MenuItem`, and the second constructs a new `MenuItem` with the specified name. In both, the items start their lives in an enabled state.

The `MenuItem` methods deal primarily with enabling/disabling items and inspecting/modifying their names.

```
String getLabel()
```

Returns the name of this item.

```
boolean isEnabled()
```

Returns `true` if this item is enabled, `false` otherwise.

```
void setEnabled(boolean isEnabled)
```

If the argument is true, this item is enabled (can respond to mouse clicks). If it is false, this item becomes disabled. Disabled items are often dimmed.

```
void setLabel(String name)
```

Sets the name of this item.

CheckboxMenuItems

A `CheckboxMenuItem` is a `MenuItem`, by inheritance. It maintains a state and a corresponding visual representation. An object of this type starts in the `false`, unchecked state and changes its state each time it is selected.

This class has three constructors.

```
CheckboxMenuItem()
CheckboxMenuItem(String name)
CheckboxMenuItem(String name, boolean state)
```

The first constructor creates a new, unnamed item in the false (unchecked) state. The second creates a named item in the false state, and the third allows you to set both the name and the state.

Along with the inherited MenuItem methods, this class includes the following methods of its own.

```
boolean getState()
void setState()
```

Gets or sets the state of this item.

PopupMenus

A PopupMenu is a Menu, with all the Menu features, that can appear when the user clicks in a Component.

There are two PopupMenu constructors.

```
PopupMenu()
PopupMenu(String name)
```

The first creates a new, unnamed Menu, and the second creates a Menu with the indicated name.

At this stage, all we can do is describe the single method of interest to us here. (We can't describe how to use the method until we've had a chance to discuss events in Chapter 6.)

```
void show(Component c, int x, int y)
```

This method causes the Menu to appear at the given location, measured in the local coordinates of the Component argument. In practice, a PopupMenu usually appears in response to a mouse click in the Component argument. It is then the job of the program to determine the Component, calculate the coordinates, and then call this method, placing the Menu where desired.

A Menu Sample

To tell the truth, the Menu classes are a lot easier to use than they are to describe. The process is really quite simple:

1. Construct a Menu.
2. Add items and separators to the Menu, disabling as necessary.

3. Repeat steps 1 and 2 as desired.
4. Construct a `MenuBar`.
5. Add all the `Menus` to the `MenuBar`.
6. Use `setMenuBar()` to attach the `MenuBar` to some `Frame`.

Take a look at the applet below and you'll see what we mean. This generates the Menu illustrated in Figure 4.5. It creates a `MenuBar`, named `mb`, with one `Menu`, `m`. `Menu m` contains six items: "New," "Open . . .," "Save," "Lose," "Randomize," and "Scatter." The item "Lose" is a submenu with four items of its own.

```java
import java.awt.*;
import java.awt.event.*; // just for the key code VK_N
import java.applet.*;

public class MenuTest extends Applet
{
    Frame myFrame = new Frame("Decisions, decisions!");
    public void init()
    {
        myFrame.setBackground(Color.white);

        // First, make the submenu.
        Menu sub = new Menu("Lose");
        sub.add("Some File");
        sub.add("Current Directory");
        sub.add("Hard Drive");
        sub.add(new CheckboxMenuItem("Mind", true));

        // Now make the main menu, adding the submenu
        // in the appropriate place.
        Menu m = new Menu("File", true);

        MenuItem itemN = new MenuItem("New");
        itemN.setShortcut(new MenuShortcut(KeyEvent.VK_N));
        m.add(itemN);

        m.add("Open...");

        m.addSeparator();

        MenuItem itemS = new MenuItem("Save");
        m.add(itemS);
        itemS.setEnabled(false);

        m.add(sub);

        m.add("Randomize");

        m.add("Scatter");

        MenuBar mb = new MenuBar();
        mb.add(m);

        // Associate the MenuBar with the frame
        myFrame.setMenuBar(mb);
```

```
        myFrame.setBounds(40, 130, 250, 130);
        myFrame.show();
    }
}
```

Review Questions

4.1 What are the purposes of the classes `MenuBar`, `Menu`, and `MenuItem`?

4.2 Why did the designers of Java make `Menu` a subclass of `MenuItem`?

4.5 Hands On

The Lablet for this chapter displays a simulation of a microwave oven. The design contains two graphics, for the oven door and the time display. It also contains ten buttons, arranged as we show in Figure 4.6.

Designing the Lablet

When we were setting up the design, we decomposed it into a collection of logically related units and then decomposed those units as needed. This is a good overall principle.

Design Tips

1. Design from the top down.
2. Don't worry about the details until you have the organization clear.
3. Defer low-level decisions as long as possible.

These tips apply equally well for both GUI design and programming.

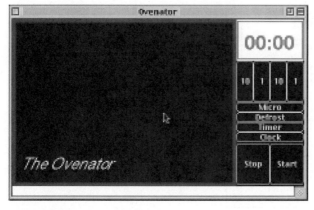

Figure 4.6

The **Ovenator** applet in action.

The visual hierarchy quickly became clear. Within the applet, we would place a control panel on the right side. The control panel would be further divided into four regions, one each for the time display, the four time buttons, the four cook mode buttons, and the two start/stop buttons. This gave us a total of five conceptual units, not counting the applet itself. Figure 4.7 illustrates the containment hierarchy, which is often called the *GUI hierarchy.*

It certainly seemed that ten buttons, five containers, and two graphics areas were entirely too many to lay out in one `init()` method. Even without counting up all the statements that would be required, we were certain that putting them all in one place would make `init()` too difficult to understand at first glance.

Programming Tip

Make life easy for the readers of your programs. Try to limit method definitions to a screen's worth of code, at most.

We could have broken the `init()` method out into a collection of smaller methods and then called each of these from `init()`, but there's an even better solution. The GUI hierarchy seems to be crying out for us to impose the obvious structure on it by breaking it up into separate classes, and that's exactly what we did.

Programming Tip

Think of design in terms of classes. Whenever you see a clearly related "chunk" of design, consider encapsulating that chunk into a class of its own.

Let's see—where does that leave us? It looks as though we'll have six classes:

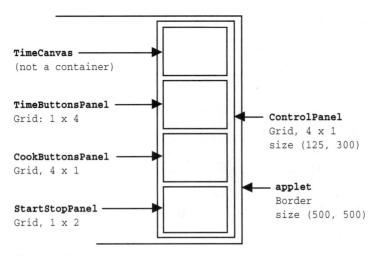

TimeCanvas
(not a container)

TimeButtonsPanel
Grid: 1 x 4

CookButtonsPanel
Grid, 4 x 1

StartStopPanel
Grid, 1 x 2

ControlPanel
Grid, 4 x 1
size (125, 300)

applet
Border
size (500, 500)

Figure 4.7

The GUI hierarchy of **Ovenator**.

▲ The applet itself, using a variable to hold a ControlPanel
▲ ControlPanel, which contains TimeCanvas, TimeButtonsPanel, CookButtonsPanel, and StartStopPanel instance variables
▲ TimeCanvas, containing nothing but a picture
▲ TimeButtonsPanel, with four instance variables for the four buttons
▲ CookButtonsPanel, also containing four buttons
▲ StartStopPanel, with its two buttons

The Lablet Code

Now we'll walk through the Lablet, pointing out sites of interest along the way. As usual, we begin with a comment block and a collection of import declarations. The applet class definition comes next. It has a single instance variable, myControls, and the expected init() and paint() methods. Did myControls *have* to be an instance variable? No—it could have been local to init(), but we put it up among the instance variables solely to make it easy to find.

Before we leave this class, we should point out that we're using a BorderLayout to place its ControlPanel on the right side. Note also how we use the dimensions of the applet when we're painting the door and its logo. By the way, we departed from our own advice here, by painting the door directly on the screen rather than using a Canvas. We did this not to be sloppy but rather to give you a chance to try using a Canvas on your own.

```
public class Ovenator extends Applet
{
    ControlPanel myControls = new ControlPanel();

    public void init()
    {
        setBackground(Color.darkGray);
        setLayout(new BorderLayout());

        add(BorderLayout.EAST, myControls);
    }

    public void paint(Graphics g)
    {
        Dimension mySize = getSize();

        g.setColor(Color.black);
        g.fill3DRect(5, 5, mySize.width - 115, mySize.height -10, true);
        g.setColor(Color.yellow);
        g.setFont(new Font("SansSerif", Font.ITALIC, 24));
        g.drawString("The Ovenator",10, mySize.height - 25);
    }
}
```

The ControlPanel class comes next. As we mentioned before, we can put the class definitions in any order in their file, so this choice is just for our convenience in reading the program. This class extends Panel, the usual choice when we're doing visual design. As before, we put the four objects it contains up as instance variables simply to make them easy to find.

Note that we use a GridLayout, arranging the four data members in a single column and that we also set the size to avoid surprises. Because ControlPanel isn't an applet, we do all our initialization in the constructor. Not only don't we have an init() method available, but we wouldn't use one even if we had—initializations belong in constructors.

```
class ControlPanel extends Panel
{
    TimeCanvas        timeDisplay = new TimeCanvas();
    TimeButtonsPanel timeButtons = new TimeButtonsPanel();
    CookButtonsPanel cookButtons = new CookButtonsPanel();
    StartStopPanel    startStop   = new StartStopPanel();

    public ControlPanel()
    {
        setBackground(Color.black);
        setForeground(Color.yellow);
        setLayout(new GridLayout(4,1));
        setSize(125,300);

        add(timeDisplay);
        add(timeButtons);
        add(cookButtons);
        add(startStop);
    }
}
```

We're now down to the bottom level of the GUI hierarchy. The TimeCanvas class is simplicity itself; all the real work is done in our override of Canvas's paint() method. In an applet that actually did something, this class would probably be a TextField, so we could change the time in a realistic way.[6]

```
class TimeCanvas extends Canvas
{
    public TimeCanvas()
    {
        setBackground(Color.white);
    }

    public void paint(Graphics g)
    {
        Dimension mySize = getSize();
        g.setColor(Color.black);
        g.draw3DRect(2, 2, mySize.width - 5, mySize.height - 5, true);
        g.setColor(Color.red);
        g.setFont(new Font("SansSerif", Font.BOLD, 30));
        g.drawString("00:00", 12, 45);
    }
}
```

All that's left are the definitions for the classes TimeButtonsPanel, CookButtonsPanel, and StartStopPanel. These are nearly identical, and they are all easy to understand. In each, the contained buttons are instance variables; they are

---

[6]That, by the way, is a somewhat difficult task, knowing only what you know now. It will be easy once you learn about threads in Chapter 11.

constructed in the class's constructor and then added to the class. It is worth noting that we're using a form of the declaration that you've seen but that we haven't discussed in much detail so far. If you have several variables of the same type, you can declare them all in one statement by following the type name with a comma-separated list of the variables.

```
class TimeButtonsPanel extends Panel
{
    Button b10Minutes = new Button("10"),
           b1Minute = new Button("1"),
           b10Seconds = new Button("10"),
           b1Second = new Button("1");

    public TimeButtonsPanel()
    {
        setLayout(new GridLayout(1,4));

        add(b10Minutes);
        add(b1Minute);
        add(b10Seconds);
        add(b1Second);
    }
}

//-------------------------------------------------------------

class CookButtonsPanel extends Panel
{
    Button bMicro = new Button("Micro"),
           bDefrost = new Button("Defrost"),
           bTimer = new Button("Timer"),
           bClock = new Button("Clock");

    public CookButtonsPanel()
    {
        setLayout(new GridLayout(4,1));

        add(bMicro);
        add(bDefrost);
        add(bTimer);
        add(bClock);
    }
}

//-------------------------------------------------------------

class StartStopPanel extends Panel
{
    Button bStop = new Button("Stop"),
           bStart = new Button("Start");

    public StartStopPanel()
    {
        setLayout(new GridLayout(1,2));

        add(bStop);
        add(bStart);
    }
}
```

4.6 Summary

■ We discussed the following classes:

BorderLayout	Menu
Canvas	MenuBar
CheckboxMenuItem	MenuComponent
Container	MenuItem
Dialog	MenuShortcut
FlowLayout	Panel
Frame	PopupMenu
GridLayout	Window

LayoutManager (an interface briefly)

■ A Container is used to group Components for visual display. A Container is a Component, by inheritance, so Containers can hold other Containers.

■ It's quite common to have a hierarchical GUI organization, with Containers nested within Containers, nested within Containers, and so on.

■ Components are added to a Container by using the Container add() method. A Container cannot contain itself, either directly or indirectly.

■ For graphic purposes, each Component (and hence each Container) has a local coordinate system, relative to its anchor point (the upper-left corner of its bounding rectangle).

■ Container is an abstract class. The instances of Container must therefore come from the AWT Container subclasses Panel, Window, Frame, and Dialog or from user-defined subclasses of Container or its subclasses.

■ Panel is a commonly used subclass of Container. Panel exists for the purpose of grouping Components in the GUI hierarchy. Panel is often subclassed for custom purposes. Applet is a subclass of Panel.

■ Each Container has its own LayoutManager describing how its Components will be displayed. The LayoutManager of a Component may be changed by the setLayout() method.

■ The AWT classes that implement LayoutManager are FlowLayout, BorderLayout, GridLayout, CardLayout, and GridBagLayout (which we didn't discuss). With the exception of GridBagLayout, all these classes have two integers that specify the horizontal and vertical gaps between the Components being laid out.

■ The FlowLayout class is the default layout for Panel (and hence for Applet). In a Container with FlowLayout, the Components are arranged in the order in which they were added: left to right within rows, with the rows arranged top to bottom.

■ BorderLayout is the default layout for Window, Frame, and Dialog. In a BorderLayout, the Container is arranged into five regions, identified by the names North, West, Center, East, and South. In this layout, Components are added by specifying the name (as a String) in the add() method call.

■ In a GridLayout, the Container is divided into a rectangular array of equal-sized cells, arranged in rows and columns. The number of rows and columns may be specified in the layout constructor.

■ Using a null argument in setLayout() will result in the Container having no

LayoutManager at all. Used with the Component methods move(), resize(), and reshape(), this permits precise and unvarying arrangement of the Components, at the expense of flexibility and possible platform-dependence.

■ The Canvas class is a Component subclass (but not a Container) that is used for drawing. It is the common choice for designing custom Components. Canvas has a paint() method, which can be overridden for drawing.

■ Window is a subclass of Container and a superclass of Frame and Dialog. A Window object appears as an unadorned rectangle that "floats" above the underlying applet or application. Window is rarely used by itself—it is much more common to use one of its subclasses or to use Window as the base for a user-defined custom class.

■ A Frame is a Window with all the ornaments of the Windows of the underlying system, such as a title and a close box.

■ A Dialog has some of the Frame ornaments, but not all. A Dialog is most often used to inform the user of some condition or to get a limited amount of information. A Dialog must have a parent Frame.

■ Whereas an applet must be run in a program like an applet runner or Web browser, a Java application is capable of executing on its own. Any class can serve as the basis for an application (though it's most common to subclass Frame). To serve as an application, a class must have a main() method.

■ A Java program may have Menus. The MenuBar class, which must be associated with a Frame, contains Menus. Menus contain MenuItems.

■ Menu is a subclass of MenuItem, permitting a Menu to have submenus.

■ A MenuItem may be enabled, so that it responds to mouse events, or disabled, so that it doesn't.

■ A CheckboxMenuItem has two states, which are indicated when the item is displayed. The state (and its visual representation) changes each time the item is selected.

4.7 Exercises

1. Why would you ever need to call either of the Container methods countComponents() or getComponentCount()? *Hint:* Think about changing the layout of the Container or adding another Component.

2. Refer to Figure 4.2.
    a. Name all the Containers.
    b. Name all the Components.
    c. In the method call _____.isAncestorOf(List2), which Container names could you put in the blank space to make the method return true?

3. Given that myPanel is of type Panel, what does this code fragment do?

```
int n = myPanel.countComponents();
Component c = myPanel.getComponent(n - 2);
myPanel.remove(c);
```

Couch your answer in simple terms; don't just tell what each statement does.

4. Which has more methods available for its use, an `Applet` object or a `Window` object?

5. What is the default alignment for `FlowLayout`? How would you change it?

6. Of the three layouts we discussed, one stands out for having default horizontal and vertical gaps that are different from the others. Which is the odd one?

7. What are the default layouts for `Panel`, `Window`, `Applet`, `Dialog`, and `Frame`, respectively?

8. Take a look at Figure 4.2 and the applet below it. Run the applet and note that it doesn't look like the figure. Obviously, the difference is due to the fact that we used the default `FlowLayout` for each `Panel`. Rewrite the applet, inserting the necessary `setLayout()` calls and modifying the arguments to the calls to `add()`, where necessary, to make the applet look like the figure.

9. Do (or redo) Exercise 21 of Chapter 3, knowing what you do now.

10. Here's the skeleton of an applet:

```
public class Layouts extends Applet
{
    Button bA = new Button("A"),
           bB = new Button("B"),
           bC = new Button("C"),
           bD = new Button("D"),
           bE = new Button("E"),
           bF = new Button("F");
    Panel  p1 = new Panel(),
           p2 = new Panel(),
           p3 = new Panel(),
           p4 = new Panel(),
           p5 = new Panel(),
           p6 = new Panel();

    public void init()
    {
        ...
    }
}
```

For each of the following parts, fill in the `init()` method so that the applet looks like the picture. There may not be just one way to make these layouts; in each part, try to find the most elegant or efficient solution.

a.
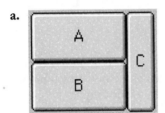

b.
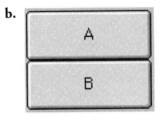

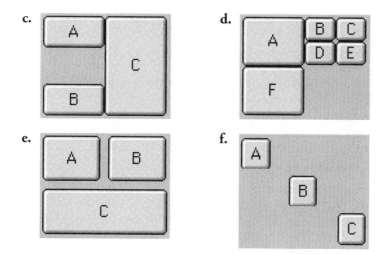

11. Write an applet that produces a display that looks *exactly* like the entire collection of pictures in Exercise 10, with part letters and grey backgrounds included. Don't use a `null` layout. (This is quite a challenging exercise.)

12. Rewrite the Chapter 3 `Gigobite` Lablet so that it doesn't get weird when the applet window is resized. (This is time-consuming but nowhere near as difficult as Exercise 11.)

13. Do Exercise 22 in Chapter 3. This time, you don't have to be especially careful to make the calculator look exactly like the screen shot. Don't waste your time with a `null` layout, and don't worry about the drop shadow.

14. Suppose you were designing a `LabeledTextField` class containing a `Label` and a `TextField`. It should look something like this:

(You don't have to paint the gray background. Some background will be provided by the browser or applet runner).

a. What constructors would you want? You can't write the constructors, because you haven't designed the class yet. All we need are the arguments you would want for them.

b. What methods would you want? As in part (a), just describe the name, return type, and arguments. In doing this part, try to anticipate what the user of your class might want. You might find it helpful to look at the methods for similar classes.

c. What member data would the class require?

d. What class should you subclass to make `LabeledTextField`?

e. Once you've answered the questions in parts (a) and (c), you can write the definitions of the constructors you designed. Do so.

f. (You'll have to do some digging here, if any of your methods in part (b) have non-`void` return types.) Write the definitions of your methods, and then write an applet that uses a `LabeledTextField` to test your class.

15. When it is time to do a `GridLayout`, Java computes the number of columns needed without regard for what you said in the constructor. The formula it uses is as follows, where *rows* is the number of rows specified in the constructor:

```
number of columns = (number of components + rows - 1) / rows
```

In doing the division, the remainder is discarded, so 8 / 3 yields 2, and 9 / 3 is 3.

a. Let the pair (c, r) denote the number of `Components` to be laid out and the number of rows specified; thus (8, 3) would mean trying to lay out 8 `Components` in 3 rows. How many columns does Java allocate in the following situations? (8, 1), (9, 3), (10, 3), (2, 6).

b. Draw the layouts for (9, 3), (10, 3), (11, 3), . . . , and describe in simple terms what happens in general.

16. Put yourself in the shoes of a `LayoutManager` and describe what you would do when asked to compute the minimum layout size of a `Container` that was using a `GridLayout`. To make life easier, assume that the numbers of rows and columns were already known. *Hint:* Look at the `getMinimumSize()` method in `Component`.

17. Exercise your creativity and come up with a specification of a useful new layout class. Try to be as detailed as we were in our descriptions of the AWT layouts.

18. Why does the `MenuBar` method `add(Menu m)` return a `Menu`? Is there any good reason why it shouldn't have a `void` return type?

19. `add()` is a popular method name.

a. Name two classes that have an `add()` method.

b. Name *all* the classes we've discussed so far that have `add()` methods.

c. (Only for the compulsive) Among all the classes we've discussed so far, what's the most frequently-occurring method name? You're allowed to count methods that differ only in their return type or argument as being distinct, but you should limit yourself to those methods we've actually mentioned in the first four chapters.

d. (Only for the *extremely* compulsive) Among *all* Java classes and methods, which method name is most popular? *Hint:* It is not one we've talked about so far.

20. *Every* Java program needs a `main()` method. Where's the `main()` hiding for applets?

21. It might be useful to have an Undo choice in both File and Edit menus in a program. Can a Java `menuItem` appear in two `Menus` at the same time?

22. Which of the following are supported by the Java environment(s) in your system?

a. Help menus

b. Tear-off menus

c. Modal dialogs

23. When discussing the Lablet, we mentioned that it would have been better to use a separate `Canvas` for drawing the oven door. Modify `Ovenator` so that it does this.

In Exercises 24–28, we'll take a first look at some GUI design principles. We'll continue these investigations in the chapters that follow.

GUI design gives you tremendous power and flexibility. Using a language like Java, you can produce programs that communicate with the user in a clear, efficient, and intuitive fashion. Power always comes with the responsibility of using it properly, though—GUI design also allows you to design a program that is inefficient, unintuitive, ugly, and irritating.

We designed the `Gigobite` Lablet for the pedagogical purpose of showing off as many of Java's widgets as we could. For a similar reason, we deliberately avoided or violated GUI design principles so that we could discuss them later (as we are doing here).

24. An interface should be *transparent,* which means that the purpose of all of its parts should be immediately obvious. Remember, what may be obvious to you may be completely opaque to someone who's never heard the acronym AWT.

a. Which parts of `Gigobite` wouldn't necessarily be obvious to the user?

b. Are there any obvious widgets that are obscurely identified? How would you fix them?

c. How logical is the placement of elements? How would you alter the design to make it clearer?

d. Is the use of color helpful or irritating? What changes would you suggest?

25. Once you've answered Exercise 24, rewrite `Gigobite` to incorporate your changes.

26. When writing any program, especially one with a complicated interface, you should *design for use.* Think carefully about all the things a user may want to do, and see that your program is capable of doing them all.

a. What tasks might a customer want to perform that would be difficult or impossible in `Gigobite`?

b. Although you can't change the action of `Gigobite` right now (it's just a layout for now, incapable of any actions), how would your answers to part (a) affect the interface?

27. A program, whether graphically oriented or not, should be *forgiving.* This means that with very few exceptions, the user should always be able to undo any action and revert to a previous state. A consequence of this guideline is that the user should never have to guess what the current state is.

a. How good is the original version of `Gigobite` at letting the user know where things presently stand? Suggest any improvements.

b. Design is an iterative process. Often, making changes to one aspect will require changes in another. If you've answered any of Exercises 24–26, have your changes influenced the forgiveness or user awareness of the program? If so, make any necessary corrections.

28. Whether or not you've completed Exercises 24–27, go back through them and do one more refinement, producing the best Gigobite you can.

4.8 Answers to Review Questions

1.1 A Container is a Component; a Container may have one or more instances of Component as its data.

1.2 Because an Applet is a Panel.

1.3 Because we can construct a new Panel. Container is an abstract class, so we can't make a new instance of a Container, only of its subclasses.

2.1 FlowLayout.

2.2 FlowLayout.

2.3 Only if the Component object is also a Container.

3.1 If you draw on a Canvas, the drawing will be placed appropriately by the LayoutManager; when you draw directly on the screen, you have little control over how the drawing will appear in relation to the other components of the program.

3.2 A Frame has all the usual ornamentation, such as borders, a title and scrollbars; a Window appears as a naked rectangle.

3.3 When a modal dialog appears, you can't do anything with the program until the dialog is dismissed. While a modeless dialog is visible, the user can still interact with other parts of the program.

3.4 A call to super() invokes the superclass constructor that's appropriate for the given arguments.

3.5 A Java application always contains a main() method definition.

4.1 A MenuBar contains Menus; a Menu contains MenuItems.

4.2 To allow programmers to create hierarchical Menus.

4.9 Class References

java.awt.BorderLayout

The default layout for Window and its subclasses, BorderLayout divides a Container into five regions: North, South, East, West, and Center.

```
class BorderLayout extends Object implements LayoutManager2
{
    //--------- Constructors ----------
◆   BorderLayout();
◆   BorderLayout(int hgap, int vgap);

    //-------- Class Constants --------
    CENTER, EAST, NORTH, SOUTH, WEST
    /* These stand for the strings with the corresponding names.
       For example, the value of BorderLayout.EAST is "East". */
```

```
//------------ Methods ------------
int getHgap();
int getVgap();
```
◆ `int setHgap();`
◆ `int setVgap();`

```
void layoutContainer(Container c)
/* Draw the argument's Components on the screen. */

Dimension maximumLayoutSize(Container c);
Dimension minimumLayoutSize(Container c);
Dimension preferredLayoutSize(Container c);
/* Return the maximum, minimum, or preferred size of the
   argument Container if it were to be laid out by this
   BorderLayout object. */
}
```

java.awt.Canvas

You'll use this class for drawing, rather than drawing on the screen. Canvas is often subclassed for creating custom Components, because it has all of the Container super-class event-handling methods.

```
class Canvas extends Component
{
    //--------- Constructor -----------
    Canvas();

    //------------ Methods ------------
```
◆ `    void paint(Graphics g);`
```
}
```

java.awt.CardLayout

Unlike the other LayoutManagers we discussed, CardLayout displays its Components one at a time, in much the same way as you'd see in a stack of index cards or a flip book. You add Components to the parent Container in more or less the usual way, but only one is visible at a time.

To add Components in this layout, you use the method with an additional String argument,

```
void add(String name, Component c)
```

The String argument will assign a name to the Component, allowing you to pick a Component for display by using its name. When Components are added in a CardLayout, they are displayed in the order in which they were added: The first Component added will be the first in visibility order.

```
class CardLayout extends Object implements LayoutManager2
{
    //--------- Constructors ----------
    CardLayout();
    CardLayout (int hgap int vgap);
```

```
//------------ Methods ------------
```
- `void first(Container parent);`
- `void last(Container parent);`
- `void next(Container parent);`
- `void previous(Container parent);`

```
/* These display the first, last, next, and previous
   Components of the parent Container in visibility order.
   Notice that this requires as its argument the Container
   with this layout. Also, you will need the CardLayout
   object itself to make this call. This means that instead
   of using an "on-the-fly" declaration like

   myContainer.setLayout(new CardLayout());

   you'll instead have to set aside a variable for the
   layout, as follows:

   CardLayout cd = new CardLayout();
   myContainer.setLayout(cd);
   ...
   cd.first(myContainer); */
```

```
int getHgap();
int getVgap();
```

```
void layoutContainer(Container c)
/* This method draws the argument's Components on the
   screen. Initially, all of the Components are visible and
   don't vanish until one is selected by first(), last(),
   next(), previous(), or show(). */
```

```
Dimension minimumLayoutSize(Container c)
Dimension preferredLayoutSize(Container c)
/* These two methods return the width and height necessary
   to place all of c's Components, using the largest width
   and height among the Components' minimum and preferred
   sizes, respectively. */
```
- `void show(Container parent, String name)`
```
/* This method displays the card with the given name. If
   there is no Component with the specified name, this
   method does nothing. */
```
```
}
```

java.awt.CheckboxMenuItem

A `CheckboxMenuItem` is a `MenuItem` with an internal two-value state. It is usually displayed as a normal menu item, with a mark (like a check) indicating whether its state is `true` or `false`.

```
class CheckboxMenuItem extends MenuItem
                       implements ItemSelectable
{
    //--------- Constructors ----------
    CheckboxMenuItem();
    CheckboxMenuItem(String label);
```
- `CheckboxMenuItem(String label, boolean state);`

```
    //------------ Methods ------------
◆   void addItemListener(ActionListener lstnr);
◆   void removeItemListener(ActionListener lstnr);
    /* As we'll see in Ch. 6, selecting a menu item generates an
       event that the program can catch and handle.

◆   boolean getState();
    void setState(boolean state);
}
```

java.awt.Container

This is the superclass of all the container classes. It is abstract, like Component, so you'll never make an instance of this. Instead, you'll use one of the subclasses (typically, Panel, Dialog, or Frame). Although we won't discuss it, you can subclass Container if you need to make a custom container.

```
abstract class Container extends Component
{
    //---------- Constructor ----------
    Container();

    //------------ Methods ------------
◆   void add(Component c);
◆   void add(Component c, int position);
◆   void add(String name, Component c);
    void doLayout();

    Component getComponent(int index);
    /* Returns the Component in the indicated position in the
       list of Components in this Container. */

    Component getComponentAt(int x, int y);
    Component getComponentAt(Point p);

    int getComponentCount();

    LayoutManager getLayout();
◆   void setLayout(LayoutManager layout);

    Dimension getMaximumSize();
    Dimension getMinimumSize();
    Dimension getPreferredSize();
        // These are overrides of Component methods (Ch. 3).

    boolean isAncestorOf(Component c);

    void paintComponents(Graphics g);
    /* Tells all the Components contained in this Container to
       paint themselves. */

    void remove(int index);
    void remove(Component c);
    void removeAll();
}
```

java.awt.Dialog

This class represents standard dialog boxes. Because they are also `Windows`, be sure to use the `Window` method `hide()` to make a `Dialog` object invisible when you dismiss it and call `Window`'s `dispose()` to make its resources available when you're finished with it.

```
class Dialog extends Window
{
    //--------- Constructors ----------
    Dialog(Frame parent);
    Dialog(Frame parent, boolean modal);
◆   Dialog(Frame parent, String title);
◆   Dialog(Frame parent, String title, boolean modal);

    //------------ Methods ------------
    String getTitle();
◆   void setTitle(String title);

    boolean isModal();
    void setModal(boolean modal);

    boolean isResizable();
    void setResizable(boolean b);

◆   void show();
}
```

java.awt.FlowLayout

The default layout for `Panel` and `Applet`, this lays out `Components` left to right, top to bottom.

```
class FlowLayout extends Object implements LayoutManager
{
    //--------- Constructors ----------
◆   FlowLayout()
◆   FlowLayout(int alignment)
    FlowLayout(int alignment, int hGap, int vGap)

    //-------- Class constants --------
    CENTER, LEFT, RIGHT

    //------------ Methods ------------
    int getAlignment();
    void setAlignment(int alignment);

    int getHgap();
    int getVgap();
    void setHgap(int h);
    void setVgap(int v);

    void layoutContainer(Container c)
    /* This method draws the argument's Components on the
       screen, using this FlowLayout's alignment and gaps. */

    Dimension minimumLayoutSize(Container c)
```

```
      Dimension preferredLayoutSize(Container c)
      /* These two methods return the width and height necessary
         to place all of c's Components in a single row, using the
         Components' minimum and preferred sizes, respectively. */
   }
```

java.awt.Frame

A Frame is a Window with the usual system-dependent ornamentation, such as a title and scrollbars. A Frame object is a Container (with default BorderLayout), so we can add to it any Components we wish.

```
class Frame extends Window implements MenuContainer
{
      //--------- Constructors ----------
      Frame();
   ◆  Frame(String title);

      //------------ Methods ------------
   ◆  void dispose();
      // An override of the Window method.

      MenuBar getMenuBar();
      String getTitle();
   ◆  void setMenuBar(MenuBar mb);
      void setTitle(String title);
      /* These pairs give access to the MenuBar and title, if any,
         associated with this Frame. */

      boolean isResizable();
      void setResizable(boolean canResize);
   }
```

java.awt.GridLayout

This lays out the components in a container in a rectangular grid. Components are placed in the grid in the order in which they are added [by add()] to the container.

```
class GridLayout extends Object implements LayoutManager2
{
      //--------- Constructors ----------
      GridLayout();
   ◆  GridLayout (int rows, int columns);
      GridLayout (int rows, int columns, int hgap, int vgap);

      //------------ Methods ------------
      int getColumns();
      int getRows();
      int getHgap();
      int getVgap();
      void setColumns(int columns);
      void setRows(int rows);
      void setHgap(int h);
      void setVgap(int v);

      void layoutContainer(Container c);
```

```
    /* This method draws the argument's Components on the
       screen. */

    Dimension minimumLayoutSize(Container c);
    Dimension preferredLayoutSize(Container c);
    /* These two methods return the width and height necessary
       to place all of c's Components, using the Components'
       minimum and preferred sizes, respectively. */

}
```

java.awt.Menu

A Menu is a collection of MenuItems (which may themselves be Menus, so we can have hierarchical arrangements of submenus, sub-submenus, and so on).

```
class Menu extends MenuItem implements MenuContainer
{
    //--------- Constructors ----------
    Menu();
◆   Menu(String name);
    Menu(String name, boolean canTearOff);

    //----------- Methods ------------
◆   void add(String name);
◆   MenuItem add(MenuItem m);

◆   MenuItem addSeparator();

    MenuItem getItem(int index)
    /* Returns the MenuItem at the given position in this Menu.
       The index value must represent a valid position in this
       Menu (i.e., between 0 and itemCount -1). */

    int getItemCount();
    /* Returns the current number of MenuItems in this Menu.
       This count does not include items in any submenus. */

    void insert(MenuItem item, int index);
    void insert(String name, int index);
    /* The first of these inserts the item in the given position
       in this Menu and the second creates a new MenuItem with
       the given name and inserts it. The index argument in
       both methods must be greater than or equal to zero. */

    void insertSeparator(String name, int index);

    boolean isTearOff();

    void remove(int index);
    /* This removes the item with the given index from this bar.
       The index must be a valid position, so we must have 0 ≤ index <
       itemCount. */

    void remove(MenuComponent m);
    /* Removes the given MenuComponent from this bar. You'll
       pass this a MenuItem. If the argument is not present in
       this menu, nothing happens. */
```

```
        void removeAll()
        /* Removes all items from this Menu. */
}
```

java.awt.MenuBar

The MenuBar class holds Menus. You use the add() method to add a Menu to the MenuBar, and you associate a MenuBar with a Frame by using the Frame method setMenuBar(MenuBar mb).

```
class MenuBar extends MenuComponent implements MenuContainer
{
    //--------- Constructors ----------
    MenuBar();

    //----------- Methods -----------
◆   Menu add(Menu m);

    Menu getHelpMenu();
    /* Returns the Menu designated as a help menu by
       setHelpMenu(), if any. */

    Menu getMenu(int index)
    /* Returns the Menu at the given position in this bar. The
       index value must represent a valid position in this bar
       and, as usual, positions are counted from zero up. */

    int getMenuCount();
    MenuItem getShortcutMenuItem(MenuShortcut s);
    /* Returns the MenuItem corresponding to the given shortcut. */

    void remove(int index);
    /* Removes the Menu with the given index from this bar. The
       index must be a valid position, so we must have 0 ≤ index <
       menucount. */

    void remove(MenuComponent m);
    /* Removes the given MenuComponent from this bar. You'll
       pass this a Menu, rather than a MenuItem. If the
       argument is not present in this bar, nothing happens. */

    void setHelpMenu(Menu m)
    /* This designates a Menu in this bar to be set in a special
       location (usually on the far right of the bar, for those
       systems that support help menus). The Menu in the
       argument must have been previously added to this bar;
       otherwise, nothing will happen. */
}
```

java.awt.MenuComponent

This abstract class is the superclass of all the Menu classes, except for MenuShortCut. As usual with abstract classes, this is a method placeholder.

```
abstract class MenuComponent extends Object
{
    //------------ Methods ------------
    Font getFont();
    String getName();
    void setFont(Font f);
    void setName(String name);

    MenuContainer getParent();
    /* Returns the MenuContainer object (a Frame) containing
       this MenuComponent. */
}
```

java.awt.MenuItem

This class describes the items that live in menus. Bear in mind that MenuItem is a superclass of Menu, so all the methods we describe here are available to Menus, too.

```
class MenuItem extends MenuComponent
{
    //--------- Constructors ----------
    MenuItem();
♦   MenuItem(String name);
♦   MenuItem(String name, MenuShortcut ms);
    /* The last constructor allows you to specify a MenuShortcut
       for this item. */

    //------------ Methods ------------
♦   void addActionListener(ActionListener lstnr);
    void removeActionListener(ActionListener lstnr);
    /* As we'll see in Ch. 6, MenuItems generate events when
       they're selected. */

    void deleteShortcut();
        // Remove the MenuShortcut for this item.

    String getLabel();
    void setLabel(String name);

    boolean isEnabled();
♦   void setEnabled(boolean isEnabled);

    String getActionCommand();
    void setActionCommand(String s);
    /* Unless you set it, the action command for this item will
       be its name. These methods are used for event handling
       (Ch. 6). */
}
```

java.awt.MenuShortcut

Objects of this class represent control-key combinations that can be used for keyboard activation of a menu item. MenuShortcut would be a really easy class to use, except for the fact that the key equivalent is represented by the key code constants that are part of the KeyEvent class, such as KeyEvent.VK_N, discussed in Chapter 6.

```
class MenuShortcut extends Object
{
     //--------- Constructors ----------
◆    MenuShortcut(int keycode);
     MenuShortcut(int keycode, boolean useShift);
     /* The first of these constructs a new MenuShortcut
        corresponding to the given keycode (see KeyEvent in Ch.6
        for a list of them). The second allows you to determine
        whether the shortcut should be activated by control-key
        or control-shift-key combinations. */

     //----------- Methods -----------
     int getKey();
        // Returns the key code for this shortcut.

     boolean usesShiftModifier();
     /* Returns true if this shortcut requires the shift key, and
        false otherwise. */
}
```

java.awt.Panel

Panel is the container of choice for laying out components. Panel and its sub-classes (such as Applet) default to FlowLayout. There is only one Panel method, addNotify(), and we won't discuss it here. Most of the work done by a Panel object is accomplished by calling its Container superclass methods.

```
class Panel extends Container
{
     //--------- Constructors ----------
◆    Panel();
◆    Panel(LayoutManager layout);
}
```

java.awt.PopupMenu

PopupMenu is almost exactly like Menu, except that it can be made to appear anywhere in a Component, rather than exclusively in a menu bar. It is associated with a Component by using the add() method of Component (see Chapter 3). Generally, a PopupMenu is made to appear when a mouse click event (Chapter 6) occurs.

```
class PopupMenu extends Menu
{
     //--------- Constructors ----------
     PopupMenu();
◆    PopupMenu(String label);

     //----------- Methods -----------
◆    void show();
}
```

`java.awt.Window`

This class is the superclass of the more commonly used `Frame` and `Dialog` classes. You generally won't use `Window` unless you're making custom dialogs, though you'll often make use of `Window` methods such as `show()`.

```
class Window extends Container
{
    //--------- Constructor -----------
    Window(Frame parent);

    //----------- Methods -----------
◆   void addWindowListener(WindowListener lstnr);
    void removeWindowListener(WindowListener lstnr);
    /* Add or remove an object that will deal with window
        events (Ch. 6). */

◆   void dispose();

    boolean isShowing();
        // Return true if this Window object is visible.

◆   void pack();
◆   void show();

    void toBack();
    void toFront();
    /* These move this Window to the back or front of the visual
        display. */
}
```

■ CHAPTER FIVE ■

JAVA LANGUAGE BASICS

You have learned all you need to know about laying out the parts necessary to make the visual portion of an applet or application. Along the way, you've learned quite a lot about the Java language itself. You know what a class is (the *semantics*, or meaning, of classes) and what a class definition looks like (the *syntax*, or rules of Java grammar). You know about variables and their declarations, and you've seen scores of method definitions and the calls necessary to invoke them. By now, you should be hankering to get to the next stage: making all the widgets in a Java program actually *do* something. Before we can teach you how to do that, though, we need to make sure you have a solid grasp of the Java language itself, and that's what we'll do in this chapter. You've seen some of this material before, so you can best think of this chapter as a combination of instruction and reference.

Objectives

In this chapter, we will

- Review the structure of a Java program.
- Discuss the *primitive types* that Java provides for your use.
- Complete our discussion of variables, talking about *access* and *scope*.
- Introduce a few statements that you haven't met before.
- Talk about some of the principles that guide efficient programming.

5.1 Primitive Types

In Java, as in many other programming languages, every piece of information has an associated *type*. The type of an object determines how much space the object will occupy in memory and how the object may be used. For example, a Panel object takes more space than an int, and it obviously makes no sense to add 2 to a Panel, even though addition makes perfect sense for ints. Each class is a type of its own, so a Panel object is considered to be a different type from a Button object or an int. In addition to all the types in the class hierarchy and those you make by extending existing types, Java provides a collection of eight *primitive* types for things like numbers and characters.

The Eight Java Primitive Types

`byte, short, int, long`	integers
`float, double`	floating-point numbers
`char`	characters
`boolean`	logical values

As we'll see shortly, there are fundamental differences between the primitive types and the class types.

Integers

Java has four types available for representing whole numbers such as 2, −54, and 3677009. These *integral types* are, in order of the sizes of numbers they represent, `byte`, `short`, `int`, and `long`. A `byte` takes up very little room in the computer's memory (only 8 binary digits), but as a consequence it is capable of representing only numbers in the range −128 to 127. A `short` integer uses twice as much space and can represent numbers in the range −32768 to 32767. When we want to represent whole numbers, we generally use the `int` type, which is four times as long as a `byte` and can represent any whole number from −2147483648 to 2147483647. Clearly, the `int` type should be sufficient for most of the programs you're likely to write, but if you need to use really big integers, the `long` integer type uses 64 binary digits. We'll leave as an exercise the problem of discovering where these ranges come from and the maximum and minimum `long` integers. For numbers that are *really* big, Java provides two classes, `BigInteger` and `BigDecimal`, which we describe in the class references at the end of the chapter.

For the primitive types, a *literal* expression is the way a specific value is written in a program. For the integral types, the rule governing the way a literal is written is quite simple:

Syntax

An integer literal must be written as [*optional sign*]*stringOfDigits*. Literals of type `long` are distinguished by a trailing L.

The following are all legal integral-type literals:

```
0 3L -200 5556556665656565L +343
```

These numbers are not Java integral-type literals:

`1,000`	(can't use commas)
`two`	(can use only digits, +, and −)

All of the primitive types have a *default value* when they are declared, unless you initialize them to some other value. For instance, the default value for integral-type variables is zero, so if you declare an `int` variable by writing

```
int total;
```

Java will set `total`'s initial value to 0, just as though you had written

```
int total = 0;
```

Caution

Don't make a habit of declaring a variable without setting its initial value. It's a bad habit to get into, because you might some day forget to set the initial value when you most emphatically didn't want it to be zero.

Floating-Point Numbers

As useful as integers are, there will be times when you need to use numbers with fractional parts, such as 3.14159 and −0.000675. The two *floating-point* types, `float` and `double`, are designed for such problems, and like the integral types, they are distinguished by the number of bits in their internal representations and, hence, by the accuracy and sizes of numbers they can represent.

To save typing when writing numbers like 0.00000000000000000012, Java allows you to use *scientific notation*, by following a number with e and an integer. The integer after the e indicates how many places to the right to shift the decimal point if the integer exponent is positive, and how many places to the left if the integer is negative. Thus the number above could be written more compactly as `0.12e-18`, or `1.2e-19`, or even `1200.0e-22`. The e actually represents multiplication by the indicated power of 10, so `3.245e2` represents 3.245×10^2, or 324.5.

A `float` number has approximately seven decimal digits of accuracy and can represent numbers as small as `1.4e-45` and as large as `3.4e+38`. For really big or small numbers, the `double` type will give you about 14 decimal places of accuracy and a range of `4.9e-324` to `1.7e+308`. As with integers, floating-point numbers have a default value of zero (0.0).

Syntax

Floating-point literals must be written in one of the following eight forms, where *digits* represents any string of the digits 0 . . . 9 :

digits	*digits* e *integer*
digits.	*digits.* e *integer*
.digits	*. digits* e *integer*
digits.digits	*digits. digits* e *integer*

We distinguish `float` literals by following the literal with the letter `f`. All floating-point numbers may have a leading + or − sign.

The following are all legal floating-point literals:

```
0    3f    .34    0.34    40.f    -12e8    -12e+8    -10.08e-13f
```

Characters

There are times when we need to manipulate information other than numbers. Java provides the `char` type to represent individual characters. Characters are written literally as a single character within single quotes, like `'X'` or `'x'` (which are considered two different characters). Internally, characters are stored using the 16-bit coding scheme known as *Unicode*, the details of which need not concern us here. Some nonprinting characters are used so often that they have been given special representations: `'\b'` is the backspace, `'\n'` is the linefeed, `'\r'` is the carriage return, and `'\t'` is the tab. Because the single quote, backslash, and (as we'll see in a moment) the double quote characters have special meanings, they also have their own representations: `'\' '`, `'\\'` and `'\" '`, respectively. Strings of more than one character are written in a program by enclosing them in double quotes (not two single quotes), as in `"This is a string"`. We'll have much more to say about character strings in Chapter 8.

Strictly speaking, the `char` type is an integral type, because `chars` are stored by their Unicode representation, a 16-bit value. For example, the character that appears to us as `'A'` is stored in Java as the number 65. The default value for the `char` type is the character with code zero, written `'\0'`. This is a nonprinting character.

The `boolean` Type

The `boolean` type has just two values, expressed by the literals `true` and `false`. We'll see shortly that just as the numeric types come with *operators*, like +, that allow us to perform arithmetic, the `boolean` type has a collection of operators that allow us to perform logical computations. The default value for `boolean` variables is `false`.

Review Questions

1.1 Name the Java primitive types.

1.2 What is the difference between a `byte` and an `int`?

1.3 Which is larger, 2338.0e5 or .02338e10?

5.2 Identifiers, Keywords, and Variables

Names of variables, methods, classes, and packages are known collectively as *identifiers*. The syntax of identifiers is simple enough:

Syntax: Identifiers

Identifiers must have the form *letter* or *letter letterNumberString*, where *letter* is any of the characters A . . . Z or a . . . z and *letterNumberString* is any collection of letters, digits (0 . . . 9), or underscores (_).[1] In addition, an identifier cannot be a Java *keyword*.

Java keywords are the built-in parts of the language. There are 50 Java keywords, all but 3 of which we'll cover in this text.[2]

Syntax: Java Keywords

abstract	default	goto	null	synchronized
boolean	do	if	package	this
break	double	implements	private	throw
byte	else	import	protected	throws
case	extends	instanceof	public	transient
catch	false	int	return	true
char	final	interface	short	try
class	finally	long	static	void
const	float	native	super	volatile
continue	for	new	switch	while

For example, the following are all valid identifiers in Java

```
x   foo   Int   button2   the_message   identifiersCanBeAsLongAsYouLike
```

We threw in the `Int` identifier to serve as a reminder that identifiers in Java are case-sensitive. We couldn't have used `int` as one of our identifiers, because `int` is a keyword. Java considers the lower- and uppercase versions of a letter as different (they have different Unicode representations), so `Int` is a perfectly legitimate identifier, although it's so close in appearance to a keyword that we do not recommend using it.

None of these are valid identifiers:

`2fold`	(Doesn't start with a letter.)
`my Panel`	(Contains an invalid character, the space.)
`final`	(It's a keyword.)

Variables

You have already seen quite a few variables in the examples we've used so far. You know that a variable is used to store information for later use, and you've seen two

---

[1]You can also use the dollar sign, $, in the `letterNumberString`, but we don't advise it.

[2]For the "language lawyers," `true`, `false`, and `null` are actually literals, not keywords.

```
class Triple
// Stores and manipulates triples of floating-point numbers.
{
  double x, y, z;          instance variables: can be used
                                here, or
                                here, or in any method in this class.
  Triple()
  {
   x = 0.0;
   y = 0.0;
   y = 0.0;
  }

  double sum()
  {
   double theSum = 0.0;    local variable: can only be used
   theSum = x + y + z;        here, in this method.
   return theSum;
  }
}
```

Figure 5.1

Instance and local variables.

different kinds of variables. *Instance variables* are declared at the class level and represent the data "owned" by an object of that class, and *local* variables are declared in a method and have meaning only within that method.

Figure 5.1 illustrates the distinction between instance and local variables.

An instance variable "belongs" to any object that is an instance of a class. If the *access* of an instance variable permits, we can inspect and modify an instance variable by using the name of the object, a dot, and the name of the variable.[3] For example, if we had made the following declaration in the method of another class,

```
Triple origin = new Triple();
```

we could then have set the x variable of origin to 2.3 by writing

```
origin.x = 2.3;
```

in much the same way as we could invoke origin's sum() method by using the "dot notation,"

```
double value = origin.sum();
```

Syntax: Instance Variables

> Instance variables of a class may be accessed by using
> *objectName.variableName*. (The last dot is the end of the sentence
> and wouldn't be part of a program.)

---
[3]We'll discuss access in a moment.

Each instance of a class has its own collection of instance variables. If `origin` and `translate` were two `Triple` instances, `origin.x` and `translate.x` would be entirely different things—one might contain `2.3` and the other might have the value `0.0`, for example.

Scope

The *scope* of an identifier is that portion of the class where the identifier may be used. As we've mentioned, a class variable, instance variable, or method name may be used anywhere in the class. A local variable, on the other hand, may be used only within the closest pair of braces, { and } that enclose the declaration—and then only in those statements within the braces that occur *after* the declaration. Here's an example:

```
class MyClass
{
    int y = -100;      // INSTANCE VARIABLE
    ...                // can use y here
    void someMethod()
    {
        ...            // can use y here, but not x
        {
            ...        // can use y here, but not x
            int x = 3; // LOCAL VARIABLE
            ...        // can use x or y here
        }
        ...            // can use y here, but not y
    }
    void someOtherMethod()
    {
        ...            // can use y here, but not x
                       // could also call someMethod() here
    }
}
```

The behavior of these variables has nothing, really, to do with whether or not they are instance or local variables. Figure 5.2 illustrates this—a variable has meaning (and can be used) from the place where it is declared down to the close brace of the innermost block that encloses the declaration.

Let's make a minor change to this example, using the *same* name for both the instance and local variables.

```
class MyClass
{
    int x = -100;
    ...
    void someMethod()
    {
        int x = 3;
        ...            // Is x -100 or 3 here?
    }
    void someOtherMethod()
    {
        ...            // Is x -100 or 3 here?
    }
}
```

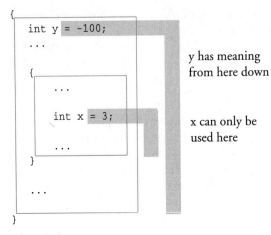

y has meaning
from here down

x can only be
used here

Figure 5.2

How scope works.

In `someOtherMethod()`, the answer is pretty clear: We're referring to the instance variable [because we can't see the local variable in `someOtherMethod()`], so its value is −100. In `someMethod()`, though, it's not clear which variable we're using at the indicated place. Should the local variable or the instance variable be more important?

Java's rule for these situations also applies in many other languages: *The most local variable is the one in force.* In this case, we say that in the indicated line, the local (value 3) variable *shadows* the less local (value −100) variable, which means that in that particular location, it is as if though the less local variable isn't even defined, as you can see in Figure 5.3.

shadow

Syntax: Resolving Scope

Java has no difficulty dealing with identically named variables. The syntactical rules follow.

1. You cannot declare two variables of the same name at the same scope level.

2. Any variable declared strictly within the scope of another with the same name will shadow the outer named variable.

This rule holds for method arguments as well. Method arguments have local scope, so they have no meaning outside of the method, and they are defined throughout the body of the method. Note that this implies you can't have a local variable in a method that has the same name as one of the method's arguments.

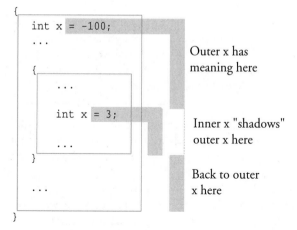

```
{
    int x = -100;
    ...
    {
        ...
        int x = 3;
        ...
    }
    ...
}
```

Outer x has
meaning here

Inner x "shadows"
outer x here

Back to outer
x here

Figure 5.3

Resolving name conflicts.

The Modifiers `static` and `final`

There are times when either it is more efficient or it makes better sense to associate a variable with an entire class, rather than having a separate copy of the variable for every instance of that class. For example, we may have a class `Circle` whose instances were intended to represent circles and perform certain computations, such as calculating areas. We'd probably need the value for *pi* to do this, but it would be silly to waste space in each `Circle` object for a copy of that value. Much better would be to set this value once and associate it with the class, rather than with all the instances of the class. We do that by using the `static` modifier, like this:

```
class Circle
{
    static double PI = 3.1415926535;
    ...
}
```

Now, just as with an instance variable, every method in this class has access to the variable `PI`. You can access a class variable from outside the class, using the dot notation, but this time you don't put an instance name in front. Rather, you use the class name itself, `Circle.PI`, in this case. Look familiar? It should—`Color.red` and `FlowLayout.RIGHT` are class variables you've already seen.[4]

---

[4]We're actually reinventing the wheel here, since the `Math` class already has a (`final static`) constant, `Math.PI`, that contains an approximation of the value of *pi*.

Syntax: `static` variables

> Class variables are distinguished from instance variables by the use of the modifier `static` at the start of their declarations. Within the class, such a variable may be accessed by its name. Outside the class, a class variable may be accessed by using the dot notation, *className.variableName.*

Methods may be `static`, too. This is commonly done in classes like `java.lang.Math` that are used only to hold methods and aren't subclassed. Such classes often have no constructors, and all their methods are `static`. We'll discuss the `Math` class in the next section.

Even if you don't know much mathematics, you probably realize that `PI` shouldn't really be a variable. After all, *pi* is fixed and we shouldn't give users of our `Circle` class the opportunity to change it. We can fix an instance of a variable forever by using the modifier `final`. In our `Circle` example, we should say

```
class Circle
{
    final static double PI = 3.1415926535;
    ...
}
```

to indicate that the class variable `PI` shouldn't act as a variable at all, but rather as a *constant*. Once we have declared `PI` this way, it is illegal to modify it by later writing an expression like this.[5]

```
Circle.PI = 3.2;     // ERROR: PI is final, so can't be changed.
```

You can define a class as `final`, too, though it's not often done. A `final` class cannot be subclassed. The `Math` and `Color` classes are final. Finally (no pun intended), if you declare a method as `final`, it means that the method cannot be overridden in any subclass.

Syntax: `final` variables

> A class variable or instance variable may be declared to be `final`, which makes it an error to change its value. The declaration of a `final` variable must include an initialization, so the declaration
>
> ```
> final int ZERO = 0;
> ```
>
> would be legal and
>
> ```
> final int ZERO;
> ```
>
> would not, in spite of the apparent default initialization of `int`s. It's common to identify final variables by using ALL_CAPS for their names.

---

[5]This actually happened. In 1897, the Indiana State Legislature, by a 67–0 vote, passed a bill that would have, as a consequence, legislated the value of pi to be 3.2! Fortunately, the bill was defeated in the Indiana Senate. For details, see

http://www.urbanlegends.com/legal/pi_indiana.html

Brief Interlude: Packages

Java allows you to group files into *packages*. The AWT classes, for example, are defined over dozens of separate files, but they are all part of the package `java.awt`. You can make packages of your own, if you wish, and import their names in just the same way as you import the names from the `java.awt` package.

To indicate that a file is part of a package, all you need to do is include the package declaration

```
package packageName;
```

as the *very first* line in your file (except, perhaps, for blank lines and comments) and then make sure that this file is in a directory or folder with the same name as the package. Suppose, for example, that we had made a couple of widgets of our own, a `GraphicButton`, and a `Slider`. For convenience, we might have put each of these in a separate file, so we might have the following file for our `GraphicButton` class definition:

```
//---------------- File GraphicButton.java ----------------
package myWidgets;

import java.awt;   // so we can use the name "Canvas"

public class GraphicButton extends Canvas
{
   ...
}
```

Similarly, the `Slider` class might reside in its own file, `Slider.java`, and might look like this:

```
//---------------- File Slider.java ----------------
package myWidgets;

import java.awt;

public class Slider extends Canvas
{
   ...
}
```

Both of these files would be placed in the directory `myWidgets`, and we could then use them in another file by importing them, like this:

```
//---------------- File Test.java ----------------
import java.applet.*;
import java.awt.*;
import myWidgets.*;   // NOTE: we get both class names here

public class Test extends Applet
{
   GraphicButton myButton;
   Slider mySlider;
   ...
}
```

anonymous package

Finally, note that our applet file doesn't have a `package` declaration. In fact, if you look back, you'll see that none of the applets or classes we've made so far have had `package` declarations. Throughout, we've been making use of the fact that Java always sets aside an *anonymous package,* into which go all of the files that don't have `package` declarations. We've been using packages all along—we just haven't generated one with a name. We haven't mentioned packages so far, but we need them now so that we can talk about *access.*

Access Modifiers

An important consideration in good programming is *information hiding.* The old observation "There are two things you don't want to watch being made: sausages and laws" could be amended with equal truth to include program design. We want to make life easy for the users of our classes, so we don't want to burden other programmers (or ourselves, for that matter) with the need to remember all the details of how we implement a class. What we'd like to do is let the users know how to use our classes in their programs, without ever giving them access to the dirty details of the variables and methods we use along the way. Doing this, we not only reduce the mental effort on the part of our fellow programmers, but, perhaps even important, we can also guarantee that outsiders won't derange the actions of our classes by interfering with things that are better left alone.

class invariant

Consider, for instance, the `Container` class. Every `Container` has to know how many `Components` it contains, so it keeps an instance variable that we might call `numComponents`. This variable is increased by 1 every time the user of the class calls `add()` and is reduced by 1 in every `remove()` call. There's an important *class invariant* at work here: "`numComponents` represents the number of `Components` in the `Container`." Imagine the chaos that could result if this variable were accessible from outside the class. A user might inadvertently set it to zero or increase it by 7. What would happen then when the time came to lay out the `Container`? We can't say for sure, but it wouldn't be pretty.

Java provides us with three declaration modifiers that allow us to specify the levels of access we will grant to *members* (class variables, instance variables, and methods).

`private` Access

The `private` modifier completely hides a member from outsiders. A `private` variable or method can be accessed by name *only within the class's methods.* The identifier is unknown to other classes, even those that `extend` the class in which it is defined.

A good rule of thumb is to make all the instance variables of a class `private`. If they need to be inspected, provide the class with *inspector methods,* and if they need to be modified, provide the class with `public` *modifier methods.* Here's an example, obtained by second-guessing how the `Container` class is defined:

```
class Container extends Component
// Our implementation of Container--not the real one.
{
    private int numComponents;
    private LayoutManager ourLayout;

    ...

    public int countComponents()
    // Inspector: The outside world can look, but not touch.
    {
        return numComponents;
    }

    public LayoutManager getLayout()
    // Inspector
    {
        return ourLayout;
    }

    public void setLayout(LayoutManager layout)
    // Modifier: Allow the user to change ourLayout
    {
        ourLayout = layout;
    }

    ...
}
```

Syntax: private

> A member can be declared to have private access by placing the modifier
> private in front of its declaration. private access means that the identifier
> is defined only within the class and can be used only in methods of this
> class. private members are *not* inherited by subclasses.

This doesn't imply that there's no way of getting at the value of a private
variable. It just means that there's no *direct* way. In the example above, if c were
some Container object, we could never legally refer to c.numComponents outside the
class, but we could still get to that value by using the inspector method call
c.countComponents(). In the example above, the class designer is saying, in effect,
"I've provided a method that allows you to look at numComponents, but I don't want
you changing it, so I haven't given you a way to do that."

Programming Tip

> Design classes on a "need to know" basis. Unless there is a compelling rea-
> son for a member to be accessed from outside a class, make the member
> private.

As with the rest of our programming tips, you can violate this guideline if there's a good reason for doing so. In the `Point` class, for example, the two instance variables x and y are `public`, which means that for a `Point` p, the data p.x and p.y can be accessed anywhere. That makes sense in this situation, because the `Point` class is little more than a way of gathering two `ints` into one object. In `Point`, inspector and modifier methods would be overkill.

Package Access

If we don't place any of the `private`, `protected`, or `public` modifiers in front of a member declaration, we are giving that member what is known as *default* or *package* access. A member with default access is visible within its own class, of course, and is visible in methods of any class in the same package.

Syntax: Package Access

A member without any access modifiers is visible anywhere within its own package but cannot be seen outside of the package where it is declared.

protected Access

If a member is given `protected` access, it is accessible anywhere within the same package and cannot be seen outside of the package, exactly as though it had default access. The difference between `protected` access and default access is that `protected` members of a class are inherited by subclasses, even if the subclass is defined in another package.

Syntax: protected

Declaring a member to be `protected` means that the identifier is defined within the package and within any subclass, whether or not the subclass is in the same package.[6]

If you design a class and suspect that it may eventually be subclassed, you can declare as `protected` any variables or methods that a subclass will need but that should be hidden from outsiders.

There is one minor quirk to this form of access that we should mention for the sake of completeness. The problem comes up only when a subclass is declared in a different package from the base class. In that case, the subclass inherits any `protected` members of the base class and can use them as its own. What it *cannot* do is access any of the `protected` members *of an instance of the base class*. We'll give an example and leave it at that, because this situation is fairly uncommon.

---

[6]You might see a related form of access, `private protected`. This access is allowed in version 1.0 but not in subsequent versions of Java, so you shouldn't use it.

Here's the base class, defined in the package `utilities`:

```
package utilities.;

class Triple
{
   protected double x, y, z;
   ...
}
```

and here's a subclass, defined in a different package:

```
package myOtherUtilities;

import utilities.*;   // so we can recognize the name "Triple"
class AlgebraicTriple extends Triple
{
   ...
   void add(Triple t)
   {
      this.x = this.x + t.x; //NO!
      ...
   }
}
```

The problem here is that `AlgebraicTriple` can certainly look at its own x variable (which it inherits from `Triple`) when we use `this.x`. It *can't*, however, inspect the x member of any superclass instances, such as `t`. This is a cause for confusion in some rare situations, but we just have to live with it.

public Access

The least restricted access is `public`. If a member is given `public` access, that member is visible anywhere, in or out of the class.

Syntax: public

A member with `public` access is visible anywhere. Constructors are nearly always `public`, and methods are generally `public` as well, except for those "helper" methods that are called only within the class. `public` members are inherited in subclasses.

Putting it all together, we have the following table.

Access	Class	Subclass	Package	Everywhere
private	✔			
(default)	✔		✔	
protected	✔	✔	✔	
public	✔	✔	✔	✔

Syntax Review: Modifiers

We've discussed five modifiers in Java: `public`, `protected`, `private`, `static`, and `final`.[7] The order in which they appear is unimportant, as long as they appear before the declaration they modify. In any declaration, at most one of `public`, `protected`, and `private` may be used.

Local variables cannot be modified.

For example, the following declarations are all equally acceptable in Java, and they all have the same result: setting the class variable `PI` to the fixed value `3.1415926535` and allowing it to be accessed by any other class, no matter where the other class is defined.

```
public static final double PI = 3.1415926535;
public final static double PI = 3.1415926535;    // our preference
static public final double PI = 3.1415926535;
static final public double PI = 3.1415926535;
final public static double PI = 3.1415926535;
final static public double PI = 3.1415926535;
```

Review Questions

2.1 What is an identifier?

2.2 What kind of variable can *never* be seen outside of its class?

2.3 What is the scope of a local variable?

2.4 Give an example of a `final static` variable from any class you've seen so far.

2.5 Arrange the access levels in order, from most restricted to least.

5.3   Operators and Expressions

In this section, we find ourselves back on familiar ground, looking at the operations Java provides for doing things like arithmetic. We'll discuss the operators first. Then we'll use the operators to produce complicated expressions and finally, in the next section, discuss how to use these expressions to write the statements that make up programs.

Numeric Operators

operand

Scattered among the example classes we've shown so far, you'll find the basic operators for manipulation of numeric information: + for addition, – for subtraction, * for multiplication, and / for division. Each of these takes an *operand* on the left and one on the right, performs the operation, and returns the value to the program. These operations—and all others, for that matter—can be combined to make

---

[7]There are two other modifiers, *transient* and *volatile*, that are outside the scope of this book.

expressions as complicated as you need, using parentheses as necessary to group subexpressions together.

Here are some examples. Let's suppose we've already declared

```
int n = 3, m = -1;
```

Then, all of the following are legitimate expressions:

```
n               // value 3
2 + n           // value 5
4 * n + m       // value 11
4 * (n + m)     // value 8
2 - n - 4       // value -5
```

Hmm. There seems to be more to this than appears at first glance. Consider the expression 4 * n + m. We have two operators here, multiplication and addition. If we do the multiplication first, 4 * n evaluates to 12, and the resulting expression, 12 + m, gives us 11. On the other hand, doing the addition first gives us 2 for the value of n + m, and then multiplication by 4 yields 8. There's a genuine ambiguity here, and Java adopts a time-honored solution—it simply legislates the problem away. Each of the Java operators has an associated *precedence.* In cases like the one above, where there are no parentheses to force a different order of evaluation, the operator with higher precedence is performed first. In this case, because multiplication has a higher precedence than addition, the multiplication is performed first. The summary section at the end of this chapter includes a complete precedence list.

precedence

What about the expression 2 - n - 4? Should we evaluate it as though it were written (2 - n) - 4 or should we do it in the order 2 - (n - 4)? In the first order the result is -5, and in the second the steps would be 2 - (3 - 4), then 2 - (-1), for a result of 3. Precedence is clearly no help here; we need another rule, for the way the implicit parentheses are placed. This rule is known as associativity, and in Java it's simple: Two-operand arithmetic operators are grouped from the left.

associativity

Semantics: Precedence and Associativity

Every Java operator has a precedence. Unless an expression is parenthesized to indicate a different order of evaluation, the operators are evaluated in order of their precedence.

If an expression contains operators of the same precedence, the order of evaluation is governed by the operators' associativity. The operators +, - , *, and / all group from the left.

As a rather complicated example, consider this expression:

```
2 * 4 - 3 + 5 * 4
```

First, the two multiplications have higher precedence than the subtraction and addition, so we have an expression with three terms:

```
(2 * 4) - 3 + (5 * 4)
```

Finally, because the operators + and – have the same precedence, we rely on their associativity to group the expression from left to right:

```
(((2 * 4) - 3) + (5 * 4))
```

Here's how the expression would be evaluated

```
(((2 * 4) - 3) + (5 * 4))
(( 8 - 3) + (5 * 4))
(  5 + (5 * 4))
(  5 + 20 )
        25
```

There are 46 Java operators, grouped into 13 levels of precedence, each operator having a defined associativity. It seems like a daunting exercise in memorization to keep all that straight, but fortunately there's an easy way out.

Programming Tip

> If there is any doubt about how to write an expression, *completely parenthesize it*. Not only will parentheses make it less likely that you'll specify the wrong order of evaluation, but it can also make the expression considerably easier to read.

We haven't used division in any of our examples in this section. There are actually two different division operators, one for integers and one for floating-point numbers. Integer division is used when both operands are integral types, and it returns the quotient, discarding any remainder and, effectively, rounding toward zero. For example, (8 / 4), (9 / 4), (10 / 4), and (11 / 4) all evaluate to 2, and (-9 / 4) yields -2. You can use the operator % to get the remainder of integer division, so (8 % 4) is 0, (9 % 4) is 1, (10 % 4) is 2, and so on. The % operator is often used to test whether one integer is evenly divisible by another, because n % m is 0 only when m divides n evenly.

Floating-point division uses the same symbol, /, but this time the quotient and fractional part are both retained, so 9.0 / 4.0 evaluates to the floating-point number 2.25.

There are no "mixed" arithmetic operators. In an expression like 9.0 / 4, the *promotion* integer 4 is first *promoted* to the floating-point equivalent, 4.0, and then the floating-point version of division is performed, yielding 2.25. Promotion is always done from "shorter" forms to longer: byte, short, and char are all promoted to int, and the promotions int → long → float → double are performed as needed to make the operands match.

There are times when you might want to do these conversions yourself. For example, the red, green, and blue components of a Color are implemented as integers in the range 0 to 255. Suppose you had a double value, amount, in the range 0.0 to 1.0, which expressed the relative amount of a color component (so 0.0 would mean none of that color and 1.0 would represent the full 255 amount). The actual color component value, then, would be an int and would have the value 255 * amount. Unfortunately, arithmetic promotion of such an expression would yield a double, not the int we want. To make the value an int, we use the *cast operator,* (*typeName*) to force the result to be an int, like this:

type casting

```
(int)(255 * amount)
```

Syntax: Type Casts

> To convert an expression to a given type, place the cast class operator in front of the expression, like this: *(typeName)expression.*
>
> *Caution:* This technique may result in the loss of data and is never allowed to convert a primitive type to a class type.

In the example above, we needed the second set of parentheses because the cast operator has the highest of all precedences. Without the second parentheses, we would just convert 255 to an int, which it is already. Be careful when type-casting. Remember that you are in effect asking Java to place a value in a chunk of memory that may not fit it, so you run the risk of losing information if you "narrow" a value from double to int, for example.

Programming Tip

> Use type casts sparingly. When you must convert types, make sure that the expression you are converting will always fit in the intended type.

There are only two more numeric operators that we need to discuss: the *increment operator,* ++, and its sibling the *decrement operator,* --. These are *unary* operators, like the negation operator, -, and the cast operator, which means that they take a single operand rather than two.

unary operator

The increment operator *may be applied only to a numeric variable* (never to an expression or a literal) and causes the value of the variable to be increased by 1. For example, if the int variable i had the value 4, then after i++ was applied, the value of i would be increased to 5. There are two different forms of the increment operator. If the operator is placed *after* the variable, the value of the variable is incremented only after it is used in an expression, whereas placing the operator *before* the variable causes the variable to be incremented before its value is used. The decrement operator works in a similar way, except that it decreases the value of its operand by 1.

To see this in action, suppose that the int variable i had the value 4. Then

```
2 * i++
```

would evaluate to 8 and would leave i with the value 5 (because the old value, 4, would be used in the expression before i was incremented), whereas

```
2 * ++i
```

would evaluate to 10 and would leave i with the value 5.

This can lead to considerable confusion. What, for instance, are we to make of an expression like this?

```
i++ + ++i
```

Programming Tip

> To lessen confusion, avoid using the increment or decrement operators in any but the simplest expressions, and *never* use more than one in an expression.

Like all unary operators, the increment and decrement operators are in the highest precedence level, and they group from the right.

The Math Class

The Math class contains a number of methods that come in handy for mathematical calculations. This class is part of the package java.lang, which is automatically imported for you in every Java program. The Math class is final, so it can't be subclassed; it has no constructors, so you can't construct a Math object; and all of its methods are static, so they must be called by using the class name before the method name, as in the expression p + Math.max(q, 0).

There are two constants in this class.

```
final static double E
final static double PI
```

Math.E is the base of the natural logarithms, 2.718281828. . . , and Math.PI is 3.141592653. . . .

We'll describe the common Math methods here. If there's a mathematical function you need (such as the arctangent) that is not mentioned here, there's a good chance you'll find it if you look through the complete documentation.

```
int abs(int x)
long abs(long x)
float abs(float x)
double abs(double x)
```

Returns the absolute value of its argument. Math.abs(3) is 3 and Math.abs(-4.009) is 4.009.

```
double ceil(double x)
```

Rounds its argument to the next highest integer. Math.ceil(3.4) is 4.0, Math.ceil(3.0) is 3.0, and Math.ceil(-2.67) returns -2.0. See also floor() and rint().

```
double cos(double x)
```

Returns the cosine of its argument, where the argument is understood to be measured in radians. `Math.cos(PI / 3.0)` returns `0.5`. See also `sin()` and `tan()`.

```
double exp(double x)
```

Returns e^x, where e here represents `Math.E`. See also `log()`.

```
double floor(double x)
```

Rounds its argument down to the next-lowest integer. `Math.floor(3.4)` is `3.0`, `Math.floor(3.0)` is also `3.0`, and `Math.floor(-2.67)` returns `-3.0`. See also `ceil()` and `rint()`.

```
double log(double x)
```

Returns the natural log of its argument. The argument must be greater than zero. See also `exp(x)`.

```
int max(int x, int y)
long max (long x, long y)
float max (float x, float y)
double max (double x, double y)
```

Return the larger of their two arguments. See `min()`.

```
int min(int x, int y)
long min (long x, long y)
float min (float x, float y)
double min (double x, double y)
```

Return the smaller of their two arguments. See `max()`.

```
double pow(double x, double y)
```

Returns the value of x^y. The argument x must be greater than zero.

```
double random()
```

This returns a number randomly chosen in the range 0.0 (included) to 1.0 (excluded), with a uniform distribution. The `java.util.Random` class, explained in the class references at the end of this chapter, contains more methods for generating "random" numbers.

```
double rint(double x)
```

Returns the double value of the integer closest to the argument. If two doubles are equally close to x (for example, if x were `10.5`), the even one is returned (`10.0`, in this case).

```
int round(float x)
long round(double x)
```

These round the argument to the nearest integral value, rounding up if the argument represents 0.5 plus an integer, so `Math.round(2.5f)` returns `3` and `Math.round(2.49)` returns `2L`.

double **sin**(double x)

Returns the sine of its argument (in radians). See `cos()` and `tan()`.

double **sqrt**(double x)

Returns the square root of its argument. The argument must be greater than or equal to zero.

double **tan**(double x)

Returns the tangent of its argument (in radians). See `cos()` and `sin()`.

Bitwise Operators (optional)

There are seven other operators available for use on integral types. For these operators, the integer isn't regarded as representing a number, but rather is considered to be just a collection of bits, and the operations apply to each of the bits in the number. These operations are useful in some special situations, and we will use them from time to time in subsequent chapters, but we'll admit that they are somewhat specialized. For that reason, you can skip this section on first reading without losing any continuity in what is yet to come in this chapter.

In Java, `ints` are represented in a form known as *32-bit, two's complement.* The "32-bit" part means that each `int` uses 32 binary digits in memory (the `byte` and `short` types use 8 and 16 digits, respectively, and `long` uses 64). As with the decimal numbers we're all accustomed to using, each position in the number represents a different value. Just as the decimal number 438 means "4 hundreds, 3 tens, and 8 ones," the digits in a *binary* representation indicate powers of some base. The only difference is that in decimal notation the positions represent powers of 10, (1, 10, 100, 1000, . . .), whereas in binary they represent powers of 2 (1, 2, 4, 8, 16, 32, 64, 128, . . .). For example, the 8-bit binary number 00001101 represents what we call 13 in decimal, as you can see by adding the position values:

```
 0    0    0    0   1   1   0   1
128   64   32   16   8   4   2   1
                     8 + 4     + 1 = 13
```

Addition in this representation is easy, because there are only two "digit" values, 0 and 1. Figure 5.4 illustrates the addition table for binary arithmetic.

The `1 + 1 = 10` entry is just the way of saying 1 + 1 = 2, in binary, because 10 is the binary equivalent of our decimal 2. In school terms, then, we have "1 plus 1 is 0, carry 1." The addition *algorithm,* or the steps we use to add, is exactly the same as it is in decimal, except that we use a different addition table. Here's an example, adding 25 + 13 in binary, with carries indicated:

+	0	1
0	0	1
1	1	10

Figure 5.4

All you need to know about binary addition.

```
      1 1 0 0 1
    0 0 0 1 1 0 0 1    (16 + 8 + 1 = 25)
  + 0 0 0 0 1 1 0 1    (8 + 4 + 1  = 13)
    0 0 1 0 0 1 1 0    (32 + 4 + 2 = 38)
```

The "two's complement" part of the description comes from the way negative numbers are represented. In this scheme, to negate a number, we first invert its bits, changing every 0 to a 1 and vice versa, and then add 1 to the result. To negate 13, for instance, in 8-bit two's complement, we would do this:

Original: `00001101`

Invert: `11110010`

Add 1: `11110011`

Thus −13 would have the representation 11110011. This is a very logical scheme—take a look at the eight numbers we can represent in 3-bit two's complement:

```
100    -4
101    -3
110    -2
111    -1
000     0
001     1
010     2
011     3
```

Note that the numbers change from top to bottom just as they would on a "binary odometer" (so 111 "rolls over" to 000, just as 999 would roll over to 000 on a decimal odometer) and that all the negative numbers are distinguished by having a 1 in the leftmost position. Note also that when we add 3 to −3 we get zero, exactly as expected. (There's a final carry, which would go into the fourth bit, if there were one. Such "overflows" are ignored in this representation.)

The unary operator ~ is the `complement` operator that inverts the bits in its argument. If b is the `byte` with value `00001101`, then ~b will yield `11110010`. The operators &, |, and ^, known as AND, OR, and XOR (for "eXclusive OR") take two operands and act on the bits according to the tables given in Figure 5.5.

&	0	1
0	0	0
1	0	1

|	0	1
0	0	1
1	1	1

^	0	1
0	0	1
1	1	0

AND   OR   XOR

Figure 5.5

The AND, OR and XOR bitwise operators.

Let's take two 8-bit bytes, `mask` and `sample`, and apply the bitwise operations to them. We've separated the bits into two groups in each computation, the group with all 0s on top and the group with all 1s.

```
  0 0 0 0 1 1 1 1   mask
& 1 0 1 0 1 1 0 1   sample
  0 0 0 0 1 1 0 1   result

  0 0 0 0 1 1 1 1
| 1 0 1 0 1 1 0 1
  1 0 1 0 1 1 1 1

  0 0 0 0 1 1 1 1
^ 1 0 1 0 1 1 0 1
  1 0 1 0 0 0 1 0
```

Look at what happens: In the AND (&) example, any pattern paired with a group of 0s in the `mask` became all 0s, and any pattern matched with a group of 1s in the `mask` stayed just as it was. *This* is why we took the time to explain the bitwise operations: They can be used to extract or set groups of bits in a number!

This idea of extracting bits by using a mask can be combined with the remaining *shift* operators to perform useful tasks. The operator `<<` takes two integral operands and returns the bits in the left operand, shifted left by the amount in the other operand, filling the resulting "holes" with 0s. For example, if `b` were a `byte` with bit pattern `00001101`, the operation `b<<3` would result in `01101000`. Similarly, the operator `>>>` returns the bit pattern shifted right by the indicated amount, again padded with zeros. Finally, the operator `>>` shifts the bits right, but this time it pads with whatever was in the leftmost bit (it "sign-extends"). Here are examples of how these operators work, with `b` having the pattern `10001101`.

```
b << 2    returns the result  00110100
b >> 2    returns the result  11100011
b >>> 2   returns the result  00100011
```

Using the bitwise operators, we can break an integer into pieces, as it were. Suppose that instead of thinking of a 32-bit integer as a number in the range $-2147483648 \ldots 2147483647$, we wanted to think of it as four 8-bit numbers, A, R, G, and B, collected into one chunk, like this:

```
  31 ... 24 23 ... 16 15 ... 9 8 ... 0
  ┌────────┬────────┬────────┬────────┐
  │   A    │   R    │   G    │   B    │  source
  └────────┴────────┴────────┴────────┘
```

To get the number in the R byte, for example, we would perform the following steps:

Step 1: Build a mask.

```
byte ALL_ONES = -1; // do you see why this is all 1s?
int mask = ALL_ONES << 16;
```

```
  31 ... 24 23 ... 16 15 ... 9 8  ... 0
  ┌────────┬────────┬────────┬────────┐
  │00000000│11111111│00000000│00000000│  mask
  └────────┴────────┴────────┴────────┘
```

Step 2: Mask out all but R.

```
int result = mask & source;
```

```
  31 ... 24 23 ... 16 15 ... 9 8  ... 0
  ┌────────┬────────┬────────┬────────┐
  │00000000│   R    │00000000│00000000│  result
  └────────┴────────┴────────┴────────┘
```

Step 3: Shift R down.

```
byte R = result >> 16;
```

```
  31 ... 24 23 ... 16 15 ... 9 8  ... 0
  ┌────────┬────────┬────────┬────────┐
  │00000000│00000000│00000000│   R    │
  └────────┴────────┴────────┴────────┘
```

This may seem like a lot of work, but we could always shorten it by eliminating some of the intermediate declarations and simply writing

```
byte ALL_ONES = -1;
byte r = ((ALL_ONES << 16) & source) >> 16;
```

Boolean Operators

We can compare numbers in Java, testing whether one is larger than or equal to another, for instance. The *comparison operators*, <, <=, ==, !=, >=, and >, take two numeric expressions as operands, evaluate them, and return a boolean value indicating the result of the comparison. They work like this:

Expression	Evaluates to `true` If and Only If
`f < g`	`f` is strictly less than `g`
`f <= g`	`f` is less than or equal to `g`
`f == g`	`f` and `g` have the same value
`f != g`	the values of `f` and `g` are unequal
`f >= g`	`f` is greater than or equal to `g`
`f > g`	`f` is strictly greater than `g`
`f < g`	`f` is strictly less than `g`

For example, if n had the value 3 and x had the value 4.8, we would have the following results:

```
n < 3                  // evaluates to false
n <= 3                 // true
n < x                  // true (n is promoted to double)
(n + 3) == 2           // false
(2 * n) != (x - 1.0)   // true
n >= n                 // true, of course
(n / 4) > 0            // false (do you see why?)
```

The comparison operators have fairly low precedence, below those of any of the arithmetic operators. This means that we can dispense with the parentheses in the examples above, because we can be sure the arithmetic will be done before any comparisons. The comparison operators group from the left, as do most of the binary operators.

Syntax Cautions

1. The order of the multicharacter operators is important: `<=` is a meaningful operator, but `=<` is not.[8]

2. You cannot put spaces in any multicharacter operator, any m ore than you ca n in wo rds: `< =` and `+ +` won't be interpreted as `<=` and `++`, and they will produce syntax errors in most contexts.

Once we can compare numbers, it would be nice to make expressions using more complicated comparisons. For example, if `sample` were a `double` variable, it might be useful to test whether `sample` was in the range 0.0 . . . 1.0. A mathematician would use the notation $0.0 \le sample \le 1.0$, but that would be completely unacceptable in Java. See why? Think about it a moment—we'll wait.

*   *   *

Got it? Java would evaluate the expression `0.0 <= sample <= 1.0` like this:

```
(0.0 <= sample) <= 1.0
```

---

[8]Although `=<` does make a pretty nice "frowny face" for e-mail messages.

because the comparison operators are left-associative. The first comparison would be perfectly okay, but the second would involve a comparison of a `boolean` value with 1.0, and the comparison operators take only *numeric* operands.

Java has several logical operators that take `boolean` operands and return a `boolean` value. Here they are, assuming that p and q are boolean expressions, variables, or literals:

Expression	Evaluates to true If and Only If
`!p`	p is `false`
`p & q`	p and q are both `true`
`p && q`	p and q are both `true`
`f | g`	either p or q is `true`(or they both are)
`f || g`	either p or q is `true`(or they both are)
`p ^ q`	p and q have different values

The unary operator `!` is called "not," `&` and `&&` are called "and," `|` and `||` are called "or," and `^` is called "exclusive or" ("xor," for short) because of their similarities to the logical operators of the same name. Now we see how to do the range checking we wanted in the above example: `sample` is in the range 0.0 ... 1.0 only when it is *both* greater than or equal to 0.0 *and* less than or equal to 1.0, so we could do the test by using the expression

```
(0.0 <= sample) && (sample <= 1.0)
```

The binary boolean operators have precedence below the arithmetic and comparison operators, so we could leave out the parentheses in this example (though we don't recommend doing so). Among the boolean operators, `!` has the highest precedence (as do all unary operators), and the binary operators have the precedence order, from highest to lowest, of `&`, `^`, `|`, `&&`, `||`.

To test your understanding of the comparison operators and the boolean connectives, you should take the time to verify the following assertions. In these examples, assume that we have made the declarations

```
int sum = 45;
int index = 30;
double r = 2.5;
boolean done = false;

(sum > 0) && (index != 0)    // true, since both subexpressions are
!(r < 10.04)                 // false (equivalent to r >= 10.4)
(sum == 45) || done          // true, since one subexpression is
done & !done                 // false (for any value of done)
(2 == 2) | done              // true (for any value of done)
```

It may appear that there's some redundancy here, because `&` and `&&` seem to do the same thing, as do `|` and `||`. The difference between the two is that `&` and `|` act like other boolean operators—Java evaluates both operands before applying the operator. In the case of AND and OR, though, that may be more work than is necessary. Because `false` AND p is `false` no matter what p is, one could evaluate the first argument in an AND expression and, if it is `false`, stop right there, in much the same way that we know 0 * x is 0, regardless of the value of x. In a similar way, knowing that the first operand of an OR expression is `true` means that the whole expression is `true` regardless of what comes later.

The operators `&&` and `||` do just this sort of "short-circuit" evaluation.

Semantics: && and ||

1. If the left operand of `&&` evaluates to `false`, the expression evaluates to `false` and the right operand isn't evaluated.

2. If the left operand of `||` evaluates to `true`, the expression evaluates to `true` and the right operand isn't evaluated.

This might seem like a minor time-saver and nothing more, but it's really much more than that. Suppose, for instance, that we needed to take some action if an average, `sum / numScores`, was greater than 85.0. We could evaluate the expression `sum / numScores > 85.0`, but that could lead to disaster if `numScores` were zero, because we're not allowed to divide by zero in Java. We could, though, use a *guard* clause, to check for the potential bad case:

```
(numScores > 0) && (sum / numScores > 85.0)
```

Now if `numScores` were zero, the first operand would evaluate to `false` and Java wouldn't even look at the second, thereby eliminating the chance of dividing by zero. We advise getting into the habit of using `&&` instead of `&` and using `||` instead of `|`.

Programming Tip

Program defensively. Expect the worst to happen (since it will, we guarantee you), and write your program to be *robust* enough not to fail when it does.

Complicated `boolean` Expressions

We don't have too much trouble analyzing complicated arithmetic expressions, but a boolean expression such as

```
(a < 100) || !((t == MAX) && ((a - MAX) > 0))
```

gives one pause. Because few of us have as much experience with boolean expressions as we do with numeric expressions, it will be helpful for you to know some of the tricks for analyzing them and generating them when you need to.

Analyzing boolean expressions is relatively simple in principle. Because any boolean expression can be only `true` or `false`, all we have to do to analyze a complicated expression is to test all possible cases (something that would clearly be impossible with integer or real expressions). One of the simplest ways to do this is to use a *truth table*. In a truth table, you begin by making columns for all possible values of the variables involved and then, in subsequent columns, use the known values to find the values of increasingly complicated expressions, until you find the value of the expression you want. There are three basic truth tables, and all the rest are made by suitable combinations of these. You already know these tables—they merely represent what you know in a tabular form.

a b	a && b		a b	a || b		a	!a
T T	T		T T	T		T	F
T F	F		T F	T		F	T
F T	F		F T	T			
F F	F		F F	F			

To find the value of an expression for a particular combination of variable values, simply find the values of the variables in the left columns (we've used T to represent true and F to represent false, to make the tables easier to write). Then read the value of the expression in its column. For example, (T && F) is F, (F \|\| T) is T, and !F is T. Note that for *n* variables, there will be 2^n rows to represent all possible combinations of values for those variables.

It is important to realize how simple life is for us when we're dealing with boolean expressions. To prove the identity $(x + y)^2 = x^2 + 2xy + y^2$ for numbers x and y, we have to resort to a moderately complex proof using algebra, because there is no way to test whether this equation is true for all of the infinitely many possible values of x and y. On the other hand, to show that the expression a && (a \|\| b) always has the same boolean value as a, all we do is write a truth table for the expression and then compare its values with those of a, like this:

a b	a || b	a && (a || b)
T T	T	T
T F	T	T
F T	T	F
F F	F	F

Note that the first and last columns are identical. In other words, we've shown that (a && (a \|\| b)) is equal to a, for any possible values of a and b. Things are simple in the world of logic, precisely because there are only two possible values for any boolean variable. A truth table is nothing more than a mechanical way of evaluating all possible cases.

To build a truth table for a more complicated expression, all you have to do is write the expression as it would be evaluated, and evaluate each row by using the values of the variables. For example, the expression

```
(a < 100) || !((t == MAX) && ((a - MAX) > 0))
```

has the form p || !(q && r), where, for ease of writing, p represents (a < 100), q represents (t == MAX), and r represents ((a - MAX) > 0). Building this up in the truth table, we have

p	q	r	q && r	!(q && r)	p || !(q && r)
T	T	T	T	F	T
T	T	F	F	T	T
T	F	T	F	T	T
T	F	F	F	T	T
F	T	T	T	F	F
F	T	F	F	T	T
F	F	T	F	T	T
F	F	F	F	T	T

It's easy to see from the last column of the truth table that this expression is false only when p is false, q is true, and r is true, so we can see that

```
(a < 100) || !((t == MAX) && ((a - MAX) > 0))
```

is false only when a >= 100, t == MAX, and a - MAX > 0.

Truth tables are very helpful when you're trying to analyze someone else's boolean expression, but what do you do when you want to build a boolean expression to correspond to conditions of your own? There are lots of logical identities, such as !(!a) == a, that any good logic text can give you (and that we'll explore in the exercises). Two classes of identities are particularly helpful to programmers.

The Distributive Laws

(p && q) || (p && r) is equivalent to p && (q || r).

(p || q) && (p || r) is equivalent to p || (q && r).

DeMorgan's Laws

!(p && q) is equivalent to (!p) || (!q).

!(p || q) is equivalent to (!p) && (!q).

You've seen numeric versions of some of these. The distributive laws allow us to "factor out" a common expression, as we do in algebra when we replace $xy + xz$ with $x(y + z)$.[9] (That 9 isn't an exponent; it's a footnote reference.) In other words, we can replace the expression

```
((t > 0) && (s <= g)) || ((t > 0) && (r != MAX + 1))
```

with the simpler one below, which is obtained by factoring out the common expression t > 0.

```
(t > 0) && ((s <= g) || (r != MAX + 1))
```

The distributive laws allow us to simplify a complicated expression, but we could always leave the expression alone if we couldn't remember the distributive laws. DeMorgan's laws, on the other hand, often tell us how to do things that we might not think of doing otherwise. We've already seen how to test whether sample is in the range 0.0 . . . 1.0. We can use

```
(0.0 <= sample) && (sample <= 1.0)
```

Now suppose we wanted to test whether sample was *not* in the desired range? We could write

```
!((0.0 <= sample) && (sample <= 1.0))
```

but this isn't particularly transparent, nor is it as simple as it could be. Realizing that DeMorgan's laws say, "The negation of an AND expression is the OR of the negation of its components," we could write the equivalent expression

```
(!(0.0 <= sample)) || (!(sample <= 1.0))
```

which is itself equivalent to the much simpler

```
(0.0 > sample) || (sample > 1.0)
```

Note, by the way, how we negated the comparison operators. We can summarize this by saying

!(a < b) is equivalent to a >= b.

!(a > b) is equivalent to a <= b.

!(a == b) is equivalent to a != b.

---

[9]We couldn't interchange the operators, though: (x + y) * (x + z) is most emphatically not the same as x + (y * z). In algebra, multiplication distributes over addition, but addition doesn't distribute over multiplication. In logic, both AND and OR distribute over the other.

Review Questions

3.1 List the numeric operators in increasing order of precedence.

3.2 List the comparison operators.

3.3 What, if anything, is the difference between the expressions 10 / 3 and 10.0 / 3.0?

5.4   Assignments and Statements

We've discussed variables and primitive types and the operators Java makes available for manipulating its primitive types. Before we go on to statements, though, there's one other collection of operators we need to discuss.

Assignments

assignment operator

One of the most important operators, if not *the* most important, is the assignment operator, =. This is the operator we use to set a variable. This operator takes two operands; the left operand *must* be a variable, and the right may be a literal, a variable, or an expression of a type that is *compatible* with the variable on the left (we'll explain assignment compatibility in a moment). Assignment has the lowest possible precedence, so in any expression, the assignment operator will always be the last to be performed, unless we use parentheses to force a different order of evaluation.

If the first argument is a variable of *primitive type,*[10] the action of v = e is to evaluate e, store that value in v, and return that value to the enclosing expression, if any.

assignment is right-associative

Alone among the two-argument operators, assignment operators are evaluated right to left. This allows us to perform "multiple assignments," like this:

```
a = b = 3
```

where a and b are, for instance, int variables.

Consider what happens when this expression is evaluated. First, because = groups from the right, the expression would be evaluated as though it were parenthesized this way:

```
(a = (b = 3))
```

side effect

The expression b = 3 would be evaluated first: b gets the value 3 as a *side effect,* and the expression returns the value 3 to the expression. Now it looks like

```
(a = 3)
```

and the process repeats: a gets the value 3, and that value is returned to the expression (where it promptly dies, because there are no further expression parts to evaluate). What has happened? In simple terms, a and b have both been set to 3.

---

[10] Remember this proviso. It is vitally important, as you'll see momentarily.

Somewhere out there, we can hear the astute reader muttering, "Aha! I can set the value of a variable inside an expression—hubba, hubba!" Yes, you can do that, writing something like

```
i = 2 * (j = 3);
```

rather than the longer

```
j = 3;
i = 2 * j;
```

But don't do it. *Never* do it. If we ever hear of you doing it, we'll track you down and erase your hard drive. This trick, beloved of C programmers, is a Very Bad Idea. The problem is although it makes nifty, compact code, it also makes code that can be exceedingly difficult to understand. If you have any doubts, tell us what the values of i, j, and k are after executing this code. You have three seconds. . . .

```
int i = 2, j = 5, k = -1;
i = j = 3 * j;
k = (j = 3) * j;
```

Once you understand assignments, they're really quite simple. You have to start with the right mental model, though. A fairly common wrong path that some people take is to think that = has something to do with an assertion of equality. It doesn't. The assignment

```
index = index + 1
```

makes utterly no sense if you think of it as saying "index is 1 more than itself." Instead, what we're really saying here is "take index's value, add 1 to it, and store the new result back in index" or, simply, "increase index by 1." The operator == tests for equality; = is used for assignment.

Using = where == was intended is a common source of confusion. It crops up in boolean expressions like

```
(final = 100) || (extraCredits > 25)
```

The intent here might be to assign an A+ grade if the final score is 100 or if more than 25 extraCredits points have been amassed. The expression is wrong, though, because it *sets* final to 100, rather than testing it. The correct expression uses the equality operator, ==, rather than the assignment:

```
(final == 100) || (extraCredits > 25)
```

You'll probably make this mistake several times. Fortunately, the Java compiler will catch it for you.[11]

---

[11]The only time you might run into trouble is when you're assigning to a boolean variable, as in (honors = true) || (extraCredits > 25). A smart compiler will still catch this and warn you about a "possible unintended assignment."

Syntactic Caution: = != ==

> Don't confuse the assignment operator and the equality operator.

Expressions to modify the value of a variable, such as i = i * 2, occur so frequently in programs that Java has a collection of shortcut assignment operators for just these situations. In each of the following examples, the expression on the left has the same effect as the one on the right.

```
v += e          is the same as          v = v + e
v -= e                                   v = v - e
v *= e                                   v = v * e
v /= e                                   v = v / e
v %= e                                   v = v % e
v <<= e                                  v = v << e
v >>= e                                  v = v >> e
v >>>= e                                 v = v >>> e
v &= e                                   v = v & e
v |= e                                   v = v | e
v ^= e                                   v = v ^ e
```

All of these operators have the same precedence and grouping as simple assignment.

Class Variables versus Primitive Variables

We've implied before that primitive types are different from class types. We mentioned that it is illegal to type-cast a primitive type to be a class type, and we threw a warning in footnote 10 to the effect that what we said about assignments applied only to primitive types. In fact, there's a *fundamental* difference between class-type variables and primitive-type variables:

> Primitive-type variables hold values; class-type variables hold addresses.

All variables are just names for storage locations in memory. The difference is what's stored in those locations. For a primitive-type variable, the associated memory location holds a value. If we execute this code, the result is easy enough to understand. In Figure 5.6, we show what's happening in memory.

```
int a = 3, b = 0;
a = b;          // a and b both contain 0
b++;            // a contains 0, b contains 1
```

Upon completion, we see that the comparison a == b would evaluate to false, because a and b obviously contain different values.

Now, let's do the same sort of thing, only this time using class-type variables. A class variable, you will recall, holds the *address* in memory where the object is located, so when we declare a new instance of that class,

```
int a = 3,
    b = 0;
```

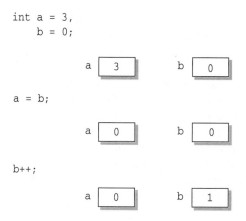

```
a = b;
```

```
b++;
```

Figure 5.6

Memory snapshot of code using primitive types.

```
Point a = new Point(3, 3),
      b = new Point(0, 0);
```

the variable just contains a reference to the object. The object itself is elsewhere in memory, at the address stored in the variable, as we indicate in Figure 5.7. This is why class types are also known as *reference types*.

reference types

If we now do an assignment,

```
a = b;
```

```
Point a = new Point(3, 3),
      b = new Point(0, 0);
```

```
a = b;
```

```
b.x++;
```

Figure 5.7

Memory snapshot of code using class types.

what happens? We've set the *address* in a to be the same as the one in b. In other words, a and b are now just two different names for the *same* object (and the object originally referred to by a is lost)! Now, if we make a change to the b object, we are also changing the a object.

alias

By making the assignment between two class variables, we've made them *aliases* for the same thing. Just as Batman gets a runny nose every time Bruce Wayne gets a cold, anything we do to a we also do to b; they are two references to the same thing.

Note now that unlike the situation with primitive-type variables, the comparison a == b evaluates as true. Two class variables are equal if and only if they refer to the same object. If two class variables refer to different objects, they will be unequal under ==, even if the objects contain identical data.

Big Semantic Cautions

> **1.** Assignment behaves very differently for class types and primitive types. Assignment for primitive types makes the values the same. Assignment for class types makes the object references identical.
>
> **2.** Equality testing also behaves very differently. Two primitive types are the same under == if their values are the same. For two class-type variables, == is true only if the variables refer to the same object.

For the purposes of assignment and type casting, primitive types and class types work in somewhat the same way. The general rule is that you can perform assignment between different types if the variable on the left is "wider" than what's on the right. In the case of primitive types, then, we would have the following situations, where d is a double and i is an int.

```
d = i              // OK: "wider" type on the left
i = d              // NO: d might not fit into i
i = (int)d         // OK: you take the risk
d = true           // NO: double and boolean are incompatible
d = (double)(true) // NO: can't even cast
```

In much the same way, you can assign a variable in a "narrower" class—that is, a subclass—to a superclass variable, but to assign in the opposite direction you need to make a type cast. In any case, you can't assign or cast across branches in the class hierarchy. For instance, suppose that we made a class MyButton that extends Button, that b was a variable of type Button, and that mb was a variable of type MyButton. We would then have the following legal and illegal assignments:

```
b = mb                    // OK: "wider" superclass on the left
mb = b                    // NO: mb "narrows" b
mb = (MyButton) b         // OK: you take the risk
b = new Point()           // NO:
b = (Button)(new Point()) // NO: can cast down, not across
```

Miscellaneous Operators

Before we leave operators, there are two more we should mention, just for the sake of completeness. The first is occasionally useful, and the second is a historical artifact inherited from Java's grandparent, C.

You can test whether a variable is a particular type by using the `instanceof` operator. This operator takes a class variable on the left and a class name on the right and returns `true` if the variable is an instance of that type or is an instance of a subclass of that type. If we continued the example above, all of the following would be legal expressions, yielding the following values:

```
b instanceof Button      // true: b is a Button
b instanceof MyButton    // false: wrong-way inheritance
mb instanceof Button     // true: mb is a Button by inheritance
mb instanceof MyButton   // true, of course
mb instanceof Object     // always true: any class is an Object
```

If the variable couldn't possibly be an instance of the indicated type, the compiler will generate an error message.

```
b instanceof Frame    // ERROR: No possible way for
                      // a Button to be a Frame
b instance of int     // ERROR: must have a class type on right
```

The *conditional operator* is unique among the Java operators in that it is a *ternary* operator, taking three operands. It looks like this:

```
booleanExpression ? expression1 : expression2
```

When the time comes to evaluate this expression, the `boolean` value of the left argument is computed. If its value is `true`, then `expression1` is evaluated, and as usual, its value is returned. On the other hand, if the boolean expression is `false`, then `expression2` is evaluated. The classic example of the conditional operator is

```
(a > b) ? a : b   // Evaluates to the larger of a and b
```

We rarely use the conditional operator. The `if` statement, which we'll cover in Chapter 6, can nearly always be used as a replacement and is easier to read.

Statements

Statements are the fundamental units of execution in a program. There are several different kinds of Java statements. *Declaration statements,* such as

```
Button clear;
private Point startpoint = new Point(45, 15), endpoint;
final int MAX = 10000;
int almostMax = MAX - 500;
```

identify new variables, specify the types they will be, indicate any other properties they may have (like `private` or `final`), and (optionally) set their initial values in an *initializer* part, occurring after the = symbol. As we mentioned, you may declare several variables of the same type in one declaration statement by placing the variables (and their initializers, if any) in a comma-separated list after the type name, as we did in the second declaration above.

Expression statements consist of an expression made into a statement by following it with a semicolon. An expression statement causes its expression to be evaluated and to perform any side effects, such as assigning a value to a variable or incrementing a variable.

```
clear = new Button("Clear");
i++;
p = q;
5; // legal, but silly, since it does nothing but evaluate 5
```

Method calls to void methods are similar to expression statements, except that their execution consists of nothing but side effects (namely, whatever happens when the object makes the call).

```
add(clear);
clear.setLabel("Really clear");
```

You've seen *return statements,* but we haven't explicitly discussed them yet. A return statement is used, in a method with non-void return type, to send the computed value back to the location where the method was called. For example, consider the method magnitude, which takes two double arguments and returns the square root of the sum of their squares.

```
double magnitude(double x, double y)
{
    double sqrSum = x * x + y * y;
    return Math.sqrt(sqrSum);
}
```

The right side of a return statement can be any expression of the type named in the header. When a return statement is encountered, it forces an immediate exit from the method. No subsequent statements in the method are executed.

A method with a non-void return type may be used anywhere in an expression where a variable of that type could appear, like this:

```
double p = 0.0266, q = 0.0909, r;
r = 28.67 * (p / 2.8 + magnitude(p, q));
```

We'll mention *empty statements* for completeness. These are statements that do nothing. You generally won't see an empty statement, unless you make a typing error like this:

```
x = x + 1;;   // NOTE the two semicolons
```

This is actually two statements: the expression statement and an empty statement between the two semicolons. With some exceptions that we'll mention in Chapter 6 and 8, empty statements are generally harmless.

The last of the statements we'll mention here (there are still a few we'll cover later) is the *group* or *compound* statement. This is any collection of statements enclosed in braces, { and } . The statement body of a method, for instance, must always be a compound statement, even if there is nothing at all between the braces. Unlike the other statements we have mentioned here, compound statements don't need to be terminated by a semicolon.

To see the importance of compound statements, we'll give you a teaser about a statement that we will explore in depth in the next chapter. The `if` statement looks like this:

```
if (booleanExpression)
    statement
```

This statement first evaluates the `booleanExpression`. If the expression evaluates to `true`, the `statement` part is then executed. If the expression is `false`, the `statement` is skipped, and execution continues with whatever comes next.

We could use this to make a counter—for instance, like this:

```
if (value > 0)
    numberOfPositives++;
```

Suppose, though, that we wanted to increment `numberOfPositives` *and* display some sort of message? The syntax of the `if` statement seems to allow for just one statement to be executed if the test succeeds. That's fine—from Java's point of view, a compound statement *is* a single statement, so we could write our `if` statement in the following form.

```
if (value > 0)
{
    numberOfPositives++;
    messageBox.setText("Found another positive');
}
```

Review Questions

4.1 What do we mean by "= != ==" and why is it important?

4.2 What can go on the left side of an assignment operator? What can go the right side?

4.3 What does `v *= 2` do?

4.4 What is the difference between the action of `a = b` when a and b are primitive types and when they are class types?

4.5 What kinds of statements have we seen so far?

5.5 Hands On

This chapter's Lablet starts off in a familiar way—we design the user interface by laying out a collection of widgets, all placed in panels and positioned by the appropriate `LayoutManagers`. This time, though, to whet your appetite for what's to come, we add an event handler that deals with button clicks, so that our Lablet actually *does* something.

Consequently, the Lablet is quite a bit more complicated than the ones earlier, because we now have to decide how the parts of our program will communicate with each other to get the job done. In this example, we've hidden all the parts of the program that deal with button clicks in a separate class, `Listener`. It is the job of the `Listener` class to detect any button clicks and call the appropriate applet methods we've made, so you don't have to concern yourself with how we handle events. All you have to do is look at the applet and observe how we've built into it the capability of dealing with the consequences of events such as a click on one of the coin or drink buttons.

Designing the Lablet, I

As usual, we began by sketching the look of our applet, placing the widgets where we wanted them. We decided to have four buttons for drink selection, arranged on the right side. On the left, we wanted three buttons to simulate insertion of nickels, dimes, and quarters, along with a coin return button. Finally, we decided to have a text display along the bottom, to keep the user informed about what is going on. In short order, we came up with a design that looked like Figure 5.8.

At that stage, we already had an inkling of the logical design, rather than just the visual design, simply by the way things were arranged. It seemed reasonable to put the four drink selection buttons in one panel. The left side dealt with a single logical portion, money handling, so we put everything on the right in a single panel. The three coin buttons were all closely related, so they deserved a subpanel of their own. We wound up placing the nine widgets into a total of four panels, as shown in Figure 5.9.

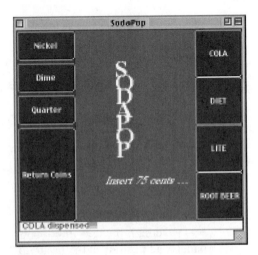

Figure 5.8

The **SodaPop** Lablet, really in action this time.

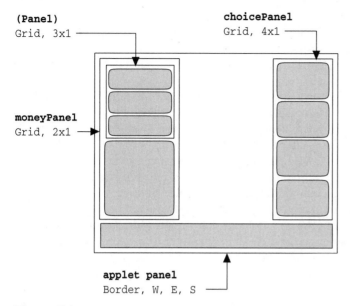

Figure 5.9

The GUI hierarchy of **SodaPop**.

We decided to make both of the major subcomponents, the choicePanel and the MoneyPanel, into classes of their own. The visual layout was easy enough. In an earlier chapter, we could have stopped there, but now we were going to add an event handler method, so the next task was to see whether we could get everything to work the way it should.

Designing the Lablet, II

The first question we asked in this phase of the design was "What does a soda machine need to know, and where does it need to know it?" In other words, we had to decide on the instance variables for our three classes. Well, what *does* our soda machine need to know? In this simple instance, it seems it only needs two things: the price of a soda and the amount of money that has been inserted so far.

Design Tip

> It is often easier to start by thinking about data, rather than methods. Once you've decided on the data, you can think about how to manipulate it.

As a first approximation, we decided that we would need two int variables, which we named amount and cost, and that these should both be instance variables of our applet itself.

Now many of the methods we needed began to be clear. Clicking on the nickel, dime, or quarter buttons should activate a method that adds the appropriate value to `amount` and updates the display text to indicate that a coin has been inserted. The coin return button was equally easy; it should call a method that displays the amount returned and then set `amount` to zero.

The only part that gave us pause was how to deal with the drink selection buttons. It wasn't that the action initiated by pressing a selection button was hard—far from it. Pressing a drink button would first cause a test to see whether the amount inserted so far was greater than or equal to the cost of a drink. If a sufficient amount had been inserted, we would simulate dispensing a soda by displaying an appropriate message and subtracting `cost` from `amount`. On the other hand, if `amount` was less than `cost`, all we'd have to do is display a message to the effect that not enough money has been inserted. How shall we do the test, though? This looks like a good time to try out the `if` statement that we introduced at the very end of the previous section. You'll see how we did it when we dive into the code.

The Lablet Code

As usual, we begin with a comment block and a collection of `import` declarations. This portion will be part of every Lablet you'll see, so we'll eliminate the description comments and the `import` declarations here and in the future.

The opening of the applet class declaration likewise holds no surprises. We declare the expected instance variables, and then in `init()` we set up the GUI. Note, though, that at the very end of `init()` we initialize the `cost` variable and one called `numberColas`, whatever that's supposed to be. (We don't want to give *everything* away here.)

```
public class SodaPop extends Applet
{
    //---------------------------- DATA ----------------------
    private MoneyPanel    money;        // for coin insertion, return
    private ChoicePanel   choices;      // for drink selection buttons
    private TextField     display;      // for status messages

    private int           amount,       // amount available
                          cost,         // price of a drink
                          numberColas;  // colas on hand

    private Listener      myListener = new Listener(this);

//--------------------- THE USUAL METHODS -----------------

public void init()
{
    setLayout(new BorderLayout());
    setBackground(Color.red);

    choices = new ChoicePanel(myListener);
    add(BorderLayout.EAST, choices);

    money = new MoneyPanel(myListener);
    add(BorderLayout.WEST, money);
```

```
display = new TextField();
display.setBackground(Color.white);
display.setForeground(Color.red);
display.setFont(new Font("SansSerif", Font.BOLD, 12));
add(BorderLayout.SOUTH, display);

cost = 75;
numberColas = 5;
}
```

We need the `paint()` method, because we are painting on the applet's frame. We could have defined a `Canvas` subclass, perhaps named `logo`, with its own `paint()` method.

```
public void paint(Graphics g)
{
   Dimension d = getSize();
   int xStart = d.width / 2 - 20;
   int yStart = d.height / 2 - 80;

   g.setFont(new Font("Serif", Font.BOLD, 36));
   g.setColor(Color.white);
   g.drawString("S", xStart, yStart);
   g.drawString("O", xStart, yStart + 20);
   g.drawString("D", xStart, yStart + 40);
   g.drawString("A", xStart, yStart + 60);
   g.drawString("P", xStart, yStart + 80);
   g.drawString("O", xStart, yStart + 100);
   g.drawString("P", xStart, yStart + 120);

   g.setFont(new Font("Serif", Font.ITALIC, 18));
   g.setColor(Color.white);
   g.drawString("Insert 75 cents ...", xStart - 20, yStart + 160);
}
```

We next come to a series of methods of our own, designed, as we just saw, to be invoked when a particular button is clicked. The `processNickelButton()` method, for example, does what we said should happen when the nickel button is pressed: It displays the message "Nickel inserted . . ." and then adds 5 to the current `amount`. The other two coin methods are the same. By the way, these methods all have default (package) access. Which access would be more appropriate?

```
void processNickelButton()
{
   display.setText("Nickel inserted...");
   amount += 5;
}

void processDimeButton()
{
   display.setText("Dime inserted...");
   amount += 10;
}

void processQuarterButton()
{
   display.setText("Quarter inserted...");
```

```
        amount += 25;
    }
```

The `processReturnButton()` method that is invoked when the coin return button is pressed has some interesting features. First, note that it has three local variables: `amountString`, `dollars`, and `pennies`. See if you can explain why we use / and % on the `amount` to initialize `dollars` and `pennies`.

```
void processReturnButton()
{
    String amountString;
    int dollars = amount / 100;
    int pennies = amount % 100;
```

The `if...else` statement that follows acts as it appears to: If the `boolean` expression `pennies < 10` is true, the first statement is executed, and if it's `false`, the second is executed. All we are doing here is applying some minor cosmetic touches to make the display look like it should.

In the code below, note that we're using the `String` concatenation operator, +, to build the `amountString` that will be displayed. Remember that Java "knows" how to convert values of primitive types to `String`s, and if it sees a class variable, it calls that class's `toString()` method, if it has one. Nearly all of the Java library classes have `toString()` methods.

```
if (pennies < 10)
{
    amountString = new String("$" + dollars + ".0" + pennies);
}
else
{
    amountString = new String("$" + dollars + "." + pennies);
}
display.setText(amountString + " returned.");
amount = 0;
}
```

Finally, when all the `String` manipulation is done, the `amountString` is sent to the `display` `Textfield`, and the `amount` variable is reset to zero, because we just gave back all the remaining money that had been inserted.

The drink selection methods all act in the same way. They use an `if` statement to check whether `amount >= cost` (that is, whether enough money has been inserted), and if the test returns `true`, the appropriate message is sent to `display` and the `cost` is deducted from the available `amount`.

The `processCola()` method is a bit more clever than its siblings. We'll ask you to explain it in the lab exercises.

```
void processColaButton()
{
    if (amount >= cost)
    {
        display.setText("COLA dispensed!!!");
        amount -= cost;
        numberColas--;
    }
```

```
    if (numberColas <= 0)
        {
            choices.disable("COLA");
        }
    }

    void processDietButton()
    {
        if (amount >= cost)
        {
            display.setText("DIET dispensed!!!");
            amount -= cost;
        }
    }

    void processLiteButton()
    {
    if (amount >= cost)
    {
        display.setText("LITE dispensed!!!");
        amount -= cost;
    }
}

void processRootButton()
    {
        if (amount >= cost)
        {
            display.setText("ROOT dispensed!!!");
            amount -= cost;
        }
    }
}
```

We're finished! The MoneyPanel and ChoicePanel classes are just more good programming—we've split off the entire panel of drink choice buttons and the panel of money-handling buttons into separate classes so that they won't further clutter the applet's init() method. As the comments indicate, these classes are just responsible for holding and laying out their buttons. With the exception of one method in the ChoicePanel class, no processing beyond that ever takes place.

```
//===================== MoneyPanel CLASS =======================
/**
 * This class is primarily for display purposes in the SodaPop
 * applet. It is, basically, a holder for the four money-related
 * buttons. It does do some event-handling in response to button
 * clicks, but for the purposes of this lab, you can ignore
 * anything that has the word "Listener" in it.
 */
class MoneyPanel extends Panel
{
    private Button    bNickel  = new Button("Nickel"),
                      bDime    = new Button("Dime"),
                      bQuarter = new Button("Quarter"),
                      bReturn  = new Button("Return Coins");

    public MoneyPanel(Listener theListener)
    {
        bNickel.addActionListener(theListener);
        bDime.addActionListener(theListener);
```

```
        bQuarter.addActionListener(theListener);
        bReturn.addActionListener(theListener);

        setBackground(Color.blue);
        setForeground(Color.white);

        setLayout(new GridLayout(2,1, 5, 5));

        Panel p = new Panel();
        p.setLayout(new GridLayout(3,1, 5, 5));
        p.add(bNickel);
        p.add(bDime);
        p.add(bQuarter);

        add(p);
        add(bReturn);
    }
}

//===================== ChoicePanel CLASS =====================
/**
 * Like the MoneyPanel class, this class is primarily a
 * holder for the four drink buttons. Again, pay no attention
 * to anything with the word "Listener" in it.
 */
class ChoicePanel extends Panel
{
    private Button bCola = new Button("COLA"),
                   bDiet = new Button("DIET"),
                   bLite = new Button("LITE"),
                   bRoot = new Button("ROOT BEER");

    public ChoicePanel(Listener theListener)
    {
        bCola.addActionListener(theListener);
        bDiet.addActionListener(theListener);
        bLite.addActionListener(theListener);
        bRoot.addActionListener(theListener);

        setBackground(Color.blue);
        setForeground(Color.white);
        setLayout(new GridLayout(4,1));

        add(bCola);
        add(bDiet);
        add(bLite);
        add(bRoot);
    }

    /**
     * This method turns off one of the buttons when called.
     */
    public void disable(String name)
    {
    if (name.equals("COLA"))
    {
        bCola.setEnabled(false);
        }
    }
}
```

The file then concludes with the definition of the `Listener` class. We won't be able to explain it until we discuss events in the next chapter, so we'll omit its description here.

5.6 **Summary**

- We introduced only one new class in this chapter. The `Math` class contains a collection of useful math routines. It is part of the `java.lang` package, so you don't have to `import` it.
- The Java primitive types are `byte`, `char`, `short`, `int`, `long`, `float`, `double`, and `boolean`.
- In order of size, the integral types are `byte` (8 bits), `char`, `short` (16 bits), `int` (32 bits), and `long` (64 bits). Each type is represented using two's complement notation, of the appropriate size.
- Integer literals have the form *optionalSign digitString*, where *digitString* consists of a string or one or more digits. Integer literals of `long` type have an L suffix.
- The floating-point numeric types are `float` (32 bits) and `double` (64 bits).
- Floating-point literals have the form *optionalSign digitDotString optionalExp*, where *digitDotString* is a string of at least one digit containing at most one decimal point, and *optionalExp* has the form e*integerLiteral*.
- The `char` type is an integral type, because characters are represented internally using a 16-bit Unicode scheme. Character literals consist of a character between single quotes or an escape code, such as `\t` for tab, enclosed in single quotes.
- The `boolean` type contains two values, represented by the literals `true` and `false`.
- Identifiers, the names for variables, methods, classes, and interfaces, all have the form *letter letterDigitString*, where *letter* is one of `A . . . z`, `a . . . z` and *letterDigitString* is any string of letters, digits (`0 . . . 9`), or underscore characters (`_`). An identifier cannot be a Java keyword.
- Variables are identifiers associated with a single instance of a class or a single value of a primitive type.
- A variable must be declared in a class. If a variable is declared in a method, it is known as a local variable and has meaning only within the nearest pair of enclosing braces. If a variable is not declared within a method, it is known as a global variable (or instance variable) and has meaning throughout its class.
- A variable name may not be used in a file before the point of its declaration.
- The scope of a variable refers to that portion of its class where its name has meaning.
- If it has the proper access, an instance variable or method may be referred to outside of its class by the form *classInstanceVariable.memberName*. Within the class in which it is declared, a method or instance variable is referenced by its name.
- A method or variable declaration may be modified by preceding its declaration by any of the keywords `static`, `final`, `private`, `protected`, or `public`. In any collection of modifiers, only one of `public`, `protected`, and `private` may be used. Local variable declarations may not be modified.

- A `static` member (instance variable or method) is associated with a class, not with any particular instance of the class.
- A `final` variable may not be modified. A class may be declared as `final`, which means that it may not be subclassed.
- A package is a grouping of files into one logical entity. A file may declare its membership in a package by using the `package` *packageName;* declaration in the first line of the file. All files in a package must be in a single directory, with the same name as the package. All files in a Java program without package declarations are grouped in a single, unnamed package, for purposes of determining access.
- Access determines the visibility of a member outside of its own class.
- A member with `private` access is visible only within its class; private members are not inherited by subclasses.
- A member declared without the modifier `public`, `protected`, or `private` is said to have default or package access and is visible anywhere within its package, but not outside.
- A member with `protected` access is visible throughout its package and cannot be accessed outside of its package, except within its subclasses.
- A `public` member is visible anywhere.
- Every one of the Java operators has an associativity governing the order of grouping when evaluating expressions. The unary operators all group from the right. Except for the assignment operators, the binary operators all group from the left. The assignment operators and the conditional `?:` group from the right.
- Don't rely on precedence when writing expressions. Use parentheses to make the order of evaluation clear.
- Numeric binary operators require both operands to be the same type. If they are not, the narrower (smaller) type will be promoted to the match the wider.
- Variables of primitive type store values, whereas variables of class type hold references to class instances.
- An expression of one type may be cast to be considered as another type by using the type-cast operator (*typeName*).
- An expression may always be cast to a wider type. For primitive numeric types, this means that it is always permissible to cast upward in the sequence `byte`, `short`, `int`, `long`, `float`, `double`. For class types, it is always permissible to cast upward in any branch of the class hierarchy. For both, casts in the other direction are allowed, but some information might be lost.
- In no case may a primitive type be cast to a class type or vice versa, and class types may not be made across branches in the class hierarchy.
- Assignment to a variable of primitive type copies a value into the variable. Assignment to a variable of class type makes the variable an alias to the other argument.
- Assignment to a wider type is allowed. Assignment with a narrower type on the left requires a type cast.

■ A frequent source of compile-time errors is confusing assignment with equality.
■ We covered the following statements: declaration, expression, method calls to void methods, return, empty, and group or compound (and `if`, briefly).
■ Every one of the Java operators has a precedence, governing the order in which operators are evaluated. The operators and their precedences are as follows, listed from highest priority (done first) to lowest. In the descriptions, any operator not identified as unary or ternary is binary (two-argument).

Precedence	Operators	Descriptions
1.	`++ --`	Increment, decrement (unary)
	`+ -`	Plus, minus (unary)
	`~`	Bitwise complement (unary)
	`!`	Boolean negation (unary)
	`(type)`	Type cast
2.	`* / %`	Multiplication, division, remainder
3.	`+ -`	Addition, subtraction
	`+`	String concatenation
4.	`<< >> >>>`	Bit shifts
5.	`< <= > >=`	Numeric comparison
	`instanceof`	Type comparison
6.	`== !=`	Equality, inequality
7.	`&`	Bitwise AND, boolean AND
8.	`^`	Bitwise XOR, boolean XOR
9.	`|`	Bitwise OR, boolean OR
10.	`&&`	Short-circuit boolean AND
11.	`||`	Short-circuit boolean OR
12.	`?:`	Conditional (ternary)
13.	`=`	Assignment
	`*= /= %=`	Assignment with operation
	`+= -=`	
	`<<= >>= >>>=`	
	`&= ^= !=`	

5.7 Exercises

1. Which of the following are legal Java literals? For those that are legal, tell what type they might be (there may not be unique answers; 1 could be a `byte` or an `int`, for example).

   a. 3
   b. 2+3
   c. "2+3"
   d. 5,280
   e. 0L
   f. 0.333333...
   g. 1e1
   h. -23.900e-0.5
   i. '\n'
   j. 4f

2. What is it about the `Math` and `Color` classes that makes it reasonable to define them as `final`? Come up with a class of your own that might be a reasonable candidate for being defined to be `final`.

3. Here is a cute use for a `static` variable:

```
class RecordKeeper
{
    public static int hits = 0;

    RecordKeeper()
    {
        hits++;
    }
    ...
}
```

Why? What's going on here?

4. Go back over `Gigobite` and look at the access levels of its members. Are they all as they should be? If not, fix those that need fixing.

5. Do Exercise 4 for the `SodaPop` Lablet. Fix all that need to be fixed and explain your reasons for each choice.

6. Consider the following class declaration:

```
class Whatever
{
    int x, y;    // call these x1 and y1
    // A
    void someMethod()
    {
        // B
        int z;
        {
            // C
            int x;    // call this x2
            // D
        }
        // E
    }
}
```

```
    // F
    void anotherMethod(int x)     // call this x3
    {
       // G
       int y;    // call this y2
       // H
    }
}
// I
```

For each of the locations A through I, tell whether the variables x1, x2, x3, y1, y2, and z would be visible, by placing a check in the appropriate cell.

	A	B	C	D	E	F	G	H	I
x1									
x2									
x3									
y1									
y2									
z									

7. Assuming that these declarations aren't local, which of the following are legal? For the illegal declarations, explain what's wrong.

a. `public int static x = 3;`
b. `private boolean isDirty;`
c. `static Button = new Button("Delete");`
d. `public final private static int MARGIN = 15;`
e. `public final double SCALE_FACTOR_X;`
f. `final public double SCALE_FACTOR_Y;`
g. `public restrooms;`
h. `private static Point anchor = new Point(15, 15);`

8. For the following numeric expressions, place parentheses to indicate the order in which they would be evaluated. Assume that all variables have been declared as ints.

a. `2 * 3 - 4`
b. `p * q / r / 3`
c. `-1 + p * (2 / q - r)`
d. `p = p * 3 - 4`
e. `7 / (double)q + 1`
f. `p++ * 3`
g. `q /= p * p << r / 2 ^ p - 1 >> q`

9. Give the Java versions of these algebraic expressions.

a. $(3p + q)(p - 2q)$

b. $\dfrac{1}{x+y} + \dfrac{1}{x-y}$

   c. $x^4 - x^3 + x^2 - x + 1$

   d. $1 + \cfrac{1}{1 + \cfrac{1}{1+x}}$

10. The `%` operator is actually defined by `p % q = p - (p / q) * q`. This definition applies to floating-point values as well. Use this definition to find the values of

   a. `13 % 3`

   b. `-13 % 3`

   c. `13 % -3`

   d. `-13 % -3`

   e. `13.0 % 3.0`

11. Suppose we have the following declarations

```
int p = 1, q = 3;
long a = 31555750L;
float f = 2.008f;
double d = 6.023e+26;
```

For the following expressions, tell the type of the result.

   a. `p - 2 * q`

   b. `2 * d`

   c. `2.0 * d`

   d. `(a - 2f) / p`

   e. `p + q + a + f + d`

   f. `p + (long)q`

   g. `d - a`

12. Which of the following expressions are not correctly formed? For those that are incorrect, explain what is wrong with them. Assume that you have the variable declarations of Exercise 11.

   a. `d << 2`

   b. `(p - a) * (d = 0)`

   c. `8`

   d. `e < 0 && 0 < e`

   e. `f++ = 2.3f`

   f. `d << 2`

13. Suppose you are interested in computing the average score for ten tests, each scored from 0 to 100 in integer amounts. Assume that the `int` variable sum contains the total of all ten scores. You want at least three decimal places of accuracy, so you decide to cast the average to a `double`. Here's the code:

```
double average = (double)(sum / 10);
```

When you try it, though, you get a surprise. What is the surprise and what is your response?

14. a. By hand, convert 31847 seconds to the form *h* hours, *m* minutes, *s* seconds, observing the usual conventions that both *m* and *s* are integers greater than or equal to 0 and less than 60.

b. Remember what you did in part (a) and imagine that you were writing a `Time` class to store and manipulate times. Suppose that the class looked like this:

```
class Time
{
    private int h,    // number of hours
            m, // number of minutes (0 .. 59)
            s; // number of seconds (0 .. 59)

    public Time(int startTime)
    // Sets h, m, and s to represent the
    // number of hours, minutes, and seconds
    // equivalent to startTime.
    {
        ...
    }
    ...
}
```

Write the constructor.

c. Write the following `Time` method.

```
public void add(Time t)
// Adds t to this Time
{
    ...
}
```

The intent here is that if this `Time` object held the values 30:47:15 (in hours:minutes:seconds) and if t held 2:24:50, the result of `add(t)` would be to set this time to 33:12:5.

d. This class has a natural candidate for a `final static int`. What is it?

e. Explain why we chose `private` access for h, m, and s.

f. Describe two more constructors and three more methods that would be useful for this class.

15. Write an expression that evaluates to `true` if the `int` variable n is odd and evaluates to `false` if n is even.

16. Consider the following code segment, where a, b, and c are ints.

```
{
    c = a % b;
    a = b;
    b = c;
}
```

If you start with some positive values in a and b and repeatedly execute this block, stopping when c is zero, what can you say about the value that winds up in a? *Hint:* Try it with a = 120, b = 25; with a = 128, b = 32; and with a = 720, b = 63.

17. Let d be a `double` variable. For what values of d is the following expression true?

```
Math.ceil(d / 3) == Math.floor(d / 3)
```

18. Write an expression that uses three int variables, a, b, and c, and returns the largest of the values of a, b, and c.

19. If a and b are ints with a < b, explain the purpose of the expression

```
floor(a + (b - a + 1) * Math.random())
```

20. Explain why the int type represents values between −2147483648 and 2147483647. Where do these two numbers come from?

21. What's the largest possible long value in Java? Express your answer
   a. In binary.
   b. Using an expression involving a power of 2.
   c. In decimal.

22. Invent a good use for using the bitwise operators | and ^ (and perhaps ~) with a mask, as we did with &.

23. a. Represent −28 as an 8-bit two's complement number.
   b. What bit pattern is the result of -28 << 2? What number does this represent?
   c. What bit pattern is the result of -28 >>> 2? What number does this represent?
   d. Try the parts above with enough samples to be able to make a reasonably simple description of what these shifts do to the values of numbers.

24. Use truth tables to verify DeMorgan's laws.

25. Express each of the following sentences as a boolean expression.
   a. *x* is greater than 10.
   b. Either *u* or *v* is smaller than 0.00001.
   c. *temp* is no farther than 1.5 away from *target*.
   d. *t* is no smaller than 3.7.
   e. Exactly one of *index* and *count* is zero.
   f. *sign* is positive, or both *x* and *y* are negative.
   g. x/y is defined and greater than 1.

26. Using DeMorgan's laws, show that you don't need AND in boolean expressions if you have NOT and OR available.

27. It happens that the operators AND, OR, and NOT are sufficient to express any boolean expression. Exercise 26 shows that just two, OR and NOT, are sufficient. Show that you can get away with just one operation, NAND, defined below, by expressing p OR q and NOT p using only NANDs.

a	*b*	*a NAND b*
T	T	F
T	F	T
F	T	T
F	F	T

28. Assume that n and m are ints and that p and q are boolean. For the valid expressions below, insert parentheses to show the order in which they would be evaluated. For the invalid ones, indicate what is wrong with them.

a. `n => 0 || p`
b. `p && ! q || p`
c. `! 2 * n < m`
d. `n && m < 0`
e. `!p || n == m`
f. `p = n == m`
g. `2 * n - m >= 3 && -3 + p * q <= q / 2`
h. `!!!!(m == n)`
i. `n < 0 && m < 0 || p`

29. In footnote 10 we mentioned that incorrectly using = instead of == might cause problems in expressions such as

```
(honors = true) || (extraCredit > 25)
```

Explain why this would not be a good way to test whether `honors` is `true` or `extraCredit` is greater than 25.

30. In the expression `x = (x == x)`, there's only one possible choice for the type of x.

a. What type must x be to make this expression legal?
b. What is the result? Write an equivalent, simpler expression.
c. Do parts (a) and (b) for the expression `(x = x) == x`. Is there now only one choice for the type of x? What is the value of the expression?
d. Which of the two expressions above is equivalent to `x = x == x` under Java's rules for evaluation of expressions?

31. Consider the following code:

```
temp = a;
a = b;
b = temp;
```

a. Assume that `temp`, `a`, and `b` have all been declared previously as `int`s. Do the kind of "memory snapshot" analysis we did in Figure 5.3 and tell, in simple terms, what this code does.
b. Redo part (a), this time assuming that all three variables have been declared previously as `Button`s. Do the same sort of thing we did in Figure 5.4. The picture for this part will, of course, look different from that of part (a), but does your "simple terms" answer change?

32. Which of the following are legal Java statements? For those that are not, explain what is wrong with them. Make whatever assumptions about variables and methods you need, trying to make the statements valid.

a. `x++;`
b. `public Point p;`
c. `p = new Point(2, 4)`
d. `p.x = Math.max(p.x, 0);`
e. `p.move(2, 2)`
f. `return (p.x < p.y);`
g. `import java.awt.*;`
h. `{5;;{int y = 0;};} ;`

> **i.** `x = y = x;`
> **j.** `if (x == 3)`
> `y++;`

33. If an instance variable of a class is accessible by `get` and `set` methods in the class, why not simply declare the variable as `public` and eliminate the two methods?

5.8 Answers to Review Questions

1.1 `byte`, `short`, `int`, `long`, `float`, `double`, `char`, and `boolean`.

1.2 The number of bits they use to represent their values (and hence the size of the numbers they can represent). An `int` is four times as long in binary as a `byte`.

1.3 Neither—they represent the same number.

2.1 The name of a package, class, method, or variable.

2.2 A local variable.

2.3 The scope of a local variable extends from its point of declaration to the close of the block (delimited by `{` and `}` braces) in which it is declared.

2.4 `Font.BOLD`, `Label.LEFT`, and `Color.black` are examples. (One can only wonder why it isn't `Color.BLACK`.)

2.5 `private`, default (package), `protected`, `public`.

3.1 `+`, `-` (the binary versions); `*`, `/`, `%`; `++`, `--`, `+`, `-` (the unary versions).

3.2 `<`, `<=`, `>`, `>=`, `==`, and `!=`.

3.3 `10 / 3` evaluates to the integer 3; `10.0 / 3.0` evaluates to the floating-point value that is as close to 3.333... as can be represented in a `float`.

4.1 The assignment operator is not the same as the comparison operator. It is important to remember the difference, because it's easy to use one operator where the other was intended.

4.2 For our purposes, the only thing that can go on the left side of an assignment is a variable. The right side can consist of any expression of a type that is compatible with the type of the variable on the left.

4.3 Replaces the value of v with twice its original value.

4.4 When a and b are primitive types, `a = b` sets the value of a to that of b. When a and b are class types, `a = b` makes a refer to b, making the two variables aliases of the same object.

4.5 Declarations, expression statements, `void` method calls, `return` statements, empty statements, and compound statements.

5.9 Class References

java.lang.Math

This class contains many mathematical functions. The class is `final`, so it can't be subclassed, and all of its methods are `static`, so they are called by using the class name rather than the name of an object. It is solely a holder for functions and constants, so it has no constructor. Don't confuse this class with the `java.math` package.

```
final class Math extends Object
{
    //-------- Class Constants --------
    final static double E = 2.7182818284590452354;
    final static double PI = 3.14158265358979323846;

    //--------- Class Methods ---------
    static int abs(int x);
    static long abs(long x);
    static float abs(float x);
    static double abs(double x);
    static double acos(double x);
    static double asin(double x);
    static double atan(double x);
    static double atan2(double x, double y);
        // These implement the inverse trig functions.

    static double ceil(double x);
    static double cos(double x);
    static double exp(double x);
    static double floor(double x);
    static double log(double x);
    static int max(int x, int y);
    static long max(long x, long y);
    static float max(float x, float y);
    static double max(double x, double y);
    static int min(int x, int y);
    static long min(long x, long y);
    static float min(float x, float y);
    static double min(double x, double y);
    static double pow(double x, double y);

    static double random();
        // See also the Random class, below.
    static double rint(double x);
    static int round(float x);
    static long round(double x);
    static double sin(double x);
    static double sqrt(double x);
    static double tan(double x);
}
```

java.util.Random

This class could be viewed as an extension of `java.lang.Math.random()` function. A `Random` object is a factory for random numbers,[12] generated by calls to `nextDouble()`, `nextInt()`, and so on. For example, you would produce a new random number generator by declaring

```
Random generator = new Random();
```

---

[12]Strictly speaking, these are *pseudo-random* numbers, because they are produced by functions that have predictable results. A sequence of such numbers "appears" random to conventional tests for true randomness.

and then call `generator.nextInt()` as often as needed to get randomly selected integers.

```
class Random extends Object

{
    //---------- Constructors ----------
    Random();
    Random(long seed);
    /* The first constructor will produce a Random object that
       gives a different sequence of numbers each time the
       program is run. If you require the same sequence each
       time, use the second constructor with a fixed seed
       argument. */

    //----------- Methods ------------
    void nextBytes(byte[] b);
    /* This fills the argument array (Ch. 8) with randomly
       selected bytes. */

    double nextDouble();
    float nextFloat();
        // These return values distributed between 0.0 and 1.0.

    int nextInt();
    long nextLong();
    /* These return a value of the appropriate type, distributed
       uniformly across their ranges of possible values. */

    double nextGaussian();
    /* This selects doubles with a Gaussian distribution having
       mean 0.0 and standard deviation 1.0. */
}
```

java.math.BigInteger

If you need *huge* integers, use this class. A `BigInteger` object has no limit on its size (except, of course, that it's limited by the amount of available memory on your computer). For brevity, we won't discuss all the methods of this class. There's a companion class in the `java.math` package, `BigDecimal`, that we won't cover here.

This class is an extension of the `java.lang.Number` class, which is discussed in Chapter 8.

```
class BigInteger extends Number
{
    //---------- Constructors ---------
    BigInteger(String value);
    BigInteger(String value, int radix);
    /* These construct a BigInteger from a string representing
       the number. The second constructor allows you to set the
       base of the string value being used (like 10 for decimal
       and 2 for binary numbers) */

    //--------- Class Methods ----------
    static BigInteger valueOf(long x);
```

```
/* Returns a BigInteger representing the same value as the
   argument. This is useful for transforming a long into a
   BigInteger */

//------------ Methods ------------
BigInteger add(BigInteger b);
BigInteger and(BigInteger b);
BigInteger divide(BigInteger b);
BigInteger min(BigInteger b);
BigInteger max(BigInteger b);
BigInteger multiply(BigInteger b);
BigInteger or(BigInteger b);
BigInteger pow(int power);
BigInteger remainder(BigInteger b);
BigInteger subtract(BigInteger b);
BigInteger xor(BigInteger b);
/* These return the result of performing the arithmetic or bitwise
   operation with this number and the specified argument as
   operands. */

BigInteger abs();
BigInteger negate();
BigInteger not();
/* Return the result of performing the unary operation on
   this BigInteger. */

int compareTo(BigInteger b);
/* Returns -1 if this number is less than b, 0 if the two
   are equal, and 1 if this number is larger than b. */

double doubleValue();
float floatValue();
int intValue();
long longValue();
/* Returns the result of converting this number into values
   of the indicated type. */

int bitLength();
// Returns the number of bits in this number.

BigInteger clearBit(int n);
BigInteger flipBit(int n);
BigInteger setBit(int n);
/* Return a BigInteger that is the same as this one with bit
   n set to 0, inverted, or set to 1, respectively. */
}
```

CHAPTER SIX

EVENTS AND ACTIONS

An important feature of many modern computer applications is that they are *event-driven.* An application like a spreadsheet or a Web browser, for example, not only spends its time doing its own work—computing new values, reading from files, and displaying information on the screen—but also keeps an eye on what's happening in the larger "world" in which it lives—watching for keyboard activities, monitoring mouse moves and clicks, and so on. Java provides a rich collection of functions to monitor and report events. Making applets responsive to the "world" of the user is the heart of event-driven programming.

Objectives

In this chapter, we will

- Introduce some Java programming constructs we'll need to handle events.
- Describe the events that are generated in the Java environment.
- Learn how to make an applet respond appropriately to events by including the necessary event-handling routines.
- Discuss event-driven programming in an object-oriented framework.
- Discuss the "delegation model" that Java uses for handling events.

6.1 More Java Programming

For the statement-level details of Java, we've adopted a "need to know" approach, discussing features as we needed them, rather than starting off by dumping the whole lot on you at the start. In this chapter, you "need to know" two new Java features: the conditional statements, `if` and `switch`, and interfaces.

The if Statement

When we write applets that are intended to respond to actions, we need to be able to test things like what kind of event it was, where it occurred, what its target `Component` was, and so on. That part isn't hard; in fact, you've already seen the boolean operators we'll need to do such tests. Once we've made the tests, though, we also have to write our programs in such a way that they take different actions, depending on the test results. So far, all the methods you've written have embodied the computer equivalent of predestination: Do the first statement, then do the next, then do the one after that, and so on; there has been no way to depart from the path of executing statements in sequence from top to bottom. What we need are some other statements that allow our programs to take different actions, depending on the results of tests we make.

The `if` statement is written like this:

```
if (boolean expression)    // (the parentheses are required)
{
    statement;                // the "controlled" statements
    statement;
    ...
}
```

Semantics: The `if` Statement

When an `if` statement is encountered, the boolean expression is evaluated. If it evaluates to `true`, the controlled statements that follow are executed, and execution passes to any subsequent statement. On the other hand, if the boolean expression is `false`, the controlled statements are skipped, as though they weren't there at all.

For example, the statement

```
if (source == order)
    displayField.setText("Button order clicked");
```

first checks whether the `source` of the event happened to be the `Button` object `order`. If it was, the message "Button order clicked" is displayed. If it wasn't, however, the `setText()` method call is ignored, and execution continues with the following statement, where, perhaps, another test is tried.

Note what seems to be a discrepancy here. The definition of the `if` statement placed the controlled statements in a block, delimited by braces, whereas in the example the braces were conspicuous by their absence. In fact, the braces are unnecessary when the `if` statement controls only a single statement. However, we're going to use braces to group the controlled part of an `if` statement, even when only one statement is being controlled. You'll see that, although it involves a bit more typing, enclosing the controlled statements in braces as a general practice is a Good Idea, because it lessens the possibility of introducing errors in your code.

Another version of the `if` statement allows us to execute one statement (simple or compound) if the test is `true` and a different one if the test is `false`. The `if...else` statement looks like this:

```
if (boolean expression)
{
    first collection of statements
}
else
{
    second collection of statements
}
```

Semantics: The `if...else` Statement

When an `if...else` statement is executed, several things happen in sequence:

1. The boolean expression is evaluated.

2. If the boolean expression evaluates to `true`, the first statements are executed.

3. If the boolean expression is `false`, the second statements are executed.

4. In either case, the program then continues with whatever comes after the `if...else` statement.

Here's a simple example:

```
if (source == colorButton1)
{
    currentColor = Color.red;    // source is colorButton1
}
else
{
    currentColor = Color.black; // source is anything else
}
```

The statement parts of an `if` or an `if...else` statement can be anything at all, even another `if` statement. We often nest `if` statements when we need to base actions on several tests, such as here:

```
if (source == colorButton1)
{
    currentColor = Color.red;
}
else
{
    //----- We enter this part only if source isn't colorButton1
    if (source == colorButton2)
    {
        currentColor = Color.blue;
    }
    else
    {
        // and we get here only if source isn't colorButton1
        // and also isn't colorButton2
        if (e.target == colorButton3)
        {
            currentColor = Color.green;
        }
        else
        {
            // The only way we can get here is if all three
            // boolean expressions evaluated to false.
            currentColor = Color.black;
        }
    }
}
```

Using these successive levels of indentation really annoys some people. If you're one of them, remember that Java ignores carriage returns and tabs in source code and doesn't require braces for single-statement controlled parts, so you could write the code above like this:

```
if (source == colorButton1)
{
    currentColor = Color.red;
}
else if (source == colorButton2)
{
    currentColor = Color.blue;
}
else if (source == colorButton3)
{
    currentColor = Color.green;
}
else
{
    currentColor = Color.black;
}
```

While we're on the subject, we should mention that we always drop the statement part of an `if` statement down to the next line and indent it. Even though it's not required by the compiler, such indentation makes code far easier to read. For example, compare these two versions of the same statement:

```
// version 1
if (x > 0) {if (y > 0) {t = 1;} else {t = 2;} }

// version 2
if (x > 0)
{
    if (y > 0)
    {
        t = 1;
    }
    else
    {
        t = 2;
    }
}
```

Few people would deny that version 2 is far easier to understand. Version 2 also points out how Java deals with a potential ambiguity inherent in the `if...else` statement and demonstrates the value of brace-delimiting the controlled part. Suppose we wrote version 2 without braces and with bad indentation, like this:

```
// version 3 (Bad! Misleading indentation)
if (x > 0)
    if (y > 0)
        t = 1; // done when x > 0 and y > 0
else
    t = 2;     // when is this done?
```

Should the `else` part be matched with the `(y > 0)` part or the `(x > 0)`? This is a genuine ambiguity, like the ambiguity we discussed earlier when Java evaluates an expression such as `2 + 3 * 4`, and the designers of Java solved it in the same way, by legislating the choice that would be made.[1]

An `else` clause is always matched to the nearest available unmatched `if`.

If we had wanted to force the statement to behave the way version 3 made it appear, we would "wall off" the inner `if` with braces, effectively terminating it before the `else`:

```
// version 4 (Different behavior from previous versions)
if (x > 0)
{
   if (y > 0)
   {
      t = 1; // done when x > 0 and y > 0
   }
}
else
{
   t = 2;    // done when x ≤ 0, regardless of y's value
}
```

Common Problems with `if`

Because the `if` statement is more complex than the other statements we've seen so far, it leaves the door open for some common programming errors. These errors can be exasperating to track down and fix, so the best remedy we can suggest is to avoid them in the first place.

Take a look at the code below. It seems simple enough—it tests the variable `x` (which is probably a `double`), and if `x` is larger than `1e38`, it displays a message on `displayField` (which is probably what sort of object?)

```
// WARNING: Bad programming here
if (x > 1e38);
{
   displayField.setText("My! What a big number!");
}
```

The problem here is that this code doesn't behave as expected. In fact, it displays the message no matter how large or small x is! Before going on, see whether you can spot the cause of the problem.

* * *

---

[1] Well, not exactly. Java was designed to have a syntax very much like C++, and C++ handles the `else` ambiguity that way. (Well, not exactly. C++ was designed to be syntactically compatible with C, so the decision really comes from C.)

Find it? A smart compiler might find it for you, even though the example code is syntactically legal. The odd behavior is caused by the semicolon after the boolean expression (x > 1e38). A semicolon, you will recall, is a statement terminator. In this case, Java expects a statement after the boolean expression and, indeed, finds one just where it should be. The only difficulty is that the statement it finds is the empty statement. In fact, the compiler treats our example code as though it were written

```
if (x > 1e38)
{
    ;    // Do nothing.
}
displayField.setText("My! What a big number!");
    // Do always!
```

In this case, if x is larger than 1e38, the empty statement part is executed and control passes down to the method call. Okay, that's more or less what we wanted to happen. However, if x is less than or equal to 1e38, the empty statement is skipped and control still passes to the method call. We've inadvertently placed the wrong statement under control of the if statement.

Caution

> The if statement does not require a semicolon terminator. There's almost no reason for a semicolon in an if statement, except for those that are needed by the individual statements controlled by the if.

Now let's make a small modification to our example. Suppose that any x value larger than 1e38 will be too big for whatever processing we do later. We decide to guard against such "bad" values by setting x to 1e38 in those cases. As mannerly programmers, though, we don't want to surprise the user by doing something behind the scenes, so we display an alert before we change the value. Our code looks like this:

```
// WARNING: More bad programming here
if (x > 1e38)
    displayField.setText("Amount too large. Using 1e38 instead");
    x = 1e38;
```

If we run the program, we discover to our dismay that x is *always* set to 1e38, no matter what its original value was. What went wrong?

*   *   *

We goofed again—we left off the braces. The only statement controlled by the if was the setText() call. Just as in the first example, the next statement, x = 1e38 is always executed. Indented properly, our code would look like this:

```
if (x > 1e38)
   displayField.setText("Amount too large. Using 1e38 instead");
x = 1e38;
```

Don't forget that indentation is only for humans. The compiler quite literally can't see extra spaces, tabs, or carriage returns, so don't be misled into thinking that indentation actually has anything to do with the workings of a program.

Caution

Don't leave off braces. It's a good idea to get into the habit of typing a pair of braces immediately after typing the boolean test expression or the keyword `else` and then going back and filling them in. It won't hurt to put a single statement inside the braces, and you'll be less likely to omit them accidentally if you adopt this habit.

Remember that except for declarations, every statement must occur in some method. This means that we always have a `return` statement available to us if we ever need to make a hasty exit from the method. You can sometimes use this feature to dispense with a cascade of nested `if...else` statements.

Suppose, for example, that we are writing a tax preparation program and that one of the methods, `taxOn()`, will take in an income amount and return the tax owed on that income. Suppose further that the tax laws dictate that incomes in the range 0 . . . 19450.00 are taxed at a 15% rate, incomes in the range 19450.01 . . . 47050.00 are taxed at 28%, incomes in the range 47050.01 . . . 97620.00 are taxed at 33%, and incomes larger than 97620.00 are taxed at 50%. We could write this method definition:

```
private double taxOn(double income)
// Example 1: Using else to control execution
{
   double tax;              // the return value
   if (income <= 19450.0)
   {
      tax = 0.15 * income;   // low income: 15% tax bracket
   }
   else if (income <= 47050.0)
   {
      tax = 0.28 * income;   // middle income: 28% tax bracket
   }
   else if (income <= 97620.0)
   {
      tax = 0.33 * income;   // well-off: 33% tax bracket
   }
   else
   {
      tax = 0.50 * income;   // rich: 50% tax bracket (ouch!)
   }
   return tax;
}
```

or we could do the following, using `return` to leave as soon as the appropriate test is satisfied.

```
private double taxOn(double income)
// Example 2: Acts like Example 1, but uses returns to break out
// of further testing.
{
   if (income <= 19450.0)
   {
      return 0.15 * income;
   }
   // Because of the return above, the only way way can get
   // here is if income > 19450.0.
   if (income <= 47050.0)
   {
      return 0.28 * income;
   }
      if (income <= 97620.0)
   {
      return 0.33 * income;
   }
   else
   {
      return 0.50 * income;
   }
}
```

This is a bit simpler than the first version, because we don't need to declare a variable to hold the amount to be returned, but it does require that you be aware of the fact that `return` forces an immediate break out of the method. We use this from from time to time, but we must alert you to the troubles you can get into if you combine these two paradigms, like this:

```
private double taxOn(double income)
// Example 3: BAD mixture of Examples 1 and 2. This doesn't
// work as expected.
{
   double tax;
   if (income <= 19450.0)
   {
      tax = 0.15 * income;
   }
   if (income <= 47050.0)
   {
      tax = 0.28 * income;
   }
   if (income <= 97620.0)
   {
      tax = 0.33 * income;
   }
   else
   {
      tax = 0.50 * income;
   }
   return tax;
}
```

If you trace the execution of this method, you'll see that it won't make low-income taxpayers very happy, because the low-income, middle-income, and well-off taxpayers are all taxed at the 33% rate. An income of 10000.00, for instance, passes all of the first three tests, so the tax is first set to 1500.00, then immediately reset to 2800.00, and finally reset to 3300.00.

Caution

> Until you are completely comfortable with the if statement, it's a good idea not to break out of an if statement by using return. Instead, make a cascade of if...else statements with a single return at the bottom.

The switch Statement

Programs use the "if *variable* == *constant*, do this, otherwise if *variable* == *constant*, do that, otherwise . . ." construct so often that it has become a feature of many programming languages, and Java is no exception. The switch statement is used to select one of several actions, depending on the value of some expression. It looks like this:

```
switch (expression)
{
case constant1:
    some statements
case constant2:
    some statements
...
default:
    some statements
}
```

The expression *must* evaluate to a char, byte, short, or int, and the constants must be literals or final variables. The default label may be omitted, but it's not a good idea, because failure of the expression value to match any of the constants will result in a run-time error.

Semantics: The switch Statement

> When a switch statement is executed, the following steps are performed in order:
>
> **1.** The expression is evaluated.
>
> **2.** Control then passes to the statement following the first case label whose constant equals the value of the expression.
>
> **3.** If none of the case constants matches the expression value, control passes to the default label.
>
> **4.** In either case, all the statements from the label to the end of the switch are executed.

It's important to note that this behavior differs from that of a collection of nested `if...else` statements. Although the look of a `switch` statement might mislead you into thinking that just the statements from one `case` label to the next will be performed, that's not the case.[2] Carefully read step 4 above, and you'll see why. Unless you take explicit action to force execution to leave the `switch` statement, *all* the statements from the `case` label to the end of the `switch` statement will be executed. If you want to separate the action of a `switch` statement into discrete units and avoid this "fall-through" behavior, you have to include a new statement, the `break`.

When a `break` statement is encountered, it forces an immediate exit from the entire `switch`, skipping any subsequent controlled statements. You will nearly always write a `switch` statement with `break`s separating the case sections. Just about the only time you won't have a `break` immediately before the next `case` label is when you want a labeled section to apply to several cases.

Semantics: The break statement

> The break statement forces an immediate exit from a `switch` statement.[3]

Here's an example of the `switch` statement in action. Suppose the variable `currentAlignment` contains a `Label` alignment value—`Label.CENTER`, for instance—and we wish to have the value of `currentAlignment` cycle through the sequence LEFT, CENTER, and RIGHT to make our label hop around in a very disturbing fashion. Because the class constants describing label alignments are represented internally as integer constants, we can use `currentAlignment` in the expression part of a `switch` statement and do the following:

```
// Local example: Don't look for this among the Lablets.
switch (currentAlignment)
{
case Label.LEFT:    // cycle left -> center
   myLabel.setAlignment(Label.CENTER);
   break;
case Label.CENTER: // cycle center -> right
   myLabel.setAlignment(Label.RIGHT);
   break;
case Label.RIGHT:  // cycle right -> left
   myLabel.setAlignment(Label.LEFT);
   break;
default:           // report error
   System.err.println("Something went wrong in label cycle");
}
```

To see the importance of the `break` statement, suppose we left them out of the example above and wrote this instead:

---

[2]However much we'd like it to be that way, it just isn't. This peculiar behavior is inherited from C and has bedeviled novice programmers for decades.

[3]Or from a *loop*, which we'll discuss in Chapter 8.

```
switch (currentAlignment)    // VERY BAD--give me a break!
{
case Label.LEFT:
   myLabel.setAlignment(Label.CENTER);
case Label.CENTER:
   myLabel.setAlignment(Label.RIGHT);
case Label.RIGHT:
   myLabel.setAlignment(Label.LEFT);
default:
   System.err.println("Something went wrong in label cycle");
}
```

This is a terrible idea. No matter what value `currentAlignment` is, execution eventually will fall through to the last statement, displaying an error message!

Caution

Leaving out a `break` statement in a `switch` is a common cause of errors.

Abstract Classes and Interfaces

Although the AWT library provides a number of geometric classes, we might find ourselves in a situation where we need more than just holders for numbers. We might, for instance, be writing a geometry package where we need to be able to find the areas of rectangles, ovals, circles, and squares and perhaps to be able to draw these objects in some program-specific way. Figure 6.1 reproduces the class hierarchy we might invent.

In this example, all of our classes are derived from the class `GeometricObject`. This class might contain data members describing an object's bounding rectangle, for example, along with other properties and methods common to all geometric

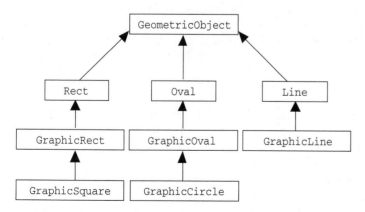

Figure 6.1

A hierarchy of geometric objects.

objects, such as a `move()` method that would shift the object's anchor to another location and an `area()` method that would compute the area of the object. It seems clear, though, that we would never want a direct instance of a `GeometricObject` in any of our programs. (What, for instance, would it mean to compute the area of a general `GeometricObject`?) Instead, we'd construct rectangles, ovals, lines, and the like and use these specific classes in our programs.

Java provides a way to indicate that a class will serve as a template for its subclasses but will never exist as specific instances on its own. An *abstract class* is declared by using the modifier `abstract` in its declaration, like this:

```
public abstract class GeometricObject
// Contains data and methods common to all its subclasses.
// Cannot be instantiated.
{
    protected Point anchor;
    protected Dimension bounds;

    public void move(int x, int y)
    {
        anchor.x = x;
        anchor.y = y;
    }
    public double area();    // Note: Empty body.
}
```

In this declaration, we've defined the `move()` method because we have all the information we need to implement it. We haven't provided a definition for `area()`, though, because the body of that method will depend on the type of object it's applied to. (The code for finding the area of a rectangle, for example, is quite different from that for finding the area of a circle.)

Syntax

> Using the `abstract` modifier in a class declaration indicates that the class cannot be instantiated. In other words, you cannot construct a `new` instance of an abstract class. In an abstract class, you can declare a method with no body, indicating that the method definition will be provided in the subclasses.

Any class with at least one empty method is automatically considered to be abstract, though it's not a bad idea to emphasize that fact by using the `abstract` modifier in the class header. A subclass of an abstract class is itself abstract unless it provides implementations of all the abstract methods of its superclass. We might have chosen to do that in our example if we had wanted another abstract class to represent one-dimensional objects such as lines, arcs, and curves.

Now, of course, any class that extends `GeometricObject` will inherit the `move()` method, and we can override the abstract `area()` method in each subclass. For example, the subclass `Rect` might have the following declaration.

```
public class Rect extends GeometricObject
{
    // The anchor and bounds fields are inherited from the
    // superclass, as is the move() method.

    public double area()
    // Override of base class method, since we can now
    // compute the area of this object.
    {
        return (double)(bounds.width * bounds.height);
    }
}
```

This use of abstract classes is fairly common. In the AWT classes, for example, `Component`, `Container`, `MenuComponent`, and `TextComponent` are all abstract.

After having made a collection of classes describing geometric objects, we might decide to incorporate them into an illustration program. As soon as we do, we see that we need to be able to draw things like rectangles and circles. Now we're faced with a problem—how to integrate the capability for drawing into our existing class structure. In Figure 6.1 we did this by modifying five of the existing classes, adding new methods like `drawGraphicRect()` and `drawGraphicLine()` to the appropriate classes.

There's something inelegant about this solution, though—we're not making good use of the existing hierarchy. It would be much better to invent a new top-level class, `DrawableObject`, with an abstract `draw()` method, and then let our five lower-level classes override the `draw()` method they inherit from `DrawableObject`. Unfortunately, that won't work.

In Java, a class may extend only one other class. Multiple inheritance is not permitted.[4]

Java does, however, provide a simple means for doing what we want. An *interface* *interface* declaration looks a lot like an abstract class declaration and acts in much the same way. In our example, we might declare the `Drawable` interface like this:

```
public interface Drawable
{
    public void draw();        // Must not have a statement body, {...} .
}
```

Syntax: `interfaces`

The declaration of an interface looks like the declaration of a class, except that the keyword `interface` is used in place of the keyword `class`. All methods of an interface must be abstract. An interface may have data fields, but they must all be `final` and `static`.

---

[4]Multiple inheritance is permitted in some other object-oriented languages, such as C++.

We would then use the `implements` clause in each of the class declarations that implement the `draw()` method. Our `Rect` class would then look like this:

```
public class Rect extends GeometricObject implements Drawable
{
   public double area()
   {
      return (double)(bounds.width * bounds.height);
   }

   public void draw()
   // Here's the method definition we promised when we said
   // this class implements Drawable.
   {
      drawRect(anchor.x, anchor.y, bounds.width, bounds.height);
   }
}
```

Semantics: `interfaces`

> A class may be declared to `implement` an interface. If it does, the class *must* provide implementations (statement bodies) for all the methods of the interface.

We may regard implementing an interface as a promise that we are going to provide definitions for all the interface's methods. In the AWT library, `LayoutManager` is an interface—you can invent your own layout scheme by writing a class that defines each of `LayoutManager`'s five abstract methods, such as `minimumLayoutSize()`.

In Figure 6.2 we illustrate how our class hierarchy would look if we used a `Drawable` interface. Comparing it with Figure 6.1, we see that the structure is no less complicated but the organization cleaner and more obvious. When we talk about Java's event model, we'll see a dozen interfaces and nearly as many abstract classes.

Unlike class inheritance, a class may implement as many interfaces as needed. We might, for example, define a `Scalable` interface that has an abstract method to

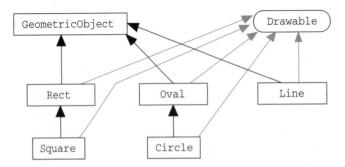

Figure 6.2

Using interfaces to clarify the **GeometricObject** hierarchy.

change the shape of an object by scaling it horizontally and vertically. Then we could declare our Rect class to be drawable and scalable by writing the header

```
public class Rect    extends GeometricObject
                     implements   Drawable,   Scalable
```

Just as with classes, we can declare a variable to be an interface type. A variable of interface type can be assigned to any other variable of a class that implements the interface. In our example, for instance, it would be perfectly legal to write

```
Circle c = new Circle();
Drawable d;
d = c;
d.draw();   // since c is a circle, it (and hence d, after the
            // assignment) knows how to draw itself.
```

This might be useful in a drawAll() method that had to display a collection of Drawable objects whose types we wouldn't know until the program was running.

Review Questions

1.1 Why does Java have an if statement?

1.2 Why do we make such a fuss about enclosing the controlled parts of an if statement in braces, even though they're not always required?

1.3 Why does a switch statement nearly always include break statements?

1.4 What can't we do with an abstract class? Why, then, do we have abstract classes?

1.5 Can a class extend more than one class?

1.6 What is the primary purpose of interfaces?

6.2   Event-Driven Programming

Although you may not have been aware of it, you've already spent a considerable amount of time generating events for a program to respond to. In the labs, you've spent a lot of time generating, editing, and running Java applets. Every time you move the mouse, scroll the contents of a window up or down, or click on a button, you generate an event that the text editor, applet runner, browser, or Java development environment had to recognize and handle appropriately. Each menu selection, keystroke, and mouse drag generates an event, and it is up to the program to decide how, or whether, to deal with it. Here we will describe the event classes and discuss the event-handling methods Java provides for our use.

Nearly all programming languages evolve over time, and Java is no exception. The first major revision of Java, version 1.1, introduced a host of new methods to the AWT classes. It also introduced some new classes and packages, but most of the changes were more or less superficial, except for the changes in event handling. In event handling we see the most significant differences between Java version 1.0 and the subsequent versions (Java 1.1 and its modifications, and Java 1.2, now known as Java 2). Fortunately (for textbook authors, at least), the 1.0 event model is no longer supported, so we can spend our time talking about a single way of dealing with events, confident that this model will be valid for at least the lifetime of this book, whether you're using a Java 2 environment or any of the 1.1.x versions.

The Delegation Model

event delegation

A Java program handles events by using what is known as a *delegation model.* In this model, there are two players, the `Component` object, such as a button, that generates events, and another object, perhaps an applet or an instance of another class, that has code for dealing with events. The salient features of this model are as follows:

▲ Any component can be the source of an event. A Button, for example, may be the source of an action event, triggered by a click.[5]
▲ Any class can be a *listener* for an event, merely through implementation of the right listener interface. For example, a class that was designed to handle a `Button`'s `ActionEvent` would merely have to implement the `ActionListener` interface, declaring the interface methods to do whatever is appropriate in response to the event.
▲ The event generated by a source `Component` is sent only to those listeners that have been *registered* with the source object. In our example, we might have a `closer` object that dealt with a click on the "Close" `Button`. The `Button`, then, would call `addActionListener(closer)` to indicate that any `ActionEvents` it generated would be sent to `closer` for handling.

> The basic idea behind the delegation model is that a source `Component` generates events that are sent to registered listener objects for handling.

Although the details of this model may appear complicated at first, the idea is actually quite simple. Let's illustrate how simple this model can be by considering an example. Our `Test` applet consists of a custom display with a red dot on a white background. The applet has two buttons that can be clicked to move the red dot left or right, respectively. The applet looks like that shown in Figure 6.3.

Let's look at the code. First, we see that we need to import a new package, `java.awt.event`. This is where most of the event-related classes live. The applet should look completely familiar by now: We begin by declaring two buttons and an instance of the `Display` class, which will be used for drawing the moveable red dot. We follow the declarations with the definition of the `init()` method, where we lay out the three components.

---

[5]Not all `Components` generate all types of events. You can cause a `Component` to be the source of event types that it doesn't normally generate, but the discussion of such event enabling is beyond the scope of our discussion here.

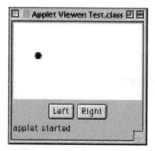

Figure 6.3

The **Test** applet.

```
import java.applet.*;
import java.awt.*;
import java.awt.event.*;    // for the event classes

public class Test extends Applet
{
    private Button    left, right;
    private Display   myDisplay;
    public void init()
    {
        setLayout(new BorderLayout());
        myDisplay = new Display();
        add(BorderLayout.CENTER, myDisplay);

        Panel p = new Panel();
        left = new Button("Left");
        p.add(left);
        right = new Button("Right");
        p.add(right);
        add(BorderLayout.SOUTH, p);

        // Register myDisplay with each button
        left.addActionListener(myDisplay);
        right.addActionListener(myDisplay);
    }
}
```

It's not until we get to the bottom of the class that we see the first unfamiliar code. The addActionListener() method belongs to the Button class (versions also belong to the List, Menu, and TextField classes) and is designed to register a listener (myDisplay) for ActionEvents, generated in this case by a click on either of the buttons. The last two statements establish connections between the two buttons—the sources of events—and the Display object that will respond to any ActionEvents that are generated by the buttons, as we illustrate in Figure 6.4.

We complete the program with the definition of the Display class. This class performs two basic functions. First, it serves as a place where we can draw a moving dot. Second, and most important for our purposes here, it contains the code necessary to catch an ActionEvent and deal with it, by repainting the dot in a new location.

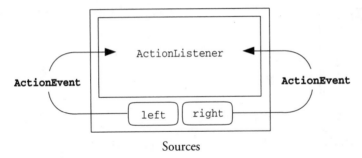

Figure 6.4

Sources and listeners for events.

We indicate that the Display class will process ActionEvents by declaring that it will implement the ActionListener interface. In other words, any Display object (such as myDisplay, up in the applet) is not only a Canvas but also an ActionListener, which means that it contains an actionPerformed() method that will be called any time a registered source generates an ActionEvent.

```
class Display extends Canvas implements ActionListener
{
private Point center;

public Display()
{
   center = new Point(50, 50);
   setBackground(Color.white);
}
```

Now we come to the actionPerformed() method. This is the method we promised to provide when we declared that this class implemented ActionListener. As for init() and paint(), we don't call this ourselves. Instead, it is called by the system whenever an ActionEvent is triggered by a registered source, like one of the two applet buttons.

Here's where we handle the button clicks, by using the getActionCommand() method belonging to the ActionEvent class and using the string to determine whether to move the dot to the left or to the right.

```
public void actionPerformed(ActionEvent e)
{
   // Get the label of the button that generated the event.
   String direction = e.getActionCommand();

   // Move the dot left or right, depending on which
   // button generated the event.
   if (direction.equals("Left"))
   {
      center.x -= 12;
   }
```

```
   else if (direction.equals("Right"))
      {
         center.x += 12;
      }
      // Since we moved the dot, force a call to paint()
      // to show it in its new position
      repaint();
   }

   /**
    * Draw the red dot.
    */
   public void paint(Graphics g)
   {
      g.setColor(Color.red);
      g.fillOval(center.x - 5, center.y - 5, 10, 10);

   }
}
```

That's all it takes: two buttons to generate events, registered with an object that implements an appropriate listener, along with the appropriate code in the listener class to deal with the events.

Syntax: Event Handling

To deal with events generated by a *source* component, a program needs

1. A declaration of the form `import java.awt.event.*;` (This is easy to forget.)

2. A *listener* object that implements all the methods of an appropriate listener interface.

3. A link between the *source* and the *listener* objects, established by a call to a `Component` method:

`source.add`*XXX*`Listener(listener);`

where *XXX* represents the type of event to be handled.

4. Code in the appropriate listener method to deal with the event.

Review Questions

2.1 What is a delegation model?

2.2 In what package do most event-related classes live?

2.3 Can a listener object be responsible for events from more than one source?

2.4 Can any type of object be the source of an event?

2.5 What method calls are used to establish the connection between an event source and its listener?

6.3   The AWTEvent **Hierarchy**

The different kinds of Java events are arranged in a hierarchy of classes, as we illustrate in Figure 6.5. This hierarchy may appear intimidating, but it's not too bad once you get used to it. There are only 11 event classes here that you would ever handle (AWTEvent and InputEvent are abstract classes, and you'll probably never deal with an EventObject), and some of those, such as FocusEvent and PaintEvent, are rarely used. In fact, in most Java programs you'll deal only with some of the ActionEvent, ItemEvent, KeyEvent, MouseEvent, and TextEvent classes, and these will be the ones we concentrate on in what follows.

Upper-Level Event Classes

The classes near the top of the event hierarchy will be of little use to you themselves. They do, however, contain some methods that will be useful when a listener needs to get information about the event it has received.

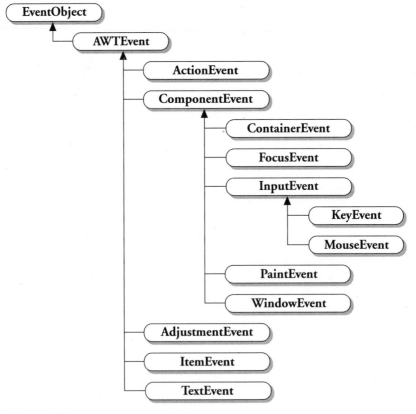

Figure 6.5

The event classes.

```
Object getSource()    // EventObject method
```

Returns the object that generated this event. Most of the time, the listener will already know the source object that generated the event, but this method could be useful in a listener that was responsible for handling events from several sources, as might happen if a listener were responsible for dealing with clicks on several buttons.

```
int getID()    // AWTEvent method
```

Returns the int constant corresponding to the type of the event. This method is sometimes useful for event classes such as MouseEvent, which contain several different types of events. The id constants you might use are

```
// MouseEvent class constants
MOUSE_CLICKED    MOUSE_DRAGGED    MOUSE_ENTERED    MOUSE_EXITED
MOUSE_MOVED      MOUSE_PRESSED    MOUSE_RELEASED

// KeyEvent class constants
KEY_PRESSED      KEY_RELEASED     KEY_TYPED
```

As with getSource(), most of the time you won't need this method, since a MouseListener, for example, will have a mouseClicked() handler to deal with mouse events with id equal to MOUSE_CLICKED.

```
Component getComponent();    // ComponentEvent method
```

Although you can call getSource() for any of the concrete (nonabstract) event classes, the subclasses of ComponentEvent, namely FocusEvent, InputEvent, KeyEvent, MouseEvent, PaintEvent, and WindowEvent, can also use getComponent() to get the source of an event.

Action Events

An ActionEvent is generated when the user clicks a Button, double-clicks an item in a List, selects a MenuItem, or presses the <Enter> key in a TextField.

```
String getActionCommand()
```

Returns a String identifying the source of the event. For Buttons, this is generally the Button's label; for List items and MenuItems, it is usually the text of the item selected; and for TextFields, it is usually the contents of the field.

```
void setActionCommand(String command)
```

This is *not* an ActionEvent method—it is a method of the Button and MenuItem classses, used to specify the command that will be returned by getActionCommand(). Although an action event triggered by a button, for example, will return the button's label string, you might want to change a button's label string when you write your applet in French. Using `setActionCommand()` will mean that your program will still work correctly even if you "internationalize" it.

```
int getModifiers()
```

Returns the mask for any modifiers that accompanied this event, as, for example, if a button click was made while the Alt key was pressed or the button was clicked by using the middle button on a three-button mouse. This would be used with the class constants `ALT_MASK`, `CTRL_MASK`, `META_MASK`, and `SHIFT_MASK`. See the related discussion at the start of the description of `InputEvents`, below, for details.

Button handling is quite simple—here's a modification of our `Test` applet from Section 6.2 that simply reports which button was clicked. We've used the French version as an illustration. If you compare this with the previous version, you'll see that here we've chosen to have the applet itself be the listener for action events, rather than using a separate class.

```
public class Test2 extends Applet implements ActionListener
{
    private Button     left, right;
    private TextField  display;

    public void init()
    {
        // Lay out the left button, the display, and the
        // right button, using the default FlowLayout.
        left = new Button("Gauche");
        add(left);
        display = new TextField(5);
        add(display);
        right = new Button("Droit");
        add(right);

        // Register this applet as the handler for each button
        left.addActionListener(this);
        right.addActionListener(this);

        // Set the action commands for each button
        left.setActionCommand("Left");
        right.setActionCommand ("Right");
    }

    public void actionPerformed(ActionEvent e)
    {
        String s = e.getActionCommand();
        if (s.equals("Left"))
        {
            display.setText(" <---");
        }
        else if (s.equals("Right"))
        {
            display.setText(" --->");
        }
    }
}x
```

Adjustment Events and Scrollbars

Scrollbars are useful widgets, not only for controlling the contents of a Canvas or TextArea, but also in their own right as controls. A scrollbar implements the Adjustable interface (which you don't have to concern yourself with unless you're going to build a custom controller, such as a dial) and generates Adjustment events. We can catch events that occur in scrollbars by trapping AdjustmentEvents and looking for an event ID matching one of the following AdjustmentEvent class constants: ADJUSTMENT_VALUE_CHANGED, UNIT_INCREMENT, UNIT_DECREMENT, BLOCK_INCREMENT, BLOCK_DECREMENT, and TRACK. We won't discuss this widget in detail; see the Class References at the end of the chapter for an explanation of the Scrollbar and AdjustmentEvent classes and the AdjustmentListener interface.

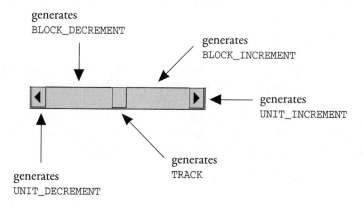

Input Events

InputEvent is an abstract superclass of the KeyEvent and MouseEvent classes. It contains several useful constants and methods dealing with modifiers to key and mouse events. First, there are four class constants, ALT_MASK, CTRL_MASK, META_MASK, and SHIFT_MASK, that represent presses of the Alt, Control, Meta, and Shift keys, respectively. To test for the presence of one of these modifiers, perform a bitwise AND of the event's modifiers and the appropriate mask. If the result is nonzero, the modifier is present. For example, to see whether a mouse event e was accompanied by pressing the Alt key, you could write

```
if ((e.getModifiers() & InputEvent.ALT_MASK) != 0)
    // The Alt modifier is present.
else
    // The Alt modifier is not present.
```

Bitwise operators and masking were covered in Section 5.3. In deciphering key and mouse events, you don't need to use these mask constants, because the InputEvent class contains four boolean *predicates* that do the same thing:

```
boolean isAltDown()
boolean isControlDown()
boolean isMetaDown()
boolean isShiftDown()
```

These methods return `true` if the corresponding modifier key accompanied the event, and `false` otherwise. The code above, for example, could be replaced by

```
if (e.isAltDown())
    // The Alt modifier is present.
else
    // The Alt modifier is not present.
```

The only time you might find you need to use masks is to detect the presence of modifiers in an `ActionEvent`, because the four predicates above aren't available to instances of `ActionEvent`.

```
int getModifiers()
```

Like the `ActionEvent` method of the same name, this method returns the mask for any modifiers that were in force when this event was generated.

We mentioned before that Java can distinguish between mouse events that came from a three-button mouse. On such a device, a click on the left button provides no modifiers, a click on the middle button sets the `ALT_MASK` bit, and a click on the right button sets the `META_MASK` modifier. For ease in readability, this class provides constants that are equivalent to the mask constants.

```
BUTTON1_MASK    // Currently unused
BUTTON2_MASK    // Equal to ALT_MASK
BUTTON3_MASK    // Equal to META_MASK
```

Item Events

An `ItemEvent` instance is generated when the user clicks a `Checkbox`, a `CheckboxMenuItem`, or a `Choice` item or single-clicks a `List` item. Note that these are all two-state objects—they have either been selected or not. All these `Component` classes share an `ItemSelectable` interface. This means that they implement the methods

```
void addItemListener(ItemListener il)
void removeItemListener(ItemListener il)
```

which we'll discuss in the next section, when we explore listeners.

Within the `ItemEvent` class, there are actually two different events, distinguished by whether the user selected or deselected the particular item. The class provides two class constants you can use to determine which subevent your listener method is using: `SELECTED` and `DESELECTED`.

```
ItemSelectable getItemSelectable()
```

Returns the `ItemSelectable` object (see above) that generated this event.

```
Object getItem()
```

Returns the item that was selected. This is usually the `String` representing the item's text or label.

```
int getStateChange()
```

Returns one of the two class constants `SELECTED` and `DESELECTED`. To test whether an `ItemEvent` instance e had been selected, for example, you could write the following test:

```
if (e.getStateChange() == ItemEvent.SELECTED)
    // The item is checked or highlighted
```

Key Events

Key events are generated when the user presses or releases a key on the keyboard. There are actually three different `KeyEvents`: a key press, a key release, and key typed, a sequence of the first two. When the user presses and releases a key on the keyboard (as opposed to an *action key,* such as a function or arrow key), all three of these events are sent. These subevents are handled by the `KeyListener` methods `keyPressed()`, `keyReleased()`, and `keyTyped()`, respectively.

There is a difference among the `KeyEvent` methods for those keys that represent characters, like A or $, and those action keys that do not. The "keyboard" events have the following available methods, among others.

```
char getKeyChar()
```

Returns the character corresponding to the key that generated this event. If the key doesn't correspond to a Unicode character (such as Shift or an arrow key), this method returns the class char constant `CHAR_UNDEFINED`.

```
boolean isActionKey()
```

Returns `true` if this key is an action key—that is, a key that doesn't correspond to a printable character—and returns `false` otherwise.

Take a look at the keyboard on the computer you use. There's a good chance you'll find a host of action keys, such as the arrows, the function keys F1 to F12, a Delete or Backspace key, and a Shift key. You might also find a keypad, often on the right, and keys for PageUp, PageDown, Home, End, NumLock, and so on. All of these keys are recognizable by Java, even though they might not be present on all keyboards, and each is associated with a "virtual key code," represented by `KeyEvent` class constants. Here's a selection of the more common action key constants:

```
VK_ALT          VK_CONTROL      VK_META      VK_SHIFT
VK_ESCAPE       VK_ENTER        VK_DELETE    VK_BACKSPACE
VK_LEFT         VK_RIGHT        VK_UP        VK_DOWN
VK_PAGE_UP      VK_PAGE_DOWN    VK_HOME      VK_END
VK_CAPS_LOCK    VK_NUM_LOCK
VK_NUMPAD0...VK_NUMPAD9
VK_F1...VK_F12
```

Once you've used `isActionKey()` to determine that the event is an action key event, you can use the following methods to detect and set the key code.

int **getKeyCode**()

Returns one of the class constants corresponding to this key. This can be used for keyboard keys, too, because there are codes for VK_A...VK_Z, VK_0...VK_9, VK_COMMA, and so on.

void **setKeyCode**(int keyCode)

Sets the key code for this key to the argument.

Mouse Events

When the mouse is clicked, moved, or otherwise manipulated, a MouseEvent is generated by the Component where the pointer was at the time. This class contains a number of class constants describing the nature of the event, such as MOUSE_CLICKED and MOUSE_DRAGGED, but you won't have much use for them, because the seven kinds of mouse events all have corresponding methods in the MouseListener and MouseMotionListener interfaces, which we'll describe in the next section.

There are some useful methods in this class, though.

int **getX**()
int **getY**()
Point **getPoint**()

These return the *x*- and *y*-coordinates of this event or the Point representation of the coordinates. All these are measured in the local coordinates of the originating Component. We use these methods in the SketchPad Lablet, for instance.

int **getClickCount**()

Returns the click count for this event (2, for example, for a double-click). There is no way to alter the time delay after which a multiple click is considered to be multiple instances of single clicks.

Text Events

TextEvents are triggered when the user has modified the contents of a TextArea or TextField or when the contents have been changed by a method like setText().

There are no methods of interest to us in this class; changes to text are trapped by the `textValueChanged()` method of the `TextListener` interface.

Review Questions

3.1 If an event handler received an `ActionEvent`, e, from a button, how could the program determine its source?
3.2 Which `Component` subclasses generate `ItemEvents`?
3.3 What types of events can a `List` generate?
3.4 What is the keycode constant for the up arrow on the keyboard?

6.4 Listeners

In the Java event model, `Components` generate events that are handled by any listener objects that have been registered with the event source. A listener is any class that implements the interface that is appropriate for the event. For example, a class that is intended to deal with action events must implement the `ActionListener` interface, and a class that deals with key events must implement all of the methods of the `KeyListener` interface.

To produce a handler for an event, you will find or build an appropriate class and have that class implement the appropriate interface. That's just what we did in the `Test` applet example that we discussed in Section 6.2. There, we had a custom component, `Display`, and we wanted it to monitor `ActionEvents` so that it would know when to move its red ball. That was easy—all we had to do was declare `Display` to implement `ActionListener`, which in this case meant nothing more than providing an implementation of the interface's `actionPerformed()` method. Then we declared an instance of our listener and registered the instance with the source. In this case, life was particularly easy for us, because the `Display` class already had all the information necessary to respond to action events. However, even in cases where we further separate the model from the view by declaring a separate class where the work goes on, the basic principle is the same.

> To design a handler for an event, you will build a class that implements the listener that is appropriate for the event and override *all* of the interface's methods.

Listener Interfaces

We're almost at the end of our description of the Java event model. With the exception of one minor but useful feature that we'll introduce in the next subsection, all we need to do is describe the listener interfaces. There are 11 of them, and we've flagged the ones we'll talk about here.

```
◆  ActionListener       // for ActionEvents
   AdjustmentListener    // for Scrollbars
   ComponentListener     // for ComponentEvents
   ContainerListener     // for ContainerEvents
   FocusListener         // for tracking focus events
◆  ItemListener          // for ItemEvents
◆  KeyListener           // for KeyEvents
◆  MouseListener         // for all mouse events except:
◆  MouseMotionListener   // MOUSE_DRAG and MOUSE_MOVE
◆  TextListener          // for TextEvents
   WindowListener        // for WindowEvents
```

ActionListener

This interface is implemented by any class that should respond to `ActionEvents`. To register an instance of `ActionListener` al, you would call the method `addActionListener(al)`. This interface has one method to override.

```
void actionPerformed(ActionEvent e)
```

Here is where you deal with any `ActionEvents` generated by sources for which this object is registered. You saw an example of this in the `Test` applet we described in Section 6.2:

```
class Display extends Canvas implements ActionListener
{
    ...
    public void actionPerformed(ActionEvent e)
    {
        ...
    }
    ...
}
```

ItemListener

This interface is used to implement listeners for the `ItemEvent` class. To register an `ItemListener` object, call `addItemListener()`. This interface has one method.

```
void itemStateChanged(ItemEvent e)
```

KeyListener

This interface is used to implement listeners for the three `KeyEvent` varieties. To register a `KeyListener` object, call `addKeyListener()`. This interface has three methods, one corresponding to each of the event varieties.

```
void keyPressed(KeyEvent e)
void keyReleased(KeyEvent e)
void keyTyped(KeyEvent e)
```

Remember the nature of interfaces—to implement an interface, you must implement every one of its empty methods. If your event-handling class isn't interested in one of these cases, you still have to implement it, even if that means putting nothing within the braces of its body, like this:

```
void keyPressed(KeyEvent e)
// We're not interested in KEY_PRESSED events.
{}
```

MouseListener

This interface is used to implement listeners for the five `MouseEvent` varieties. To register a `MouseListener` object, call `addMouseListener()`. This interface has five methods.

```
void mouseClicked(MouseEvent e)
void mouseEntered(MouseEvent e)
void mouseExited(MouseEvent e)
void mousePressed(MouseEvent e)
void mouseReleased(MouseEvent e)
```

MouseMotionListener

This interface should be folded into `MouseListener`. It's not, though, because `MOUSE_DRAG` and `MOUSE_MOVE` are fundamentally different from the other mouse events, if only because these two are far more computationally expensive than the others. To register a `MouseMotionListener` with a `Component`, call `addMouseMotionListener()`. This interface requires you to override two methods:

```
void mouseMoved(MouseMovedEvent e)
void mouseDragged(MouseMovedEvent e)
```

TextListener

This interface is quite simple. It receives events that indicate that the text of a `TextField` or `TextArea` has been changed. To register a `TextListener` object, call `addTextListener()`. This interface has one method.

```
void textValueChanged(TextEvent e)
```

Adapters

As you know, when a class declares that it implements an interface, it is promising to provide implementations for all the interface methods. Some of the listener interfaces, such as `MouseListener`, may contain several methods you wouldn't be interested in implementing. For such interfaces, Java provides seven abstract *adapter classes*. Each of these classes implements the appropriate listener interface, using methods with a no-statement body, { }, rather than an empty statement body. The advantage of this approach is that these classes allow you to subclass them and implement only the methods that are of interest to your listener.

For example, here's an adapter subclass that implements only the MOUSE_RELEASED event handler:

```
class Worker extends MouseAdapter
{
    public void mouseReleased(MouseEvent e)
    {
        // Do something
    }
}
```

The other mouse event handlers are here, by inheritance, but they don't do anything, which for our purposes is just fine. The adapter classes are

```
ComponentAdapter
ContainerAdapter
FocusAdapter
KeyAdapter
MouseAdapter
MouseMotionAdapter
WindowAdapter
```

Review Questions

4.1 Could a Button register several different listener objects for its ActionEvents?

4.2 Suppose a class has exactly two methods. How do we know that that class couldn't possibly implement the KeyListener interface?

4.3 Of the listener interfaces we discussed, which has the most methods?

4.4 Why would you want to use an adapter class?

6.5 Hands On

There are two Lablets for this chapter. The first, GalaEvents, tracks and displays the events that are generated by a typical GUI program. The (optional) second, Sketch-Pad, makes use of the mouse events to implement a simple drawing program.

The GalaEvents Lablet

Chapter 3's Lablet, Gigobite, demonstrated the major widgets available to an applet. Of course, Gigobite was somewhat limited in that none of its lists, text areas, buttons, choices, or checkboxes did much of anything. In GalaEvents we extend Gigobite so that we can inspect the events that take place when the user interacts with its widgets.

The first part of the applet tracks the six mouse events. Whenever any mouse event is detected, the type of the event and its coordinates are displayed. We also include a handler for KeyTyped events, an actionPerformed() method to detect and display any events generated by a double-click on any of the three lists or a click on the order button, and an ItemStateChanged() method to detect clicks on the checkbox, the sizes choice object, and the lists.

Take the time right now for a quick scan of the code. Where are all the widgets? Aha! They're all declared in the Gigobite applet, so by declaring GalaEvents to be a subclass of Gigobite, we get all the widgets and methods of Gigobite free. What we've done here is often called the *model/view* approach. We've made a clean separation between the GUI portion in Gigogite (the view) and the active portion in GalaEvents (the model). Adopting this approach allows us to modify the way a program *looks* without having to concern ourselves unduly with the details of how it *acts*, and vice versa.

model/ view approach

The program begins with a declaration of a boolean constant, VERBOSE. Because mouse events are generated every time the user moves the mouse, the program's event reporting can become annoyingly full of mouse event reports. Setting VERBOSE to false turns off all mouse reporting, by the simple expedient of not registering any mouse event handler. The constructor for GalaEvents does the expected initialization, registering the appropriate listeners with the widgets by indicating that this class will contain all the listener interface methods.

```
public class GalaEvents    extends    Gigobite
                           implements  MouseListener,
                                       MouseMotionListener,
                                       KeyListener,
                                       ActionListener,
                                       ItemListener
{
   private final boolean VERBOSE = true;

   public GalaEvents()
   {
      if (VERBOSE)  // Turn mouse reporting on or off.
      {
         addMouseListener(this);
         addMouseMotionListener(this);
      }
      addKeyListener(this);

      order.addActionListener(this);
      sandwiches.addActionListener(this);
      drinks.addActionListener(this);
      sides.addActionListener(this);

      superSize.addItemListener(this);
      sizes.addItemListener(this);
      sandwiches.addItemListener(this);
      drinks.addItemListener(this);
      sides.addItemListener(this);
   }
```

We next come to the implementation of the five methods promised by the `MouseListener` interface and the two that are needed to implement the `MouseMotionListener` interface. Note that all of these methods do their reporting by calls to `System.out.println()` methods. The `System` class, part of the `java.lang` package, has an instance variable, `out`, that is used to display messages on what is known as the *standard output,* typically a frame where text can appear by the `println()` or `print()` methods.

```
//----------------- MouseListener METHODS -----------------

public void mouseClicked(MouseEvent e)
{
    System.out.println("MOUSE_CLICKED at " + e.getX() + ", " + e.getY());
}

public void mouseEntered(MouseEvent e)
{
    System.out.println("MOUSE_ENTERED at " + e.getX() + ", " + e.getY());
}

public void mouseExited(MouseEvent e)
{
    System.out.println("MOUSE_EXITED at " + e.getX() + ", " + e.getY());
}

public void mousePressed(MouseEvent e)
{
    System.out.println("MOUSE_PRESSED at " + e.getX() + ", " + e.getY());
}

public void mouseReleased(MouseEvent e)
{
    System.out.println("MOUSE_RELEASED at " + e.getX() + ", " + e.getY());
}

//--------------- MouseMotionListener METHODS ---------------

public void mouseDragged(MouseEvent e)
{
    System.out.println("MOUSE_DRAGGED to " + e.getX() + ", " + e.getY());
}

public void mouseMoved(MouseEvent e)
{
    System.out.println("MOUSE_MOVED to " + e.getX() + ", " + e.getY());
}
```

The `KeyListener` interface requires us to implement three methods, as we do here, even if we have no intention of handing some of the events. You can see that we're interested only in reporting `KeyTyped` events, so we provide empty bodies for the other two types of key events.

```
public void keyPressed(KeyEvent e)
{ }

public void keyReleased(KeyEvent e)
{ }
```

```
public void keyTyped(KeyEvent e)
{
   System.out.println("KEY_TYPED: " + e.getKeyChar());
}
```

The `actionPerformed()` method is a bit more complicated than the ones we've seen so far, because `ActionEvents` can be generated by several sources in this program: the `order` button or the `sandwiches`, `drinks`, or `sides` lists.

```
public void actionPerformed(ActionEvent e)
{
   Object source = e.getSource();
   if (source == order)
   {
      System.out.println("ACTION: order button clicked");
   }
   else if (source == sandwiches)
   {
      System.out.println("ACTION: Sandwich chosen: " +
                          sandwiches.getSelectedItem());
   }
   else if (source == drinks)
   {
      System.out.println("ACTION: Drink chosen: " +
                          drinks.getSelectedItem());
   }
   else if (source == sides)
   {
      System.out.println("ACTION: Side order chosen: " +
                          sides.getSelectedItem());
   }
}
```

The `itemStateChanged()` method of the `ItemListener` class is the most complicated of our methods, for two reasons. First, there are five components in our program that can generate `ItemEvents`: the `superSize` checkbox, the `sizes` choice object, and the three lists. The other reason why this method is complicated is that we are building the report string for events from the lists in several stages: First we report the name of the list that generated the event, then we get the name of the item clicked (using a method of our own), and finally we indicate whether the item was selected or deselected.

```
public void itemStateChanged(ItemEvent e)
{
   Object source = e.getSource();
   if (source == superSize)    // We're in the Checkbox
   {
      if (e.getStateChange() == ItemEvent.SELECTED)
      {
         System.out.println("ITEM: Supersize selected");
      }
      else
      {
         System.out.println("ITEM: Supersize deselected");
      }
   }
```

```
    else if (source == sizes)    // We're in the Choice
    {
        System.out.println("Size choice made: " + e.getItem());
    }
    else                         // We're in one of the Lists
    {
        // First, find out which list generated the event
        String message = "ITEM: ";
        if (source == sandwiches)
        {
            message += "Sandwich ";
        }
        else if (source == drinks)
        {
            message += "Drink ";
        }
        else if (source == sides)
        {
            message += "Side order ";
        }
        // Then, get the name of the item chosen and append
        // it to the message.
        Integer n = (Integer)(e.getItem());
        message += source.getItem(n.intValue());

        // Finally, determine if the item was
        // selected or deselected.
        if (e.getStateChange() == ItemEvent.SELECTED)
        {
            message += " selected";
        }
        else
        {
            message += " deselected";
        }
        System.out.println(message);
    }
}
```

We had to go through a bit of arcana to get the name of the item chosen, because when called by an event that comes from a List, getItem() returns the Object equivalent of the *index* of the item in the list, not its name. We'll discuss the Integer class in Chapter 8.

The SketchPad Lablet (optional)

In this Lablet, we go beyond merely reporting events to using them in a constructive fashion. SketchPad is a simple drawing program that works in two different modes: The user can draw curves freehand, using the mouse, or can have more precise directional control over the drawing keys by extending the curve up, down, left, or right by using the arrow keys.

In spite of the fact that this Lablet has fewer events to deal with than GalaEvents, you'll discover that it is conceptually more complicated. The main reason for the complexity is that we no longer handle all of the events in the applet. Instead, we use `SketchPad` as a motivation for a discussion of adapter classes, designing two such classes to handle mouse and mouse motion events. As useful as adapters are, you'll discover that they introduce some problems, especially in communication between the component that generates an event and the adapter object that handles it. For that reason, we've flagged this section as optional—for many programs, it suffices to let the applet or application handle all of its events, as we did in `GalaEvents`. Doing so isn't always the most elegant solution, but it has the decided advantage of simplicity.

The visual design of the applet, illustrated in Figure 6.6, is almost trivial. We have a "Clear" button at the top, to erase the drawing, and we have a group of four radio buttons at the bottom, to set the current drawing color. The region between the two is for a `Display` object of our own design, where all the drawing will take place.

Considering what the user will do with the Lablet gives us five kinds of events: action events from the Clear button, item events from the checkboxes, key events from the arrow keys to draw small line segments, mouse events from mouse presses to start a new curve, and mouse motion events generated by the user dragging the mouse to draw a curve. It seems to make sense to let the applet handle the first two, because they are generated by its own components, and to let the `Display` deal with the key and mouse events that directly affect the drawing—and that's just what we do.

We'll need at least two classes, the applet and its display, so we'll start by discussing the applet. The class definition begins in the now-familiar way, with the class header and declarations of the instance variables. The applet is going to handle button and checkbox clicks, so we make sure that our class implements the `ActionListener` and `ItemListener` interfaces. We also declare an instance of our `Display` class, which, as in the `Test` applet we discussed earlier, will be an extension of `Canvas`.

Figure 6.6

Drawing with **SketchPad**.

```
public class SketchPad extends Applet
                      implements   ActionListener,
                                   ItemListener
{
    private Button     clear;
    private Checkbox   color1,
                       color2,
                       color3,
                       color4;
    private Display    myDisplay;
```

There's not much surprising about the init() method, either. We construct new instances of our Button and the four Checkboxes and lay them out, using a CheckboxGroup to make the checkboxes into radio buttons and placing them in a panel of their own. We then construct a new Display object and place it in the center of the applet.

```
public void init()
{
    setLayout(new BorderLayout());

    clear = new Button("Clear");
    add("North", clear);
    Panel controls = new Panel();
    controls.setBackground(Color.lightGray);

    CheckboxGroup grp = new CheckboxGroup();
    color1 = new Checkbox("Red", grp, false);
    controls.add(color1);
    color2 = new Checkbox("Green", grp, false);
    controls.add(color2);
    color3 = new Checkbox("Blue", grp, false);
    controls.add(color3);
    color4 = new Checkbox("Black", grp, true);
    controls.add(color4);
    add("South", controls);

    myDisplay = new Display();
    add("Center", myDisplay);

    myDisplay.requestFocus();
```

There's only one part of the code that needs explanation before we get around to registering the widgets with the applet as event listener, and that's the requestFocus() call. If you think about a program that had two TextFields, you'll see that it is not obvious which one should get the text when the user starts typing. Java deals with keyboard activities by sending key clicks to the component that has *focus*. The user customarily gives focus to a text component by clicking on it, but you can also program focus to go to a component by calling the Component method requestFocus(), as we do here. Without this statement, the display would never "see" any keys clicked by the user.

input
focus

```
    clear.addActionListener(this);
    color1.addItemListener(this);
    color2.addItemListener(this);
    color3.addItemListener(this);
    color4.addItemListener(this);
}
```

As we promised when we said that the applet would implement `ActionListener`, we have to implement an `actionPerformed()` method. This is simplicity itself, because we have only one source for `ActionEvents`. All we need to do in response to a click on the `clear` button is tell the display to erase itself and recapture focus (we took it away when we clicked the mouse on the button).

```
public void actionPerformed(ActionEvent e)
{
    myDisplay.erase();

    myDisplay.requestFocus();
}
```

The sole `ItemListener` method is a bit more complicated, because we have to determine which checkbox generated the `ItemEvent`. We use the `getItem()` method to get the label of the checkbox and a cascade of `if...else` statements to tell the display to set its drawing color appropriately. Having done that, we're finished with the applet definition.

```
public void itemStateChanged(ItemEvent e)
{
    String label = "" + e.getItem();
    if (label.equals("Red"))
    {
        myDisplay.setColor(Color.red);
    }
    else if (label.equals("Green"))
    {
        myDisplay.setColor(Color.green);
    }
    else if (label.equals("Blue"))
    {
        myDisplay.setColor(Color.blue);
    }
    else
    {
        myDisplay.setColor(Color.black);
    }

    myDisplay.requestFocus();
    }
}
```

The real work in this program is delegated to the `Display` class. The drawing it has to do is accomplished by keeping track of two points, the start point and end point of a small line segment. Each time the user drags the mouse or presses an arrow key, a new value will be recorded in `endPoint`. The class will then draw a line between the `startPoint` and the `endPoint` and finally will set the new value of `startPoint` to be the same as that of `endPoint`, getting ready to draw the next segment in response to the next mouse drag or arrow key click event.

When we look at the class header, we get our first surprise. Why haven't we indicated that this class is going to implement `MouseListener` and `MouseMotionListener`? We haven't because we aren't going to let the class handle these events. Instead, we're going to use instances of adapter classes. One of them, `Clicker`, is used in the data declarations, as the type of an instance variable, named `mouser`, that will deal with mouse events. Here's surprise number two: The adapter object that deals with mouse drags isn't listed here because it doesn't even have a name! As if things weren't weird enough, we should call your attention to something else that at first looks like an error—for some reason, `endPoint` has package access, rather than the `private` access it should have. If all this makes you feel like Dorothy did when she dropped into Oz, be patient; all will be made clear shortly.

```
class Display    extends      Canvas
                 implements   KeyListener
{
    // where we'll start drawing
    private final   Point    START = new Point(5, 25);

    private         Point    startPoint = new Point();
                    Point    endPoint = new Point();

    private         Color    currentColor = Color.black;
    private         Clicker  mouser = new Clicker(this);
```

As usual with all classes that aren't applets, we begin with a constructor, the job of which is to do all the necessary initialization. Here we get the explanation of our second surprise. Look at the `add...Listener()` calls. The first one indicates that this class will handle key events, the second indicates that our `mouser` object will be responsible for mouse clicks, and the third explains why we didn't have to declare a named instance variable to deal with mouse drags. We're constructing a new, *anonymous* instance of the `Dragger` class and using that unnamed critter as the handler for `MouseMotion` events! Had we desired, we could have done the same thing for both mouse-related event handlers, eliminating `mouser` from the instance variables altogether.

```
public Display()
{
    resetPoints(START);

    addKeyListener(this);
    addMouseListener(mouser);
    addMouseMotionListener(new Dragger());

    setBackground(Color.white);
}
```

Okay, we have two objects to handle events: mouser for mouse clicks and an object-without-a-name for mouse drags. We'll come back to them shortly, but first we have some ordinary, unsurprising method definitions to get through. Both erase() and setColor(), you'll recall, are called from the applet, in the actionPerformed() and itemStateChanged() methods, respectively. Their actions are just what you'd expect: erase() erases the display and sets the start points and end points to a default value, and setColor() sets the current drawing color to whatever's in the argument. resetPoints() is just a utility method called in the constructor, erase(), and Dragger's mouseDragged() method.

```java
public void erase()
{
    Graphics g = getGraphics();
    g.setColor(Color.white);

    Dimension size = getSize();
    g.fillRect(0, 0, size.width, size.height);
    g.dispose();

    resetPoints(START);
}

public void setColor(Color c)
{
    currentColor = c;
}

public void resetPoints(Point p)
{
    startPoint.setLocation(p);
    endPoint.setLocation(p);
}
```

The update() and paint() methods do the drawing. When a component needs to be repainted, the system calls update(), passing it a Graphics object. Normally, update() erases the component and then calls paint(), but in this program, that would destroy whatever had already been drawn. To keep our drawing on this canvas, we have to override update() so that it just calls paint() and doesn't do any erasing. As you'll see in Chapter 12, this override of update() is done quite often. All that paint() has to do is draw a line between startPoint and endPoint and then reset startPoint to get ready for the next call.

```java
public void update(Graphics g)
{
    paint(g);
}

public void paint(Graphics g)
{
    g.setColor(currentColor);
    g.drawLine(startPoint.x, startPoint.y, endPoint.x, endPoint.y);

    startPoint.setLocation(endPoint);
}
```

We've seen the KeyListener methods before, in GalaEvents. Of course, because we have implemented the interface, we need to include all three of its methods, even though we need only one of them here. We'll see almost immediately how to deal with this apparent waste of code.

```java
public void keyPressed(KeyEvent e)
{
    endPoint.setLocation(startPoint);

    switch (e.getKeyCode())
    {
    case KeyEvent.VK_LEFT:
        endPoint.x -= 5; break;
    case KeyEvent.VK_RIGHT:
        endPoint.x += 5; break;
    case KeyEvent.VK_UP:
        endPoint.y -= 5; break;
    case KeyEvent.VK_DOWN:
        endPoint.y += 5; break;
    default:
        return;    // Ignore presses on any other keys.
    }
    repaint();    // force a redraw of the new segment
}

public void keyTyped(KeyEvent e)
{ }

public void keyReleased(KeyEvent e)
{ }
```

Whoa! What's this? We have the Dragger class we've been expecting, but it's defined *inside* the Display class!

```java
private class Dragger extends MouseMotionAdapter
{
    public void mouseDragged(MouseEvent e)
    {
        endPoint.setLocation(e.getPoint());
        repaint();
    }
}
}
```

member
class

We've never seen a class defined inside another, but it turns out that such *member classes,* as they are called, have been perfectly acceptable to all versions of Java since version 1.1. We'll have more to say about member classes in a moment, but ignoring its peculiar placement, note what we have here. Because Dragger extends MouseAdapter, it means that instead of providing empty implementation of the mouseMoved() method we're not interested in, all we have to do is write the one we need, mouseDragged(). This is a tidy solution and one we should have applied for the key events we just described.

Using member classes makes a lot of sense, once you think about it. If you have a class that's tightly coupled to another, as we have here, it seems reasonable to allow the helper class to be defined inside another. Dragger, after all, exists solely to deal with mouse drag events of the Display class, so it probably shouldn't even have an independent existence.

One of the nicest features of member classes is that a member class *should* have access to all the data and methods of its parent class. This would make communication with the parent class very simple, if it worked. Unfortunately, although the standard says that this should be true, a very common compiler bug doesn't allow a member class to have access to the parent class's private data. That, by the way, explains the third surprise we encountered above: We had to make endPoint nonprivate, because otherwise Dragger couldn't have seen it.

Last of all, we come to the other common way of using adapter classes. This time, we use a familiar external class. We have a real saving here—the MouseListener interface requires five methods, so using an adapter class saves us four empty methods in this case. Note, however, that because this class is external to Display, we have to send its constructor a reference to the Display object it will report to by sending the reference along when we create a new Clicker. That's what we did in the Display class declaration

```
private Clicker mouser = new Clicker(this);
```

Sending a reference to the Display allows us to make a *callback,* when our Clicker object detects a mouse press event and has to tell its Display (which it knows as owner) to call its resetPoints() method.

callback

```
class Clicker extends MouseAdapter
{
    private Display owner;

    public Clicker(Display who)
    {
        owner = who;
    }

    public void mousePressed(MouseEvent e)
    {
        owner.resetPoints(e.getPoint());
    }
}
```

Finished at last! There's a lot going on in the SketchPad program: The applet deals with action and item events itself, and its Display instance deals with key events while leaving the task of dealing with mouse-related events to an instance (mouser) of an external class and an anonymous instance of an internal class. Which technique is best? It depends. The simplest is certainly to have a class implement a listener for events that it or its components generate. The problem, especially for the big listener interfaces such as MouseListener and KeyListener, is that you may be forced to write empty methods, an admittedly inelegant solution.

Adapter classes allow you to implement a listener and write just the methods you need. The downside is that member classes take a bit of getting used to (especially if they're constructed anonymously), whereas using an instance of an external adapter class can complicate communication between the event source and the object that serves as the event destination. As so often happens, there's no "best" answer; all you can do is let experience be your guide.

Review Question

5.1 Does an inner class have to be associated with an anonymous instance?

6.6   Summary

■ The `if` statement has the following form:

```
if (boolean expression)    // the parentheses are required,
{                          // braces are a Good Idea
    statements             // the "controlled" statements
}
```

In execution, the boolean expression is evaluated, and if its value is true, the controlled statement is executed. If the boolean expression evaluates to false, the controlled statement is not executed.

■ The `if` statement may also have an `else` clause:

```
if (boolean expression)
{
    statements
}
else
{
    other statements
}
```

In this variant, the `statements` are executed if the boolean expression is `true`, and the `other statements` are executed if the boolean expression is false.

■ In either of the `if` statements, the controlled statement or statements can be any Java statement whatsoever, including compound statements and other `if` statements. Braces aren't required if only a single statement is controlled, but we advise using them in any case.

■ The `else` clause is always logically associated with the nearest unmatched `if` (much like open and close braces).

■ The `switch` statement takes the following form:

```
switch (expression)
{
case constant1:
    some statements
case constant2:
    some statements
...
default:    // optional
    some statements
}
```

The expression is evaluated, and execution skips down to the first `case` label with a matching constant. Execution then proceeds through all subsequent statements to the end of the statement.

- In a `switch` statement, the expression must evaluate to a primitive type, and the `case` constants must be literals or `final` variables of a type compatible with the value of the expression.

- The `break` statement causes an immediate exit from a `switch` statement and is commonly used to avoid "falling through" the rest of the controlled statements.

- It is also possible to break out of a `switch` statement by using `returns`. This option should be used with care.

- The `default` label in a `switch` statement indicates a default match for values of the expression that fail to match any of the `case` constants. The `default` label is optional, but it is a good idea to have one in any `switch` statement, because failure to match a `case` constant in the absence of a `default` label will generate a run-time error.

- A class may be declared to be abstract by using the `abstract` modifier. Abstract classes cannot be instantiated with `new`. Generally, abstract classes are used as templates and are intended to be subclassed.

- Whether the `abstract` modifier is present or not, any class that has a method with a missing body (or any class that inherits a method with a missing body) is automatically considered abstract. A method is declared to have a missing body by following its signature with a semicolon, as, for example,

```
void draw();
```

- A Java class can `extend` only one other class. Multiple inheritance is not allowed in Java.

- An interface is declared as follows:

```
optionalModifiers interface Name
{
    final static variable declarations

    declarations of methods with empty bodies
}
```

- A class may implement an interface by using an `implements` clause in its declaration, like this:

```
class MyClass implements MyInterface
{
    ...
}
```

A class that implements an interface must provide overrides of all the interface methods, even if their bodies have no statements, using { } for the method body.

- A class may implement an arbitrary number of interfaces, using a comma-separated list of interface names in the `implements` clause.

■ An event source registers one or more listeners, and these listeners implement the appropriate interface methods to handle the source's events.

■ Any Component can be the source of an event, and any class whatsoever can be a listener.

■ There are 14 event classes:

```
EventObject
    AWTEvent            (abstract)
        ActionEvent
        ComponentEvent
            ContainerEvent
            FocusEvent
            InputEvent    (abstract)
                KeyEvent
                MouseEvent
            PaintEvent
            WindowEvent
        AdjustmentEvent
        ItemEvent
        TextEvent
```

■ To respond to an event from a source Component, a program must (1) supply an object that implements a listener for the event, (2) register the source with the handler by calling the appropriate add...Listener() method, and (3) provide code in the listener interface method to deal with the event.

■ The MouseEvent, KeyEvent, and ItemEvent classes are further broken down into subsidiary events:

```
// MouseEvents
MOUSE_CLICKED    MOUSE_DRAGGED    MOUSE_ENTERED
MOUSE_EXITED
MOUSE_MOVED      MOUSE_PRESSED    MOUSE_RELEASED
// KeyEvents
KEY_PRESSED      KEY_RELEASED     KEY_TYPED
// ItemEvents
SELECTED         DESELECTED
```

■ An ActionEvent is generated when the user clicks a Button, double-clicks an item in a List, selects a MenuItem, or presses the <Enter> key in a TextField.

■ InputEvent is an abstract superclass of the KeyEvent and MouseEvent classes. This class has methods and constants that can be used to detect the presence of the modifier keys Alt, Control, Meta, and Shift.

■ An ItemEvent instance is generated when the user selects a Checkbox, a CheckboxMenuItem, or a Choice item or single-clicks a List item.

■ Key events are generated when the user presses or releases a key on the keyboard. In order for a Component to receive key presses, the Component must have focus.

■ There are two classes of key events. Keyboard events are associated with the alphanumeric keys on the keyboard, and action keys, like the arrows, do not have char equivalents.

■ There are seven MouseEvents:

```
MOUSE_CLICKED    MOUSE_DRAGGED    MOUSE_ENTERED
MOUSE_EXITED
MOUSE_MOVED      MOUSE_PRESSED    MOUSE_RELEASED
```

■ There are eleven listener interfaces:

```
ActionListener          // for ActionEvents
AdjustmentListener      // for Scrollbars
ComponentListener       // for ComponentEvents
ContainerListener       // for ContainerEvents
FocusListener           // for tracking focus events
ItemListener            // for ItemEvents
KeyListener             // for KeyEvents
MouseListener           // for all mouse events except:
MouseMotionListener     // MOUSE_DRAG and MOUSE_MOVE
TextListener            // for TextEvents
WindowListener          // for WindowEvents
```

■ Each listener interface contains empty methods that can be used to deal with events of a particular kind. When a class implements a listener interface, it must provide all of the methods of the interface, even if they will never be called.

■ An adapter is a class that implements a listener, providing empty methods for all the listener methods. Using a user-defined subclass of an adapter class allows the programmer to override only those listener methods that will be needed.

■ A class can be defined inside another class. Such member classes are commonly used to implement adapter class extensions.

6.7 Exercises

1. Fill in the blanks. In order not to give you any extra clues, we haven't indented the statements or provided our usual braces.

```
if (a > 1)
if (m <= 0)
```
This is executed when _____.
```
else
```
This is executed when _____.
```
else
```
This is executed when _____.

2. In the following code fragments, there are a number of boxes. Into which boxes could we put semicolons without causing syntax errors? Of the "legal" boxes, which are unlikely to receive semicolons and which *must* have semicolons?

a. if ☐ (x != 0 ☐) ☐
```
    {
        a /= x ☐
    }
```
b. if ☐ (n % 2 == 1) ☐
```
    {
        n = 3 * n + 1 ☐
    }
    else ☐
    {
        n = n / 2 ☐
    }
```

3. In part (b) of Exercise 2, if you put the semicolons where they "should" be and execute the statement repeatedly for various starting values of n, what happens? Try it repeatedly for n = 32, 7, and 25. This is known as the *Collatz function,* and nobody has yet been able to show that it eventually reaches 1 for all starting values of n. If you'd like a chance at fame, try showing that it does or finding a value of n for which it never reaches 1.

4. Suppose that E1 and E2 are `boolean` expressions and S is a statement. What is the difference between these two statements, if any?

```
if (E1 && E2)        if (E1)
{                    {
    S                    if (E2)
}                        {
                             S
                         }
                     }
```

5. If we use the `return` statement to break out of a related collection of tests, we must be careful to order the tests from most restrictive to least. What would be the action of this version of the `taxOn()` method?

```
private double taxOn(double income)
{
    if (income <= 47050.0)
        return 0.28 * income;
    if (income <= 19450.0)
        return 0.15 * income;
    if (income <= 97620.0)
        return 0.33 * income;
    else
        return 0.38 * income;
}
```

6. Write the body of the method

```
boolean isOrdered(int x, int y, int z)
```

that returns `true` if x, y, and z are in numeric order—namely if $x \leq y \leq z$—and returns `false` if they are not.

7. Write the body of the method

```
boolean isSum(int x, int y, int z)
```

that returns `true` if any one of x, y, and z is equal to the sum of the other two and returns `false` if they are not.

8. In a quadratic equation, such as $ax^2 + bx + c = 0$, we are given the coefficients *a*, *b*, and *c* and are to find all values of *x* that make the equation true. The nature of the solution depends on the values of *a*, *b*, and *c* as follows:

If $a = 0$ and $b \neq 0$, then there is one solution.

If $a = 0$ and $b = 0$, then there are no solutions if $c \neq 0$, and all *x* values are solutions if $c = 0$.

If $a \neq 0$, let *d* denote $b^2 - 4ac$. If $d < 0$, then there are two complex solutions. If $d = 0$, then there are two identical real solutions. If $d > 0$, then there are two unequal real solutions.

Write a method

```
void quadratic(double a, double b, double c)
```

that will take three coefficients and display (using `System.out.println`) the nature of the solutions of the quadratic equation that has these coefficients.

9. Look at the `actionPerformed()` handler in `SketchPad`. The portion

```
if (label.equals("Red"))
{
    currentColor = Color.red;
}
else if label.equals("Green"))
{
    currentColor = Color.blue;
}
else if (label.equals("Blue"))
{
    currentColor = Color.green;
}
else
{
    currentColor = Color.black;
}
```

looks like a natural candidate for a `switch` statement. Why didn't we use one?

10. Which `Components` can generate `ActionEvents`?

11. Why isn't there an `ActionAdapter` class?

12. For most applets, we don't need to trap `WINDOW_CLOSING` or `WINDOW_CLOSED` events, because the applet runner or browser will handle that for us. We do need to trap these events, though, whenever we make windows of our own. Here's an example, using what is just about the simplest application you can write:

```
import java.awt.*;
import java.awt.event.*;

public class WinTest extends Frame
{
    public WinTest()
    {
        add("Center", new Label("Just a label"));
        addWindowListener(new Closer());
    }

    private class Closer extends WindowAdapter
    {
        public void windowClosing(WindowEvent e)
        {
            Window me = e.getWindow();
            me.dispose();
        }

        public void windowClosed(WindowEvent e)
        {
            System.exit(0);
        }
    }

    public static void main(String[] args)
```

```
      {
         Frame f = new WinTest();
         f.setBounds(50, 50, 100, 100);
         f.show();
      }
   }
```

To see the difference between the two events and how they are handled by your application runner, try some experiments.

a. Run it as it is written. Do whatever is necessary in your environment to make the window go away. Record what happens.

b. Comment out the addWindowListener() call so that your program no longer responds to any window events. Record what happens and explain any differences between this program and the one in part (a).

c. The call System.exit() terminates the running of a Java program. Move this call from the windowClosed() method and make it the last line of the windowClosing() method. Explain any differences in behavior that you observe.

13. We've said that a button generates ActionEvents. That's true enough, but it doesn't mean that a Button object can't generate other events. A Button, after all, is a Component by inheritance, and any Component can generate mouse events. Use this fact to make an applet with a single button and have the applet trap MOUSE_ENTERED events so that every time the user moves the pointer over the button to click it, the applet moves the button to a randomly selected new location. This can be a very amusing program to demonstrate.

14. Modify the Test applet of Section 6.2 so that it uses a List to control the Display. The List will have two items, "Left" and "Right." Double-clicking on one of the items should move the dot in the indicated direction. Does this modification require any modification of Display?

15. Extend the Test applet of Section 6.2 so that it also uses the up and down arrow keys to increase and decrease the size of the dot.

16. Write an applet with a List and a TextField. Each time the user double-clicks on a List item, the name of that item will appear in the TextField, and the item will be deleted from the list. *Hint:* Look at GalaEvents to see how to get the item's string.

a. Try doing this exercise by placing the actionPerformed() handler in the applet itself.

b. Try doing this exercise by subclassing List to make a new class, DiminishingList, that implements ActionListener. Have the actionPerformed() handler in your new class do the item deletion. You'll have to figure out how the deleted item's name will get passed into the TextField.

c. Do both parts (a) and (b) and discuss which was easier to write and which was easier to understand. Would your answers be different if the applet contained ten such lists?

17. Look at Chapter 5's SodaPop Lablet. Can the event handling there be simplified, or is it good as it stands? Explain your response.

18. At the very end of the discussion of GalaEvents, we mentioned that getItem(), when called by an event that came from a List, returns the Object equivalent of the *index* of the item in the list, rather than its name. This makes sense, once you think about it. Why?

19. We mentioned that different Java environments post events differently. Augment the GalaEvents Lablet so that it tracks *all* Java events for all of its components. For a particular environment, do you see any events that could be posted but are not? If you can, run your augmented program in several environments and see whether there are any differences. With luck, we will be able to eliminate this question from subsequent editions of this book, but for now you'll just have to be patient with the inconsistencies, and test your applets in as many environments as possible if you intend to release them to the public.

20. Make a table, where the columns correspond to the the Java Components and the rows to the event types. In each cell of the table, put a check if the Component can generate the event. Remember that double-clicking a List item generates an ActionEvent.

6.8   **Answers to Review Questions**

1.1 To allow the program to take different paths of execution, depending on the state of its information at a given time.

1.2 To reduce the chance of making logic errors when writing programs.

1.3 Because of its peculiar behavior of "falling through" every statement after the matching case.

1.4 It's impossible to make a new instance of an abstract class. Abstract classes are commonly used as holders for methods that will be used by their derived classes (as was the case with TextComponent, for example).

1.5 No, unless you count the classes above it in the inheritance hierarchy.

1.6 To get around the problem of Java's lack of multiple inheritance.

2.1 The term *delegation model* refers to the way Java handles events, by registering a source component with one or more listener objects. Historical note: Java 1.0 didn't use a delegation model.

2.2 java.awt.event.

2.3 Certainly. Look at the Test applet.

2.4 No, only Component subclasses.

2.5 source.addSomeKindOfListener(listener);

3.1 By calling e.getSource() to get the Object that generated the event or e.getActionCommand() to get the button's label text.

3.2 Checkbox, CheckboxMenuItem, Choice, and List.

3.3 ActionEvent (from a double-click on an item) and ItemEvent (from a single click).

3.4 VK_UP.

4.1 Yes. That's an advantage of the delegation model.

4.2 The KeyListener interface has three methods. Any class implementing that interface would have to implement keyPressed(), keyReleased(), and keyTyped(), along with any of its own methods.

4.3 `MouseListener`. `WindowListener` is larger, but we discuss that only in the Class References below.

4.4 To avoid having to write listener methods with no-statement bodies for event types you are not interested in handling.

5.1 No; you could used a named instance variable just as well.

6.9   Class References

java.awt.event.ActionEvent

An `ActionEvent` is generated when the user clicks a `Button`, double-clicks an item in a `List`, selects a `MenuItem`, or presses the `<Enter>` key in a `TextField`. This class contains two constructors, but as with most of the event class constructors, you won't generally use them, and we won't discuss them because they're beyond the scope of this text.

```
class ActionEvent extends AWTEvent
{
    //-------- Class Constants --------
    final static int ALT_MASK;
    final static int CTRL_MASK;
    final static int META_MASK;
    final static int SHIFT_MASK;

    //------------ Methods ------------
◆   String getActionCommand();
◆   int getModifiers();
}
```

java.awt.event.ActionListener

This interface must be implemented by any class wishing to respond to `ActionEvents`.

```
abstract interface ActionEvent extends EventListener
{
    //------------ Method ------------
◆   abstract void actionPerformed(ActionEvent e);
}
```

java.awt.event.AdjustmentEvent

An `AdjustmentEvent` is triggered when the user manipulates a scrollbar. The event IDs `ADJUSTMENT_VALUE_CHANGED` and `TRACK` are similar, but `TRACK` is like `MOUSE_MOVED`, in that `TRACK`-type events are usually generated sequentially.

```
class AdjustmentEvent extends AWTEvent
{
    //-------- Class Constants --------
    final static int ADJUSTMENT_VALUE_CHANGED;
    final static int BLOCK_DECREMENT;
```

```
    final static int BLOCK_INCREMENT;
    final static int TRACK;
    final static int UNIT_DECREMENT;
    final static int UNIT_INCREMENT;

    //------------ Methods ------------
    int getAdjustMentType();
    int getValue();
}
```

java.awt.event.AdjustmentListener

This interface must be implemented by any class wishing to respond to AdjustmentEvents.

```
abstract interface AdjustmentListener extends EventListener
{
    //------------ Method -------------
    abstract void adjustmentValueChanged(AdjustmentEvent e);
}
```

java.awt.AWTEvent

Note that this is *not* part of the java.awt.event package. For our purposes, the main utility of this class is that its getID() method can be used in any of its sub-classes to determine the particular type of an event. You won't generally use this class, because registering a listener with a source will ensure that the listener gets the right type of event.

```
abstract class AWTEvent extends EventObject
{
    //------------ Methods ------------
    int getID();
}
```

java.awt.event.ComponentEvent

This class is the superclass, directly or indirectly, of FocusEvent, KeyEvent, MouseEvent, PaintEvent, and WindowEvent. You won't use most of this class, but you will probably use one of its methods quite frequently.

```
class ComponentEvent extends AWTEvent
{
    //------------ Methods ------------
◆   Component getComponent();
}
```

java.util.EventObject

This class is also not part of the java.awt.event package. This is the topmost class in the event hierarchy, and it has only one method of use to us. getSource() returns the Object that generated the event, which is very handy when a handler has to determine which of several possible Components generated an event.

```
class EventObject extends Object
{
    //------------ Methods ------------
◆   Object getSource();
}
```

java.awt.event.FocusAdapter

This class provides no-statement implementations of the two FocusListener methods.

```
abstract class FocusAdapter extends Object
                            implements    FocusListener
{
    //------------ Methods ------------
    void focusGained(FocusEvent e);
    void focusLost(FocusEvent e);
}
```

java.awt.event.FocusEvent

A FocusEvent is generated when a Component gains or loses input focus. You might use events of this class to take some special action when the user clicks on a TextField, for instance. To determine what Component gained or lost focus, you can use the ComponentEvent class's getComponent() method. For events of this type, the AWTEvent method getID() will return one of two class constants, FOCUS_GAINED or FOCUS_LOST.

```
class FocusEvent extends ComponentEvent
{
    //-------- Class Constants --------
    final static int FOCUS_GAINED;
    final static int FOCUS_LOST;

    //------------ Methods ------------
    boolean isTemporary();
    /* Returns true if the loss of focus is temporary, which
       might happen when the user does something like pulling
       down a menu. */
}
```

java.awt.event.FocusListener

This interface must be implemented by any class wishing to respond to FocusEvents.

```
abstract interface FocusListener extends EventListener
{
    //------------ Method -------------
    abstract void focusGained(FocusEvent e);
    abstract void focusLost(FocusEvent e);
}
```

java.awt.event.InputEvent

This is an abstract superclass of MouseEvent and KeyEvent. Because it extends ComponentEvent, you can use the ComponentEvent method getComponent() to determine which component generated this event. For events of this type, the AWTEvent method getID() will return one of class constants described below, which can then be used to determine the presence or absence of any accompanying modifiers.

```
abstract class InputEvent extends ComponentEvent
{
    //-------- Class Constants --------
    final static int ALT_MASK;
    final static int CTRL_MASK;
    final static int META_MASK;
    final static int SHIFT_MASK;
    final static int BUTTON1_MASK;
    final static int BUTTON2_MASK;
    final static int BUTTON3_MASK;

    //------------ Methods ------------
    int getModifiers();
    boolean isAltDown();
    boolean isControlDown();
    boolean isMetaDown();
    boolean isShiftDown();
}
```

java.awt.event.ItemEvent

An ItemEvent instance is generated when the user selects a Checkbox, a CheckboxMenuItem, or a Choice item or single-clicks a List item. You can determine the nature of the event by calling getStateChange() and comparing the returned value to one of the two class constants.

```
class ItemEvent extends AWTEvent
{
    //-------- Class Constants --------
    final static int DESELECTED;
    final static int SELECTED;

    //------------ Methods ------------
 ◆  Object getItem();
 ◆  int getStateChange();
}
```

java.awt.event.ItemListener

This interface must be implemented by any class wishing to respond to InputEvents.

```
abstract interface ItemListener extends EventListener
{
    //------------ Method -------------
 ◆  abstract void itemStateChanged(ItemEvent e);
}
```

`java.awt.event.KeyAdapter`

This class provides no-statement implementations of the three `KeyListener` methods.

```
abstract class KeyAdapter extends Object
                          implements FocusListener
{
    //------------ Methods ------------
◆   void keyPressed(KeyEvent e);
◆   void keyReleased(KeyEvent e);
◆   void keytyped(KeyEvent e);
}
```

`java.awt.event.KeyEvent`

A `KeyEvent` is generated when a keyboard key is pressed or released. This class contains a large number of class constants for numeric equivalents of keyboard keys, most of which we list here. These key codes are also used in the `MenuShortcut` class, which is described in Chapter 4.

```
class KeyEvent extends InputEvent
{
    //-------- Class Constants --------
    // (all are final static)
    VK_A, ..., VK_Z, VK_0, ..., VK_9,
    VK_NUMPAD0, ..., VK_NUMPAD9,
    VK_SPACE, VK_BACK_SPACE, VK_DELETE, VK_ENTER, VK_TAB,
    VK_ESCAPE, VK_ALT, VK_CONTROL, VK_META, VK_SHIFT,
    VK_CAPS_LOCK,
    VK_F1, ..., VK_F12,
    VK_PAGE_DOWN, VK_PAGE_UP, VK_END, VK_HOME,
    VK_UP, VK_DOWN, VK_LEFT, VK_RIGHT,
    VK_ADD, VK_SUBTRACT, VK_MULTIPLY, VK_DIVIDE,
    VK_PERIOD, VK_COMMA, VK_SLASH, VK_BACK_SLASH,
    VK_QUOTE, VK_BACK_QUOTE, VK_OPEN_BRACKET,
    VK_CLOSE_BRACKET, VK_EQUALS, VK_SEMICOLON

    //------------ Methods ------------
    char getKeyChar();
    void setKeyChar(char c);
    /* The latter method could be used to change the key value
       that generated this event. Any changes you make will
       appear in the Component (like a TextArea) in which the
       event was generated */

◆   int getKeyCode();
    void setkeyCode(int code);

◆   boolean isActionKey();

    int setModifiers(int mask);
    /* This allows you to change the modifiers that accompanied
       this event. For example, you might want to do this to
       add a Shift modifier to this event, thereby changing the
       character to uppercase. This class inherits the
       companion method getModifiers() from its superclass
       InputEvent. */
}
```

java.awt.event.KeyListener

This interface must be implemented by any class wishing to respond to KeyEvents.

```
abstract interface KeyListener extends EventListener
{
   //------------ Method -------------
♦  abstract void keyPressed(KeyEvent e);
♦  abstract void keyReleased(KeyEvent e);
♦  abstract void keyTyped(KeyEvent e);
}
```

java.awt.event.MouseAdapter

This class provides no-statement implementations of the five MouseListener methods.

```
abstract class MouseAdapter extends Object
                            implements MouseListener
{
   //------------ Methods ------------
♦  void mouseClicked(MouseEvent e);
♦  void mouseEntered(MouseEvent e);
♦  void mouseExited(MouseEvent e);
♦  void mousePressed(MouseEvent e);
♦  void mouseReleased(MouseEvent e);
}
```

java.awt.event.MouseMotionAdapter

This class provides no-statement implementations of the two MouseMotionListener methods.

```
abstract class MouseMotionAdapter extends Object
                                  implements FocusListener
{
   //------------ Methods ------------
♦  void mouseDragged(MouseEvent e);
♦  void mouseMoved(MouseEvent e);
}
```

java.awt.event.MouseEvent

A KeyEvent occurs when the user clicks or moves the mouse. A call to getID() will return one of the class constants.

```
class MouseEvent extends InputEvent
{
   //-------- Class Constants --------
   // (all are final static)
   MOUSE_CLICKED, MOUSE_DRAGGED, MOUSE_ENTERED,
   MOUSE_EXITED, MOUSE_MOVED, MOUSE_PRESSED,
   MOUSE_RELEASED

   //------------ Methods ------------
   char getClickCount();
```

```
◆     Point getPoint()
      int getX();
      int getY();
}
```

java.awt.event.MouseListener

This interface must be implemented by any class wishing to respond to the five MouseEvents types that don't concern mouse motion.

```
abstract interface MouseListener extends EventListener
{
      //------------ Method -------------
◆     abstract void mouseClicked(MouseEvent e);
◆     abstract void mouseEntered(MouseEvent e);
◆     abstract void mouseExited(MouseEvent e);
◆     abstract void mousePressed(MouseEvent e);
◆     abstract void mouseReleased(MouseEvent e);
}
```

java.awt.event.MouseMotionListener

This interface must be implemented by any class wishing to respond to the two mouse motion events.

```
abstract interface MouseMotionListener extends EventListener
{
      //------------ Method -------------
◆     abstract void mouseDragged(MouseEvent e);
◆     abstract void mouseMoved(MouseEvent e);
}
```

java.awt.Scrollbar

Although you won't generally make stand-alone instances of scrollbars, they can sometimes be handy as controls. Their real use, of course, comes from scrolling the contents of a frame or text area. There's an AWT class we don't discuss here, ScrollPane, that makes scrolling a display quite easy.

```
class Scrollbar extends Component implements Adjustable
{
      //--------- Constructors ----------
      Scrollbar();
      Scrollbar(int orientation);
      Scrollbar(int orientation, int value, int visible,
            int min, int max);
      /* A scrollbar has several private members: its orientation
         (Scrollbar.HORIZONTAL or Scrollbar.VERTICAL), its
         current value, and its minimum and maximum possible
         values, all of which can be initialized by the
         constructors. */

      //-------- Class Constants --------
      final static int HORIZONTAL;
      final static int VERTICAL;
```

```
//------------ Methods ------------
void addAdjustmentListener(AdjustmentListener lstnr);
void removeAdjustmentListener(AdjustmentListener lstnr);

int getBlockIncrement();
int getUnitIncrement();
void setBlockIncrement(int incr);
void setUnitIncrement(int incr);
/* These get/set pairs allow access to the amount of change
   due to clicks in the "page up" and "line up" portions of
   this scrollbar. */

int getMaximum();
int getMinimum();
int getValue();
void setMaximum(int value);
void setMinimum(int value);
void setValue(int value);
void setValues(int value, int visible, int min, int max);
/* These pairs allow you to inspect and modify this
   scrollbar's maximum, minimum, and current values. */

int getVisibleAmount();
void setVisibleAmount(int value);
/* In some systems, the "thumb," or slider part of a
   scrollbar can vary its size, often to reflect the
   relative amount of a scrollable panel that is currently
   visible. These methods allow the program to
   inspect and modify the slider's width. */
}
```

java.awt.event.TextEvent

A TextEvent occurs whenever the text in a TextComponent is changed. There is nothing of interest to us in this class.

java.awt.event.TextListener

This interface must be implemented by any class wishing to respond to a TextEvent. Within this method, use getSource() to determine what Component generated the event.

```
abstract interface TextListener extends EventListener
{
    //------------ Method ------------
    abstract void textValueChanged(TextEvent e);
}
```

java.awt.event.WindowAdapter

This class provides no-statement implementations of the seven WindowListener methods. See the WindowListener class for descriptions of these methods.

```
abstract class WindowAdapter extends Object
                             implements WindowListener
```

```
{
    //------------ Methods ------------
    void windowActivated(WindowEvent e);
    void windowDeactivated(WindowEvent e);
    void windowOpened(WindowEvent e);
◆   void windowClosed(WindowEvent e);
    void windowClosing(WindowEvent e);
    void windowIconified(WindowEvent e);
    void windowDeiconified(WindowEvent e);
}
```

java.awt.event.WindowEvent

There are a number of things a user or a program can do to a window, and many of these trigger events. First, a window may become active or may be deactivated by the window being brought to the front or sent behind another. In many systems, it is possible to *iconify* a window, by shrinking it to a small representation, or to *deiconify* it, by expanding it from its iconified state. A WINDOW_OPENED event is generated when a window first appears, a WINDOW_CLOSING event is generated when the user tries to close a window, and a WINDOW_CLOSED event is generated when the window finally has been closed. As usual, getID() will return the class constant that describes the type of event.

The only method of interest to us is getWindow(), which returns the Window object that generated this event.

```
class WindowEvent extends ComponentEvent
{
    //-------- Class Constants --------
    final static int WINDOW_ACTIVATED;
    final static int WINDOW_CLOSED;
    final static int WINDOW_CLOSING;
    final static int WINDOW_DEACTIVATED;
    final static int WINDOW_DEICONIFIED;
    final static int WINDOW_ICONIFIED;
    final static int WINDOW_OPENED;

    //------------ Methods ------------
◆   Window getWindow();
        // Returns the Window that generated this event.
}
```

java.awt.event.WindowListener

This interface must be implemented by any class wishing to respond to WindowEvents.

```
abstract interface WindowListener extends EventListener
{
    //------------ Methods ------------
    void windowActivated(WindowEvent e);
    void windowDeactivated(WindowEvent e);
    void windowOpened(WindowEvent e);
◆   void windowClosed(WindowEvent e);
    void windowClosing(WindowEvent e);
    void windowIconified(WindowEvent e);
    void windowDeiconified(WindowEvent e);
}
```

CHAPTER SEVEN

METHODICAL PROGRAMMING

You've seen a lot of Java details so far. You know that a Java program is made up of a collection of classes and that classes contain variables for storing information and methods for manipulating this information. You know that an object communicates with another by asking the recipient to invoke one of its methods. You've seen a significant portion of the AWT class hierarchy and you've seen how to use these classes and interfaces to produce the visual design of an applet or application.

In other words, you have a large collection of tools. In fact, except for a few features that we'll cover in the next chapter, you have almost everything you need to build all but the most arcane Java programs.

Having the tools is necessary for writing programs. However, it's not sufficient. As with other crafts, to become proficient you need to know how to use the tools. Having a complete collection of classes, methods, and statements won't make you a programmer, any more than having a complete collection of brushes, paints, palette knives, and solvents will make you an artist. In both cases, you need to have a plan to guide you when you find yourself staring at that blank canvas, wondering "Where do I go from here?" In this chapter, we'll design a complex program and show you how we got from imprecise description to working program.

Objectives

In this chapter, we will

- Use an extended programming exercise to illustrate the strategies of effective program design.
- Discuss designing from the top down, starting with a decision about what classes to use.
- See how decisions about classes suggest what methods to include in the classes.
- Talk about the nature of methods, their arguments, their return values, and their statement bodies.
- Show how decisions about methods suggest what statements they require.

7.1 Method Recap

Because we'll be building quite a few methods in the pages that follow, it would be a good idea to review what we know about methods and lay down some of the syntactic and semantic rules governing methods.

Method Signatures

The *header* of a method is what you see in the first line of the method declaration. Here are some examples:

```
void init()                             // from Applet
boolean isEnabled()                     // from Component
void addItem(String name)               // from List
void addItem(String name, int index)    // also from List
String toString()                       // from Color, Component,
                                        // and over forty other
                                        // classes
```

The *signature* of a method consists of the *name* of the method and the *argument list*. The signature of a method is used by the compiler to determine which method to call. A class may not have two methods with the same signature (if that were allowed, there would be no way for the compiler to determine which method should actually be called).

The return type is a primitive type name (like `boolean`), a class name (like `String`), or the literal `void`. The return type tells the compiler what type of information will be returned by the method. If the return type is `void`, the expression does its thing when called and returns, not passing anything back to the program. If the return type is not `void`, the method sends back some information to the program, to be used where it was called, just as a variable of that type would be. For example, `isEnabled()` has a `boolean` return type and so could be used in any expression that expects a `boolean` value, such as

```
if (myButton.isEnabled())    // okay: A boolean is returned here.
{
   myButton.setEnabled(false);
}
```

The controlled statement in the example above illustrates how we use a method with a `void` return type. The `setEnabled()` method couldn't be used in a complex expression that expected some value, but it can be called by a simple expression statement. In effect, the expression statement `myButton.setEnabled(false);` is like `index++;` in that both statements tell the system "Do this, and don't do anything with the value that's returned, if any."

The name that appears in the method signature can be any legal Java identifier, as long as it isn't a keyword, such as `if` or `class`. In the samples above, you'll note that there are two methods in `List` that have the same name. That's perfectly acceptable—the compiler will be able to tell which is which by the fact that the two methods have different signatures (because their argument lists are different).

The argument list of a method consists of a pair of parentheses containing either nothing or one or more *TypeName argumentName* pairs, separated by commas. These argument descriptions look a lot like variable declarations. As you'll see shortly, they look like declarations because they act that way. However, you can't use the shortcut form that you can use with variable declarations. The signature

```
double average(double x, y)    // NO!
```

is illegal, because each argument must be paired with a type name. In Java, you can't set an initial value for an argument, either, so this would be unacceptable to the compiler:[1]

```
void sleep(int x = 0)        //NO!
```

Calling Methods

Every method belongs to a class. In Java there are no "free methods" that are declared outside of classes. This means that every instance of a class has a set of methods that it can call into action, just as we did above when the `Button` instance `myButton` called the `Component` method `setEnabled()`. As in the example above, an instance of a class can call one of its methods, or any accessible method of a superclass, by using the form *instanceName.methodName(arguments)*. For example, the following are all legal calls (to methods with `void` return types):

```
myButton.setEnabled(true); // from the Component superclass
myButton.setLabel("OK");   // setLabel() is a Button method
```

whereas the following are not:

```
myButton.add(x);   // NO. There are add() methods in Container,
                   // Menu, MenuBar, and Rectangle, but these
                   // aren't Button superclasses.
myButton.erase();  // NO. Who ever heard of erase()?
```

As you would expect, access plays a role here. An object can call any methods of its own class, the `public` methods of any other class, any default access of any class in the same package, and the `protected` methods of any of its superclasses. An object cannot call a `private` method of any class but its own.

If a method has a non-`void` return type, a call to it can be used anywhere in an expression where a value of that type could be used, as we mentioned. For example, `getLabel()` is a `Button` method that returns a `String`, so we could use a call to `getLabel()` in any expression where a `String` would be allowed, such as

```
myButton.getLabel() + " is the label"
```

Similarly, `myButton` has access, by inheritance, to the `Component` method `location()` that returns a `Point`. Because the x field of `Point` is `public`, and hence accessible everywhere, we could write the expression

```
3 + myButton.location().x
```

This is a little complicated, so let's unpack it. The dot notation isn't, strictly speaking, an operator in Java, though it acts like one.[2] If we think of the dot as an

---

[1] This is known as a *default argument*, and it is legal in some languages, including C++.

[2] The dot *is* an operator in C and C++.

operator, it would have the highest possible precedence and would group from the left. With that in mind, the compiler would evaluate the expression above as

```
( 3 + ( ( myButton.location() ).x ) )
```

which would become

```
( 3 + ( someAnonymousPoint.x ) )
```

and then something like

```
( 3 + 78 )
```

which would finally yield

```
81
```

This order of evaluation works equally well for cascaded method calls, like this mess,

```
myButton.getParent().countComponents()
```

which gets the `Container` of `myButton` and then calls that `Container`'s `countComponents()` method, thus finding how many other widgets share `myButton`'s `Container`. It's not a good idea to string too many method calls together with dots—the result is hard to read. Much better is to introduce temporary local variables:

```
Container c = myButton.getParent();
int numComponents = c.countComponents();
```

However, if you ever see a sequence like the one above, just start grouping from the left and keep going until you run out of dots.

For the sake of simplicity, a call to a method *from within the same class* doesn't need an instance name in front. If you want to make it obvious that you're calling one of the class's methods, you can use the synonym `this`, which means "this object." Here's an example that includes both ways of calling a method from the same class.

```
class PairOfInts
{
    private int x, y;

    public PairOfInts(int x, int y)
    // We need "this" here, to distinguish between the instance
    // variables and the constructor arguments.
    {
        this.x = x;
        this.y = y;
    }
```

```
public void flop()
// Changes (x, y) to (-y, x)
{
    int temp = -y;
    y = x;
    x = temp;
}

public void flip()
{
    flop();        // Note: no object name in front of call.
    this.flop();   // Same effect, but emphasizing we're
                   // calling the flop() method of
                   // this class.
}
}
```

Arguments

The arguments of a method provide the means by which information may be sent from the calling context to the method.

Definition

> The *formal arguments* (also known as *parameters*) of a method are those that appear in the method definition. The *actual arguments* are those that are used in the method call. The actual arguments must match the formal arguments in number and order, and the types must be compatible (which we'll explain below).

Consider, for example, the `Point` method,

```
void translate(int x, int y)
```

We can "second guess" what the definition of this method must look like:

```
void translate(int x, int y)
// Remember, Point has two int instance variables, x and y.
{
    this.x += x;    // Add the x argument to this x value
    this.y += y;    // Add the y argument to this y value
}
```

When this method is called, perhaps like this,

```
int deltaY = 10;
myPoint.translate(5, deltaY);
```

what happens, in effect, is that the compiler inserts invisible initializations for the argument values that are done first:

```
void translate(int x, int y)
{
   x = 5;            // Initialize the first argument.
   y = deltaY;       // Initialize the second argument.

   this.x += x;      // Add the x argument to this x value.
   this.y += y;      // Add the y argument to this y value.
}
```

> When a method is called, the first thing that happens is that the actual arguments in the call are used to initialize the corresponding formal arguments in the method declaration.

This hidden initialization has some important consequences. The first consequence is that the actual arguments don't have to be the same type as the corresponding formal arguments. As long as the formal argument type is "wider" than the actual argument, the initialization will work just fine. For example,

```
byte dY = 10;
myPoint.translate(5, dY);
```

is perfectly acceptable, because we can always initialize the int argument y by using a byte, with no loss of information. However, we can't use a wider type in the actual argument, like this,

```
double largeDY = 1.0098e14;
myPoint.translate(5, largeDY)
```

because the hidden initialization

```
x = largeDY;
```

wouldn't be allowed (we can't force a double into an int).

> A formal argument may be initialized with an actual argument of another type, as long as the formal argument is "wider" than the actual argument.

To help you remember this, just keep in mind that a method with a double argument may be called using any numeric type, because double is wider than any of the other numeric types. Refer to Section 5.4 for more information on this kind of type compatibility.

For arguments of class type, we have similar considerations: A formal argument of a given class type can be called using actual arguments of that class or any subclass. For example, the Container method

```
void add(Component c)
```

could be called by myPanel (which is a Container, of course) in any of the following forms:

```
myPanel.add(theButton);     // Button is a Component
myPanel.add(theLabel);      // Label is a Component
myPanel.add(theWindow);     // Window is a Container is a Component
```

However, none of these calls would be allowed, unless you made a type cast:

```
myPanel.add(theMenu);       // Menu isn't a Component subclass
myPanel.add(theObject);     // Object is a Component superclass
myPanel.add(theInt);        // int isn't even a class type
```

The memory aid here is that if the formal argument is `Object`, you can use an instance of any class in the method call.

Value Arguments, Reference Arguments

Another consequence of the "hidden initialization" that takes place at the start of any method invocation is that methods act differently on *value arguments* (that is, arguments of a primitive type) than on *reference arguments* (arguments of class type). Remember that variables of primitive type hold values, whereas variables of class type hold addresses in memory where member data may be found.

Let's see how methods act on value arguments first. Consider a class with a helper method `swap(int x, int y)`. Interchanging two values is a common operation in many programs, and that's what `swap()` is supposed to do. If `swap()` is called with two variables containing 3 and 2, for example, after the call we want the variables to contain 2 and 3, respectively

```
class SomeClass
{
    public someMethod()
    {
        int a = 3;
        int b = 2;
        swap(a, b);
        // Now what are a and b?
    }

    private void swap(int x, int y)
    // Interchange the values of the arguments. NOT!
    {
        int temp = x;
        x = y;
        y = x;
    }
}
```

Figure 7.1 shows what happens when `swap(a, b)` is called, with a containing the value 3 and b containing the value 2. The first thing that happens is that the formal arguments, x and y, are initialized to the corresponding value of the actual arguments in the "hidden initialization" step. Then, in the three statements of the method, the local variable temp is set to x's value, 3, x gets the value, 2, of y, and finally, y is set to the value saved in temp. Perfect! The values in x and y are indeed interchanged.

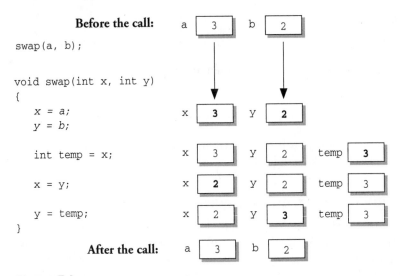

Figure 7.1

Trying, and failing, to modify value arguments.

However, this swapping never shows up in a and b. As far as we can tell, swap() has no effect! That's because all the work swap() does is performed on the *local* copies, x and y, of its arguments. The actual arguments are never touched. Indeed, this is always the case.

> A method *cannot* modify the values of primitive type arguments.

When the method returns, the arguments x and y, and the local variable temp are lost, and the variables a and b used in the method call have their original values. You can think of value arguments as *read-only*; they pass information in to the method, but that's all.

The situation is quite different for reference arguments. In Figure 7.2 we illustrate the action of a slightly different swap() method. In this case, the method has an argument of type Point and is designed to interchange the values of the Point's x and y fields. When this method is called, with some Point q as its actual argument, the "hidden initialization" sets the formal argument p to refer to q. Now p and q are *aliases* for the same object, because the addresses they contain are the same.

The method statements then interchange the values of the x and y fields, just as they did in our first example. This time, though, when the method returns, p and temp both vanish, as usual, and q persists, *with the changed fields!* Note that we really haven't changed q—it still has the same address as before. We have, though, modified the data in the object to which q refers. You can think of the fields of a refer-

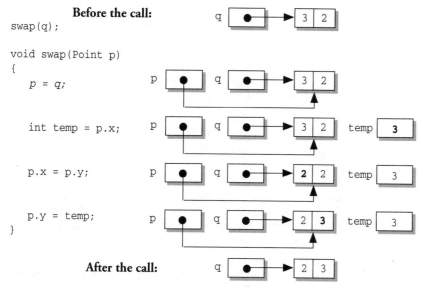

Figure 7.2

Successfully modifying the fields of a reference argument.

ence argument as *read-write*; they can be used to pass information both in and out of a method.

A method *can* modify the fields of class type arguments.

Review Questions

1.1 What is a method signature?
1.2 What is the relationship between methods and classes?
1.3 What are formal and actual arguments? How are they related?
1.4 Can a method change the values of its arguments?

7.2 Step 1: Specification

The task that will occupy us throughout this chapter can be stated simply enough: "Build an ATM." That's not much of a description, though. Most of the time, you'll be given more details than we have here, but we're making a point. No matter how precisely a programming problem is phrased, the description will nearly always be incomplete. There will invariably be questions that need to be answered: Should this ATM be a simulation, or is it intended to control a real piece of equipment? When writing our program, should we consider saving and retrieving account information, or should we just design the "front end" that the user will see? What *is* an ATM?

Advice: Look Before You Leap

> Before you start doing anything with a programming task, make sure you know what you're supposed to do.

If the programming task occurs in a professional environment, you'll probably want to meet the client and clarify what he or she expects; in a classroom setting, your instructor will be your client; and for a program task you set yourself, you'll be the client, of course. In this case, we are the clients, so we can do whatever we want, subject only to the requirement that it provide you with a useful experience. Let's see how we can fill in the details of our project.

An automatic teller machine (ATM) is basically a remote terminal connected to a bank's computer. It has a store of cash that is used to fulfill requests for withdrawals, and it can be used to accept and record deposits from bank clients, as well. You don't yet know how to store information in files that persist after the program quits, so we decided to do just a simulation of the front end and to produce an applet that will look like the real ATMs you find in stores and parking lots.

The next thing we did was go around our town and take a look at some actual ATMs. (We were ready for a break, anyhow, and this "field research" was a good excuse.) We discovered that all four ATMs in Clinton, New York[3] looked pretty much the same: They had a display window and a numeric keypad for entering cash amounts, and most had a control panel of buttons labeled "Clear," "Enter," "Deposit," and Withdrawal." Of course, they had other parts, such as the slot where the cash came out, that we noted but didn't intend to simulate.

We finally had a pretty good idea of what we were trying to accomplish. In a more complicated task, we would certainly write down the specifications rather than relying on our memory. This requirement goes without saying in the world of commercial programming: Not only is it an aid to design, but it also eliminates some nasty surprises down the road when, after nine months of work, you show your design to the client, only to be told, "This isn't anything like what we agreed on."

Specification

To specify our program, we need to describe how it will look and also how it will work. We generally concentrate on the look first—it is generally the easier of the two tasks, and it also often serves to clarify questions about how the program should behave.

Advice: First Impressions Are Most Important

> Design the visual aspect of your program first; then describe how it will act.

---

[3]If you deduce from this that Clinton is a small town, you're quite right.

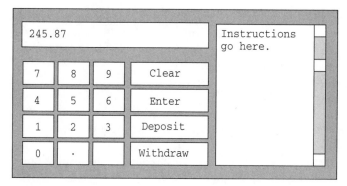

Figure 7.3

ATM visual design.

In this example, for instance, we can stare at the picture of our program and pretend we are using it, asking questions like "What should happen in the other components when the user presses the Deposit button?"

After not too much thought, we arrived at the layout illustrated in Figure 7.3. It seems to have all the features we need, including the last-minute addition of a `TextArea` for instructions to the user. We decided to add that, rather than placing instructions in the `TextField`, because we thought that we might need more than a single line for some instructions.

Things get a little more complicated when it comes to specifying the action of our program, but it's still not to hard to get started.

1. Opening mode: Show instructions, "Press Deposit or Withdraw buttons to make a transaction. Press Clear to end this session." Disable Enter button. Go to (2).

2. a. If Clear button pressed, show instruction "Thank you for doing business with us. Have a nice day." and then append opening instructions from (1).

   b. If Deposit button pressed, go to Deposit mode (3).

   c. If Withdraw button pressed, go to Withdraw mode (5).

   d. Ignore any keypad events.

3. Deposit mode: Show instructions, "Please key in amount of deposit and then press Enter to confirm. If you make a mistake, press clear and re-key the amount and then press Enter to complete your deposit." Enable Enter button, disable Deposit and Withdraw buttons. Go to (4).

4. a. If Clear button pressed, clear display.

   b. Send keypad presses to display.

   c. If Enter button pressed, and display is 0 or blank, show instruction, "You must enter a nonzero amount for your deposit," and append original deposit instructions.

   d. If Enter button is pressed and there is a nonzero amount in display, show confirmation message and go back to opening mode (1).

5. Withdrawal mode: Show instructions, "Please key in amount of withdrawal and then press Enter to confirm. If you make a mistake, press clear and re-key the amount and then press Enter to complete your deposit." Enable Enter button, disable Deposit and Withdraw buttons. Go to (6).

6. a. If Clear button pressed, clear display.

   b. Send keypad presses to display.

   c. If Enter button pressed, and display is 0 or blank, show instruction, "You must enter a nonzero amount for your withdrawal," and append original withdrawal instructions.

   d. If Enter button is pressed and there is a nonzero amount in display, show confirmation message and go back to opening mode (1).

Once we finished the action description, we found we also had a list of questions: "Should we keep track of the amount the customer has available?" "Should we check the available amount before allowing a withdrawal?" "In a real ATM, withdrawals must be in multiples of some minimum amount, like ten dollars. Should we enforce that here, too?" "Should we allow the user another option, to check his or her available funds?" These are all good questions, and the answer to all of them should probably be "Yes," but none of them seems to stand in the way of our design, so we leave them for later. We might actually do the same thing in a commercial project—get things partially up and running, so we could verify with the client that our design is acceptable so far (a technique known as *rapid prototyping*). Because we ourselves are the clients, we'll allow these questions to go unanswered for the moment, but we put them on a list so that we won't forget to come back to them.

Advice: Know Where You Are

> At each step, go back over what you have and note any changes that should be made. Don't be afraid to suggest changes that seem worthwhile.

Review Questions

2.1 What three modes can our ATM be in?

2.2 In simple terms, what is the purpose of the Clear button?

2.3 What actions by users could prompt a gentle reminder that they did something wrong?

7.3   Step 2: Determine the Classes

With a GUI design, the next step is to decide what classes you need to achieve the look you've decided on. In our program, we have 11 keypad buttons, 4 control buttons, a field for numeric amounts, and a text area for instructions.

The first thing we notice is that the keypad seems to be a single logical unit. In addition, not only is it the most complicated part of our program, but it also seems to be something we might want to use in other programs. It seems like we might be well served if we made a separate `Keypad` class. This has two important advantages: It gives us a widget we could reuse, and it allows us to think of it as a single conceptual unit, rather than having to keep track of 11 separate buttons.

Advice: Clump Logically

> If you have a collection of objects that serve similar purposes, consider collecting them into a single class. If you think the collection might be useful in other programs, don't just *consider* collecting them into a class—do it.

Remember that a Java program is just a collection of classes. In the first pass, *let the visual design suggest the classes.*

Layout

Now it is time to examine our design closely and see how we can make it look the way we want. We're down to seven widgets: The four control buttons, the `Keypad`, the numeric field, and the instruction text area. Given the advice about grouping, it's clear that the control buttons should be grouped together, but it's not clear that it's worth placing them in their own class. Instead, we'll use a `Panel` with a `GridLayout` to place them in our program.

Advice: Clump, Clump, Clump Visually

> Do GUI design from the bottom up, collecting widgets into containers, collecting the containers into larger containers, and so on.

We now have just four things to deal with: a `Keypad` instance, a `Panel` with the control buttons, a numeric field, and an instruction `TextArea`. See how easy design is when we clump things together? Now go back to the visual design in Figure 7.1 and start drawing nested rectangles to collect things. It seems that we want to place the `Keypad` and the control button `Panel` in another `Panel`, and because they won't necessarily be the same size, we'll use a `BorderLayout` for that `Panel`.

Now we're down to just *three* objects: (1) the `Panel` containing the `Keypad` and the control `Panel`, (2) the number field, and (3) the `TextArea`. The number field and the other `Panel` seem to need a `Panel` of their own, with `BorderLayout`, again, because the objects almost certainly won't be the same size. Finally, we take our big `Panel` and the `TextArea` and lay them out in the applet. Note that this is the first time we have used the word *applet*. This program was a natural candidate to show in a browser, so we decided to make it an applet. Figure 7.4 shows our design, laid out into `Panels`.

Now, for the first time, we can sit down and write code. We know how tempting it is to hop right in and start coding, but we strongly discourage it. Unless you

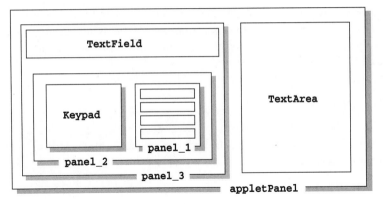

Figure 7.4
ATM GUI hierarchy.

are *very* good at keeping track of a host of details or you are doing a "toy" program, coding without having first considered design is a prescription for disaster.

Advice: Design, Then Code

The longer you can put off coding, the better off you'll be in the long run.

The first pass through the code went quickly enough. It took perhaps ten minutes to write our applet and compile it. The expected host of compile errors greeted us, because we had typed "KeyPad" in a couple of places, instead of "Keypad." Those were easy enough to find; we were expecting errors from typing.

Advice: Let the Compiler Help

If you haven't already, get into the compile/catch errors/fix errors/compile cycle. Many times, the compiler will point you directly to the error. If that fails, start looking backwards in the code from the point where the error finally surfaced.

Once the applet compiled, we ran it, only to discover that the TextArea filled the entire applet. Not only had we not specified the number of columns in the TextArea, but we had also set the size of the applet too small. We noted that, fixed the errors, and tried again.

Advice: Consider Keeping a Bug Log

It may slow you down a bit, but it is generally useful to record the errors you found and how you fixed them. This useful learning device is vitally important for larger programs so that you can keep track of the changes from one version to the next.

We fixed the `TextArea` constructor call and compiled the applet again. This time there were no errors (good typing on our part), but when we ran it, we discovered that the widgets were too closely packed. That was an easy fix—we just added some `hgap` and `vgap` values in the layout constructor calls.

Finally, our code looked like the following. Note, by the way, that we initialized all of our instance variables when we declared them, rather than using `new` in the `init()` method. We could have done the initialization in either location, but we decided that initializing the widgets inside `init()` would make that method even more cumbersome than it already was.

Advice: Keep Methods Short

If you have to scroll to get from the top to the bottom of a method, it's probably too long to be understood at first glance. Consider writing some `private` helper methods to pull out some of the code.

```java
import java.applet.*;
import java.awt.*;
import java.awt.event.*;

public class ATM extends Applet implements ActionListener
{
    private TextField  display = new TextField();
    private Keypad     pad = new Keypad();
    private Button     clear = new Button("Clear"),
                       enter = new Button("Enter"),
                       deposit = new Button("Deposit"),
                       withdraw = new Button("Withdraw");
    private TextArea   help = new TextArea(6, 20);

    public void init()
    {
        // Build the control button panel.
        Panel p1 = new Panel();
        p1.setLayout(new GridLayout(4, 1, 0, 3));
        p1.add(clear);
        p1.add(enter);
        p1.add(deposit);
        p1.add(withdraw);

        // Put the keypad and the control panel together
        Panel p2 = new Panel();
        p2.setLayout(new BorderLayout(3, 0));
        p2.add(BorderLayout.CENTER, pad);
        p2.add(BorderLayout.EAST, p1);

        // Put the display field with the keypad-control
        // panel
        Panel p3 = new Panel();
        p3.setLayout(new BorderLayout());
        p3.add(BorderLayout.NORTH, display);
        p3.add(BorderLayout.CENTER, p2);

        // Put the TextArea with everything we've included
        // so far.
```

```
        // Note, we use the optional "this." here to make
        // it clear that we're dealing with this applet.
        this.setLayout(new BorderLayout(5, 0));
        this.add(BorderLayout.CENTER, p3);
        this.add(BorderLayout.EAST, help);
        this.setBackground(Color.lightGray);
    }
}

//-------------------------------------------------------------

class Keypad extends Panel
// This will eventually be a panel of numeric buttons.
{
    private Label message;

    public Keypad()
    {
        message = new Label("The keypad");
        add(message);
        setBackground(Color.white);
    }
}
```

Finally, note that our `Keypad` class is just a *stub*. We didn't need to concern ourselves with its details yet, so we just wrote a class that did nothing but serve as a placeholder.

Advice: Write What's Necessary, and No More

If a class isn't absolutely required yet, just write a stub. (See "Design, Then Code.")

After swatting all the design bugs, typos, and logic errors, we finally came up with a layout that reflected our original specification exactly. To see how close we came, compare Figures 7.3 and 7.5.

Filling in the Details

Once the large-scale design was satisfactory, it was time to go back and do the layout part of the `Keypad` class. We declared the 11 buttons as instance variables and laid them out in the constructor, using the `GridLayout` we had decided on previously. It turned out to be a bit more complicated than we expected, because we decided to emulate a standard keypad, using a wider button on the bottom for the "0" key.

```
class Keypad extends Panel
{
    private Button b0, b1, b2, b3, b4, b5, b6,
                   b7, b8, b9, bPoint;

    public Keypad()
    {
```

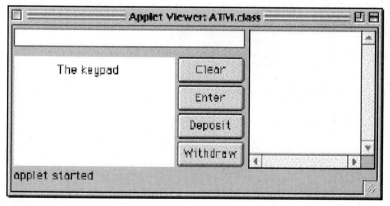

Figure 7.5

The ATM applet, stage 1.

```
setLayout(new GridLayout(4, 1, 4, 4));

// Top row: 7, 8, 9 keys
Panel p1 = new Panel();
p1.setLayout(new GridLayout(1, 3, 4, 4));
b7 = new Button("7");
p1.add(b7);
b8 = new Button("8");
p1.add(b8);
b9 = new Button("9");
p1.add(b9);
add(p1);

// Second row: 4, 5, 6 keys
Panel p2 = new Panel();
p2.setLayout(new GridLayout(1, 3, 4, 4));
b4 = new Button("4");
p2.add(b4);
b5 = new Button("5");
p2.add(b5);
b6 = new Button("6");
p2.add(b6);
add(p2);

// Third row: 1, 2, 3 keys
Panel p3 = new Panel();
p3.setLayout(new GridLayout(1, 3, 4, 4));
b1 = new Button("1");
p3.add(b1);
b2 = new Button("2");
p3.add(b2);
b3 = new Button("3");
p3.add(b3);
add(p3);

// Bottom row: fat zero button, skinny point button
Panel p4 = new Panel();
```

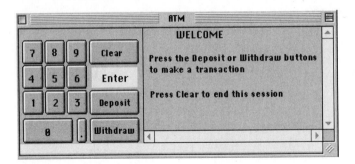

Figure 7.6

The ATM applet, layout complete.

```
    p4.setLayout(new BorderLayout(7, 4));
    b0 = new Button("0");
    p4.add(BorderLayout.CENTER, b0);
    bPoint = new Button(".");
    p4.add(BorderLayout.EAST, bPoint);
    add(p4);
  }
}
```

We were on a roll—the applet compiled without errors the first time we tried. Unfortunately, it looked all wrong, because we had not only reversed the numbers for rows and columns in the GridLayout constructor but also added the buttons in the wrong order. Fortunately, both of these logic errors were easy to identify and fix. It took several more iterations of fiddling to get the width of the applet and the number of columns in the TextArea to be such that the keypad buttons weren't too narrow or too wide. Finally, though, everything looked right, as we show in the screen shot in Figure 7.6, and we were ready to make our applet *do* something.

Review Questions

3.1 At the topmost level, what components are contained in our applet?
3.2 Why did we decide to separate the keypad into a class of its own?
3.3 In Figure 7.6, what mode is the applet in?

7.4 Step 3: Determine the Methods

The next step in the process of making our program is the most time-consuming and the trickiest. We made the visual arrangement and that suggested some of the classes we would need, such as the Keypad class. The next step was to look closely at the classes and see what they suggested about the methods (and member data) we needed.

The best place to start this stage is, of course, at the action specifications. In our example, it seemed that there was a clear division into *modes*: The applet behaves in one way at the start, it behaves in another way when a deposit is being made, and it behaves in another way (though much as it does in deposit mode) when the user is making a withdrawal. With this in mind, we can think of the control buttons as initiating transitions between modes

We won't make a big issue about this part of our design, because it is somewhat specialized. With experience, you'll find that this modal behavior is common to many programs, but it is certainly not a universal feature.

Top-Level Decomposition

In our case, it seems that the program needed to "know" what mode it was in (for example, the help message that is displayed will differ depending on the current mode). How did we do that? It seemed clear that we would need an instance variable to keep track of the current mode. If there were just two modes, we could use a boolean variable, inModeA, but in our program we needed to have a data member capable of expressing one of *three* values, not just of two. A common way of dealing with this is to establish three constants and make a variable of the appropriate type that will be given only these constants as its value. This is a technique that you've already seen in some of the AWT classes. The alignment of the text in a Label, for instance, is always one of the integer values given by CENTER, LEFT, or RIGHT.

That's what we did here. We established three constants, START_MODE, DEPOSIT_MODE, and WITHDRAW_MODE, and used them to set and modify the value of the instance variable mode, like this:

```
public class ATM extends Applet
{
    private final int    START_MODE = 0,
                         DEPOSIT_MODE = 1,
                         WITHDRAW_MODE = 2;
    private int mode;

    ...
}
```

We could do even more, though. It was pretty clear that when the program started, the first thing we'd need to do after laying out the components was display the introductory message, set the mode to START_MODE, and disable the Enter button. Those activities were obviously related—they would all be performed in an indivisible unit. This should sound a mental bell, because that's a clear requirement for collecting the statements into a method.

Advice: Clump Activities

If you find a collection of activities that are always performed as a unit, put them in a method and call the method to perform the activities.

We collected all the opening preamble into a method, introStart(), and put a call to it at the end of our init() method. Because introStart() was just a "helper" method and wouldn't ever be called from outside the applet, we gave introStart() private access. Finally, while we were at it, we made some similar methods, introDeposit() and introWithdraw(), to handle entries into deposit or withdrawal mode. Here's the applet as it looked at that stage:

```
public class ATM extends Applet
{
    private final int   START_MODE = 0,
                        DEPOSIT_MODE = 1,
                        WITHDRAW_MODE = 2;
    private      int    mode = START_MODE;

    ...

    public void init()
    {
        ...

        introStart(); // NEW: Enter start mode when we begin
    }

    public void actionPerformed(ActionEvent e)
    // Just a stub, for now.
    { }

    private void introStart()
    // Do the initialization needed to enter start mode.
    {
        help.setText("            W E L C O M E\n\n");
        help.appendText("Press the Deposit or Withdraw buttons\n");
        help.appendText("to make a transaction.\n\n");
        help.appendText("Press Clear to end this session.");

        display.setText("");
        clear.setEnabled(true);
        enter.setEnabled(false);
        deposit.setEnabled(true);
        withdraw.setEnabled(true);
    }

    private void introDeposit()
    // Do the initialization needed to enter deposit mode.
    {
        help.setText("            D E P O S I T\n\n");
        help.appendText("Key in the amount of your deposit ");
        help.appendText("and then press Enter to finish.\n\n");
        help.appendText("If you make a mistake, press Clear, ");
        help.appendText("key in the amount again, ");
        help.appendText("and then press Enter. ");

        display.setText("");
        clear.setEnabled(true);
        enter.setEnabled(true);
        deposit.setEnabled(false);
        withdraw.setEnabled(false);
    }
```

```
private void introWithdraw()
// Do the initialization needed to enter withdrawal mode.
{
    help.setText("        W I T H D R A W A L\n\n");
    help.appendText("Key in the amount of your withdrawal ");
    help.appendText("and then press Enter to finish.\n\n");
    help.appendText("If you make a mistake, press Clear, ");
    help.appendText("key in the amount again, ");
    help.appendText("and then press Enter. ");

    display.setText("");
    clear.setEnabled(true);
    enter.setEnabled(true);
    deposit.setEnabled(false);
    withdraw.setEnabled(false);
}
}
```

Note also that we included a stub for the `actionPerformed()` method. We weren't ready to deal with it, so we just marked it for later refinement.

Advice: Write What's Necessary, and No More (II)

"Use stubs while designing" applies to methods as well as classes.

Of course, we tested our applet. The first time, the introductory message wasn't spaced well and it all ran together, so we added some `\n` newline characters in the message strings to force the text to drop to the next line. We also replaced the `introStart()` call in `init()` with calls to the other two methods, just so we could check that they displayed as they should.

Advice: Never Stray Too Far from a Working Program

Try to write your program in such a way that after every few additions and changes you'll be able to compile and run it.

The reason why we always try to test our program after making a few changes is that this strategy *localizes* the inevitable errors. If you test after adding a method and suddenly find that the program doesn't work correctly, the odds are excellent that you'll be able to blame the errors on your new code and will be able to find them quickly. It's a common bad habit to get so involved in coding that hours pass before you do a test run. You'll certainly encounter some errors, and then you'll have to try to find their source among hundreds of lines of code, scattered in dozens of locations throughout your program. Trust us, this is not fun.

Filling in the Details, Again

With the top-level actions complete, we could now start to fill in any stubs we left. In this case, that meant the `actionPerformed()` method. This was complicated, because the results of clicking on the various buttons depended on the current mode.

We decided to use our top-level organization to organize the `actionPerformed()` handler, breaking it into three distinct parts depending on the mode.

Initially, the method looked like this:

```
public void actionPerformed(ActionEvent e)
{
    switch (mode)
    {
    case START_MODE:
        // Deal with clicks on the Deposit, Withdraw,
        // and Clear buttons
    case DEPOSIT_MODE:
        // Deal with clicks on the Enter and Clear
        // buttons, and the keypad
    case WITHDRAW_MODE:
        // Deal with clicks on the Enter and Clear
        // buttons, and the keypad
    }
}
```

Note how closely this organization reflects the action specification we made originally. The form of this method looks like an outline, as it should.

Advice: Make Your Code Self-Documenting

> The organization of a method's code should be so logically coherent that the organization makes the purpose clear, even without comments. If you find that you need extensive comments to explain what's going on, you should probably rethink your design.

Again, note that we had arranged things so that we could fill in each part and test it before going on to the next. The START_MODE section just involved checking whether the Deposit or the Withdraw button was clicked, and then switching to the appropriate mode by calling either `introDeposit()` or `introWithdraw()`, respectively.

The other two modes, though, had some details that we wanted to defer considering until later. We couldn't have handled a press of the Enter button in either mode, because we hadn't implemented the keypad, so there was no way of checking whether the amount entered was greater than zero. As usual, then, we just invented some new stub methods and put calls to them in the appropriate locations, arriving at the code below. This use of calls to stub methods is very convenient— when the time came to fill in the stubs, we'd never even have to look at the `action()` handler.

```
public class ATM extends Applet
{
    // (Declarations and init() deleted for brevity.)

    public void actionPerformed(ActionEvent e)
    {
        Object source = e.getSource();
        switch (mode)
```

```
        {
    case START_MODE:
        if (source == deposit)
        {
            mode = DEPOSIT_MODE;
            introDeposit();
        }
        else if (source == withdraw)
        {
            mode = WITHDRAW_MODE;
            introWithdraw();
        }
        else if (source == clear)
        {
            //*** FILL IN LATER
        }
        else if (source == enter)
        {
            mode = START_MODE;
            introStart();
        }
        break;
    case DEPOSIT_MODE:
        if (source == enter)
        {
            handleDeposit();
        }
        else if (source == clear)
        {
            display.setText("");
        }
        else
        {
            //*** KEYPAD CLICK--DO LATER
        }
        break;
    case WITHDRAW_MODE:
        if (source == enter)
        {
            handleWithdrawal();
        }
        else if (source == clear)
        {
            display.setText("");
        }
        else
        {
            //*** KEYPAD CLICK--DO LATER
        }
    }
}

// (introStart(), introDposit(), and introWithdraw() deleted
// for clarity.)

/**
 * A deposit request has been made. Check whether the amount
 * in display is nonzero. If so, just go back to start mode.
 * If not, display a help message.
 */
```

```
    private void handleDeposit()
    {
        introStart();    //*** FILL IN LATER
    }

    /**
     * A withdrawal request has been made. Check whether the
     * amount in display is nonzero. If so, just go back to start
     * mode. If not, display a help message.
     */
    private void handleWithdrawal()
    {
        introStart();    // FILL IN LATER
    }
}
```

Did we test the new changes? You bet. We must have been getting better with practice, because there were no compile errors, and everything worked exactly as we expected it to.

Review Questions

4.1 What's a stub?

4.2 How did we keep track of what mode the program was in?

4.3 Why do we urge you to compile and test your programs frequently when writing them?

7.5   Step 3, Continued

We had put off completing the Keypad class as long as we could. The applet was running perfectly, but it didn't respond to keypad events. We needed a way of passing keypad button clicks on to the applet's actionPerformed() handler so that we could then send the appropriate digit or decimal point to the display field.

Here was where we encountered the first real problem, one that's fairly common when communicating between classes. First of all, the applet's actionPerformed() handler should have been able to look for the keypad button that was clicked by using the usual dot notation to find the button within the pad object, like this:

```
if (source == pad.b0)
    // the b0 button in the pad was clicked
```

But it couldn't, because we made the buttons private members of the Keypad class. Of course, this has an easy fix—just change the access of the 11 buttons to public. And that's just what we'd do if we had no intention of ever using the Keypad class in another program. However, Keypad seemed to be useful enough to be saved for future use, so we had to think about making it so useful and robust enough that we'd be willing to put our names on it.

If we had changed our design and made the buttons public, we would have left the door open for some programmer to do this:

```
Keypad myPad = new Keypad();
...
myPad.b0.setLabel("zero");
```

Suddenly, if that occurred, the class would no longer work as specified. The `Keypad` class is supposed to have buttons with labels consisting of the digits "0" through "9" and the decimal point, ".". The intention is that a program using this class would be able to send the label string to another object, to represent part of a number. Now, though, the program might result in setting a numeric string to "37zero", rather than the "370" that was expected. This, clearly, could lead to all sorts of unpleasant errors.

The second part of this problem was that there was no easy way to register a listener for the pad buttons, because a `KeyPad` object wouldn't know about what object was going to do the action listening.

The fix was surprisingly easy and appealingly clever. Why not write our own version of `addActionListener()`, so that any class that wanted to listen to the pad's buttons could simply register, thereby listening to all 11 buttons at once, *regardless* of the fact that the buttons are `private` members of the class. This would be a completely new method, not an override, because `KeyPad` is a `Panel`, and none of the `Panel` superclasses has a method with this signature.

```
class Keypad extends Panel
{
    // (Button declarations and constructor omitted)

    public void addActionListener(ActionListener listener)
    {
        b0.addActionListener(listener);
        b1.addActionListener(listener);
        b2.addActionListener(listener);
        b3.addActionListener(listener);
        b4.addActionListener(listener);
        b5.addActionListener(listener);
        b6.addActionListener(listener);
        b7.addActionListener(listener);
        b8.addActionListener(listener);
        b9.addActionListener(listener);
        bPoint.addActionListener(listener);
    }
}
```

After patting ourselves on the back for being so clever, we tested our changes by putting in a call to `setText()` in the appropriate place in the applet's `actionPerformed()` handler. It worked like a charm.

```
else if (source == pad)
{
    String name = ((Button)source).getLabel();
    display.setText(name);
}
```

Would it have been reasonable to expect you to discover this trick on your own? Of course not. Would it be reasonable to expect you to recall having seen this trick when you need it in the future? Yes, indeed, just as we would expect an athlete or actor to learn by studying what others do.

Advice: Learn from Others

Coming up with something brand new is *hard*. It's much easier to acquire a stock of patterns and techniques that you can apply when you need them.[4]

A New Class

Only one more major task remained: designing the interactions of the applet with its `display` field. This occurred in four places, all originating within the applet's `actionPerformed()` handler. The pair of methods `handleDeposit()` and `handleWithdraw()` both needed to check whether `display` contained a positive number, and the two places where an event originated from the keypad needed to append the new string to the end of the display.

What, exactly, did the display have to do? Thinking about it, we came up with this list.

1. Initialize itself to contain the empty `String`.
2. Append a digit or decimal point to the right end of its text.
3. Be able to report whether it contained the representation of a positive number.
4. Clear itself to contain the empty `String`.
5. At all times, contain either the empty `String` or the representation of a legal number (nothing like "`34.2.117`", for example.)

The last item in the list made us stop and think. It seemed as though we were looking at something that was "like" a `TextField` but more specialized. It seemed, in fact, that we had come across another candidate for a class of its own. Thinking some more, we realized that a numeric field class could be put to good use in other applications. That settled it—we would invent a new `NumField` class and use it in our applet.

How should we design our new class? The same way we design any new class, by first deciding what methods it should have. It's convenient to ask two questions at this stage: "What would users like to know?" and "What kinds of modifications would users want to make?" The nice part about the early stage of class design is that we can let the class declaration serve as our outline. Here's what we came up with—a compileable class declaration full of method stubs.

```
class NumField extends TextField
{
    // Member data will go here

    // Constructors will go here
```

---

[4]The fact that experience can substitute for brilliance is one of the comforts of aging.

```
//------------ Inspector ------------

/**
 * Returns the value represented by this field's text,
 * or zero, if the text is empty or just contains a minus sign.
 */
public double getValue()
{
    return 0.0; // FIX.  We have this here only
                // because a method with a non-void
                // return type must return something.
}

//------------ Modifiers ------------

/**
 * Set the text to be the empty String.
 */
public void clear()
{
    //*** LATER
}

/**
 * Set the text to represent the double value of the argument.
 */
public void setValue(double d)
{
    //*** LATER
}

/**
 * Append the character c to the end of the text.
 * We check that this method will result
 * in a legal number representation, and do nothing
 * if the char to be appended would result in an
 * invalid number representation.
 */
public void append(char c)
{
    //*** LATER
}

/**
 * Append the first character of s to the end of the text.
 */
public void append(String s)
{
    //*** LATER
}

/**
 * Override of the TextComponent method. We don't want to
 * allow the user to change the text arbitrarily.
 */
public void setText(String s)
{ }
}
```

You may have noticed that we included methods here, such as `setValue()`, that wouldn't be used in our program. We could have left them out if we were never going to use this class anywhere else, but we wanted to make this class useful in a potentially wide range of settings.

Advice: Build in Generality

> When designing a class someone else might use, try to anticipate what the other programmer might want.

The flip side of this advice is that it's easy to go overboard, designing in a host of methods that might be used only once in a hundred programs. This is a practice that in larger contexts leads to bloated commercial applications that require at least 50 megabytes of memory and 500 megabytes of hard disk space.

Now we walked our way down the list of methods, filling them in as we went.

```
public double getValue()
```

See the Class References for further details on wrapper classes.

This one wasn't simple. How were we to convert the text `String` to a `double`? We had to head to the documentation for this one. Eventually, though, we found what we needed. Each of the primitive types has an associated class, known as a *wrapper class*. These are intended for situations where we need to convert a primitive type into a reference type, but the important part here is that the `Double` wrapper class has a constructor that takes a `String` argument and converts it into a `Double`. The class also has a method, `doubleValue()`, that converts a capital-D `Double` to a lowercase-d primitive `double`. We then had a two-step conversion that would do what we wanted. Finally, we had to remember that the text might be empty, and for those instances we decided to return `0`.

```java
public double getValue()
{
    if ((getText().equals("")) || (getText().equals("-")))
    {
        return 0.0;
    }
    else
    // Here's the two-step conversion, from String
    // to Double, and then from Double to double
    {
        Double d = new Double(this.getText());
        return d.doubleValue();
    }
}
```

Advice: Look It Up

> If there's something you need to do, the chances are that Java has methods to do it. Rummaging through the documentation can be instructive, as well as useful.

public void **setValue**(double d)

This took another trip to the documentation. The String class method valueOf() returns a String representing the value of its argument, and that was exactly what we needed. Note that we had to call the superclass's setText() method, because we had overridden our own to do nothing.

```
public void setValue(double d)
{
    super.setText(String.valueOf(d));
}
```

public void **clear**()

Trivial. All we had to do was use the parent class's setText() method, with the empty string, "", as argument. Or so we thought. . . .

```
public void clear()
{
    super.setText("");
}
```

public void **append**(char c)

This seemed simple at first. All we needed was to get the text as a String, use the + concatenation operator to add the character to the end of the text, and set the text to be the new value, like this:

```
public void append(char c)
// NOT the final version--does no legality checking
{
    super.setText(this.getText() + c);
}
```

The problem, as we noted in the comment, is that this did no checking for legality. The user could have appended g just as easily as 7. In keeping with our advice on putting off coding as long as possible, we invented a method, isLegal(char c), that returns true if and only if the character c could be legally appended to the current text. Now our method looked like this:

```
public void append(char c)
// STILL NOT the final version
{
    if (isLegal(c))
        super.setText(this.getText() + c);
}
```

The problem here was that although isLegal() could check whether c was a digit or a decimal point, the decimal point is legal only if there's not already one in the text. We needed a boolean instance variable, hasDecimalPoint, that keeps track of whether we have seen a decimal point. This will be used in isLegal(), and we'll set it in this method, rather than in `isLegal()`, because the job of that method is only to test a character. Finally, we were finished:

```
public void append(char c)
// FINAL VERSION (sort of, see the exercises)
{
    if (isLegal(c))
    {
        if (c == '.')
            hasDecimalPoint = true;
        super.setText(this.getText() + c);
    }
}
```

Advice: Listen to the Code

Just as we let the design suggest the classes and the classes suggest the methods, the methods can often suggest the variables they will require.

public void **append**(String s)

This method does almost the same thing as the previous one, but it accepts a `String` argument rather than a `char`. This method is the one we would use in our applet, because the `Keypad`-generated action event returns the button label as a `String`, like `"4"`, for instance. We didn't know how to extract the first character from a `String` (well, all right, we did, but we pretended we didn't), so we went back to the documentation again and found the `String` method `charAt(int i)` that returns the character at position `i`, counted from `0`, as usual. Now our method looked like this:

```
public void append(String s)
// NOT the final version
{
    char c = s.charAt(0);    // get the leftmost character
    if (isLegal(c))
    {
        if (c == '.')
            hasDecimalPoint = true;
        super.setText(this.getText() + c);
    }
}
```

What a waste! We had two methods that differed by a single statement. There's a much shorter way to write this, by calling the `char` version from within the `String` one:

```
public void append(String s)
// FINAL VERSION (perhaps, see the exercises)
{
    char c = s.charAt(0);    // get the leftmost character
    append(c);
}
```

Advice: Avoid Multiply Redundant Duplication!

> If you find you've written two chunks of code that are nearly identical, consider encapsulating them as methods. If they are already methods, see whether you can call one to implement the other.

public void **setText**(String s)

Whenever you extend a class by inheritance, you are specializing it. There is always a chance that some methods of the parent class would give the user power to do something you don't want, and that's exactly what happened here. We certainly didn't want the user to be able to make arbitrary changes to our text, so we over-rode the parent[5] method here, turning it into a "do-nothing" method. This, by the way, is why we were so careful about calling super.setText() in the other methods in this class. If we hadn't, we would have been calling the Keypad version, which would do nothing.

```
public void setText(String s)
{
}
```

private boolean **isLegal**(char c)

We were down to the last of our methods, the one that tests for the legality of a character. We had two things to test: whether the character represented a digit (always legal) and whether it was the decimal point (legal only when hasDecimalPoint is false). Note that we made use of the Character wrapper class method isDigit(), which returns true if and only if its argument is one of the digit characters 0 through 9.

```
private boolean isLegal(char c)
{
    if (Character.isDigit(c))
        return true;
    else if ((c == '.') && !hasDecimalPoint)
        return true;
    else
        return false;
}
```

All that remained was to fill in the constructors and any member data we discovered along the way. The member data was easy: The only new variable we discovered we needed when designing the NumField methods was the boolean variable hasDecimalPoint. It had to be an instance variable, because it was used in isLegal(), set in append(), and—Oops!—it needed to be reset to false in clear(). We were lucky to have thought of that, rather than having it turn up to bedevil us later.

---

[5]Grandparent, actually; the setText() method belongs to TextComponent, not Textfield.

The constructors are mirrors of those of the parent class. One is the default, and the other allows us to set the width of this field. Note that we did the same thing here as we did with `append()`—we implemented the simpler one with a call to the complex one.

```
public NumField()
{
    this(8);        // Call our other constructor.
}

public NumField(int cols)
{
    super(cols);    // Call the TextField constructor.
    this.setText("");
    this.setEditable(false);
    hasDecimalPoint = false;
}
```

It is worth mentioning that this isn't always a good idea. Method calls involve a fair amount of computational overhead, so if there is a very time-sensitive routine to implement, you will be better off duplicating code than making a method call. In this applet, though, any call to a `NumField` constructor will be done only once, and `append()` will have to wait eons (in computer time) for the user to hit a key. As you'll see if you continue your studies, this trade-off between space (of code in memory) and time (of execution) is quite common in many areas of computer science.

That's it—the `NumField` class was complete. Here it is.

```
package Utilities;
//================================================================
//   PROJECT:           _programming.java_
//   FILE:              Keypad.java
//   PURPOSE:           Chapter 7 demo program, NumField class
//   VERSION:           1.0
//   TARGET:            Java 1.1 and above
//   UPDATE HISTORY:    1.0    11/2/98
//================================================================


//--------------------------- IMPORTS ---------------------------

import java.awt.*;

//======================= NumField CLASS =======================+

/**
 * A NumField stores and displays the text representation of
 * a floating-point number. We've designed this class so that
 * at any time, its display is either empty or contains a
 * legal representation of a floating-point number.
 */
public class NumField extends TextField
{
    boolean hasDecimalPoint = false;

    /**
     * Default constructor--build a NumField eight columns wide,
     * initially empty.
     */
```

```java
public NumField()
{
    super(8);                   // Call the superclass constructor.
    super.setText("");
    setEditable(false);     // Don't let the user in.
    hasDecimalPoint = false;
    setBackground(Color.white);
}

/**
 * Returns the value represented by this field's text,
 * or zero, if the text is empty or just contains a minus sign.
 */
public double getValue()
{
    if ((getText().equals("")) || (getText().equals("-")))
    {
        return 0.0;
    }
    else
    {
        Double d = new Double(getText());
        return d.doubleValue();
    }
}

/**
 * Set the text to represent the double value of the argument.
 */
public void setValue(double d)
{
    super.setText(String.valueOf(d));
}

/**
 * Set the text to be the empty String.
 */
public void clear()
{
    super.setText("");
    hasDecimalPoint = false;
}

/**
 * Append the character c to the end of the text.
 * We check that this method will result
 * in a legal number representation, and do nothing
 * if the char to be appended would result in an
 * invalid number representation.
 */
public void append(char c)
{
    if (isLegal(c))
    {
        if (c == '.')
        {
            hasDecimalPoint = true;
        }

        if ((getText()).equals("0"))
        {
```

```
                super.setText("");
            }

        super.setText(getText() + c);
    }
}

/**
 * Append the first character of s to the end of the text.
 * This uses the other version of append() to ensure
 * the representation is valid.
 */
public void append(String s)
{
    char c = s.charAt(0);
    append(c);
}

/**
 * Override of the TextComponent method. We don't want to
 * allow the user to change the text arbitrarily.
 */
public void setText(String s)
{ }

//------------- Utility -------------

/**
 * Returns true if and only if c could legally be appended to
 * the end of the text. In other words, return true
 * (1) if c is a digit, or (2) if c would be the only decimal
 * point in the text representation, or (3) if c is '-' and the
 * current text is 0 or empty.
 */
private boolean isLegal(char c)
{
    if (Character.isDigit(c))
    {
        return true;
    }
    else if (c == '.')
    {
        return !hasDecimalPoint;
    }
    else if ((c == '-') &&
        ((getText().equals("")) || (getText().equals("0"))))
    {
        return true;
    }
    else
    {
        return false;
    }
}
}
```

We took a bit of a chance here, finishing up the whole class without trying it out, so before we went much further, we put it to the test. In fact, we were so close to the end that putting in the code to test our NumField class resulted in a substantially complete applet. All we had to do was change TextField to NumField in the declarations, make a few modifications to the action() handler, and fill in the handleDeposit() and handleWithdrawal() methods, like this:

```java
public class ATM extends Applet
{
    // (Some declarations omitted.)

    private NumField   display = new NumField();

    // (More declarations and init() omitted.)

    public void actionPerformed(ActionEvent e)
    {
        Object source = e.getSource();
        switch (mode)
        {
        case START_MODE:
            // (Omitted.)

        case DEPOSIT_MODE:
            if (source == enter)
            {
                handleDeposit();
            }
            else if (source == clear)
            {
                display.clear();
            }
            else
            {
                String name = ((Button)source).getLabel();
                display.append(name);
            }
            break;

        case WITHDRAW_MODE:
            // (Almost exactly the same as DEPOSIT_MODE)
        }
    }

    // (introStart(), introDeposit(), introWithdraw() omitted.)

    private void handleDeposit()
    {
        if (display.getValue() == 0.0)
        {
            // display an error message
        }
        else
        {
            mode = START_MODE;
            introStart();
        }
    }

    private void handleWithdrawal()
    {
        // (Almost the same as handleDeposit())
    }
```

Cleanup

At this stage, the only part we had left undone was addressing how to let the customer quit. The specifications stated that in start mode the user could click the Clear button to leave. We didn't want to shut the applet down, so we decided that clicking the Clear button would bring up another help message, thanking the user for his or her business and (the new part) indicating that clicking the Enter button would start the whole process up again. To implement this, all we had to do was add a call to a new method, doQuit(), defined as shown below, and add a clause to the applet's action() handler to deal with the Enter button click.

```
public void actionPerformed(ActionEvent e)
{
    Object source = e.getSource();
    switch (mode)
    {
    case START_MODE:
        if (source == deposit)
        {
            mode = DEPOSIT_MODE;
            introDeposit();
        }
        else if (source == withdraw)
        {
            mode = WITHDRAW_MODE;
            introWithdraw();
        }
        else if (source == clear)
        {
            doQuit();
        }
        else if (source == enter)
        {
            mode = START_MODE;
            introStart();
        }
        break;
        ...
    }
    ...

private void doQuit()
{
    help.setText("Thank you for your business.\n\n");
    help.appendText("Have a nice day.\n\n\n");
    help.appendText("Press the Enter button to start.");

    display.clear();      // So the next customer can't see
                          // what happened during this session.
    clear.disable();
    enter.enable();
    deposit.disable();
    withdraw.disable();
}
```

We did one final round of tests, first imitating an ordinary user making ordinary transactions, and then trying to be as idiotic as possible. Everything seemed to work as it should. Of course, testing isn't going to guarantee that a program is correct. In the words of Edsger Dijkstra, "Testing can reveal the presence of errors, but never their absence." The parts of a program can interact in complicated and unexpected ways, but fortunately for us, our design was solid from the start. The way we built our program resulted in a collection of more or less self-contained units: the applet itself and the `Keypad` and `NumField` classes. Each of these three classes was further made up of methods, none of which was too large to comprehend at a glance. We had to make sure that the methods interacted smoothly, and that was a major task only in the ATM class, with its eight instance variables. We took the time to look at each place where the mode was changed, to make sure that the buttons were enabled and disabled as they should be, and we made sure that the transitions between modes were being performed correctly.

Everything looked good, but while we were reading the code, we noticed that there was some unnecessary duplication. Several of the help messages contained exactly the same text,

```
and then press Enter to finish.

If you make a mistake, press Clear,
key in the amount again,
and then press Enter.
```

so we pulled those calls to `help.appendText()` out and placed them in a new method, `showGeneralMessage()`.

Finally, we went over the code one more time. There were some typos in the comments that the compiler didn't catch, of course. We had been putting comments in as we wrote the code, but we hadn't included a block of header comments at the beginning of the file, so we did that, too.

Advice: Writing Is Rewriting

Once your program is running satisfactorily, go back over the code. Is it clear? Is it well documented? Can it be streamlined? Can it be cleaned up? Edit, edit, edit!

Finally, we were finished. From start to finish, the project took three days to produce 490 lines of code (counting blank lines). A hundred-plus lines of code per day is pretty good, especially considering that the program and the chapter were being written more or less in parallel. There were still lots of things that we could have done. We mentioned some of them at the end of Section 7.1:

▲ Keep track of the amount in the user's account.
▲ Don't allow withdrawals if the user doesn't have sufficient funds.

▲ Allow withdrawals only in multiples of some fixed minimum amount, such as ten dollars.

▲ Allow the user to determine how much is in his or her account.

▲ Require the user to enter his or her PIN (personal identification number) before starting a session.

These are all interesting features and should all be part of the program. The real goal of this project, though, was to produce a program we could use as the centerpiece of the chapter, and we decided that what we had was sufficient.

Closing Advice

Programs are never finished, only released.

Review Questions

5.1 How did we get the KeyPad buttons registered with the applet listener?

5.2 Why did we include methods such as setValue() in NumField, when we knew we were never going to use them in the program?

5.3 How do you get a double value from a String representation of a number?

5.4 What made NumField's append() methods tricky?

7.6 The ATM Applet

```
//=================================================================
//   PROJECT:            _programming.java_
//   FILE:               ATM.java
//   PURPOSE:            Chapter 7 demo program, final version
//   VERSION:            2.0
//   TARGET:             Java 1.1 and above
//   UPDATE HISTORY:     2.0    11/2/98    new event model
//                       1.0     7/4/96
//=================================================================


//--------------------------- IMPORTS ----------------------------

import java.applet.*;
import java.awt.*;
import java.awt.event.*;
import Utilities.*;     // Our own package, for the Keypad and
                        // NumField classes


//========================= ATM CLASS =========================

/**
 * This applet simulates the action of an automatic teller
 * machine, consisting of a keypad, a collection of control
 * buttons, a numeric display field, and a text area for
 * instructions.
 * See _programming.java_, Chapter 7, for details and
 * specification.
 */
```

```java
public class ATM extends Applet implements ActionListener
{
    private final int    START_MODE = 0,
                         DEPOSIT_MODE = 1,
                         WITHDRAW_MODE = 2;
    private int          mode = START_MODE;

    private NumField     display = new NumField();
    private Keypad       pad = new Keypad();
    private Button       clear = new Button("Clear"),
                         enter = new Button("Enter"),
                         deposit = new Button("Deposit"),
                         withdraw = new Button("Withdraw");
    private TextArea     help = new TextArea(6, 35);

    public void init()
    {
        Panel p1 = new Panel();
        p1.setLayout(new GridLayout(4, 1, 0, 3));
        p1.add(clear);
        p1.add(enter);
        p1.add(deposit);
        p1.add(withdraw);

        Panel p2 = new Panel();
        p2.setLayout(new BorderLayout(3, 0));
        p2.add(BorderLayout.CENTER, pad);
        p2.add(BorderLayout.EAST, p1);

        Panel p3 = new Panel();
        p3.setLayout(new BorderLayout());
        p3.add(BorderLayout.NORTH, display);
        p3.add(BorderLayout.CENTER, p2);

        this.setLayout(new BorderLayout(5, 5));
        this.add(BorderLayout.CENTER, p3);
        this.add(BorderLayout.EAST, help);
        help.setEditable(false);
        this.setBackground(Color.lightGray);

        clear.addActionListener(this);
        enter.addActionListener(this);
        deposit.addActionListener(this);
        withdraw.addActionListener(this);
        pad.addActionListener(this);

        introStart();
    }

    public void actionPerformed(ActionEvent e)
    {
        Object source = e.getSource();
        switch (mode)
        {
        case START_MODE:
            if (source == deposit)
            {
                mode = DEPOSIT_MODE;
                introDeposit();
            }
```

```
            else if (source == withdraw)
            {
                mode = WITHDRAW_MODE;
                introWithdraw();
            }
            else if (source == clear)
            {
                doQuit();
            }
            else if (source == enter)
            {
                mode = START_MODE;
                introStart();
            }
            break;

    case DEPOSIT_MODE:
            if (source == enter)
            {
                handleDeposit();
            }
            else if (source == clear)
            {
                display.clear();
            }
            else if (source == pad)
            {
                String name = ((Button)source).getLabel();
                display.append(name);
            }
            break;

    case WITHDRAW_MODE:
            if (source == enter)
            {
                handleWithdrawal();
            }
            else if (source == clear)
            {
                display.clear();
            }
            else if (source == pad)
            {
                String name = ((Button)source).getLabel();
                display.append(name);
            }
            break;
    }
}

private void introStart()
{
    help.setText("             W E L C O M E\n\n");
    help.appendText("Press the Deposit or Withdraw buttons\n");
    help.appendText("to make a transaction.\n\n");
    help.appendText("Press Clear to end this session.");

    display.clear();
    clear.setEnabled(true);
    enter.setEnabled(false);
```

```
        deposit.setEnabled(true);
        withdraw.setEnabled(true);
    }

    private void introDeposit()
    {
        help.setText("                 D E P O S I T\n\n");
        help.appendText("Key in the amount of your deposit\n");
        showGeneralMessage();

        display.clear();
        clear.setEnabled(true);
        enter.setEnabled(true);
        deposit.setEnabled(false);
        withdraw.setEnabled(false);
    }

    private void introWithdraw()
    {
        help.setText("                 W I T H D R A W A L\n\n");
        help.appendText("Key in the amount of your withdrawal\n");
        showGeneralMessage();

        display.clear();
        clear.setEnabled(true);
        enter.setEnabled(true);
        deposit.setEnabled(false);
        withdraw.setEnabled(false);
    }

    /**
     * A deposit request has been made. Check whether the amount
     * in display is nonzero. If so, just go back to start mode.
     * If not, display a help message.
     */
    private void handleDeposit()
    {
        if (display.getValue() == 0.0)
        {
            help.setText("*** oops! The amount can't " + " be
                        zero\n\n");
            help.appendText("Key in the amount of your deposit\n");
            showGeneralMessage();
        }
        else
        {
            mode = START_MODE;
            introStart();
        }
    }

    /**
     * A withdrawal request has been made. Check whether the
     * amount in display is nonzero. If so, just go back to start
     * mode. If not, display a help message.
     */
    private void handleWithdrawal()
    {
        if (display.getValue() == 0.0)
        {
```

```
                    help.setText("*** oops! The amount can't " + " be
                              zero\n\n");
                    help.appendText("Key in the amount of " + " your
                              withdrawal\n");
                    showGeneralMessage();
                }
                else
                {
                    mode = START_MODE;
                    introStart();
                }
        }

        private void doQuit()
        {
            help.setText("Thank you for your business.\n\n");
            help.appendText("Have a nice day.\n\n\n");
            help appendText("Press the Enter button to start.");

            display.clear();
            clear.setEnabled(false);
            enter.setEnabled(true);
            deposit.setEnabled(false);
            withdraw.setEnabled(false);
        }

        private void showGeneralMessage()
        {
            help.appendText("and then press Enter to finish.\n\n");
            help.appendText("If you make a mistake, press Clear,\n");
            help.appendText("key in your amount again,\n");
            help.appendText("and then press Enter. ");
        }
}

package Utilities;
//================================================================
//  PROJECT:             _programming.java_
//  FILE:                Keypad.java
//  PURPOSE:             Chapter 7 demo program, Keypad class
//  VERSION:             1.0
//  TARGET:              Java 1.1 and above
//  UPDATE HISTORY:      1.0    11/2/98
//================================================================

//------------------------- IMPORTS ----------------------------

import java.awt.*;
import java.awt.event.*;

//======================= Keypad CLASS =======================

/**
 * A Keypad object contains eleven buttons, representing
 * the digits 0 through 9 and the decimal point. When
 * another class uses a Keypad object, an appropriate
 * ActionListener must be provided to the Keypad
 * constructor, by calling addActionListener().
 * We have to invent our own method for registering
```

```
 * the buttons, since the Panel class doesn't have an
 * addActionListener() method.
 */
public class Keypad extends Panel
{
    private Button b0, b1, b2, b3, b4, b5, b6,
                     b7, b8, b9, bPoint;
    /**
     * Construct a Keypad object by laying out
     * the buttons.
     */

    public Keypad()
    {
        setLayout(new GridLayout(4, 1, 4, 4));

        // Top row: 7, 8, 9 keys
        Panel p1 = new Panel();
        p1.setLayout(new GridLayout(1, 3, 4, 4));
        b7 = new Button("7");
        p1.add(b7);
        b8 = new Button("8");
        p1.add(b8);
        b9 = new Button("9");
        p1.add(b9);
        add(p1);

        // Second row: 4, 5, 6 keys
        Panel p2 = new Panel();
        p2.setLayout(new GridLayout(1, 3, 4, 4));
        b4 = new Button("4");
        p2.add(b4);
        b5 = new Button("5");
        p2.add(b5);
        b6 = new Button("6");
        p2.add(b6);
        add(p2);

        // Third row: 1, 2, 3 keys
        Panel p3 = new Panel();
        p3.setLayout(new GridLayout(1, 3, 4, 4));
        b1 = new Button("1");
        p3.add(b1);
        b2 = new Button("2");
        p3.add(b2);
        b3 = new Button("3");
        p3.add(b3);
        add(p3);

        // Bottom row: fat zero button, skinny point button
        Panel p4 = new Panel();
        p4.setLayout(new BorderLayout(7, 4));
        b0 = new Button("0");
        p4.add(BorderLayout.CENTER, b0);
        bPoint = new Button(".");
        p4.add(BorderLayout.EAST, bPoint);
        add(p4);
    }
```

```
/**
 * Register all of the buttons as sources for
 * ActionEvents to be handled by the ActionListener
 * provided in the argument.
 */
public void addActionListener(ActionListener listener)
{
    b0.addActionListener(listener);
    b1.addActionListener(listener);
    b2.addActionListener(listener);
    b3.addActionListener(listener);
    b4.addActionListener(listener);
    b5.addActionListener(listener);
    b6.addActionListener(listener);
    b7.addActionListener(listener);
    b8.addActionListener(listener);
    b9.addActionListener(listener);
    bPoint.addActionListener(listener);
}
}
```

To avoid duplication, we haven't included the `Utilities.Numfield` class here; we provided a complete listing of the finished version in the previous section.

7.7 Hands On

Design a four-function calculator. We'll give you some hints in the lab exercises, but it's high time you completed a real applet on your own. We've made it easy for you, though—notice that the calculator contains some very familiar pieces that you might want to borrow from the ATM example (see Figure 7.7). In general, of

Figure 7.7

The **Calculator** Lablet.

course, you would cite borrowed code, just as you would cite material quoted from other sources in a research paper. In a for-sale program, you'd go even further and get explicit permission from the author or owner. In this exercise, you have our blessing—use the `Keypad` and `NumField` classes and modify them as you see fit (we don't want a flood of e-mail requests for permission).

7.8 Summary

- Every method is defined within a class. There are no "free methods" in Java.
- The signature of a method consists of the name of the method and the argument list. The name of a method can be any legal Java identifier that is not a keyword. The argument list is a pair of parentheses containing a (possibly empty) comma-separated list of the form "typeName identifier."
- The compiler uses signatures to determine which method is invoked by a method call.
- A class may not have two methods with the same signature.
- The return type of a method appears before the signature in a method declaration. The return type can be a primitive type, a class type, or the keyword `void`.
- A method is called by using an instance of the method's class (or a subclass), such as

```
button1.hide();
```

- A method with a `void` return type is almost invariably called within an expression statement, such as

```
myPanel.add(button1);
```

- A call to a method with a non-`void` return type may be used anywhere a value of that type may appear.
- If a method returns a class type, the method call may be used where an instance of that type would be appropriate, such as

```
myButton.getParent().countComponents();
```

- For syntactic purposes, the dot token acts as though it were a left-associative operator with precedence higher than any other.
- A call to a method from within the same class does not require an instance name and a dot before the call. To underscore the fact that the method call is being made by the instance itself, the word `this` is a synonym for the instance.
- The keyword `this` is used to distinguish members from nonmembers of the same name, as in

```
this.x += x;   // two different "x" variables in use here
```

- When a method call is made, the actual arguments in the method call are used to initialize the formal arguments in the method definition.
- The formal argument must be of a type that is at least as wide as the type of the actual argument. For the numeric primitive types, for example, `double` is wider

than `float`, which is wider than `long`, which is wider than `int`. For class types, a class is wider than its subclasses.

- A method cannot modify the values of primitive type arguments.
- A method can modify the fields of class type arguments.
- For designing a Java program, a useful strategy is
  - Let the visual design suggest the classes.
  - Let the classes suggest the methods.
  - Let the methods dictate their statements.
- Before you begin writing a program, specify its look and its action as carefully as you can.
- Design the visual aspect of your program first.
- If you have a collection of objects that serve similar purposes, consider collecting them into a single class.
- Do GUI layout from the bottom up, collecting widgets into containers, collecting the containers into larger containers, and so on.
- The longer you can put off coding, the better off you'll be in the long run.
- Use the compiler as a tool for catching errors in syntax.
- If you have to scroll to get from the top to the bottom of a method, it is probably too long to be understood at first glance. Consider writing some `private` helper methods to pull out some of the code.
- If a class or method isn't absolutely required at any stage in the design process, just write a stub.
- Test your program frequently while writing code. Try to write your program in such a way that after every few additions and changes, you'll be able to compile and run it.
- If you find a collection of activities that are always performed as a unit, put them in a method and call the method to perform the activities.
- Try to make your code as self-documenting as possible.
- Look at the code of other programs; try to learn from what others have done.
- When designing a class someone else might use, try to anticipate what the other programmer might want.
- The primitive types all have associated wrapper classes, designed for situations when you need to use primitive types as though they were reference types.
- The wrapper classes are `Boolean`, `Character`, `Double`, `Float`, `Integer`, and `Long`. We'll discuss these classes in detail in the Class References at the end of the chapter. The wrapper classes have useful methods for converting from one type to another.
- Become familiar with the online documentation of the Java classes and methods. You can find the version 1.1 documentation at

  `http://java.sun.com/products/jdk/1.1/docs/api/packages.html`

- Just as we let the design suggest the classes and the classes suggest the methods, the methods can often suggest the variables they will require.
- If you find you've written two chunks of code that are nearly identical, consider

encapsulating them as methods. If they are already methods, see whether you can call one to implement the other.

■ Once your program is running satisfactorily, go back over the code. Is it clear? Is it well documented? Can it be streamlined? Can it be cleaned up? Edit, edit, edit!

■ Writing a program needn't be an intimidating process if you approach it systematically and carefully.

7.9 Exercises

1. Which of the following method headers are correctly formed? For those that are incorrect, explain what is wrong with them.

a. `real findInt()`

b. `char convert(x, y, z)`

c. `Point increase()`

d. `int return(double n)`

e. `void a()`

f. `function F(x : int): int`

g. `double randomNumber(void)`

h. `Component convert(Container c)`

i. `void convert(int x = 0)`

2. For the method declared as `void check(Container c, int t)`, which of the following types could be used as actual arguments? For example, in part (a) the choice `(Button int)` means that we are asking whether this method could be called with actual arguments `(myButton, 3)`. For the arguments that are not allowed, explain what is wrong with them.

a. `(Button int)`

b. `(int Button)`

c. `(Component int)`

d. `(Panel double)`

e. `(Container)`

f. `(boolean)`

g. `()`

h. `(Label byte)`

i. `(Object byte)`

3. The following two methods have different signatures, so they could be declared in the same class. It wouldn't be a good idea to declare them both, though.

```
void sum(double x, int y)
void sum(int x, double y)
```

a. Which would be invoked if we called `sum(r, s)` with variable r of type `long` and s of type `int`?

b. Here's the problem: Suppose we called `sum(p, q)` with p and q both of type `int`. Which of the above methods *could* be called?

c. Try it—run this applet. What happens? Why?

```
public class Test extends Applet
{
    private     int p = 3;
    private int q = 2;

    private TextField display = new TextField(20);

    public void init()
    {
        add(display);
        sum(p, q);
    }

    public void sum(double x, int y)
    {
        display.setText("The double/int one");
    }

    public void sum(int x, double y)
    {
        display.setText("The int/double one");
    }
}
```

4. Build the longest sequence of cascaded method calls you can, starting with the Button object myButton. Just to make this a challenging problem, you are allowed to use only one copy of each method, so you can't answer

```
myButton.getParent().getParent().getParent()
```

5. Consider the method declared as follows:

```
Point pick(Point p, Point q)
{
    if ((p.y >= q.y) && (p.x >= q.x))
        return p;
    else
        return q;
}
```

Assume we had the following code in another method in the same class.

```
// Assume Points a and b had already been declared.
Point origin = new Point(0, 0);
pick(a, b) = origin;
```

    a. Would this code be legal?
    b. What would it do?

6. Redo Exercise 5 with the following method:

```
int pick(int p, int q)
{
    if (p >= q)
        return p;
    else
        return q;
}
```

and the following code:

```
// Assume ints a and b had already been declared.
int origin = 0;
pick(a, b) = origin;
```

    a. Would this code be legal?

    b. What would it do?

7. One of the following tasks can be done and one can't.

    (1) Write a method `void stretch(int x)` that doubles the value of its argument.

    (2) Write a method `void stretch(Dimension d)` that doubles the height and width of its argument.

    a. Which can be done and which can't? Explain.

    b. Produce the code for the method that can be written.

8. Change the layout of our ATM, placing the `TextArea` *above* the `display` field, rather than on the righthand side of the applet.

9. In designing the ATM applet, we made an assumption that is quite common when moving a real-world task to the computer—we made our program look and act like the real thing. An important difference between physical objects and computer programs is the *plasticity* of programs: We can design programs to look and act in any way we wish. You have dozens of widgets available to you—use what you know to improve the user interface of the applet. In other words, draw and explain the action of a better interface, indicating why your design is better than the existing one.

10. Why didn't we make a separate class for the help text?

11. We could have pulled out much of the code of the ATM `actionPerformed()` handler into three methods:

```
private boolean startAction(Event e)

private boolean depositAction(Event e)

private boolean withdrawAction(Event e)
```

    a. Write these three methods, and write the modified `actionPerformed()` handler that would use them.

    b. Explain whether this is a worthwhile modification.

12. The `actionPerformed()` handler of the ATM class must deal with clicks on the keypad and any of the four control buttons. It is currently arranged first by mode and then by the event targets within each mode.

    a. Change the organization so that the method first checks the target of the event and then bases its action on the mode. In other words, the handler should have five major divisions corresponding to the possible targets.

    b. Is the new organization clearer than the original? Explain.

    c. In which organization would it be easier to add a new button to the applet, perhaps a "Funds" button that checked the amount in the user's account?

13. Look at the visual appearance of the `Keypad` class. We have laid out the buttons in what might be called "calculator order," with 7, 8, 9 in the top row. Now take a look at the keypad of a telephone. You'll note that the order is reversed—on telephones (and on most ATMs too), the top row contains 1, 2, 3. It would be useful to implement either order, so let's do it.

a. Make `Keypad` an abstract class and from it derive two new subclasses, `CalcPad` and `PhonePad`. For each of these, push as much functionality as you can up to the base `Keypad` class.

b. Don't subclass `Keypad`. Instead, change the constructors so that they take an `int` argument equal to one of two class constants, `KeyPad.PHONE` or `KeyPad.CALC`, and arrange the keys accordingly. You may also decide to have a default arrangement for use in constructors that don't use the order argument.

c. Discuss the advantages and disadvantages of each approach. There are two important criteria here: Which is easier for another programmer to use, and which is easier for another programmer to read and modify?

14. If the `Keypad` keys were laid out in a 4-by-3 grid, there would be room for the 11 buttons and for one more. Rewrite `KeyPad` so that it lays out its buttons in a simple grid (no fat zero button), and add one or more constructors that take a `String` argument representing the label to be used on the extra button.

15. Many computer games use the keypad to control movement, with the 8 key for moving up, the 4 key for moving left, the 6 key for moving right, and the 2 key for moving down. Modify the `Test` applet of Section 6.2 so that the movement of the dot is controlled by a `Keypad` object.

16. The `setValue()` method of `NumField` could be written without using the `String` method `valueOf()`. How? Hint: +.

17. Will `append()` methods of `NumField` allow the user to place the characters 04 in `Display`? If they will, fix them so that they won't; if they won't, explain why.

18. Does `append(String)` work correctly if the argument is the empty string? If not, how would you guard against this eventuality?

19. We could augment `NumField` by adding a method

```
void add(double d)
```

that would add `d` to the number in the text, replacing it with the new sum.

a. Write this method and add it to the class.

b. Comment on whether this is a change that *should* be made.

c. It would be silly to add this method without adding at least three more. What are they? Which of the three would be more complicated to implement than the others?

20. Here is a list of features we could have added to the ATM applet but didn't. Think about how you would add them to the program, and rank them in increasing order of how difficult you think they would be to include.

a. Keep track of the amount in the user's account. Assume that each user starts with five hundred (dollars, francs, lire, pesos, pounds, yen, or whatever your currency of choice happens to be).

b. Don't allow withdrawals if the user doesn't have sufficient funds.

c. Allow withdrawals only in multiples of some fixed minimum amount, such as ten.

d. Allow the user to determine how much is in his or her account.

e. Require the user to enter his or her PIN (personal identification number) before starting a session.

f. Make the display show exactly two digits after the decimal point.

21. (a–f). Implement the changes indicated in the preceding exercise.

22. Implement (and test, of course) the modifications to the ATM applet we listed in Exercise 19.

23. There are 21 Advice aphorisms in this chapter. If you had to pick the five most important ones to impart to a novice programmer, which would they be? Provide pithy and eloquent justifications for your choices.

7.10   Answers to Review Questions

1.1 The method name and its (formal) arguments.

1.2 A method can be defined only within some class.

1.3 The formal arguments of a method are the ones used in its definition; the actual arguments are the literals, variables, or expressions used when calling the method. The actual arguments must match the formal arguments in number and order, and the values of the actual arguments must be compatible with the types of the corresponding formal arguments.

1.4 No. A method can change the values of (accessible) instance variables of arguments of class type, but the arguments themselves cannot be changed, no matter what you do.

2.1 Start mode, deposit mode, and withdrawal mode.

2.2 To undo or complete a transaction.

2.3 Attempting to deposit or withdraw a zero amount.

3.1 A text area for instructions and a panel for everything else.

3.2 First, it was complicated and logically coherent and so belonged in a class of its own. Second, it looked to be of general enough use that we might want to have a class we could reuse in another program.

3.3 Start mode.

4.1 A method or class that contains just enough to allow it to be compiled.

4.2 With an `int` variable, `mode`, whose value was always equal to one of the class constants `START_MODE`, `DEPOSIT_MODE`, or `WITHDRAW_MODE`.

4.3 It localizes errors to be in or related to the small portion of code you just produced, making the process of tracking down errors easier.

5.1 By defining our own addActionListener() method for KeyPad.

5.2 Because it appeared that `NumField` might be useful in other programs, we tried to anticipate other features we might want it to have.

5.3 By a two-step process: (1) Use the `Double` constructor to make a `Double` from a `String`. (2) Use the `Double` method `doubleValue()` to convert from a `Double` to a (lowercase-d) `double`.

5.4 First, we had to disallow appending of any characters except those that could be part of a legitimate representation of a number. Second, we had to make sure the displayed number never had more than one decimal point.

7.11 Class References

java.lang.Boolean

This class is a "wrapper" around a value of boolean type. It is used when you need an Object equivalent of the primitive boolean type.

```
class Boolean extends Object
{
    //---------- Constructors ----------
◆   Boolean(boolean b);
    Boolean(String s);
    /*  The first constructor creates a new Boolean object
        corresponding to the argument. The second creates a TRUE
        Boolean if the argument (ignoring case) is "true", and
        creates a FALSE Boolean otherwise. */

    //-------- Class Constants ---------
    final static Boolean TRUE;
    final static Boolean FALSE;
    /*  These are the equivalents of the literals true and false.
        Note that Boolean.TRUE is not compatible with the boolean
        literal true. */

    //------------ Methods ------------
    boolean equals(Object b);
    /*  Returns true if b is Boolean and has the same value as
        this object, otherwise returns false. */
◆   boolean booleanValue();
        // Returns the boolean value represented by this object.
}
```

java.lang.Character

This class is a "wrapper" around a value of char type. It is used when you need an Object equivalent of the primitive char type. This class is fairly complicated—we'll discuss only some of it here. The overwhelming majority of methods in this class are class methods, used to test a property of an ordinary char. For example, if c were a char variable, you could test whether its value was an uppercase letter by calling Character.isUpperCase(c).

```
class Character extends Object
{
    //---------- Constructors ----------
    Character(char c);
    /*  Create a new Character object corresponding to the
        argument. */

    //-------- Class Methods ----------
◆   static boolean isDigit(char c);
◆   static boolean isLetter(char c);
    static boolean isLetterOrDigit(char c);
◆   static boolean isLowerCase(char c);
◆   static boolean isUpperCase(char c);
```

```
static boolean isSpaceChar(char c);
static boolean isWhiteSpace(char c);
/*  These test the argument for the presence or absence of
    the property named. */

static char toLowerCase(char c);
static char toUpperCase(char c);
/*  If the argument has a representation in the case
    indicated, a copy of the argument in the indicated case
    is returned. If there is no corresponding character in
    the case desired, a copy of the argument is returned. */

//------------ Methods -------------
boolean equals(Object c);
/*  Returns true if c is Character and has the same value as
    this object, otherwise returns false. */

char charValue();
    // Returns the char value represented by this object.
}
```

java.lang.Double

This class is a "wrapper" around a value of double type. It is used when you need an Object equivalent of the primitive double type.

```
class Double extends Number
{
    //---------- Constructors ----------
    Double(double d);
    /*  Create a new Double object corresponding to the
        argument. */

    Double(String s) throws NumberFormatException;
    /*  If s is a valid representation of a double value, this
        constructs a Double with value equal to that represented
        by the argument. If the argument doesn't represent a
        legal double, an exception (Ch. 9) is thrown. */

//--------- Class Methods ----------
    static String toString(double d);
        // Returns a String representing the value of the argument.

    static Double valueOf(String s) throws NumberFormatException;
    /*  If s is a valid representation of a double value, this
        constructs a Double with value equal to that represented
        by the argument. If the argument doesn't represent a
        legal double, an exception (Ch. 9) is thrown. */

    //------------ Methods -------------
    boolean equals(Object d);
    /*  Returns true if d is a Double and has the same value as
        this object, otherwise returns false. */

    double doubleValue();
        // Returns the double value represented by this object.
}
```

java.lang.Integer

This class is a "wrapper" around a value of int type. It is used when you need an Object equivalent of the primitive int type.

```
class Integer extends Number
{
    //---------- Constructors ----------
    Integer(int n);
    Integer(String s) throws NumberFormatException;
        //  These act like their Double equivalents.

    //--------- Class Methods ----------
◆   static String toString(int n);
    static Integer valueOf(String s) throws NumberFormatException;
        //  These act like their Double equivalents.

◆   static int parseInt(String s) throws NumberFormatException;
    /*  This useful class method converts the argument to the int
        it represents. If the String doesn't represent a legal
        int, this throws an exception (Ch 9). */

    //------------ Methods -------------
    boolean equals(Object n);
    /*  Returns true if n is an Integer and has the same value as
        this object, otherwise returns false. */

    double doubleValue();
    float floatValue();
◆   int intValue();
    long longValue();
    long shortValue();
    /*  These return the value represented by this object, cast
        to the appropriate type. */.
}
```

java.lang.Number

This is the abstract superclass of all the numeric-type wrapper classes: Byte, Double, Float, Integer, Long, and Short. Its primary function is as a holder for the conversion methods that are implemented by its subclasses.

```
abstract class Integer extends Object
{
    //------------ Methods -------------
    abstract byte byteValue();
    abstract double doubleValue();
    abstract float floatValue();
    abstract int intValue();
    abstract long longValue();
    abstract short shortValue();
}
```

■ CHAPTER EIGHT ■

COLLECTIONS

Java's data types come in two forms. The primitive types, such as int, float, char, and boolean, all represent single values, whereas a class is a *compound type* in that an object of a class may have several data members, rather than just one. In this chapter, we will introduce a new compound type, the array, and its big brother, Vector. We'll also discuss the String class in more detail, because a String may be thought of as having the same sort of structure as an array of characters.

Objectives

In this chapter, we will

■ Introduce some more Java programming constructs that we'll need to manipulate arrays.
■ Discuss Java's array type.
■ Investigate some ways of sorting a list of numbers.
■ Discuss the Vector class.
■ Describe the String class and show how to use String objects.

8.1 Loops

Before we begin talking about arrays, we need to introduce some more Java programming details. In Chapter 5, we saw that we could use if and switch statements to control the order of execution of a program on the basis of information about the state of a program's variables at run-time. When we are writing programs, it quickly becomes obvious that it would be useful to be able to repeat a sequence of statements, something we can't do (at least not conveniently) with what we've seen so far. Fortunately, Java provides us with three different ways to perform such *loops*, as they are known.

Consider, for instance, a simple financial problem: If you invest some money at a given annual interest rate, how many years will it take for your money to double? Knowing only what we do now (and assuming we didn't know how to solve the problem mathematically), this would be a forbidding task. Finding the amount of money at the end of a year for a given interest rate r is easy enough: If we start the year with an amount a, at the end of the year we have our original amount plus the interest, ar, for a total of $a + ar$, which is $a(1 + r)$. The problem, though, is that we have to keep repeating the "multiply by $1 + r$" step until we've at least doubled our original amount. We might have to write something like this:

```
// Assume we have a double variable, rate, containing the interest
// rate, like 0.05 for 5%

double amountSoFar = 1.0;
int years = 0;

// Compute the amount at the end of the first year
amountSoFar = (1 + rate) * amountSoFar;
years++;
if (amountSoFar >= 2.0)
    System.out.println("It took " + years + " to double");
else
{
    // Compute the amount at the end of the second year
    amountSoFar = (1 + rate) * amountSoFar;
    years++;
    if (amountSoFar >= 2.0)
        System.out.println("It took " + years + " to double");
    else
    {
        // Compute the amount at the end of the third year
        amountSoFar = (1 + rate) * amountSoFar;
        years++;
        if (amountSoFar >= 2.0)

        // ... and so on
```

Obviously, this is a Very Bad Idea, if for no other reason than that we have absolutely no idea how many `if` tests we'd have to write. Clearly, what we need is a way to write code that does something like this:

```
double amountSoFar = 1.0;
int years = 0;

// keep doing this:
{
    amountSoFar = (1 + rate) * amountSoFar;
    years++;
} // as long as (amountSoFar < 2.0);

System.out.println("It took " + years + " years to double");
```

The do Loop

Java has just what we need for cases like this. In fact, the language construct is almost an exact mirror of the "keep doing this . . . as long as some condition is satisfied" form that we saw we would need in the example above. In actual code, we would write the fragment this way:

```
double amountSoFar = 1.0;
int years = 0;
```

```
do
{
    amountSoFar = (1 + rate) * amountSoFar;
    years++;
} while (amountSoFar < 2.0);
System.out.println("It took " + years + " years to double");
```

The do loop is written

```
do
{
    statement              // one or more statements here
} while (boolean expression);   // We need the semicolon here
```

It causes the statement to be executed repeatedly, as long as the boolean expression evaluates to true. The exit test is performed at the end of each loop iteration. As with the if statement, the braces are not required if the loop controls only a single statement, but we advise using them in all cases.

Note the location of the *exit* test at the bottom of the loop. This means that the loop body of a do loop will always be performed at least once, prior to the first test. There are times, however when we want the loop test to be performed first rather than last. When that happens, we have a second loop form we can use.

exit test

The while Loop

Suppose we changed our financial problem slightly. This time, instead of finding out how long it would take to double our money, we want to determine how long it will take for an initial investment to grow to an amount greater than or equal a certain goal amount. This time we have to make the test before we add the interest and increment the year, because we have to allow for the possibility that the initial amount was actually larger than the goal. Here's the code to do this:

```
// assume we have the following double variables:
// amount, representing the amount at the start of any year
// goal, representing the desired amount
// rate, representing the interest rate

int years = 0;
while (amount < goal)
{
    amount = (1 + rate) * amount;
    years++;
}
if (years == 0)
    System.out.println("Lucky you, you already have your goal");
else
    System.out.println("It will take " + years + " years to get there");
```

The `while` loop is written

```
while (boolean expression)
{
   statement        // one or more statements here
}                   // Note, no semicolon needed
```

It causes the statement to be executed repeatedly, as long as the boolean expression is `true`. The exit test is performed at the start of each loop iteration. As with the `if` statement, we recommend the braces, even though they're not required if the loop body consists of a single statement.

Note that unlike the `do` loop, a `while` loop needs no terminating semicolon; the termination at the end of the statement body already provides the compiler with all the information it needs (either from a semicolon or from a brace) to determine where the statement ends.

The `for` Loop

The `do` and `while` loops are especially useful in cases where we don't know at the time of writing how many times the loop will be executed. Often, though, we will know exactly how many times we wish to loop. This happens so frequently that many languages include a special loop statement that uses a counter variable and increments the counter by 1 at each iteration, testing the counter value against an upper limit each time.

To see this in action, let's make one more modification to our financial problem. This time, we want to produce a table that will tell, for a given interest rate and a given starting investment, how much money we will have at the end of each year, for a given number of years. Here's what the code would look like:

```
// assume we have the following double variables:
// amount, representing the amount at the start of any year
// rate, representing the interest rate
// and an int, numYears, indicating how many years
// we will run our simulation

for (int y = 1; y <= numYears; y++)
{
   amount = (1 + rate) * amount;
   System.out.println("Year " + y + " amount = "+ amount + "\n");
}
```

The `for` loop is written

```
for (initStatement; testExpression; iterationExpression)
{
   statement                  // one or more statements
}
```

This does the following things:

1. It performs the `initStatement` (if any) once, before starting the loop.

2. The `testExpression` is evaluated at the start of each pass through the loop. If it is `false`, control passes out of the loop, down to the next statement after the loop.

3. If the `testExpression` is true, the loop body statement is performed.

4. After the loop body statement is performed, the `iterationExpression` (if any) is executed.

5. Finally, control passes back to step 2.

We could write the equivalent of the `for` statement using a `while` loop. (We'll explain the need for the extra braces in the "Common Problems with Loops" section that follows.)

```
{
    initStatement;
    while (testExpression)
    {
        statement;
        iterationExpression;
    }
}
```

It is possible to do some fancy things in a `for` loop, but in the vast majority of cases the three parts of the `for` statement (the `initStatement`, the `testExpression`, and the `iterationStatement`) take very simple forms:

```
for (int index = startValue; index <= finalValue; index++)
```

In this form, the loop iterates with `index` equal to `startValue`, `startValue + 1`, `startValue + 2`, and so on, up to `finalValue`, just as we did in our financial example above.

Just as we saw with `if` statements, the statement body of a loop can be any statement whatsoever, even another loop. For example, if instead of compounding interest once a year, we could equally well compound it monthly. To do this, we divide the interest rate by 12 and do the computations 12 times a year. In general, if interest is compounded `periodsPerYear` times each year, our table-generating code takes the following form:

```
for (int y = 1; y <= numYears; y++)
// loop through the years
{
    // for each year, loop through the compounding periods
    for (int p = 1; p <= periodsPerYear; p++)
    {
        amount = (1 + rate / periodsPerYear) * amount;
    }
    System.out.println("Year " + y + " amount = " + amount);
}
```

> Remember that every statement in a loop is executed completely for each iteration. Thus if we have one loop within another, the inner loop gets executed completely for each pass through the outer loop. In simple terms, the inner loop iterates most rapidly.

In the example above, with `numYears` equal to 5 and `periodsPerYear` equal to 2, the (y, p) values that would be used would be, in order or execution, (1, 1), (1, 2), (2, 1), (2, 2), (3, 1), (3, 2), (4, 1), (4, 2), (5, 1), (5, 2).

Common Problems with Loops

Consider this perfectly reasonable-seeming code segment:

```
// computes the sum 1 + 2 + ... + n. NOT!
int sum = 0;
for (int i = 1; i <= n; i++);
{
    sum += i;
}
```

What is the value of `sum` when this loop terminates? Surprisingly, this piece of code won't even compile! Can you spot the error? Take a close look—we'll wait.

*   *   *

There are two problems here, both caused by the semicolon immediately after the header of the loop. By placing the semicolon where we did, we were actually giving the loop an empty body. When the code is indented to show what really was going on, we have

```
int sum = 0;
for (int i = 1; i <= n; i++)
    ;               // perfectly good statement: "do nothing"
{
    sum += i;    // disaster!
}
```

> Be careful not to place a semicolon at the end of a loop header. Doing so will give the loop an empty body, not the statement or statements you expect to be iterated.

If it were permitted to execute, this loop would iterate n times, doing nothing each time. It actually wouldn't execute at all, though, because there's another problem here. The variables declared in the `for` statement's header or body have meaning *only* within the loop itself. When the compiler got to `sum += i`, it would be out of the `for` loop and so it would look for the declaration of a variable named `i`. If it had seen one earlier in the same block of code, a compile error would result; Java syntax forbids a variable declared in a loop header to have the same name as any outer variable of the same type. If no variable i had been declared earlier, Java would still generate an error during compilation, because every identifier has to be declared before it is used. (This explains why we needed the extra braces in the example on page 339.)

> Any variable declared within a for loop has meaning only within the loop.[1] The name of a variable declared in the loop header cannot be the same as that of any variable of the same type that is in an enclosing scope.

Here is another common problem is encountered in loops like this, a slight modification of the one we saw earlier:

```
double amountSoFar = 1.0;
int years = 0;
do
{
    amountSoFar = (1 + rate) * amountSoFar;
    years++;
} while (amountSoFar != 2.0);
System.out.println("It took " + years + " to double");
```

Look at the loop test: amountSoFar != 2.0. The intent is that as long as the amount hasn't doubled, we'll keep iterating. What will happen when this code executes? Think about it before going on.

*   *   *

It's very likely that it will look as though the program has frozen up. Nothing apparent will happen at all, because the loop will keep iterating and never satisfy the exit condition—namely, that amountSoFar will be *exactly* 2.0. This is a common source of error and is very hard to track down unless you know where to look.

Caution

> Whenever you design a loop, make very sure that the test expression will eventually become false, no matter what happens. If your program gets hung up in the middle of processing, there's an excellent chance it has gotten stuck in what's known as an "infinite loop," never satisfying the exit condition.

Review Questions

1.1 What is the primary difference between a while loop and a do loop?

---

[1] C and C++ programmers, take note. This is different in Java.

1.2 If n is greater than for some int n, how many passes through the loop will be made when its header is written like this?

```
for (int i = 0; i < n; i++)
```

1.3 Redo the exercise above, assuming n is −1. The question we're getting at here is "How does a for loop work when the test expression is initially false?"

8.2 Arrays

Like classes, arrays allow us to group information in a single logical unit. Arrays, however, differ from classes in three fundamental ways. First, the elements contained in an array must all be of the same type. Second, the elements in an array are *indexed* from 0 to some upper limit, so the elements of an array are accessed by number rather than by a distinct member name. Finally, although arrays have operations to inspect and manipulate their data just as classes do, you cannot add methods of your own to the array type, because arrays cannot be subclassed. In a sense, then, arrays fall somewhere between primitive types and classes.

An array is nothing more than an indexed list of elements of the same type. The *base type*—that is, the elements stored in the array—can be any type whatsoever. We can have an array of doubles, an array of Buttons, and even, as we'll see shortly, an array of arrays. In Figure 8.1 we show how an array of five doubles would be arranged.

Note that the indices begin at zero. This may seem a peculiar way to enumerate the elements in a list, but it simply is one of those historical accidents we have to live with.

> In any array of size N, the indices lie in the range 0, 1, . . . , N − 1.

Declaring Arrays

As with any Java variable, we have to declare an array before we use it. Declaring array variables is a trifle more complicated than declaring primitive types, because we need to indicate to the compiler that the variable is an array, and we also need to specify the base type of its elements. We indicate the base type as we do in any

0	1	2	3	4
3.01	−44.2	5.2e−9	0.0	0.0012

Figure 8.1

An array of five **double** values.

declaration, by putting it first, and we indicate that the variable represents an array by including a pair of square brackets. Java allows us to do this in two ways: by placing the square brackets after the variable name or by placing them after the type name, like this

```
double readings[];      // These declarations are both legal.
double[] readings;
```

Declaring an array, like declaring a class variable, simply tells the compiler what type the variable is. It doesn't allocate any space in memory for the array, nor does it initialize any of the elements in the array. To initialize an array variable, we must do the same thing we do when we initialize a class variable—use the new operator. In the example above, for instance, we could set aside space in memory for the array readings by writing

```
readings = new double[5];    // readings is an array with 5 zeros.
```

This initialization would set aside room in memory for five double values and would set them to the default value for doubles, namely 0.0. Most of the time, we would do the declaration and the initialization at the same time by writing

```
double readings[] = new double[5];
```

Caution

> It's a common mistake to declare an array without eventually initializing it. Get in the habit of doing both at the same time whenever you can.

Of course, we may not be satisfied with the default values for the elements in an array. If we know in advance what the element values will be, Java allows us to specify them, in a manner similar to the way we can specify the initial value of a primitive type. The only difference is that we use braces to group a comma-separated list values. For example, to initialize the array in Figure 8.1, we could write

```
double readings[] = {3.01, -44.2, 5.2e-9, 0.0, 0.0012} ;
```

Note that in this example, we don't use the new operator and we don't specify the size of the array. Java will call new for us and will use the size of the list to determine the size of the array. Although the example above used constant values for the initialization list, we could also compute the values "on the fly," like this:

```
double angles[] = {0.0, Math.PI / 3, 2 * Math.PI / 3, Math.PI} ;
```

If we are using class elements for the base type of an array, we can do the same sort of initializing, placing in the list the expressions we would use to initialize any single variable of the base type, as in this example:

```
Button controls[] = {new Button("Left"), new Button("Up"),
                     new Button("Down"), new Button("Right")} ;
```

Accessing Array Elements

Once we have declared and initialized an array variable, we may inspect and modify its elements by using the variable name followed by a pair of square brackets containing an integer expression. The integer expression is evaluated, and the result will be the index value of the element to be accessed. For example, readings[2] will refer to the index-2 element of the array readings (the element containing 5.2e-9, in our example). Note that readings[2] will be the third element in the array, because indices start at zero.

> Don't forget that arrays in Java begin with index 0. This means that an array declared by int value[] = new int[3] will have elements value[0], value[1], and value[2] and that value[2] will be the third element in the array.

An element in an array can be used any way an ordinary variable of that type can be used. For example, given the declaration at the beginning, all of the subsequent statements are legal:

```
int value[] = new int[3];
value[0] = 34;
value[1] = 2 * value[0]++;
value[2] = 2 * value[1] - value[0];
if ((value[0] < value[1]) && (value[1] < value[2]))
    System.out.println("The list is in sorted order");
int sum = 0;
for (int i = 0; i < 3; i++)
{
    sum += value[i];
}
```

As the last line above indicates, the contents of the square bracket can be any integer-valued expression. We could equally well write value[j + 2 * k], for instance, as long as the expression j + 2 * k evaluated to 0, 1, or 2. If it didn't, Java would detect that at run-time and generate an error. If you have C or C++ experience, you'll notice that Java is better behaved than you're used to; it does *range checking* and will tell you if you are trying to access an element by using an index that's out of the allowable range for the array in question (such as value[-1] or value[677], for example).

range checking

Arrays and Loops

Loops and arrays are natural companions. Often, we will use a loop to perform the same actions on each element of an array. We saw that in the last two lines of the example above, where we computed the sum of all the elements in an array.

```
int sum = 0;                    // Initialize sum to zero.
for (int i = 0; i < 3; i++)     // For every element in the array...
{
    sum += value[i];            // add that element to the sum.
}
```

As a slightly more involved example, suppose we wanted to find the index of the smallest element at or after index `start`. To do this, we would keep track of the index, `minIndex`, of the smallest element we had seen so far, and for each element in the array from `start` to the end of the array, we would compare that element to the element in position `minIndex`. If the current element was smaller than the smallest we had seen so far, we would mark its location as the next `minIndex`. This *linear search*, where we inspect each array element, in order, until some condition is met, is a very important programming idiom. Here's what it would look like as a method:

linear search idiom

```
int mindex(int[] theArray, int start)
// Returns the index of the smallest element at or after the
// index start.
{
    int minIndex = start;
    for (int i = start; i < theArray.length; i++)
    {
        // For each index in the array...
        if (theArray[i] < theArray[minIndex])
        {
            // Found a new smallest value, so record its index.
            minIndex = i;
        }
    }
    return minIndex;
}
```

A couple of things are worth noting here. First, you can see that we can pass an array as a method argument simply by making what looks like a declaration in the argument list, as we did when we wrote `int[] theArray`. Second, in the loop header, we made use of an instance variable, `length`, that every array has. The `length` field, as you might expect, contains the length of the array—namely, one more than the highest legal array index.

length field of an array

> Arrays are like classes in that if an array is used as a method argument, the elements of the array may be modified by the method.

When using loops in general, and particularly when using loops with arrays, we have to be especially careful. The smallest mistake in writing loops can lead to methods that don't work as we expect them to or, worse still, don't work at all. We'll point out some of the most common problems with loops by considering several attempts to solve the following problem.

Write a method int prefixSum(int[] a) that will return the sum of the elements in a, up to but not including the first negative number. For example, if the array argument contains {0, 9, 4, 0, 4, –3, 2, 1, 1, –8, 3}, the method will return the sum 0 + 9 + 4 + 0 + 4 = 17.

Here's our first attempt:

```
int prefixSum(int[] a)
// Attempt 1. WRONG
{
   int i = 0,
       sum = 0;
   do
   {
       sum += a[i];
   } while (a[i] >= 0);
   return sum;
}
```

This is dismal. Unless a[0] is negative, it will never leave the loop, because we never increase the index i. We said it before, but it's important enough to bear repetition.

Caution

When you design a loop, make very sure that there's *always* a way out.

It's a good idea to ask yourself, "Under what conditions should I leave the loop?" Then negating that condition will provide the loop control expression. In our case, there are *two* conditions that will cause us to leave the loop: when we encounter a negative value for a[i] *or* when i is greater than or equal to a.length, indicating that we've run out of array elements to inspect. (Note that we missed the latter condition completely in attempt 1.) Our exit condition is then

```
(a[i] < 0) || (i >= a.length)
```

so its negation, the expression that keeps us in the loop, is

```
(a[i] >= 0) && (i < a.length)
```

Or is it? No! We need i < a.length as a *guard* for the first clause; otherwise, we'll run the risk of trying to access an element with a bad index. The correct control condition is

```
(i < a.length) && (a[i] >= 0)
```

Caution

Unless you are certain that you're looking at a legal index in an array, guard the access with a test against the upper and lower possible index values.

Here's the next attempt, this time with the right control expression.

```
int prefixSum(int[] a)
// Attempt 2.  STILL WRONG
{
    int i = 0,
        sum = 0;
    do
    {
        sum += a[i];
        i++;
    } while ((i < a.length) && (a[i] >= 0));
    return sum;
}
```

This is better, but it still won't work right. The problem here is that we're adding the element a[i] *before* we test whether it's negative. This is a classic off-by-one error—our sum will include the negative "sentinel" value and therefore will be smaller than it should be. We need to rearrange the loop so that we test a[i] *before* we add it in, like this:

off-by-one error

```
int prefixSum(int[] a)
// Attempt 3. CORRECT, finally
{
    int i = 0,
        sum = 0;
    while ((i < a.length) && (a[i] >= 0))
    {
        sum += a[i];
        i++;
    }
    return sum;
}
```

Finally, let's take a look at one more attempt, this time using a for loop.

```
int prefixSum(int[] a)
// Attempt 4. CORRECT but inelegant
{
    int sum = 0;
    for (int i = 0; i < a.length; i++)
    {
        if (a[i] < 0)
            return sum;
        else
            sum += a[i];
    }
    return sum; // We got all the way to the end
                // without seeing a negative value.
}
```

This is correct, but we're doing two things we shouldn't do. First, we're using an extra test statement inside the loop body, which makes our code that much more complicated and that much harder to read. Second, we're using a return statement to break out of the loop. Such an "emergency exit" is acceptable in some cases, but generally it should be reserved for just that—emergencies. It's much clearer if we write the loop so that the exit is controlled by the loop control, like this:

```
int prefixSum(int[] a)
// Attempt 5.  CORRECT, and tidier (but we slightly prefer version 3)
{
    int sum = 0;
    for (int i = 0; (i < a.length) && (a[i] >= 0); i++)
    {
        sum += a[i];
    }
    return sum;
}
```

Advice

> Loops that are controlled by counting (that is, loops that are known to iterate a fixed number of times) are best written with a for statement. Loops that are controlled by some logical condition (that is, loops that will iterate as long as some condition is satisfied) should be written with while or do loops. If there is a possibility that the loop's body will never be executed, use a while loop. If the body must be executed at least once, consider using a do loop.

Multidimensional Arrays

In some programming languages, arrays are not limited to a single dimension. A two-dimensional array, for example, can be considered to be arranged in tabular form, with each element identified by two indices, one for the row and one for the column. Java, like its ancestors C and C++, does not provide direct support for multidimensional arrays, in part because it doesn't need to. The elements of an array can be any type at all, so we can make a two-dimensional array, for example, by making an array of arrays. Consider, for instance, how we would make a 3 × 4 table. We could make the declaration

```
double table[][] = new double[4][3];
```

which would declare table to be an array of arrays and initialize it to a four-element array, each element of which was itself a three-element array, as we illustrate in Figure 8.2.

The initialization syntax is, we'll admit, a trifle confusing. You can take comfort in the knowledge that it really doesn't matter how you think of such declarations (Is the 4 the number of rows or the number of columns?) as long as you pick one interpretation and stick to it consistently.

We could, of course, do the same sort of thing to make three-dimensional arrays, or arrays with arbitrarily large dimensionality (though the pictures get pretty hard to draw beyond two dimensions). We can initialize multidimensional arrays with a list of values, much as we did with one-dimensional arrays. To fill the table above, for example, we could instead make the declaration initialization

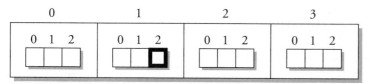

This is the way the array is arranged in memory

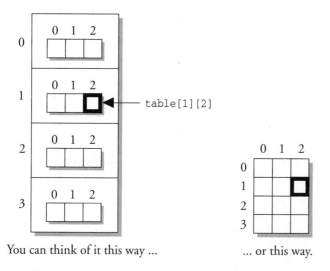

You can think of it this way ...   ... or this way.

Figure 8.2

Three ways to think of an array **double[4][3]**.

```
double table[][] = {{0.0, 0.1, 0.2} , {1.0, 1.1, 1.2} ,
                    {2.0, 2.1, 2.2} , {3.1, 3.0, 3.2} } ;
```

To inspect all the elements in a multidimensional array, we commonly use several loops, one inside another. For instance, suppose we wanted to find the row and column of the smallest element in a two-dimensional array of doubles. We could modify our mindex() example, presented earlier, to search through each column of each row, like this:

```
/**
 * Return a point containing the row and column indices where a
 * minimal element in the array argument is found.
 */
Point mindex2D(double[][] a)
{
    Point location = new Point();
    double minSoFar = a[0][0];
    // Iterate down the rows
    for (int row = 0; row < a.length; row++)
```

```
    {
        // For each row, iterate across the columns in that row
        for (int col = 0; col < a[row].length; col++)
        {
            if (a[row][col] < minSoFar)
            {
                location.x = row;
                location.y = col;
                minSoFar = a[row][col]
            }
        }
    }
    return location;
}
```

Recall that nested loops have the property that the innermost loop goes through a complete cycle for each iteration of the outer loop. In our example, then, we would inspect the elements of the array a in the order a[0][0], a[0][1], a[0][2], …, a[1][0], a[1][1], a[1][2], … , a[2][0], a[2][1], a[2][2], … and so on.

Here's another example of inspecting every element in a two-dimensional array. This time, we want to find the *minimax* element—that is, the smallest of all the row maxima. For example, in the array

2	7	5
8	4	1
1	2	**3**

the maximal elements in each row are, respectively, 7, 8, and 3, and the minimal element among the maxima is 3. Here's how we could do this:

```
/**
 * Return the smallest of all the row maxima in the argument
 * array.
 */
int minimax(int[][] a)
{
    int minimaxSoFar = a[0][0];

    // Iterate down the rows
    for (int row = 0; row < a.length; row++)
    {
        // Record the largest element so far in this row.
        int thisRowMax = a[row][0];
        // Find the largest element in this row.
        for (int col = 0; col < a[row].length; col++)
        {
            if (a[row][col] > thisRowMax)
            {
                thisRowMax = a[row][col]
            }
        }

        // Done with this row; see if we've found a new
        // smallest max.
```

```
        if (thisRowMax < minimaxSoFar)
        {
            minimaxSoFar = thisRowMax;
        }
    }
    // We've finished looking at all the array elements,
    // so send back the answer.
    return minimaxSoFar;
}
```

Finally, a potentially useful feature of Java arrays is that because of the way they are declared, they need not be "rectangular" (see Figure 8.3). If we wish, we could defer the initialization of the "inner" pieces by not specifying their sizes. If we had made the declarations

```
double pyramid[][] = new double[4][];
pyramid [0] = new double[1];
pyramid [1] = new double[3];
pyramid [2] = new double[5];
pyramid [3] = new double[7];
```

we would have created a structure with one element in the first row, three elements in the second, five elements in the third, and seven elements in the last row. Such a structure is sometimes called a "ragged array."

Heterogeneous Arrays

We said before that the elements of an array must all be of the same type. That's true enough, but it shouldn't stop you from making a *heterogeneous array*, whose elements are of different types, when you need to. Consider the following applet, for example.

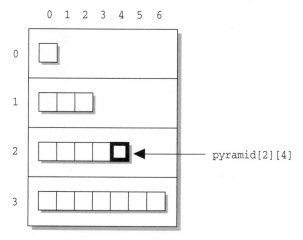

Figure 8.3

Java arrays need not be rectangular.

```
public class Test extends Applet
{
    private Component[] c = new Component[3];

    public void init()
    {
        c[0] = new Button("button");
        c[1] = new Label("label");
        c[2] = new TextField("text");

        for (int i = 0; i < 3; i++)
            this.add(c[i]);
    }
}
```

The array c, you will observe, contains a Button, a Label, and a TextField. Well, that's the way it appears to us, at least. In fact, as far as the compiler is concerned, all of the elements are the same type, Component. Because Component is a wider type than Button, Label, and TextField (that is, because Component is a superclass of all three of these), we can initialize any of c[0], c[1], and c[2] to instances of the subclasses, which is exactly what we did in the applet.

In the above example, the only tricky part would come from our trying to have one of the c[i]s call a method that wasn't a Component method. For example, if we wanted to set the label of the Button c[0], we couldn't make this call:

```
c[0].setLabel("OK");
```

because setLabel() isn't a Component method. Instead, we'd have to make an explicit type cast,

```
((Button)c[0]).setLabel("OK"); // see footnote[2]
```

Although you generally wouldn't use a heterogeneous array in a situation like the applet above, they do come in handy. Suppose, for instance, that we were making a program to keep track of employee records. We might have a collection of classes like this:

```
abstract class Employee
{
    static final double DEDUCTION = 35;    // applies to everyone
    abstract double getPay();
    ...
}

class Salaried extends Employee
{
    private double salary;
    ...
    double getPay()
    {
```

---

[2]We need the parentheses because the dot binds more tightly than the cast operator, and we have to perform the cast *before* we use the dot to call the method.

```
            return salary - DEDUCTION;
      }
}

class Hourly extends Employee
{
   private double hourlyRate;
   private double hoursWorked;
   ...
   double getPay()
   {
      return hourlyRate * hoursWorked - DEDUCTION;
   }
}
```

We could then set up an array containing all the workers by declaring

```
Employee[] emps = new Employee[3];    // a small company
```

Then we could initialize c[0] to be a new Salaried employee and c[1] and c[2] to be new Hourly employees, for instance, all in the same array. Now to compute the total payroll, we could use a loop to iterate through the array:

```
double totalPayroll = 0.0;
for (int i = 0; i < 3; i++)
{
   totalPayroll += emps[i].getPay();
}
```

We don't need to do any type casting here. Because Employee is a class with an abstract getPay() method, the system will look at the type of each element at runtime and decide which getPay() method would be appropriate to call.

We could even do the same thing with the primitive types, but first we'd have to change them to class types by using the wrapper classes we mentioned in the last chapter. For example, if we wanted to put the int 34, the double 6.2e+2, and the float 2.008f into one array, we could use the wrapper classes Integer, Double, and Float to make new class instances of these numbers and then use the Number superclass to make our array, like this:

```
Number[] nums = new Number[3];
Integer i = new Integer(34);
Double d = new Double(6.2e+2);
Float f = new Float(2.008f);
nums[0] = i;
nums[1] = d;
nums[2] = f;
```

Each of the numeric wrapper classes has a method doubleValue() overriding Number's abstract doubleValue() method, so, just as we did with employees, we could add the elements of nums like this:

```
double sum = 0.0;
for (int i = 0; i < 3; i++)
{
   sum += nums[i].doubleValue();
}
```

Review Questions

2.1 What is the usual way of visiting all elements of an array a?

2.2 Can an array be composed of elements of different types?

2.3 How would you refer to the last element in an array a?

2.4 Explain the difference between the declarations

```
int a[];     and     int b[] = new int[3];
```

2.5 In simple terms, what do we mean by the "linear search idiom"?

8.3 Sorting

As long as we are doing examples of array processing, we may as well include one more, one that illustrates a common task: sorting the elements in an array. The problems of sorting and searching an array for a particular value constitute a large research topic in computer science; the standard reference on these problems is over 700 pages long!

Selection Sort

You've already seen a searching algorithm: `mindex()` inspected each element in an array and returned the index where an element of minimal size is located. We can use the code of `mindex()` to build a method that sorts. The method we will construct will take an array as its sole argument and will rearrange the array's elements so that they are in sorted order, from smallest to largest. The algorithm we will use is very simple—though not particularly efficient—and is known as *Selection Sort* (see Figure 8.4). In this scheme, suppose that at some step all the elements from indices 0 to i-1 are already in their final sorted order. We will then use `mindex()` to find the index of the smallest element in the array from position i to the end. Having found the location of the smallest remaining element, we will swap it with the

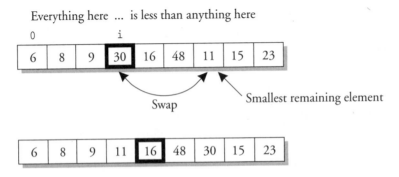

Figure 8.4

One pass of Selection Sort.

one in position i. Thus, at each stage, we start with the sorted elements in positions 0 to i-1 and end with the sorted elements in positions 0 to i. Repeating this, we will eventually have the entire array in sorted order.

Figure 8.5 illustrates the action of Selection Sort on the array that initially contains the values (15, 23, 8, 30, 16, 48, 11, 6, 9). Note that after each pass, the highlighted element has been replaced with the smallest value at or after the highlighted location.

```
/*
 * Sorts the array argument's elements in increasing order.
 */
void selectionSort(int[] a)
{
    for (int i = 0; i < a.length - 1; i++)
    {
        // Find the index of the smallest element in
        // a at or after position i.
        int minPos = mindex(a, i);

        // Swap current element with the smallest remaining.
        int temp = a[i];
        a[i] = a[minPos];
        a[minPos] = temp;
    }
}
```

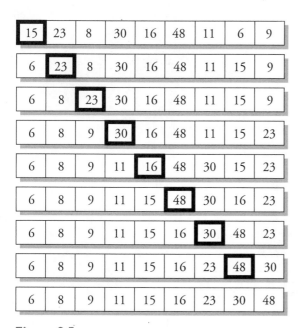

Figure 8.5

Selection Sort in action.

Insertion Sort

Selection Sort is by no means the only possible way to sort a list of objects. If you're a card player, think for a moment about the algorithm you use to sort a hand of cards. Many people use a manual version of Selection Sort, but another common way of arranging cards is to work from left to right and, for each card encountered, to place that card in its proper place among the cards to its left. In this scheme, as in Selection Sort, the elements to the left of the current position are in sorted order, but unlike Selection Sort, the elements in the left segment may not be in their final positions. This algorithm is known as *Insertion Sort*, and in Figure 8.6 we show what happens in one pass.

At the start of the pass, we save the value of the current element. Then we walk our way down the array, shifting each element that is larger than the saved element up one position, and stop when we find an element that is smaller than the saved value (or when we find ourselves at the start of the array). Finally, we place the saved element where it belongs.

```
/*
 * Sorts the array argument's elements in increasing order.
 */
public void InsertionSort(int[]
{
    for (int i = 1; i < a.length; i++)
    // For every element except the leftmost one,
    // insert it where it belongs in the sorted segment
    // to its left.
    {
        int currentValue = a[i],
            index = i;
        // Walk down from the current position, i,
        // shifting up every element larger than temp.
        while ((index >= 1) && (currentValue < a[index - 1]))
```

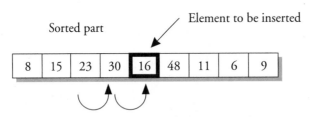

Figure 8.6

One pass of Insertion Sort.

```
        {
            a[index] = a[index - 1];
            index--;
        }
        // Now we know where currentValue belongs,
        // so put it there.
        a[index] = currentValue;
    }
}
```

Figure 8.7 shows how Insertion Sort rearranges the same array we used in Figure 8.5. Note that some of the passes (the first, third, and fifth, in this example) have no work to do after the first comparison, because the element to be inserted happens to be larger than any of those to its left and so is already where it belongs. This "short-circuit" feature, where some passes have only one comparison to do, differs sharply from the situation in Selection Sort, where we always have to do the same number of comparisons to find the minimal element, regardless of how the data is arranged. Insertion Sort is particularly efficient when the initial array is very nearly sorted, as you can see by considering how it would act in the limiting case, when the initial array happens already to be arranged in sorted order. In that lucky case, for an array of size N, Selection Sort will make (as always) $1 + 2 + \cdots + (N - 1)$ com-

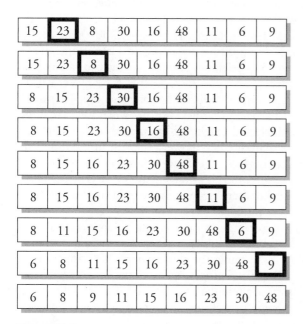

Figure 8.7

Insertion Sort in action.

parisons (why?), whereas Insertion Sort will make only $N - 1$. To see what this means in practice, consider that on a perfectly sorted list of $N = 1000$ elements, Selection Sort will make 499,500 comparisons, compared to the 999 that Insertion Sort would make.

We should be honest and point out that although Insertion Sort can use far fewer comparisons than Selection Sort (and uses about half as many comparisons in the "average" case), when we consider the number of data moves each of the algorithms makes, Selection Sort clearly has the edge. At each pass, Selection sort makes only one swap, to place the minimal element at the current position, whereas Insertion Sort may have to do a lot of data moves if the current element is smaller than nearly all the elements to its left. As with many problems in computer science, there's no "best" choice in this case: If you have reason to believe the input data is nearly sorted to begin with, Insertion Sort is clearly the winner, but if the number of data moves is important (if, for example, the data elements are very large and hence will take significant time to copy), then Selection Sort is to be preferred.

Quicksort

Although there may be no clear reason to pick either Insertion Sort or Selection Sort to sort an array, there are good reasons to choose *neither*. We'll conclude our introduction to sorting by considering one more sorting technique, one that generally runs far faster than either of the two we've covered so far. Let's begin with the observation that Insertion Sort is inefficient primarily because it moves the data so slowly, shifting an element by only one position per step. We'd be in much better shape if we could find a way, as we do in Selection Sort, of moving the data near its ultimate resting place more rapidly.

Suppose that we had a list of numbers we wished to sort, and suppose further that we were willing to settle for "partial" sortedness, so that when we were done, the list would be rearranged into a left and a right sublist, in such a way that every element in the left sublist was less than or equal to every element in the right sublist. For example, starting with the list 4, 5, 2, 1, 3, we might be content to wind up with the rearrangement 3, 1, 2; 5, 4. In this arrangement, every element in the left sublist 3, 1, 2 is less than or equal to every element in the right sublist 5, 4. Does this lead to anything useful? You bet it does.

Note that the left sublist is in its correct position. The individual *elements* of the sublist aren't where they should be, but the sublist itself is. The same property, of course, holds for the right sublist. Now comes the clever part: What happens if we apply the same "rearrange into two sublists" process again, to the left and right sublists? Nothing we do to either sublist alters the fact that the lists are where they should be, and every time we apply the partial sort to a sublist, we'll wind up with two smaller sublists, each of which is in its correct position. For example, the sublist 3, 1, 2 might get rearranged to be 2, 1; 3 and the right sublist must necessarily become the two smaller lists 4; 5. Now our entire list looks like 2, 1; 3; 4; 5. That's almost perfectly sorted, and it becomes perfectly sorted as soon as we do the last

original list

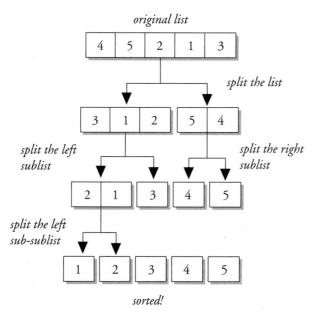

Figure 8.8

QuickSort in action.

partial sort on the sublist 2, 1. We illustrate this algorithm, which is called *Quick-Sort*, in Figure 8.8.

Quicksort is almost too good to be true. Because the elements in every sublist are no further from their correct—sorted—positions than the size of the sublist, as long as we can guarantee that at every stage a sublist will be split into two nonempty sub-sublists, we will eventually wind up with a collection of lists of size one, each of which consists of a single element in its correct position.

The real beauty of this scheme, though, comes from the elegant way we can write it as a method. Quicksort illustrates a common programming idiom known as *divide and conquer:* Solve a problem by breaking it into two or more smaller instances and solving the instances separately. Often, you can write the definition of a method to solve a problem by *using calls to itself* on smaller instances, and that's exactly what we do here:

divide and conquer idiom

```
/**
 * Sort the list in array a, from positions [start] to [end].
 */
void quickSort(int[] a, int start, int end)
{
    // We have nothing to do if start == end, since a
    // one-element list is already sorted.
```

```
    if (start < end)
    {
        // Rearrange (somehow) a into two subarrays, from
        // a[start] to a[split] and from a[split+1] to a[end],
        // in such a way that every element in the left part is
        // less than or equal to every element in the right part.
        int split = partition(a, start, end);

        // Now sort the left sublist
        quickSort(a, start, split);

        // and sort the right sublist.
        quickSort(a, split + 1, end);
    }
}
```

recursion   There's nothing illegal in Java about a method that calls itself. Such *recursive* methods, as they are known, are in fact rather common. Consider, for example, the Component method getPreferredSize(), which returns the Dimension that this component would "like" to be, using its current layout manager. A component might contain other components, so we would compute its preferred size by some calculation involving the preferred sizes of all the components it contains, thus defining getPreferredSize() by a number of calls to c.getPreferredSize(), for each component c that this component might contain.

As we mentioned before, Quicksort seems too simple to be right, but on the basis of our understanding of recursion, it seems as though it has to work. Quick-Sort clearly works correctly on lists with a single element (that's known as the *base case*, the way out of the routine), and if it sorts lists of size smaller than *n*, it will certainly work on lists of size *n* (that's the *recursive case*, after we invoke partition() to produce the two sublists).

Of course, all the real work of QuickSort() is done by the helper method partition(). The idea behind partition() is also rather clever: We work our way inward from positions start and end, and every time we find a pair of elements that are in the wrong sublists, we swap them.

```
/**
 * Rearrange the portion of the array a so that each element
 * in a[start] ... a[split] is less than or equal to each element
 * in a[split+1] ... a[end], and return the index "split."
 */
int partition(int[] a, int start, int end)
{
    // Start with two indices, top and bottom, just
    // outside of the list we're partitioning.
    int bottom = start - 1,
        top = end + 1;

    // Pick a value pivot. We'll rearrange the list by putting
    // on the left all values <= pivot and on the right all
    // values >= pivot.
    int pivot = a[start];

    // Walk bottom and top towards each other, using them
    // to swap array elements as we go, and stopping when
    // bottom and top pass each other.
```

```
while (bottom < top)
{
    // Walk up until you find an element that's
    // not in its correct sublist.
    do
    {
        bottom++;
    } while (a[bottom] < pivot);

    // Walk down until you find an element that's
    // not in its correct sublist.
    do
    {
        top--;
    } while (a[top] > pivot);

    // Swap a[bottom] and a[top], thus putting
    // the values in the correct sublists.
    int temp = a[bottom];
    a[bottom] = a[top]
    a[top] = temp;
}
// Undo the last swap, that took place after the bottom
// and top indices passed each other.
int temp = a[bottom];
a[bottom] = a[top]
a[top] = temp;

// Finally, return the split index.
return top.
}
```

Figure 8.9 illustrates how partition() works on the list 4, 5, 2, 1, 3. After two swaps it is finished, having produced the sublists 3, 1, 2 and 5, 4.

As if it weren't enough for QuickSort to be elegant and simple, we get another benefit as well: Except for very small lists, QuickSort is considerably faster than either Selection Sort or Insertion Sort. We coded and ran all three on the same data sets and found that for lists of 1000 elements, QuickSort averaged about 8 times faster than Insertion Sort (and 18 times faster than Selection Sort). The speed difference, becomes more pronounced the larger the lists are: On lists of 2000 elements, QuickSort beat Insertion Sort by a factor of better than 17.7, and for lists of size 4000, QuickSort was over 30 times faster than Insertion Sort! Think of it this way: For really large lists, you might have time to go out for coffee while QuickSort was running, but for Insertion Sort or Selection Sort, you'd have time to go to Colombia and pick the beans.

Review Questions

3.1 How would you describe Selection Sort to someone who had never seen it?
3.2 Selection Sort and Insertion Sort are similar in that at any intermediate step, some initial portion of the array is in sorted order. In which of the two sorts are the initial elements actually in their ultimate resting places?
3.3 What do we mean by a recursive definition?

Begin with `pivot` = 4, the starting element.

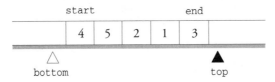

Move bottom up and top down, until we
find `a[bottom]` ≥ `pivot` and `a[top]` ≤ `pivot`.

Swap the elements and continue moving `bottom`
and `top` until we find another pair to swap.

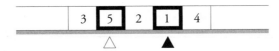

Swap the elements and keep moving.
We stop when `bottom` and `top` pass each other.

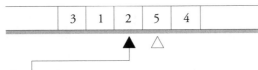

Done; return the top index.

Figure 8.9

Tracing the action of **partition()**.

8.4 Vectors

Arrays are exceedingly useful; indeed, it would be a rare medium-to-large program that didn't use arrays in some form or another. You've seen that arrays have several strong "selling points"—they're easy to use, and they're natural candidates for any collection of information that can be thought of in list-like order, with a first element, a second, a third, and so on.

The disadvantages of arrays arise, paradoxically, from the fact that they are so useful. You don't have to write too many programs using arrays before you hear yourself wishing, "If only there were an easy way of doing. . . ." The problem is that arrays, as they come "off the shelf," are exceptionally handy data containers, but they don't do much more than that. Arrays can't grow or shrink; there's no easy way of inserting a new element in an array without overwriting an element that's already there; there's no easy way to remove an element from an array while leaving the other elements unchanged; and there's no built-in way of determining whether an array contains a particular element.

The Vector Class

The Vector class, in the java.util package, was designed in response to the "wish lists" that come from experience with arrays. A Vector object is a linear collection of elements, indexed 0, 1, 2 . . . , just like an array. Vectors differ from arrays in three important ways. First, unlike arrays, vectors are *dynamic*—their size can be modified at any time. The second difference is that there is only one choice for the element type: A Vector object is always a container of elements of Object type. The third difference between arrays and vectors is that the Vector class comes with an extensive suite of powerful methods for manipulating the underlying array and its elements. We'll cover the basics of the Vector class in this section and will provide a more thorough description in the Class References at the end of this chapter.

There are three constructors for this class:

```
Vector(int initialCapacity, int capacityIncrement);
Vector(int initialCapacity);
Vector();
```

Think of a vector as an array into which you can place Objects. At first, there is nothing useful in the array, even though there is a *capacity* to store a certain number of Objects. As you place objects in the array, its logical *size* will increase, until such time as the size has increased to be the same as the capacity. Then, in order for us to add a new object to the array, its capacity must increase. The first constructor above allows you to set the initial capacity and the amount by which the capacity will increase when necessary. For example, if you declare a new vector by

```
Vector v = new Vector(3, 5);
```

The vector v will initially have room for three objects. If you then call v.addElement() three times, three objects will be placed in the vector, filling it to capacity. If you then try to add a new element, the vector must grow to make room for it, which it will do by increasing the capacity by the capacityIncrement. In this case, the result will be a bigger internal array with 3 + 5 = 8 available spaces and with valid data in the first four, in positions 0 through 3, as we illustrate in Figure 8.10.

initialCapacity must be greater than 0, and capacityIncrement must be greater than or equal to 0. If capacityIncrement is 0, when the time comes to grow the internal array, its capacity will be increased to twice the current size. If capacityIncrement isn't specified (as in the second two constructors), it will default to zero, and if initialCapacity isn't specified in the last constructor, it will default to a capacity of 10.

```
Vector v = new Vector(3, 5);
```

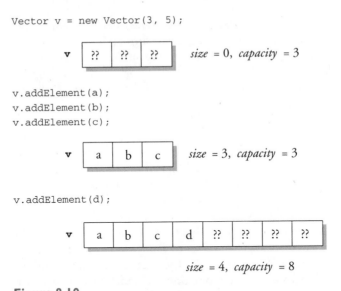

```
v.addElement(a);
v.addElement(b);
v.addElement(c);
```

```
v.addElement(d);
```

Figure 8.10

The effect of growth on size and capacity of a vector.

Inspectors

There are several methods that can be used to inspect the state of a Vector object and its contents. Like nearly all of the Vector methods, these are final, which you'll recall means that they can't be redefined in any Vector subclass you might define.

```
int size()
int capacity()
```

These return the size (the number of valid objects in the internal array) and the capacity (the length of the internal array) of this vector.

```
boolean isEmpty()
```

Returns true if this vector contains no valid elements (that is, if a call to size() would return 0).

```
boolean contains(Object obj)
```

Returns true if this vector contains at least one reference to the argument object, and false if it doesn't.

```
int indexOf(Object obj)
int indexOf(Object obj, int start)
```

The first of these returns the index in the internal array of the first instance of the argument, if any, and returns –1 if the argument object is not contained in this vector. The second method acts much like the first, except that it returns the index of the first instance of the object at or after the *start* position, and returns -1 if there is no instance of the argument in positions start, . . . , size() - 1. The start index must be a valid index (that is, start ≥ 0 and start < size()).

```
Object firstElement()
Object lastElement()
```

Return a reference to the first or last elements in this vector—namely, the object in position 0 or the element in position size() - 1, respectively. These methods will generate errors if the vector is empty.

```
Object elementAt(int index)
```

Perhaps the most often used method in this class, this returns a reference to the element in position index. Of course, the argument must be a valid index, satisfying the conditions we mentioned above. This is the Vector equivalent of the [] operator, so v.elementAt(2) returns the object in position 2—namely, the third from the start.

Modifiers

The rest of the Vector methods that we will discuss here modify the object that calls them.

```
void setElementAt(Object obj, int index)
```

This places the object in the argument at the specified position, replacing whatever was there. As usual, the specified index must be valid, which means that it must be greater than or equal to zero and less than the size of this vector.

```
void addElement(Object obj)
```

This adds the argument object to the end of the vector, increasing the size by 1 and growing the internal array if necessary.

```
void insertElementAt(Object obj, int index)
```

This nifty method saves a lot of programmer effort. It places the argument object in the specified position, first shifting all elements in later positions up by one. For example, if the vector v initially contained {A, B, C}, then after a call to v.insertElementAt(X, 1), v would contain {A, X, B, C} , shifting B, C, and D up one position and placing X in the resulting "hole." The index must be greater than or equal to zero and less than or equal to size(). Note that this means that

```
v.insertElementAt(X, v.size());
```

has the same effect as

```
v.addElement(X);
```

If the vector is full to capacity, this method first grows the array to make room for the new element.

void **removeElementAt**(int index)

The companion method to insertElementAt(), this removes the element at the specified index by shifting all subsequent elements down by one position. As expected, the index must be a valid one in the vector. For example, if the vector v originally contained {A, B, C, D, E, F}, then after a call to v.removeElementAt(1), v would contain {A, C, D, E, F}.

void **removeAllElements**()

Removes all elements in this vector, making the size equal to 0.

void **ensureCapacity**(int newCapacity)

This has no effect on the size of this vector, but it does grow the internal array, if necessary, to a capacity at least as large as that specified by the argument. You might use this if you were going to insert several new elements and wanted to make sure there was room for the new elements, rather than leaving the growth to the insertion method.

void **trimToSize**()

Makes the capacity equal to the current size. You might use this to ensure that this vector wasn't taking up any unnecessary space in memory.

When to Use Vectors

Because vectors can do everything that arrays can, and lots more, is there any good reason *not* to use vectors and thus ignore arrays completely? Well, no, except in very special cases. Using a Vector instead of an array introduces fairly little penalty, in terms of either memory usage or performance, and it gives you access to a host of useful methods. None of the Vector methods would be particularly difficult to invent for ordinary arrays, but why bother, if they're already built in for you?

Just about the only problem with vectors is that the elements are Objects. This means that you may or may not have to do a little work to place something in a vector, and you *will* have a bit of work to do to get an element out of a vector. For class-type elements, life is simple. Object is the superclass of all classes, so to add a Button to a vector, you'd just put it in, like this:

```
Button b = new Button("Click me");
Vector v = new Vector();
v.addElement(b);
```

To get it out later, though, recall that elementAt() returns an Object, so you'd have to cast the result to a Button, like this:

```
Button stored = (Button)(v.elementAt(0));
```

For nonclass types, you have extra work to do at both ends. First, you have to convert the primitive type to the appropriate wrapper class, so if n were an int, for instance, you'd first have to convert it to an Integer instance, like this:

```
v.addElement(new Integer(n));
```

and to get it out, you'd have to get the object, cast it to an Integer, and then use the Integer method intValue(), to get the int you wanted:

```
Integer temporaryInteger = (Integer)(v.elementAt(1));
int whatWeReallyWanted = temporaryInteger.intValue();
```

This is cumbersome, even if you encapsulate the ugly code in a method of your own devising, such as int getIntAt(Vector v, int index). The conclusion is that if you don't need the methods Vector provides *and* you don't want to spend time thinking about type conversions, use arrays. For any other purpose, though, it generally makes sense to use Vectors instead.

Review Questions

4.1 Can you make a class of your own that extends Vector? If so, can you then redefine the Vector methods in your new class?

4.2 Assuming that v is a Vector, explain under what circumstances it would be an error to call v.removeElementAt(i); *regardless* of the value of i.

4.3 Which of the Vector methods we have discussed might increase the capacity of a vector? Which might decrease the capacity?

4.4 Can you have a Vector whose elements are Vectors?

8.5 Strings

The String class is part of the java.lang package, which means that it is already known to the compiler without the need for you to write a special import declaration to get its names into your programs. You've seen quite a few examples of the String class already. In the Lablets and the sample code in this book, we've used dozens of String literals, written as any sequence of characters between quotes, such as, for example, "This is a string". Combining the appearance of a String literal with what you've learned in this chapter, you might guess that a String is represented internally as an array of chars, and you'd be exactly right. The String class, though, is both more and less powerful than just an array of characters.

First, like Vector, the String class contains a large collection of methods that allow you to do things with its instances. Just as with arrays, you can find the length of a String and can inspect the character in a given position. This class also has methods with no corresponding array equivalents, such as the ability to search a String for a match with another String. In spite of all this power, there are things you can do with arrays of characters that you can't do with Strings. One thing you can't do is change a String. Once a String instance has been created, there is no way to change its characters or its length. This is done primarily in the interest of efficiency: Knowing that String objects cannot change gives the designers of Java compilers the ability to use internal data structures that optimize the efficiency of the String methods and conserve space in memory.

> Unlike other classes, Strings are *immutable*. Once a String instance has been created, it cannot be changed.

Another difference between the String class and most of the rest of the Java classes is that String is a final class—you cannot subclass String. Again, this is dictated largely by the need for efficiency.

The String Class

We won't cover all the details of the String class. It would be worth your time to read what we consider to be the most important and useful features of String and then take a look at the documentation for a taste of String arcana.

There are quite a few String constructors, most of which we won't discuss here. The first, and most common, does much of its work behind the scenes. You can construct a String simply by initializing it to a literal in a declaration, like this:

```
String myString = "Brand new string";
```

Note that there's no new operator in this declaration. As with the array initialization using a brace-enclosed list of data, the compiler will invoke whatever is needed to build a new String containing the literal and make sure that myString gets the right reference address. We should remark here that a String literal can't be broken over several lines in the source code. If you have a very long literal, you should break it into pieces, using the concatenation operator,

```
String myString = "This is an exceptionally long string. In"
                + "fact, it won't even fit on a single line,"
                + "but rather has to be broken over three."
```

The other constructors are more like the constructors you've seen, and like other constructors, they are invoked in declarations by using new.

String(String s)

A copy constructor, this constructs a new String containing the same characters and having the same length as the argument.

String(char[] c)

This is a conversion constructor. Given an array of chars, it constructs a new String containing those characters. For instance, if we had declared and filled an array of chars like this,

```
char[] myChars = {'A', ' ', 's', 't', 'r', 'i', 'n', 'g'} ;
```

we could then use this array to initialize a `String` by

```
String myString = new String(myChars);
```

This constructor is often used with `toCharArray()`, which we describe below.

Access and Comparison

We'll begin our discussion of the `String` methods by looking at the methods that allow you to get information about a `String` and compare two `Strings`. In what follows, we'll use the following example `Strings`:

s = "alphabet"   and   t = "answer"

char **charAt**(int i)

Returns the character at position `i` in this `String`. The argument must be a valid position in this `String`, so it must be greater than or equal to 0 and less than the length of this `String`. For our example, `s.charAt(2)` returns `'p'`.

int **compareTo**(String s)

This method compares this `String` with the argument `String`, using what is known as *lexicographic order*. This ordering is an extension of the underlying order on characters. For the standard characters we're used to in English (the ASCII ordering of characters, as it is called[3]), this is

```
<space> ! " # $ % & ' ( ) * + , - . / 0 1 2 3 4 5 6 7 8 9 : ; < =
> ? @ A B C D E F G H I J K L M N O P Q R S T U V W X Y Z [ \ ] ^
_ ` a b c d e f g h i j k l m n o p q r s t u v w x y z { | } ~
```

This order is extended to `Strings` in accordance with the following rules:

1. Starting at the left, compare the strings character by character, stopping at the first pair of characters that differ, or when you run out of characters in one or both `Strings`, whichever comes first.
2. If you find two different characters, return the difference of their codes. Thus in the comparison `s.compareTo(t)` we find that `"alphabet"` first differs from `"answer"` in the index-1 position and `'l'` is two places earlier in character order than `'n'`, so the call `s.compareTo(t)` would return 2. Similarly, we would find that `t.compareTo(s)` would return -2.
3. If the method runs out of characters before finding a mismatch, it returns the difference in the lengths of the `Strings`, so `s.compareTo("alpha")` would return $8 - 5$, or 3.

---

[3]ASCII stands for "American Standard Code for Information Interchange." The first 128 Unicode characters are exactly the ASCII characters.

If `compareTo()` returns a negative value, we say that this `String` is less than the argument. Some consequences of this ordering are (1) the empty string is less than any other, (2) `"BRAIN"` is less than `"BRAWN"` (unfortunately) and (3) `"BEE"` is less than `"BEEKEEPER"`. See the discussion of `equals()`.

```
boolean endsWith(String st)
```

Returns `true` if and only if this `String` ends with the argument `String`. For example, `s.endsWith("bet")` returns `true`, and the method call `s.endsWith("beta")` would return `false`. See the companion method `startsWith()`.

```
boolean equals(Object obj)
boolean equalsIgnoreCase(Object obj)
```

The first of these returns `true` if and only if this `String` and the argument (which must be a `String`) have equal contents (that is, if `compareTo()` would return 0). The second method acts like `equals()` but counts upper- and lowercase letters as equal, so the call `s.equalsIgnoreCase("AlPhAbEt")` would return true.

```
int indexOf(char c)
int indexOf(char c, int start)
int indexOf(String st)
int indexOf(String st, int start)
```

All of these return the index (counting from 0, of course) of the first location where the argument `char` or `String` is found, and return `-1` if the indicated `char` or `String` isn't found in this `String`. If an `int` argument is specified, the search returns the first index where a match is found, at or after the `start` index. For example,

```
s.indexOf('a')         // returns 0
s.indexOf('a', 2)      // returns 4
s.indexOf("pha")       // returns 2
s.indexOf("pha", 4)    // returns -1
```

```
int length()
```

Returns the length (the number of characters) of this `String`. For our example `String`s, `s.length()` returns 8, and `t.length()` returns 6.

```
boolean startsWith(String st)
```

Returns `true` if and only if this `String` starts with the argument `String`. For example, `s.startsWith("alp")` returns `true`, and the method call `s.startsWith(t)` would return `false`. See `endsWith()`.

```
char[] toCharArray()
```

Constructs and returns a new array of `char`s, having the same length as this `String` and the same characters. This is commonly used to do `String` manipulations that aren't provided by the class, like this:

```
String manipulator(String original)
{
    // First, build the array from the String
    char[] myChars = original.toCharArray();

    // (Then, do something with the array myChars)
    // Finally, build a new String from the modified array
    // and return it.
    return new String(myChars);

}
```

Builders

Although you can't modify a String instance, the class provides methods that allow you to make a new String from an existing one. These methods all have String return types.

```
String concat(String st)
```

Returns a new String that is the concatenation of this String and the argument. For example, s.concat("ical") returns the String "alphabetical". This method is equivalent in its action to the concatenation operator +.

```
String replace(char original, char replacement)
```

Returns the String that results from replacing every instance of original in this String with replacement. For instance, a call to s.replace('a', 'e') returns the new String "elphebet". If no instances of original are found in this String, a reference to this String itself is returned.

```
String substring(int start)
String substring(int start, int end)
```

Return a new String containing the characters in this String from position start to the end of this String, or from position start to (but not including) position end, respectively. The index start must be nonnegative, and it cannot be larger than the length of this String. The index end must satisfy the same conditions and must also be greater than start. Here are some examples:

```
s.substring(5)

// returns "bet"
s.substring(8)

// returns "" (the empty String)
s.substring(0, 5)
// returns "alpha"
s.substring(2, 3)
// returns "p"

String toLowerCase()
String toUpperCase()
```

Return a new `String` made by converting each letter in this `String` to lower- or uppercase, respectively These methods convert only the characters that have Unicode lower- or uppercase equivalents. For our purposes, that means letters and not numbers or other characters.

```
String trim()
```

Returns a new `String` made from this one by removing all leading and trailing whitespace (blanks, tabs, and returns, for example).

Using Strings for Conversion

It's quite common for a Java program to store and display its information in `String` form—we do this all the time in the `TextFields` and the `TextAreas` of an applet. As a result, we often find ourselves in the position of having to convert an `int`, for instance, to a `String`, placing the result in a `TextField` for the user to see, and then later having to convert that `String` back to an `int`. The `String` class has methods for converting objects to `Strings`, but we have to look elsewhere for conversions in the opposite direction.

All Java classes have a method, `toString()`, that can be used to return a `String` representation of an instance, because the ultimate superclass, `Object`, has a `toString()` method. `Object`'s `toString()` method doesn't do anything, but many of the built-in Java classes provide overrides of this method. Typically, calling `someInstance.toString()` returns a `String` that contains useful information about the object `someInstance`, perhaps its label, location, or size. For example, if `display` is a `TextField` and you do this

```
Point p = new Point(10, 30);
display.setText(p.toString());
```

you'll find that `display` gets the text `"java.awt.Point[x=10,y=30]"`. You don't even need the explicit call to `toString()` that we used above; when the compiler sees a class instance as one of the operands of the concatenation operator `+`, it will automatically insert a call to `toString()`. In other words, we could have written the code above as

```
Point p = new Point(10, 30);
display.setText("Information: " + p);
```

or, to accomplish exactly the same thing as the first example, we could have used the empty `String`, like this:

```
Point p = new Point(10, 30);
display.setText("" + p);
```

It's not a bad idea to include an override of `toString()` in classes you write. This can be handy for providing debugging information.

The primitive types don't have `toString()` methods, of course, because they're not classes. However, the `String` class contains `static` methods that accomplish the same thing:

```
static String valueOf(boolean b)
static String valueOf(char c)
static String valueOf(int i)
static String valueOf(long l)
static String valueOf(float f)
static String valueOf(double d)
```

All of these methods return a `String` representation of their arguments, so we could execute this code

```
double d = 266.0909;
boolean b = (d > 0.0);
display.setText(String.valueOf(b) + " " + String.valueOf(d));
```

and find that `display` contains the text `"true 266.0909"`.

As with `toString()` for classes, Java will insert the necessary calls to `valueOf()` in `String` concatenation expressions, so we could equally well have written the above code as

```
double d = 266.0909;
boolean b = (d > 0.0);
display.setText(b + " " + d);
```

The only care you have to exercise when doing this kind of conversion is to make sure you are forcing `String` concatenation by including at least one guaranteed `String` operand. For example, the call

```
display.setText(b + d);
```

would be wrong on two counts: We can't add a `boolean` and a `double`, and even if we somehow could, the result almost certainly wouldn't be a `String` and so couldn't be used as an argument to `setText()`.

> The easiest way to convert an object or a primitive type to a `String` is to use concatenation with the empty `String`, `"" + x`, and let the compiler insert the necessary call to `toString()` or `valueOf()`, as appropriate.

To convert in the other direction, from `String` to a primitive type, we need to use the wrapper classes `Boolean`, `Character`, `Integer`, `Float`, `Long`, and `Double` as intermediaries, as we discussed in Chapter 7.

Review Questions

5.1 Why does Java provide a `String` class when we could simply use arrays of chars?

5.2 If s is a `String`, how can you change its size?

5.3 Arrange the following strings in lexicographic order: `"book"`, `"Bookmark"`, `"Bookkeeper"`, `"Book"`.

5.4 Can a `String` literal contain a double quote?

5.5 How would you get the third character from the left in a `String` s?

8.6 Hands On

This chapter's Lablet is an example of what is known as *algorithm visualization*. Knowing how to code a sorting routine is a far cry from having an intuitive understanding of how it works. Although the analytical part of your brain can think of sorting in terms of making comparisons and moving data, we shouldn't neglect the part that sees patterns in the data movements. Thanks to Java's graphical features, we can design an applet that shows how a sorting algorithm looks in action.

Figure 8.11 shows what it looks like when running. The main portion of the applet is a collection of lines drawn so that their length is proportional to the size of the data. At the bottom there are three controls: a Reset button, which generates new random data values, a Sort button, which starts the sorting process, and a Choice object, which allows the user to select a particular sorting algorithm to observe.

Designing the Lablet

By now, you should have no problem coming up with the layout for Sortmeister: We place the display Canvas subclass in the center region of a BorderLayout and add the control Panel to the South, thereby reserving a large open region in which to draw the lines.

The active part of the applet is a bit more complicated than the visual design, but not intimidatingly so (except for the inclusion of some techniques, for the animation, that we won't discuss until Chapter 11). We'll keep the data to be sorted in an array, of course, and the Reset button will shuffle the data in the array into a ran-

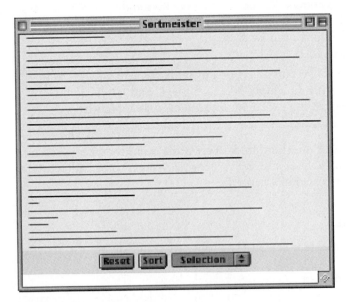

Figure 8.11

Sortmeister, ready to go.

dom order. The Sort button will invoke the sorting algorithm selected in the Choice object, which will cause the display Canvas to redraw the lines in accordance with the way the algorithm moves the data around.

The visible activity of this program is the responsibility of the Display class. The main entry to this class will be a draw() method that indicates which two lines will be highlighted in different colors and causes the display to repaint itself, using the current data values to determine the lengths of the lines.

Exploring the Lablet

As usual, we won't discuss the import declarations and the opening comments, because they have nothing new to show us. The declaration of the applet class begins with the usual collection of constant and instance variable declarations.

```
public class Sortmeister extends    Applet
                          implements ActionListener,
                                     ItemListener,
                                     Runnable // ignore for now
{
   private final int  SIZE = 30;       // number of data values
   private final int  DELAY_MS = 150;  // pause length

   private int        data[];          // data to be sorted
   private Button     reset,           // to reset the data
                      sort;            // to perform the sort
   private Choice     sortChoice;      // how to sort
   private String     sortName;        // name of the sort
   private Display    display;         // where we draw
   private Thread     runner = null;   // ignore for now
```

We wanted to make the applet as general as we could, so we declared an int constant, SIZE, to hold the size of the data array. In simple terms, SIZE determines how many lines we'll have in our applet. The constant DELAY_MS controls the delay between updates of the applet—the larger this value is, the slower the sorting routines will appear to run. You might find you have to tweak this value, depending on how fast your computer is.

The instance variables are the ones you would expect. We've already mentioned the data array; note that we have set aside space only for references to this array and haven't yet made any space in memory for it. The variable sortName will hold one of the strings "Selection" or "Quick", to indicate the algorithm we'll use to do the sorting. The widgets reset, sort, and sortChoice will, as we have indicated, control the action of the applet. Finally, the animation will be controlled by a Thread object, which we won't discuss here. We'll cover threads in Chapter 11.

The init() method should be familiar enough. The only thing we do here that you haven't seen in other applets is to initialize the data array.

```
public void init()
{
   setLayout(new BorderLayout());

   data = new int[SIZE];       // Create the array.
```

```
    // Lay the controls out in their own panel

    Panel p = new Panel();
    p.setBackground(new Color(212, 212, 255));
    reset = new Button("Reset");
    sort = new Button("Sort");
    sortChoice = new Choice();
    sortChoice.addItem("Selection");
    sortChoice.addItem("Quick");
    p.add(reset);
    p.add(sort);
    p.add(sortChoice);
    add(BorderLayout.SOUTH, p);

    // Create the display Canvas and add it to the applet

    display = new Display(data);
    display.setBackground(new Color(255, 255, 212));
    add(BorderLayout.CENTER, display);

    // Register the buttons and the Choice object

    sortChoice.addItemListener(this);
    reset.addActionListener(this);
    sort.addActionListener(this);

    // Set the default sort method and initialize the data

    sortName = "Selection";
    shuffle(data);
    display.repaint();
}
```

We'll explain the shuffle() method shortly; it fills the data array with a random rearrangement of the numbers 1, 2, 3 . . ..

The next things we see are the two event-handling methods. The actionPerformed() method handles a click on the Reset button by shuffling the data array and asking the display to repaint itself. The Sort button does some things we won't be ready to discuss in detail until later, but in essence it just starts the animation of the sorting algorithm. The itemStateChanged() method is simplicity itself. It sets the sortName variable to the name chosen in the sortChoice object.

```
public void actionPerformed(ActionEvent e)
{
    String cmd = e.getActionCommand();
    if (cmd.equals("Reset"))    // Reshuffle and show the data.
    {
        shuffle(data);
        display.repaint();
    }
    else                        // Do the sorting (Huh?  How?).
    {
        if (runner != null)
        {
            runner.stop();
        }
```

```
        runner = new Thread(this);
        runner.start();      // This does some things and
                             // then calls run().
    }
}

public void itemStateChanged(ItemEvent e)
{
    sortName = "" + e.getItem();
}
```

The shuffle() method is nice. It begins by using a for loop to fill the data array with the numbers 1, 2, . . ., length, in order. It then makes another pass through the array, this time swapping the element in position i with a randomly chosen element at or after position i. We explore this method in more detail in the lab exercises.

```
private void shuffle(int[] a)
{
    for (int i = 0; i < a.length; i++)
    {
        a[i] = i + 1;
    }
    for (int i = 0; i < a.length - 1; i++)
    {
        // Pick a random index in the range i ... a.length - 1.
        int index = i + (int)(Math.random() * (a.length - i));

        // Swap a[i] and a[index].
        int temp = a[i];
        a[i] = a[index];
        a[index] = temp;
    }
}
```

The animation thread starts its work by calling the doSort() method. As you can see, all this does is call one of the sorting methods, depending on the string stored in sortName.

```
private void doSort()
{
    if (sortName.equals("Selection"))
    {
        selectionSort(data);
    }
    else if (sortName.equals("Quick"))
    {
        quickSort(data, 0, data.length - 1);
    }
}
```

We've already discussed the two sorting algorithms. The only difference between the originals and the versions here is the inclusion of several calls to the stall() method. This method stops the animation briefly (for the amount of milliseconds given in the DELAY_MS constant) and highlights the lines in the display that correspond to the indices in the arguments, if any. To give a good idea of the relative speed of the two sort algorithms, we insert a call to stall() at each comparison or data move operation.

```java
private void selectionSort(int[] a)
{
    for (int i = 0; i < a.length - 1; i++)
    {
        int minPos = i;

        for (int j = i + 1; j < a.length; j++)
        {
            if (a[j] < a[minPos])
                minPos = j;

            stall(i, j);
        }

        int temp = a[i];
        a[i] = a[minPos];
        a[minPos] = temp;

        stall(i, minPos);
    }
    stall(-1, -1);
}

private void quickSort(int[] a, int start, int end)
{
    if (start < end)
    {
        // Rearrange the array into two subranges.
        int split = partition(a, start, end);

        // Sort each subrange.
        quickSort(a, start, split);
        quickSort(a, split + 1, end);
    }
    stall(-1, -1);
}

private int partition(int[] a, int start, int end)
{
    int bottom = start - 1,
        top = end + 1;
    int pivot = a[start];

    while (bottom < top)
    {
        do
        {
            bottom++;
            stall(start, bottom);
        } while(a[bottom] < pivot);
        do
        {
            top--;
            stall(start, top);
        } while(a[top] > pivot);
```

```
        int temp = a[bottom];
        a[bottom] = a[top];
        a[top] = temp;

        stall(bottom, top);
    }
    int temp = a[bottom];
    a[bottom] = a[top];
    a[top] = temp;

    stall(bottom, top);
    return top;
}
```

The class declaration concludes with the two thread-related methods, neither of which we're prepared to discuss at this time, but which we list for completeness.

```
    private void stall(int i, int j)
    {
        display.draw(i, j);
        try
        {
            Thread.sleep(DELAY_MS);
        }
        catch(InterruptedException e)
        { }
    }

    public void run()
    {
        doSort();
    }
}
```

All of the drawing takes place in an instance of the Display class. As we've done several times before, we do our drawing on a subclass of Canvas. The important part of the data declaration is that the Display class keeps a reference to the applet's data array and that this reference is set by the constructor. We need to do this, of course, because otherwise a Display object would have no idea what data it is supposed to represent by the lines it draws.

```
class Display extends Canvas
{
    private final int INSET = 10;  // size of the margins

    private int[] data;        // the data to be displayed
    private int   swapIndex,    // index of blue line
                  compareIndex; // index of the green line

    public Display(int[] a)
    {
        data = a;
    }
```

The other two instance variables, swapIndex and compareIndex, are used by the drawing routine to determine that the lines corresponding to the data in these two locations in the array should be drawn in different colors from the others, so that it is easier for the observer to tell what the sort algorithms are actually doing.

```
public void draw(int i, int j)
{
    swapIndex = i;
    compareIndex = j;
    repaint();
}
```

As we mentioned in the discussion of Sortmeister in Chapter 6, the update() method normally does its thing by erasing the component and calling paint(). Here, we override update() so that it doesn't do any erasing. We could have left update() in its usual form, but, as you'll see in the lab exercises, doing so introduces an annoying flicker into the animation.

```
public void update(Graphics g)
{
    paint(g);
}
```

As often happens, the real work in this class is done in the paint() method. The first part of this method computes the scale values that will be used to draw the lines. To find the vertical separation between the lines, we get the height of the canvas and divide by the number of lines to be drawn. That, of course, we can get by using data.length. For example, if the height of this object was 150 pixels and we had to display 30 lines, we would draw them 150 / 30 = 5 pixels apart. That's what unitY represents. Similarly, because we know that the largest possible data value is data.length, we know that each unit of data will correspond to the available horizontal dimension (minus twice the INSET, to give us some margins) divided by data.length, which we store in the local variable unitX.

```
public void paint(Graphics g)
{
    Dimension size = getSize();
    int unitY = size.height / data.length;
    double unitX = (size.width - 2.0 * INSET) / data.length;
```

When the time comes to draw the lines, we walk our way through the data array, and for each index, i, we erase the old line by drawing a background-colored line across the full width of the display.

```
for (int i = 0; i < data.length; i++)
{
    int y = unitY / 2 + i * unitY;
    // Erase the old i-th line.
    g.setColor(getBackground());
    g.drawLine(INSET, y,
            INSET + (int)(unitX * data.length), y);
```

Now all that's left is to draw the new line. If the index, i, matches swapIndex, we draw the line in red; if the index matches compareIndex, we draw it in green;

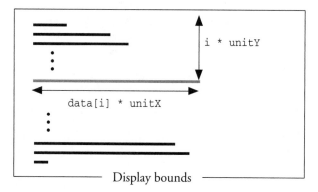

Figure 8.12

Drawing the **i**-th line.

and we draw any other line in black. Each line's vertical position will be proportional to i, and its horizontal extent will be proportional to data[i], as shown in Figure 8.12.

```
// Draw the new i-th line.
if (i == swapIndex)
{
    g.setColor(Color.red);
}
else if (i == compareIndex)
{
    g.setColor(Color.green);
}
else
{
    g.setColor(Color.black);
}
g.drawLine(INSET, y,
        INSET + (int)(unitX * data[i]), y);
        }
    }
}
```

Review Questions

6.1 In Sortmeister, what sequence of method calls causes the sorting to take place? We're looking for an answer like "foo() calls bar(), which calls baz(), which actually does the sorting."

6.2 What events are handled by the classes Sortmeister and Display?

6.3 Why does the Display class have a reference to the applet's data[] array?

6.4 Why didn't we use a Vector to store the data?

8.7 Summary

■ The do loop is written

```
do
{
    statements
}
while (boolean expression);   // We need the semicolon here
```

It causes the statement or statements to be executed repeatedly, as long as the boolean expression is true. The exit test is performed at the end of each loop iteration.

■ The while loop is written

```
while (boolean expression)
{
    statements
}
```

It causes the statement or statements to be executed repeatedly, as long as the boolean expression is true. The exit test is performed at the start of each loop iteration.

■ The for loop is written

```
for (initStatement; testExpression; iterationExpression)
{
    statements
}
```

This does the following things:

1. It performs the initStatement (if any) once, before starting the loop.
2. The testExpression is evaluated at the start of each pass through the loop. If it is false, control passes out of the loop, down to the next statement after the loop.
3. If the testExpression is true, the loop body statement or statements are performed.
4. After the loop body is performed, the iterationExpression (if any) is executed.
5. Finally, control passes back to step 2.

■ In each of the loop statements, the statement body can be any statement, simple or compound.
■ If the statement body of a loop is another loop, the inner loop iterates most rapidly.
■ There is almost never a good reason to place a semicolon immediately after a loop header.
■ Any variable declared within a for loop has local scope: It has meaning only within the loop and must not have the same name as any other variable of the same type in an enclosing scope.

- Whenever you design a loop, make very sure the test expression will eventually become false, no matter what happens.
- Loops that are controlled by counting (that is, loops that are known to iterate a fixed number of times) are best written with a for statement. Loops that are controlled by some logical condition (that is, loops that will iterate as long as some condition is satisfied) should be written with a while loop or a do loop. If there is a possibility that the loop's body will never be executed, use a while loop. If the body must be executed at least once, consider using a do loop.
- An array is an indexed list of elements of the same type.
- Java arrays always begin with index 0.
- An array in Java may be declared in two equivalent forms:

  ```
  typeName variableName[];
  typeName[] variableName;
  ```

- An array declaration does not allocate space in memory for the array. To do that, the array must be initialized by

  ```
  variableName = new typeName[integerValue];
  ```

- It's a good idea to combine declaration and initialization of arrays, like this,

  ```
  double[] myArray = new double[10];
  ```

- Remember that array indices begin at 0. Declaring

  ```
  int[] nums = new int[4];
  ```

  constructs an array with elements nums[0], nums[1], nums[2], and nums[3].
- An array's elements may be initialized by providing their values within a comma-separated list enclosed within braces, as in

  ```
  nums = {2, 100, -3, 8} ;
  ```

- You can initialize an array and let the compiler determine its size, as in

  ```
  int[] nums = {2, 100, -3, 8} ;
  ```

- The initialization form works for classes, as in

  ```
  Button controls[] = {new Button("Left"), new Button("Up"),
                       new Button("Down"), new Button("Right")} ;
  ```

- Once we have declared and initialized an array variable, we may inspect and modify its elements by using the variable name followed by a pair of square brackets containing an integer expression.
- Java will check the legality of array indices at run-time and will generate an error if the value of the expression within the square brackets is less than 0 or greater than or equal to the length of the array.
- Every array has a public field, length, that contains the number of elements in the array.
- An array element may be used anywhere a variable of the base type may be used.
- An extremely common use of loops is to iterate through the elements of an array.

■ Arrays are like classes in that if an array is used as a method argument, the elements of the array may be modified by the method.

■ In Java you can implement a multidimensional array by using an array of arrays, like this:

```
double table[][] = new double[4][3];
```

■ To initialize a multidimensional array, you can use nested initializations, such as

```
double table[][] = {{0.0, 0.1, 0.2} , {1.0, 1.1, 1.2} ,
                    {2.0, 2.1, 2.2} , {3.1, 3.0, 3.2} } ;
```

■ Using inheritance, you can make an array of objects whose elements are of different types, as long as all types are subclasses of the element type.

■ In Selection Sort, the element in position i is found by searching all the elements in positions $j \geq i$ for the smallest. This smallest element is then swapped with the element at position i.

■ The invariant property of Selection Sort is that at the end of iteration i, all the elements in positions at or before i are in their correct locations.

■ Insertion Sort is performed by inserting the element in position i in sorted order among the earlier positions.

■ The invariant property in Insertion Sort is that at the end of iteration i, all the elements in positions at or before i are in sorted order.

■ Selection Sort and Insertion Sort both require no more than a fixed multiple of N^2 steps to sort a list of N elements.

■ Quicksort is a recursive sorting routine that works by splitting a portion of an array into left and right subarrays so that everything in the left subarray is less than or equal to everything in the right subarray. It then recursively sorts each subarray.

■ Quicksort is, in general, more efficient than either Selection Sort or Insertion Sort.

■ The `Vector` class is a generalization of Java's built-in arrays. A `Vector` instance behaves like an array of `Objects` and contains a number of methods for manipulating its data.

■ A vector is implemented using an internal array of `Objects`. The elements contained in a vector occupy consecutive positions in the internal array, starting at position 0.

■ The size of a vector is the number of data elements it contains; the capacity of a vector is the length of its internal array—that is, the maximum number of elements it could contain.

■ Because the underlying element type of a vector is `Object`, it is generally necessary to perform a type cast to extract an element from a Vector.

■ A `String` instance is a list of characters. Once it has been created, a `String` cannot be modified. The `String` class is a final class—it cannot be subclassed.

■ There is an order on `Strings`, derived from the underlying order on Unicode characters. In this lexicographic order, the empty `String` is less than any other, `"BRAIN"` is less than `"BRAWN"`, and `"BEE"` is less than `"BEEKEEPER"`.

- Strings may be manipulated by generating an array of chars from the String, manipulating that array, and creating a new String result from the array.
- Every class has a method toString() that can convert an instance of that class to a String representation. For primitive types, the static String method valueOf() will convert a primitive type value to a String representation.
- The wrapper classes Boolean, Character, Integer, Float, Long, and Double contain methods that can be used to convert appropriately formed Strings to instances of the corresponding wrapper class type.

8.8 Exercises

1. In the following segments, identify and correct any syntax errors. Don't worry about whether the code does anything useful. You're interested here only in whether the segments will compile. You may assume that all variables have been declared and initialized.

a.
```
while n != -1
    sum = sum + n;
    n--;
```

b.
```
do
{
    n--;
} while ((n > 0) && (n % 2 != 0))
```

c.
```
do
{
    g += g;
}
while (h <= 0);
```

d.
```
for (int i = 0; i < 10;)
{
    s *= 2;
}
```

2. Once you've made the necessary corrections in the segments of Exercise 1, tell which loops, if any, may never terminate.

3. The for loops you've seen so far all increase the index variable by 1 at each iteration. There are times, though, that you might want other sequences. Write for loops where the index variable takes the following values.

    a. 10, 9, 8, 7, 6, 5, 4, 3, 2, 1
    b. 1, 2, 4, 8, 16, 32, 64, 128, 256, 512
    c. 1, 4, 13, 40, 121, 364, 1093

4. Assume that s is a statement and that b is a boolean expression.

    a. Using a while statement and anything else you might need, write the equivalent of

```
do
{
    s
} while (b);
```

b. Using a do statement and anything else you might need, write the equivalent of

```
while (b)
{
    S
}
```

5. Write a method `double power(double x, int n)` that returns x^n.
    a. Assume that n will always be greater than or equal to 0.
    b. Don't assume that n will always be greater than or equal to 0.

6. Write a method `int sumOdds(int n)` that will return the sum of the first n odd integers. For example, if n is 4, the method would return $1 + 3 + 5 + 7 = 16$. If n is less than or equal to 0, the method should return 0.

7. (Tricky) Do Exercise 6 without using a loop.

8. Look at the attempts to write `prefixSum()` on pages 364–368. For the following new attempts, comment on whether they are correct and, if so, on whether they are clearer or less clear than Attempt 3.

    a.
```
int prefixSum(int[] a)
{
    int sum = 0;
    for (int i = 0; (a[i] >= 0) && (i < a.length); i++)
    {
        sum += a[i];
    }
    return sum;
}
```

    b.
```
int prefixSum(int[] a)
{
    int i = 0,
        sum = 0;
    boolean done = false;
    do
    {
        if ((i < a.length) && (a[i] >= 0))
        {
            sum += a[i];
        }
        else
        {
            done = true;
        }
    } while (!done);
    return sum;
}
```

    c.
```
int prefixSum(int[] a)
{
    int i = 0,
        sum = 0;
    while (true)
    {
        if ((i < a.length) && (a[i] >= 0))
        {
            sum += a[i++];
        }
        else
```

```
        {
            return sum;
        }
    }
}
```

9. In each of the following loops, how often is the statement s executed?

a.
```
for (int i = 0; i < 5; i++)
{
    for (int j = 0; j < 5; j++)
    {
        s;
    }
}
```

b.
```
for (int i = 0; i < 5; i++)
{
    for (int j = i; j < 5; j++)
    {
        s;
    }
}
```

c.
```
for (int i = 0; i < 5; i++)
{
    for (int j = i; j < 5 - i; j++)
    {
        s;
    }
}
```

10. We can find the square root of a nonnegative number n without using the Math routine sqrt() by performing the following segment:

```
double a = n;
while (Math.abs(a * a - n) > 1.0e-8)
{
    a = a - (a * a - n) / (2.0 * a);
}
```

In this segment, we do the loop until the answer a has a square that is within 0.00000001 of n. This technique is known as *Newton's method,* and the nice part about it is how fast it works. Try it. Write the current value of a at each iteration and see how many iterations it takes to compute the square root of 100 to eight decimal places. Try it again, this time to find the square root of 10,000.

11. (Tricky) The *harmonic series* $1 + 1/2 + 1/3 + 1/4 + \cdots + 1/n$ increases without limit as n increases. Eventually, for example, it will become larger than 30. We could find out how many terms it would take for the series to become larger than 30 by writing

```
double sum = 0.0;
int n = 0;
do
{
    n++;
    sum += 1.0 / n;
} while (sum < 30.0);
System.out.println("It took " + n + " terms to get over 30.");
```

This won't work, though. Why?

12. The following loop takes a binary number, n, assumed to be composed only of the digits 0 and 1, and sets num equal to the decimal equivalent of n, so if n was 1101, the loop would set num to 13. Fill in the boolean expression to control the loop.

```
int num = 0;
int power = 1;
while (_____)
{
    digit = n % 10; // Get the rightmost digit of n.
    num += power * digit;
    power = 2 * power;
    n = n / 10; // Remove the rightmost digit from n.
}
```

13. Write the method int digits(int n) that counts the number of digits in n. *Hint:* Look at Exercise 12.

14. a. Write the method

```
int reverse(int n)
```

that reverses n, so that reverse(4723) returns 3247. This is a tricky problem. It involves extracting the digits from the right of n and building the reverse using these digits as they come in. Look at Exercise 12 for a hint.

b. Use reverse() to write the method

```
boolean isPalindrome(int n)
```

that returns true if and only if n is a *palindrome*—that is, if n reads the same from left to right as from right to left, as do 454 and 3333.

c. An interesting problem is the following: Take a starting number, *n*, add it to its reverse, and continue this process until the result is a palindrome. For example, starting with 95, we add it to its reverse to get 95 + 59 = 154. Adding *this* to its reverse, we get 154 + 451 = 605. Adding this to its reverse, we have 605 + 506 = 1111, which is a palindrome, after three iterations. Write a program to count the number of iterations this process takes to produce a palindrome, and try it for some starting values. You might want to use the long type, instead of ints, because the numbers can get pretty big. For example, starting with value 98 takes 24 iterations and results in the palindrome 8,813,200,023,188, which won't fit in an int. Don't even think about trying it on 295—if that ever results in a palindrome, the result is over two million digits long. Does the process always result in a palindrome for any starting value?

15. The following method is supposed to return the index of the first instance of repeated numbers in an array of ints. For example, when given the array {2, 8, 6, 6, 10, 6, 7, 7, 7, 3, 9} , the method would return 2, the index of the start of the 6, 6 pair. The method is to return –1 if there are no adjacent equal numbers. The method below doesn't work correctly. Why?

```
int firstRepeat(int[] a)
{
    int i = 0;
    while ((i < a.length - 1) && (a[i] != a[i + 1]))
    {
        i++;
    }

    if (a[i] != a[i + 1])
    {
        return -1;
    }
    else
    {
        return i;
    }
}
```

16. Quicksort is most efficient when each partition splits the array segment into two pieces of nearly equal size. For the version of `partition()` we presented, what kind of split do we get if the original array happens to be in sorted order already?

17. As we mentioned in Exercise 14, a palindrome is a number or string that reads the same left-to-right as it does right-to-left. Complete the following recursive definition: "Any string of length ____ is automatically a palindrome. For longer strings s, we can say that s is a palindrome if _____ and _____."

18. The following two recursive functions both compute x raised to the power n, for n ≥ 0. Describe what each does when given x = 2.0, n = 13. Which is more efficient, in terms of using fewer recursive calls to complete the calculation?

```
double power1(double x, int n)
{
    if (n == 0)
    {
        return 1.0;
    }
    else
    {
        return x * power1(x, n - 1);
    }
}
```

```
double power2(double x, int n)
{
    if (n == 0)
    {
        return 1.0;
    }
    else if (n % 2 == 1)
    {
        return x * power2(x * x, n / 2);
    }
    else
    {
        return power2(x * x, n / 2);
    }
}
```

19. What would be displayed by the call process("alligator", 0) for the function below? What would happen if we reversed the order of the two statements in the if statement? What would happen if we removed the if statement and kept the two others?

```
void process(String s, int i)
{
    if (i < s.length())
    {
        process(s, i + 1);
        System.out.print(s.charAt(i));
    }
}
```

20. For any list of numbers, we can measure how far each element is from its correct location by simply taking the absolute value of the difference between its index and its place in sorted order. For example, in the list 15, 23, 8, 30, 16, 48, 11, 6, 9, element 15 is in index 0 and it would be in position 4 when the list was finally sorted, so 15 is $| 0 - 4 | = 4$ places from where it should be.

We can extend this to a measure of the "unsortedness" of a list by adding the differences we computed above for each element. For example, here's a list and the "misplacement numbers" for each element.

Element	15	23	8	30	16	48	11	6	9
Index	0	1	2	3	4	5	6	7	8
Sorted index	4	6	1	7	5	8	3	0	2
Difference	4	5	1	4	1	3	3	7	6

Adding the bottom row, we can say that the list has unsortedness $4 + 5 + 1 + 4 + 1 + 3 + 3 + 7 + 6 = 34$.

a. What is the unsortedness of a sorted list?

b. For a list with 9 elements, like the one above, what is the largest possible value the unsortedness number can be?

c. (Hard) Prove that the unsortedness number of a list of size n is always less than or equal to $n^2 / 2$.

21. For the illustrations of Selection Sort and Insertion Sort in Figures 8.5 and 8.7, give the unsortedness (defined in Exercise 20) of the list at each step. Generally speaking, both of the sorting methods reduce the unsortedness number, but they do so in different ways. In one of the methods, for instance, the unsortedness number of the list tends to decrease slowly at first and then much more rapidly at the end. Come up with some "high-level" descriptions of how each of Selection Sort and Insertion Sort affects the unsortedness number of a list.

22. Each of the following pictures illustrates a sorting algorithm at an intermediate stage, as we might see while watching the Sortmeister Lablet. Identify each as Selection Sort, Insertion Sort, or Quicksort. Explain the reasons for your choices.

a.

b.

c.

23. Rewrite `selectionSort()`, assuming that the data is stored in a `Vector` rather than in an array.

24. Let's try to second-guess how the `Vector` class is implemented. Suppose that the definition of `Vector` looks like this:

```
class Vector extends Object implements Cloneable
{
    // the capacity increment
    protected int capacityIncrement = 0;
    // the number of valid elements in the array (the size)
    protected int elementCount = 0;
    // storage for the vector elements
    protected Object elementData[] = null;

    // Constructors and methods go here
}
```

Using just the instance variables specified, write the code for the following `Vector` operations, as though you were filling in the class definition.

    a. The default constructor `Vector()`

    b. `removeAllElements()`

    c. `removeElementAt(int index)`

25. Some of the `Vector` member functions are easy to write using calls to other member functions.

    a. Write `contains()`, assuming that someone else has already written `indexOf()`.

    b. Find another example of a `Vector` member function that's easy to write by calling a member function.

    c. Why do you suppose the designers of the `Vector` class included methods, such as `isEmpty()`, that are trivial to define in terms of other `Vector` methods?

26. The following method is supposed to remove the elements in positions 0, 2, 4, . . . from a Vector:

```
void discardEveryOther(Vector v)
{
    for (int i = 0; i < v.size(); i += 2)
    {
        v.removeElementAt(i);
    }
}
```

a. It doesn't work as specified. What happens if it is applied to the Vector that originally contains {3, 6, 9, 12, 15} ?

b. Rewrite the method so that it works correctly.

27. Suppose that s is the String "flabbergasted" and that t is the String "berg". What are the values of the following expressions?

   a. s.indexOf('s')
   b. s.indexOf(t)
   c. s.lastIndexOf('e')
   d. length(s.concat(s))
   e. s.indexOf(s.substring(1, 4))
   f. s.compareTo(s)
   g. s.compareTo(t)
   h. t.compareTo(s)
   i. s.compareTo(s.concat(t))
   j. valueOf(s.equals(t))
   k. s.substring(0, 2) + s.substring(2)

28. For the String method

```
getChars(int start, int end, char[] chars, int cStart),
```

what conditions on start, end, the length of the string, the length of the array, and the value of cStart must be satisfied for the call to succeed?

29. Rewrite Insertion Sort so that it sorts an array of Strings.

30. *Planit reduction* transforms English words into a coded form using the following rules, in order.

   (1) Replace each character in the word using the following rules:

      A, E, I, O, U, Y → A
      B, F, P, V → B
      C, G, K, J, Q, S, X, Z → C
      D, T → D
      H, W → H
      L → L
      M, N → M
      R → R

   (2) For any consonant that's followed by an H, eliminate the H. Thus DH would be replaced by D, for instance.

   (3) Replace any repeated sequence of consonants by a single instance. For example, MM would be replaced by M.

(4) Finally, eliminate all the A's.

For example, the planit reduction of THINNING is

$$THINNING \rightarrow DHAMMAMC, \text{ after step 1}$$
$$\rightarrow DAMMAMC, \text{ after step 2}$$
$$\rightarrow DAMAMC, \text{ after step 3}$$
$$\rightarrow DMMC, \text{ after step 4}$$

Planit reduction is useful in automated dictionaries, because variant spellings often have the same Planit reduction. Write a program to perform Planit reduction, and test it on the strings THEIR, THERE, THEYRE, and EITHER.

31. Write a program that will take a text string and produce a classified ad by deleting all lowercase vowels. For example, given the following source string (in a `TextArea`, for instance)

> 1989 Ferrari Testarossa. Auto, air, awesome stereo.
> Some minor body damage, mostly small holes.
> Contact Sonny, this paper, box MH1765.

the program will produce

> 1989 Frrr Tstrss. At, r, wsm str.
> Sm mnr bdy dmg, mstly smll hls.
> Cntct Snny, ths ppr, bx MH1765.

(Clearly, this algorithm needs some fixing. We particularly like what happens to "Ferrari" and "air.")

32. a. Write a method,

```
String numToWord(String s)
```

that takes a `String` argument representing an integer between 0 and 9999 and returns the word equivalent. For example, for `s = "423"`, the method would return the `String "four hundred twenty-three"`.

b. Use `numToWord()` in an applet that gets a `String` from the user and replaces the numbers with words. For example, the sentence "John had 130 hogs that he traded for 4091 guinea pigs." would produce the output "John had one hundred thirty hogs that he traded for four thousand ninety-one guinea pigs."

33. Write the method `String reverse(String s)` that returns the reverse of its argument, producing "rotagilla" from "alligator", for instance.

34. a. Write a method,

```
boolean isPalindrome(String s)
```

that returns `true` if and only if the argument is a *palindrome*—that is, it is the same as its reverse, like "pop" and "toot."

b. Extend `isPalindrome()` so that it ignores all nonletters and isn't sensitive to case, so, for example, it would recognize "Madam, I'm Adam." as a palindrome.

35. A simple way of encoding a message is the *railfence cypher*. In this scheme, we first make a string from the original by extracting all the characters in the even positions and then append the string we get from the original's odd-index characters. For example, in the string `"FOOLEDYOUDIDNTI"` we have the even-position characters `"FOEYUINI"` and the odd-position characters `"OLDODDT"`. Concatenating these gives the encoded string `"FOEYUINIOLDODDT"`.

a. Write a method that takes a `String` argument and returns the string that results from applying the railfence cypher.

b. The railfence cypher has the interesting property that if it is applied repeatedly to a string, the original string is eventually produced. The number of repetitions needed to get back to the original depends on the length of the string. For instance, for strings of length 2, one iteration of the cypher obviously leaves the string unchanged; for strings of length 32, five iterations suffice, whereas for strings of length 30, it takes 28 iterations. Write a program to investigate the number of iterations of the railfence cypher it takes to bring a string back to its original form. What conclusions can you draw?

8.9   Answers to Review Questions

1.1 A `while` loop performs its test at the start of each loop iteration; a `do` loop performs its test at the end of each loop iteration.

1.2 `n`.

1.3 If the loop test is initially false, a `for` loop will do nothing. In that respect, a `for` loop behaves like a `while` loop.

2.1 With a `for` loop that looks like this:

```
for (int i = 0; i < a.length; i++)
{
    // Do something with a[i].
}
```

2.2 Strictly speaking, no. However, if the element type is a class type, `T`, then the elements can be instances of any subclass of `T`.

2.3 `a[a.length - 1]`.

2.4 The first declares a as an array of `int`s; the second declares b as an array of `int`s *and* sets aside enough room in memory for the three `int`s that will compose b's elements.

2.5 Start from some location in the array and iterate through consecutive elements until some condition is satisfied.

3.1 "Starting at the beginning location and moving up one position each time, find the smallest element at or after the current location, and swap the smallest element found with the current element."

3.2 Selection Sort.

3.3 A recursive definition is one that uses the term to be defined as part of its definition. For methods, a recursive method is one that includes one or more calls to itself.

4.1 Yes, but you can't override the `Vector` methods [except for `clone()`] in a subclass.

4.2 If `v` were empty.

4.3 `addElement()`, `insertElementAt()`, and `ensureCapacity()` might increase the capacity of a vector; `trimToSize()` might decrease the capacity.

4.4 Sure. A `Vector` is an `Object`, so a `Vector` can have `Vectors` as its elements.

5.1 The `String` class contains many useful methods that aren't available for arrays of `chars`.

5.2 You can't. Like arrays (and unlike vectors), once a `String` object has been constructed, it is impossible to change its size.

5.3 `"Book"`, `"Bookkeeper"`, `"Bookmark"`, `"book"`.

5.4 Yes, but it has to be represented by the special character literal `\"`, as in `"Answer \"yes\" or \"no\" to this question"`.

5.5 `s.charAt(2)`.

6.1 `actionPerformed()` calls `start()`, which (invisibly) calls `run()`, which calls `doSort()`, which calls either of `selectionSort()` or `quickSort()`, where the sorting takes place.

6.2 `Sortmeister` deals with `ActionEvents` from its two buttons and with `ItemEvents` from its `Choice` object; `Display` does no event handling.

6.3 Without a reference to the applet's `data` array, `Display` would have no way of knowing what data values it must represent by lines.

6.4 Because we didn't want to deal with type casts to get the `ints` in and out of `data`, and because we didn't need any of the `Vector` methods.

8.10 Class References

`java.lang.String`

A `String` may be regarded as an array of characters. Once a `String` object is created, it cannot be modified. Along with the other constructors, a `String` may be initialized by a literal, as in `String message = "Hello";`. A number of these methods will throw exceptions (Ch. 9) that will bring your program to a screeching halt if provided with bad arguments.

```
class String extends Object
{

    //--------- Constructors ----------
    String(String s)
            throws NullPointerException;
    String(char[] c)
            throws NullPointerException;

    String()
        // Create an empty String, i.e., one with length 0.

    //--------- Class methods ---------
    static String valueOf(Object obj);
    static String valueOf(boolean b);
    static String valueOf(char c);
    static String valueOf(char[] c)
            throws NullPointerException;
```

```
◆  static String valueOf(int i);
   static String valueOf(long l);
   static String valueOf(float f);
◆  static String valueOf(double d);


   //------------ Methods ------------
◆  char charAt(int i)
         throws IndexOutOfBoundsException;
◆  int compareTo(String s)
         throws NullPointerException;
   boolean endsWith(String st)
         throws NullPointerException;
◆  boolean equals(Object obj);
   boolean equalsIgnoreCase(Object obj);

   void getChars(int start, int end, char[] c, int cStart)
         throws NullPointerException, IndexOutOfBoundsException;
   /*  This is one of those uncommon String methods that
       modifies the contents of one of its arguments. This
       fills the char array c with the characters in this
       String, from position start to (but not including)
       position end. The argument cStart specifies where in the
       c array the copying should begin. There is a complicated
       precondition for this method to work without error. See
       the simpler version toCharArray(), below. */
   int indexOf(char c);
   int indexOf(char c, int start);
   int indexOf(String st)
         throws NullPointerException;
   int indexOf(String st, int start)
         throws NullPointerException;
   int lastIndexOf(char c);
   int lastIndexOf (char c, int start);
   int lastIndexOf (String st)
         throws NullPointerException;
   int lastIndexOf (String st, int start)
         throws NullPointerException;
   /*  These are the "backwards" versions of the indexOf()
       methods, in that they begin their searches at the end or
       at a specified position and search towards the beginning
       of the string. */

◆  int length();
   boolean startsWith(String st)
         throws NullPointerException;
◆  char[] toCharArray();

   String concat(String st)
         throws NullPointerException;
   String replace(char original, char replacement);
   String substring(int start)
         throws IndexOutOfBoundsException;
◆  String substring(int start, int end)
         throws IndexOutOfBoundsException;
   String toLowerCase();
   String toUpperCase();
   String trim();
}
```

java.util.Vector

As we explained in the chapter, this class behaves much like an array of Objects, with the addition of a number of useful methods. A Vector instance contains an internal array, where all the data is stored, and you should be aware of the distinction between the *capacity* of the internal array (its length) and the *size* of the data set contained in the array. The data elements will always occupy a contiguous range of positions, from 0 to size − 1, and it will always be the case that size ≤ capacity. Note that some of these methods will throw exceptions (Chapter 9), if called with invalid arguments.

```
class Vector extends Object implements Cloneable
{
        //-------- Protected data ---------
        protected int capacityIncrement;
        protected int elementCount;
        protected Object[] elementData;
        /*  These are available to any Vector subclasses.
            capacityIncrement is the amount by which capacity will
            increase when the vector needs to be grown, elementCount
            is the current number of valid elements in this vector
            (i.e., its size), and elementData is the Object array
            where the data is stored. */

        //--------- Constructors ----------
        Vector(int initialCapacity, int capacityIncrement);
        Vector(int initialCapacity);
        Vector();

        //----------- Inspectors ----------
        final int capacity();

        Object clone()
        /*  This is the only nonfinal method in this class. It
            constructs and returns a copy of this vector. This is
            the method promised by implementing the Cloneable
            interface, saying, in effect, "This is a class for which
            we can make copies of its instances." */

        final void copyInto(Object someArray[])
               throws IndexOutOfBoundsException;
        /*  Copy the contents of this vector, in order, into the
            array provided in the argument. The array provided must
            be at least as large as the size of this vector. */

◆    final boolean contains(Object obj);
◆    final Object elementAt(int index)
               throws IndexOutOfBoundsException;
        final Object firstElement()
               throws NoSuchElementException;
◆    final int indexOf(Object obj);
        final int indexOf(Object obj, int start)
               throws IndexOutOfBoundsException;
        final boolean isEmpty();
        final Object lastElement()
               throws NoSuchElementException;
```

```
      final int lastIndexOf(Object obj);
      final int lastIndexOf(Object obj, int start)
            throws IndexOutOfBoundsException;
      /*  These methods act like indexOf(), except that they search
          for the argument object from the end of the vector or a
          start position downwards towards the 0 position. */
◆  final int size();

      //------------ Modifiers ----------
◆  final void addElement(Object obj);
◆  final void ensureCapacity(int newCapacity);
◆  final void insertElementAt(Object obj, int index)
            throws IndexOutOfBoundsException;
◆  final void removeElementAt(int index)
            throws IndexOutOfBoundsException;
      final void removeAllElements();
◆  final void setElementAt(Object obj, int index)
            throws IndexOutOfBoundsException;

      final void setSize(int newSize);
      /*  Change the (logical) size of this vector. If the new
          size is smaller than the current size, discard all the
          elements in positions at or after the argument, and if
          the new size is larger than the current size, then grow
          the vector if necessary and fill the new elements with
          null references. */

◆  final void trimToSize();
}
```

CHAPTER NINE

EXCEPTIONS

An inescapable fact of life is that *things go wrong*. This fact raises its ugly head so often during the execution of programs that we seriously considered adding a subtitle to the title of this chapter: "When bad things happen to good programs." Even if you design a program with utmost care, verifying that every method works exactly as it should and that all the classes coordinate their actions smoothly, there will still be things that can cause your beautifully wrought code to go down in flames. Consider, for example, that you have no control over how your classes will be used (or misused) by other programmers, and you can't possibly guarantee that every user of your program will know precisely what you expect them to do. Fortunately, Java provides powerful error-handling facilities that can be used to make your programs respond gracefully when the inevitable excrement hits the ventilator.

Objectives

In this chapter, we will

- Introduce the Exception classes.
- Review some methods that can generate exceptions.
- Discuss Java's techniques for dealing with exceptions.
- Show you how to invent exceptions of your own.

9.1 Exceptions

Some things that can go wrong during the execution of a program can't possibly be detected at compile-time. Suppose, for instance, your program includes the statement

```
offset = x / n;
```

for int variables offset, x, and y. Now, there's not a thing wrong with this statement from the compiler's point of view—it's a garden-variety expression statement. However, during execution of the program, it might happen that n has the value 0. This is an exceptional state of affairs, because there's no reasonable way to define int division by zero. Java then indicates that something problematic has happened by *throwing an exception*. In effect, what then happens is that an internal alarm bell goes off, indicating to the run-time system that emergency action must be taken. The system then immediately halts its normal mode of execution and goes off looking for help. With luck, the system will find some code in your program that will *catch* the exception and deal with it, perhaps by displaying an error message or taking some other action, such as setting `offset` to some default value. Once the exception has been caught, the alarm bell is silenced and the system picks up execution at a location after the block that contained the offending statement.

Notice how this technique differs from the error handling you're used to. In the old way, you would write code to head off the error before it occurred, probably by writing a guard like this:

```
if (n > 0)      // Guard against division by 0.
   offset = x / n;    // normal action
else
   offset = 10;       // error-state action
```

Using exceptions, however, you would allow the unusual situation to be noted and take steps elsewhere in your program to deal with it. As so often happens in programming, there's not a simple reason to prefer one strategy over the other. You'll see shortly that both techniques for dealing with exceptional situations have their advantages and disadvantages.

Exception Subclasses

Scattered through the Java packages, you'll find sixty or more exception classes. All these classes are derived from the class `Exception`, which is itself a subclass of `Throwable`, as we illustrate in Figure 9.1. The `Throwable` class is also a superclass of

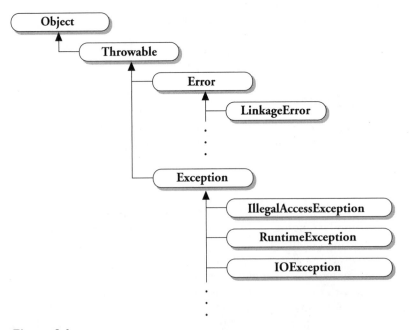

Figure 9.1

Part of the **Throwable** hierarchy.

`Error` and its subclasses. We won't discuss dealing with errors, because they usually arise from situations, such as running out of memory, that are beyond the power of your program to handle.

Exceptions, on the other hand, are used to indicate situations that you generally will be able to handle, such as trying to access a character in an illegal `String` location. Below we list some of the more common `Exception` subclasses.

`java.lang.`**`ArithmeticException`**

Indicates that something, such as division by zero, has gone wrong in an arithmetic expression.

`java.lang.`**`ArrayIndexOutOfBoundsException`**

Indicates that an attempt has been made to access an element in an invalid index in an array (less than 0 or greater than or equal to the array length, for instance).

`java.lang.`**`ArrayStoreException`**

Indicates that an attempt has been made to place an element of the wrong type into an array.

`java.io.`**`EOFException`**

Indicates that an end-of-file mark has been seen. We'll talk about files and the `java.io` package in Chapter 10.

`java.io.`**`FileNotFoundException`**

Indicates that a reference has been made to a file that could not be found.

`java.lang.`**`IllegalArgumentException`**

Indicates a method call with an invalid argument. This is the parent class of `IllegalThreadStateException` and `NumberFormatException`.

`java.lang.`**`IllegalThreadStateException`**

Indicates that a thread is in an inappropriate state for some method call. We'll explain threads in Chapter 11.

`java.lang.`**`IndexOutOfBoundsException`**

This is the parent class of `ArrayIndexOutOfBoundsException` and `StringIndexOutOfBoundsException`. It indicates that an index is out of bounds.

`java.lang.`**`InterruptedException`**

Indicates that execution of some process been interrupted.

`java.io.`**`InterruptedIOException`**

Indicates that an input or output operation has been interrupted.

`java.io.`**`IOException`**

Indicates a general input/output exception.

`java.net.`**`MalformedURLException`**

Indicates an improperly formed URL. We'll discuss the `java.net` package in Chapter 12.

`java.lang.`**`NegativeArraySizeException`**

Indicates that an attempt has been made to declare an array with a negative size specification.

`java.lang.`**`NullPointerException`**

Indicates that a class method is being called by an object instance that is currently `null`.

`java.lang.`**`NumberFormatException`**

Indicates that an illegal number format is being used, often as the argument to a method.

`java.lang.`**`StringIndexOutOfBoundsException`**

Indicates that an attempt has been made to use an inappropriate `String` index.

The `Exception` class itself is very simple. It consists only of two constructors:

```
Exception()
Exception(String message)
```

These both construct a new `Exception` instance, of course. The second constructor allows you to specify a message string as part of the instance. This string could be used to provide details about the nature of the exception, for example. To retrieve the message, you can use the parent class `Throwable`'s method `getMessage()`, which returns the message, if any, associated with the exception. You generally won't construct a new `Exception`—instead, you'll use one of the subclass constructors, with or without a message `String`. As you'll see shortly, you can subclass `Exception` to make exceptions of your own, defining your own constructors.

Methods That Throw Exceptions

Many of the methods we've discussed throw exceptions. Because we have not made use of that fact until now, it's clear that a Java program doesn't have to deal with exceptions, but now that you know they exist, we'll provide a fairly complete list of the methods we've covered that throw exceptions.

Choice:

```
void add(String s)
void addItem(String s)
```

Throw a `NullPointerException` if the argument is `null` (that is, if it hasn't been initialized).

```
String getItem()
void insert(String item, int index)
void remove(String item)
void select(int index)
```

Throw an `IllegalArgumentException` if the index is out of range or the argument of `remove()` is not in this `Choice`.

Container:

```
void add(Component c)
```

Throws an `IllegalArgumentException` if you attempt to add this `Container` to itself. All of the various `Component add()` methods have this property.

Dialog:

```
Dialog(Frame parent)
```

All the `Dialog` constructors throw an `IllegalArgumentException` if the parent argument is `null`.

Double:

```
static Double valueOf(String s)
```

Throws a `NumberFormatException` if the argument doesn't represent a valid double.

Float:

```
static Float valueOf(String s)
```

Throws a `NumberFormatException` if the argument doesn't represent a valid float.

Integer:

```
static int parseInt(String s)
static Integer valueOf(String s)
```

Throw a `NumberFormatException` if the argument doesn't represent a valid `int`. We haven't talked about `parseInt()` yet, though we will shortly.

Label:

```
void setAlignment(int alg)
```

Throws an `IllegalArgumentException` if the argument isn't one of the class constants `Label.LEFT`, `Label.CENTER`, or `Label.RIGHT`.

List:

```
void remove(String item)
```

Throws an `IllegalArgumentException` if the `item` argument isn't in this `List`.

Long:

```
static long parseLong(String s)
static long valueOf(String s)
```

Throw a `NumberFormatException` if the argument doesn't represent a valid `long`.

String:

```
String(String s)
String(char[] c)
int compareTo(String s)
String concat(String s)
boolean endsWith(String s)
int indexOf(String s)
int lastIndexOf(String s)
boolean startsWith(String s)
```

Throw a `NullPointerException` if the argument is `null`.

```
char charAt(int index)
void getChars(int start, int end, char[] c, int cStart)
String substring(int index)
String substring(int start, int end)
```

Throw a `StringIndexOutOfBoundsException` if one or more of the arguments doesn't represent a valid index in this `String`. In addition, `getChars()` throws a `NullPointerException` if the array argument is `null`.

TextArea:

```
void setColumns(int c)
void setRows(int r)
```

Throw an `IllegalArgumentException` if the argument is negative. The `TextField` method `setColumns()` also does this.

Vector:

```
void copyInto(Object[] array)
Object elementAt(int index)
int indexOf(Object obj, int start)
void insertElementAt(Object obj, int index)
int lastIndexOf(Object obj, int start)
void setElementAt(Object obj, int index)
void removeElementAt(int index)
```

Throw an `IndexOutOfBoundsException` if the index isn't valid for the size of this vector or, in the case of `copyInto()`, if the argument array is smaller than the size of this vector.

```
Object firstElement()
Object lastElement()
```

Throw a `NoSuchElementException` if this vector is empty.

Review Questions

1.1 Tell what exception would be thrown by the statement

```
int n = intArray[-10];
```

1.2 Give a statement that would cause a `NumberFormatException` to be thrown.

9.2　Handling Exceptions

Although the process of dealing with exceptions in Java includes some nit-picky details, the basic idea is very simple: You indicate your intention to handle an exception by marking the block where the exception could be raised, and then you include some code that will be called into action only when the need to deal with the exception arises. If the exception doesn't arise, Java simply ignores the extra code.

try and catch

The keyword `try` is used before a *block* of statements (that is, a collection of zero or more statements within braces) that can throw an exception. Putting `try` before a block of code indicates that you have the intention of handling some or all of the exceptions that are thrown within the block. If no exceptions are raised while the statements in the block are being executed, no special action is taken, just as though the `try` weren't there.[1]

Syntax: try Block

A `try` block is written like this:

```
try
{
    // Code that might raise an exception.
}
```

Once you've indicated by a `try` block that you intend to handle some exceptions, the next step is to follow the `try` block with one or `catch` clauses. A `catch` clause consists of a segment of code that looks very much like a method declaration, with a formal argument and a statement body enclosed in braces:

---

[1] We're simplifying things just a bit here. You'll see why when we talk about the `finally` clause at the end of this section.

Syntax: catch Clause

A catch clause is written like this:

```
catch (ExceptionType variable)
{
    // code to handle the exception, perhaps using variable
    // The variable has meaning only within this block.
}
```

If no exception is raised during execution of a try block, its associated catch clauses are skipped. If, however, an exception is raised in the try block and there is a subsequent catch clause that is compatible with the exception type, control immediately passes out of the try block to the appropriate catch clause. The statements in the catch block are then executed, and control passes to the first statement after the try block (ignoring any subsequent catch clauses). The division-by-zero example we used in Section 9.1 would be handled like this:

```
try
{
    offset = x / n;
    // anything from here down will be ignored if n is 0.
}
catch (ArithmeticException e)
{
    offset = 10;
}
// Here's where execution picks up again after handling the
// exception.
```

A couple of important facts are worth mentioning here. First, note that because of the semantics of try...catch, you can assume that if a statement in the try block is executed, none of the previous statements raised any exceptions, because once control passes out of a try block it doesn't return.[2] Second, the catch clauses are examined from the top down, stopping at the first one that has an argument compatible with the exception thrown (in the usual sense of argument compatibility) and skipping all subsequent clauses. This means that you should list your catch clauses in order from most specific to least. For example, the following code would be a waste of effort, because the second catch clause would never be executed.

```
try
{
    ...
}
catch (Exception e)          // This argument type is assignment
                             // compatible with every exception,
```

---

[2]Unless control enters the block from the top at a later time in the usual course of execution, as it might in a loop, for example.

```
   {
       ...
   }
   catch (ArithmeticException e)  // so this would never be used.
   {
       ...
   }
```

A try block must be immediately followed by one or more `catch` clauses, and neither can exist on its own—you can't write a `try` block without following it with a `catch` clause, and you can't write a collection of `catch` clauses without an immediately preceding `try` block.

Exception Propagation

Suppose an exception occurs outside of a `try` block or within a `try` block that is not associated with a `catch` clause of a compatible kind. What happens to the exception then?

If an exception is raised within a `try` block, the system first looks for an associated `catch` clause that can handle it. If none of the `catch` arguments are assignment compatible with the exception (that is, none are superclasses of the exception), the system looks for an enclosing `try...catch` pair. For example, because any statement can appear in a `try` block, the program might look like this:

```
try
{
    ...
    try
    {
        // exception raised here
    }
    catch (SomeException e)
    {
        // but not caught here
    }
}
catch (SomeOtherException e)
{
        // so look here
}
```

This search continues until it comes to the block enclosing the entire method body. If no compatible `catch` clause is found, the search is widened to include the block containing the method call, like this:

```
void oops()
{
    try
    {
        // exception generated
    }
    catch (SomeException e)
```

```
        {
            // but not caught
        }
    }
    ...

    // We're in some other method here, where the original
    // call was made to oops(), the method that caused the exception
    // in the first place.
    try
    {
        oops();     // Exception generated by this call
                    // wasn't caught in oops(),
    }
    catch (SomeOtherException e)
    {
                    // so look here, after having looked in
                    // the code of oops().
    }
```

If there still isn't a match, the process continues, outward through blocks and backward through method calls (and their enclosing blocks), until a catch clause can be found. The same sort of behavior applies to an exception that is not raised within a try block—the search begins at the block enclosing the offending statement and continues outward and back through method calls until the system finds a handler for the exception.

Eventually, a handler for the exception is guaranteed to be found. Where? In the Java environment itself. This is because, if you trace backward through the method calls that got you to a statement, sooner or later you'll find a method that Java itself called, because *it is impossible to run an applet or application except through a call made by Java*. Think about it: An application begins execution at main(), and an applet begins with init() [or a similar call, to paint(), for instance]. Do you make those calls? No. The Java environment does.

Of course, if you haven't provided an exception handler somewhere along the line, Java will terminate the program. That's not always a bad idea. If a method is called by an object that hasn't been initialized, for example, there's really nothing you can do about the resulting NullPointerException, so it's best not to catch it at all and simply to let the program die a horrible death.

Throwing Exceptions

There will be times when you want to generate an exception under your control, rather than passively sitting back and letting Java generate them for you. You can do that by using a throw statement.

Syntax: throw **Statement**

A throw statement has the following form:

throw *exceptionInstance;*

When a `throw` statement is executed, the `exceptionInstance` is sent off to the run-time environment, in just the same way as an exception is generated by Java when it encounters something like an array index out of bounds. Your program could then use a `try...catch` collection to deal with the exception in the usual way. Suppose, for instance, that we had a sequence of statements that required the variable n to be even in order to work correctly. You might deal with this precondition by throwing an appropriate exception, like this:

```
// n gets set to some value here
try
{
    if (n % 2 == 1)      // n is odd
        throw new ArithmeticException();
    else
        // The code that requires n to be even is here
}
catch (ArithmeticException e)
{
    // Deal with odd values of n here.
}
```

This is a somewhat contrived example, we'll admit. It would be far simpler to place the code dealing with odd n right inside the first `if` clause, replacing the `throw` statement, and to eliminate the `try...catch` construct entirely. You still might want to do it as shown, though, if the "odd n" case were rare and the code for dealing with it were extensive. In that case, putting the exceptional part within the `if` statement would just obscure the sense of what goes on in the vast majority of situations, forcing the reader to wade through dozens of lines before realizing, "Oh, this stuff will almost never be done—why did I have to waste time reading it here?"

> A good use for exceptions is to isolate complicated code that deals with unlikely occurrences. Doing so can make a program easier to read.

When you are designing a method that may throw an exception, you have two choices: You can use a `try...catch` to deal with the exception within the method, or you can let the exception go uncaught and rely on the propagation mechanisms to catch the exception elsewhere. If you take the latter course and let the exception propagate out of the method, you should (and in some cases you *must*) indicate to the compiler that your method may perhaps throw an exception that it isn't going to catch itself. This is done by using a `throws` clause in the method header.

Syntax: `throws` Clause

> A throws clause may be appended to a method header, like this:
>
> ```
> void myMethod() throws ExceptionType1, ExceptionType2
> ```
>
> A `throws` clause may name as many `Exception` types as necessary, separating their names by commas.

Here's an example, a method that indicates it could throw one of two kinds of exceptions, either an `IllegalArgumentException` that is explicitly thrown by one of the statements or a `NullPointerException` that is thrown by `equals()` if the invoking `String` instance is `null`.

```
String wantCookie(String s) throws IllegalArgumentException,
                                    NullPointerException
{
    if (s.equals("Cookie"))
        return "Thanks!";
    else
        throw new IllegalArgumentException("Me want Cookie!");
        // Don't need a return, since you can't get here.
}
```

In fact, this method doesn't actually need the `throws` clause. Java makes a distinction between what are known as "checked" and "unchecked" exceptions and has different requirements for each. A "checked" exception is one that *must* be declared in a `throws` clause if it could be thrown and not caught within the method. If the method does not declare that the exception will be thrown, the statement that could cause the exception must be placed in a `try` block with an appropriate `catch` clause later. Of the checked exceptions, the ones that you'll be likely to see are

▲ `InterruptedException`
▲ The file exceptions—that is, the subclasses of `IOException`
▲ Those that you invent yourself by subclassing `Exception`

The subclasses of `RuntimeException`, which constitute the most common exceptions, are "unchecked" and do *not* have to be mentioned in a `throws` clause or handled by a `try` block. These include

▲ `ArithmeticException`
▲ `IllegalArgumentException`
▲ `NumberFormatException`
▲ `IndexOutOfBoundsException` and its two subclasses, `ArrayIndexOutOfBounds` and `StringIndexOutOfBounds`
▲ `NullPointerException`
▲ Those that you invent yourself by subclassing `RuntimeException`

In making this distinction, the designers of Java were guided by the fact that it would be very difficult for a programmer to remember every possible exception that could be thrown by every statement in a method and then include all of them in a `throws` clause. Thus they reserved compile-time checking for those that were rare, easy to locate, and serious.

Advice

Make life easy on yourself. Use a `throws` clause only if a method will throw (and not catch) one of the checked exceptions.

Here's an example of *not* using a `throws` clause. We've designed a subclass, `IntTextField`, of `TextField`. Our intention here is that an `IntTextField` object will contain only a text string that could represent a legal integer. This means that we have to override the superclass's `setText()` method to ensure that the user of this class won't try making a call to the `setText()` method of this class by using an argument like `"two"`.

We do this by using the `Integer` wrapper class method

```
static int parseInt(String s)
```

This method checks the `String` argument to determine whether it is a legal representation of an `int`, such as `"278"`. If it is, the method returns the corresponding `int` value, and if it isn't, the method throws a `NumberFormatException`. Note that we don't catch the exception, first because it's not clear what we would do with it if we did catch it,[3] and second because a bad number format is such a serious violation of the `IntTextField` specification that the user of this class should probably be informed that a mistake was made.

```
class IntTextField extends TextField
{
    ...

    public void setText(String s)
    // NOTE: This method will throw a NumberFormatException if
    // the argument string does not represent a legal int.
    {
        int dummy = Integer.parseInt(s);
        super.setText(s); // Okay--set the text
    }
}
```

This, by the way, is a case where we *couldn't* use a `throws` clause even if we wanted to. Doing so would produce a compilation error, for somewhat subtle language design reasons:

> A method override cannot be declared with a `throws` clause that names exceptions not thrown by the parent method.

In our example, the superclass `setText()` method doesn't throw any exceptions, so it would be a syntax error for us to have a `throws` clause in our override.

Prophylactic Programming

A good program is *robust*, which is to say that it handles unusual situations by taking appropriate action rather than going down in flames. As we mentioned, there

---

[3]Somewhat like the situation of a dog chasing a car.

are basically two ways to deal with run-time problems: Make sure they don't happen in the first place, or let them happen and then deal with the problem.

The first strategy is often implemented by recognizing a potential problem and guarding against it, often by using a test in an `if` statement. The second strategy, of course, is to write a program so that the problem situation will raise an exception and then to catch the exception and handle it. We'll illustrate the difference between these two approaches by considering the method `mindex()` that we introduced in Chapter 8.

```
int mindex(int[] theArray, int start)
// Returns the index of the smallest element at or after the
// index start.
{
    int minIndex = start;
    for (int i = start; i < theArray.length; i++)
    {
        if (theArray[i] < theArray[minIndex])
        {
            minIndex = i;
        }
    }
    return minIndex;
}
```

Whenever we design any method, we should always ask, "What is expected to be true when this method is called?" The statement of what must be true at the start of a method (or any section of code, for that matter) is known as the *precondition*. In the case of `mindex()`, the precondition is simple—the array argument must represent a valid array, and `start` must be a valid index within the array.

The next question we should ask is "Is there any action this method can take to recover if the precondition is violated?" In our example, the answer is both "yes" and "no." If the array argument hasn't yet been initialized, there's nothing `mindex()` can do to recover. Because a method with a non-`void` return must return a value no matter what, there's not even a way to return a default value, such as 0, because doing so would violate the *postcondition*, which is to say the condition that is assumed to be true when the method is complete. In our case, the postcondition is that the `int` returned is the position in the array where a smallest element is to be found, and because there is no legal position in a `null` array, no possible return value could satisfy the postcondition. In short, if the array argument is `null`, we can't even complete the method. In this case, it's best to let the `NullPointerException` occur, thereby aborting the method.

Advice

> If there's no possible way of handling a potential error, raise an exception.

In our example, the `NullPointerException` will be thrown for us, though we could throw one ourselves, if we wished, providing a diagnostic error message,

```
int mindex(int[] theArray, int start)
{
    if (theArray == null)
        throw new NullPointerException("null array in mindex()");
    ...
}
```

For the other part of our precondition, if the argument start isn't a valid index in the array, we can recover, although we have to change the precondition slightly. If the start index is negative, we can simply set it to 0, and if start is greater than the last array index, we can simply make start the last index. We don't need exceptions for this; we can handle everything internally. Our method now looks like this, where we have also specifically listed the pre- and postconditions:

```
int mindex(int[] theArray, int start)
// Pre: theArray has been initialized.
// Post: (1) if start < the length of the array, returns the index
// of a minimal element at or after position start.  (2) if
// start >= the length of the array, returns the last index in the
// array.
{
    // NEW--make sure the index is valid
    if (start < 0)
    {
        start = 0;
    }
    if (start >= theArray.length)
    {
        return theArray.length - 1;      // can leave immediately
    }

    int minIndex = start;
    for (int i = start; i < theArray.length; i++)
    // For each index in the array...
    {
        if (theArray[i] < theArray[minIndex])
        // Found a new smallest value, so record its index.
        {
            minIndex = i;
        }
    }
    return minIndex;
}
```

Advice

If you can handle an error simply, do so without raising an exception.

One of the most important reasons for using exceptions sparingly is that compared to using an if statement to detect and handle the bad situations, the process of throwing and catching exceptions is *slow*, often extremely so. In many environments, it takes hundreds of times longer to throw and catch an exception than it does to use an if statement to do the same thing locally. We'll explore this in the exercises.

Advice

Reserve exceptions for exceptional circumstances.

Finally, `finally`

The `finally` clause is used for activities that should be performed whether or not an exception was thrown and caught.

Syntax: `finally`

The `finally` clause looks like this:

```
finally
{
    // Cleanup code.
}
```

A `try` block can have at most one `finally` clause, and it must appear immediately after the last `catch` clause. If a `try` block has a `finally` clause, it need not have any `catch` clauses. Like `catch`, a `finally` clause must be associated with a `try` block.

The block of a `finally` clause is guaranteed to be executed, no matter how control leaves its `try` block. If none of the `catch` clauses is executed, the `finally` clause is executed after the `try` block. If one of the `catch` clauses is executed, the `finally` clause is executed after completion of the `catch`. The `finally` clause is executed even if the `try` or `catch` portions contain `break` or `return` statements.[4]

A `finally` clause is generally used for cleanup purposes. For example, a `Graphics`, `Frame`, or `Window` object ties up a considerable amount of system resources, so it's good programming manners to free up those resources explicitly by calling the `dispose()` method, like this:

```
void myMethod()
{
    Graphics g = this.getGraphics();
    try
    {
        ...
    }
    finally
    {
        g.dispose();
    }
}
```

Sooner or later g would be disposed by the Java environment, no matter what we did. All we are doing here is making sure it gets freed up as soon as possible.

---

[4]Or a `continue` statement, which causes execution to skip down to the bottom of an enclosing loop.

Review Questions

2.1 Are the braces in a `try` block required or optional?

2.2 How many catch clauses can follow a `try` block?

2.3 If a statement follows a `try...catch` collection, what can you be certain of when the statement executes?

2.4 Does a `throw` statement have to be enclosed in a `try` block?

2.5 What is a checked exception?

9.3   Your Very Own Exceptions

In spite of the wealth of exception types Java provides, there will be times when you want to invent exceptions of your own to signal situations not covered by any of the predefined `Exception` classes. You do this by subclassing `Exception`, if you want a checked exception, or `RuntimeException`, if you want to invent an unchecked exception.

Programmer-defined exceptions are treated just like any others, except, of course, that you have to throw them yourself. In the Lablet for this chapter, we have two exception types of our own design. One of them, `MissingData`, is intended to be thrown when one or more of the applet's `Textfields` are empty. The declaration is simple enough:

```
class MissingData extends Exception
// Thrown by the processSubmitButton() method when one or more
// of the data fields are empty.
{
    public MissingData()
    {
        super();
    }
    public MissingData(String s)
    {
        super(s);
    }
}
```

In both the constructors, all we need to do is call the appropriate superclass constructor. (We actually don't need the first constructor, because Java will call the default superclass constructor for us, but we include it to make our intent obvious to the reader.)

The `MissingData` exception is thrown within a utility method,

```
private void processSubmitButton() throws MissingData
// Make sure all data is filled in before submitting the order.
{
    if ((custName.getText().equals(EMPTY)) ||
        (custStreet.getText().equals(EMPTY)) ||
        // (six more clauses omitted here)
        (order.getText().equals(EMPTY))      )
    {
        throw new MissingData("Must enter data in all fields");
    }
```

```
    else // Data is all there, so submit the order.
    {
        order.appendText(CRLF + "  *** ORDER PLACED ***");
    }
}
```

Note that we had to use a throws clause in the header, because MissingData is a checked exception.

Finally (no pun intended), the exception that was generated and thrown in processSubmitButton() is caught by the applet's actionPerformed() handler.

```
...
else if (source == bSubmit)
{
    try
    {
        processSubmitButton();
    }
    catch (MissingData ex)        // Some data was missing
    {
        order.appendText("*** " + ex.getMessage() + CRLF);
    }
}
```

You can see here how we make use of the message field of Exception, by calling getMessage() to retrieve the message "Must enter data in all fields" and display it to the user.

Review Questions

3.1 Here's an interesting idea for an exception class of your own design—an exception that would be thrown if a method was called with too many or too few arguments: WrongNumberOfArgumentsException. Is this a reasonable suggestion?

3.2 Can you subclass an exception class that you invented?

9.4 Hands On

This chapter's Lablet, OrderPlease (Figure 9.2), is an online ordering program quite similar in purpose to Chapter 2's Gigobite. The main difference is that here we also get information about the customer, such as name, address, and credit card data, and, as a well-behaved electronic order form should, we check for errors in the customer information before processing the order.

As you would expect, we'll use exceptions to handle correctness checking. As an added pedagogical bonus, we'll also make use of an auxiliary class to manage the complexity of this applet in a way you'll find useful in other situations.

Designing the Lablet

The visual design of our applet is simple, once we've collected the various parts into functional units. We have five main parts: the customer information (name, address,

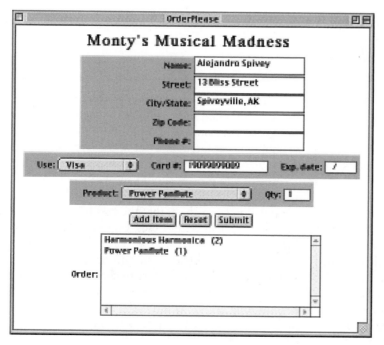

Figure 9.2

The **OrderPlease** applet.

phone number, and so on); the usual credit card information (card type, number, and expiration data); a unit for ordering items (item description and quantity ordered); three buttons to add a new item to the order, clear the order form, and submit an order; and finally a text area where information about the current order is displayed.

The action of the applet is concentrated entirely in the three buttons. The "Add Item" button will add the name of the current selection in the productChoice widget and the number of such items desired to the order display. The "Reset" button will cause all the text in the customer information part and in the order display to be cleared. Finally, the "Submit" button will just display a message that the order has been submitted. Of course, this last action would be much more complicated in a real order form, because we would have to get all the customer, credit card, and order information and send it back to the host computer.

We will deal with button clicks in an actionPerformed() handler where each button click will invoke one of the utility methods processAddItemButton(), processResetButton(), and processSubmitButton().

The bulk of the work done by each of these three methods will deal with handling possible errors on the part of the customer.

Arrogant, Patronizing, and Syntactically Incorrect Definition That, in Spite of Its Faults, Still Contains a Grain of Truth

```
"User" == "Idiot".
```

In spite of the fact that error detection will require some extra work on our part, we should always keep in mind that a program serves the user, not the other way around. Good user interface design is, fundamentally, nothing more than good manners embodied in code—we should never forget that one of the most important parts of a user-centered program is to make the user feel comfortable, no matter what he or she might do. For our part, the design process should always include consideration of what might go wrong and how the program will deal with problems.

In `processAddItemButton()`, we will need to check that the user has indicated a valid number of items in the `custQuantity` field. The "Reset" button will require no special checking on our part, but the method `processSubmitButton()` will at least have to verify that all the fields have been filled before submitting the order. In a "real" application, we might even devote the time necessary to check that the fields have valid information. While checking that a name or address is valid is probably beyond the current state of programming art, we could certainly check that a zip code, telephone number, or credit card number is correctly formed. These latter checks, in fact, make good lab exercises, as you'll see.

Exploring `OrderPlease`

We begin our exploration of the Lablet at the end and then work our way back to the start. At the end of the file, we declare two subclasses of `Exception`; they are `IllegalQuantity` and `MissingData`. We will throw an instance of the former when our program discovers that the quantity of a certain item has been specified to be zero or less, and we'll throw a `MissingData` exception if we discover that the user has neglected to fill in a field like name or credit card number. As usual with `Exception` subclasses, these declarations consist of nothing more than definitions of the two possible constructors.

```java
/**
 * This is thrown by the doAddItem() method when the number
 * of items isn't positive.
 */
class IllegalQuantity extends Exception
{
    public IllegalQuantity()
    {
        super();
    }

    public IllegalQuantity(String s)
    {
        super(s);
    }
}
```

```
/**
 * Thrown by the processSubmitButton() method when one or more
 * of the data fields are empty.
 */
class MissingData extends Exception
{
    public MissingData()
    {
        super();
    }

    public MissingData(String s)
    {
        super(s);
    }
}
```

The next class has nothing to do with exceptions but illustrates a tidy way of dealing with a complicated collection of widgets. In our applet there are ten labels, not counting the title. We could have included each of them in the applet itself, making them local to init(), because they're never used anywhere else. However, init() is complicated enough already, what with eight TextFields, two Choices, three Buttons, and a TextArea.

What we did instead was collect all the Label instances into a single class, Labels, and then generate a new instance of that class, which we named label, in init(). The result was that init() was shortened by nine lines and the only price we had to pay was to remember to refer to each label by using the instance name and a dot, as in label.name and label.street. You should skip down to the applet's init() method to see what we mean.

```
/**
 * The sole purpose of this class is to encapsulate the labels used
 * in the OrderPlease applet.
 */
class Labels
{
    // Since this class is private within the applet, we can get
    // away with giving these variables package access.
    Label    name,
             street,
             cityState,
             zip,
             phone,
             ccName,
             ccNum,
             ccExp,
             product,
             quantity,
             order;

    /**
     * All the constructor has to do is initialize the labels.
     */
    public Labels()
    {
        name =        new Label("Name:", Label.RIGHT);
```

```
    street =    new Label("Street:", Label.RIGHT);
    cityState = new Label("City/State:", Label.RIGHT);
    zip =       new Label("Zip Code:", Label.RIGHT);
    phone =     new Label("Phone #:", Label.RIGHT);
    ccName =    new Label("Use:", Label.RIGHT);
    ccNum =     new Label("Card #:", Label.RIGHT);
    ccExp =     new Label("Exp. date:", Label.RIGHT);
    product =   new Label("Product:", Label.RIGHT);
    quantity =  new Label("Qty:", Label.RIGHT);
    order =     new Label("Order:", Label.RIGHT);
  }
}
```

At the top of the file we come to the applet itself. We begin with the declaration of two `String` constants, for an empty `String` and a carriage return/line feed combination, and follow with declarations of the various widget instances.

```
/**
 * This applet implements a simple order form, using exceptions
 * to catch some of the possible input errors the user might make.
 */
public class OrderPlease  extends Applet
                          implements  ActionListener
{
    private final String    EMPTY = new String(),
                            CRLF = new String("\n");

    private Label   title = new Label("Monty's Musical Madness");

    private TextField   custName = new TextField(20),
                        custStreet = new TextField(20),
                        custCityState = new TextField(20),
                        custZip = new TextField(20),
                        custPhone = new TextField(20),
                        custCC = new TextField(15),
                        custExp = new TextField("  /  ",5),
                        custQuantity = new TextField(4);

    private Labels      label = new Labels();

    private Choice      ccChoice = new Choice(),
                        productChoice = new Choice();

    private Button      bAddItem = new Button("Add Item"),
                        bReset = new Button("Reset"),
                        bSubmit = new Button("Submit");

    private TextArea    order = new TextArea(6,40);
```

The `init()` method does nothing but lay out the various widgets and perform whatever event registry is needed. Here you can see how we used the `Labels` class to replace eight `Label` declarations by a single initialization of a `Labels` object. This method is longer than we would have liked, but there's not much we can do about that for an applet as complicated as this one.

```java
public void init()
{
    title.setForeground(Color.red);
    title.setFont(new Font("TimesRoman", Font.BOLD, 24));
    add(title);

    //----- p1 is the panel that holds the basic
    //----- customer information.

    Panel p1 = new Panel();
    p1.setBackground(Color.cyan);
    p1.setLayout(new GridLayout(5,2, 6, 2));

    p1.add(label.name);
    custName.setBackground(Color.white);
    p1.add(custName);

    p1.add(label.street);
    custStreet.setBackground(Color.white);
    p1.add(custStreet);

    p1.add(label.cityState);
    custCityState.setBackground(Color.white);
    p1.add(custCityState);

    p1.add(label.zip);
    custZip.setBackground(Color.white);
    p1.add(custZip);

    p1.add(label.phone);
    custPhone.setBackground(Color.white);
    p1.add(custPhone);

    add(p1);

    //----- p2 is the credit card information panel.

    Panel p2 = new Panel();
    p2.setBackground(Color.cyan);

    ccChoice.addItem("Visa");
    ccChoice.addItem("AMEX");
    ccChoice.addItem("MasterCard");
    ccChoice.addItem("Discover");

    p2.add(label.ccName);
    ccChoice.setBackground(Color.white);
    p2.add(ccChoice);

    p2.add(label.ccNum);
    custCC.setBackground(Color.white);
    p2.add(custCC);

    p2.add(label.ccExp);
    custExp.setBackground(Color.white);
    p2.add(custExp);

    add(p2);
```

```
//----- p3 is the product panel.

Panel p3 = new Panel();
p3.setBackground(Color.cyan);

productChoice.addItem("Amazing Accordian");
productChoice.addItem("Harmonious Harmonica");
productChoice.addItem("Dapper Drum Set");
productChoice.addItem("Going Going Gong!");
productChoice.addItem("Trump No Trumpet");
productChoice.addItem("Kabloowie Kazooie!");
productChoice.addItem("Power Panflute");
productChoice.addItem("Supersizer Synthesizer");
productChoice.addItem("Zany Zither");

p3.add(label.product);
productChoice.setBackground(Color.white);
p3.add(productChoice);

p3.add(label.quantity);
custQuantity.setBackground(Color.white);
p3.add(custQuantity);

add(p3);

//----- Panel p4a is the button panel.

Panel p4a = new Panel();
p4a.add(bAddItem);
p4a.add(bReset);
p4a.add(bSubmit);

// Register the three buttons
bAddItem.addActionListener(this);
bReset.addActionListener(this);
bSubmit.addActionListener(this);

//----- p4b holds the information about the current order.

Panel p4b = new Panel();
p4b.add(label.order);
p4b.add(order);

//----- p4 holds the button panel and the info panel

Panel p4 = new Panel();
p4.setLayout(new BorderLayout());
p4.add("North", p4a);
p4.add("Center", p4b);

add(p4);
}
```

The heart of the applet, as so often happens, is the `actionPerformed()` method. Here we respond to clicks on any of the three buttons by calling a helper method. You'll see that the `processSubmitButton()` might throw a `MissingData` exception if one or more of the fields have not been filled in, so we catch that exception here and deal with it by displaying an error message in the `order` `TextArea`. Because `order` is an applet instance variable, and hence is accessible within `processSubmitButton()`, we could also have dealt with the missing data problem within the method itself, not using an exception at all. That, in fact, would have been a better choice, but we ignored our own advice in order to show you how exceptions are raised and handled.

```
/**
 * This action routine not only responds to the button clicks
 * for processing the order information, but also catches the
 * possible MissingData exception thrown by method
 * processSubmitButton().
 */
public void actionPerformed(ActionEvent e)
{
    Object source = e.getSource();
    if (source == bAddItem)
    {
        processAddItemButton();
    }
    else if (source == bReset)
    {
        processResetButton();
    }
    else if (source == bSubmit)
    {
        try
        {
            processSubmitButton();
        }
        catch (MissingData ex) // Some data was missing
        {
            order.appendText("*** " + ex.getMessage() + CRLF);
        }
    }
}
```

The `processAddItemButton()` method handles its own exceptions and illustrates two points. First, we find ourselves in a situation where not using an exception would entail a considerable amount of extra work, namely checking that the text in the `custQuantity` field represents a legitimate integer. Although we could write the code necessary to check that a `String` represents a legal `int`, it wouldn't be pleasant to write, especially when the `Integer` class method `parseInt()` will do it for us.

The second point we wanted to illustrate is that we have a `try` block with two associated `catch` clauses. The first catches a `NumberFormatException`, and the second catches the possibility that the quantity is less than or equal to zero (it would make no sense for the customer to request –3 accordions, for example). In both cases, the `catch` clause just displays an error message.

```
/**
 * Before adding a new item to the order, this method first
 * checks that the quantity entered in the custQuantity
 * Textfield is (1) an integer and (2) greater than zero.
 * CALLED BY: actionPerformed()
 */
```

```
private void processAddItemButton()
{
    try
    {
        // This might throw a NumberFormatException
        int quantity = Integer.parseInt(custQuantity.getText());
        // This might throw our own IllegalQuantity exception
        doAddItem(quantity);
    }
    catch (NumberFormatException ex) // not an integer.
    {
        order.appendText("*** Must provide an integer value" + CRLF);
        order.appendText("*** in the quantity field" + CRLF);
    }
    catch (IllegalQuantity ex)      // not positive.
    {
        order.appendText("*** " + ex.getMessage() + CRLF);
        order.appendText("*** in the quantity field" + CRLF);
    }
}
```

The `doAddItem()` method is a helper for `processAddItemButton()`. It checks that the quantity of items is one or more and throws one of our `IllegalQuantity` exceptions if it is not. If the quantity is positive, the method appends the item and its quantity to the order text. Take a look back at the `processAddItemButton()` method. You'll see that by placing a call to this method within a `try` block, after a call to `Integer.parseInt()`, we have guaranteed that this method will be called with a valid integer argument.

```
/**
 * Try to add the current item to the order, checking that the
 * number entered was positive.
 * CALLED BY: processAddItemButton()
 * THROWS: IllegalQuantity
 */
private void doAddItem(int quant) throws IllegalQuantity
{
    if (quant < 1)
    {
        throw new IllegalQuantity("Must have a positive" + " amount");
    }
    else // Quantity is OK, so go ahead and add the item.
    {
        order.appendText("" + productChoice.getSelectedItem()
                        + " (" + custQuantity.getText()
                        + ")" + CRLF);
    }
}
```

The `processResetButton()` method is trivial—all it has to do is clear all the TextFields.

```
/**
 * Clear all the data fields.
 * CALLED BY: actionPerformed()
 */
```

```
private void processResetButton()
{
    custName.setText(EMPTY);
    custStreet.setText(EMPTY);
    custCityState.setText(EMPTY);
    custZip.setText(EMPTY);
    custPhone.setText(EMPTY);
    custCC.setText(EMPTY);
    custQuantity.setText(EMPTY);
    custExp.setText("  /  ");
    order.setText(EMPTY);
}
```

The last method in this class is `processSubmitButton()`, called by the `actionPerformed()` handler. This first checks whether all the `Textfields` have some data, and if one or more don't, it terminates abruptly by throwing a `MissingData` exception. If all the fields have data, this method just displays a message that the order has been submitted.

```
/**
 * Make sure all data is filled in before submitting the order.
 * CALLED BY: actionPerformed()
 * THROWS: MissingData
 */
private void processSubmitButton() throws MissingData
{
    if (     (custName.getText().equals(EMPTY))
        ||   (custStreet.getText().equals(EMPTY))
        ||   (custCityState.getText().equals(EMPTY))
        ||   (custZip.getText().equals(EMPTY))
        ||   (custPhone.getText().equals(EMPTY))
        ||   (custCC.getText().equals(EMPTY))
        ||   (custQuantity.getText().equals(EMPTY))
        ||   (custExp.getText().equals("  /  "))
             (order.getText().equals(EMPTY))      )
    {
        throw new MissingData("Must enter data in all fields");
    }
    else // Data is all there, so submit the order.
    {
        order.appendText(CRLF + "  ***  ORDER PLACED  ***");
    }
}
}
```

Review Questions

4.1 There's a `MissingData` exception that may be thrown in the Lablet. Where is it thrown and where is it caught?

4.2 Along with the `MissingData` and `IllegalQuantity` exceptions that we define ourselves, there's a predefined exception that appears in the Lablet. What is it, where is it thrown, and where is it caught?

9.5 Summary

- The `Exception` class has no methods and only two constructors. One constructor takes no arguments, and the other takes a `String` argument specifying a message that can be retrieved by using the method `getMessage()`, which belongs to `Exception`'s superclass `Throwable`.

- When an exception is thrown, the Java runtime environment immediately suspends its normal mode of execution and looks for a way of dealing with the exception.

- To indicate that a block of code may throw exceptions that your program will attempt to handle, preface the block with the keyword `try`, like this:

```
try
{
    // Code that might raise an exception.
}
```

- A `try` block must be immediately followed by one or more `catch` clauses (or a `finally` clause) of the following form:

```
catch (ExceptionType variable)
{
    // code to handle the exception
}
```

- If no exception is raised during execution of a `try` block, its associated `catch` clauses are skipped. If an exception is raised in the `try` block and there is a subsequent `catch` clause that is assignment compatible with the exception type, control immediately passes out of the `try` block to the appropriate `catch` clause.

- Once control leaves a `try` block, it does not return after executing a `catch` or `finally` clause.

- If an exception is thrown, the system looks for catch blocks by moving outward through enclosing blocks until all of the method has been searched. Then it moves back to the location of the method call and through its enclosing block structure, and so on. If no catch is found that is compatible with the exception, the exception will eventually be caught by the run-time environment.

- A `finally` clause is executed when control passes out of a `try` block, whether through an exception or through a `return`, `break`, or `continue` statement. Like `catch`, a `finally` clause must be associated with a `try` block. A `finally` clause must appear after the last `catch` clause associated with its `try` block.

- `finally` clauses are generally used for cleanup purposes.

- The `throw` statement throws an instance of an exception. It has the following form:

```
throw exceptionInstance;
```

- If a method does not catch an exception, you can indicate that to the compiler by using a `throws` clause at the end of the method header:

```
returnType methodSignature throws listOfExceptionTypes
```

- **RuntimeException** and its subclasses do not need to be mentioned in a `throws` clause and do not need to be thrown within a `try` block. All other exceptions do.
- A method override cannot be declared with a `throws` clause that names exceptions not thrown by the parent method.
- If there is no possible way of handling a potential error, raise an exception.
- If you can handle an error simply, do so without raising an exception.
- Reserve exceptions for exceptional circumstances. Do not use them for routine checking that could be better done with an internal test—using an `if` statement, for example.
- You can declare your own exceptions, usually by subclassing `Exception` (for a checked exception) or `RuntimeException` (if you don't care whether the exception will be checked by the compiler for an enclosing `try` block or `throws` clause).

9.6 Exercises

1. We mentioned that there's no meaningful way to define `int` division by zero. Why? Pick one or more ways of defining division by zero and show that each eventually leads to an inconsistency in the way we would expect arithmetic to work.

2. If you were to write the declaration

```
int[] myArray = new array[5.5];
```

would that statement raise an exception at run-time, or could it be caught earlier, during compilation?

3. Unfortunately, at the time of this writing, some Java run-time environments do not raise all the exceptions we listed in Section 9.1. Write an applet that deliberately raises exceptional conditions, such as division by zero and out-of-range indices in arrays and strings. Which are caught by your system and which are ignored?

4. You've gotten all the way to Chapter 9 and haven't yet seen a true/false exercise. Just for variety, here's one. Tell whether each of the following statements is true or false. Warning: Some of these are tricky.

    a. Every `try` block must be followed by at least one `catch` clause.

    b. Every `catch` clause must be associated with a `try` block.

    c. A `try` block may have two associated `catch` clauses.

    d. A `try` block may have two associated `finally` clauses.

    e. If a `try` block controls just one statement, that statement does not need to be enclosed in braces.

    f. A `try` block may be nested within another `try` block.

    g. A `catch` clause may appear within another `catch` clause.

5. In Section 9.1 we listed a number of exceptions that are thrown by methods we have discussed. Which of them are checked exceptions and which are not?

6. Complete the definition of the `IntTextField` class.

7. What's wrong here?

```
try
{
    // something
}
catch (StringIndexOutOfBoundsException e)
{
    ...
    int errorCount = 1;
}
finally
{
    if (errorCount > 0)
        // do something
    else
        // do something else
}
```

8. Here's a method that takes an array, source, and fills another array, destination, with all the nonzero elements in source, in their original order. For example, if source contained {34, 0, 0, 9, 17, 0, 22}, destination would contain {34, 9, 17, 22} when the method completes. Upon completion, the method will return the number of nonzero elements it saw.

```
int copyNonzero(int[] source, int[] destination)
{
    int j = 0;
    for (int i = 0; i < source.length; i++)
        if (source[i] != 0)
        {
            destination[j] = source[i];
            j++;
        }
    return j;
}
```

a. What is the precondition for this method?

b. Which parts of the precondition can the method handle itself, and which are beyond the method's ability to handle?

c. Write the method so that it handles all the problems it can and throws appropriate exceptions for the ones it can't.

d. Describe the best postcondition you can for this method.

9. Here's the method we used in the text to illustrate the use of the finally clause.

```
void myMethod()
{
    Graphics g = this.getGraphics();
    try
    {
        ...
    }
    finally
    {
        g.dispose();
    }
}
```

There may be a problem here that we didn't mention. Suppose some statement in the `try` block generates a `NullPointerException` that the method is incapable of handling. We still want to dispose of the Graphics object `g`, but after we have done so, the exception hasn't gone away. Do we need to take any special action to pass the exception out of the method, and if so, what do we have to do?

10. Suppose that any of `method1()`, `method2()`, and `method3()` might throw an `ArithmeticException` and that we want to take different actions to handle the exception, depending on its source. Suppose our error-handling was done like this:

```
try
{
    method1();
    method2();
    method3();
}
catch (ArithmeticException e)
{
    ...
}
```

How could we identify the method that threw the exception? You're not allowed to take the easy way out and enclose each of the method calls in its own `try` block. *Hint:* Consider modifying the methods, too.

11. We mentioned that exceptions take much longer to raise and handle than equivalent local tests. Now let's see how large the difference is. Try the following applet, which uses the `Date` class to measure the time, in milliseconds, that it takes to handle several thousand out-of-bounds `String` accesses.

```
import java.applet.*;
import java.awt.*;
import java.util.*;   // for the Date class

public class Test extends Applet
{
    private TextField display = new TextField(10);

    public void init()
    {
        add(display);
        char c = 'a';
        String s = "Sample";
        Date dStart = new Date();
        long timeStart = dStart.getTime();
        for (int i = 0; i < 50000; i++)
        {
            try
            {
                char c = s.charAt(i);
            }
            catch (StringIndexOutOfBoundsException e)
            { }
        }
        Date dEnd = new Date();
        long timeElapsed = dEnd.getTime() - timeStart;
        display.setText("" + timeElapsed);
    }
}
```

Now replace the body of the for loop with this equivalent block and compare the running times of the two versions. It would be instructive to do this exercise in several different Java environments, if possible. If you can, you'll see why.

```
{
    if (i < s.length())
    {
        c = s.charAt(i);
    }
}
```

9.7 Answers to Review Questions

1.1 NegativeArraySizeException.

1.2 Integer i = Integer.valueOf("two"); is one example.

2.1 Required.

2.2 At least one (unless there's an associated finally block), and as many more as you need.

2.3 That no exception was thrown within the try block.

2.4 No.

2.5 An exception, such as IndexOutOfBoundsException, that does not have to be captured by a try...catch combination and does not have to be mentioned in a throws clause in a method header.

3.1 This is a silly idea, for two reasons. First, it's not obvious how one would detect when to throw it, and second, the compiler will catch mismatched arguments with no effort on your part.

3.2 Certainly.

4.1 MissingData is thrown in processSubmitButton() and is caught in the actionPerformed() method.

4.2 NumberFormatException is thrown by the call to parseInt() in the processAddItemButton() method and is caught immediately below.

9.8 Class References

There's no need to explain any of the exception classes in detail, because each consists of nothing but a pair of constructors. Consequently, we'll simply list the most common ones, in hierarchical order, where each class is understood to be a subclass of the nearest one above it at an outer level of indentation. (Thus, for example, RuntimeException is a subclass of Exception.)

```
java.lang.Exception
    java.lang.InterruptedException
    java.lang.RuntimeException
        java.lang.ArithmeticException
        java.lang.ArrayStoreException
        java.lang.IllegalArgumentException
            java.lang.IllegalThreadStateException
            java.lang.NumberFormatException
```

```
java.lang.IndexOutOfBoundsException
    java.lang.ArrayIndexOutOfBoundsException
    java.lang.StringIndexOutOfBoundsException
java.lang.NegativeArraySizeException
java.lang.NullPointerException
java.io.IOException
    java.io.EOFException
    java.io.FileNotFoundException
    java.io.InterruptedIOException
    java.net.MalformedURLException
```

CHAPTER TEN

INPUT/OUTPUT

Up to now, none of the programs you have written have had any long-term memory. When your programs complete their intended tasks and quit, all the information they have saved is lost forever, gone to that great bit bucket in the sky. Clearly, if computers are to have any real practical use, there must be some way to store their results in a more or less permanent form. Consider the Java compiler that you have been using. In this case, there are two things that need to be stored permanently: your source code and the resulting object code. We could dispense with the object code and recompile the source code every time it's needed, but it would be an incredible bother to enter your source code, test and run it, quit for the day, and have to re-enter the same source code the next day.

All modern programming languages have the ability to save the output of a program in an external file that may reside on a hard disk, for instance. Once the file is written to the disk (or tape, or compact disk, or any of a number of other media), it may be read at a later date and used as input for a program—either the same program that generated the file in the first place or an entirely different program. In this chapter, we will discuss the classes Java provides for file input and output.

Objectives

In this chapter, we will

- Introduce Java's stream types.
- Use streams to read from and write to files.
- Discuss Java's security measures and see how they determine how much access they provide to the environment's file structure.
- Use what you've learned to build a functional word processor.

10.1 Streams

Java input and output are accomplished by using the *stream* classes InputStream and OutputStream and their subclasses, some of which we illustrate in Figure 10.1, along with the File class. These classes are all found in the java.io package. A stream in Java is an ordered sequence of objects and a collection of methods that allow you to extract an object from the stream (*read* it from the stream) and add a new object to the stream (*write* it to the stream). Although we'll be primarily concerned with reading from and writing to files that reside on an external source, such as a floppy disk or a hard drive, Java streams may be associated with other data sources, such as a String or an array of bytes in memory.

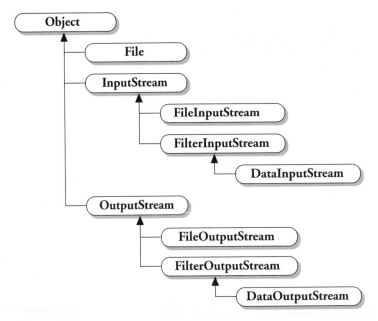

Figure 10.1

Part of the stream hierarchy.

The Classes `InputStream` and `OutputStream`

The basis for input and output in Java is the pair of abstract classes `InputStream` and `OutputStream`. Because they are abstract, you cannot construct an instance of either of these classes, but they provide the basic operations common to all of their subclasses. These classes reside at the top of their respective hierarchies, so they provide limited functionality for input and output; more sophisticated methods are provided by their subclasses. In fact, the input and output methods of these two classes are limited to reading and writing single bytes or arrays of bytes.

An `InputStream` object provides a source of bytes that your program may read. You'll note that all of the methods listed below may throw an `IOException`. This might happen in response to a number of conditions—for example, if the source of bytes has become unavailable because a disk has been ejected or has become corrupted.

It's important to realize that `InputStreams` differ from most other Java data structures in that the access methods `read()` have the side effect of removing the byte or bytes read, rather than just copying them (Figure 10.2).

```
int available() throws IOException
```

This returns 0. Overrides of this method in subclasses may return an integer that indicates how many bytes are currently available to be read.

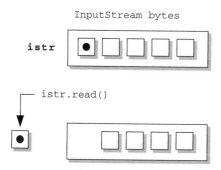

InputStream bytes

istr

istr.read()

Figure 10.2

Reading from a stream removes what was read.

```
void close() throws IOException
```

Streams consume a fair amount of system resources. This method frees up the resources and, as a consequence, makes further input operations impossible. You should always close an InputStream object when you're finished using it.

```
int read() throws IOException
```

This abstract method is intended to be overridden by subclasses of this class. Where it is implemented, it extracts and returns the next available byte from this stream. The byte value is a number from 0 to 255, and if there are no bytes currently available in this object, the method returns −1.

```
int read(byte[] bArray) throws IOException, NullPointerException
```

Reads bytes from this stream and transfers them into the argument array. This method attempts to fill the entire array and returns the actual number of bytes read. It throws a NullPointerException if the array has not been initialized.

```
int read(byte[] bArray, int offset, int length)
    throws IOException, NullPointerException, IndexOutOfBoundsException
```

Reads bytes into the array, starting at bArray[offset] and continuing until length bytes have been transferred or no bytes remain. This method returns the actual number of bytes transferred. It is not hard to come up with the conditions that would cause this method to throw an IndexOutOfBoundsException. We leave that as an exercise.

```
long skip(long n) throws IOException
```

Discards the specified number of bytes from this stream, just as though they had been read. This method returns the actual number of bytes discarded, because, for instance, there may not be n bytes available in this stream.

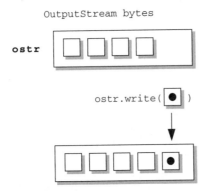

OutputStream bytes

ostr

ostr.write(●)

Figure 10.3

Writing to an **OutputStream** (compare with Figure 10.2).

The OutputStream class (Figure 10.3) is the companion class to InputStream. An instance of OutputStream provides a destination where your program may write one or more bytes. Note, by the way, that we can think of bytes being written to one end of a stream and read from the other. This will be useful to bear in mind when we discuss files, because the same sequence of bytes can be used for both input and output streams.

```
void close() throws IOException
```

Like the InputStream method of the same name, this method closes this OutputStream. Once closed, no further operations may be performed on this stream. You should close an OutputStream as soon as you are finished with it.

```
void flush() throws IOException
```

This does nothing. In some subclasses of OutputStream, though, objects are stored temporarily in a *buffer* before being written to the stream. For those classes, flush() causes all buffered objects to be written to the stream immediately.

```
void write(int n) throws IOException
```

Writes the low-order eight bits of n to the stream, ignoring the other twenty-four bits. For example, write(781) would write the byte 00001101 to the stream, because 781 is 00000000 00000000 00000011 00001101 in binary.

```
void write(byte[] bArray)
    throws IOException, NullPointerException
```

Writes the bytes bArray[0], bArray[1], . . . in that order, to the stream.

```
int write(byte[] bArray, int offset, int length)
    throws IOException, NullPointerException, IndexOutOfBoundsException
```

Writes the bytes bArray[offset], bArray[offset + 1], ..., bArray[offset + length - 1] to the stream.

The Classes `DataInputStream` and `DataOutputStream`

The `DataInputStream` and `DataOutputStream` classes are so useful that you would write them yourself if they weren't provided in the `java.io` package. In nearly all applications that need input or output, you will want to do much more than simply read and write bytes. For example, it would be far nicer to be able to read an `int` from a stream by calling one method, `readInt()`, than it would to read four bytes from an `InputStream` and convert them into an `int` yourself.

The two classes we'll discuss in this section may be regarded as wrapper classes for `InputStream` and `OutputStream`. `DataInputStream` and `DataOutputStream` have access to all the methods of their parent classes, and they add the extra functionality necessary to read or write any of Java's primitive types.[1]

The class `DataInputStream` has a single constructor.

`DataInputStream`(InputStream in)

This constructs a new `DataInputStream`, using the `InputStream` argument as the source of its bytes.

`DataInputStream` provides a complete suite of methods for reading primitive types. These methods are all `final`, so you can't override them if you make your own subclass of `DataInputStream`. As with the `InputStream` methods, all of these may throw an `IOException` (if they're called on a closed stream, for example) and although we don't mention it in the individual descriptions, all of these methods except `skipBytes()` will throw an `EOFException` if the end of file is reached before all the needed information has been read.

All of these methods are compatible with the `write()` methods of `DataOutputStream`. Thus, for example, the bytes written by `writeInt()` will be converted correctly when they are read by `readInt()`.

boolean **readBoolean**() throws IOException

Values of `boolean` type are stored in streams as a single byte, with the value 0 representing `false` and any nonzero value representing `true`. This method reads a single byte from the stream and returns the corresponding boolean value.

byte **readByte**() throws IOException

Reads and returns a single byte. The byte value is considered to be *signed*, so it may represent any value between −128 and 127.

char **readChar**() throws IOException

---

[1] Though we needn't go into details here, the wrapper class methods come from the fact that they implement the interfaces `DataInput` and `DataOutput`.

Extracts two bytes and returns the corresponding Unicode character.

```
double readDouble() throws IOException
```

Reads eight bytes and returns the corresponding `double` value.

```
float readFloat() throws IOException
```

Reads four bytes and returns the corresponding `float` value.

```
int readFully(byte[] bArray)
    throws IOException, NullPointerException
int readFully(byte[] bArray, int offset, int length)
    throws IOException, NullPointerException,
        IndexOutOfBoundsException
```

These methods read data from this stream into an array of bytes. For details, see the descriptions of the `read()` methods of `InputStream`.

```
int readInt() throws IOException
```

Reads four bytes and returns the corresponding `int` value.

```
long readLong() throws IOException
```

Reads eight bytes and returns the corresponding `long` value.

```
short readShort() throws IOException
```

Reads two bytes and returns the corresponding `short` value.

```
void skipBytes(int n) throws IOException
```

Discards n bytes from this stream. This method may discard fewer than the desired number of bytes if there aren't enough available in the stream. In any case, it will return the number of bytes discarded.

As we mentioned, the `DataOutputStream` class provides writing methods that are compatible with the reading methods of `DataInputStream`. This means that you don't have to worry about how `writeInt()` actually stores an `int` in four bytes. All that matters is that if the `int` was written by `writeInt()`, those four bytes will give the same value when `readInt()` is called.

There is a single `DataOutputStream` constructor.

```
DataOutputStream(OutputStream in)
```

This constructs a new `DataOutputStream`, using the `OutputStream` argument as the destination of its bytes.

The methods of this class are given below. Some of the descriptions are self-evident and have been omitted. For details about the number of bytes each type requires, see the descriptions of the corresponding `read()` methods of `DataInputStream`. As with `DataInputStream`, most of these methods are `final`.

```
void flush() throws IOException
```

Like the `OutputStream` method of the same name, this causes immediate writing of any buffered output.

```
int size()
```

Returns the number of bytes written to this stream so far.

```
void write(int n) throws IOException
```

This is an implementation of the abstract `write()` method of `OutputStream`. It writes the low-order eight bits of the argument.

```
int write(byte[] b, int offset, int length)
    throws IOException, NullPointerException,
        IndexOutOfBoundsException
```

Writes the bytes

```
b[offset], b[offset + 1], . . . , b[offset + length - 1]
```

to the stream. This is an override of the similar method in `OutputStream`.

```
void writeBoolean(boolean b) throws IOException
void writeByte(int n) throws IOException
```

Write the low-order eight bits of n to the stream.

```
void writeBytes(String s) throws IOException
```

Writes s to this stream, using one byte for each character in the argument `String`. To use this with `readLine()`, make sure the argument is terminated by a newline character. You'll often call this method like this:

```
ostr.writeBytes(myString + "\n");
```

```
void writeChar(int n) throws IOException
```

Writes the low-order two bytes of the argument to this stream. Most of the time, you'll call this method with a `char` argument, which is, of course, compatible with the wider `int` type.

```
void writeChars(String s) throws IOException
```

This method acts as `writeBytes()` does, except that it uses two bytes for each character in the `String` argument. If you use this method in conjunction with `readLine()`, which expects a single byte for each character, you may get strange results.

```
void writeDouble(double d) throws IOException
void writeFloat(float f) throws IOException
void writeInt(int n) throws IOException
void writeLong(long l) throws IOException
void writeShort(int n) throws IOException
```

Write the low-order two bytes of n to this stream.

Review Questions

1.1 The important stream methods transfer information between a stream and the program that uses it. In which direction does the transfer proceed in a *read* method, from program to stream or from stream to program?

1.2 You don't need many of the InputStream methods if you are using a DataInputStream, because the latter class's methods can do most of the reading operations of InputStream. Which InputStream methods *are* important if you are using a DataInputStream?

1.3 What is the difference between the DataOutputStream methods writeChars() and writeBytes()?

10.2   File I/O

The term *file* is an abstraction representing the information that's physically stored on some device like a floppy disk. We can think of a file as any collection of information that is logically related, such as the text and formatting tags in an HTML document or the bytes in a compiled program. Fortunately for us, the hardware-specific details of how the information in a file is stored on a device and how it can be located is handled by the *operating system* of the computer.

Java further isolates us from the details of the operating system by providing us with two fundamental stream classes, along with a few other classes that make file input and output fairly painless.[2] In this section and the next, we'll start with a simple problem in file input and output and then gradually introduce and add features that illustrate the things a well-behaved program does with files.

The FileInputStream and FileOutputStream Classes

To use a file as a source of bytes for reading or as a destination to which to write, Java provides the FileInputStream and FileOutputStream classes. These are subclasses of InputStream and OutputStream, respectively, and they provide the same primitive reading and writing capabilities as their parent classes.

FileInputStream has three constructors, two of which are of interest to us here.

```
FileInputStream(String filename)
    throws FileNotFoundException, SecurityException
FileInputStream(File f)
    throws FileNotFoundException, SecurityException
```

The first of these creates a new FileInputStream attached to the file with a name specified by its argument, and the second creates a new instance attached to the specified File argument. We'll talk about the File class shortly. We'll talk about the SecurityManager class and SecurityExceptions in Section 10.4.

This class has the following methods, which are either implementations or

---

[2]At least when we can do file I/O at all. You'll see what we mean in Section 10.4.

overrides of methods in `InputStream` (where you should look for the method descriptions).

```
int available() throws IOException
void close() throws IOException
int read() throws IOException
int read(byte[] bArray) throws IOException, NullPointerException
int read(byte[] bArray, int offset, int length)
    throws IOException, NullPointerException,IndexOutOfBoundsException
long skip(long n) throws IOException
```

`FileOutputStream` is defined quite similarly to `FileInputStream`, in that it has two constructors and its methods are implementations or overrides of the similarly named methods of the parent class `OutputStream`.

```
FileOutputStream(String filename)
    throws FileNotFoundException, SecurityException
FileOutputStream(File f)
    throws FileNotFoundException, SecurityException

void close() throws IOException
void write(int n) throws IOException
void write(byte[] bArray)
    throws IOException, NullPointerException
int write(byte[] bArray, int offset, int length)
    throws IOException, NullPointerException,IndexOutOfBoundsException
```

A `FileInputStream` is an `InputStream` by inheritance, so it can be used as the actual argument in the constructor of `DataInputStream`. By wrapping a `FileInputStream` in a `DataInputStream`, we can use the methods of `DataInputStream` to read any of the primitive types from a file. To open a file with a specified name this way, all you need to do is write

```
FileInputStream fstr = new FileInputStream(name);
DataInputStream in = new DataInputStream(fstr);
```

or you could eliminate the step of making a `FileInputStream` variable and simply gang the two constructors together, like this:

```
DataInputStream in = new DataInputStream(new FileInputStream(name));
```

If you want to write to a file, you can do the same sort of thing to wrap a `FileOutputStream` inside a `DataOutputStream`:

```
FileOutputStream fstr = new FileOutputStream(name);
DataOutputStream out = new DataOutputStream(fstr);
```

I/O for Primitive Types

Once you have constructed a `FileOutputStream` and used it to construct a `DataInputStream`, you have all the `write()` methods of the latter class. As an example, the method that follows shows how you would make a new file named

"Sample," write a `String`, a `double`, and an `int` to it, and then close the file that was created.

```
void buildMyFile(String s, double d, int n)
{
   // First, attach the file to a DataOutputStream.
   FileOutputStream fstr = new FileOutputStream("Sample");
   DataOutputStream out = new DataOutputStream(fstr);

   // Now, write the information.
   out.writeInt(s.length());
   out.writeChars(s);
   out.writeDouble(d);
   out.writeInt(n);

   // We're done, so close the stream.
   out.close();
}
```

After all the preliminaries it took to get to this point, we suspect you'd agree that this is a pretty simple process. The only part that needs explanation is why we bothered to write the length of the String s before we wrote the string. We need to do this, because although we can write a String as a list of characters using `writeChars()`, there's no corresponding way of reading a string except character by character. For that we need to know how many characters we'll have to read. At any rate, once we're finished, our file looks like this:

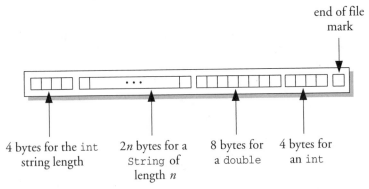

4 bytes for the int string length

$2n$ bytes for a String of length n

8 bytes for a double

4 bytes for an int

The end-of-file mark in the accompanying illustration is just a conceptual convenience indicating that Java has a way of knowing where the file ends, either by counting bytes or by using a special character. It's not a "real" byte in the sense that you could read it or, in fact, inspect it in any way.

If you could use a text editor to open the file "Sample," you'd see the string, preceded and followed by a bunch of unrecognizable junk. The junk would be the `double` and the `int`; those values are stored in a `DataInputStream` in their binary representations, not in their character equivalents.[3] This makes inspecting the file

---

[3]If you ever need to write primitive types as strings of characters, you can use the `PrintWriter` class. This provides methods for writing information in textual rather than binary form.

once it has been built somewhat difficult, but it actually makes our life easier. Suppose that a DataOutputStream stored numbers as strings of characters. How would you interpret the string "34.091667" if you knew it represented a double followed by an int? Should it be interpreted as 34.0 and 91667 or as 34.091 and 667? The nice part of using a *fixed-length representation* for all primitive types is that there is no ambiguity—the first eight bytes are the double, and the next four are the int.

Reading the file "Sample" is equally easy. Since, conceptually, we write to a file by appending new material to the right and we read by removing data from the left, we would read the length int first, followed by the chars of the string, by the double, and finally by the int.

Fundamental Principle of File I/O

Read 'em like you wrote 'em.

Here's how we would read the data from the file:

```
String s;
double d;
int n;
...
void readMyFile()
{
   // First, attach the file to a DataInputStream.
   FileInputStream fstr = new FileInputStream("Sample");
   DataInputStream in = new DataInputStream(fstr);

   // Now, read the information, in the order it was written.

   // First, read the string length and use that to build
   // an array of chars for the string. Then, read the chars
   // and use them to construct the string.
   int len = in.readInt();
   char[] buffer = new char[len];
   for (int i = 0; i < len; i++)
   {
      buffer[i] = in.readChar();
   }
   s = new String(buffer);

   // Now, get the rest of the data.
   d = in.readDouble();
   n = in.ReadInt();

   // We're done, so close the stream.
   in.close();
}
```

You can see now why we wrote the length of the String before we wrote its chars. Without it, we would have no way of knowing how many of the subsequent bytes should be interpreted, in pairs, as chars. In other words, we would have no way of knowing where the String stopped and the double began.

I/O for Class Types

It's not much more difficult to read and write class types than it is to do I/O on the primitive types—all you do is apply the appropriate `DataInputStream` or `DataOutputStream` methods to the class's member data. It is often convenient to provide a class with methods that can be used to do the reading and writing, as we do below with the methods `readFrom()` and `writeTo()`.[4]

```
class Record
{
    private String s;
    private double d;
    private int n;

    public Record(String s, double d, int n)
    {
        this.s = new String(s);
        this.d = d;
        this.n = n;
        this.s = s;
    }

    public void readFrom(DataInputStream in) throws IOException
    // Try to read the data from "in." If something goes wrong,
    // we can't handle it, so just pass the IOException along.
    {
        int len = in.readInt();
        char[] buffer = new char[len];
        for (int i = 0; i < len; i++)
        {
            buffer[i] = in.readChar();
        }
        s = new String(buffer);
        d = in.readDouble();
        n = in.readInt();
    }

    public void writeTo(DataOutputStream out) throws IOException
    // Try to write the data to "out." As with reading, if
    // something goes wrong, pass the exception to the calling
    // routine.
    {
        out.writeInt(s.length());
        out.writeBytes(s);
        out.writeDouble(d);
        out.writeInt(n);
    }
}
```

Then we could use this `Record` class in an applet or application by constructing the appropriate stream and using it for input or output. To write a file "Sample2" containing one `Record` object, we could do this:

---

[4]We should admit that we're making things more complicated here than they need to be. The classes `ObjectInputStream` and `ObjectOutputStream` are designed for reading and writing many kinds of class objects without your having to worry about how their member data are represented. We decided not to discuss them, though, because life is complicated enough with just what we'll cover here.

```
Record myRecord = new Record("Thursday", 34.09, 1667);
...
private void doSave()
{
    try
    {
        FileOutputStream fstr = new FileOutputStream("Sample2");
        DataOutputStream out = new DataOutputStream(fstr);
        myRecord.writeTo(out);
        out.close();
    }
    catch (IOException ex)
    // Just display the exception.
    {
        System.err.println(ex);
    }
}
```

To get the saved value from the file "Sample2" and use it to set the fields of myRecord, we could call the method defined like this:

```
private void doOpen()
{
    try
    {
        FileInputStream fstr = new FileInputStream("Sample2");
        DataInputStream in = new DataInputStream(fstr);
        myRecord.readFrom(in);
        in.close();
    }
    catch (IOException ex)
    {
        System.err.println(ex);
    }
}
```

Headers

Now suppose that we wanted to write and later read not just a single Record object but an entire collection of such objects. We might, for instance, have set up an array of Records, like this:

```
Record[] rArray = new Record[10];
rArray [0] = new Record("first", 3.00787, 442);
rArray [1] = new Record("second", 0.02768, -5);
rArray [2] = new Record("third", -4.30117e2, 0);
int numRecs = 3;
```

It certainly wouldn't be hard to write these to a file; all we'd have to do is have each of the three array elements call its writeTo() method. The problem comes when we try to read the elements back, perhaps in another program. How do we know how many Records are stored in the file?

An elegant solution is to store the number of records in the file itself, using a single int at the start to hold the number of Records that follow, just as we did when writing a String. What we've done is make what is known as a *file header*—some

A `Record` object's file representation

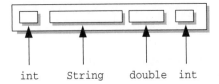

    int   String   double int

A file of `Record`s, with header

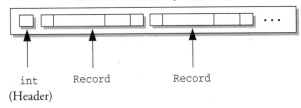

  int   Record   Record
(Header)

Figure 10.4

A typical file structure.

extra data in the file that provides information about the file itself, as we illustrate in Figure 10.4.

Using a file with a header that stores the number of records, our doSave() and doOpen() methods now would look like this:

```
private void doSave()
{
   try
   {
      FileOutputStream fstr = new FileOutputStream("Sample3");
      DataOutputStream out = new DataOutputStream(fstr);

      // Write the header.
      out.writeInt(numRecs);

      // Write the rest of the Records
      for (int i = 0; i < numRecs; i++)
         r[i].writeTo(out);
      out.close();
   }
   catch (IOException ex)
   {
      System.err.println(ex);
   }
}

private void doOpen()
{
   try
   {
      FileInputStream fstr = new FileInputStream("Sample3");
      DataInputStream in = new DataInputStream(fstr);
```

```
        // Read the header value.
        numRecs = in.readInt();

        // Read the Records, now that we know how many we have.
        for (int i = 0; i < numRecs; i++)
            r[i].readFrom(in);

        in.close();
    }
    catch (IOException ex)
    {
        System.err.println(ex);
    }
}
```

Using a header to store the number of records in a file is indeed elegant, but you can't guarantee that every program that would make a file of Records will be that helpful. If the file just consisted of a collection of Records, how would you know how many elements the file contained? It turns out that you don't need to know. A simple way of reading all the elements from such a file is just to keep reading until you run out of things to read. If any of the read() methods of DataInputStream encounter the end of the stream before they have enough bytes to complete their operation, they will throw an EOFException. All we have to do is catch that exception and realize that it means we've read everything there is in the file. Our doOpen() method would then take the following form:

```
private void doOpen()
{
    try
    {
        FileInputStream fstr = new FileInputStream("Sample4");
        DataInputStream in = new DataInputStream(fstr);

        numRecs = 0;

        while (true)
        // We're counting on an EOFException to be thrown
        // eventually, to get us out of this never-ending loop.
        {
            r[numRecs].readFrom(in);
            numRecs++;
        }
        in.close();
    }
    catch (EOFException ex)
    {
        // Nothing needed here, since we expected this exception
        // to be thrown eventually.
    }
    catch (IOException ex)
    // Catch any other unexpected behavior.
    {
        System.err.println(ex);
    }
}
```

Review Questions

2.1 If you look at the definition of the DataInputStream constructor in the previous section, you'll see that it takes an InputStream as an argument. How, then, can we use a FileInputStream as an argument to construct a new DataInputStream?

2.2 What is the basic idea about the order of reading information from a file?

2.3 DataOutPutStream is capable only of writing primitive types. How can we use the class to write class types to a stream?

2.4 What is a file header?

10.3 Advanced File I/O

As you just saw, writing to files and reading from files is basically quite simple. There are, however, some things we'd like to be able to do with files that go beyond the basics. In this section, we'll introduce some new classes that permit us to do with files the things that a robust and sophisticated program should do.

Filtering File Names

You may have seen some applications that limit the files you can open to a certain type. A paint program, for example, might restrict you to opening files that contain graphical images. The FilenameFilter interface gives you a means of doing this. A class that implements FilenameFilter will provide the code for a single method:

```
boolean accept(File directory, String name)
```

Returns true if the file in the given directory and having the given name is one that should appear in a list of files or a file dialog box.

When we talk about the File and FileDialog classes, you'll see how they can use a class that implements FilenameFilter. Here's an example of such a class, which filters out any file whose name doesn't end with a ".txt" extension.

```
class TxtFilter implements FilenameFilter
{
    // Doesn't need a constructor, since we let Java
    // provide a default constructor for us.

    public boolean accept(File dir, String name)
    {
        if (name.endsWith(".txt"))
            return true;
        else
            return false;
    }
}
```

The File Class

Lots of things can go wrong when we try to open a file. The file name we provide in the FileInputStream or FileOutputStream may not be the name of any file; it might be the name of a directory, rather than a data file, or it might be the name of a file to which we are denied access for security reasons. The constructors for these two streams will throw a `FileNotFoundException` if the associated file can't be opened, but we might want to know about the validity of a file *before* we attempt to open it.

The `File` class has several methods that allow us to get information about a file. To construct a new `File` object, you give the constructor the `String` representing the name of the file.[5] The `File` instance will be created even if the name doesn't represent a valid file—this is handy, because we can then use methods of the `File` class to test whether the name really does refer to a file.

Below, we list some of the `File` methods, omitting some that are beyond the scope of this discussion. Each of the methods listed below may throw a `SecurityException` if the current `SecurityManager` will not permit the operation. We'll talk about security in Java in Section 10.4.

```
boolean canRead()
```

Returns `true` if this file can be read; otherwise, returns `false`.

```
boolean canWrite()
```

Returns `true` if this file can be written; otherwise, returns `false`.

```
boolean delete()
```

Attempts to delete this file. This method returns `true` if the deletion succeeded and returns `false` if the file wasn't deleted. You might use this in a program if the user was trying to write a file with a name that already existed. The program might then ask something like "A file with this name already exists. Delete it?" and then call `delete()` if the user answered in the affirmative.

```
boolean equals(Object ob)
```

Returns `true` if the argument is a file with the same name as this one; otherwise, returns `false`.

```
boolean exists()
```

Returns `true` if this object exists (i.e., there is a file or directory with the same name as this file); otherwise, returns `false`.

```
boolean isDirectory()
```

Returns `true` if this object is a directory; otherwise, returns `false`.

```
boolean isFile()
```

Returns `true` if this object is a data file; otherwise, returns `false`.

---

[5]Actually, the string is the *path name* of the file, relative to the directory where the Java interpreter is located. We won't discuss the intricacies of path names in any detail.

```
long lastModified()
```

Returns a number representing the last modification time of this file. This number may have no correspondence to clock time. All you can be sure of is that if you compare the numbers for two files, the one with larger number was modified later.

```
long length()
```

Returns the number of bytes in this file.

```
String[] list()
String[] list(FileNameFilter f)
```

If this file is a data file, these methods return a `null` array. If this file is a directory, they return an array containing the names of all the files the directory contains. These methods only list the top-level files in this directory—they don't look in any directories that this directory might contain.

The second of these methods allows you to specify a `FileNameFilter` to limit the files that appear in the list. For example, we could use the filter we declared at the start of this section to limit the list of files to those with names ending in ".txt".

```
String[] items;
File myFile;
...
TxtFilter filter = new TxtFilter();
items = myFile.list(filter);
```

Below, we present an example that uses some of the `File` methods. The primary task of `makeInputStream()` is to encapsulate the construction of a new `FileInputStream` and wrap it in a `DataInputStream`. As a bonus, this method also first checks whether the `FileInputStream` constructor should be able to complete its task, by seeing whether a file with the given name exists, is a data file, and can be read. If any of these conditions are not met, the method throws a `FileNotFoundException` of its own, providing a diagnostic message about the reason for failure.

```
private DataInputStream makeInputStream(String name)
    throws FileNotFoundException
{
    // Get information about the file, if any,
    // with the specified name.
    File f = new File(name);

    if (!f.exists())     // Does the file exist?
        throw new FileNotFoundException("\"" + name + "\" doesn\'t exist");

    if (!f.isFile())     // Is it a data file?
        throw new FileNotFoundException("\"" + name + "\" isn\'t a file");

    if (!f.canRead())    // Can we read from this file?
        throw new FileNotFoundException("\"" + name + "\" can\'t be read");

    // If we get this far, we can attach a new
    // DataInputStream to the file,
```

```
      // and that's just what we do.
      FileInputStream fs = new FileInputStream(name);
      DataInputStream source = new DataInputStream(fs);
      return source;
}
```

Now we could modify our doOpen() method so that it begins by calling makeInputStream(). If that call doesn't throw an exception, we know that we can try to read from the file. If makeInputStream() happens to throw one of our FileNotFoundExceptions, we can take some action based on the message we gave the exception when we threw it.

```
private void doOpen()
{
   try
   {
      DataInputStream in = makeInputStream(name);

      numRecs = in.readInt();
      for (int i = 0; i < numRecs; i++)
         r[i].readFrom(in);

      in.close();
   }
   catch (FileNotFoundException ex)
   {
      String s = ex.getMessage();
      if (s.endsWith("doesn\'t exist"))
         // Take some action.
      else if (s.endsWith("isn\'t a file"))
         // Take some other action.
      else if (s.endsWith("can\'t be read"))
         // Take yet another action.
      else
         System.err.println(ex);
   }
   catch (IOException ex)
   {
      System.err.println(ex);
   }
}
```

The FileDialog Class

In the footnote on page 449 we said we weren't going to discuss the details of how to deal with the native file system's path conventions. We don't have to, because for most user-oriented programs we can use Java's FileDialog class to provide users with the familiar file selection dialog boxes, thereby eliminating any need for them (or you, for that matter) to know how to specify the location of a file. Figure 10.5 illustrates a typical file dialog box. The appearance of a file dialog depends on the system in which it appears, but all file dialogs do the same thing: They allow the user to find or specify a file, and they then return the path name of the chosen file for the program to use.

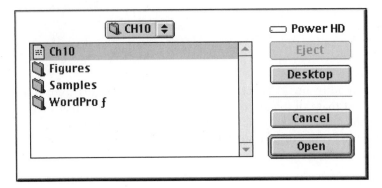

Figure 10.5

A LOAD file dialog box.

The `FileDialog` class is part of the `java.awt` package. It is a subclass of `Dialog`, which we discussed in Section 4.3. File dialogs are modal, which you may recall means that they trap all events the user might generate until the dialog is put away.

There are two class constants in the `FileDialog` class. These constants, `FileDialog.LOAD` and `FileDialog.SAVE`, are used in one of the constructors to indicate whether the dialog is to be used to locate a file for reading, like the example in Figure 10.5, or whether to specify a file for writing, like the one illustrated in Figure 10.6.

There are three constructors for a `FileDialog`. All three require a `Frame` argument, specifying the parent of the `FileDialog`. As a result, it is easier to construct a

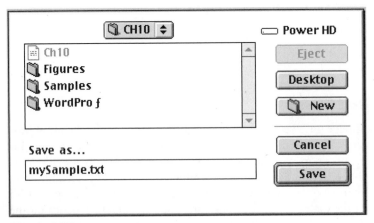

Figure 10.6

A SAVE file dialog box.

`FileDialog` from within an application than from within an applet; a Java application is generally made by subclassing `Frame`. This, as you'll see in Section 10.4, is not much of a hardship, because file access from applets is problematic at best.

FileDialog(Frame parent)
FileDialog(Frame parent, String mssg)
FileDialog(Frame parent, String mssg, int mode)

The first constructor creates a new `FileDialog` with no message string (which would appear as the dialog title or as a label within the dialog), in LOAD mode. The second constructor allows you to specify the message for a LOAD dialog, and the third allows you to specify both the message and the mode. The mode must be either `FileDialog.LOAD` or `FileDialog.SAVE`.

The `FileDialog` methods allow you to get the file information the user provided and to set the initial information displayed in the dialog. All of the `set()` methods must be called before the dialog is shown.

String **getDirectory**()

Returns a `String` representing the directory selected by the user.

String **getFile**()

Returns the name of the selected file.

FilenameFilter **getFilenameFilter**()

Returns the `FilenameFilter` associated with this dialog. This method returns `null` if this dialog has no `FilenameFilter`.

int **getMode**()

Returns the current mode of this `FileDialog`. The returned value will be one of the constants `FileDialog.LOAD` or `FileDialog.SAVE`.

void **setDirectory**(String dir)

Allows you to set the opening directory—that is, the one the user will see when the dialog comes up.

void **setFile**(String name)

Allows you to set the opening file name. This would be used to produce a default file name in a SAVE mode dialog.

void **setFilenameFilter**(FilenameFilter filter)

Sets the `FilenameFilter` of this dialog to be the one specified in the argument. The files that appear in the dialog window will be only those for which the filter's `accept()` method returns `true`. Unfortunately, you may find that your Java environment won't filter the names that appear in the dialog.

```
void setMode(int mode)
```

Allows you to set the mode of this dialog.

If we were interested only in reading and writing files in the current directory (that is, where the Java interpreter resided), we wouldn't have to bother with the directory information. However, we can't guarantee that the user won't choose to open a file elsewhere in the file system, so we need to use the directory to construct the complete file name. For example, as this chapter was being written, it was located in the directory

```
/power HD/Books/programming.java/text
```

and had the name Ch10, so the complete name for this chapter would be made by concatenating the directory, the separator character (which can be found in the File class constant File.separator), and the file name:

```
"/power HD/Books/programming.java/text" + "/" + "Ch10"
```

Fortunately, we never have to see these details. We can get the information from the FileDialog, use it to build the file name, and then use the name to construct a FileInputStream or FileOutputStream. The following code might be executed after the user selected Open from the File menu, for example.

```
// Build the dialog.
FileDialog fd = new FileDialog(this, "Open...", FileDialog.LOAD);

// Bring it up. As with any modal dialog, execution blocks at this
// point, until the user puts the dialog away.
fd.show();

// Make the complete file name.
String fdir = fd.getDirectory();

String fname = fd.getFile();
String name = fdir + File.separator + fname;

// Be polite and free up the dialog's system resources.
fd.dispose();

// Now we can use the name to make a FileInputStream.
FileInputStream = new FileInputStream(name);
```

We should actually be more careful here, because the getFile() method returns a null String if the user puts the dialog away by clicking the Cancel button. It would be safer to test first, like this:

```
FileDialog fd = new FileDialog(this, "Open...", FileDialog.LOAD);
fd.show();
String fdir = fd.getDirectory();
String fname = fd.getFile();
fd.dispose();
```

```
if (fname != null)
{
    String name = fdir + File.separator + fname;
    FileInputStream = new FileInputStream(name);
    ...
}
else
    // Take some action in response to a user cancellation.
```

Review Questions

3.1 Why is the `File` class so far up in the `java.io` class hierarchy?

3.2 How can you determine the number of bytes in a file?

3.3 Why is it harder to use a `FileDialog` in an applet than in an application?

3.4 How can we avoid having to know the exact path name of a file we want to open?

10.4 Security, Applets, and Applications

Almost from the beginning, Java was designed with the Worldwide Web in mind. The operating assumption was that a Java applet would reside on a *host* system and would be downloaded over the Net to a *client* computer. Once it had been copied to the client system, the applet would then be run by a Java-enabled Web browser. The last thing in the world the Java design team wanted was to put a loaded gun in the hands of a malicious applet designer, so Java was designed from the start with security in mind.

Consider some of the things that could happen if a hostile program were allowed to execute on the client system. The program might do any of the following:

▲ Destroy or alter files.

▲ Damage the client system's directory structure.

▲ Get information about the client system, such as user name, e-mail account information, or passwords, and pass it back to the host system.

▲ Get file system information, such as directory contents, and send it to the host system.

▲ Damage other executable programs, causing them to malfunction or not to work at all.

▲ Introduce viruses into the client system.

▲ Consume so many system resources that the client machine slows to a crawl or can't do anything at all.

▲ Steal data or programs from the client.

▲ "Spoof" the client by appearing to be a trusted program and then acting in a dangerous or annoying fashion.

As you'll see, Java does quite a lot to protect against these and other forms of dangerous behavior by applets, and Web browsers typically add their own security measures on top of the precautions Java takes. The resulting protections aren't perfect—it's theoretically impossible to protect against every eventuality—but we can say that Java is at least as secure as other programming languages and far more secure than many. The theme of this section, though, is not so much security in Java as the implications these security measures have on what your applets are allowed to do with files and what they're forbidden to do.

Java Security

People have known for centuries that security is enhanced by adopting a multi-layer approach: If a potential danger slips through one level, there's still a chance it will be caught at the next. Java embodies this approach by providing four levels of protection, which we'll explain by using metaphors from a hypothetical action movie.

First, *the Java language itself is safe.* By not having explicit access to memory addresses (through what are known as *pointers* in other languages), Java programs cannot search arbitrary locations in memory. This same memory protection is enforced by array bounds checking. If a program could set up an array and then access array indices far outside of the array bounds, a program could do what is known as "core fishing," making probes into memory locations outside of those allocated to the program to see what's stored in memory. In our movie, this means that access to the top-secret government installation is restricted to humans. No ultra-powerful alien cyborgs that can bash down the doors and no supernatural beings that can phase through walls are permitted.

Second, before running an applet, Java passes the compiled code through a *bytecode verifier,* to make sure that the code is legitimate Java and doesn't contain any viruses, for instance. The next scene in the movie shows the visitor passing through a metal detector and being subjected to ID checks, fingerprinting, and retina scans to make sure that Doctor Jones isn't carrying any weapons and is who she claims to be.

Third, applets that come across the Net are handled by the *applet class loader,* which assigns the applet its own limited area of memory and makes sure it obeys access restrictions. The class loader also makes sure that an applet doesn't replace any of the standard Java classes with versions of its own. Doctor Jones has gotten in from the outside, but she is restricted to visiting Level Five. All the doors to the other levels are locked.

Finally, every applet runs under a *security manager,* which monitors any attempts to access the rest of the system and throws a `SecurityException` when the applet attempts an action that is deemed to be insecure. Having gotten into Level Five, Doctor Jones finds herself accompanied by an armed guard wherever she goes. She can walk around Level Five to her heart's content, but the guard will block any attempt she makes to open one of the closed doors or look in a locked file cabinet.

We'll be interested mainly in the last level, because the `SecurityManager` instance assigned to an applet controls access to the file system. We'll see that our movie metaphor, like all metaphors, is only a partial reflection of reality.

Applet Security

When an applet is loaded, either by an applet runner or by a Web browser, the application uses its own `SecurityManager` instance to monitor the applet while it is running. In general (though not always), the `SecurityManager` is initialized to make a distinction between applets that come across the Net, assuming they are not to be trusted, and applets that are loaded from the client's local file system, which are treated as being somewhat more trustworthy.

If an applet is loaded from the Net, it is generally not allowed to

▲ Read or write files on the local file system.
▲ Delete any files on the local file system.
▲ Get any information about local files or directories, or even check whether they exist.
▲ Make a new directory on the local system.
▲ Rename or move any files on the local file system.

Some applet runners allow you to establish an *access control list* that name files and directories to which applets may have access, but you can usually be guided by the following observation:

Advice: Local File Access

Assume that any applet you write will be denied access to the client's file system.

Applet runners are designed with an eye toward applet development, so for applets that reside on the same system as the applet runner, the rules are often relaxed. If you write an applet that accesses files on your own computer, you will probably discover that you can do most of the file operations you want.[6]

On the other hand, Web browsers generally don't distinguish between local applets and applets that they load over the Net, and they generally deny both any access to the local file system. This, of course, makes a Web browser a less than ideal vehicle for testing applets that do any file access. For example, you shouldn't expect an applet to be able to put up a `FileDialog` within a Web browser, because doing so would allow the applet to get information about the local file system from a trusting but naive user.

Note that nothing we've said would have any impact on an applet such as `Gigobite` or `OrderPlease`. Both of these get information from the user (but *not* from the user's file system) and could be expanded to send the order information back to the host file system, from which the applet originated. Denying access to the host file system would severely limit the usefulness of many applets, so such access is generally allowed.

---

[6]Though you will probably not be allowed to use the `File` class's `delete()` method.

Advice: Access to the Host System

> You may generally assume that an applet will be allowed access to files on the host system.

Note that everything we've said so far concerns applets rather than Java applications. This is because the security restrictions imposed on applets differ markedly from those imposed on applications.

Security of Java Applications

There is none! A Java application is a stand-alone program and has the same access to the system on which it is running as any other program. For an application, the client system is the same as the host system, and the user takes the same chances with a Java application as he or she would with any "off the shelf" software such as a Web browser, a spreadsheet, a word processor, or a game. Of course, the safety features of the language itself are still in place, but as far as files are concerned, an application can do whatever it wants.

For programs that must deal with files, the conclusion is obvious. Unless you're writing a program that must be run from within a browser, such as our ordering Lablets, write it as an application rather than an applet.

This isn't a burdensome restriction, because there is very little difference between the code that makes up an applet and the code that makes up an equivalent application. (You saw this in the discussion of the `DialogAppTest` application in Chapter 4.) Though there are some minor details to take care of, you can usually change an applet to an application, and vice versa, by using these equivalences:

1. An application extends `Frame`; an applet extends `Applet`.
2. An application is initialized within its constructor; an applet does its initialization in its `init()` method.
3. An application has a `main()` method; an applet doesn't.

The following list shows applets and applications in parallel. You can see the equivalences in each line.

Applet Version	*Application Version*
``public class Foo extends Applet
{
    // Variables
    public void init()
    {
        // Code
    }
    // Methods
}``` | ```public class Foo extends Frame
{
    // Same variables
    public Foo()
    {
        // Same code
    }
    // Same methods

    public static void
        main(String[] args)``` |

Applet Version	Application Version

```
                                    {
                                        Frame f = new Foo();
                                        f.show();
                                    }
                                }
```

As an example, we'll provide an application that uses `FileDialogs` and shows the complete path name of the file the user selected. You should recognize much of this code from the example we provided at the end of Section 10.3. All we've done here is wrap the code in an application with some widgets.

```java
import java.awt.*;
import java.awt.event.*;
import java.io.File;

public class Test extends Frame implements ActionListener
{
    private TextField   display;      // to display path information
    private Button      loadBttn,     // brings up LOAD dialog
                        saveBttn;     // brings up SAVE dialog

    public Test()
    // Lay out the widgets and register the buttons.
    {
        display = new TextField(20);
        add("Center", display);
        Panel p = new Panel();
        loadBttn = new Button("Load");
        p.add(loadBttn);
        saveBttn = new Button("Save");
        p.add(saveBttn);
        add("South", p);

        loadBttn.addActionListener(this);
        saveBttn.addActionListener(this);
    }

    public void actionPerformed(ActionEvent e)
    // Handle clicks on either of the buttons.
    {
        Object source = e.getSource();
        if (source == loadBttn)
        {
            FileDialog fd = new FileDialog(this, "Open...",
                                    FileDialog.LOAD);
            fd.show();
            String fdir = fd.getDirectory();
            String fname = fd.getFile();
            fd.dispose();
            if (fname != null)
            {
                String name = fdir + File.separator + fname;
                display.setText(name);
            }
        }
```

```
        else if (source == saveBttn)
        {
           FileDialog fd = new FileDialog(this, "Save...",
                                          FileDialog.SAVE);
           fd.show();
           String fdir = fd.getDirectory();
           String fname = fd.getFile();
           fd.dispose();
           if (fname != null)
           {
              String name = fdir + File.separator + fname;
                 display.setText(name);
           }
        }
     }

     public static void main(String[] args)
     {
        Frame f = new Test();
        f.setBounds(20, 20, 400, 200);
        f.show();
     }
  }
```

Review Questions

4.1 Why are the security restrictions on applets so tight as effectively to deny applets any access to the client machine's file system?

4.2 What method is required in an application?

4.3 What are the major code differences between applets and applications?

10.5 Hands On

Perhaps the most surprising part of this chapter's Lablet is how short it is. It's a tribute to the power of Java that in just over three hundred lines of code, we've managed to build a functioning word processor. Admittedly, WordPro lacks many of the features we've come to associate with its commercial cousins: It has no formatting capabilities such as tab and margin settings, the text is limited to a single typeface in a single style, and we can't embed graphics in a WordPro document. However, it does have the ability to open any text document and save a document to a file, and it can do the usual cut, copy, and paste operations. If you wanted, you could use WordPro to write and edit your Java programs or compose a letter to a friend. As you'll see when you do the lab exercises, you can even use WordPro to inspect its own source code!

Designing the Lablet

As you can see in Figure 10.7, the WordPro application is visually quite simple.[7] It has two Menus, File and Edit; a central TextArea where the text is displayed; and a TextField at the bottom that is used for status messages.

---

[7]When you run WordPro, it won't necessarily look quite like this, because your system may display frames and menus differently.

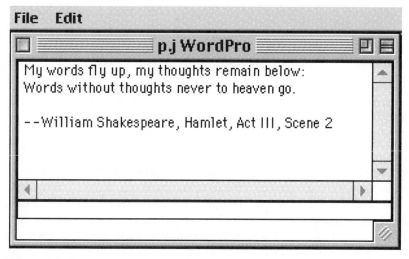

Figure 10.7

The **WordPro** interface.

You've had enough experience by now that you can probably anticipate what we did to make the WordPro interface. We constructed two Menus and added the necessary MenuItems (as you can see in Figure 10.8), and we used the default BorderLayout of Frame to put the TextArea in the center and the TextField in the south region. The Frame, of course, came from the fact that WordPro is an application, not an applet.

The active part of the Lablet is based entirely on the items in the two menus, so we can begin this stage by specifying what should happen when the user selects each of the menu items. Specifying these actions was easy—all we had to do was look at what a real word processor does. In the list that follows, we've described the

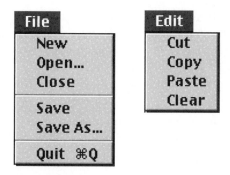

Figure 10.8

WordPro's File and Edit menus.

actions WordPro currently takes, along with some hints about what a good program should do.

File Menu Items

New: Clears the text in the TextArea and clears the current file name, if any. *Enhancements:* A user-friendly application should first ask the user whether he or she wants to save the current text. A sophisticated program would keep the current text and bring up a new editing frame for the new text.

Open: Brings up a FileDialog in LOAD mode. If the user cancels the dialog, displays a message to that effect in the status box and takes no further action. If, on the other hand, the user selects a file to open, the text is cleared and replaced by the contents of the opened file. The number of characters read is displayed in the status field. *Enhancement:* As with New, we should give the user a chance to save the current text before it is replaced, or take the sophisticated option of opening the file in a new frame.

Close: Not implemented in WordPro. *Enhancement:* A sophisticated program would close the front frame, after first asking the user whether he or she wants to save the frame's contents to a file. A really sophisticated program would keep track of whether the text in the frame was "dirty" (that is, whether it had been modified since the last save) and would not bother the user by asking whether to save text that wasn't dirty.

Save: First, checks whether we have a name for the current file. If we do, just writes the text to the current file. If we don't have a current file name, brings up a FileDialog in SAVE mode and allows the user to select a file where the text should be saved. The number of characters written is displayed in the status field. *Enhancement:* We should make sure that we have write permission and that we're not trying to write to a directory. Most of the time, because of the way FileDialog works on most systems, the latter condition won't occur.

Save As: Not implemented. We leave to you the task of figuring out what choosing this item should do.

Quit: Exit the application. *Enhancement:* If there's any text, we should give the user the option of saving it before quitting. A sophisticated program would ask whether to save only if the text was dirty. A very sophisticated program with multiple frames would ask this question for every dirty frame.

Edit Menu Items

Cut: Copy the selected text to a "clipboard" String and then delete the selected text.

Copy: Replace the clipboard text with the current selection without changing the text in the TextArea.

Delete: Delete the selected text without saving it to the clipboard.

Paste: Insert the text in the clipboard, if any, at the location of the cursor in the text area.

To implement these actions, we'll design `private` utility methods for nearly every menu choice. In fact, if you stop to think about it, the only portions of `WordPro` that have to be `public` are the `actionPerformed()` handler and the `main()` method (which must be `public`). We made the constructor `public` out of habit. It doesn't have to be, because it will never be called from outside the `WordPro` class, but it might be if we ever made a subclass of this application.

Introducing `WordPro`

We begin with the usual collection of instance variables. The `String` `clipboard` will be used to save text that is cut or copied, so that we'll have it for subsequent paste operations.

The `init()` method does the usual layout—we build the menus and add their items, and we add the `text` and `display` widgets.

```
public class WordPro extends Frame implements ActionListener
{
    private String      clipBoard = new String();
    private String      fileName  = new String();
    private TextArea     text     = new TextArea("", 20,80,
                                    TextArea.SCROLLBARS_VERTICAL_ONLY);
    private TextField    display   = new TextField(15);

    public WordPro()
    {
        setTitle("p.j WordPro");
        setFont(new Font("SansSerif", Font.PLAIN, 12));
        MenuBar mbar = new MenuBar();

        // Define and add the File menu to the menu bar.

        Menu mf = new Menu("File");
        mf.add(new MenuItem("New"));
        mf.add(new MenuItem("Open..."));
        mf.add(new MenuItem("Close"));
        mf.addSeparator();
        mf.add(new MenuItem("Save"));
        mf.add(new MenuItem("Save As..."));
        mf.addSeparator();
        mf.add(new MenuItem("Quit", new MenuShortcut(KeyEvent.VK_Q)));
        mbar.add(mf);

        // Define and add the Edit menu to the menu bar.

        Menu med = new Menu("Edit");
        med.add(new MenuItem("Cut"));
        med.add(new MenuItem("Copy"));
```

```
        med.add(new MenuItem("Paste"));
        med.add(new MenuItem("Clear"));
        mbar.add(med);

        // Attach the menu bar and add the text area and display
        // to our frame. Remember, frames use Border layout.

        setMenuBar(mbar);
        add(BorderLayout.CENTER, text);
        add(BorderLayout.SOUTH, display);

        // Register the two menus as sources of action events and
        // register the application as a source of window events,
        // to be handled by our member class WindowMinder,
        // defined below.

        mf.addActionListener(this);
        med.addActionListener(this);
        addWindowListener(new WindowMinder(this));
    }
```

The real work begins with the `actionPerformed()` handler. As we mentioned when discussing the design of this Lablet, we respond to most of the menu selections by invoking one or more appropriate helper methods.

```
public void actionPerformed(ActionEvent e)
{
    String itemText = e.getActionCommand();
    if (itemText.equals("Quit"))
    {
        this.dispose();
        System.exit(0);
    }
    else if (itemText.equals("New"))
    {
        clearText();
        fileName = "";
    }
    else if (itemText.equals("Open..."))
    {
        doOpen();
    }
    else if (itemText.equals("Save"))
    {
        doSave();
    }
    else if (itemText.equals("Cut"))
    {
        doCopy();
        doClear();
    }
    else if (itemText.equals("Copy"))
    {
        doCopy();
    }
    else if (itemText.equals("Paste"))
    {
        doPaste();
    }
```

```
    else if (itemText.equals("Clear"))
    {
        doClear();
    }
}
```

The next thing we see is one of those member classes we introduced back in the SketchPad Lablet of Chapter 6. We're interested only in WindowClosing events (as any polite application should), so we subclass WindowAdapter here so that we won't have to implement all seven of the WindowListener methods. In this application, all we do is exit the program. Things would be slightly different if we were doing the sophisticated version, because we would want to destroy the frame and not exit from the program.

```
private class WindowMinder extends WindowAdapter
{
    private Window owner;

    /**
     * Construct a new WindowMinder object by recording
     * a reference to the application to which it belongs.
     */
    public WindowMinder(Window theWindow)
    {
        owner = theWindow;
    }

    /**
     * Handle a request by the user to close the
     * application's window by freeing up the window's
     * resources and quitting.
     */
    public void windowClosing(WindowEvent e)
    {
        if (e.getSource() == owner)
        {
            owner.dispose();
            System.exit(0);
        }
    }
}
```

File Commands

When the user selects Open from the File menu, the actionPerformed() method invokes the doOpen() method. You've seen this method in several guises already—we put up a LOAD FileDialog, and when control returns from the dialog, we check that the user selected a file. If not, we leave immediately.

```
private void doOpen()
{
    FileDialog myFD = new FileDialog(this,"Open...", FileDialog.LOAD);
    myFD.show();

    // Get the file name chosen by the user.
```

```
String name = myFD.getFile();
String dir = myFD.getDirectory();
fileName = dir + File.separator + name;
myFD.dispose();
if (name == null)
{
   display.setText("Open operation cancelled");
   return;
}
```

If the user hasn't canceled the operation, we assume (dangerously) that the selected file is valid, so we clear the current text and read from the file into the text. We first read the number of characters in the file. Next we read the rest of the file into an array of chars and then use that array to build a String, which we place in the TextArea.

```
clearText();
try
{
   FileInputStream fis = new FileInputStream(fileName);
   DataInputStream inStream = new DataInputStream(fis);

   int len = inStream.readInt();
   char[] buffer = new char[len];
   for (int i = 0; i < len; i++)
   {
      buffer[i] = inStream.readChar();
   }

      text.setText(new String(buffer));
   inStream.close();
   display.setText(len + " chars read from " + fileName);
}
catch (IOException e)
{
   display.setText("" + e);
   return;
}
}
}
```

The doSave() method is very similar to the doOpen() method. We do a little more here than we did in doOpen(), though, because we first check whether fileName is the empty String. If it is, it means that the user hasn't gotten the text from a file, so we put up a SAVE dialog to get a name for the file to be saved. As we did in doOpen(), we also check whether the user has canceled the save operation. We leave this method if that happened.

```
private void doSave()
{
   // If we don't have a file name, get one.
   if (fileName.equals(""))
   {
      FileDialog myFD = new FileDialog(this,"Save as...",
                              FileDialog.SAVE);
      myFD.show();

      // Get the file name chosen by the user.
```

```
        String name = myFD.getFile();
        String dir = myFD.getDirectory();
        fileName = dir + File.separator + name;
        myFD.dispose();
        if (name == null)
        {
            // User canceled the save dialog.
            display.setText("Save operation canceled");
            return;
        }
    }
```

If the user hasn't canceled the operation, we assume (again, dangerously) that the selected file is suitable for writing. We get the entire text `String` and write its length and then write the string to the file, using the `DataOutputStream` method `writeChars()`.

```
    String theText = text.getText();
    try
    {
        FileOutputStream fos = new FileOutputStream(fileName);
        DataOutputStream outStream = new DataOutputStream(fos);

        // Write the entire contents of the text to
        // the file.

        outStream.writeInt(theText.length());
        outStream.writeChars(theText);
        outStream.close();
        display.setText(theText.length() + " chars written to " +
                    fileName);
    }
    catch (IOException e)
    {
        display.setText("" + e);
        return;
    }
    }
}
```

The `clearText()` utility is called by `doOpen()` and by the New choice of the `actionPerformed()` method. We encapsulate it as a method just so that we can use a descriptive name in the two locations where it's called. This makes the code somewhat easier to read, at the expense of another method call. Because this operation will occur so infrequently, we decided that the expense of a method call was justified in the interest of clarity.

```
private void clearText()
{
    text.setText("");
}
```

Edit Commands

We're finished with the file operations, so we can turn our attention to the actions that take place when the user selects an option from the Edit menu. We get a lot of help from Java here; a `TextArea` automatically handles the details of highlighting any selections we make, recording the positions of the start and end of the selected text. As we have noted, several of the editing operations use a `String`, which we called `clipBoard`, to hold selected text for copying and pasting.

The `doCopy()` method is called when the user selects the Cut or Copy items from the Edit menu. All we have to do here is copy the selected text to the `clipBoard`. The `doPaste()` operation is not much more complicated. All we have to do is replace the selected text with the contents of the clipboard, using the `replaceText()` method of the `String` class.

```
private void doCopy()
{
    clipBoard = new String(text.getSelectedText());
}

private void doPaste()
{
    text.replaceText(clipBoard, text.getSelectionStart(),
                     text.getSelectionEnd());
}
```

The `doDelete()` method is called when the user selects Cut or Delete from the Edit menu. We delete the selected text in a three-step process. First, we use the `String` methods `getSelectionStart()` and `substring()` to make a temporary copy of everything before the selected portion. Second, we use `getSelectionEnd()` and `substring()` to get everything after the selection. Finally, we concatenate these two substrings and replace the text with the result, thereby removing the selected portion. Works like a charm!

```
private void doClear()
{
    // String "all" holds our text temporarily so that we can
    // operate on it.

    String all = new String(text.getText());
    String s1 = new String(all.substring(0, text.getSelectionStart()));
    String s2 = new String(all.substring(text.getSelectionEnd()));
    text.setText(s1 + s2);
}
```

The `doPaste()` method is simple. All we have to do is replace the selected text with the contents of the clipboard, using the `replaceText()` method of the `String` class.

```
private void doPaste()
// Replace the current selection with the contents of
// the clipboard
{
    text.replaceText(clipBoard, text.getSelectionStart(),
                     text.getSelectionEnd());
}
```

Finishing up

We finish our class declaration with the usual boilerplate code that's part of most Java applications. The `main()` method here is more or less standard for applications. We construct a `Frame` for the application by invoking the `WordPro` constructor, we size the frame suitably, and we show it. Once that's done, all the program has to do is wait for the `actionPerformed()` handler to deal with events triggered by menu selections.

```
public static void main(String args[])
{
    Frame myFrame = new WordPro();
    myFrame.setSize(400,300);
    myFrame.show();
}
}
```

Review Questions

5.1 What is the purpose of the internal `WindowMinder` class?

5.2 In the `doOpen()` method, we bring up a file dialog box. How do we determine whether the user clicked the Cancel button (or its equivalent)?

5.3 Do the Edit operations do any file manipulation?

10.6 Summary

- A stream is an ordered sequence of objects and a collection of methods that allow you to extract an object from the stream (that is, to *read* it from the stream) and add a new object to the stream (to *write* it to the stream).
- The abstract class `InputStream` is the basis for all streams that serve as a source of data to be read. This class contains methods for byte-level input.
- The abstract class `OutputStream` is the basis for all streams that serve as a destination for data to be written. As with `InputStream`, the methods of this class support byte-level output.
- Conceptually, information is read from one end of a stream and written to another.
- The streams we have discussed may be opened for reading or writing, but not both. (The `RandomAccessFile` stream can be opened in both modes.)
- The `DataInputStream` subclass of `InputStream` provides methods for reading all of Java's primitive types.
- A `DataInputStream` is constructed by supplying any `InputStream` instance. The resulting `DataInputStream` then provides all of its operations in addition to those of the `InputStream` instance it encloses.
- The `DataOutputStream` class is a companion to `DataInputStream` in that any value written by a `DataOutputStream` method can be read by the corresponding `DataInputStream` method.

- Because of the way streams are read and written, the information in any stream constructed by a sequence of write operations can be extracted by the corresponding sequence of read operations.
- A file is any collection of information that is logically related and stored on a physical device, such as a floppy disk, hard drive, magnetic tape, or compact disk.
- File input is accomplished through the `FileInputStream` class. This is a subclass of `InputStream`, so a `FileInputStream` can be used in the constructor of a `DataInputStream` instance to provide routines for reading any primitive type from a file.
- The class `FileOutputStream` is the companion of `FileInputStream`. As with input, it is common to wrap a `FileOutputStream` inside an instance of `DataOutputStream`.
- It is generally easy to perform I/O on class instances by reading or writing the primitive types that constitute the instance's member data.
- A header is a collection of information at the start of a stream. A typical use of headers is to store the number of records that follow in the stream.
- Most of the stream read methods will throw an `EOFException` if they reach the end of the stream before completing the read operation. A common way of reading from files is to keep reading until the `EOFException` is thrown.
- The `FilenameFilter` interface includes a single method, `accept()`. A class that implements `FilenameFilter` provides an implementation of `accept()` to determine whether a file name will be accepted or not. This interface is used with the `File` method `list()` and (perhaps, depending on the Java environment) with the `FileDialog` method `setFilenameFilter()`.
- An instance of the `File` class is constructed by supplying a file name. This class contains a number of useful methods for finding information about files.
- `FileDialog` is a subclass of `Dialog`. It is used to allow the user to select a file and to return the name of the file and the name of the file's directory.
- A `FileDialog` instance may be in one of two modes, LOAD and SAVE. The only difference is in the appearance of the resulting dialog.
- In most cases, applets have no access to the client file system.
- It is usually safe to assume that an applet will have access to its own host file system.
- There are no limitations on the file system access a Java application has, except those that are in force for all other programs on the system.

10.7 Exercises

1. Under what circumstances will the `InputStream` method

```
int read(byte[] bArray, int offset, int length)
```

throw an `IndexOutOfBoundsException`?

2. Suppose the bytes in a stream object `out` are written by calling

```
out.write(a);
out.write(b);
out.write(c);
```

Then suppose those bytes are later used as the basis of another stream, in, and are read by the segment

```
x = in.read();
y = in.read();
z = in.read();
```

What are the values of x, y, and z?

3. To give you an idea of how useful the wrapper classes DataInputStream and DataOutputStream are, consider what you would have to do if you were limited to byte-level operations.

   a. Suppose you read four bytes into an array b[0], b[1], b[2], b[3]. Write a code segment that would convert these bytes to an int, with b[0] as the high-order eight bits and b[3] as the low-order bits. You might make good use of the bit-level operations we mentioned in Section 5.3.

   b. Reverse the process and show how you would convert an int to four bytes and write them to a stream, in such a way that the result would be compatible with the read operation of part (a).

4. Here's the last doOpen() method from Section 10.2. Recall that it reads Records until it runs out of things to read. There's nothing syntactically wrong with this method, but it could cause problems at run-time. What could happen and how would you prevent it?

```
private void doOpen()
{
    try
    {
        FileInputStream fstr = new FileInputStream("Sample4");
        DataInputStream in = new DataInputStream(fstr);

        numRecs = 0;
        while (true)
        {
            r[numRecs].readFrom(in);
            numRecs++;
        }
        in.close();
    }
    catch (EOFException ex)
    {
    }
    catch (IOException ex)
    {
        System.err.println(ex);
    }
}
```

5. Write the method

```
void copy(FileInputStream src, FileOutputStream dest)
```

which will copy src into dest. You may assume that the two file streams have been constructed and are both valid. Note that neither of the arguments are wrapped in DataInputStream and DataOutputStream classes, so you are just copying bytes.

6. Modify the `copy()` method of Exercise 5 so that before copying, it checks whether the argument streams are valid for reading and writing. If either or both of the files are invalid, throw a `FileNotFoundException` with an appropriate message.

7. Change the `copy()` method of Exercise 5 to

```
void append(FileInputStream src, FileOutputStream dest)
```

which will append the bytes of `src` to the end of `dest`.

8. Give the class declarations for each of the following data structures and describe briefly how you would write instances of these classes to a file. You might find it helpful to use some auxiliary classes.

    a. A class list of students, including their names and scores (integers in the range 0 . . . 20) on each of five quizzes, two exams (integers in the range 0 . . . 100) and a final (integer in the range 0 . . . 300).

    b. The current state of a game of chess (those of you who aren't chess players will have to do a little more work than those who are).

    c. A black and white picture. You may assume that the picture is 200 pixels wide and 150 pixels high and that each pixel is either black or white.

    d. A black and white picture of arbitrary size.

9. Suppose you had a file of `doubles` that had been generated by using the method `writeDouble()` from `DataOutputStream`. If you needed to read all the elements from the file, how could you tell how many `doubles` the file contained?

10. How would you sort a file of `ints`, assuming that there was enough room in memory to store the entire file in an array?

11. How would you sort a file of `ints`, assuming that only half of them would fit in memory? This is a hard problem, and there are several correct answers.

12. Suppose you had two files of `ints`, each of which was sorted in order from smallest to largest. Write a method that would *merge* the two files into one, sorted in increasing order. For example, the merge of files containing 3, 15, 18, 25, 39 and 4, 7, 22, 41, 44 would be 3, 4, 7, 15, 18, 22, 25, 39, 41, 44.

13. Write an application that will open a file (which you may assume contains text only) and count the number of instances of each letter, treating upper- and lower-case letters as identical. The method should ignore any character that is not A . . . Z or a . . . z.

14. Suppose that the `OrderPlease` Lablet of Chapter 9 was to be modified to write a completed order to a file. We haven't discussed the naming conventions for files on remote machines, so just describe the structure of the file for an order and how you would write it.

15. Assume that you have three classes, A, B, and C, and that each has its own `readFrom()` and `writeTo()` methods. Explain what you would do to create a file containing a mixture of instances of these classes in such a way that it could be read by a program that didn't know ahead of time the types of the elements in the file, except that they would be either A, B, or C. A typical file, for example, might contain

```
b1, b2, a1, b3, c1, a2, c2, c3, c4, b4, c5, a3
```

where the a's are of type A, the b's are of type B, and the c's are of type C.

16. Write a method `long size(File f)` that acts like this:

- If f doesn't exist, it returns 0.
- If f is a data file, it returns the length of the file.
- If f is a directory, it returns the sum of the sizes of all files in the directory.

You will make use of the `File` methods `list()` and `length()`, among others. This can be an exceptionally difficult problem. However, a true understanding of the fact that a method definition can include calls to itself changes the problem from exceptionally difficult to almost trivial.

10.8 Answers to Review Questions

1.1 From stream to program.

1.2 `close()`, in particular.

1.3 Both take a `String` argument, but `writeChars()` writes the two-byte Unicode value of each character in the string, whereas `writeBytes()` writes a single byte for each character in the string.

2.1 By inheritance, a `FileInputStream` is an `InputStream` and so is compatible with arguments of type `InputStream`.

2.2 Read the information from a stream in the same order in which it was written.

2.3 Directly or indirectly, nearly all information in a class is of primitive type, so we just write the values of the primitives. (For which types of data is this *not* true?)

2.4 Some extra information (such as the number of values that follow), written at the head of a file.

3.1 It's sufficiently general that it doesn't logically belong any lower in the hierarchy than it is.

3.2 If f is a `File`, then `f.length()` will return the file size in bytes.

3.3 It's much easier to determine the parent `Frame` in an application than it is in an applet.

3.4 That's why file dialogs were invented.

4.1 Because an applet may be loaded onto a client machine from an untrusted source.

4.2 `public static void main()`.

4.3 Though it's not the only way to do things, we've been writing each of our applications as a subclass of `Frame`. In addition, the `init()` method of an applet is often replaced by the constructor in an application, and, of course, an application has a `main()` method that isn't necessary for an applet.

5.1 To shut things down when the user closes the application frame.

5.2 By checking whether or not the string returned by `myFD.getFile()` is `null`.

5.3 No.

10.9 Class References

Here we provide some of the many classes in the java.io package. Some of the ones we don't talk about here (such as PrintStream) are useful but beyond the scope of this book; some, such as FilterInputStream and FilterOutputStream, are mentioned briefly in the chapter body but aren't necessary for the programs you'll be writing.

java.io.DataInput

This is an interface implemented by DataInputStream (and RandomAccessFile, which we don't discuss here). It contains methods for reading primitive types. All of the methods here throw IOExceptions.

```
abstract interface DataInput
{
    //----------- Methods -------------
    abstract boolean readBoolean();
    abstract byte readByte();
    abstract char readChar();
    abstract double readDouble();
    abstract float readFloat();
    abstract void readFully(byte[] b);
    abstract int readInt();
    abstract String readLine();
    abstract long readLong();
    abstract short readShort();
    abstract int skipBytes(int n);
}
```

java.io.DataInputStream

This class contains implementations of the InputStream methods used to read primitive types. Each of the methods here can throw an IOException. Note that all methods in this class are final.

```
class DataInputStream extends FilterInputStream
                      implements DataInput
{
    //--------- Constructor -----------
    DataInputStream(InputStream in);

    //----------- Methods -------------
◆   final void read(byte[] b);
    final boolean readBoolean();
    final byte readByte();
◆   final char readChar();
◆   final double readDouble();
    final float readFloat();
    final void readFully(byte[] b);
◆   final int readInt();
    final long readLong();
    final short readShort();
◆   final int skipBytes(int n);
}
```

java.io.DataOutput

This is an interface implemented by DataOutputStream (and RandomAccessFile). It contains methods for writing primitive types. All of the methods here throw IOExceptions. See the companion interface DataInput.

```
abstract interface DataOutput
{
    //---------- Methods ------------
    abstract void write(int n);
    abstract void write(byte[] b);
    abstract void writeBoolean(boolean b);
    abstract void writeByte(int n);
    abstract void writeBytes(String s);
    abstract void writeChar(int n);
    abstract void writeChars(String s);
    abstract void writeDouble(double d);
    abstract void writeFloat(float f);
    abstract void writeInt(int i);
    abstract void writeLong(long l);
    abstract void writeShort(short s);
}
```

java.io.DataOutputStream

This class contains implementations of the OutputStream methods used to write primitive types. Each of the methods here can throw an IOException. Note that nearly all methods in this class are final.

```
class DataOutputStream extends FilterOutputStream
                       implements DataOutput
{
    //--------- Constructor -----------
    DataOutputStream(OutputStream out);

    //---------- Methods ------------
    void flush();
    final int size();
    final void write(int n);
    final void write(byte[] b);
    final void writeBoolean(boolean b);
    final void writeByte(int n);
    final void writeBytes(String s);
 ◆  final void writeChar(int n);
 ◆  final void writeChars(String s);
 ◆  final void writeDouble(double d);
    final void writeFloat(float f);
 ◆  final void writeInt(int i);
    final void writeLong(long l);
    final void writeShort(short s);
}
```

java.io.File

This class contains methods for dealing with file information such as accessability, file names, and directory names. Unlike many other classes in this package, none of the methods mentioned here throw any exceptions.

```
class File extends Object
{
    //--------- Constructor -----------
    File(String path);
    File(String path, String name);
    File(File directory, String name);

    //------- Class constants ---------
    final static String pathSeparator;
    final static char pathSeparatorChar;
    final static String separator;
    final static char separatorChar;

    //----------- Methods -------------
◆   boolean canRead();
◆   boolean canWrite();
    boolean delete();
    boolean equals(Object ob);
◆   boolean exists();
    boolean isDirectory();
◆   boolean isFile();
    long lastModified();
◆   long length();
    String[] list();
    String[] list(FileNameFilter f);
}
```

java.awt.FileDialog

A FileDialog instance is a system-specific "Open" or "Save" dialog box. Except for its special look and its methods, this is just another dialog, with all the inherited Dialog methods. See Chapter 4 for a discussion of the Dialog superclass, and note that this class is *not* defined in the java.io package.

```
class FileDialog extends Dialog
{
    //--------- Constructor -----------
    FileDialog(Frame parent);
    FileDialog(Frame parent, String name);
    FileDialog(Frame parent, String name, int type);

    //------- Class constants ---------
    final static int LOAD;
    final static int SAVE;

    //----------- Methods -------------
◆   String getDirectory();
◆   String getFile();
    FilenameFilter getFilenameFilter();
    int getMode();
◆   void setDirectory(String dir);
    void setFile(String name);
    void setFilenameFilter(FilenameFilter filter);
    void setMode(int mode);
}
```

java.io.FileInputStream

A `FileInputStream` is an `InputStream` that is associated with a `File` object. As usual, all the methods can throw an `IOException`, along with the other exceptions noted.

```
class FileInputStream extends InputStream
{
    //--------- Constructors ----------
    FileInputStream(String name) throws FileNotFoundException;
    FileInputStream(File f) throws FileNotFoundException;

    //----------- Methods -------------
    int available();
    void close();
    int read();
    int read(byte[] bArray) throws NullPointerException;
    int read(byte[] bArray, int offset, int length)
        throws NullPointerException,
            IndexOutOfBoundsException
    long skip(long n);
}
```

java.io.FileNameFilter

This interface contains a single method. Objects implementing this interface can be used in file dialogs to filter just files that have a particular extension, are readable, and so on.

```
abstract interface FileNameFilter
{
    //----------- Method --------------
◆   abstract boolean accept(File f, String s);
}
```

java.io.FileOutputStream

A `FileOutputStream` is an `OutputStream` that is associated with a `File` object. As usual, all the methods can throw `IOExceptions`, along with the other exceptions noted.

```
class FileOutputStream extends OutputStream
{
    //--------- Constructors ----------
    FileOutputStream (File f);
    FileOutputStream (String name);

    //----------- Methods -------------
    void close();
    void write(int n);
    void write(byte[] bArray) throws NullPointerException;
    int write(byte[] bArray, int offset, int length)
        throws NullPointerException,
            IndexOutOfBoundsException;
}
```

java.io.InputStream

This is an abstract superclass of all the input stream classes. All of the methods here throw IOExceptions, along with the other exceptions noted.

```
abstract class InputStream extends Object
{
    //--------- Constructor -----------
    InputStream();

    //----------- Methods ------------
    int available();
♦   void close();
    abstract int read();
    int read(byte[] bArray)
        throws NullPointerException;
    int read(byte[] bArray, int offset, int length)
        throws NullPointerException,
               IndexOutOfBoundsException;
    long skip(long n);
}
```

java.io.OutputStream

This is an abstract superclass of all the output stream classes. All of the methods here throw IOExceptions, along with the other exceptions noted.

```
abstract class OutputStream extends Object
{
    //--------- Constructor -----------
    OutputStream();

    //----------- Methods ------------
♦   void close();
    void flush();
    abstract void write(int n);
    void write(byte[] bArray)
        throws NullPointerException;
    int write(byte[] bArray, int offset, int length)
        throws NullPointerException,
               IndexOutOfBoundsException;
}
```

THREADS

"Time," it is said, "is what keeps everything from happening at once." There are few domains that are more rigidly time-constrained than the activities that take place within a computer. A single processor executes the instructions of a program sequentially, employing what is known as the *fetch–execute cycle.* At each iteration of this cycle, the next program instruction is fetched from memory, and that statement is used to determine the action of the machine. Having fetched and executed one statement, the cycle begins again at the next instruction, and it continues in the same manner until the program halts. The fetch–execute cycle is implemented in an orderly fashion by endowing the computer with a sense of time.

Each computer includes a clock at the heart of its circuitry, marking off the steps of the fetch-execute cycle like an electronic metronome. Thus we can envision the action of the computer as an elaborate dance with thousands of performers, choreographed by the program and conducted by the clock, at a rate of millions of steps per second.[1]

The problem with this approach is that there are often situations where we want several things to happen in our programs simultaneously. For instance, we would like to be able to click buttons while our program is doing other processing, such as updating the screen. Oh—we already can, can't we? We can because the Java environment creates the *illusion* of simultaneity by slicing two or more tasks into small pieces, executing one task for a moment, then executing part of another, returning to the first, and so on. The computer is still doing one thing at a time, but it works so fast that it seems to us that several things are going on concurrently.

Modern languages such as Java enable us to exploit this time-slicing feature in our programs by specifying *threads* of execution. Using threads, we'll be able to split off the execution of parts of our programs and imagine that the separate parts are capable of executing simultaneously, without ever having to concern ourselves with the invisible details of how this *multiprogramming* or *multithreading*, as it's called, is actually being implemented by the underlying system.

Objectives

In this chapter, we will

- Discuss the concept of independent threads of execution in a program.
- Introduce the `Thread` class and the `Runnable` interface.
- Show how threads may be grouped.

---

[1] With the right equipment, it is actually possible to hear or see this dance, because the circuits of a computer emit faint but detectable radio signals.

■ Discuss some problems that may arise from concurrent execution and introduce techniques for synchronizing threads.

■ Build a digital alarm clock, using threads and the time-related classes Java provides.

11.1   Threaded Execution

You've gotten through ten chapters so far and haven't seen threads. One might be tempted to think that a programmer could lead a happy and productive life without ever worrying about separating execution into several pieces. Well, let's take a look at a simple task and try to do it knowing only what you know now. Here's the assignment:

Write an applet that draws an animated picture of a ball bouncing back and forth across the screen. Provide a toggle button that will allow the user to start and stop the animation.

That sounds simple enough. We'll set up a Canvas for the drawing and a Button to control the animation, as illustrated in Figure 11.1. The button will begin life with the label "Start," and each time it is clicked, it will toggle its label between "Start" and "Stop." In good object-oriented practice, we'll make a separate Ball class that will know how to draw() itself on the Canvas and move() to another location.

The initial part of the applet is simplicity itself,

```
// BOUNCING BALL APPLET, VERSION 1
public class Bouncer1 extends Applet implements ActionListener
{
    private Canvas display = new Canvas();
    private Button startStop = new Button("Start");
    private Ball   ball = null;
```

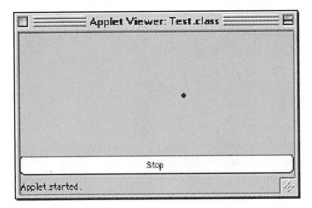

Figure 11.1

The Bouncing Ball applet, as it should appear.

```
public void init()
{
    setLayout(new BorderLayout());
    add("South", startStop);
    add("Center", display);
    startStop.addActionListener(this);
}
```

The `actionPerformed()` method is only slightly more difficult. The only event it deals with is a click on the `startStop` button. If its label is "Start," we change it to "Stop" and start the ball bouncing, by constructing a new Ball instance and moving it, as long as the button label is "Stop." Once the user clicks on the "Stop" button, it will change its name, thereby stopping the loop.

```
public void actionPerformed(ActionEvent e)
{
    if (startStop.getLabel().equals("Start"))
    {
        startStop.setLabel("Stop");

        //------------- Bounce the ball -------------
        ball = new Ball(display);
        ball.draw();
        while (startStop.getLabel().equals("Stop"))
        {
            ball.move();
        }
    }
    else
    {
        startStop.setLabel("Start");
    }
}
```

The `Ball` class likewise has few surprises. A `Ball` knows what `Canvas` to use to draw itself, and its x- and y-coordinates, along with how far to move at each step. The only new part is that we draw the ball in what is known as `XORMode`. This painting mode has the nice property that drawing an object over itself will erase the object. You'll note that the `move()` method checks for collisions with invisible boundaries at x = 10 and x = 290 and reverses the direction variable `increment` if it detects a collision.

painting in XOR mode

```
class Ball
{
    private Canvas theCanvas; // where to draw
    private int x, y;         // the ball coordinates
    private double velocity;  // speed of the ball

    public Ball(Canvas c)
    {
        theCanvas = c;
        x = 150;
        y = (int)(10 + 100 * Math.random());
        velocity = 0.6 + Math.round(2.5 * Math.random());
    }
```

```
public void draw()
// Draw a filled circle at (x, y). Since we've set
// the drawing mode to XOR, drawing a ball twice at
// the same location will erase it.
{
    Graphics g = theCanvas.getGraphics();
    g.setXORMode(Color.black);
    g.fillOval(x, y, 5, 5);
    g.dispose();
}

public void move()
{
    // Do a "nothing" loop to slow the ball down.
    for (int i = 0; i < 10000; i++)
        ;
    // Erase the old image,
    draw();

    // move the ball, checking for bounces,
    if ((x <= 10) || (x >= 290))
    {
        velocity = -velocity;
    }
    x = (int)(Math.round(x + velocity));
    // and draw the ball in its new location.
    draw();
}
}
```

We encourage you to take a moment and enter and run this applet. Be advised, though, that there is a good chance that it will misbehave. The result will depend on the system you're using, but once the ball starts up, there probably won't be a thing you can do to stop it. Not only won't the button work, but it may not even be possible for you to quit the applet runner or browser you're using.

The problem is that the "tight loop" we highlighted in the actionPerformed() method is hogging all the computer's attention. As long as the ball is bouncing in the loop, nothing else can happen. All of the button clicks are piling up in the event queue (if they're even being received at all), and the system can't find the time to get to them. In technical terms, the processor and the GUI resources are *shared resources,* needed by the applet and the environment within which it is running, and the applet is starving the system by not letting it into the resource it needs.

starvation

If you stop to think about it, you'll see that there isn't even a good place to put the loop. The actionPerformed() method clearly isn't a good choice; as long as the loop is running, control never gets out of the first if clause, so the user never gets a chance to change the button label in the second clause. We can't put the loop in the init() method, either; if the loop ever were to finish, control would pass out of the method and never return. Where else could the loop go? In a paint() method? No, that wouldn't work either, for reasons we'll leave it to you to articulate. It seems we're stuck. With the tools you have at your disposal, it seems that there simply is no way to write a program to do what we need. Basically, we need another place for the animation to go, and we need to be able to iterate the loop in such a way that the rest of the program can still have an occasional chance to do its own work.

The Basics of the `Thread` Class

A thread represents an independent sequence of action in a program. If you're used to thinking of the execution of a program as though you were running your finger down the code from statement to statement, perhaps jumping backwards to the start of a loop, or jumping from one place to another in response to a method call, you'll have a good model of a thread, the applet thread. You can, however, have several fingers following the action. In practice, the fingers never move simultaneously—one finger may execute several statements and then pause while the other traces through the code in another location—but this alternation happens so rapidly that you may as well think of them as both working at the same time.

The `Thread` class is part of the `java.lang` package. It has a moderate number of constructors and methods, many of which we'll have to defer discussing until later. For now, there is one constructor and four methods that will be of interest to us.

`Thread``()`

Creates a new thread. In our finger metaphor, a new finger has been raised, but it hasn't yet pointed at any location in the code.

The `Thread` methods that we'll use now include one class method and three instance methods.

`static void `**`sleep`**`(long ms) throws InterruptedException`

Halts the execution of the current thread for approximately the given number of milliseconds. This useful method gives other threads a chance to execute while the current thread is sleeping. The `Thread.sleep()` method throws an `InterruptedException` in case the sleeping thread is interrupted by another. This won't happen often, but because `InterruptedException` is a checked exception,[2] we have to use a `try/catch` pair whenever we call `Thread.sleep()`, even though we don't do anything in the `catch` clause. There's no guarantee that `sleep()` will pause a thread for *exactly* the indicated number of milliseconds; the run-time system will do the best it can, but it may be a bit off.

`void `**`start`**`() throws IllegalThreadStateException`

Starts this thread. This is where you'll do any initialization that has to take place before the thread begins running. This method calls `run()` when it is finished with the initialization you've given it. The finger has been set down in the code of this method, and almost immediately hops to the `run()` method. This method may throw an `IllegalThreadStateException`. This is an unchecked exception—we'll talk about thread states in Section 11.3.

`void `**`run`**`()`

Begins execution of this thread. This method is the heart of any thread. It is where the thread does its work. Here's the home for the finger, as you'll soon see.

---

[2]See Section 9.2 for a review of checked and unchecked exceptions.

You'll rarely call run() yourself. Instead, you'll call start() and let it call run() for you.

```
final void stop() throws SecurityException
```

This stops the execution of the thread. Metaphorically, the moving finger stops here and goes away. Note that this method is final—you can't override it for your own purposes. You won't see the unchecked SecurityException unless you do something the SecurityManager determines is forbidden, like trying to stop a thread that doesn't belong to you.

For simple threads, you may not need to call stop(), but you will certainly need to call start() and write your own run() method.

Fundamental Principle of Threads

A thread executes in a run() method.

There are two standard ways of dealing with threads in a program. The first is to make a subclass of Thread and provide a run() method in the class. The second is to create an instance of Thread and provide an external run() method in which the Thread instance may execute. Let's apply the first technique to our bouncing ball exercise. The only modifications we have to make to the Ball class are to make it a subclass of Thread and give it a run() method.

```
// BOUNCING BALL APPLET, VERSION 2 MODIFICATIONS
class Ball extends Thread
{
    // No changes in the instance variables and the constructor.

    public void run()
    {
        draw();
        while (true)
        {
            move();
            try
            {
                sleep(10);
            }
            catch (InterruptedException e)
            { }
        }
    }

    // No changes in draw() and move().
}
```

We've taken the animation loop out of the applet and put it in our run() method. This solves the "Where do we put the loop" problem we mentioned before: The loop has a natural home in the run() method. The only other part worth mentioning here is that we used the Thread sleep() method to pause this thread for 10 milliseconds. This is a much nicer way of slowing down the motion of the ball than the "do nothing" loop we had in `Bouncer1`. When we do this, the `Ball` thread actually surrenders control for a hundredth of a second in each loop iteration, which is plenty of time for any other threads to get useful things done. In particular, it allows the applet thread to call the `stop()` method for this thread, terminating its execution. This explains why we could get away with the never-ending `while(true)` loop in the `run()` method. We let the thread run until it is stopped externally by the user pressing the "Stop" button.

> A well-mannered thread will always call the class method `Thread.sleep()` in its `run()` method to give other threads a chance to execute.

The applet also requires very few changes. In fact, all we have to do is change the `actionPerformed()` method, by moving the animation loop out and replacing it with calls to the `Thread` methods `start()` and `stop()`. Note that the `Ball` class doesn't override these two methods—we're using the `start()` and `stop()` methods of the `Thread` superclass.

```
// BOUNCING BALL APPLET, VERSION 2 MODIFICATIONS
public void actionPerformed(ActionEvent e)
{
    if (startStop.getLabel().equals("Start"))
    {
        startStop.setLabel("Stop");

        ball = new Ball(display);
        ball.start();
    }
    else
    {
        startStop.rtStop.setLabel("Start");
        ball.stop();
        display.repaint();
    }
}
```

The `Runnable` Interface

Suppose that for some reason `Ball` was a `final` class, so we couldn't subclass it, or suppose `Ball` needed access to private information in the applet. How would we find a home for the animation loop then? The other standard way of using threads is to provide an external `run()` method, using the `Runnable` interface, declared in the `java.lang` package.

This interface contains a single method,

```
void run()
```

By declaring a class to implement `Runnable`, you are promising to provide an implementation of that method so that any threads you declare in that class will have a place to execute.

Two Ways of Running Threads

1. Declare a class that is a subclass of `Thread`, and override the `Thread` method `run()` in the class. Run instances of that class.

2. Declare a class that implements `Runnable`, provide an implementation of `run()`, and use that to run any threads you declare.

Think of these two strategies in terms of you (a class) looking for a place to change clothes and get a night's sleep (perform some actions). In the first strategy, you're a camper carrying your own tent [your own `run()` method] and in the second, you're checking into a hotel room [using an external `run()` method]. This is quite similar to the way we can handle events: We can extend an adapter class, or we can declare that a class implements the appropriate listener interface. We can illustrate the interface idiom by again modifying our bouncing ball example.

In this version, the applet class implements `Runnable` and provides a `run()` method, in which we bounce the `ball` instance. We must declare a `Thread` for the animation in this version, because our modified `Ball` class isn't a `Thread` itself.

```
// BOUNCING BALL APPLET, VERSION 3 MODIFICATIONS
public class Test extends Applet implements Runnable
{
    // no changes to other instance variables
    private Thread ballThread = null;

    // init() is unchanged

    public void run()
    {
        ball.draw();
        while (true)
        {
            ball.move();
            try
            {
                Thread.sleep(10);
            }
            catch (InterruptedException e)
            { }
        }
    }
}
```

Note that we use a different version of the `Thread` constructor in the `actionPerformed()` method. This version requires a `Runnable` object as an argument so that the new `Thread` will know where to look for its `run()` method. In this example, the `run()` method is in the applet, so we use the applet's synonym `this` for the argument.

```
public void actionPerformed(ActionEvent e)
{
```

```
      if (startStop.getLabel().equals("Start"))
      {
         startStop.setLabel("Stop");

         ball = new Ball(display);
         ballThread = new Thread(this);
         ballThread.start();
      }
      else
      {
         startStop.setLabel("Start");
         ballThread.stop();
         display.repaint();
      }
   }
}

class Ball
{
   // no other changes
}
```

Before we leave this example, we should point out that we don't have to limit ourselves to a single animation thread. In fact, we can have as many threads in a program as we want. We could modify our Bouncing Ball applet so that it has several balls on screen at once by spawning a new thread each time the user clicked the button. We'll change the version 3 applet by changing the start/stop button to one that simply spawns a new thread. In the new version, we remove the `ball` and `ballThread` instance variables, constructing a new thread in the `action()` handler and a new ball at the start of the `run()` method.

In the new version, we don't have to modify the `Ball` class. Aside from removing the two instance variables, the only changes that we make are in the applet's `run()` and `actionPerformed()` methods.

```
// BOUNCING BALL APPLET, VERSION 4 MODIFICATIONS
public void run()
{
   Ball ball = new Ball(display);
   ball.draw();
   while (true)
   {
      ball.move();
      try
      {
         Thread.sleep(10);
      }
      catch (InterruptedException e)
      { }
   }
}

public void actionPerformed(ActionEvent e)
{
   Thread ballThread = new Thread(this);
   ballThread.start();
}
```

Grouping Threads

It's quite possible for a moderately complicated program to have dozens of threads alive at any time. It would be very useful in such cases to be able to provide some overall organization to the mass of threads, and Java does just that with the ThreadGroup class, which is part of the java.lang package. By collecting threads into a ThreadGroup, we can apply some operations to the entire group, rather than having to apply the operation to each thread individually.

Every thread is contained in exactly one ThreadGroup. With the exception of the top-level "system" ThreadGroup, every group is contained in another, known as its *parent*.

There are two constructors for this class.

```
ThreadGroup(String name)
     throws SecurityException
ThreadGroup(ThreadGroup parent, String name)
     throws NullPointerException, SecurityException
```

These construct a ThreadGroup containing no threads. The first constructor makes a ThreadGroup whose parent is the group containing the current thread. The second constructor allows you to specify the ThreadGroup in which this new ThreadGroup will be contained. The second constructor will throw a NullPointerException if the parent ThreadGroup hasn't yet been initialized. Both constructors allow you to specify a name for the new ThreadGroup.

There are quite a few methods for this class; we'll list only the most important here and cover some of the rest in the Class References at the end of this chapter.

```
final void resume() throws SecurityException
```

Calls resume() on all threads in this group and its subgroups. We'll talk about the Thread method resume() in the next section.

```
final void stop() throws SecurityException
```

Stops all threads in this group and its subgroups. Note that ThreadGroup doesn't have a matching start() method.

```
final void suspend() throws SecurityException
```

Suspends all threads in this group and its subgroups. We'll talk about the Thread method suspend() in the next section.

Finally, there are two Thread constructors and a Thread method that deal with thread groups.

```
Thread(ThreadGroup parent, Runnable target)
     throws SecurityException
Thread(ThreadGroup parent, String name)
     throws SecurityException
```

Constructs a new thread belonging to the specified parent ThreadGroup. The target argument in the first constructor specifies the object that contains the run()

method for this Thread. The second constructor is used for thread subclasses that contain their own run() methods. The name argument allows you to give this new Thread a name (see the Thread summary at the end of the chapter for details about naming threads). If you don't specify a group to which a new Thread belongs, Java will put it in a default group.

ThreadGroup **getThreadGroup**()

Returns the group to which this thread belongs. Recall that every Thread belongs to some ThreadGroup.

In version 5 of our Bouncing Ball applet, we've included a new ThreadGroup to contain all the ball threads. The "Stop" button kills all threads in the "Balls" ThreadGroup. If you try to run this applet, you may discover that the SecurityManager under which the applet runs won't let you construct a new ThreadGroup.

```
// BOUNCING BALL APPLET, VERSION 5 MODIFICATIONS
public class Bouncer5 extends Applet implements Runnable
{
    private Canvas display = new Canvas();
    private Button newBttn = new Button("New"),
                  stopBttn = new Button("Stop");

    private Thread     ballThread = null;
    private ThreadGroup tg = new ThreadGroup("Balls");

    // init() and run() omitted
    public boolean action(Event e, Object arg)
    {
        if (e.target == newBttn)
        {
            ballThread = new Thread(tg, this);
            ballThread.start();
            return true;
        }
        else
        if (e.target == stopBttn)
        {
            tg.stop(); // Kill all threads in this group
            display.repaint();
            return true;
        }
        else
            return false;
    }
}
```

Review Questions

1.1 What is a thread?

1.2 What method is required for a thread to execute? When do you call it?

1.3 Why do we use the Thread.sleep() method?

1.4 What are the two different techniques for threaded execution?

1.5 Can two threads share a single run() method?

11.2 Threads and Applets

It would be instructive for you to try running `Bouncer4` or `Bouncer5`. In particular, run the applet in a browser and create a dozen or so balls. Then, without quitting the browser, switch to a program with which you're familiar, such as a word processor, and see whether you notice any difference in its behavior. There's a good chance you will—your program may seem quite sluggish. The reason is pretty clear: The dozen ball threads are still running in the background, and your program has to share computational resources with all of them. You might notice the same problem even if you didn't open a new program and just went to another page in the browser. What we need is a way to stop a thread from running once the browser leaves the page containing the applet.

There are two `Applet` methods that will help us do what we want. Like `init()` and `paint()`, these are methods you can't call yourself. They are called for you by the browser.

```
void start()
```

This method is called each time the page containing the applet appears. Unlike `init()`, which is done only once, when the applet is loaded, `start()` may be called many times during the life of the applet. Be careful here. In spite of the similarity in name, this method has nothing to do with the `Thread` method `start()`.

```
void stop()
```

Called when the page containing the applet is replaced by another. You would usually override this method to suspend or stop any threads that are currently active. The warning above applies here, too: Don't confuse this with the `Thread` method `stop()`.

The usual way of using these two methods to do something like this:

```
public class MyApplet extends Applet implements Runnable
{
   ...
   Thread myThread = null;
   ...
   public void run()
   {
      // Do something.
   }

   public void start()        // the Applet method
   {
      if (myThread == null)
      {
         myThread = new Thread(this);
         myThread.start(); // the Thread method
      }
   }

   public void stop()         // the Applet method
   {
      if (myThread != null)
      {
```

```
        myThread.stop();  // the Thread method
        myThread = null;
      }
    }
}
```

Here, we're using `null` for two purposes. It serves as a flag to indicate whether a thread has been started (we'd get a `NullPointerException` if we tried to stop a `null` thread), and it hastens reclamation of the dead thread's resources after it has been stopped.

If we didn't want to kill a thread when the applet page was replaced, we could use a gentler pair of `Thread` methods.

`final void` **suspend**`() throws SecurityException`

Stops the execution of this `Thread`. This method acts in a manner similar to `Thread.sleep()`, except that the thread stays suspended until a call is made to `stop()` (which will wake it up and kill it, if you'll permit a somewhat gruesome description) or to `resume()`. If a thread has already been suspended, calling `suspend()` has no effect.

`final void` **resume**`() throws SecurityException`

If this thread has been suspended, it starts execution again, at the place where it was suspended. If this thread is currently executing, the method has no effect. As we mentioned when we discussed the `Thread` method `stop()`, this method [and suspend()] may throw `SecurityExceptions`, but you don't have to check for them, and you'll probably never see them.

Here's an example of the difference between start/stop and suspend/resume. We begin with a simple `Thread` extension that counts from 0 to 99, displaying the count in an external `TextField` and sleeping for a second between display updates.

```
class Counter extends Thread
{
    private TextField theField; // where to write the value

    public Counter(TextField t)
    {
        theField = t;
    }

    public void run()
    {
        for (int i = 0; i < 100; i++)
        {
            theField.setText("" + i);
            try
            {
                sleep(1000);
            }
            catch (InterruptedException e)
            { }
        }
    }
}
```

In the applet, we set up an array of three `Counters` and three `TextFields` in which they will write. We start all three `Counters` in the `init()` method, but we take different actions for each thread in the applet's `start()` and `stop()` methods. The thread `c[0]` is started and stopped, the thread `c[1]` is suspended and resumed, and we take no special action for `c[2]`, simply letting it run.

```
public class StartStopTest extends Applet
{
    private Counter[]   c = new Counter[3];
    private TextField[] t = new TextField[3];

    public void init()
    {
        for (int i = 0; i < 3; i++)
        {
            t[i] = new TextField(5);
            add(t[i]);
            c[i] = new Counter(t[i]);
            c[i].start();
        }
    }

    public void start()
    {
        if (c[0] == null)
        {
            c[0] = new Counter(t[0]);
            c[0].start();
        }
        c[1].resume();
    }

    public void stop()
    {
        if (c[0] != null)
        {
            c[0].stop();
            c[0] = null;
        }
        c[1].suspend();
    }
}
```

If you run this applet in a browser, you'll see that the three `TextFields` will be incremented more or less in step. After about 15 seconds or so, they might have the values 15, 15, and 15. If we then direct the browser to another page and stare at that page for a while before returning to the applet's page, we might see the values 0, 15, and 45 in the fields for `c[0]`, `c[1]`, and `c[2]`. The 0 shows that the `c[0]` thread was killed and reborn, the 15 reflects the fact that `c[1]` was suspended at 15 while we were away, and the 45 derives from the fact that all the time we were looking at the other page, the `c[2]` thread was still merrily counting away in the background.

> It's generally a bad idea to let a thread keep running after an applet has stopped. An applet that declares threads should have a `stop()` method that either kills or suspends each of its threads.

Review Questions

2.1 When is the `Applet` class's `start()` method called? What method call will you often place in a definition of `start()`?

2.2 If a thread has been suspended, how can you have it resume execution?

11.3 Synchronizing Threads

Once you have a program with threads, life can get a bit complicated. Consider the following simple-seeming description.

> *Thread A and thread B share a* `TextField`, `display`. *Thread A repeatedly does some calculation resulting in an* `int` *and places the text equivalents in* `display`. *Thread B repeatedly gets the text from* `display` *and converts it to an* `int` *for its own calculations.*

When the program is running, the system will swap execution between A and B. How this happens varies from environment to environment and is completely beyond your control.

Fundamental Principle of Thread Execution

> You cannot assume *anything* about the order of execution of two or more threads.

The system might run one thread to completion before starting the other; it might run one thread through three statements before running the other for one statement; and it might even let one thread get halfway through a statement, suspend it, and start the other. Once you realize that you can't know how execution will be interleaved between A and B, you become aware of several ugly scenarios.

1. Thread A gets partly through updating `display`, and then execution switches to B. The result is that B might get garbage when it tries to inspect `display`.

2. Thread A puts new information in `display` before B has inspected the old value. The old value is lost.

3. Thread B gets a value and then gets back to `display` before A has sent in a new value. The old value is used twice.

Scenario 1 calls for *mutual exclusion*—the two processes should not be allowed simultaneous access to the shared `display` resource—whereas scenarios 2 and 3 require *serialization*—each process must wait until the other finishes using the shared resource.

It's important to note that these scenarios are problematic only because threads A and B both access the `display` object. If the code executed by A and the code executed by B never made reference to a shared object, A and B could both go their way in any order the run-time system decided, and the order of execution would have no effect on the result of the program.

mutual
exclusion
and
serialization

> If two threads never communicate or share information, you don't have to worry about synchronizing them. If they do, you do.

Synchronization and Mutual Exclusion

The first problem we have to deal with is eliminating the possibility that two or more threads might try to access an object at the same time. Java deals with this problem by using what are known as *monitors*. Monitors are implemented by providing each object with a *lock*. Once a thread acquires a lock for an object, no other thread can acquire the lock until the original thread surrenders it. In Java, the keyword synchronized is used to identify a method or other segment of code associated with an object's lock.

monitors and locks

To identify a method associated with an object's lock, we use the synchronized keyword in the method header, like this:

```
class MyClass
{
    ...
    public synchronized void doThis()
    {
        ...
    }
    public synchronized void doThat()
    {
        ...
    }
    public void doTheOther()
    {
        ...
    }
}
```

MyClass has three methods, two of which are synchronized and one of which is not. Suppose that foo was an instance of MyClass, declared like this:

```
MyClass foo = new MyClass();
```

and suppose also that none of the foo methods had yet been called. Now, if foo.doThis() were called, the current thread would acquire foo's lock, and no other thread could complete a call to any of foo's synchronized methods until the original thread left the doThis() method. Whether the lock had been acquired or not, any thread could enter the nonsynchronized doTheOther() method. In Figure 11.2, we illustrate a typical situation, using a heavy line to indicate which thread currently has foo's lock.

> If a thread enters a synchronized method of an object, no other thread can enter any of that object's synchronized methods until the first thread leaves the method.

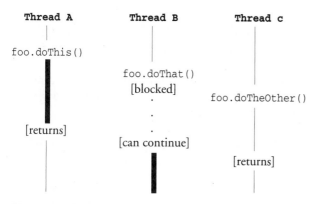

Figure 11.2

Acquiring and releasing locks on an object.

What makes this process work is that acquiring and releasing a lock are *atomic* actions; a thread cannot be preempted by the system while it is doing either of these operations. In other words, when a synchronized method is called, you can be sure that one of two things will happen: Either the thread will be able to enter the method, thereby acquiring the lock for the object, or the thread will block and not enter the method until the object's lock has been released.

You can synchronize a block of code, as well. The statement

synchronized (*expression*)
  statement or block of statements

requires that the *expression* evaluate to an object (not a primitive type). The thread executing this statement will then either acquire that object's lock and execute the controlled statements or block its execution until it acquires the object's lock.

Synchronization solves the first of our problems, enforcing mutual exclusion.

> To guarantee that two threads don't try to access an object simultaneously, synchronize the methods or code that accesses that object.

As you might expect, several of the methods of the standard Java classes are synchronized. The Component methods disable() and enable(), for instance, are synchronized, because we wouldn't want one thread to try to disable a Button while another was trying to enable it. Doing so might result in a button that was dimmed but still responded to mouse clicks. For similar reasons, the add() and remove() methods of MenuBar are synchronized.

The wait() and notify() Methods

You saw that synchronization allows us to deal with the mutual exclusion problem, but we haven't yet addressed the problem of serialization—the fact that a thread may have to wait for a resource until another thread has done something to it. Consider our example from the start of this section: Thread A places integers in display, but before depositing a new value, it should wait until B has had a chance to get the old one.

It would be easy enough for the two threads to communicate, once we realize that they could use the display field for more than just sending and receiving integers. One possible solution would be to use an empty text string:

1. The sender, thread A, would wait until display was empty before sending an int.
2. The receiver, thread B, would wait until display had a number. Then it would get that number and empty the field.

This protocol wouldn't even be hard to implement. We could just use a pair of empty loops so that the two threads would "spin their wheels" until display was in the necessary state.

```
public synchronized int getInt()
{
    while (display.getText().equals(""))
        ;
    // The only way we can get to this point is if there's
    // some text, so we get it and convert it to an int.
    int n = ...

    display.setText("");     // Signal that we've gotten the value,
    return n;                // and send it back
}

public synchronized void setInt(int n)
{
    while (!display.getText().equals(""))
        ;
    // The only way we can get to this point is if the
    // text is empty, so we can now send the int.
    display.setText("" + n);
}
```

Unfortunately, this may not work. Recall the fundamental principle of thread execution: *You can't guarantee anything about how the order of execution of two threads will be interleaved.* Suppose, for example, that thread B gets into getInt() before A gets into setInt(). B will hog the processor while it loops, waiting for something to be placed into display. As long as B is looping, of course, A never gets a chance to put something in display, so there's a chance that B will never get out of its loop. As far as anyone could tell, it would appear that the program had locked up, which in fact it would have. It doesn't even help if A gets in first—as an exercise, we ask you to come up with a scenario in which the program still wouldn't work as it should.

What we need is a way to make a thread block until some situation has occurred and then wake up and continue execution. There are three methods that allow us to do this. They're found—of all places—in the `Object` class. All three may throw an unchecked `IllegalMonitorStateException`, which you won't have to worry about unless you call one of these methods without having acquired the object's lock.

> Call `wait()`, `notify()`, and `notifyAll()` only within synchronized methods or code.

Because these three methods are called only within a synchronized method or block of code, they all deal with the associated object's lock.

```
final void wait() throws IllegalMonitorStateException,
                         InterruptedException
```

This method causes the current thread to suspend execution and give up its lock on the object where the call was made. The thread doesn't give up any other locks it may possess. The thread remains suspended until it is awakened by `notify()` or `notifyAll()`. It is then free to try to reacquire its lock. If it does, it picks up execution where it left off; if it doesn't, it remains blocked until it acquires the lock again.

```
final void notify() throws IllegalMonitorStateException
```

This awakens some thread that has been suspended on this object by a `wait()` call. If several threads have been blocked by `wait()` calls for this object, you cannot predict which will be awakened.

```
final void notifyAll() throws IllegalMonitorStateException
```

Awakens all threads that have been suspended by `wait()` calls for this object.

> If a thread has been suspended by `wait()` and then awakened by `notify()` or `notifyAll()`, it has to compete for a lock before it can continue execution.

In the following applet, we provide an implementation of our reader/writer problem. We first declare a class `IntField` to serve as our display. The only reason why we declared this class, rather than just using a `TextField`, was so that we could provide it with the synchronized methods `getInt()` and `setInt()`.

```
class IntField extends TextField
{
    public IntField()
    {
        super("", 15);
    }
    public synchronized int getInt()
            throws InterruptedException
    {
```

```
        while (getText().equals(""))
        {
            wait();
        }
        int n = -1;
        String s = getText();
        try
        {
            n = Integer.parseInt(s);
        }
        catch (NumberFormatException e)
        { }
        // Delay a second so we can see what's happening.
        Thread.sleep(1000);
        setText("");
        notify();
        return n;
    }

    public synchronized void setInt(int n)
            throws InterruptedException
    {
        while (!getText().equals(""))
        {
            wait();
        }
        setText("" + n);
        notify();
    }
}
```

The classes `Reader` and `Writer` are subclasses of `Thread`. The `run()` method of `Reader` just gets the values in the `IntField` and sums them, whereas the `run()` method of `Writer` just generates the successive odd integers 1, 3, 5 . . . , 19 and places them in the field. The only detail we haven't mentioned yet is that `Writer` signals the end of its task by placing the *sentinel* value –1 in the field, and `Reader` uses that as a signal for it to report the sum it has found.

sentinel

```
class Writer extends Thread
{
    private IntField f;

    public Writer(IntField f)
    {
        this.f = f;
    }

    public void run()
    {
        try
        {
            for (int i = 0; i < 10; i++)
            {
                f.setInt(2 * i + 1);
                sleep(500);
            }
            f.setInt(-1);          // Signal completion.
        }
```

```
            catch (InterruptedException e)
            { }
        }
}

class Reader extends Thread
{
    private IntField f;

    public Reader(IntField f)
    {
        this.f = f;
    }

    public void run()
    {
        int n = 0;
        int sum = 0;
        try
        {
            n = f.getInt();
            while (n >= 0)
            {
                sum += n;
                sleep(1000);
                n = f.getInt();
            }
            f.setInt(sum);    // Report the result.
        }
        catch (InterruptedException e)
        { }
    }
}
```

We use these three classes in a very simple applet, containing an IntField and a Button that, when clicked, starts the two threads.

```
public class ReaderWriter extends Applet implements ActionListener
{
    private IntField   display = new IntField();
    private Button     startBttn = new Button("Start");

    private Writer     w = new Writer(display);
    private Reader     r = new Reader(display);

    public void init()
    {
        add(display);
        add(startBttn);
        startBttn.addActionListener(this);
    }

    public void actionPerformed(ActionEvent e)
    {
        w.start();
        r.start();
    }
}
```

Priorities

As you have seen several times so far, there are lots of things going on in the background while a Java program is running. One of these background processes is the *thread scheduler*. It's the job of the thread scheduler to decide which thread to run when, for example, the current thread is suspended by wait() or sleep().

Although the details of how the thread scheduler makes its decisions vary from one system to another, there are a few things you can count on. First, every thread in a Java program has a *priority*, expressed as an integer from 1 to 10. It is generally true that when deciding which thread to run, the thread scheduler will choose to run the thread with highest priority. This doesn't mean that the scheduler will wake up a sleeping thread, nor will it revive a thread that has been suspended by wait() but hasn't yet heard a notify(). It does, though, mean that if two threads are capable of being run, the one with higher priority will be favored to run next.

The Thread class contains three class constants that you can use to refer to priorities:

```
final static int MIN_PRIORITY = 1;
final static int NORM_PRIORITY = 5;
final static int MAX_PRIORITY = 10;
```

You can inspect or modify the priority of a thread by using a pair of Thread instance methods.

```
final int getPriority()
```

Returns the priority of this thread.

```
final void setPriority(int p) throws SecurityException,
                                     IllegalArgumentException
```

Sets the priority of this thread to the value specified in the argument (assuming that the SecurityManager will permit such an operation). If the argument is smaller than MIN_PRIORITY or larger than MAX_PRIORITY, this method will throw an IllegalArgumentException. The priority of a thread cannot be larger than the maximum permitted priority of its thread group.

Each ThreadGroup has a maximum priority value for all of its threads. This value can be set and inspected by the following methods.

```
final int getMaxPriority()
final void setMaxPriority(int p) throws SecurityException,
                                       IllegalArgumentException
```

You can adjust the priority of a thread to suit the needs of your program. A thread that does some relatively unimportant task could be given a low priority, for instance. It's usually a bad idea to give a task a priority of MAX_PRIORITY, because doing so might lock out other important threads (such as the applet thread itself).

The applet below inspects all currently active threads while it's running. It is interesting to run this in several different environments—the default priorities given to the applet thread and the thread "Mine" vary quite a bit from system to system. See the Class References section for a description of the `Thread` class method `activeCount()`.

```java
public class ThreadInspector extends Applet implements Runnable
{
    private TextArea    display = new TextArea(8, 70);
    private Thread      mine = new Thread(this, "Mine");

    public void init()
    {
        mine.start();
        add(display);
        report();
    }

    public void run()
    {
        for (int i = 0; i < 4; i++)
        {
            try
            {
                Thread.sleep(2500);
                report();
            }
            catch (InterruptedException e)
            { }
        }
        display.appendText("Stopped!");
    }

    private void report()
    {
        display.setText("");
        // Make an array of Threads and fill it with the
        // currently active threads.
        Thread[] t = new Thread[10];
        Thread.enumerate(t);

        for (int i = 0; i < Thread.activeCount(); i++)
        {
            display.appendText(t[i].getPriority()
                               + "    "
                               + t[i].getName() + "\n");
        }
    }
}
```

Review Questions

3.1 What is the fundamental principle of thread execution?

3.2 When do you *not* need to worry about synchronizing two threads?

3.3 Are locks associated primarily with methods, classes, or objects?

11.4 On Time

In the Lablet for this chapter, we'll make use of threads to implement a digital clock. Because we will be displaying the time, we'll be able to make good use of several of Java's library classes that deal with the complicated details of keeping track of the correct time and displaying it properly. The details of time keeping are quite complex. Not only do the formats for specifying the time vary from country to country, but there are also several different standards for specifying the "official" time, depending on whether you are using an atomic clock as a standard or basing time computations on the durations of Earth's rotation about its axis and the time required to complete a revolution around the Sun. Fortunately, the classes `Date`, `Calendar`, and `GregorianCalendar` in the `java.util` package handle all the details for us; unfortunately, because of the details involved, these classes are somewhat complex.

The `Date` Class

The simplest of the three classes we'll discuss, the `Date` class is used primarily as a clock for measuring seconds. In Java, time is measured in thousandths of seconds since the beginning of the "epoch," which was arbitrarily chosen to be the start of January 1, 1970.[3] Since its introduction in version 1.0, many of the methods in this class have become deprecated[4] in favor of methods in the `Calendar` class.

Two constructors in this class will be of use to us.

```
Date()
Date(long time)
```

The first creates a new `Date` object representing the time on the local machine at the moment of its creation; the second allows the user to set the time represented.

Among the methods that have not been deprecated, we find the following five.

```
boolean after(Date when)
boolean before(Date when)
boolean equals(Object obj)
```

The first two return `true` if this object represents a time after (or before) that represented by the argument; otherwise, they return `false`. The third is an override of the `Object` method of the same name and is designed to return `true` if the argument is a Date object that represents the same time as this and otherwise to return `false`.

---

[3]Because Java stores time as a `long` value, there will come a time when the value will overflow the 64 bits in a `long`, leading to Java's equivalent of a "Y2K" problem. That should happen about the year 292,000,000, give or take a few millennia.

[4]A technical term meaning "poo-poohed."

```
long getTime()
void setTime(long time)
```

This pair allows you to get access to the internal value used to store the time represented by this object. We used these functions in the Sortmeister lab exercises when we measured the running time of a sorting algorithm. The usual form for such a timing idiom is

```
Date start = new Date();

// Do something

Date finish = new Date();
// Compute how long in seconds it took to "do something."
double elapsed = (finish.getTime() - start.getTime()) / 1000.0;
```

The Calendar Class

The Calendar class, like Date, represents time. This class has a large number of methods to express time in years, months, weeks, days, hours, minutes, and seconds. You can't construct a Calendar object, because it's an abstract class. Instead, you'll make an instance of the concrete GregorianCalendar class and use some of this parent class's methods.

The idiom for accessing the fields of this class is rather clever. Because of the large number of possible ways of slicing up time, the designers avoided the proliferation of methods such as getYear(), getDay(), and getSecond(), by providing a number of class constants that can be used by a single method, such as get(), to specify which field to inspect. These field constants include

```
YEAR, MONTH, WEEK_OF_YEAR, WEEK_OF_MONTH, DATE,
DAY_OF_MONTH, DAY_OF_YEAR, AM_PM, HOUR, HOUR_OF_DAY,
MINUTE, SECOND, MILLISECOND
```

In addition to the field constants, there are a number of constants (final static, like the field constants) that represent values of the fields:

```
JANUARY, FEBRUARY, MARCH, APRIL, MAY, JUNE, JULY, AUGUST,
SEPTEMBER, OCTOBER, NOVEMBER, DECEMBER, SUNDAY, MONDAY,
TUESDAY, WEDNESDAY, THURSDAY, FRIDAY, SATURDAY, AM, PM
```

Much like the Graphics class, you won't construct a Calendar instance for use in your programs. Instead, you'll call the following class method.

```
static Calendar getInstance()
```

This returns a new Calendar object, initialized to represent the current system time.

The instance methods of this class deal with conversions between the internal representation of time and the more human-usable forms.

```
final int get(int field)
final void set(int field, int value)
```

This pair provides access to the individual fields of this object, using the field constants we mentioned above. For example, to determine the current number of minutes on the clock represented by the `Calendar` object `when`, you would call

```
int minutes = when.get(Calendar.MINUTE);
```

and to set this field to zero, you could write

```
when.set(Calendar.MINUTE, 0);
```

```
final Date getTime()
final void setTime(Date when)
```

These functions allow you to convert this `Calendar` object to a `Date` object and to set this object to the time corresponding to a `Date` object.

There are quite a few methods that we have omitted here, either because you won't have much use for them or because they're abstract and are designed to be overridden by methods in a subclass, like the one we're about to describe.

The `GregorianCalendar` Class

This is a concrete subclass of `Calendar`. It represents time using the Christian calendar familiar in many locales. This calendar was introduced by Pope Gregory XIII to correct some errors in the older Julian calendar. It reset the date October 5, 1582, to be October 15, 1582, and codified the counting of leap years. Unless you are writing programs dealing with sixteenth-century times, this discontinuity in the calendar shouldn't concern you.

There are seven constructors in this class. Two that will be of use to you are

```
GregorianCalendar()
GregorianCalendar(int year, int month, int date,
                  int hour, int minute, int second)
```

The first makes a new calendar, initialized to the current system time. The second constructor allows you to specify the date and time represented by this object.

Along with the methods inherited from `Calendar`, this class provides overrides of the parent class's abstract methods.

```
void add(int field, int amount)
```

This adds the specified amount to the indicated field, incrementing or decrementing the higher fields as necessary. For example, if this calendar represented the time 10:55:23, a call to `add(Calendar.MINUTE, 8)` would have the effect of changing this object's time to 11:02:23.

```
boolean after(Object when)
boolean before(Object when)
boolean equals(Object when)
```

Like the `Date` methods of the same names, these return `true` if this argument is a `GregorianCalendar` and represents a time that is, respectively, after, before, or equal to that represented by the argument; it returns `false` otherwise.

Object **clone**()

Returns a new GregorianCalendar that represents the same time as this object.

boolean **isLeapYear**(int year)

Returns true if the argument is a leap year and returns false if it is not.

void **roll**(int field, boolean up)

Increases or decreases the value of the specified field by 1, depending on whether the second argument is true or false, respectively. Unlike add(), this method does not affect any other fields.

Review Questions

4.1 As far as Java is concerned, when did time start?

4.2 How precise is Java time?

4.3 What is the main use for the Date class?

4.4 Once a GregorianCalendar instance has been created, does its time ever change?

4.5 What is the main difference between add() and roll()?

11.5 Hands On

The TickTock Lablet is a simple digital alarm clock. It displays the system time in hours, minutes, and seconds and is updated often enough that it is never off from the system time by more than a second. As you'll see, we get a lot of help here from the Date and GregorianCalendar classes we discussed in Section 11.4. This is also a program that makes use of threads (but you probably expected that, given that it's the Lablet for the thread chapter).

In addition to displaying the current time, our clock has an alarm feature. The user can set the time when the alarm is to go off and can turn off the alarm once it has been set.

Designing the Lablet, I: The TickTock User's Manual

Designing a consumer electronics device, even in simulation, can be surprisingly difficult. If you've ever struggled with programming a VCR, you've seen evidence that coming up with a good design isn't easy, even for experts. In fact, if you specify the action of a device for general use and find the process easy, there's a good chance that you're either *very* good or have missed the point somewhere. We'll shortly provide the User's Manual for our clock, but before we do, we should be honest and mention that we had trouble with the design ourselves. In fact, what you see is the third major revision of the Lablet. Each of the first two revisions worked, but we discarded them and started anew after asking ourselves, "Would this be usable right out of the box, or would we have to hire extra people to answer the help lines?"[5]

Finally, though, we settled on the final design and wrote the User's Manual:

Welcome!

Thanks for using TickTock™, another fine product of Rick and Stu's Applet Mill®. TickTock is a fully functional digital alarm clock, and a lot more. You can not only use TickTock as it comes, but you can also configure it to your own needs, just by following the simple guidelines in the Lab Manual that came with your purchase. In this User's Manual, we'll take a look at your new product and show you how you can get the most out of it. To learn how to change TickTock into a visual sorting demonstration or an online order form, just take a look at the Lab Manual.

Product Hint. If you want to become a true master of TickTock, we suggest you look at *programming.java* (Brooks Cole Publishing Co., Belmont, CA). This book makes a tasteful gift, as well, for those hard-to-satisfy relatives and friends.

System Requirements

TickTock™ is system-independent. You can run it on any computer that has a Java-aware Web browser or applet runner installed.

Getting Started

When you start TickTock, it will look like this:

There are two basic parts to TickTock: the Time Display™, where the time is displayed, and the Control Panel™, which contains the control buttons.

---

[5]Authorial rant: Many companies would do well to ask themselves this question before their product hits the stores.

TickTock starts in Time Mode: The Time Display shows the current system time. In Time Mode, TickTock is a clock—it's as simple as that! You'll notice that only one of the buttons in the Control Panel is active. Clicking on the "Alarm" button will take you out of Time Mode and into Alarm Mode.

The Alarm

When you press the "Alarm" button, the Control Panel changes to look like this:

When you see this configuration, you know you're in Alarm Mode and can set the alarm. You do this by clicking on the "Hour+" and "Minute+" buttons. Each of these advances the hour or minute portion of the Time Display. Once you've changed the Time Display to the time you want the alarm to go off, just press the "Set" button. You'll return to Time Mode, and the Time Display will revert to showing the system time, as usual. That's all there is to it!

Back in Time Mode, you can tell that the alarm has been set, because the "Off" button will be active:

Once the alarm has been set, it will go off at the indicated time, turning the display from green to red.[6] To turn off the alarm, just click on the "Off" button. The display will turn back to green, and the "Off" button will be disabled until you go back to Alarm Mode (by clicking the "Alarm" button) and set the alarm again.

Designing the Lablet, II: Meeting the Specifications

As amusing as it was to write the User's Manual, we had to settle down eventually and build the applet. The look of the applet dictated the first stage of design, as usual. We needed a display for the time and four buttons. We decided to write our own class for the display; there was no way to get the look we wanted from a TextField (mainly because we couldn't have two sizes for text). Because we would be drawing the time string, we made our Timer class a subclass of Canvas.

---

[6]Our engineers plan to add an audible alarm, but first they need to find out how by looking in Chapter 12. When this feature is added to Ticktock 3.0, all registered users will be able to participate in our upgrade program.

The next step was to write the applet. We wanted to let the applet design dictate the methods we would include in `Timer`, so we deliberately deferred writing the `Timer` class. We knew that we would need a thread to control the time display, because we wanted the time to be updated independently of whatever else the applet was doing. Deciding where to put the thread was more or less a matter of preference. We had two choices:

1. Make the thread an instance variable of the applet and put the thread's `run()` method in the applet itself. This choice would require that we declare the applet to implement the `Runnable` interface.

2. Put the thread and its `run()` method in `Timer`. This brought up a problem we hadn't encountered so far. We couldn't make `Timer` a subclass of `Thread`, since it was already a subclass of `Canvas`, and Java doesn't allow multiple inheritance. In this case, the solution was to do with `Timer` what we did with the applet in the preceding option—we would declare `Timer` to implement the `Runnable` interface, give it its own thread, and write a `run()` method for the thread.

Because `Timer` wouldn't need access to any of the applet's data, there was no clear reason to prefer one solution over the other. We tossed a coin and decided to implement the second strategy.

Now the applet started to take shape. Keeping in mind that this applet might be used in a browser, we wrote `start()` and `stop()` overrides to start and stop the timer when we visited or left the page containing the applet. Having done that, all we had to do was fill in the applet's `actionPerformed()` method. Here's what we came up with for the four buttons:

bMode: The leftmost button. When it is clicked, we first look at its label.

> **"Alarm":** The user wants to set the alarm. Enable the "Hour+" and "Min+" buttons and change the label of this button to "Set." Tell the timer to go to alarm mode.

> **"Set":** The user has set the alarm. Disable the "Hour+" and Min+" buttons and enable the "Off" button. Tell the timer to return to time mode.

bHr: Tell the timer to increment the hour part of its display by 1.

bMin: Tell the timer to increment the minute by 1.

bOff: Disable the "Off" button. Tell the timer to turn its alarm off.

We now knew what the `Timer` class had to do. It needed its own thread, of course, and it needed to keep instance variables for the hour, minute, and second to display, along with the alarm hour and minute. It needed to know whether it was in time mode and whether its alarm had been set. It needed `start()` and `stop()` methods and a `run()` method for its thread. It needed a method to instruct it to switch between time and alarm modes, along with one to set its alarm. It also needed methods to set its alarm hour and minute, and it needed to be able to paint() itself. In the words of the User's Manual, "That's all there is to it!" Let's take a look at the result.

The Applet

We begin with the usual import declarations. We need to import java.util for the GregorianCalendar and Date classes we'll use to maintain the clock, the displayed time, and the alarm.

```
import java.applet.*;
import java.awt.*;
import java.awt.event.*;
import java.util.*;
```

The start of the applet declaration is easy enough to understand. We declare the Timer instance we'll use, along with the four buttons, and lay everything out in the init() method.

```
public class TickTock extends Applet implements ActionListener
{
    private Timer    timeDisplay;    // the clock

    private Button   bMode,          // toggle the mode
                     bHr,            // increment the alarm hour
                     bMin,           // increment the alarm minute
                     bOff;           // turn off the alarm

    public void init()
    {
        setLayout(new BorderLayout());

        Panel p = new Panel();
        bMode = new Button("Alarm");
        bHr = new Button("Hour+");
        bMin = new Button("Min+");
        bOff = new Button("OFF");
        p.add(bMode);
        p.add(bHr);
        p.add(bMin);
        p.add(bOff);
        add("South", p);

        bHr.setEnabled(false);
        bMin.setEnabled(false);
        bOff.setEnabled(false);
        timeDisplay = new Timer();
        add("Center", timeDisplay);

        bMode.addActionListener(this);
        bHr.addActionListener(this);
        bMin.addActionListener(this);
        bOff.addActionListener(this);
    }
```

The start() and stop() methods just call the methods of the same names in the Timer class. In this program, we just stop the timer when the user leaves the page containing the applet so that its thread doesn't keep running (at the expense of other threads) when the timer isn't visible.

```
/**
 * Called each time the browser returns to the page containing
 * this applet.
 */
public void start()
{
    timeDisplay.start();
}

/**
 * Called when the browser leaves the page containing this
 * applet.
 */
public void stop()
{
    timeDisplay.stop();
}
```

We've described what the actionPerformed() method has to do—a click in the mode button does different things, depending on whether the user is about to change the alarm settings or is setting the alarm and returning to time mode. Aside from disabling and enabling the buttons as needed, this method just calls the set-TimeMode(), incrementAlarmHour(), incrementAlarmMinute(), and setAlarm() methods of the Timer instance.

```
public void actionPerformed(ActionEvent e)
{
    Object source = e.getSource();
    if (source == bMode)
    // The user has changed from time to alarm mode or
    // vice versa.
    {
        if (bMode.getLabel().equals("Alarm"))
        // Get things ready for the user to set the alarm.
        {
            bMode.setLabel(" Set ");
            bHr.setEnabled(true);
            bMin.setEnabled(true);
            timeDisplay.setTimeMode(false);
        }
        else
        // Set the alarm to the time the user set
        // and then return to clock mode.
        {
            // Tell the timer to set its alarm,
            timeDisplay.setAlarm(true);

            // and reset our widgets back to time mode.
            bMode.setLabel("Alarm");
            bHr.setEnabled(false);
            bMin.setEnabled(false);
            bOff.setEnabled(true);
            timeDisplay.setTimeMode(true);
        }
    }
```

```
        else if (source == bHr)
        // Increment the hour part of the display.
        {
            timeDisplay.incrementAlarmHour();
        }
        else if (source == bMin)
        // Increment the minute part of the display.
        {
            timeDisplay.incrementAlarmMinute();
        }
        else if (source == bOff)
        // Tell the timer to turn its alarm off.
        {
            timeDisplay.setAlarm(false);
            bOff.setEnabled(false);
        }
    }
}
```

The Timer Class

As you can see, the `Timer` class declaration begins with the instance variables for its thread of execution, three `GregorianCalendar`s (for the alarm, the current time, and the time displayed), and two boolean variables, describing on whether the alarm has been set and on whether we are in time mode. The constructor just sets the background color, initializes the three clocks, and sets the display thread to `null` so that it will be initialized in the class's `start()` method.

```
class Timer extends Canvas implements Runnable
{
    private Thread            clockThread; // the thread
    private GregorianCalendar alarm,       // alarm time
                              clock,       // current time
                              showing;     // displayed time
    private boolean           alarmSet = false,
                              timeMode = true;

    public Timer()
    {
        setBackground(Color.black);
        alarm = new GregorianCalendar();
        clock = new GregorianCalendar();
        showing = new GregorianCalendar();
        clockThread = null;
    }
```

The `start()` and `stop()` methods are called externally when the applet needs to start and stop the clock.

```
public void start()
{
    if (clockThread == null)
    {
        clockThread = new Thread(this);
        clockThread.start();
    }
}
```

```
public void stop()
{
   if (clockThread != null)
   {
      clockThread.stop();
      clockThread = null;
   }
}
```

The thread, of course, spends its time in this class's run() method. As long as the thread is active, we update the time shown by changing our clock to reflect the current time and sending the new time to be displayed. If we happen to be in alarm mode, we just send the alarm instance to be displayed. The updateTime() method we call here just displays the time represented by the argument (the clock or the alarm).

```
public void run()
{
   while (clockThread != null)
   {
      if (timeMode)
      // We're in time mode, so just update the clock with
      // the current time.
      {
         clock.setTime(new Date());
         updateTime(clock);
      }
      else
      // We're in alarm-setting mode now, so ask the timer
      // to show its alarm setting, for possible changes
      // by the user.
      {
         updateTime(alarm);
      }
      try
      // clockThread politely sleeps here.
      {
         Thread.sleep(500);
      }
      catch (InterruptedException e)
      { }
   }
}
```

The paint() method is fairly complex. We generate an appropriate "A.M" or "P.M." string, adjust the hour if needed (GregorianCalendar uses a zero base for hours, representing 12:00:00 as 00:00:00) We also use two local variables, minSep and secSep, to contain either just a semicolon separator or, if the minutes or seconds are less than ten, a semicolon and a leading zero.

We set the horizontal offset to compensate for a one- or two-digit hour, and we set the drawing color to red if the alarm has been triggered. Finally, we build a string representing the time and draw it in the appropriate color.

```
public void paint(Graphics g)
{
   String minSep = ":";   // separator for hh:mm
```

```java
    String secSep = ":";    // separator for mm:ss
    String ampm = " ";      // "A.M." or "P.M."

    // Make the String for A.M./P.M.
    if (showing.get(Calendar.AM_PM) == Calendar.AM)
    {
        ampm = ampm + "A.M.";
    }
    else
    {
        ampm = ampm + "P.M.";
    }

    // Correct for hour = 0
    int hour = showing.get(Calendar.HOUR);
    if (hour == 0)
    {
        hour = 12;
    }

    // Insert leading zeros into the time, if necessary
    if (showing.get(Calendar.MINUTE) < 10)
    {
        minSep = minSep + "0";
    }
    if (showing.get(Calendar.SECOND) < 10)
    {
        secSep = secSep + "0";
    }

    // Set the horizontal offset to compensate for a
    // one- or two-digit hour.
    int offset;
    if (hour >= 10)
    {
        offset = 10;
    }
    else
    {
        offset = 30;
    }

    // Finally, draw the time string in the
    // appropriate color.
    if (alarmTriggered())
    {
        g.setColor(Color.red);
    }
    else
    {
        g.setColor(Color.green);
    }
    g.setFont(new Font("SansSerif",Font.BOLD,36));
    g.drawString("" + hour
                    + minSep + showing.get(Calendar.MINUTE)
                    + secSep + showing.get(Calendar.SECOND),
                 offset, 50);
    g.setFont(new Font("SansSerif", Font.BOLD, 24));
    g.drawString(ampm, 175, 50);
}
```

The `updateTime()` method is called by `run()`, as we saw. It just sets the displayed timer to be the argument (either the clock or the alarm) and forces a call to `paint()` to show the new time. The frequent calls to this method cause a slight flicker from frequent redrawing. In the next chapter, we'll discuss ways to deal with this annoyance.

```
private void updateTime(GregorianCalendar c)
{
    showing = c;
    repaint();
}
```

The methods that deal with the alarm are all short and simple. We provide methods to set the time mode, enable or disable the alarm, and set the alarm hours and seconds.

```
/**
 * Set the time mode to time (if the argument is true)
 * or alarm (if the argument is false).
 */
public void setTimeMode(boolean timeMode)
{
    this.timeMode = timeMode;
}

/**
 * If the argument is true, enable the alarm. If the
 * argument is false, disable the alarm.
 */
public void setAlarm(boolean isOn)
{
    alarmSet = isOn;
}

/**
 * Increase the alarm hour setting by 1, making sure
 * that 0 <= aHour < 24.
 */
public void incrementAlarmHour()
{
    aHour++;
    if (aHour == 24)
    {
        aHour = 0;
    }
    updateTime(aHour, aMinute, 0);
}

/**
 * Increase the alarm minute setting by 1, making sure
 * that 0 <= aMinute < 60.
 */
public void incrementAlarmMinute()
{
    aMinute++;
    if (aMinute == 60)
    {
        aMinute = 0;
    }
    updateTime(aHour, aMinute, 0);
}
```

The private method `alarmTriggered()` is a utility called in `paint()` to determine whether we should paint the display string in red or green. We tell whether the alarm should go off (alarm has been set, and the current time is later than the alarm setting) and return the appropriate value. It would be tempting to use the `GregorianCalendar` method `after()` to make our test, but we can't because we don't want to consider the other fields of our calendars, such as day (particularly), month, and year, in deciding whether the alarm time is before or after the clock time.

```
private boolean alarmTriggered()
{
   if (!alarmSet)
   {
      return false;
   }
   if ((clock.get(Calendar.AM_PM) == Calendar.AM)
    && (alarm.get(Calendar.AM_PM) == Calendar.PM))
   {
      return false;
   }
   else if ((clock.get(Calendar.AM_PM) == Calendar.PM)
        && (alarm.get(Calendar.AM_PM) == Calendar.AM))
   {
      return true;
   }
   // Now we know we're in the same half-day.
   if (clock.get(Calendar.HOUR) < alarm.get(Calendar.HOUR))
   {
      return false;
   }
   else if (clock.get(Calendar.HOUR) > alarm.get(Calendar.HOUR))
   {
      return true;
   }
   // Now we know we're in the same hour.
   if (clock.get(Calendar.MINUTE) < alarm.get(Calendar.MINUTE))
   {
      return false;
   }
   else
   {
      return true;
   }
}
}
```

Review Questions

5.1 Why did we have `Timer` implement `Runnable`, rather than simply making it a subclass of `Thread`?

5.2 What is the primary activity performed by `clockThread`?

11.6 Summary

■ We discussed the following classes:

`Applet` [for the methods `start()` and `stop()`]

`Calendar`

`Date`

`GregorianCalendar`

`Object` [for the methods `wait()`, `notify()`, and `notifyAll()`]

`Runnable` (interface)

`Thread`

`ThreadGroup`

■ A thread represents an independent sequence of action in a program. A program can have arbitrarily many threads.

■ A thread requires a `run()` method. A thread executes in its `run()` method.

■ There are two standard ways of dealing with threads in a program. The first is to make a subclass of `Thread` and provide a `run()` method in the class. The second is to create an instance of `Thread` and provide an external `run()` method in which the `Thread` instance may execute.

■ The fundamental thread methods are `start()` which you can override and call, `run()`, which you'll always override and never call, and `stop()`, which you may call, but can't override.

■ The class method `Thread.sleep()` suspends the current thread for the specified number of milliseconds.

■ To give other threads a chance to execute, a well-mannered thread will always call the class method `Thread.sleep()` or `yield()` in its `run()` method.

■ If you declare a class to implement the `Runnable` interface, you must provide a `run()` method in the class (unless it's also declared to be `abstract`). The `run()` method may then be used for the class's threads.

■ Threads may be declared to be part of a `ThreadGroup`. Each thread is in some `ThreadGroup`. If you declare a thread without specifying a `ThreadGroup`, the thread will be assigned to the group containing the currently executing thread. A thread may be a member of only one `ThreadGroup`.

■ With the exception of the top-level group, every `ThreadGroup` belongs to another. A `ThreadGroup` may not belong to itself.

■ The `Applet` method `init()` is called once, when the applet is loaded by the browser.

■ The `Applet` method `start()` is called whenever the browser opens the page containing the applet. Unlike `init()`, `start()` may be invoked several times during the applet's life. Like `init()`, you don't call `start()` yourself—the system makes the call for you.

■ The `Applet` method `stop()` is called when the browser leaves the page containing the applet.

■ The `Applet` `start()` and `stop()` methods are often used to call the `Thread` methods `start()` and `stop()` for the threads in the applet.

■ The `stop()` method kills its thread. To keep the thread but stop it from executing, use the `suspend()` method to put the thread to sleep, and use `resume()` to wake it up.

■ A thread may continue to execute long after the applet has quit. It's good practice eventually to stop any thread you declare, unless you are sure it will reach the end of its `run()` method.

■ You cannot assume anything about the order of execution of two or more threads. That's up to the thread scheduler and is beyond your control.

■ Every object has an associated lock. A thread that enters a `synchronized` method or block belonging to an object acquires the lock for the object, and no other thread can enter any of the object's synchronized portions until the thread that has the lock leaves the synchronized segment.

■ To guarantee that two threads don't try to access an object simultaneously, `synchronize` the methods or code that accesses that object.

■ The `wait()`, `notify()`, and `notifyAll()` methods of `Object` must appear within code that has been synchronized.

■ The `wait()` method suspends the action of the thread and forces it to give up its lock.

■ The `notify()` method wakes up some waiting thread, allowing it to compete for the lock it surrendered. Once the thread reacquires its lock, it continues from where it left off.

■ The `notifyAll()` method wakes up all the threads waiting for the lock on the object.

■ Every thread in a Java program has a *priority*, expressed as an integer from 1 to 10. When deciding which thread to run, the thread scheduler usually chooses to run the thread with highest priority.

11.7 Exercises

1. In the `Bouncer` applets, versions 2 through 5, does increasing the argument of `sleep()` slow down or speed up the motion of the balls? Explain.

2. Change `Bouncer5` so that each ball's direction has a *y*-component as well as an *x*-component. In other words, allow the balls to move in a diagonal direction and bounce off the top and bottom as well as off the left and right walls. This exercise has nothing to do with threads, but it makes the applet more fun to watch.

3. Change `Bouncer5` by assigning the second ball's thread a different priority than the others. Describe what changes you see, if any, and explain your findings.

    a. Do this by assigning the second thread a priority that is 1 more than the priority of the first ball's thread.

    b. Do this by assigning the second thread a priority of `MAX_PRIORITY`.

    c. Do this by assigning the second thread a priority of `MIN_PRIORITY`.

4. In `Bouncer5`, how could you check whether a ball was about to collide with another?

5. Change `Bouncer5` so that the balls collide realistically. This exercise is best when combined with Exercise 2. This is quite difficult, even if you know about conservation of energy and momentum.

6. Look at the `StartStopTest` applet at the end of Section 11.2. As written, it uses a `Counter` class, declared as a subclass of `Thread`. Rewrite it using our other strategy; that is, have the applet implement `Runnable`, declare three threads in the applet, and declare a single `run()` method for all three threads. You won't need the `Counter` class. Compare your result with the original, and comment on which is easier to understand.

7. Why are `wait()`, `notify()`, and `notifyAll()` methods of the `Object` class?

8. Look through the documentation of the `java.awt` package and find an example of a `synchronized` method that we didn't mention. Explain why the method you found is declared to be `synchronized`.

9. Generally, a `run()` method is not declared to be `synchronized`. Why?

10. Look at the `ReaderWriter` example applet we presented at the end of Section 11.3. Explain why it would not be a good idea to move the `getInt()` method into `Reader` and to move `setInt()` into the `Writer` class.

11. Would the `ReaderWriter` applet work correctly if we modified it by adding one or more additional `Writers`?

   a. Explain why or why not.

   b. Modify `ReaderWriter` so that it uses two `Writers`.

12. All of the communication between threads we've talked about use a shared resource, such as the `display` field we used in `ReaderWriter`. Another means of communication is to have one thread call a method of another. In `ReaderWriter`, for example, we didn't really need `display`, except to show the final result. Instead, we could have the `Writer` send its new value by calling a method belonging to `Reader`. Modify `ReaderWriter` so that the two threads communicate by calling each other's methods. (There will still be problems of synchronization to address.)

13. Suppose that three threads all shared a `run()` method and that within `run()` there was a call to a method `doSomething()`. Suppose also that the three threads were represented by the variables `thread1`, `thread2`, and `thread3`. The nature of `doSomething()` is that `thread1` is always allowed to enter the method, `thread2` cannot enter the method until `thread1` has entered and returned, and `thread3` cannot enter the method until `thread2` has entered and returned. Write `doSomething()`.

14. Simulate the action of a car wash. There is a single wash bay and a driveway capable of holding a fixed number of cars. The cars arrive at unpredictable intervals (perhaps by the user clicking a button to generate a new car), and each car will always spend the same amount of time in the wash bay. If the driveway is full, an entering car will simply leave. You don't have to write a complete applet, but you should describe the threads you will use and show what their `run()` method or methods would look like. You should also describe any auxiliary variables you need.

15. A common thread problem is that of *deadlock,* when one thread has resource A and needs resource B to continue, while another thread has resource B and needs resource A to continue. Consider, for example, the problem of a number of people trying to cross a river by using a series of stepping stones. If two people try to cross in different directions, they might arrive at the middle with each standing on a stone that the other needs.

   a. Come up with *two* strategies the river crossers could use to avoid deadlock.

b. For each of your strategies, tell whether they could lead to the possibility of *starvation*—the chance that some person may never be able to cross the river.

c. Come up with a strategy that avoids both starvation and deadlock.

16. Here's a possible way of simulating the river-crossing problem of Exercise 15. We might represent the stones as an array of boolean values, along with two methods, moveEast() and moveWest(), that are to be used by the threads attempting to cross the river.

```
class SteppingStones
{
   private boolean[] stone = new boolean[10];

   public SteppingStones()
   {
      for (int i = 0; i < 10; i++)
      stone[i] = false;
   }

public synchronized void moveEast(int n)
{
   // If n equals 9, indicate that the thread has
   // successfully crossed to the east bank.
   // If stone[n+1] is false, set it to true and
   // set stone[n] to false, indicating that the thread
   // has moved one step east.
   // If stone[n+1] is true, the thread can't move,
   // since its destination stone is occupied.
}

public synchronized void moveWest()
{
   // If n is 0, indicate that the thread has
   // successfully crossed to the west bank.
   // Otherwise, act like moveEast(), except that
   // we look at stone[n-1].
}
```

A thread is constructed with an initial direction: 1 for an east destination and –1 for a destination on the west bank. The run() method for each thread is

```
public void run()
{
   int current, destination;
   if (direction == 1)
   {
      current -1;
      destination = 9;
   }
   else
   {
      current = 10;
      destination = 0;
   }
   while (current != destination)
      if (direction == 1)
         // try to call theStones.moveEast()
      else
         // try to call theStones.moveWest()
}
```

Implement your best strategy from Exercise 15. Before you start, here are some questions you should ask yourself: Where should most of the decision making go; in the `move()` methods or in `run()`? How should the `SteppingStones` class communicate to the threads whether a move was successful?

17. A classic scheduling problem is the *dining philosopher's problem.* In this problem, there are *n* philosophers sitting around a circular table. Each philosopher is sitting in front of a bowl of food. Between each pair of bowls there is a single chopstick, as illustrated below for the case *n* = 4.

At any time, a philosopher is either eating, talking, or hungry. A talking philosopher eventually gets hungry. A hungry philosopher tries to pick up the chopsticks to her left and right (our philosophers are all women). These are two distinct actions and can't be done simultaneously. If a hungry philosopher gets both chopsticks, she eats for an unpredictable length of time, drops the chopsticks, and starts talking. If a hungry philosopher doesn't get both chopsticks, she stays hungry. The problem is to come up with a strategy that can be applied to all philosophers so that each gets to eat eventually. For each of the following strategies, tell whether they will be successful. For the ones that will not be successful, give a sequence of philosopher actions that will either result in a deadlock or starve one of the diners.

    a. Each hungry philosopher will first try to pick up the chopstick on her left.

    b. Each philosopher is assigned a number, 1, 2, . . . , *n,* and they are arranged sequentially around the table. An odd-numbered hungry philosopher will first try to pick up the chopstick on her left, and an even-numbered hungry philosopher will first try to pick up the chopstick on her right.

    c. A hungry philosopher will pick up a chopstick only if both are available.

    d. If more than one philosopher is hungry at any time, the waiters forceably restrain all but one from trying to pick up the chopsticks.

18. Write an applet that displays an animation of the dining philosophers problem.

    a. Use one of the strategies above.

    b. Come up with a fair solution (if none of the above strategies are fair) and implement it.

    c. To see one solution, point your browser to

        `http://java.sun.com/applets/contest/DiningPhilosophers/index.html`

19. Go back to the Chapter 8 lablet `Sortmeister`, and modify it so that it shows two animations side by side, one running Selection Sort and the other running Shellsort on the same data. This is a moderately complicated exercise, but you'll find it extremely instructive to watch the two sorting routines run in parallel.

11.8 Answers to Review Questions

1.1 A place to put an independent unit of execution of a program.

1.2 `run()`. You don't call it. That's what `start()` is for.

1.3 To suspend execution of the current thread temporarily, in order to give other threads a chance to execute.

1.4 Either subclass `Thread` or have a class that implements the `Runnable` interface.

1.5 Sure; look at versions 4 and 5 of the bouncing ball example.

2.1 When the page containing the applet becomes visible. The `start()` method of an applet is a good place to put a call to the `start()` method belonging to the `Thread` class.

2.2 Call `resume()` on the thread.

3.1 You can never assume anything about the order of execution of two threads.

3.2 If they don't share any resources.

3.3 All three, really, but a lock is "owned by" an object.

4.1 00:00:00, January 1, 1970.

4.2 Java measures time in milliseconds (thousandths of a second).

4.3 As a stopwatch.

4.4 No, not unless the program changes it.

4.5 They both change the values of a `Calendar` field, but `add()` "carries" any changes over to the next higher field, whereas `roll()` doesn't.

5.1 We couldn't have `Timer` subclass `Thread`, because it subclassed `Canvas`, and Java doesn't permit multiple inheritance.

5.2 It spends most of its time sleeping. It spends most of its brief awake time calling `updateTime()`, with the clock as argument.

11.9 Class References

`java.util.Calendar`

This abstract class represents dates and times.

```
abstract class Calendar extends Object implements Cloneable
{
    //-------- Class Constants --------
    // (all are final static)
    YEAR, MONTH, WEEK_OF_YEAR, WEEK_OF_MONTH, DATE,
    DAY_OF_MONTH, DAY_OF_YEAR, AM_PM, HOUR, HOUR_OF_DAY,
    MINUTE, SECOND, MILLISECOND

    JANUARY, FEBRUARY, MARCH, APRIL, MAY, JUNE, JULY,
    AUGUST, SEPTEMBER, OCTOBER, NOVEMBER, DECEMBER,
    SUNDAY, MONDAY, TUESDAY, WEDNESDAY, THURSDAY, FRIDAY,
    SATURDAY, AM, PM

    //--------- Constructors ----------
    protected Calendar();
    /* You'd use this only if you were implementing your own
        subclass of Calendar (for an Incan calendar, for
        example). */
```

```
        //--------- Class Method -----------
        static synchronized getInstance();

        //----------- Methods -------------
        abstract void add(int field, int value);
        abstract boolean after(Object when);
        abstract boolean before(Object when);
        final void clear();
        final void clear(int field);
        /* These clear all the fields of this object, or clear a
           particular field. The fields will then be invalid, in
           the sense that they no longer correspond to the internal
           time in milliseconds. To get valid values in the fields,
           you would then call the protected method complete(). */

        Object clone();
        abstract boolean equals(Object when);
   ◆    final Date getTime();
   ◆    final void setTime(Date time);
        abstract void roll(int field, boolean up);
        /* These act like the corresponding methods in
           GregorianCalendar. */

   ◆    final void set(int field, int value);
        final void set(int year, int month, int date);
        final void set(int year, int month, int date,
                       int hour, int minute);
        final void set(int year, int month, int date,
                       int hour, int minute, int second);

        //------- Protected Methods --------
        protected void complete();
        /* Compute the internal time, using the field values, and
           then reset the fields to the values corresponding to the
           new time. */

        protected void computeFields();
        /* Use the current internal time in milliseconds to update
           all the fields. */

        protected long getTimeInMillis();
        protected void setTimeInMillis(long time);
        // Inspect or modify the internal time.
   }
```

java.util.Date

A Date object represents times. Although it was originally intended to handle both dates and times, much of the functionality of this class has been subsumed in the Calendar class, leaving this class with a number of methods that may vanish in later versions of Java and with some, which we list below, that have to do primarily with elapsed time.

```
class Date extends Object implements Cloneable
{
    //--------- Constructors ----------
    Date();
    Date(long ms);
```

```
//----------- Methods -------------
boolean after(Date d);
boolean before(Date d);
boolean equals(Date d);
```

◆ ```
long getTime();
void setTime(long ms);
```

```
//------ Deprecated Methods --------
int getDate();
int getMonth();
int getDay();
int getHours();
int getMinutes();
int getSeconds();

void setDate(int date);
void setYear(int year);
void setMonth(int month);
void setDay(int day);
void setHours(int hrs);
void setMinutes(int mins);
void setSeconds(int secs);
}
```

java.util.GregorianCalendar

This is a concrete subclass of Calendar. It represents time using the Christian calendar familiar in many locales.

```
class GregorianCalendar extends Calendar
{
    //--------- Constructors ----------
    GregorianCalendar();
    GregorianCalendar(int year, int month, int date);
    GregorianCalendar(int year, int month, int date,
                      int hour, int minute);
    GregorianCalendar(int year, int month, int date,
                      int hour, int minute, int second);

    //----------- Methods -------------
```
◆ ```
    void add(int field, int amount)
        throws IllegalArgumentException;
```
◆ `    boolean after(Object when);`
◆ `    boolean before(Object when);`
◆ ```
    boolean equals(Object when);
    Object clone();
    boolean isLeapYear(int year);
    void roll(int field, boolean up);
        throws IllegalArgumentException;
    /* Note that add() and roll() will throw an exception if the
       field argument isn't one of the Calendar field constants.
     */
}
```
```

java.lang.Runnable

This interface contains the run() method required by any Thread.

```
interface Runnable
{
    //----------- Methods -------------
♦   abstract void run();
}
```

java.lang.Thread

A Thread represents a single thread of execution in a program. In addition to the methods listed here, you will often use the Object methods notify(), notifyAll(), and wait() to control synchronization among threads, and you may need the Applet methods start() and stop() as points from which you will start, stop, suspend, or resume the threads in the program.

```
class Thread extends Object implements Runnable
{
    //--------- Constructors -----------
    Thread();
    Thread(Runnable target);
    Thread(ThreadGroup g, Runnable target);
    Thread(String name);
    Thread(ThreadGroup g, String name);
    Thread(Runnable target, String name);
    Thread(ThreadGroup g, Runnable target, String name);

    //------- Class constants ---------
    final static int MAX_PRIORITY;
    final static int MIN_PRIORITY;
    final static int NORM_PRIORITY;

    //-------- Class Methods ----------
    static int activeCount();
    /* Returns the number of threads in the ThreadGroup to
       which the current Thread belongs. */

    static Thread currentThread()
    /* Returns the current thread, i.e., the one that was active
       when this method was called. */

    static void enumerate(Thread[] t)
    /* Sets the argument to an array containing all threads in
       this thread's group, and any subgroups of the group. */

♦   static void sleep(long ms) throws InterruptedException

    static void yield(long ms)
    /* This causes the current thread to surrender its
       execution. Doing so may allow another thread to be
       selected for execution. All this method does is give
       other threads the possibility of running--the system may
       decide to run another thread or simply revive the old
       current thread. This is another way a thread can be
       polite--rather than calling sleep(), you can call yield()
       to give other threads a chance to execute. */
```

```
//----------- Methods -------------
final String getName()
/* Returns the name of this Thread, or null if no name has
   been specified. */

final String getPriority()
final ThreadGroup getThreadGroup()

final boolean isAlive()
/* Returns true if this thread has been started and has not
   yet died, as a result either of stop() being called or of
   completing its run() method. */

final void join()
   throws InterruptedException
final synchronized void join(long ms)
   throws InterruptedException
/* The first method causes the current thread to suspend its
   execution until this thread has finished, either by being
   stopped or by completing its run() method. The second
   method waits the current thread until this thread has
   completed or the indicated number of milliseconds have
   elapsed. These are useful when the current thread spawns
   another and has to wait for the new thread to complete
   before it can continue. */

♦  final void resume() throws SecurityException
   void run()

   final void setName(String name) throws SecurityException
      // Sets the name of this Thread.

   final void setPriority(int p) throws SecurityException,
                                        IllegalArgumentException

♦  synchronized void start(int p) throws IllegalThreadStateException

♦  final void stop() throws SecurityException
♦  final void suspend() throws SecurityException
}
```

java.lang.ThreadGroup

A ThreadGroup represents a collection of threads, along with methods for manipulating the threads it contains. A ThreadGroup is a *recursive* structure, in that it may also contain other ThreadGroups.

```
class ThreadGroup extends Object
{
   //--------- Constructors ----------
   ThreadGroup(String name);
   ThreadGroup(ThreadGroup parent, String name)
      throws NullPointerException, SecurityException;

   //----------- Methods -------------
   int activeCount();
   int activeGroupCount();
```

```
   /* The first of these returns the total number of threads in
      this group and all its subgroups. The second returns the
      total number of groups in this group and all of its
      subgroups. */

final void destroy() throws SecurityException;
/* This method destroys this group. Before you call this,
   you must have stopped all the threads it contains. */

void enumerate(Thread[] threads);
void enumerate (Thread[] threads, boolean recurse);
void enumerate (ThreadGroup[] groups);
void enumerate (ThreadGroup[] groups, boolean recurse);
/* These methods fill arrays of threads or thread groups so
   that they contain all of the threads or thread groups in
   this group and all of its subgroups. If the boolean
   argument is false, only the threads or groups in this
   group will be enumerated, ignoring any in this group's
   subgroups. */

final int getMaxPriority();
final void setMaxPriority(int max);
/* These return or set the largest priority of any thread in
   this group. setMaxPriority() will not change the priority
   of any threads that are currently in this group. */

final String getName();
/* Returns the name of this group, if it has one, or null,
   if it doesn't. */

final ThreadGroup getParent();
/* Returns the parent ThreadGroup of this group or null
   if this group is the top-level system group. */

   final boolean parentOf(ThreadGroup g);
/* Returns true if and only if the argument is equal to this
   ThreadGroup or is a parent of this group. */

◆  final void resume() throws SecurityException;
◆  final void stop() throws SecurityException;
◆  final void suspend() throws SecurityException;
}
```

CHAPTER TWELVE

APPLETS IN CYBERSPACE

We've mentioned several times that applets are designed to be run in a Web browser, as part of an HTML document. As anyone with even a modicum of Net surfing experience knows, the Worldwide Web is a vast collection of information, organized into millions of pages distributed among hundreds of thousands of computers. An applet can be as much a part of this world of information as the Web page in which it lives. It can access graphical images, sounds, and other data on remote computers, it can use and manipulate this data, and it can receive input information from the HTML document that calls it into action. In this, our final chapter, we'll show you how to make your applets into first-class Web citizens.

Objectives

In this chapter, we will

- See how information can be sent to an applet, and how an applet can discover the context in which it is running.
- Show how applets can use sounds and images.
- Discuss image manipulation.
- Continue our discussion of animation that we began in Chapter 11.
- Complete our discussion of programming in general and Java programming in particular by investigating a Lablet that is as close to an "industrial-strength" program as we can make it.

12.1   Setting the Scene

If an applet is intended to be accessed from a Web page, the HTML document that describes the page will contain a reference to the applet, using the HTML tag `<APPLET>`. The applet doesn't really "live" in the HTML document, any more than an image does. Instead, the `<APPLET>` tag will contain the address of the location where the applet's `.class` file or files may be found.

When a user "goes to" a Web page, by clicking on a link, for example, what happens is that the user's local computer finds the host computer where the desired page is located and sends a request to the host computer to send a copy of the page to the local system. Once the HTML document reaches the local system, the local Web browser takes over and attempts to lay out the page by interpreting the embedded HTML tags. Some of these tags, like `<HR>`, instruct the browser to do layout actions that can be accomplished locally, such as placing a horizontal rule on the display.

Some of the tags, though, might require the browser to send off a request for further information. This might happen if the tag contained a reference to an image or an applet that was stored on another computer. In that case, the browser would instruct the local system to do the same sort of thing it did when the page was first loaded—go off to another computer and ask it to send a copy of the necessary information, such as the image or applet.

This process is fast, but you've probably seen that it's not instantaneous. You've almost certainly had the experience of waiting while your computer loads the images, sounds, movies, and applets needed by a Web page. The amazing thing about this process, though, is that it works at all. At any instant, there are hundreds of thousands of computers throughout the world all doing the same thing, locating files on other computers and transferring them back and forth. What makes this process work more or less invisibly to the users is that every single file available on the Internet is uniquely identified by a name, known as its *uniform resource locator*, or URL, for short.

URLs

A uniform resource locator is a string, divided into four parts: the *protocol*, the *host name*, the *path name*, and the name of the resource, usually a file.

A URL has the form

```
protocol://host name/path name/file name
```

The protocol identifies the format to be used for transfer of this information. The protocol you'll see most frequently is `http`, short for *hypertext transfer protocol*. This is the format for all Worldwide Web documents. Other formats include `file`, for a file on the local system, `ftp`, for files on an FTP (*file transfer protocol*) server, and `gopher`, for files using the Gopher protocol.

The host name is a hierarchical listing of *domains*, separated by periods, such as `cs.hamilton.edu` and `java.sun.com`. The domains that make up a host name are listed in increasing order of generality. For example, the host name `java.sun.com` represents the computer named `java` in the wider domain of all systems at the `sun` location (all the computers at Sun Microsystems), which is itself located in the top-level `com` domain of all commercial institutions. You may find an optional *port number* as part of a host name, as in

```
www.somewhere.com:8080
```

and you may have seen a host name in the *dotted quad* format, consisting of four integers (from 0 to 255) separated by periods, as in

```
150.209.8.36
```

Once the host computer has been located, the path name describes where in the system's file structure the resource may be found. The path name is also hierarchical but is listed in decreasing order of generality—that is, in the order of directory then subdirectory. For example, the Java 1.1 documentation is found in

```
products/jdk/1.1/docs/api
```

which indicates that the pages are found in the top-level `products` directory, which contains the subdirectory `jdk`, which contains the 1.1 sub-sub-directory, which contains the `docs` three-times-subdirectory, which, finally, contains the `api` subdirectory at the very bottom.

Once the protocol, host name, and path name have been specified, the file within the lowest directory is identified by its name. Putting all the parts together, at the time of this writing, the description of all the available Java 1.1 packages—packages.html—has the full URL

```
http://java.sun.com/products/jdk/1.1/docs/api/packages.html
```

This is quite a chunk of text. There will be times, though, when you don't need the entire URL to specify a file. A *partial* or *relative* URL is a shorter form in which part of the address is implied, rather than stated explicitly. For instance, in the context of the URL above, the partial URL `tree.html` would refer to the file of that name in the last-named directory just as well as would the full, or *absolute*, URL

```
http://java.sun.com/products/jdk/1.1/docs/api/tree.html
```

We can also refer to files in subdirectories of the current directory by continuing the path and ending with the file name. If there were a directory within `api` named `foo` (there isn't, but we can pretend there is), containing the page `hello.html`, we could refer to it relative to the `api` directory by using

```
foo/hello.html
```

instead of using the absolute URL

```
http://java.sun.com/products/jdk/1.1/docs/api/foo/hello.html
```

Finally, we can also go upwards in the directory structure, by placing one or more slash characters before a path name. For example, relative to the URL

```
http://java.sun.com/products/jdk/1.1/docs/api/tree.html
```

the partial URL

```
/boo/notes.html
```

with an initial slash would indicate that the address begins one level higher in the directory structure (namely, in the `docs` directory), so the corresponding absolute URL would be

```
http://java.sun.com/products/jdk/1.1/docs/boo/notes.html
```

The URL class in the package `java.net` is used to construct and inspect URLs in an applet or application. This class is commonly used by applets that load images or sounds from the host computer. There are four constructors for this class; each throws a `MalformedURLException` if the information provided is not sufficient to create a legal URL. This is a checked exception, so you'll have to enclose calls to these constructors in a `try` block.

URL(String name)

Constructs a URL object from the absolute name given in the argument.

URL(URL base, String relative)

Constructs a URL object from the name given in the argument, relative to the specified base URL.

URL(String protocol, String host, String file)

Constructs a URL from the information provided. For example, we might construct a URL by

```
URL theURL = new URL("http", "www.host.com", "images/ball.gif");
URL(String protocol, String host, int port, String file)
```

Acts like the constructor above, except that it also allows you to specify the port.

There are four URL methods you might find useful in case you wish to extract one of the parts of a URL object.

String **getFile**()

Returns the string describing the path name and file name of this URL.

String **getHost**()

Returns the string describing the host name of this URL.

int **getPort**()

Returns the port number of this URL.

String **getProtocol**()

Returns the string describing the protocol in use for this URL.

The Applet Class, Revisited

The `java.applet` package contains the `Applet` class and three interfaces: `AppletContext`, `AppletStub`, and `AudioClip`. An applet interacts with its environment by calling some `Applet` methods we'll discuss in this section. Many of these methods work by calling `AppletContext` methods of the same name, in effect asking the browser or applet runner to do the work. The `AppletContext` and `AudioClip` interfaces are implemented by the applet viewer or browser that's actually responsible for running the applet. Unless you are writing your own applet viewer, there's very little chance you'll ever need `AppletStub`, and we won't discuss it here.

The Class References at the end of Chapter 2 contain a description of the `Applet` class; we're finally ready for a more thorough description of some of the `Applet` methods. The first two methods we'll cover are used to get information about where the applet and its HTML document reside on the host file system. This information is important, because an applet often requires data, such as sounds and graphical images, that are stored on the host system. When an applet is loaded into a local computer, then, there must be a way for the applet to request that the needed data be loaded from the host computer.

URL **getCodeBase**()

Returns the URL of the directory that contains this applet's `.class` file.

URL **getDocumentBase**()

Returns the URL of the current HTML document.

In the file structure illustrated in Figure 12.1, suppose that `page1.html` contained an `<APPLET>` tag referring to the applet whose compiled bytecode was in the file `Button1.class`. Then, within the `Button1` applet, the statement

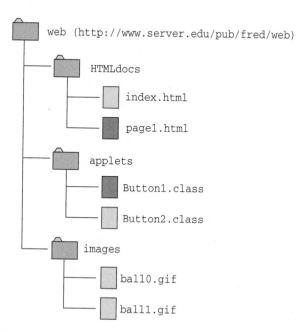

Figure 12.1

An example of a portion of a file structure.

```
URL appURL = this.getCodeBase();
```

would set `appURL` to correspond to the URL

```
http://www.server.edu/pub/fred/web/applets/
```

and the statement

```
URL docURL = this.getDocumentBase();
```

would set `docURL` to correspond to the URL

```
http://www.server.edu/pub/fred/web/HTMLdocs/page1.html
```

The URL class is commonly used in combination with Applet methods to load images and sounds. These are often stored on the host computer and referenced by addresses relative to the applet or the HTML document that uses the applet.

```
AudioClip getAudioClip(URL absolute)
AudioClip getAudioClip(URL base, String relative)
```

These methods return an AudioClip object that is located at the indicated URL. We'll discuss the AudioClip interface in Section 12.2. The first of these methods takes a String argument representing an absolute URL, and the second uses a base URL and an address relative to that URL to determine where the AudioClip is located.

```
Image getImage(URL u)
Image getImage(URL base, String relative)
```

These methods return a reference to the Image stored at the specified absolute or relative URL.

In the example of Figure 12.1, for instance, the image `ball0.gif` has the relative URL

```
/images/ball0.gif
```

with respect to both the code and the document, so we could load the image `ball0.gif` into our applet by doing this:

```
URL ballURL = new URL(getCodeBase(), "/images/ball0.gif");
Image ball = getImage(ballURL);
```

or by using this shorter but perhaps more opaque statement

```
Image ball = getImage(getCodeBase(), "/images/ball0.gif");
```

There are seven more methods of interest to us in the Applet class. We'll list them here for completeness and discuss getAppletContext() and getParameter() in detail shortly.

```
AppletContext getAppletContext()
```

Returns the AppletContext object associated with this applet.

```
String getAppletInfo()
```

You'll override this method to return a `String` containing information about this applet. Although most browsers and applet runners don't call this method at present, it is designed for potential use in an environment that would provide an "About this applet" menu choice. You might want to override this method to return copyright information, for example.

```
String getParameter(String name)
```

The `<APPLET>` tag allows you to specify information that the applet might need. This list of *parameters* consists of certain named pieces of information, somewhat like variables. This method returns the `String` value of the parameter with the specified name or, if no parameter with the given name has been supplied, returns the `null String`.

```
String[][] getParameterInfo()
```

Returns an arbitrarily long array of triples of strings, each consisting of the parameter name, its type, and its description. You will override this to provide a complete description of the parameters your applet uses.

```
void play(URL absolute)
void play(URL base, String relative)
```

These load and play the `AudioClip` at the given absolute or relative URL.

```
void showStatus(String message)
```

Displays the `String` argument in the applet runner's or browser's status bar. This method is most commonly used to display the status of an operation, as, for example, "Image loading complete." Because the environment uses the status bar for its own purposes, you should use this method only for incidental information, understanding that it may vanish quite rapidly. You may have seen the status bar used to irritating effect by an applet that hogs it for worthless messages, such as "This is my first applet. Isn't it way cool?" Don't do that. Users depend on the status bar for information about links in an HTML document and will hate you if you parade your ego where they are looking for useful information.

The `AppletContext` Interface

The `AppletContext` instance of an applet is "owned" by the applet runner or browser in which an applet is running. This instance provides a means by which the applet can communicate with the outside world. The `AppletContext` interface is abstract—the methods it names are all implemented by the program that runs your applets. This interface contains some methods that have the same names as the `Applet` methods we've mentioned:

```
AudioClip getAudioClip(URL absolute)
Image getImage(URL absolute)
void showStatus(String message)
```

In addition, there are some methods that you might call, once you've gotten the AppletContext instance associated with the environment, by using the Applet method getAppletContext().

```
Applet getApplet(String name)
```

Returns a reference to an applet with the given name. The applet named must be on the same HTML page as the applet where the method call takes place. This provides you with a limited amount of interapplet communication. Suppose, for instance, that an HTML page contained two applets, "Tick" and "Tock," and that "Tock" was of type Timer and had a public method reset(). Then, from within "Tick," we could make a call to "Tock" by using the appropriate type cast:

```
Timer otherApplet = (Timer)getAppletContext().getApplet("Tock");
otherApplet.reset();
```

The name argument in this method can be either the class name or the name given by the name attribute of the <APPLET> tag (which we'll discuss almost immediately). This method returns null if the applet can't be found, so be careful to get the name right.

```
void showDocument(URL absolute)
void showDocument(URL base, String relative)
```

These request the environment to show the document with the absolute or relative URL specified. The environment is allowed to ignore this request, as might happen, for example, in an applet runner that's not equipped to display an HTML document. We could use this in a Web browser, though, to tell the browser to load another page. We do this in the Lablet, where you'll find the following code:

```
// destURL has previously been set to the URL of a Web page
getAppletContext().showDocument(destURL);
```

Applet Parameters, Applet Attributes

Communication between applets and the world of the Web can work in both directions. In particular, an HTML document can send information to any of the applets it contains. In the Lablet, for instance, we construct a GraphicButton class and use it in an applet that displays a widget that acts like a regular button but looks nicer. Like an ordinary AWT Button, a GraphicButton has a setLabel() method, but it's of no use to the HTML document containing the applet, because HTML has no way of accessing the methods of its applets.

The <APPLET> tag, though, provides Web page designers with a way of sending information to an applet, as long as the applet has indicated that it is interested in the information. This is done by using the <PARAM> tag within the <APPLET> element. The Lablet for this chapter, for example, appears within a Web page and is specified by the following <APPLET> tag.

```
<APPLET    code = "GraphicButtoner.class"
           width = 82
           height = 27
           align = left>
    <PARAM name = "pattern" value = "bttn*.gif">
    <PARAM name = "numPix" value = "2">
    <PARAM name = "label" value = "Home">
    <PARAM name = "destURL"   value = "http://www.bogus.edu/">
</APPLET>
```

Each of the <PARAM> elements has two required attributes: the name of the parameter and a string representing its value. In the example above, for instance, the parameter name "label" is paired with the value "Home". The GraphicButtoner applet contains a String instance variable, theLabel, and this variable is set within the applet's init() method by the statement

```
theLabel = getParameter("label");
```

This method looks in the <APPLET> element for a parameter with the name "label" and, if it finds one, returns the String value of the parameter with that name. In this case, the value (and hence the String used for the button label) is "Home".

> The Applet method getParameter(String name) looks for a parameter with the given name among the <PARAM> elements of the <APPLET> element. If it finds a matching name, the method returns the value of that parameter. If there is no parameter with the given name, getParameter() returns null.

This can be extremely handy. A Web page author needs only to know the parameter names and can then match those names with values to customize the applet, without knowing any Java at all!

While we're on the subject, we should explain the rest of the <APPLET> tag—namely, the attributes, such as code, width, height, and align, that appear in the example above. There are three required attributes:

code = the name of the applet's class file

width = the width, in pixels, that the browser allocates for the applet on its page

height = the height, in pixels, that the browser allocates for the applet

There are several optional attributes you can include, as well:

codebase = the URL where the applet's class file is located. This is used if the class file isn't in the same directory as the applet.

name = the name you give the applet. This is useful if you have two applets of the same type on a page.

alt = a string that will appear if the browser can't load the applet or isn't equipped to deal with Java.

align = any one of these words: left, right, top, bottom, middle. These determine the placement of the applet on the page.

vspace = the amount of vertical padding, in pixels, that the browser will place above and below the applet.

hspace = the amount of horizontal padding, in pixels, that the browser will place to the left and right of the applet.

Review Questions

1.1 What are the four parts of a URL?

1.2 In which package is the URL class located?

1.3 What is the difference between the Applet methods getCodeBase() and getDocumentBase()?

1.4 Of what use is an APPLET parameter?

12.2   Lights, Camera, . . .

Once you know how to locate resources on the Web, you're ready to load sounds and images and use them in your applets. We'll take care of sounds first (they're fairly simple) and then spend most of this section talking about creating, using, and manipulating images.

Audio Clips

There are a bewildering number of formats for storing sounds in digital form. Web browsers deal with this proliferation of formats by using *helper applications*. When a browser encounters a sound file it needs to play, it first looks in the header of the file to determine its format and then checks whether it has a program it can call to play the sound. If it can't find an appropriate helper application, the browser may put up a dialog box, asking the user to select a program that can play the file, and if the user can't find the right program, the browser simply ignores the request and doesn't play the sound.

This strategy would clearly violate Java's design principle of platform independence, so there is only one sound format a Java environment is guaranteed to recognize, the AU format. This means that if you find a sound you want to use and it's in WAV or SND format, for example, you'll have to find a program that will convert the sound file into AU format before you can use it.

Once you have a file with the right format, though, playing it is simple. First, you will use the Applet method getAudioClip() to load the sound. This returns an

AudioClip instance associated with the sound file whose URL you specified in the method's argument. The AudioClip interface contains three methods you will use for handling sounds.

void **play**()

Plays this AudioClip from start to finish.

void **loop**()

Plays this AudioClip continuously. Once it reaches the end of the file, it returns to the beginning and starts over.

void **stop**()

Stops playing this AudioClip. It's important that you stop any sound you play, especially if you are looping it. Failure to do so will keep the sound playing, even when the user leaves the Web page containing the applet. Needless to say, this can be quite annoying.

Suppose, for instance, that you have a sound file "gong.au" that is stored in the same directory as the class file for the applet. To play this sound, here's all you have to do:

```
AudioClip gongClip = getAudioClip(getCodeBase(), "gong.au");
if (gongClip != null)      // We were able to load it,
{
    gongClip.play();       // so now play it.
}
```

To be safe, you'd also stop the sound in the applet's stop() method:

```
public void stop()
{
    if (gongClip != null)    // It's still playing,
    {
        gongClip.stop();     // so stop it.
    }
    ...
}
```

Image Basics

You've seen how to use the Graphics class's methods to do simple drawing. In theory, at least, you could use drawRect(), drawOval(), drawLine(), and the like to produce any picture you want. In practice, of course, you'd never want to draw the Mona Lisa this way—even if you had the necessary skill, it would require thousands of Graphics method calls. It would be far easier to render the picture in a paint program or use a scanner to convert an existing image to digital form and then somehow load the image and draw it where you wanted.

Java's Image class provides support for loading, manipulating, and displaying images. Fortunately for us, the problem of multiple formats that we mentioned when talking about audio files is nowhere near as serious for images. There are two widely used formats for images on the Web, known as GIF and JPEG, and Java supports both.

Although Java's support for sounds is quite limited, it provides an intimidatingly complex and powerful set of classes for image manipulation. Besides the `Image` class in `java.awt`, the package `java.awt.image` contains 11 classes and 3 interfaces devoted to image manipulation. Fortunately, if all you want to do is display an image in an applet, the process is quite simple. First, you use the `Applet` method

```
Image getImage(URL base, String relative)
```

to associate an `Image` object with the GIF or JPEG file at the specified URL, and then all you have to do is use the `Graphics` method

```
boolean drawImage(Image im, int x, int y, ImageObserver ob)
```

to load and then draw the `Image` instance, anchored at coordinates (x, y). We'll have more to say about the `ImageObserver` interface later, but for this simple use all we need to know is that the `Component` class implements `ImageObserver`, so we can use `this` applet as our `ImageObserver`. Below, we present an applet that gets an image and displays it. The result is illustrated in Figure 12.2.

```java
import java.applet.*;
import java.awt.*;

public class ImageTest1 extends Applet
{
    Image asteroids;
```

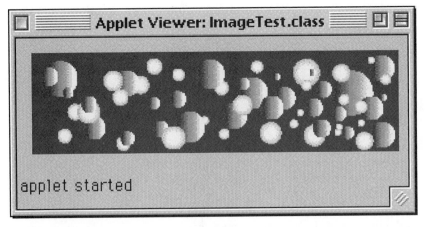

Figure 12.2

An image displayed in an applet.

```
    public void init()
    {
        asteroids = getImage(getCodeBase(), "aster.gif");
    }

    public void paint(Graphics g)
    {
        g.drawImage(asteroids, 10, 10, this);
    }
}
```

Note, by the way, that we're doing something a bit unusual here. The drawImage() method returns a boolean value, indicating whether it was able to load and draw the image. When we make the call, though, we never make use of the return value. In a fancier program, we might use the return value to discover whether the image was successfully drawn before doing something else.

The Graphics method drawImage() comes in quite a few forms. These methods allow you to place the image where you want, crop it, scale it, and perform other manipulations. Each of these methods returns true if the image has been completely drawn; otherwise, each returns false.

```
boolean drawImage(Image im, int x, int y, ImageObserver ob)
```

We've just seen this method. It loads and draws the image, with its upper left corner at (x, y), measured in the Graphics object's local coordinates.

```
boolean drawImage(Image im, int x, int y, int width, int height,
            ImageObserver ob)
```

This acts like the method above, except that it scales the image to fit the given width and height. This may take a *long* time to complete—most of the time, you should instead use getScaledInstance() to scale the image first. We'll discuss this further when we cover the Image class.

```
boolean drawImage(Image im, int x, int y, Color bgColor,
            ImageObserver ob)
```

Some graphics formats, such as GIF89A, allow you to specify that one color will be transparent. This method allows you to specify a background color that will show through any transparent parts of the image.

```
boolean drawImage(Image im, int x, int y, int width, int height,
            Color bgColor, ImageObserver ob)
```

This method allows you to set the width, height, and background color.

```
boolean drawImage(Image im, int dx1, int dy1, int dx2, dy2, int sx1,
            sy1, int sx2, int sy2, ImageObserver ob)
```

The coordinates (sx1, sy1) and (sx2, sy2) determine the corners of a rectangle in the image, and (dx1, dy1) and (dx2, dy2) determine the corners of a rectangle in the Graphics drawing region. This method draws the portion of the image within the specified source (s-) rectangle in the destination (d-) rectangle in this Graphics object. If the corners don't correspond, the image will be reflected when drawn. If the source rectangle is larger than the destination rectangle, the image will be cropped to fit, and if the source rectangle is smaller than the destination rectangle (as it is in Figure 12.3), the image rectangle will be scaled to fit.

```
boolean drawImage(Image im, int dx1, int dy1, int dx2, dy2,
                  int sx1, sy1, int sx2, int sy2, Color bgColor
                  ImageObserver ob)
```

This acts like the preceding method, but it also allows you to specify the background color that will show through any transparent parts of the image.

The Image class is fairly simple. It has no constructor you can call; you have to get an Image instance by calling the Applet method getImage() or the Component method createImage(). This class contains five class constants that are used in getScaledInstance():

SCALE_AREA_AVERAGING: use a particular slow but nice scaling scheme.

SCALE_DEFAULT: use the default scaling algorithm.

SCALE_FAST: prefer speed over a nice result.

SCALE_REPLICATE: use a particular fast but not pretty scaling scheme.

SCALE_SMOOTH: prefer a nice result over speed.

```
void flush()
```

This method forces this image to be reloaded the next time it is drawn, rather than allowing the system to reuse the original image without reloading. You would use this if you expected the source image to be changed over time, as it might be if the original was made from a real-time video source.

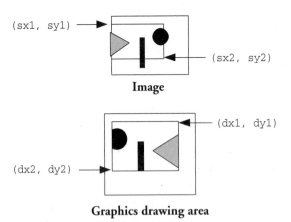

Figure 12.3

Scaling and reflecting with **drawImage()**.

Graphics **getGraphics**()

Returns a Graphics instance associated with this image. This can be used only with an image that came from the Component createImage() method; you cannot use this with images that came from a remote source through getImage(). This is useful for drawing on "offscreen images," as you'll see.

int **getHeight**(ImageObserver ob)

Asks the ImageObserver for the height of this image. If this image hasn't been completely loaded, the ImageObserver may not yet have enough information to report the height and will signal that by returning −1.

int **getWidth**(ImageObserver ob)

As with getHeight(), this returns the width of this image, if known, and returns −1 if the width isn't known yet.

Image **getScaledInstance**(int w, int h, int hints)

Returns an image made from this image, scaled to width w and height h, using the scaling scheme specified by the constant, like Image.SCALE_FAST, in the hints argument.

ImageProducer **getSource**()

Every image is associated with an ImageProducer, as you'll see. This method returns the ImageProducer that is the source of bits in this image.

Drawing Offscreen

When drawing to the screen, we rely on Component's paint() method to make sure the screen is properly updated. If we're doing a complicated drawing, though, it may take a noticeable amount of time for paint() to refresh the screen completely. A common method for dealing with this problem is known as *double buffering*. In this technique, the drawing is done on an Image instance. Once the image is complete, we display the whole thing at once by calling drawImage() within our paint() method. This generally makes the drawing process appear much smoother, which can be a big advantage when doing animation.

double buffering

Double Buffering

1. Use the Component method createImage(int w, int h) to construct an Image instance of width w and height h.

2. Use the Image method getGraphics() to get a Graphics instance associated with the image.

3. Use the Graphics object to do all the drawing.

4. Call drawImage() to display the image on the screen.

In the applet below, we illustrate a simple use of double buffering. The result is pictured in Figure 12.4.

```java
import java.applet.*;
import java.awt.*;

public class ImageTest2 extends Applet
{
    Image offscreen;
    public void init()
    {
        // Step 1: Get an image for our drawing.
        offscreen = createImage(200, 50);

        // Step 2: Get a Graphics instance and use that
        // for drawing.
        Graphics g = offscreen.getGraphics();
        doComplexDrawing(g);

        g.dispose();
    }

    public void paint(Graphics g)
    // Step 3: Copy our offscreen image to the screen.
    {
        g.drawImage(offscreen, 10, 10, this);
    }

    private void doComplexDrawing (Graphics g)
    {
        g.setColor(Color.white);
        g.fillRect(0, 0, 200, 50);
        g.setColor(Color.black);
        g.drawRect(1, 1, 198, 48);
        g.setColor(Color.red);
        g.drawRect(2, 2, 196, 46);
        g.setColor(Color.pink);
        g.drawRect(3, 3, 194, 44);
        g.setColor(Color.black);
        for (int i = 0; i < 11; i++)
        {
            g.drawLine(5, 45 - 4 * i, 195, 5 + 4 * i);
        }
    }
}
```

Image Processing Prerequisites

Java provides extraordinarily powerful image processing facilities. Many of the operations we can perform on images, though, are beyond the scope of this book. We'll give you a taste of what you can do with images by talking about one simple form of an *image filter* that can be used to modify the colors of an image. There are many more things you can do with image filters, such as rotating an image, blurring it, and fading between one image and another. If that sort of thing sounds exciting, we encourage you to look at the online documentation and search the Web for samples.

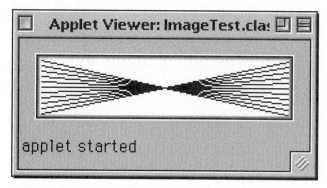

Figure 12.4

Offscreen drawing with **ImageTest2**.

Before we get to image filtering, there are some preliminary topics we need to cover. We'll first take a closer look at the Color class, which we introduced in Chapter 2, and while doing that we'll provide a quick review of *hexadecimal* representation of integers.

An instance of the Color class represents a color, as you know. There are many different ways of representing colors in a computer, but they all use some sort of numeric code.[1] One of the color models that Java uses is to divide a color into its red, green, and blue components, in much the same way as a color television does. Each of these components is represented by an integer from 0 (component is turned off) to 255 (component is at maximal brightness). For example, the color with (R, G, B) components (0, 0, 0) is black, (128, 128, 128) represents a medium gray, and (255, 175, 175) represents pink, because we're adding some more red to the light gray we'd have from (175, 175, 175).

We can represent the numbers from 0 to 255 in binary[2] using no more than eight bits (a byte, in other words), so we can pack all three components into a single 32-bit int and still have eight bits to spare.[3] In this compressed representation, the red component occupies bits 23 to 16, the green component is in bits 15 to 8, and the blue component takes up bits 7 to 0, as we illustrate in Figure 12.5. Pink, for instance, would have 11111111 in the red component, because 255 in binary is 11111111, and the green and blue components would both contain the bits 10101111, the representation for the decimal number 175 (= 128 + 32 + 8 + 4 + 2 + 1).

The binary representation of pink, 111111111010111111010, is too cumbersome to use, even if we strip off the leading zeros. The decimal equivalent, 16756655, is tedious to calculate and hides all the information about the components. A more

---

[1] Because it would be difficult to paint a bit in memory red, for instance.

[2] We introduced binary representation of integers in Chapter 5.

[3] The high-order eight bits are used to express *transparency*, as you'll see.

Components   (255,   175,   175)

                31   24 23   16 15   8 7   0

Memory | 00000000 | 11111111 | 10101111 | 10101111 |

Binary   00000000111111111010111110101111

              0000 0000 1111 1111 1010 1111 1010 1111

Hex   0   0   f   f   a   f   a   f

Hexadecimal literal   0x00ffafaf

Figure 12.5

Representations of `Color.pink`.

compact way of representing binary numbers is to collect the bits into groups of four and assign a code to each group. With four bits, we can represent the numbers 0 to 15, so we use the "digits" 0 . . . , 9 and a . . . , f for each group. This is known as *hexadecimal* (or base-16) notation.

Hexadecimal "Digits"

0000 → 0	0001 → 1	0010 → 2	0011 → 3
0100 → 4	0101 → 5	0110 → 6	0111 → 7
1000 → 8	1001 → 9	1010 → a	1011 → b
1100 → c	1101 → d	1110 → e	1111 → f

Now we can express a 32-bit number using just 8 hexadecimal digits. We can use this representation in a Java program by appending 0x in front of a hexadecimal number, so we can say that `Color.pink` can be represented by the hex (for short) literal 0x00ffafaf, or 0xffafaf, or, because we can use uppercase letters in this representation, 0XFFAFAF. Note how easily we can determine the color components: There's ff of red, af of green, and af of blue.

The `Color` class has three constructors.

`Color`(int r, int g, int b)

Constructs a new `Color` instance with the given red, green, and blue components. These arguments should be integers in the range 0 . . . , 255.

`Color`(int rgb)

Constructs a new `Color` instance from the specified compressed integer. For example, `Color(0xffafaf)` and `Color(16756655)` will both construct a new `Color.pink` instance.

Color(float r, float g, float b)

Constructs a new `Color` instance using `float` values between 0.0 and 1.0 to represent the intensities of the components, where 0.0 represents none of the component and 1.0 represents the maximal value of the component. For example, because 175/255 is approximately equal to 0.68627, we could construct a color close to `Color.pink` by calling `Color(1.0f, 0.68627f, 0.68627f)`.

The `Color` methods allow you to inspect the components of a color, convert `String` names to the associated `Color` instances, and do some simple modifications to colors.

```
static Color getColor(String name)
static Color getColor(String name, Color default)
static Color getColor(String name, int default)
```

Return a `Color` instance corresponding to the name. The first method returns `null` if the name does not match one of the `Color` class constants `black`, `blue`, `cyan`, `darkGray`, `gray`, `green`, `lightGray`, `magenta`, `orange`, `pink`, `red`, `white`, or `yellow` (or a color defined among the system properties, which we won't discuss here). The second and third methods return the default color or the color represented by the integer, if the name doesn't match a color constant name. Note that these are static methods and so would be called by using `Color.` in front, rather than a `Color` instance.

```
int getBlue()
int getGreen()
int getRed()
```

Return an integer in the range 0 . . . , 255, representing the value of the indicated component of this color.

```
int getRGB()
```

Returns an integer with the components in the low-order three bytes.

As an example of using the `Color` class, we present a simple applet that allows the user to set the components of a color and see what the color looks like. Figure 12.6 shows the applet in action. The user enters the (R, G, B) component values in the three fields at the top and then clicks the Set button to see a rectangle painted with the corresponding color. You'll have to take our word for the fact that (150, 50, 80) is a pleasant burgundy.

The applet is so easy to understand that we can present it with almost no commentary. Do take note, though, of the very last line,

```
return n & 0xff;
```

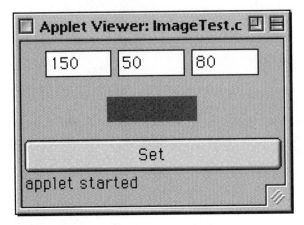

Figure 12.6

The color picker in action.

What we're doing here is using the hex value ff as a *mask*. 0xff, you will recall, is the integer with 24 high-order zeros and 8 ones in the low-order byte. When we take the bitwise AND of this mask and the integer n, the result is the number in n with its topmost 24 bits set to zero. In other words, we're forcing the return value to be in the required range 0 . . . , 255. Bear this in mind—we'll do some more bit-level manipulation of color values when we talk about image filters.

```
public class ColorPicker extends Applet implements ActionListener
{
    private TextField    redF = new TextField(4),
                         greenF = new TextField(4),
                         blueF = new TextField(4);
    private Button       setB = new Button("Set");
    private Color        paintColor = Color.white;

    public void init()
    {
        setLayout(new BorderLayout());
        Panel p = new Panel();
        p.add(redF);
        p.add(greenF);
        p.add(blueF);
        add("North", p);
        add("South", setB);

        setB.addActionListener(this);
    }

    public void paint(Graphics g)
    {
        g.setColor(paintColor);
        g.fillRect(65, 30, 70, 30);
    }
```

```
public void actionPerformed(ActionEvent e)
{
    int r = getComponent(redF);
    int g = getComponent(greenF);
    int b = getComponent(blueF);
    paintColor = new Color(r, g, b);
    repaint();
}

private int getComponent(TextField t)
{
    int n = 0;
    String s = t.getText();
    try
    {
        n = Integer.parseInt(s);
    }
    catch (NumberFormatException e)
    {
        return 0;
    }
    return n & 0xff;
}
}
```

Image Processing, Behind the Scenes

The Image class contains seven methods, which makes it a small-to-medium-sized class, when compared with its AWT brethren. Image is larger than Panel, about the same size as Point and Dialog, and far smaller than Component. The relative simplicity of Image, though, is misleading. All the real work of dealing with images is handled by the classes within the java.awt.image package, and that, as we mentioned earlier, is big, with 11 classes and 3 interfaces.

The complexity behind image processing is due, first, to the fact that the java.awt.image package provides a rich collection of classes we can use for image processing, but even more to the fact that the designers of Java had to deal with two inescapable facts: Images are big and the Net is slow. If you consider that a 2-inch by 1-inch picture might consume 40,000 bytes just for the raw pixel data, you can see that even a fast computer might take a while to manipulate every pixel of the image. In addition, with a 56K modem commonly in use today, it would take over 5 seconds, in the best of circumstances, just to get the information from a remote source.[4] We'll discuss some of what goes on when an image is loaded, processed, and displayed, and (fortunately) we'll see that Java takes care of most of the work for us.

An image begins with an ImageProducer. An object implementing this interface takes a source of data—from memory or a remote source over the Net, for instance—and produces an array of ints, representing the pixels of the image.

---

[4]Although images are typically compressed to take up less space (and hence to load faster), the point still remains that loading images takes time, as anyone who has waited for a Web page to load can attest.

When you call `getImage()` or `createImage()`, Java will generate an `ImageProducer` for you, whose job it is to start gathering pixels.[5] The fact to keep in mind here is that the producer is almost certainly working faster than the data is arriving, so not all of the pixels of the image may be available at any time. You'll need to use `ImageProducer`s, but you may never implement one.

If you've indicated that you want an image, you'll almost certainly want to do something with it, such as drawing it by calling `drawImage()`. When you do that, Java will designate an `ImageConsumer` for you. The responsibility of an `ImageConsumer` is to do something with the bits an `ImageProducer` is generating. Every `ImageConsumer` is registered with some `ImageProducer`, and as the producer generates some more image bits, it periodically calls one of the consumer's methods to pass the new data along. As in real life, the producer runs the show, notifying all of its registered consumers as information about the image become available. You won't need to make much use of the `ImageConsumer` interface, and you'll almost certainly never implement one.

If you've called `drawImage()`, the system will spawn a new thread for loading and displaying the image. In that thread, the producer is generating new pixels from the source and calling the consumer's methods to pass them along. The consumer, in its turn, is preparing the pixels for painting on the screen, often row by row. While this is going on, the consumer is being watched by an `ImageObserver`. The job of the `ImageObserver` is to observe what the consumer does and report to the rest of the program.

The `ImageObserver` interface consists of a single method.

```
boolean imageUpdate(Image im, int flags, int x, int y, int w, int h)
```

This method is called periodically by the `ImageConsumer`; you won't call it yourself. The consumer indicates the image it's preparing, the (x, y) coordinates of the upper left corner of the prepared part of the image, and the width and height of the portion of the pixel array it has prepared so far. The `flags` integer contains information about the status of the image being prepared. This method returns `true` if this `ImageObserver` is interested in getting further updates from the consumer and returns `false` if it knows everything it needs to know about the image.

The flags argument represents a collection of constants, chosen from the following list (where we've omitted some of the less important items).

ABORT	Loading has been halted, perhaps temporarily.
ALLBITS	All of the bits of the image are now available.
ERROR	Loading has been halted and can't continue.
HEIGHT	The height of the image is known. A call to `im.getHeight()` will return the correct height of the image.

---

[5]The `ImageProducer` won't start working until it's told to, often by a subsequent call to `drawImage()`, but you needn't be concerned about that.

SOMEBITS   Part of the image has been loaded and prepared. If this flag is set, the x, y, w, and h arguments will contain the anchor, width, and height of the rectangle enclosing the prepared part of the image.

WIDTH   The width of the image is now known.

You can test these flags by forming the bitwise AND of the flags argument and the appropriate constant. For example, the expression

```
flags & ImageObserver.ALLBITS
```

will evaluate to 0 if all the bits of the image haven't yet been processed and will be nonzero if all the bits are available.

The Component class implements ImageObserver, as we've said, so most widgets can be used as ImageObservers. The Component version just calls repaint(), to paint as much of the image as has been prepared. This means that ImageTest1, which you saw on page 538, might appear to take its own sweet time drawing the image. In fact, it's drawing as fast as it can—as soon as the default consumer has some more pixels prepared, it calls the applet's imageUpdate(), which forces a repaint() call.

You might want to wait until the image is completely loaded before trying to draw it. In that case, you could override the imageUpdate() method, as we do in the applet that follows.

```
import java.applet.*;
import java.awt.*;
import java.awt.image.ImageObserver;

public class ImageTest3 extends Applet
{
    private Image   asteroids;
    private boolean ready = false;

    public void init()
    {
        asteroids = getImage(getCodeBase(), "aster.gif");
        prepareImage(asteroids, this);
    }

    public boolean imageUpdate(Image img, int flags,
                               int x, int y,
                               int width, int height)
    {
        if ((flags & ImageObserver.ALLBITS) != 0)
        // All the bits have been loaded.
        {
            ready = true;   // Set the ready flag,
            repaint();      // force a call to paint(),
            return false;   // and tell the consumer we're done
        }
        else
        // Indicate that further updates are needed.
        {
            return true;
        }
    }
```

```
public void paint(Graphics g)
// Don't even try to draw the image until it's been loaded.
{
    if (ready)
    {
        g.drawImage(asteroids, 10, 10, this);
    }
}
}
```

The `Component` method `prepareImage()` that we called in the `init()` method forces loading to start. We need that here, because normally Java won't try to load an image until `drawImage()` is called, and we enclosed `drawImage()` within an `if` statement that guaranteed it wouldn't be called. Another way to deal with this is to realize that `drawImage()` returns `true` if the image has been fully drawn. We could eliminate the `ready` flag and just write

```
public void paint(Graphics g)
{
    if (!g.drawImage(asteroids, 10, 10, this))
    {
        showStatus("Loading...");
    }
    else
    {
        showStatus("Loading complete");
    }
}
```

forcing `drawImage()` to be called in the `if` test. This is less elegant than the first way.

Delaying drawing by writing our own `imageUpdate()` is simple enough if we have only one image to handle. It's not as nice if we have multiple images. In Section 12.3 we'll discuss another way of waiting for images to load.

Image Filters

An image filter allows you to manipulate an image. With the appropriate `ImageFilter` object, you can fade or blur an image, scale or crop it, rotate or reflect it, and change its colors—in fact, you can do anything with an image that your programming skill permits. As you might expect, some forms of image filters are quite complicated to write and are beyond our scope here.

We can, however, do a lot with a class that is quite easy to use. The `RGBImageFilter` class is a subclass of `ImageFilter`, one in which the same operation is performed on every pixel of an image. The operations permitted in this class and its subclasses are purely local, in the sense that they may only modify the colors of each pixel and may not inspect any other pixel while doing their modifications.

We can't use an `RGBImageFilter` to rotate or crop an image, but there are still many interesting things we can do. For example, we can *invert* the colors of an image like a photographic negative, as we illustrate in Figure 12.7.

To invert a color, we subtract each of its components from 255. A pure green,

Figure 12.7

An image and its inverse.

with components (0, 255, 0), would turn into magenta, with components (255, 0, 255). The medium gray (128, 128, 128) would undergo almost no change, except for an imperceptible darkening, as its components became (127, 127, 127). We can make an `InvertFilter` to do this by subclassing `RGBImageFilter`, as we do below.

There are a few things to note about our new class. First, image pixels are slightly different from colors, in that the high-order byte is actually used. In the `int` representing one of an image's pixels, bits 24 to 31 store the *transparency* (also called the *alpha* value). This determines how much of the background will show through the image. A value of 0 means the pixel will be completely transparent, a value of 128 will let approximately half of the background show through, and a value of 255 will make the pixel completely opaque.

Note also the helper method `flip()`. This method is supplied with an `int` argument, `source`, and `offset` value. This method first gets the byte by shifting `source` down by the given `offset` and then masking it with `0xff`. It then subtracts that byte from 255 and shifts it back into its original position.

Once we've inverted the red, green, and blue bytes, we OR them together to produce the inverted pixel and then return it. That's all it takes—the parent class takes care of calling the `filterRGB()` method for each pixel in the image.

See Section 5.3 for more details on shifting and masking.

```
/**
 * An RGBImageFilter is a simplified filter that performs the same
 * action on all pixels.
 * To extend such a filter, all that's necessary is to add a
 * constructor (if needed) and override the filterRGB() method.
 */
class InvertFilter extends RGBImageFilter
{
    public int filterRGB(int x, int y, int pix)
    // The arguments x and y are needed by the base class filter,
    // even though they aren't used here.
    {
        int a = pix & 0xff000000;  // Just mask the alpha value.
```

```
        int r = flip(pix, 16);      // Invert each component.
        int g = flip(pix, 8);
        int b = flip(pix, 0);
        return a | r | g | b;       // Reassemble the components
                                    // into a pixel and return it
    }

    private int flip(int source, int offset)
    {
        int component = (source >> offset) & 0xff;
        return (255 - component) << offset;
    }
}
```

Defining an image filter, especially a simple one that is a subclass of the class RGBImageFilter, is conceptually much easier than using one. The applet ImageTest4 loads an image and displays it. When the user presses the mouse button, the applet displays the inverted image, and when the user releases the button, the original image is again displayed.

The complicated part of this applet is all in the init() method:

```
original = getImage(getCodeBase(), "start.gif");
ImageFilter f = new InvertFilter();
ImageProducer p = new FilteredImageSource(original.getSource(), f);
inverse = createImage(p);
theImage = original;
```

The class FilteredImageSource implements ImageProducer. It uses an Image-Producer, which we get from original.getSource(), and an ImageFilter, which in this case is an instance of our InvertFilter, to generate a new producer, p. We then make an image from this producer by calling the Component method createImage(), this time with the producer as argument.

In simple terms, the original image producer sends pixels to the filter (which implements ImageConsumer), and the filtered image is used to construct the producer FilteredImageSource.

```
import java.awt.*;
import java.applet.*;
import java.awt.event.*;
import java.awt.image.*;

public class ImageTest4 extends Applet
{
    // These have package access so the inner class can see them.
    Image   original,  // the original image
            inverse,   // the inverted image
            theImage;  //the image to display

    public void init()
    {
        original = getImage(getCodeBase(), "start.gif");
        theImage = original;

        // Produce the inverted image
        ImageFilter f = new InvertFilter();
```

```
        ImageProducer p = new FilteredImageSource(original.getSource(),
          f);
        inverse = createImage(p);

        addMouseListener(new Mouser());
    }

    public void update(Graphics g)
    {
        g.drawImage(theImage, 0, 0, this);
    }

    // A member class to handle mousePressed and
    // mouseReleased events (as we did in SketchPad in Chapter 6).
    private class Mouser extends MouseAdapter
    {
        public void mousePressed(MouseEvent e)
        {
            theImage = inverse;
            repaint();
        }

        public void mouseReleased(MouseEvent e)
        {
            theImage = original;
            repaint();
        }
    }
}
```

If you run this applet, you'll probably discover that the first time you click the mouse button, the inverted image takes a while to appear. This is because the InvertFilter takes quite a lot of time to produce the inverted image. You might also discover that it takes a noticeable amount of time to load and display the original image, as well. These delays aren't particularly bothersome in this applet, but they could be annoying in time-sensitive applications, such as those that use animation. In the next section, we'll discuss some techniques for dealing with these delays.

Review Questions

2.1 If you loop() an AudioClip, what else should you do?
2.2 How do you draw an Image?
2.3 How do you draw to an offscreen image? Why would you do this?
2.4 What is the job of an ImageProducer? Of an ImageObserver?
2.5 When would you construct a new RGBImageFilter?

12.3 Action!

Drawing static images is useful, but there will be times when you want your images to be more active. In this section, we'll discuss animation and give you some tips on making your programs draw as smoothly as possible. Before we do that, though, we'll introduce a custom widget that we'll use for all of our drawing.

Preliminaries: Drawing on a Canvas

We've already mentioned that it is generally better for a program to do its drawing on a `Canvas` than to draw directly on the applet panel or application frame. First, it's good program design, because we're making a separate class for a collection of logically related operations. Second, doing all our drawing on a separate object simplifies the applet or application: The program's top level can concentrate on management and not be cluttered up with a lot of code for drawing. Finally, having a separate target for drawing provides us with a class we might want to use in other programs. In fact, that's just what we're going to do in this section. We'll write four different applets, but each of them will use the same class as a place for drawing.

Drawing Tip

> Except in the simplest programs, if you're going to do much drawing, it's a good idea to declare a `Canvas` or make a `Canvas` subclass of your own to draw on.

Our `Display` class is a subclass of `Canvas`. It will have a background image that it generates internally and will have the capability of drawing a foreground image on top of the background. We begin, as usual, with a collection of instance variable declarations.

```
class Display extends Canvas
{
    private Image    background,      // the background image
                     other = null;    // an image to be drawn on top
                                      // of the background
    private int x, y;                 // where to draw the
                                      // foreground image
    private boolean initialized = false;
```

We need the `initialized` variable for a somewhat obscure reason. A `Component` instance has a height and width, but these aren't known at the time the object is declared. In fact, they aren't known until layout is complete, and that may not be until the applet or application is painted the first time. A `Display` object needs to know its height and width before that it can create the background image, so we defer creating the background until the `initialized` flag indicates that the height and width are known.

Our `showImage()` method adds a new foreground image to this class and forces it to be drawn at a specified location. Note that it would be easy enough to extend this so that we could have an array of foreground images, rather than just one.

```
public void showImage(Image im, int x, int y)
{
    other = im;
    this.x = x;
    this.y = y;
    repaint();
}
```

The `paint()` method is pretty much what you'd expect. After checking that initialization is complete, it draws the background first and then draws the foreground image, if any, on top. If initialization hasn't been done, we check whether we have the width and height, and if so, we make the background image and set the `initialized` flag.

We override `update()` here, too, forcing it just to paint, rather than doing the default erasing-then-painting. This is very important—with the default `update()`, the canvas would have an extremely annoying flicker as it was repainted, because almost none of the drawing is done in the background color.

```
public void paint(Graphics g)
{
    if (initialized)
    {
        g.drawImage(background, 0, 0, this);
        if (other != null)
        {
            g.drawImage(other, x, y, this);
        }
    }
    else if ((getSize().width > 0) && (getSize().height > 0))
    {
        background = makeBackground();
        initialized = true;
    }
}

public void update(Graphics g)
{
    paint(g);
}
```

Drawing Tip

> When drawing a fixed background on a component, consider overriding that component's `update()` method so that it doesn't erase the background.

The `makeBackground()` method is called once, when we find that we know the width and height of this `Display` instance. This method draws `steps` rectangles, filling the canvas from top to bottom. Each band is filled with a shade of blue, ranging from darkest at the top to pure blue at the bottom. As a result, the background appears to shade smoothly from black to blue as you look down the display. Note that we're constructing an offscreen image here. As a result, we only have to do the separate drawing calls once, to construct the image in the first place. Then, all we have to do in the `paint()` method is make a single call to `drawImage()`. If our background were more complicated, you'd notice a marked gain in smoothness, because the background would be repainted all at once, rather than through a sequence of separate drawing calls.

Drawing Tip

If you have a complicated picture that has to be drawn repeatedly, draw it to an offscreen image first and then call `drawImage()` when you need to display the picture.

```
private Image makeBackground()
{
    int     width = getSize().width,
            height = getSize().height,
            steps = 32,
            yIncrement = height / steps;

    Image img = createImage(width, height);
    Graphics g = img.getGraphics();

    g.setColor(Color.blue);
    g.fillRect(0, 0, width, height);
    for (int i = 0; i < steps; i++)
    {
        Color bg = new Color(0, 0, (255 / steps) * i);
        g.setColor(bg);
        g.fillRect(0, i * yIncrement, width, yIncrement);
    }
    g.dispose();
    return img;
}
}
```

Animation Preamble

Animation in Java is done in the same way as in other programming languages. The technique predates the computer by at least two hundred years: Display a sequence of closely related images fast enough that the eye and brain blend them together to give the illusion of motion. Human physiology works in our favor here—ten images per second, more or less, is enough to fool the eye and brain into accepting the discrete images as a smooth stream. That's all you really need to know about the subject; all the rest is just technical details, with just enough programming thrown in to make the discussion worth pursuing here. Before we begin, though, we beg your indulgence while we make a short digression.

<RANT>

Animation is a powerful, attractive, and—in Java—easy technique. It is also one of the principal reasons why some people have misgivings about Java. Mastery of a tool like animation should always include knowing when to use it and when to avoid its use. Jittering text and bouncing heads are perfectly fine if all you want to do is show off your mastery and share what you've learned (as we do in this book). When writing applications and applets for public consumption, though, you should never lose sight of the fact that computer programs are means of communication and that this communication can be irritating and annoying just as easily as it can be effective and engaging. If you write an applet and the ani-

mation detracts from the contents of the page it lives in, leave the animation out, no matter how nifty it is.
`</RANT>`

There, we feel much better. Now let's get back to work.

Loading Images: The `MediaTracker` Class

Because we do animation by displaying a sequence of images, it would be a good idea to make sure that all the images are available before we start trying to display them. You've seen that we can use the `ImageObserver` method `updateImage()` to block execution until an image has been loaded. With some more work, you could modify this technique so that it applied to several images, but it's generally not worth the effort, because the `java.awt` package contains the `MediaTracker` class that is specifically designed for watching the status of multiple images while they're being loaded.

There are four class constants in `MediaTracker`. They are returned by the `statusAll()` and `statusID()` methods.

ABORTED	Loading of the image has been halted for some reason. It may be possible to continue later.
COMPLETE	The image has been loaded.
ERRORED	Loading has been halted with no possibility of continuing.
LOADING	The image is being loaded.

There is one constructor in this class,

MediaTracker(Component c)

Creates a new `MediaTracker` instance. The argument is the `Component` that will serve as the destination of the images. You will nearly always use `this` as the constructor argument.

There are quite a few `MediaTracker` methods. Below, we list the ones that will be of interest to us here.

void **addImage**(Image im, int id)

Registers the argument image for observation by this `MediaTracker`. The `id` argument is used to assign the image to a group if you want to monitor the loading of different images in different ways. You can assign the same `id` to several images.

boolean **checkAll**()
boolean **checkAll**(boolean load)

Return `true` if all images registered with this tracker have finished loading, either successfully or in error. If the `load` argument is `true`, this will start to load any image that hasn't begun loading yet.

```
boolean checkID(int id)
boolean checkID(int id, boolean load)
```

These methods act like the `checkAll()` methods, except that they check only the images with a given `id`.

```
boolean isErrorAny()
boolean isErrorID()
```

Return `true` if any image (or any image with the given `id`) encountered an error while loading.

```
void removeImage(Image im)
void removeImage(Image im, int id)
```

Remove all instances of the specified image (or all instances with the given `id`). These methods were introduced for efficiency, because a `MediaTracker` continues to monitor images even after they have been loaded.

```
int statusAll(boolean load)
int statusID(int id, boolean load)
```

Return the bitwise `OR` of the status constants for all registered images (or all images with the specified `id`).

```
void waitForAll() throws InterruptedException
void waitForID(int id) throws InterruptedException
```

These methods block the current thread until all images have been loaded (or until all images with the specified `id` have been loaded.

Here's an example of using a `MediaTracker`. In this example, we have four images in a directory `"ships"` that are named `"ship0.gif"`, `"ship1.gif"`, `"ship2.gif"`, and `"ship3.gif"`. We want to load them into an array of `Images`, named `ships[]`. We assign each image a separate `id`, and we load them sequentially, using `waitForID()` to block until each is loaded. If any of the images fails to load, we display a status message to that effect and return the value `false`. If all the images load successfully, we display a message and return `true`.

```
private boolean loadImages()
{
    showStatus("Loading images...");
    MediaTracker tracker = new MediaTracker(this);
    for (int i = 0; i < 4; i++)
    {
        ship[i] = getImage(getCodeBase(),
                       "ships/ship" + i + ".gif");
        tracker.addImage(ship[i], i);
        try
        {
            tracker.waitForID(i);
        }
        catch (InterruptedException e)
        { }
        if (tracker.isErrorID(i))
```

```
            {
                showStatus("Failed to load image " + i);
                return false;
            }
        }
        showStatus("Images loaded");
        return true;
    }
```

Animation I: Starting Out

In our first animation example, we display a cartoon-y UFO on an evening sky. The UFO hovers, while in classic 1950s style, its lights cycle through a sequence of colors. Figure 12.8 illustrates one frame of the animation.

The applet that displays our visitor uses the `Display` class we discussed earlier and the `loadImages()` method.

```java
import java.applet.*;
import java.awt.*;

public class AnimationTest1 extends Applet implements Runnable
{
    private Image[] shipImg = new Image[4];
    private Image   background;
    private Thread  animator = null;
    private int     x = 80,
                    y = 40,
                    currentShip = 0;
    private Display display;

    public void init()
    {
        if (!loadImages())
        {
            showStatus("Couldn't continue");
            System.exit(0);
        }

        display = new Display();
        setLayout(new BorderLayout());
        add("Center", display);
    }
```

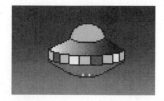

Figure 12.8

Visitors from Cydonia.

```
public void start()
{
    if (animator == null)
    {
        animator = new Thread(this);
        animator.start();
    }
}
```

As typically happens, we do the animation in a separate thread. All we have to do in the `run()` method for the `animator` thread is cycle through the indices of the `shipImg[]` array and call `display.showImage()` to draw the current ship image. Note that the animator thread is a good citizen and sleeps occasionally.

```
public void run()
{
    while (animator != null)
    {
        if (currentShip == 3)
        {
            currentShip = 0;
        }
        else
        {
            currentShip++;
        }

        display.showImage(shipImg[currentShip], x, y);
        try
        {
            Thread.sleep(200);
        }
        catch (InterruptedException e)
        { }
    }
}

public void stop()
{
    if (animator != null)
    {
        animator.stop();
        animator = null;
    }
}

public void update(Graphics g)
// Remember, a call to paint() calls paint() on the components
// contained in this applet.
{
    paint(g);
}

// private boolean loadImages() omitted
}
// class Display omitted
```

Animation II: Better Design

The next pass at our program looks to the user exactly like the first. The difference under the hood is that we've split the ship off into a class of its own, running the animation, rather than having the applet run the animation. Again, we're removing some of the complexity from the animation and putting it where it belongs, in a Ship instance. There's no need for the managing applet to know any of the details of what the ship does with its running lights. After all, as far as the applet is concerned, the ship may as well be a static image.

The only tricky part about separating the ship from the applet is that the ship needs to know where to draw itself. We provide this information to the ship via its constructor, sending it a callback reference to the display, as well as an array of images and its location on the display canvas.

Most of the Ship class code is taken directly from the AnimationTest1 applet. Note that we've tried to make the class as general as possible by allowing the user to use an arbitrary number of images.

```
class Ship extends Thread
{
    private Image[]     image;
    private int         numImages,
                        currentImage = 0,
                        x, y;
    private Display     display;

    public Ship(Image[] images, int numImages,
                Display display, int x, int y)
    {
        this.numImages = numImages;
        image = new Image[numImages];
        for (int i = 0; i < numImages; i++)
        {
            image[i] = images[i];
        }
        this.display = display;
        this.x = x;
        this.y = y;
    }

    public void moveTo(int x, int y)
    // We don't use this yet, but it seems reasonable that
    // sooner or later we'll want to move the ship. After
    // all, we don't want to frighten the natives unnecessarily.
    {
        this.x = x;
        this.y = y;
        display.showImage(image[currentImage], x, y);
    }

    public void run()
    {
        while (true)
        {
```

```
            if (currentImage == numImages - 1)
            {
                currentImage = 0;
            }
            else
            {
                currentImage++;
            }

            display.showImage(image[currentImage], x, y);
            try
            {
                Thread.sleep(200);
            }
            catch (InterruptedException e)
            { }
        }
    }
}
```

By moving the animation to the Ship class, we've simplified the applet. It no longer needs to implement Runnable, so we remove the run() method and construct and start the Ship thread in the applet's start() method. The applet now has a more managerial air, as it should, because it delegates the display and animation operations to the Display and Ship classes.

```
public class AnimationTest2 extends Applet
{
    // Other declarations omitted

    private Ship    theShip = null;

    // init() omitted--same as in AnimationTest1

    public void start()
    {
        if (theShip == null)
        {
            theShip = new Ship(shipImg, 4, display, x, y);
            theShip.start();
        }
    }

    public void stop()
    {
        if (theShip != null)
        {
            theShip.stop();
            theShip = null;
        }
    }

    // update(), loadImages() omitted--no changes
}
// class Display omitted
```

Animation III: Moving the Ship

In the third version of our program, the ship moves in response to mouse clicks. When the user clicks the mouse, the ship heads in the direction of the point where the mouse was clicked. Because of our design, changing the applet to move the ship requires no modification of the Display and Ship classes.

We change the applet back to implementing the Runnable interface, because the ship movement will be in a separate thread, mover.

```
public class AnimationTest3 extends Applet implements Runnable
{
    int destinationX = 80,
        destinationY = 40;
    private Image[] shipImg = new Image[4];
    private double  currentX = 80.0,
                    currentY = 40.0,
                    velocityX = 0.0,
                    velocityY = 0.0;
    private Thread mover = null;
    private Display display;
    private Ship    theShip = null;

    // init() omitted
```

Because we have two threads at work here, one to animate the running lights and one to move the ship, we start and stop both threads in the applet's start() and stop() methods. In a more complex program, we could save some lines of code by placing all the threads in a single ThreadGroup and starting and stopping them as a group, but that's hardly worth the effort here.

```
    public void start()
    {
        if (theShip == null)
        {
            theShip = new Ship(shipImg, 4, display,
                               destinationX, destinationY);
            theShip.start();
        }
        if (mover == null)
        {
            mover = new Thread(this);
            mover.start();
        }
    }

    public void stop()
    {
        if (theShip != null)
        {
            theShip.stop();
            theShip = null;
        }
```

```
      if (mover != null)
      {
          mover.stop();
          mover = null;
      }
}
```

The `run()` method for the mover thread repeatedly calls the helper method `computeNextMove()` and uses `moveTo()` to move the ship to its new location and draw it on the display.

```
public void run()
{
    while (mover != null)
    {
        Point p = computeNextMove();
        theShip.moveTo(p.x, p.y);
        try
        {
            Thread.sleep(125);
        }
        catch (InterruptedException e)
        { }
    }
}
// update() omitted
```

The sole event handler in this applet just records where the mouse event occurred and calls the helper method `setVelocity()` to determine the new values of the velocity components `velocityX` and `velocityY`. To avoid implementing all five of the `MouseEvent` handlers, we use an internal member class that extends `MouseAdapter`, as we did in the `InvertFilter` example earlier.

```
private class Mouser extends MouseAdapter
{
    public void mouseReleased(MouseEvent e)
    {
        destinationX = e.getX();
        destinationY = e.getY();
        setVelocity();
    }
}
```

To move the ship, all we do at each step is add `velocityX` to the current x-coordinate, `currentX`, and likewise add `velocityY` to `currentY`.

```
private Point computeNextMove()
{
    currentX = currentX + velocityX;
    currentY = currentY + velocityY;
    int x = (int)Math.round(currentX);
    int y = (int)Math.round(currentY);
    return new Point(x, y);
}
```

The only tricky part of this applet is computing the new velocity components when the user clicks the mouse. As illustrated in Figure 12.9, we let `deltaX` and `deltaY` represent the differences in the *x*- and *y*-coordinates of the current point and the destination point. We then scale these distances, by multiplying them by `2.0 / distance`, where `distance` represents the distance between the current and destination points. By doing this, we guarantee that the ship's velocity will always be 2.0 pixels per move, more or less.

Finally, recall that because of a common compiler bug, we can't make this method `private`, as we'd like; if it were, the member class `Mouser` couldn't access it.

```
void setVelocity()
{
    double deltaX = destinationX - currentX;
    double deltaY = destinationY - currentY;
    double distance = Math.sqrt(deltaX * deltaX
                                + deltaY * deltaY);
    if (distance < 2.0)
    {
        velocityX = 0.0;
        velocityY = 0.0;
    }
    else
    {
        velocityX = 2.0 * deltaX / distance;
        velocityY = 2.0 * deltaY / distance;
    }
}

    // loadImages() omitted
}
// class Display omitted
// class Ship omitted
```

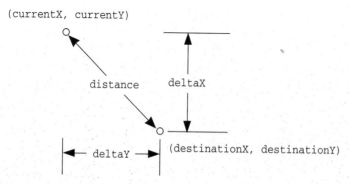

(currentX, currentY)

distance   deltaX

deltaY   (destinationX, destinationY)

Figure 12.9

Computing the ship's velocity.

Animation IV: Clipping

If you stop to think about it, you'll realize that there's a lot of unnecessary drawing being done in our applet. When the ship moves, we obviously have to erase the old image (which we do by painting over it with the background image) and draw the new image, but there is a lot of Display real estate that never needs to be touched. In fact, all we really have to do at each ship move is repaint the rectangle that encloses the old and the new ship images, as we illustrate in Figure 12.10. In the figure, oldR is the bounding rectangle of the old image, and newR is the bounding rectangle of the new image.

The Graphics method clipRect() takes as its arguments the x, y, width, and height of a rectangle, and it limits drawing to the parts of that rectangle that lie within the total drawing area of the associated component.[6] In our final modification of AnimationTest, we changed Display's update() method so that it clipped the drawing region to the smallest rectangle that contained the changes.

Drawing Tip

If your drawing is going to take place on only a small portion of the total drawing area, consider clipping the Graphics context to the part of the region you need.

```
public void update(Graphics g)
{
    oldR = newR;
    if (other != null)
    {
        newR = new Rectangle(x, y, other.getWidth(this),
                             other.getHeight(this));
        Rectangle clip = oldR.union(newR);
        g.clipRect(clip.x, clip.y, clip.width, clip.height);
    }
    paint(g);
}
```

The only thing you need to keep in mind when clipping is that once you have set the clip rectangle for a Graphics instance, you can't increase its size. This isn't a problem here; we are doing all our clipping in the update() method, and every time update() is called, it is provided with an entirely new Graphics object.

Review Questions

3.1 Why do we override update(), rather than using the default one that comes with Component?

---

[6]Or at least it should. When testing the animation applets on several platforms, we discovered that some run-time environments aren't as careful about clipping as they should be. By now, you may have noticed this lack of adherence to standards several times.

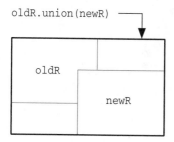

oldR.union(newR)

Figure 12.10

Computing the clipping rectangle.

3.2 How do you register an image with a `MediaTracker`? How do you then check that a registered image has been loaded?

3.3 `AnimationTest3` uses two threads of its own. What do they do?

3.4 What do we mean by "clipping?" Why do we do it?

12.4   Hands On

In our culminating Lablet, we use almost every major subject you've learned so far. Along with the customary language details, we have HTML, classes, inheritance, packages, arrays, exceptions, threads, graphics, URLs, applet parameters, and animation, to name just a few. There's no file manipulation, and we have no dialogs or menus, but those are just about the only things we *don't* use. This multiplicity of features wasn't so much a deliberate choice on our part as a natural consequence of designing any moderately complicated program. You've seen a lot of tools so far; some are specific to Java, and many others are part of good programming in any language. Becoming a competent programmer is in large measure nothing but acquiring mastery of the tools and techniques of the craft, because you can be sure that most programs you write will require bits and pieces of everything you know.

We've tried to see that each of our Lablets and all of our example code are models of good practice, and we took special care in this Lablet to make it as close to an industrial-strength program as we could. There are a few programming techniques in this Lablet that we'll need to explain, and a few omissions we left for you to fill in, in the lab exercises, but you can assess your mastery of programming by looking through the Lablet code now and seeing whether you can read and understand it easily.

Designing the Lablet

Our goal with this example was to design two applets and two classes that a Web page designer could use to place custom buttons on the page, as we illustrate in Figure 12.11.

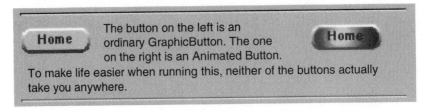

The button on the left is an ordinary GraphicButton. The one on the right is an Animated Button. To make life easier when running this, neither of the buttons actually take you anywhere.

Figure 12.11

Two custom buttons embedded in a Web page.

One of the applets, `GraphicButtoner`, constructs and implements a static `GraphicButton`. A `GraphicButton` acts just like an ordinary button, but it uses two images to represent its normal up state and the down state that it takes when the user presses the mouse button while the pointer is over the button. The applet is responsible for getting the information necessary to construct the button, such as the two images, the button label, and the URL of the page where the browser will go when the button is clicked. Once the applet has this information, it lays out the button and then just sits back and waits for a button click.

The other applet, `AnimatedButtoner`, acts just like `GraphicButtoner`, except that it produces an `AnimatedButton` instance. `AnimatedButton` is a subclass of `GraphicButton`, the only major difference being that an `AnimatedButton` cycles through several images when in its up state, to give an animated appearance.

Exploring the `GraphicButtoner` Applet

We've omitted most of the `import` declarations and comments in our Lablet explorations so far. This time, though, we kept them in. First, we wanted to point out that we used a package of our own, named "myWidgets," to organize our two button classes. Remember that to make a package of your own, all you need to do is head each class declaration with a `package` declaration and then put the compiled class file in the directory with the same name as the package.

We kept the comments in so that you could see what a moderately thorough job of documentation looks like. When writing documentation for a program, you should write for someone who is a competent programmer but is seeing your program for the very first time. At the very minimum, the header comments should explain what the program does, what information is necessary to use it, and any notes about behavior that is not immediately obvious.

```
//================================================================
//   PROJECT:        _programming.java_
//   FILE:           GraphicButtoner.java
//   PURPOSE:        Chapter 12 lablet
//   VERSION:        2.0
//   TARGET:         Java 1.1 and above
//   UPDATE HISTORY  2.0    12/4/98    new event model
//                   1.0     8/1/97
//================================================================
```

```
//------------------------- NOTES -----------------------------
/*
    To use this applet, place the files "GraphicButtoner.class" and
    "GraphicButton.class" in the same directory or folder as the
    HTML document, along with two gifs, representing the down and
    up images of the button.
    Then, embed the following HTML (with appropriate values) in the
    main document:
    <APPLET code = "GraphicButtoner.class" width = 82 height = 27>
        <PARAM name = "pattern" value = "bttn*.gif">
        <PARAM name = "numPix"  value = "2">
        <PARAM name = "label"   value = "Home">
        <PARAM name = "destURL" value = "some URL">
    </APPLET>

PARAMETERS:
        pattern (REQUIRED): The name template of the button pictures.
            In the example above, the pictures would be named
            "bttn0.gif" and "bttn1.gif". The picture numbered 0
            will be used for the down picture. For best results,
            these gifs should be the size specified in the WIDTH
            and HEIGHT arguments. If this argument isn't present
            or is malformed, the applet will default to using an
            ordinary button instead of a GraphicButton.
        numPix (OPTIONAL): The number of pictures. This must be
            at least 2 and will default to 2 if missing,
            incorrectly written, or too small.
        label (OPTIONAL): The name that will appear in the
            button. The label will be centered in the button,
            so if it is too long, you may have to adjust the
            WIDTH and HEIGHT arguments (the class will shrink
            the images to fit the label, but it can't grow them
            beyond the applet size).
        destURL (OPTIONAL): If specified and valid, this is the
            destination the browser will go to when the button
            is clicked.
*/
//------------------------- IMPORTS -----------------------------

import java.applet.*;
import java.awt.*;
import java.awt.event.*;
import java.net.*;       // for URL and MalformedURLException
import myWidgets.*;      // for GraphicButton
```

The class declaration begins with declarations of the instance variables and the init() method. In init(), we get the applet parameters and lay out the single button. This method does most of its work by calling helper methods to decode the parameters and load the images. For example, numPix is an integer variable, but its parameter is, like all parameters, a string. To avoid cluttering up init(), we wrote a method, getIntParameter(), that gets the value of the parameter with the specified name, converts it to an int, and returns the value. You've seen a simple version of loadImages() already. This returns true if all the images eventually load successfully. If they do, we construct a GraphicButton, and if they don't, we default to constructing an ordinary button; thus the applet always does something, even if it's not quite what the user wanted.

```
//==================== GraphicButtoner CLASS =====================
/**
 * This applet is designed to place a custom button in a Web
 * document.
 */
public class GraphicButtoner   extends Applet
                               implements  ActionListener
{
    private GraphicButton  theButton;
    private Button         backupButton;
    private Image[]        images;
    private int            numImgs;
    private String         theLabel;
    private URL            destURL;

    /**
     * Get the images, construct the GraphicButton, lay it out
     * as the only component in the applet, and register it as a
     * source of ActionEvents.
     */
    public void init()
    {
        // Get all the parameters, sometimes using our own
        // utilities (see below).
        String pattern = getParameter("pattern");
        numImgs = getIntParameter("numPix", 2);
        if (numImgs < 2)
        {
            numImgs = 2;
        }
        theLabel = getParameter("label");
        destURL  = getURLParameter("destURL", null);

        // Construct the button and add it to the applet.
        images = new Image[numImgs];
        Dimension size = getSize();
        if (loadImages(pattern))
        {
            theButton = new GraphicButton(images, theLabel);
            theButton.setSize(size.width, size.height);
            add(theButton);
            theButton.addActionListener(this);
        }
        else
        // Failed to make a GraphicButton, so default to an
        // ordinary Button.
        {
            backupButton = new Button(theLabel);
            backupButton.setSize(size.width, size.height - 4);
            add(backupButton);
            backupButton.addActionListener(this);
        }
    }

    /**
     * Handle a mouse click in the graphic or default button by
     * sending the browser to the URL given by the applet
     * parameter.
     */
    public void actionPerformed(ActionEvent e)
```

```
    {
        Object source = e.getSource();
        if (((source == theButton) || (source == backupButton))
            && (destURL != null))
        {
            getAppletContext().showDocument(destURL);
        }
    }
}
```

We do a little more in this version of `loadImages()` than we did in the version in Section 12.3. Here the method is given a `String` argument representing the pattern of the image names. We require the user to ensure that all the button images have the same relative URLs, differing only by the image number, such as `"bttn0.gif"` and `"bttn1.gif"`, and to pass the pattern, with `'*'` where the numbers are, as a parameter. The method uses this pattern to generate the image URLs and then loads them, as usual.

```
/**
 * Get the images with the given pattern name and load them
 * into the images[] array.
 * RETURNS: true if and only if all images were successfully
 * loaded.
 */
private boolean loadImages(String pattern)
{
    // First, parse the pattern, splitting it into the base
    // part, before '*', and the extension part, after '*'.
    // For example, "bttn*.gif" would split into the base
    // string "bttn" and extension string ".gif".
    String  base,
            extension;
    int starIndex = pattern.indexOf('*');
    try
    {
        base = pattern.substring(0, starIndex);
        extension = pattern.substring(starIndex + 1);
    }
    catch (IndexOutOfBoundsException e)
    {
        showStatus("Bad pattern parameter");
        return false;
    }

    // Wait for the images to load, and signal by returning
    // false if any are broken.
    showStatus("Loading images...");
    MediaTracker tracker = new MediaTracker(this);
    for (int i = 0; i < numImgs; i++)
    {
        images[i] = getImage(getCodeBase(),
                            base + i + extension);
        tracker.addImage(images[i], i);
        try
        {
            tracker.waitForID(i);
        }
        catch (InterruptedException e)
        { }
```

```
        if (tracker.isErrorID(i))
        {
            showStatus("Failed to load image " + i);
            return false;
        }
    }
    showStatus("Images loaded");
    return true;    // Indicate that loading was successful.
}
```

We discussed the getParameterInfo() and getAppletInfo() methods in Section 12.1. The applet would work perfectly well without them, but they're methods that a well-mannered applet should have, and it doesn't cost a lot of programming effort to put them in.

```
/**
 * RETURNS: an arbitrarily long array of three strings, one for
 * each the applet expects. The strings describe,
 * respectively, the parameter name, its type, and its
 * description.
 */
public String[][] getParameterInfo()
{
    String[][] aboutParams = {
        {"pattern", "String", "base*extension"},
        {"numPix",  "int",    "number of images"},
        {"label",   "String", "button label"},
        {"destURL", "URL",    "destination when clicked"} };
    return aboutParams;
}

/**
 * RETURNS: a String giving information about the applet. A
 * browser might use this in an About box.
 */
public String getAppletInfo()
{
    return "Graphic Button applet. Copyright 1997,"
        + " Rick Decker";
}
```

The applet concludes with the two helper methods that are used by init() to get the parameters. Each tries to convert the String parameter value to the correct type and returns the value if it succeeds and a default value if conversion fails. As usual, we're trying to make our program as robust as possible, anticipating errors that might happen and dealing with them so that they don't cause disaster.

```
/**
 * Try to get the parameter with the given name. If there's no
 * such parameter or if the value is incorrectly formatted,
 * return the given default value.
 * RETURNS: an int corresponding to the parameter, or the
 * default value, if the parameter doesn't represent a legal
 * int
 * CALLED BY: init()
 */
private int getIntParameter(String paramName, int defaultValue)
```

```
{
    try
    {
        return (Integer.parseInt(getParameter(paramName)));
    }
    catch (NumberFormatException e)
    {
        return defaultValue;
    }
}

/**
 * Like getIntParameter, except that here we're getting a URL.
 * RETURNS: a URL object corresponding to the parameter, or the
 * default value, if the parameter is malformed
 * CALLED BY: init()
 */
private URL getURLParameter(String paramName, URL defaultValue)
{
    try
    {
        return (new URL(getParameter(paramName)));
    }
    catch (MalformedURLException e)
    {
        return defaultValue;
    }
}
}
```

Exploring the `GraphicButton` Class

Our `GraphicButton` has two images and a label. It generates `actionEvents` when clicked, and its label can be set and inspected, just like a regular button. It also has a refinement that AWT buttons lack: Moving the cursor over the button highlights its label in red, and moving the cursor away sets the label back to its original color.

A button that changes its look when the pointer moves over it is called a *rollover* button.

```
package myWidgets;

//===================================================================
//   PROJECT:          _programming.java_
//   FILE:             GraphicButton.java
//   PURPOSE:          Chapter 12 lablet
//   VERSION:          2.0
//   TARGET:           Java 1.1 and above
//   UPDATE HISTORY:   2.0      12/4/98      new event model
//                     1.0      8/1/97
//===================================================================

//--------------------------- NOTES ---------------------------
/*
    Here's how to use a GraphicButton:

    INITIALIZATION
        To construct a GraphicButton, supply the constructor with
        an array of two images, and an optional label. In the
        array of images, image[0] should be the down image and
        image[1] the up.
```

```
            NOTE: While not required, it's a good idea for the images
            to be the same size. This class uses the size of the down
            image to center the label.

        EVENT HANDLING
            A GraphicButton object responds to MOUSE_ENTERED and
            MOUSE_EXITED events by highlighting and de-highlighting its
            label. It responds to MOUSE_PRESSED and MOUSE_RELEASED
            events by redrawing the button
            in its appropriate state (down or up, respectively).

            We've implemented an addActionListener() method, so when
            a GraphicButton processes a MOUSE_RELEASED event, it
            sends a new ActionEvent to all registered listeners, just
            like an ordinary AWT Button.

        INSPECTORS, MODIFIERS
            getLabel(): Returns the label string.
            setLabel(): Sets the label string to the argument and
                        resizes this object to fit.
  */

//-------------------------- IMPORTS --------------------------

import java.awt.*;
import java.awt.event.*;
```

A `GraphicButton` needs references to the two images passed to it by the constructor. It also needs to know its visible width and height, which it computes on the basis of the width and height of its label. Note that these are not the dimensions of the button canvas itself—the button may take up more space than it appears to.

```
/**
 * A GraphicButton has the same functionality as an ordinary AWT
 * button: it responds to mouse clicks by generating ActionEvents,
 * and it keeps track of all listeners that have registered
 * themselves. The primary difference is that it uses images for
 * its up and down displays.
 */
public class GraphicButton extends Canvas implements MouseListener
{
    private final int       LABEL_INSET  = 15;
    private final Color      UP_COLOR     = Color.darkGray;
    private final Color      DOWN_COLOR   = Color.white;
    private final Color      HILITE_COLOR = Color.red;

    protected   Image[] theImage;    // 0 -> is down, 1 -> is up
    private String    theLabel;
    private int       thisWidth,
                      thisHeight,
                      labelBase;
    // a list of all the registered listeners
    private ActionListener listeners = null;
    protected   int        curImage = 1;

//---------- Constructors and initialization utility ---------
/**
 * Construct a GraphicButton with two images and a label.
 */
```

```
public GraphicButton(Image[] imgs, String label)
{
    theLabel = label;
    theImage = imgs;

    setFont(new Font("SansSerif", Font.BOLD, 10));
    fitLabel();
    addMouseListener(this);
}

/**
 *  Construct a GraphicButton with two images and no label.
 */
public GraphicButton(Image[] imgs)
{
    this(imgs, ""); // Call the other constructor.
}
```

To compute the height and width of the visible portion of the button, we need to know the width of its label text. The FontMetrics class keeps track of the sizes of the various parts of text in a particular font. A String is drawn by giving the coordinates of its *anchor*, which is a point on the *baseline* at the left edge of the text. A FontMetrics instance associated with a font has access to the methods getAscent(), getDescent(), and stringWidth(), among others.

The getAscent() method returns the maximal height, in pixels above the baseline, of any character in the font. Note that this might be larger than the height of a particular string (it wouldn't be the correct ascent of "stop", for example, because that string has no uppercase letters), but there's nothing we can do about that—there is no method to get the ascent of a particular string. Similarly, the method getDescent() returns the maximal height in pixels below the baseline that any character in the font can be. We're better off on width: The method stringWidth() computes and returns the width of a given string in the font associated with the FontMetrics object. The fitLabel() method uses the height of the down button image, the LABEL_INSET constant, and the FontMetrics methods to decide the width and height of the visible portion of the button, along with the y-coordinate, labelBase, of the anchor. We leave it as an exercise to determine how this is accomplished.

```
/**
 * Size the button so that there is a LABEL_INSET pixel inset
 * on each side of the label and the label is centered
 * vertically in the button.
```

```
    */
    private void fitLabel()
    {
        thisHeight = theImage[0].getHeight(this) - 4;

        if (!theLabel.equals(""))
        {
            FontMetrics fm = getFontMetrics(getFont());
            thisWidth = 2 * LABEL_INSET + fm.stringWidth(theLabel);
            labelBase = (thisHeight + fm.getAscent()
                            - fm.getDescent()) / 2;
        }
        else
        {
            thisWidth = 3 * LABEL_INSET;
        }
    }
```

A `GraphicButton` deals with four mouse events and consumes all of them. A `mousePressed` event causes the button to be repainted in its down state, by setting `curImage` to 0 and then calling for a repaint, which will draw the down image `theImage[0]`. A `mouseReleased` event will cause the button to be redrawn in its up state and send along a new `action` event, because that's the only event an AWT button triggers. The `mouseEntered` and `mouseExited` events redraw the label in its new colors.

We have to be a little tricky here to get our `GraphicButton` to act like an AWT Button. A `Canvas` subclass like this generates mouse events, so we can handle all the mouse events internally, merely by implementing the `MouseListener` methods. Unfortunately, `Canvas` doesn't generate `ActionEvents`, as a Button does, so we can't just catch them and pass them along to the registered listeners. Instead, we use the `AWTEventMulticaster` class defined in the `java.awt` package. An object of this type keeps a list of all the registered listeners and can tell them to implement their appropriate event-handling methods. In this program, when we get a `mouseReleased` event, we build a new `ActionEvent` of our own and use the `AWTEventMulticaster` instance to invoke the `actionPerformed()` method for each of its listeners.

```
/**
 * Register a new listener for action events that we'll trigger
 * from this object. The AWTEventMulticaster keeps track of all
 * the listeners that have registered with this object and will
 * broadcast any event we want to all the listeners.
 */
public synchronized void addActionListener(ActionListener who)
{
    // "listeners" is a chain of registered listeners.
    // This statement adds the argument to the chain.
    listeners = AWTEventMulticaster.add(listeners, who);
}

/**
 * Change the button state to down.
 */
```

```
public void mousePressed(MouseEvent e)
{
    curImage = 0;
    repaint();
}

/**
 * Change the button state to up and send an action event
 * to all registered listeners.
 */
public void mouseReleased(MouseEvent e)
{
    curImage = 1;
    repaint();

    // Make a new action event to send out,
    ActionEvent ae = new ActionEvent(this, ActionEvent.ACTION_PERFORMED,
                                     theLabel);
    // and let the AWTEventMulticaster tell each registered
    // listener to activate its own actionPerformed() method
    // on the new event.
    listeners.actionPerformed(ae);
}

/**
 * Do nothing in response to a mouse click, since we
 * have already done all the necessary handling in the
 * mousePressed() and mouseReleased() methods.
 */
public void mouseClicked(MouseEvent e)
{ }

/**
 * Deal with a MOUSE_ENTERED event by highlighting the label of
 * the button.
 */
public void mouseEntered(MouseEvent e)
{
    Graphics g = getGraphics();
    g.setColor(HILITE_COLOR);
    g.drawString(theLabel, LABEL_INSET, labelBase);
}

/**
 * Turn off highlighting when the mouse leaves this object.
 */
public void mouseExited(MouseEvent e)
{
    paintLabel(this.getGraphics());
}
```

The paint() method scales the button image to the width and height that were calculated by fitLabel() and draws the label at the anchor point (LABEL_INSET, labelBase), in the appropriate color. We didn't need to override update() here, but doing so does no harm, and we'll need the override in the subclass AnimatedButton.

```
/**
 * For flicker-free animation in the AnimatedButton subclass.
 */
public void update(Graphics g)
{
    paint(g);
}

/**
 * Redraw the image and paint the label on top of it.
 */
public void paint(Graphics g)
{
    g.drawImage(theImage[curImage], 0, 0, thisWidth, thisHeight,
                this);
    if (!theLabel.equals(""))
    {
        paintLabel(g);
    }
}

/**
 * Paint the label in the appropriate color.
 * CALLED BY: mouseExited(), paint()
 */
private void paintLabel(Graphics g)
{
    if (curImage > 0)
    {
        g.setColor(UP_COLOR);
    }
    else
    {
        g.setColor(DOWN_COLOR);
    }
    g.drawString(theLabel, LABEL_INSET, labelBase);
}
```

The class declaration concludes with the inspector method getLabel() and the modifier setLabel(), neither of which needs explanation.

```
/**
 * Return a copy of the label string.
 */
public String getLabel()
{
    return new String(theLabel);
}

/**
 * Set the label text, center it, and update the drawing.
 */
public void setLabel(String s)
{
    theLabel = s;
    fitLabel();
    repaint();
}
}
```

Exploring the `AnimatedButton` Class

The `AnimatedButton` class is very simple, because nearly all of the work is done by the `GraphicButton` superclass. All this class has to do, as a result, is handle the animation. It does that by implementing the `Runnable` interface, which means implementing a `run()` method for its animation thread.

The class has an instance variable, `delayTime`, that is supplied in the constructor and controls the speed of animation by setting the amount of time the animation thread sleeps at each iteration of the loop in `run()`. The only other thing we need to track is whether the animation is moving up or down through the images. For five images, for instance, the animation would cycle through image numbers 1, 2, 3, 4, 3, 2, 1, 2, 3, 4 . . . , so although we don't need to know what to do when the current image is at either end of the cycle, we do need to know what to do when we're in the middle of the image sequence. Note, by the way, that we animate only when the button is in its up state—that explains why we use image 0 for the down state.

```
package myWidgets;

//==================================================================
//   PROJECT:        _programming.java_
//   FILE:           AnimatedButton.java
//   PURPOSE:        Chapter 12 lablet
//   VERSION:        2.0
//   TARGET:         Java 1.1 and above
//   UPDATE HISTORY:    2.0     12/4/98       new event model
//                      1.0     7/28/97
//==================================================================

//-------------------------- IMPORTS --------------------------

import java.awt.*;

//==================== AnimatedButton CLASS ====================
/**
 * This class implements an animated version of GraphicButton.
 * images[0] is the down picture--the rest are for the animated up
 * state. Requires at least three images for animation.
 */
public class AnimatedButton  extends    GraphicButton
                             implements Runnable
{
   private long     delayTime;
   private Thread   myThread;
   private boolean  goingDown = false;
```

The constructors and the `start()` and `stop()` methods are simple and—by now, we hope—easy to understand. We'll leave explanation of the details of the `run()` method for the lab exercises.

```java
public AnimatedButton(Image[] imgs, String label, long delayMs)
{
    super(imgs, label);
    delayTime = delayMs;
    myThread = new Thread(this);
    myThread.start();
}

public AnimatedButton(Image[] imgs, long delayMs)
{
    this(imgs, "", delayMs);
}

//-------------------- Thread handlers -----------------------

/**
 * Start the animation thread.
 */
public void start()
{
    if (myThread == null)
    {
        myThread = new Thread(this);
        myThread.start();
    }
}

/**
 * Cycle through the up pictures when needed.
 */
public void run()
{
    while (myThread != null)
    {
        try
        {
            Thread.sleep(delayTime);
        }
        catch (InterruptedException e)
        { }

        // Do nothing this turn if this button is down or if
        // no animation is possible.
        if ((curImage == 0) || (theImage.length == 2))
        {
            continue;
        }

        if (goingDown)
        {
            if (curImage == 1)
            {
                curImage++;
                goingDown = false;
            }
            else
            {
                curImage--;
            }
        }
```

```
        else
        {
            if (curImage == theImage.length - 1)
            {
                curImage--;
                goingDown = true;
            }
            else
            {
                curImage++;
            }
        }
        repaint();
    }
}

/**
 * Stop the animation thread.
 */
public void stop()
{
    if ((myThread != null) && myThread.isAlive())
    {
        myThread.stop();
    }
    myThread = null;
}
}
```

We didn't list the `AnimatedButtoner` applet that runs an `AnimatedButton`, because it is almost exactly the same as the `GraphicButtoner` applet. The only significant difference between the two is that they construct different types of buttons.

Finally, the HTML

To complete the Lablet, the chapter, and the book, all we have to do is show the HTML that the Web browser will use to display the two buttons and the text surrounding them. You can see that we use two `<APPLET>` tags, one for each button. In each we supply the necessary parameters.

```
<HTML>
    <HEAD>
        <TITLE>Button Test Page</TITLE>
    </HEAD>

    <BODY>
    <HR>
    <APPLET code = "GraphicButtoner.class" width = 82 height = 27
            align = left>
        <PARAM name = "pattern" value = "bttn*.gif">
        <PARAM name = "numPix" value = "2">
        <PARAM name = "label" value = "Home">
        <PARAM name = "destURL" value = "http://www.bogus.edu/">
    </APPLET>
    <APPLET CODE = "AnimatedButtoner.class" width = 82 height = 27
            align = right>
```

```
        <PARAM name = "pattern" value = "animate/ab*.gif">
        <PARAM name = "numPix" value = "11">
        <PARAM name = "label" value = "Home">
        <PARAM name = "destURL" value = "http://www.alsobogus.org/">
    </APPLET>
    The button on the left is an ordinary GraphicButton. The one
    on the right is an AnimatedButton. To make life easier when
    running this, neither of the buttons actually takes you
    anywhere.
    <HR>
    <A href = "GraphicButtoner.java">See the source.</A>
    </BODY>
</HTML>
```

12.5   Summary

■ We discussed the following classes:

Applet	
AppletContext	(interface)
AudioClip	(interface)
Color	
Component	
FilteredImageSource	
FontMetrics	(briefly)
Graphics	
Image	
ImageConsumer	(interface)
ImageObserver	(interface)
ImageProducer	(interface)
MediaTracker	
RGBImageFilter	
URL	

■ A URL has the form `protocol://hostName/pathName/fileName`. The protocol identifies the file format (such as `http`), the hostName identifies the computer (such as `java.sun.com`), and the fileName identifies the location (such as `products/jdk/1.1/docs/api/Package-java.awt.html`) of the file in the host's directory structure.

■ URLs can be expressed as absolute or as relative to a given directory.

■ The `URL` class can construct a URL from a string and has methods for extracting the protocol, hostName, and fileName from a given URL.

■ The `Applet` methods `getCodeBase()` and `getDocumentBase()` are used to get the URL of an applet's `.class` file or the URL of the HTML document referring to the applet.

- The `Applet` methods `getAudioClip()` and `getImage()` are used to initiate the process of loading a sound or an image into an applet.

- An applet may use parameters specified in the `<APPLET>` element of an HTML document. The `Applet` method `getParameter()` returns the value `String` of the parameter with the specified name.

- An applet has an `AppletContext`, which refers to the context in which the applet is running. The `AppletContext` method `showDocument()` requests the context to load the document with the specified URL.

- The `<APPLET>` element requires the attributes `code`, `width`, and `height` and may use the optional attributes `codebase`, `alt`, `align`, `vspace`, and `hspace`.

- An `AudioClip` file must be in AU format. The methods `play()` and `stop()` play the sound and stop it, respectively.

- Once an `Image` has been identified by `getImage()`, it can be drawn by the `Graphics` method `drawImage()`. A call to `getImage()` does not initiate loading. Loading will begin when a request comes to use the image—by drawing it, for example.

- To force an image to load, call the `Component` method `prepareImage()`.

- The Image methods `getGraphics()`, `getHeight()`, and `getWidth()` can be used to get a `Graphics` instance associated with the image and to get the height and width of the image. These might not yield reliable results if the image hasn't been fully loaded at the time of the call.

- To use an offscreen image, create a new instance by `createImage()`, get its `Graphics` context, and use the `Graphics` instance methods to draw on the image. The image can then be displayed by `drawImage()`.

- If you have a complicated picture that has to be drawn repeatedly, draw it to an offscreen image first and then call `drawImage()` when you need to display the picture.

- A `Color` instance represents a color by specifying its red, green, and blue components. A value of 0 represents none of that component, and a value of 255 represents the maximum brightness of that component.

- It is often convenient to use hexadecimal notation to construct or manipulate a `Color`. A hexadecimal literal begins with the characters `0x`, so the literal `0xffafaf` could be used to construct the `Color.pink` color.

- When an image is drawn, an `ImageObserver` instance is created to monitor the loading of the image. `Component` implements `ImageObserver`, so you will generally use `this` to refer to the default `ImageObserver` in a `drawImage()` call. You can override the sole `ImageObserver` method `imageUpdate()` to do your own observing of the progress of an image.

- An `ImageFilter` object is used to modify the pixels of an image. The `RGBImageFilter` is a simple subclass of `ImageFilter` that performs the same color modification on each pixel of an image.

- To use an `ImageFilter`, supply one to a `FilteredImageSource`, along with an image producer [usually obtained by calling `getSource()`]. A `FilteredImageSource` is an image producer, so you can then use it as an argument to `createImage()` to create a new filtered image.

■ The high-order byte of an image pixel represents the amount of transparency of that pixel, with 0 denoting a transparent pixel and 255 representing an opaque pixel.

■ It's generally a good idea to do drawing on a `Canvas` or a `Canvas` subclass.

■ When drawing a fixed background on a component, consider overriding that component's `update()` method so that it doesn't erase the background.

■ To do animation, display a sequence of closely related images fast enough that the eye and brain blend them together to give the illusion of motion. This is almost always done in a separate thread.

■ The `MediaTracker` class is designed for watching the status of multiple images while they are being loaded. An image is registered with a `MediaTracker` by calling `addImage()`. The methods `waitForAll()` and `waitForID()` block the current thread until all images (or the images with the specified `id`) are loaded.

■ The `Graphics` method `clipRect()` takes as its arguments the `x`, `y`, `width`, and `height` of a rectangle, and it limits drawing to the parts of that rectangle that lie within the total drawing area of the associated component.

■ If your drawing is going to take place on only a small portion of the total drawing area, consider clipping the `Graphics` context to the part of the region you need.

■ The `FontMetrics` class keeps track of the sizes of the various parts of text in a particular font, such as the ascent, descent, and height of the text. The method `stringWidth()` can be used to compute the width of a `String` in a particular font.

■ If you got this far, take a moment to reflect on what you've learned and congratulate yourself on your diligence and effort.

12.6 Exercises

1. Consider the URL

```
http://www.server.org/pub/docs/joubert/index.html
```

Give the absolute URLs that correspond to the following relative URLs.

   a. `page2.html`
   b. `art/rainbowBar.gif`
   c. `/misc/MyApplet.class`
   d. `//admin/recs/july92/index.html`

2. In the file structure of Exercise 1, how would `MyApplet` load the image `rainbowBar.gif`?

3. In the `SketchPad` Lablet of Chapter 6, resizing the applet window causes the drawing to vanish, because resizing the window forces a call to `paint()` and thus loses all the old drawing. You can fix this problem by double buffering, using an offscreen image that mirrors what was drawn on the screen. In other words, you could write the program so that every drawing call was done twice, once to the screen and once to the offscreen image. Then, when the time came to update the screen, all you would have to do is copy the offscreen image to the screen. Modify `SketchPad` so that it does this double buffering.

4. What are the conventional names for the colors with the following (R, G, B) components?
  a. (128, 0, 128)
  b. (230, 230, 90)
  c. (30, 90, 30)
  d. (255, 0, 255)
  e. (255, 255, 0)
  f. (0, 255, 255)
  g. (255, 128, 0)

5. Convert each of the colors in Exercise 4 to its integer equivalent, expressed in hexadecimal form.

6. Show that 16756655 is indeed the decimal representation of `Color.pink`.

7. Come up with the best (R, G, B) values you can for the following colors. You may have to do a bit of research for this question.
  a. Aubergine
  b. Heliotrope
  c. Taupe
  d. Teal

8. Consider the following method.

```
public Color mystery(Color c)
{
    int n = c.getRGB();
    int x = (n & 0x0000ff00) << 8;
    int y = (n & 0x000000ff) << 8;
    int z = (n & 0x00ff0000) >> 16;
    return new Color(x + y + z);
}
```

  a. What color does this method return if the argument color corresponds to the integer `0x00ff8000`?
  b. What is the result of `mystery(mystery(mystery(myColor)))`?
  c. We deliberately made this method incomprehensible to make this exercise more challenging. Use the `getRed()`, `getGreen()`, and `getBlue()` methods to make `mystery()` less mysterious.

9. If you look at `ImageTest3`, you'll notice that it consists of the methods `init()`, `imageUpdate()`, and `paint()`, none of which you call yourself. Trace the action of `ImageTest3`, describing who calls the methods in what order. Remember, there are a lot of implicit players: the run-time system, an `ImageProducer`, an `ImageConsumer`, and an `ImageObserver`.

10. Remove the call to `prepareImage()` from `ImageTest3` and run it. Nothing will happen. Give a careful explanation of the reason why, explaining the circularity involved.

11. In `InvertFilter`, we used bitwise `OR` to combine the masked component values into a pixel. Could we have added them instead? Explain why or why not.

12. Consider the problem of making an image filter that will take an image and gray it out. An easy way to do this is to take each of the red, green, and blue components of a pixel and average each with 128.

a. Give the values that would result if this scheme were applied to the components 255, 128, and 0.

b. Write a `FadeFilter` class that will do this.

c. Modify `ImageTest4` so that it uses your `FadeFilter` rather than an `InvertFilter`.

13. Because a `FilteredImageSource` takes an `ImageProducer` as one of its arguments and returns an `ImageProducer` as a result, you should be able to chain two filters together to produce a new one.

a. Try it. Modify `ImageTest4` so that it takes an image and applies an `InvertFilter` first and then applies the `FadeFilter` of Exercise 12.

b. Would the result of part (a) be different if you applied the filters in the opposite order? Explain.

c. What would happen if you chained two `InvertFilters` together?

14. We can't use an `RGBImageFilter` to blend two images, but we can simulate a blend by making a `TransparencyFilter` that sets the transparency of each pixel of an image to some value less than 255 and then drawing the filtered image on top of another. Try it.

15. At 72 pixels per inch and 4 bytes per pixel, how much memory would be required to store the pixels of a 2-inch by 1-inch image?

16. Run `AnimationTest1` with and without the override of the `update()` method in `Display`. Explain the differences you see.

17. We designed the `Ship` class used in the animation applets as a subclass of `Thread`. The other way of doing this would have been to have the `Ship` class contain a `Thread` and then have `Ship` implement `Runnable`.

a. Rewrite `Ship` this way.

b. Discuss the advantages or disadvantages of this approach, compared to the original.

18. The `GraphicButton` and `AnimatedButton` classes don't have quite all the functionality of real buttons. In particular, we need some way of indicating visually what happens when we call the `Component` method `disable()` on our buttons.

a. Rewrite `GraphicButton` so that it has an override of `disable()`. This should not only keep the button from generating action events (does it already?) but should also dim the button (see Exercise 12 for a way to do that). Of course, you should also write an override of `enable()` to make the button active and restore it to its original appearance.

b. Repeat part (a) for the `AnimatedButton` class. In this case, a call to `disable()` should also turn off the button's animation.

19. Write the utility method

```
boolean getBooleanParameter(String name, boolean default)
```

that will look for the parameter with the given name. If there is no parameter with the specified name, the method should return the `default` value. It should also return the `default` value if there is a parameter with the right name but the value was neither of false or true. If there is a parameter with the specified name and the value is `true` or `false`, it should return the boolean value equivalent to the value string. Your method should treat value strings such as `"True"`, `"true"`, and `"TRUE"` as corresponding to `true`. (*Hint:* Use the `String` method `toLowerCase()`.)

20. In the `fitLabel()` method of `GraphicButton`, explain what is being done in the calculation of `labelBase`. Suppose, for example, that `thisHeight` was 30, that the font's ascent was 8, and that its descent was 4. How much space would be above the label and how much would be below the label?

12.7   Answers to Review Questions

1.1 The protocol, host, path, and resource.

1.2 `java.net`.

1.3 `getCodeBase()` returns the URL of the directory where the applet's `.class` file is located; `getDocumentBase()` returns the URL of the directory containing the current HTML document.

1.4 An `APPLET` parameter provides a means by which information in an HTML document may be passed to an applet.

2.1 `stop()` it.

2.2 Use the `Graphics` method `drawImage()`.

2.3 Use `createImage()` to make a target for drawing; call the image's `getGraphics()` method to get a `Graphics` instance; use the instance to draw; call `drawImage()` to display the image. You would use this technique to smooth the drawing process.

2.4 An `ImageProducer` uses an external source to produce the bits in an image, for eventual use by some consumer. An `ImageObserver` monitors the consumer's use of the image bits.

2.5 Never—it's an abstract class. You would, however, construct an instance of a subclass you had designed.

3.1 To lessen flicker when repainting.

3.2 Call the `ImageTracker add()` method, using the image as an argument. Call `checkID()`.

3.3 One controls the animation of the ship's running lights (required by Intergalactic Navigation Commission rules), and the other controls the ship's motion.

3.4 Clipping limits drawing to a specified rectangle. It's a way to save time when only a portion of an image needs to be redrawn.

12.8   Class References

`java.applet.AppletContext`

This interface allows a program access to the context in which it is running.

```
abstract interface AppletContext
{
    //------------ Methods ------------
    abstract Applet getApplet(String name);
    abstract AudioClip getAudioClip(URL location);
```

```
◆   abstract Image getImage(URL location);
    abstract void showDocument(URL location);
◆   abstract void showDocument(URL directory, String name);
◆   abstract void showStatus(String message);
}
```

java.applet.AudioClip

This interface contains methods that deal with playing sounds. The sounds must be stored in AU format.

```
abstract interface AudioClip
{
    //------------ Methods ------------
    abstract void loop();
◆   abstract void play();
◆   abstract void stop();
}
```

java.awt.AWTEventMulticaster

An AWTEventMulticaster is a list of event listeners. It is used to facilitate event handling when you wish to implement a custom component. To implement an add***Listener() method for a custom component that didn't support events of type ***, you would get the listener argument and call the Class method add() to add the argument to the end of this list. In a similar way, remove() would be used to remove a listener from this list.

This class implements all of the event listeners, which implies that it contains all their methods. When an AWTEventMulticaster calls one of the listener methods, it causes that method to be called by all of the listeners in its list. In the descriptions below, *** indicates any of Action, Adjustment, Component, Container, Focus, Item, Key, Mouse, MouseMotion, Text, and Window. If two or more *** wildcards appear in a single definition, they must be the same. (Thus, for example, you can't add an ActionListener to a list of KeyListeners.)

```
class AWTEventMulticaster    extends Object
                             implements ***Listener
{
    //---------- Constructor ----------
    protected AWTEventMulticaster(EventListener a, EventListener b);
    /*  You won't make a new instance of this class, as a rule.
        Instead, to initialize a list, you begin with a null
        instance of the appropriate type. For example, to make a
        list of actionListeners, you would begin with

        ActionListener myList = null;

        Then, to add the ActionListener lstnr, you would make the
        method call

        myList = AWTEventMulticaster.add(myList, lstnr);      */
```

```
     //--------- Class Methods ---------
◆   static ***Listener add(***Listener list, ***Listener added);
     static ***Listener remove(***Listener list,
                         ***Listener removed);
     /*  Both of these return the list itself, i.e., a reference to
         the first argument. */

     //------------ Methods ------------
◆   void actionPerformed(ActionEvent e);
◆   // (all other listener methods omitted)
◆   void windowOpened(WindowEvent e);
}
```

java.awt.image.FilteredImageSource

FilteredImageSource is used in conjunction with an ImageFilter to provide a producer for the bits that come from the filter. There are five instance methods in this class, but you generally will not use any of them. The only part of this class we'll discuss is the constructor.

```
class FilteredImageSource     extends Object
                              implements ImageProducer
{
     //---------- Constructor ----------
◆   FilteredImageSource(ImageProducer origin, ImageFilter filter);
     /*  Construct a new instance, almost certainly to be used
         subsequently as an ImageProducer. In simple terms, this
         object is an ImageProducer that takes bits from another
         producer, origin, passes them through the filter, and
         sends the filtered bits out. To use this, you would
         write code like this:

     Image origin = getImage(from somewhere);
     ImageFilter f = new FilterOfSomeKind();
     ImageProducer p = new FilteredImageSource(origin.getSource(), f);

     Image theFilteredImage = createImage(p); */
}
```

java.awt.FontMetrics

The FontMetrics class keeps track of the sizes of the various parts of text in a particular font. Because this is an abstract class, you won't construct a new instance of it. Instead, you'll use the Graphics or Component method's getFontmetrics() to return an instance of the FontMetrics class associated with the current Font.

```
abstract class FontMetrics extends Object
{
     //------------ Methods ------------
     int charWidth();
     /*  Returns the advance width of the character specified in
         the argument. The advance width is the number of pixels
         one would move from the left edge of the character to the
         start of the next character. Roughly speaking, the
```

advance width is the width of the character plus the
amount of space allowed between characters. */

```
int charsWidth(char[] chars, int start, int length)
        throws ArrayIndexOutOfBoundsException;
/* Returns the total advance width of the characters in the
   array, starting at position start and containing length
   characters. This throws an exception if either offset or
   length is invalid for the array. */
```

```
◆   int getAscent();
◆   int getDescent();
    int getMaxAscent();
    int getMaxDescent();
    /* The first two return the height in pixels from the
       baseline to the top or bottom of the largest characters
       in the font. The second two return the largest ascent or
       descent for characters with modifications. For
       example, a capital letter with an umlaut added on top may
       have an ascent larger than the value returned by
       getAscent(). */
```

```
◆   int getHeight();
    /* Returns the recommended space between baselines, the sum
       of ascent, descent, and leading. */
```

```
    int getLeading();
    /* Returns the leading, the vertical space between lines of
       text. */
```

```
◆   int getMaxAdvance();
    /* Returns the largest advance width of any character in this
       font. See charWidth() for an explanation of advance
       width. */
```

```
◆   int stringWidth(String s);
    /* Returns the width of the argument when displayed in this
       font. */
}
```

java.awt.Image

This class represents a displayable image. Because this is an abstract class, you won't
construct a new `Image` instance. Instead, you'll use the `Applet` method `getImage()`
or the `Component` method `createImage()` to return an `Image` instance for you to use.

```
abstract class Image extends Object
{
    //-------- Class Constants --------
    final static SCALE_AREA_AVERAGING;
    final static SCALE_DEFAULT;
    final static SCALE_FAST;
    final static SCALE_REPLICATE;
    final static SCALE_SMOOTH;
```

```
     //------------ Methods ------------
     void flush();
     Graphics getGraphics();
◆    int getHeight(ImageObserver ob);
◆    Image getScaledInstance(int w, int h, int hints);
◆    ImageProducer getSource();
◆    int getWidth(ImageObserver ob);
     }
```

java.awt.image.ImageConsumer

We include this interface for the sake of completeness; unless you're going to be doing some sophisticated image manipulation, you'll never directly use (or even refer to) this class. The methods of ImageConsumer are invoked behind the scenes by some ImageProducer with which this instance is registered.

```
abstract interface ImageConsumer
{
     // (Description omitted)
}
```

java.awt.image.ImageObserver

This interface contains one method, which is used to monitor the progress of an image as it is being loaded. Component implements this interface, and you will generally call imageUpdate() through some Component object.

```
abstract interface ImageObserver
{
     //-------- Class Constants --------
     final static int ABORT;
     final static int ALLBITS;
     final static int ERROR;
     final static int FRAMEBITS;
     final static int HEIGHT;
     final static int PROPERTIES;
     final static int SOMEBITS;
     final static int WIDTH;

     //------------ Method ------------
◆    abstract boolean imageUpdate(Image img, int flags,
                    int x, int y, int width, int height);
}
```

java.awt.image.ImageProducer

A class implements this interface if it is intended to get an image from some source and produce bits that can be used by some ImageConsumer. Typically, for instance, an ImageProducer, p, will be used to produce an Image by calling the Component method `createImage(p)`. You won't generally call any of the methods of any class that implements this interface, and you'll almost never implement the methods of this interface in a class of your own.

```
abstract interface ImageProducer
{
    // (Description omitted)
}
```

java.awt.MediaTracker

A MediaTracker object is used to monitor the loading of one or more images.

```
class MediaTracker extends Object
{
    //---------- Constructor -----------
    MediaTracker(Component c);

    //-------- Class Constants --------
    final static ABORTED;
    final static COMPLETE;
    final static ERRORED;
    final static LOADING;

    //------------ Methods ------------
♦   void addImage(Image im, int id);
    boolean checkAll();
    boolean checkAll(boolean load);
    boolean checkID(int id);
    boolean checkID(int id, boolean load);
    boolean isErrorAny();
♦   boolean isErrorID();
    void removeImage(Image im);
    void removeImage(Image im, int id);
    int statusAll(boolean load);
    int statusID(int id, boolean load);
♦   void waitForAll() throws InterruptedException;
♦   void waitForID(int id) throws InterruptedException;
}
```

java.awt.image.RGBImageFilter

The RGBImageFilter class is a subclass of ImageFilter, in which the same operation is performed on every pixel of an image. Of the seven methods in this class, you will generally use just one when you define a subclass to do your own filtering. The other methods are beyond the scope of this book.

```
abstract class RGBImageFilter extends ImageFilter
{
    //---------- Constructor -----------
    RGBImageFilter(Component c);

    //------------ Method ------------
    abstract int filterRGB(int x, int y, int pix);
}
```

java.net.URL

This class represents a uniform resource locator (URL)—namely, an Internet address.

```
final class URL extends Object
{
    //---------- Constructors ----------
    URL(String name);
    URL(URL base, String relative);
    URL(String protocol, String host, String file);
    URL(String protocol, String host, int port, String file);

    //------------ Methods ------------
    String getFile();
    String getHost();
    int getPort();
    String getProtocol();
}
```

GLOSSARY

abstract class A class for which it is impossible to construct an object, either because the class is defined using the keyword `abstract` or because one or more of its methods is defined without a statement body. An abstract class, like `Component`, is intended to serve as the parent class of one or more derived classes, which will provide implementations of the empty methods in the abstract parent. Similar to, but not identical to, an *interface*.

access The property of a class, method, or variable that determines whether it may be used by subclasses, classes in other packages, or by another class. Java has four access levels: private, package, protected, and public. Related to, but higher-level than, *scope*.

actual argument The information sent to a method when the method is called. See *argument*.

adapter class A class that modifies the programmer-visible portion of another class, interface, or primitive type. Typical examples include `MouseAdapter` and `Integer`. Also known as a wrapper class.

alias A variable that refers to the same object as another. Only class-type variables can be aliases of each other.

algorithm A sequence of instructions, capable of being performed by a computer, that performs some actions and eventually halts.

applet A Java program designed to be run within a Web browser or similar shell.

applet parameter Information, presented in an `<APPLET>` tag in an HTML document, that can be read by the applet.

application A more traditional program than an applet, designed to be capable of executing on its own.

argument A piece of data that is sent to a method when the method is called. The arguments that appear in the method definition are known as the formal arguments and the corresponding values that appear in the method call are known as the actual arguments.

argument list The comma-separated list of type/name pairs that appears as part of a method definition.

assembler/assembly language An assembler is a program that converts input in assembly language to output in machine language. Usually, a single statement in assembly language is translated to a single machine language instruction, so we may regard assembly language as a human-readable code for machine language.

assignment   An operator that sets the value or reference of one of its arguments, according to the value or reference of its other. For example, the expression x = 3 evaluates to 3 and sets the value of x to 3 as a *side-effect*.

associativity   The order of evaluation of repeated instances of an operator. For example, subtraction is left-associative, so 5 - 4 - 3 would be evaluated as if it were written ((5 - 4) - 3), while assignment is right-associative, so x = y = 3 would be evaluated as if it were written (x = (y = 3)). In Java, all the binary operators except the assignments are left-associative, all the unary operators are right-associative.

binary operator   An operator, like * or &&, that requires two operands.

binary representation   Any form of encoding data as a collection of *bits*. Commonly used to refer to a specific scheme for representing integers as a sum of powers of 2, using 0 and 1 as "digits."

bit   The smallest unit of data, capable of taking on one of two values, often represented as 0 and 1.

boolean   A logical type, representing either of the values true or false. Named in honor of George Boole, a nineteenth century logician.

byte   Eight bits. A byte can represent any of 256 possible values. Often, the fundamental unit of organization of computer memories.

bytecode   The output of a Java compiler. The bytecode is then translated and executed by the Java interpreter for a particular system. In theory, the bytecode of a Java program should produce essentially the same result regardless of the system on which it is interpreted.

C   A programming language developed in the early 1970s by Dennis Ritchie at Bell Laboratories. The "grandparent" language of Java.

C++   A programming language developed by Bjarne Stroustrup in the latter half of the 1980s. Originally called C with Classes, C++ is an object-oriented extension of C. The "parent" language of Java, in that Java is syntactically quite similar to C++.

call   An invocation of a method. When a method is called, the flow of execution jumps to the method and continues there until a return statement or the end of the method is encountered, at which time execution jumps back to the place of the call.

callback   A method or object of one class that is registered with another (often at construction), so it can be called or used at a later time.

case-sensitive   A property of a language that upper- and lowercase versions of the same letter will be regarded as different. Java is case-sensitive, in that the variables sum and Sum would be regarded as different, while HTML is case-insensitive, so the tags <APPLET>, <applet>, and <ApPlEt> are considered to be identical.

cast An explicit change in the type of a variable's value, as in `myInt = (int)myDouble`. Related to *promotion* of a value, like the implicit type change in the expression `myDouble = myInt`.

class A description of the data and methods for manipulating the data of each object of its type. A class may be regarded as a blueprint or prototype for each of its objects.

class invariant An assertion that is always true for all of objects of that class, as "the instance variable `count` is greater than or equal to zero."

class method/variable A method or variable that belongs to a class, rather than to each object of the class. In Java, class methods and variable are designated by using the keyword `static`. See also *instance variable*.

comment A portion of a program that provides information to the reader of the source code, but which is ignored by the compiler or interpreter.

compiler A program that takes source code as input and produces object code in another language as output. A Java compiler translates Java source code into *byte-code*. See also *interpreter*.

constant A variable with the value that cannot be modified while running. A variable in Java is made constant by using the keyword `final` as part of its declaration.

constructor An optional part of the definition of a class, a constructor describes how an object of the class will be initialized. A constructor in Java is defined somewhat like a method, but its definition may not specify a return type and must have the same name as the class.

coordinates The horizontal and vertical location of a point in a component. Coordinates are measured from the upper-left corner of a component (local coordinates) or of the display screen (global coordinates).

debugging The process of finding and correcting errors in a program. The most painful part of the programming process, lessened but never eliminated by careful practices.

declaration A statement that establishes storage for a variable and may optionally set an initial state for the variable's data.

definition That portion of a program that describes the data and action of a class or method. Java source code files consist of nothing but class definitions, `import` declarations, and comments.

deprecated A feature of an earlier version of Java, but which may not be supported in future versions. Generally applied to classes, methods, or variables.

derived class A class that inherits some or all of the methods and instance variables of another. In a class definition `class B extends A`, `B` is a derived class of `A`.

divide and conquer   A design idiom in which a program is solved by breaking it into one or more parts, getting a solution to each part and combining the partial solutions into a solution to the original problem. Often implemented recursively. Quicksort is a divide and conquer algorithm.

error   The failure of a program to perform as intended. A compile-time error is caused by failure to conform to the grammatical rules of the language (like omitting a semicolon), a run-time error is caused by a situation that makes further execution impossible (like division by zero), and a logic error is caused by a failure to meet the specified design (like a program that should sort an array but which instead leaves the array unchanged).

event   Usually, an action that is generated by some user interaction with a program, such as clicking a button or moving the mouse.

event delegation   The model of dealing with events in which an event is sent to a method (event handler) of one or more objects in a program that have been registered as being capable of taking appropriate action.

field   In Java, a synonym for instance or (less often) class variable.

focus   A property of components in a Java program, indicating that a component is capable of responding to key events. For example, on many systems the visual indication that a text field has focus is that the field contains a blinking insertion cursor.

formal argument   One of the placeholders for information sent to a method. See *argument.*

front end   That part of a program that is visible to the outside world. For example, in a program that made a logical separation of the user interface and the processing portion, the user interface part would be called the front end.

function   Commonly used as a synonym for method. In some languages, a distinction is made between functions, which have non-`void` return types, and procedures, which have `void` return types.

guard   A statement or expression that shields subsequent code from potential errors. For example, in `((b != 0) && (a / b > 10))`, the first clause guards against possible division by zero in the second clause.

GUI   Graphic User Interface. The part of a program that is visible to the user when the program is running.

HTML   Hypertext markup language. HTML is the collection of markup tags, like `<APPLET>`, that are used by Web browsers to control the display of text, graphics, and sounds.

IDE   Integrated Development Environment. A program used to facilitate the programming process, usually by providing in a single package a text editor, compiler, debugger, and a means of executing programs.

identifier   The name of a class, method, argument, or variable.

immutable   An immutable object cannot be changed once it has been constructed. In Java, strings are immutable.

import   A form of declaration indicating that a type defined in another package may be used in a program merely by specifying its name.

inheritance   The feature of object-oriented languages that permits one class to have the data and methods of another, as if they were explicitly written as part of the inheriting class. See also *derived class*.

inspector   Generally, a method used to determine the value of one of an object's instance variables, without modifying the value of the variable. Often given a name starting with "get," as in `getLabel ()`. See also *modifier*.

instance variable   A variable in a class that is part of each object of the class. Distinguished from a class variable, which is a single variable that is shared by all objects of the class.

instantiation   The process of setting aside storage for an object and setting the initial states of some or all of its data. See also *constructor*.

interface   A Java feature somewhat like a class, but with empty implementations of all its methods. If a class implements an interface, it must provide statement bodies (even if they have no statements) for all methods in the interface. The event listeners are all interfaces.

interpreter   A program that translates source code into object code on a statement-by-statement basis, interleaving execution of the object code with the translation process. This differs from a *compiler*, which translates all of the source code before execution.

I/O   Short for Input/Output.

keyword   A word that has a predefined meaning in a programming language. In Java, "if," "return," and "int" are examples of keywords.

library   A collection of useful classes or (in languages other than Java) methods. See also *package*.

literal   A representation in source code of a value of a primitive, String, or `null` type. For example, 3.08 is a double literal and "foo" is a String literal.

linear search   A common programming idiom in which a collection of information like an array is inspected in linear order until some condition is satisfied.

local variable   A variable that is declared in the body of a method, as distinguished from *instance variable*. Local variable declarations may not include *modifiers*.

loop   A segment of code that is intended to be executed repeatedly. The three Java loop constructs are the `do`, `while`, and `for` loops.

member class   A class which is defined within the body of another class.

method   One of the active parts of a class. A method is a named collection of code that is executed by calling its name, somewhat like invoking a demon in creepy fantasy stories.

model/view   A program designed strategy that emphasizes the separation of the internal representation of information (the model) from the accessible or visible form (the view) derived from the model.

modifier   (1) A keyword that is applied to the definition of a method or a variable. The Java modifiers are `private`, `protected`, `public`, `final`, `static`, and two we didn't discuss, `transient` and `volatile`. (2) A key, such as Shift or Control, that can be pressed in combination with another.

multiple inheritance   The situation in which a class inherits the variables and methods of two or more other classes, neither of which is a *superclass* of the other. Allowed in some languages, like C++, but not permitted in Java.

mutual exclusion   The process of permitting only one process or thread at a time to have access to a shared resource, like a variable.

null   The only class-type literal. A null object is one which is in an uninitialized state.

object   An instance of a class.

object code   The code produced by a compiler from a source code input.

object-oriented   The programming or design paradigm that is based on the notions of objects as instances of classes that are related by inheritance.

operator   A language feature that takes one or more pieces of information, manipulates them in some way, and returns a result. Differs syntactically from a method in that the information to be used is not presented as an argument list. + and <= are examples of operators.

operand   The information used by an operator. In the expression 3 / 6, the numbers 3 and 6 are the operands used by the / operator.

overload   The use of the same name for two or more methods or constructors in a class, such as `void setLocation(iint x, int y)` and `void setLocation(Point p)`.

override   A redefinition of a parent class method in a derived class or of an interface method in a class that implements the interface. Common overrides are those of `init()`, `paint()`, and `actionPerformed()`.

package   In Java, a directory containing files of class definitions. The names of classes in a package may be used in another file by using the `import` declaration.

parameter   (1) See argument. Some authors make a distinction between the terms *argument* and *parameter*, using the former to denote an actual argument and the latter to denote a formal argument. (2) See *applet parameter*.

pixel   A contraction of "picture element;" refers to a single displayable point in an image or a single dot in a visual display like a computer monitor.

postcondition   A logical assertion that is required to be true after execution of a segment of code, as, for example, "Array a contains all of the elements it did originally, rearranged in numeric order from smallest to largest."

precedence   The order in which operators in an expression will be evaluated, in the absence of parentheses. For example, in Java multiplication has higher precedence than addition, so the expression 2 + 3 * 4 will be evaluated by performing the multiplication before the addition, yielding the result 14.

precondition   A logical assertion that is required to be true before execution of a segment of code, as, for example, "Array a has been declared and holds at least N nonnegative ints."

predicate   A method that returns a *boolean* value. Such methods are often given names starting with "is," as isVisible().

primitive type   A type of information in a Java program that is not an instance of a class. The Java primitive types are byte, char, short, int, long, float, double, and boolean.

procedure   In some languages other than Java, used to refer to the equivalent of what we would call a method with a void return type.

promotion   The (often implicit) act of considering information of one type as if it were a wider type. For example, the expression 3 + 2.817 would be evaluated by promoting the int 3 to a double, yielding the double result 5.817. See also *cast*.

rapid prototyping   A program design technique in which the first code produced is a limited-function version for the purpose of assessing its usability, appearance, and eventual functionality.

range-checking   The process used in Java to check that the index used in an array access represents a legitimate position in the array. Some languages do no range checking, sacrificing safety for efficiency.

recursion   (1) A call to a method, either directly or indirectly as part of executing the same method's code. (2) More generally, a recursive definition is one which uses a term as part of its own definition (see *recursion*).

reference argument   In Java, a method argument of class type, rather than of primitive type. Roughly speaking, a reference argument may be thought of as an address, rather than a value. See also *value argument*.

reference type   In Java, a synonym for class type. More generally applied and far more confusing in some other languages.

return type   The specification of the type of information, if any, returned by a method to the place where it was called.

RGB   A form of representation of colors which uses three values to represent the red, green, and blue components of the color.

scope   The scope of a variable is that portion of a program where the variable has meaning and may be used.

semantics   The meaning and action of a programming language feature, as opposed to its *syntax*, which refers to the way the feature must be written, according to the grammatical rules of the language.

serialization   (1) Limiting access to a shared resource by one process or thread until another process had finished with it. (2) A form of I/O for objects that is very handy but beyond the scope of this book.

side-effect   An action taken by an operator or method beyond simply returning a value. For example, the expression x++ returns the value of x and then increments that value as a side-effect.

signature   The name and list of argument types of a method. A class may not have two methods with the same signature.

source code   The input to a compiler or interpreter. A programmer is a device that turns coffee and junk food into source code.

statement   The fundamental execution of a program. Java statements include expression statements, compound statements, empty statements, do, while, and for loops, and if, break, return, switch, throw, and try statements.

stub   A method definition that has an empty or trivial body. Often used in program development to establish the organization of a program while deferring detailed implementation until later.

subclass, superclass   Terms describing containment under inheritance. In the definition class A extends B {/* . . . */}, class A is a subclass of B and B is a superclass of A. In this example, B is a *wider type* than A since every A object is also a B, by inheritance.

syntax   The grammatical rules governing the way a language feature must be written. See also *semantics*. In English, the example by Noam Chomsky, "Colorless green ideas sleep furiously" is syntactically correct, but semantically meaningless.

tag   The basic constituent of HTML. A tag consists of an HTML keyword and other optional information, enclosed in < and > brackets.

truth table   A means of determining the behavior of a boolean expression by using a tabular representation of all possible combinations of values of the variables that make up the expression.

type   The type of a variable is characterized by the set of values the variable can represent and the operations that can be performed on it. Java types are broadly divided into the eight primitive types and everything else (the class types).

type cast, typecast   (See *cast*.)

unary operator   An operator, like ++, that takes a single operand.

URL   Uniform Resource Locator. For example, the address of a Web document and the protocol to be used for transmitting and receiving the document.

value argument   In Java, an argument of primitive type. More generally, an argument that is treated in a method by first making a local copy and then manipulating the copy. A value argument is not modified after the method completes execution.

variable   A name in a program, representing a location where information of a given type may be stored. There are three kinds of variables in Java: *class variables*, *instance variables*, and *local variables*.

wider type   Type W is wider than type N if every N can be considered to be a W but there may be Ws that aren't Ns. For example, double is a wider type than int, since there's a reasonable interpretation of any int as a double, but there are doubles, like 3.5, that have no reasonable interpretations as ints. See also *superclass*.

wrapper class   (See *adapter class*.)

INDEX